FREIGHT TERMINALS AND TRAINS

BY
JOHN A. DROEGE

INTRODUCTION BY JOHN ARMSTRONG

National Model Railroad Association

Introduction, copyright National Model Railroad Association, 1998
Second Printing 2012
Printed and bound in the United States of America
Signature Book Printing, www.sbpbooks.com

ISBN # 0-9647050-2-8

Front Cover Information: Chesapeake and Ohio's Peach Creek, West Virginia freight terminal, January 1946
Photo courtesy of C&O Historical Society

Cover design by Gerry Leone

National Model Railroad Association
4121 Cromwell Road - Chattanooga, Tennessee 37421

Freight Terminals & Trains
An Introduction by John Armstrong

John A. Droege -- An Appreciation

Who would expect to find a railroader in a 1930s edition of *Who's Who Among North American Authors*? Perhaps an academic personage turned company historian, but an operating man schooled only by rising through the ranks from telegrapher to general manager? Not likely....

Nevertheless, among the professors, novelists and clergymen there is one, identified in the accompanying biography only as "v.p. and gen. mgr." of an unidentified railroad. And who was this person? John Albert Droege, author of two classic rail texts, *Freight Terminals and Trains* (1912, 1925) and *Passenger Terminals and Trains* (1917).

J. A. Droege

Born in 1861 in Deer Park, Maryland, Droege (pronounced Droh' ghee) was hired as a telegrapher on the Baltimore and Ohio Railroad, right out of high school. Booming around the South on the Chesapeake and Ohio; East Tennessee, Virginia & Georgia (later, Southern Railway) and Norfolk and Western, he advanced steadily from operator, stenographer, yardmaster, dispatcher and chief dispatcher to trainmaster.

In 1899, at the age of 38, he moved north with his family to become trainmaster for the Lehigh Valley's busy Jersey City and Perth Amboy waterfront terminals. Within a year the Valley promoted him to superintendent of its Pennsylvania and New York Division in the remote railroad town of Sayre, Pennsylvania.

Five years later he moved to the New Haven Railroad as superintendent of its Providence Division. While there, he somehow found time to write a book on yards and terminals. The 450 page first edition of *Freight Terminals and Trains* was published by McGraw-Hill in 1912. Five years later, while still general superintendent for the New Haven, he wrote the companion volume, *Passenger Terminals and Trains*.

Just before his promotion in 1925 to general manager of all New Haven operations, Droege updated *Freight Terminals and Trains*. This second edition, reflecting changes in the freight transportation scene during the previous 12 years, was expanded to 573 pages. It included new chapters on main-line electrification and the early steps in integrating motor-truck transport with railroading.

But just what do we know about the personality and outlook of this railroader/scholar/ author?

His books reveal him to be a well-read and pragmatic man. His strong opinions are based on broad personal experience and are coupled with a deep sense of responsibility for the effect his work could have on the actions of others. As he notes in the book's preface, "in a field in which there is such diversity of opinion, and where 'standard practice' is yet to be established, it seems advisable to include all possible information and to quote freely from the views of experts, both those confirming and opposing the views of the author."

A distinguishing feature of Droege's books is their balanced inclusiveness. As an expensive but indispensable element of all railroads, terminals and the people who plan and operate them, are clearly his focus. However, the operation of the freight trains also receives considerable attention.

In his writing, consideration for the railroad's bottom line is always evident. Droege evaluates such factors as the cost of unfortunate characteristics of an existing yard in terms of the capitalized cost of improvements that could be supported by engine, car and crew cost savings realized in operation. Dissertations on deficiencies and opportunities for improvement are made pleasantly readable by anecdotal, but to-the-point, illustrations from Droege's own experiences.

Much of the challenge facing a railroad's operating forces is in meeting the demands of its traffic department. The challenge stems from deficiencies -- in both quantity and quality -- in the tools provided by the engineering and mechanical departments (tracks, rolling stock and facilities). Droege's extensive experience shows in his thoughtful and constructive criticisms, with primary blame often reserved for general management's misallocation of resources.

As a yardmaster, Droege knew how crucial it was that all incoming traffic be properly handled. As a chief dispatcher, he also knew how crucial the functioning of a single engine terminal could be to the flow of an entire region. As a division superintendent, he appreciated the importance of a trainmasters resilience in coping with the crises that frequently occurred whenever traffic was at its heaviest and weather at its worst. In considering how a railroad should best be run, Droege left few skeletons in the closet.

An across-the-board student of railroading, Droege evidently remained a hands-on manager as well. Modestly mentioned as "contributions of the author" are two incidents. First he kept expensive yard crews productive by arranging to swap switchers, on the spot, with freshly-fueled replacements. Second, he planned a somewhat daring elevated service track from which locomotives could drop their ashes directly into cars below.

While it might be expected that *Freight Terminals and Trains* would be limited mostly to nut and bolt considerations, Droege recognized that people make a railroad go, as shown by his discussions of the qualities that distinguish good from merely adequate yardmasters, freight agents and engine terminal foremen. Without taking sides, he also presents arguments for and against the 30-year-old Brown system of discipline, based on merits and demerits, rather than suspensions. In his generally progressive tone, Droege's attitude in such management issues closely resembles that of the Baltimore and Ohio's Daniel Willard.

Perhaps because of his experience as a stenographer, Droege came down most sharply on the endless flow of letters and memoranda of query and explanation exchanged among railroad officers who, he felt should instead be thinking of better ways to run the railroad. This plague he would fight by white-lining (marking for scrapping) typewriters as well as outdated rolling stock.

In 1929 Droege became a vice-president at the New Haven. A year later, he was given responsibility for the railroads New England Transport highway subsidiary. In 1931, after 51 years of railroading -- 27 with the New Haven -- he retired at the age of 70. He died in Florida in 1961, just short of his 101st birthday. Railroading was truly fortunate to have had a man of such vision and ability.

Model Railroading via Droege

What does *Freight Terminals and Trains* offer today's model railroader? We might as well face it -- a big part of creating a model railroad is R&D. Research is conducted so as to understand what we are trying to represent in miniature. Development (typically by a series of disappointments -- or even disasters -- and eventual recoveries) is carried out to push us beyond our initial grasp of modeling. Droege's text provides us with a vast array of information on what freight terminals and trains are like, why they are that way, and how railroaders can or should run them.

For example, we are likely to look for track diagrams of yards and terminals that can fit into our limited space. Droege leads off with a section on track construction and maintenance. He sets forth recommended practices with respect to turnout selection and geometry, track center spacing and ladder angles.

We find that fanning out to the desired number of tracks in as short a distance as possible is just as much a problem for the 12" = 1' people, as it is for the modeler. We are told how much sharpening the ladder angle can help, and we receive specific guidance on one of the biggest length-savers, "three-way" turnouts. Because of differences between the characteristics of model and full-size rolling stock the numbers are different -- No. 7s are considered the minimum -- but the principle still applies.

As for yard track diagrams, the book presents 46 examples, some of "track plan" simplicity and compactness. More are representations of larger yards or terminal complexes. They are useful, but simply too big for direct use in laying out trackage of typical model railroad proportions.

The accompanying text, however, greatly rewards the reader by explaining why the tracks and facilities they serve are so arranged. *Freight Terminals and Trains* suggests, by principle and example, what tracks can and can not be shortened, reduced in number, shared with other functions or omitted in reducing particular railroad operations to basement size.

Freight Terminals

According to the dictionary, a terminal is "a railway facility, not necessarily at the terminus (end) of the line, for assembling, assorting, classifying and relaying trains." On the other hand, a freight terminal is defined as "an arrangement of terminal facilities for handling freight." Costly and non-revenue producing as the freight terminal is, without it there can be no railroad because there will be no profitable line-haul.

By putting *Terminals* first in the title, Droege gives proper recognition to what he considers an often ignored part of the railroad plant. To compete with existing or proposed lines, tracks were extended toward new traffic sources. As a result, the railroad's resources were often too depleted to acquire expensive, close-in real estate and to install well-designed terminal trackage adequate for the anticipated increase in business. This taxed the ingenuity of the next generation of managers -- even on the most successful lines -- in coping with costly yard congestion. Doesn't that have a familiar ring, when in the absence of adequate staging trackage you have to sneak cars off shelves or out of boxes to make up your dream train for a few minutes of running!

Fig. 1 Chicago, Milwaukee & St. Paul Milwaukee, WI freight terminal, May 14, 1919. (CM&StP Photo)

Droege's recommendations for yard design are not presented in a 1-2-3, cookbook format, but rather expressed in more general and useful terms. Besides emphasizing the need during the planning phases for close coordination between the engineering and operating departments, he points out the desirability of including input from the traffic department that is out lining up new business. Without the traffic departments input, the new facility could easily be designed and built based upon the current volume of traffic, rather than the anticipated future volume. This is simply long-term management. In modeling terms, it means keeping an eye on the car types in the stock of unbuilt kits when deciding what traffic source should go into that uncommitted corner area.

A great strength of the book is its in-depth discussion of inland and waterside storage, loading, and unloading facilities. More than a third of the book is devoted to these facilities, from country cattle-chutes, freight houses and grain elevators to the most massive coal and ore piers. Plans and diagrams, many not readily available elsewhere, are detailed enough for track- and space-allocating purposes. With reasonable ingenuity, the complex structures themselves can be credibly modeled.

But they're so BIG! As has often been noted, much of model railroading consists of condensing reality without losing its essence. With this material on too-big prototypes available, we have the incentive to allocate more space for such potent traffic-generators, but also the basis for determining the limits of "selective compression" in working out facilities that will fit on a layout while retaining essential operational capabilities.

For example, consider the team tracks where cars are loaded and unloaded by customers who do not have their own sidings. From an operational standpoint, this is simple and highly productive. They can be any size, from one track-one car, on up. Droege provides abundant data on design alternatives, such as track-center and roadway spacing, approach curvature, crane service, and more as larger ones are contemplated.

Handling Less Than Car Load Freight

About 20 percent of the book relates to the handling of less than carload (L.C.L.) freight. This was a large part of most railroads operations until the final years of the steam era. The car movements they generated were often the backbone of switch-crew and local-freight duties.

Some of Droege's examples may suggest novel but authentic approaches to designing more operation in less space. The two-level freight house found in some cramped, hilly urban areas is a start, but how about tracks on the fourth floor! Faced with a model-like cramped space and an out-of-sync elevation situation after coming across the Mononga-hela River into Pittsburgh, the Wabash conceived such a building, with elevators bringing freight up and down from street level.

More commonplace in the larger cities were separate freight houses. One was for outbound freight which was loaded into cars near the end of the work day and the other for freight inbound which was held for pick-up. For modelers, this presents an opportunity for additional daily moves as cars, emptied at one house, are spotted for loading at the other.

As befits Droege's direct experiences of moving freight in and out of both sides of Manhattan, (as Lehigh Valley's trainmaster at Jersey City and later as general manager of New Haven's western divisions, including operations on Long Island) there is extensive discussion and illustration of waterside terminals and their traffic. Car floats being of less impractical modeling length than most ocean or lake freighters, such operations can make an interesting addition to a layout.

For the ultimate in compactness, consider those team-track and freight-house enclaves served only by water. They were so constrained by the limits of high-priced real estate as to warrant circular loading docks surrounded by two concentric tracks of snap-track radius (90 feet!) and around which cars were uncoupled and individually hauled.

One chapter is devoted to freight transfers -- facilities where L.C.L., arriving from various freight houses in "trap" or "ferry" boxcars, is sorted by destination and re-loaded into "package" cars containing shipments for a single destination. The hectic activity within the transfer does not have to be modeled. However, as another facet of transportation simulation, the timely placing and subsequent routing of the package cars can be duplicated. Spacewise, the advantage of the transfer is that, with railcar loading on both sides, no width need be "wasted" for a wagon or truck driveway.

Classification Yards

The longest chapter in the book concerns classification yards. Here is where modeling requires the greatest degree of condensation. Not only are major classification yards 30 to 60 tracks wide, but, with associated arrival and departure appendages, their three or four mile length exceeds that of most of our main lines. Fortunately, sorting cars into a half dozen, or so, tracks of lengths compatible with our freight trains can still give much of the feel and fascination of the classification process.

Droege discusses, in some depth and with strong feelings, the three ways in which classification can, and was, being done. First was "flat" or "tail" switching, in which the switch engine pushes the string of cars to be classified onto the appointed classification tracks. Second was "summit", "hump" or "gravity" switching in which cars roll downward to their destinations under the control of car riders manning the hand brakes. The third switching option was "poling."

The distinction between flat and summit, or gravity switching is readily appreciated. The speed and cost advantages of the latter are understandable, well documented and applauded by Droege. For many train-watchers, one of the most fascinating sights in all of railroading is a hump yard in action. Here are seen several cuts of cars simultaneously coasting to their different destinations at a steady two or three mile per hour pace, punctuated by periodic impacts as they couple with other cars standing on their appointed tracks.

Fig. 2 Through a system of levers, a **car retarder** applies an equal amount of pressure to each side of the wheel rim slowing down the car. Norfolk & Western's Portsmouth, OH yard. (Gary Rings photo)

And what about a "poling" operation? Still quite popular at the time of Droege's 1925 second edition, its reported efficiency, in comparison to that of flat switching, was strongly supported by the author. Poling requires a second track, parallel to a ladder track that is connected directly to all the body, or classification tracks. A switcher on this track propells each cut by engaging a ten-foot pole diagonally against the poling socket at the rear corner of a car. The action is snappy, since the engine does not have to accelerate the whole string of cars and then pull them back before shoving the next cut.

Lifting the pole into place was both tricky and hazardous. Where poling was a routine procedure it was usual to provide a poling car with a swinging boom. The boom would be positioned against the target car by a man on the footboard. Since the push phase must end as the car peels away from the ladder track onto a body track, the car must be kicked just hard enough to coast the rest of the way to coupling. Wherever possible, poling yards were laid out with a slight slope in one direction so as to aid the classification process.

Space and trackage-wise, modeling a hump or poling yard may not be a great problem. For a poling operation, the only addition is an extra track alongside the ladder for the switcher. In the design of both prototype and model hump yards, the goal is to fan out to the required number of tracks as quickly as possible, and Droege discusses the pros and cons of various ladder arrangements.

With today's slippery, plastic, pointed-axle trucks, the rolling friction of model cars approaches that of the prototype. They may start to roll on about that same half or third of one percent grade. However, the trick is to keep them moving smoothly through turnouts, around curves, over less than perfect trackage and on the level. The laws of physics governing the ratio of inertia of moving objects to their velocity decree that a car must be traveling about (for HO scale) nine times faster. If we are to achieve that "several-cars-in-motion" fascination some artificial assistance will be necessary. A gentle breeze? Undertrack magnets? Psychokinetics? The choice is left to the modeler, but the result should be well worth it.

Droege provides abundant background on other aspects of yard design and operation. He discusses such matters as the hazards and delays that occur whenever switchmen and riders must cross busy tracks and the hump gradient needed to keep cars out of each other's way.

Along with the classification yard go the functions of receiving and departure, typically aligned end-to-end with the classification "bowl" into something far too long for most layouts. Doubling or tripling classified blocks into a departing consist within the classification yard itself is something quite prototypical. This is especially true if the terminal is in an urban area where a separate departure yard would involve prohibitive political opposition or costs. In the model, the less-avoidable arrival yard is likely to shrink to a single switch-lead alongside the main. This is not a significant problem since we are unlikely to be so prototypical as to tie up the track by delaying the start of humping to represent the time required to bleed off brake cylinders, car-by-car.

There are terminal functions, other than classification by destination to be kept in mind. These include holding (for perishable loads awaiting sale and routing), icing, cleaning, seasonal storage, or repair. Droege advises to store cars on tracks outside the high-cost downtown yard area. Model translation: build more shelves if you can't put more single-ended car-storage trackage underneath somewhere.

Engine Terminals

The most vital adjunct to the yard is the engine terminal. With decades of experience on all that can go wrong, Droege gives detailed recommendations that are useful to anyone designing a prototypically-ideal facility. For example, he tells you to locate the pole holding the land end of the electrical power connection to the turntable away from the enginehouse. In the event of a fire, this may be the key to saving as many engines as possible.

A useful check list for anyone planning an engine terminal is a presentation of the time and costs of the many sub-tasks involved in turning a steam locomotive. The relative complexity and importance of the principal components of the facility can also be judged by the space allocated to each in the book: engine house -- 26 pages; coaling -- 20 pages (including factors associated with burning anthracite, bituminous or a mixture); supplying sand -- 3 pages; and ash handling -- 10 pages! (Perhaps we modelers tend to downplay the difficulty of coping with the residue of combustion.)

Freight Trains

The *Trains* aspect of the book's title is primarily covered in two chapters. One chapter deals with the effect of freight train makeup, powering, scheduling and dispatching on transportation efficiency once the goods are aboard. The second describes the operation of time freights. Much of the discussion concerns optimizing the movement of traffic systemwide -- that is, over several divisions.

Model railroads with a single yard are not affected by one of the principal philosophical questions Droege raises. Should cars be assembled to get the train on the road to the next division point as promptly as possible, or should they first be assembled in the blocks so they can travel to their destinations without further classification? The answer, when you consider the urgency of the traffic and the capacity of the yards and their congestion, is, of course, that depends. The chapter on time freight discusses the practicality of classifying time-sensitive traffic to destination so that main trackers can pass intact through one or more division points.

What this does suggest is that in selecting an actual or free-lance segment to model, a subdivision point in which some trains are classified but others pass through unscathed is a good choice. We then have the option of intricate switching when that appeals and the relaxation of uninterrupted main-line running when it doesn't.

How People Run the Railroad

We already use such "railroady" titles and job classifications as superintendent, clerk and paymaster in our National Model Railroad Association organizations, as well as dispatcher, operator, engineer, conductor and brakeman in our model-scale operations. All this is done with varying degrees of authenticity, as dictated by differences in scale and purpose. Not only does *Freight Terminals and Trains* help make our modeling more realistic, but Droege's description of the characteristics of a good yardmaster, trainmaster and enginehouse foreman shows us how capable and dedicated people, working together, can make a railroad run better.

Likewise, in what might seem improbable places, there are many nuggets of information that suggest worthwhile offshoots from more conventional modeling. For example, consider the 13-page chapter, Weighing Freight. Much of it is devoted to platform scales for the freight house. This probably interests only those who are superdetailing and illuminating their building interiors. On the other hand, the location, characteristics and use of track scales not only affect yard design and switching and routing patterns, but effects also show up in other chapters. In attempting to compare the efficiency of yard operations, a higher percentage of cars that require weighing will handicap a terminal if management judges it on the simple basis of cars in and out (Droege says this is unwise). For the small area a scale house adds, it can be a potent action-generator in any scale.

So, keep browsing -- it can be worthwhile.

Freight Terminals and Trains -- Then & Now

Since 1925 when John Droege so definitively set forth the state of the art, what has transpired in the world of freight terminals and trains?

In many aspects, the changes in terminals wrought by the evolution in railroad technology and traffic patterns have been profound. For example, intermodal ("piggyback") freight terminals, virtually non-existent in the 1920's have gone through two generations of design. In the process they have become the largest single class of carload-originating facilities.

In other respects, terminals and trains have evolved only in minor detail since 1925, remaining largely similar in principle and general configuration. For example:

- The geometry of turnouts and ladder trackage remains essentially the same.

- Yard and switch crews still pick up and set out cars, individually, or in blocks, as required.

- Out on the road, as parallel routes are abandoned or severed, trains must still have second or passing tracks to get past each other, although with centralized traffic control single-track routes routinely carry tonnage that would have taxed double or triple-track lines of yesteryear.

- Many of the largest classification yard complexes are gone, but their essential functions remain, taken over by similar installations hundreds of miles away.

- Downtown industrial trackage has disappeared, along with the establishments it served that have died or have been moved to less congested or environmentally restricted sites.

Surprisingly, one number long considered a measure of the relative significance of yard and other subsidiary trackage, has remained remarkably constant. On major U. S. railroads, the ratio of total mileage of track -- first, second, third, siding, yard and terminal -- to the mileage of line has remained between 1.64 and 1.68 to 1 since the late 1920's. More than half the line mileage -- including branches with relatively little siding and yard trackage -- has either been taken over by short lines or abandoned. The remaining multi-track main lines, many of which have been reduced to single track, now carry heavier tonnage and require more supporting trackage.

With short-haul traffic largely shifting to trucks over this same period, the tonnage of rail freight has risen only about 20 percent. However, because of the longer average haul, the ton-mile total is up by 300 percent. Since each ton is loaded and unloaded only once, terminal facilities, whether railroad or shipper owned, represent a smaller part of the freight-moving plant. Over the longer haul, typically involving movement over several routes, efficient classification and interchange yards still remain essential.

Over the period, of course, evolution has not occurred at a steady rate, and the nature of change in handling different commodities has varied greatly. Rapid changes in rail traffic patterns have, in many cases, been driven as much by advances in freight car capabilities or loading and unloading facilities as by changes in sources, production methods, or overall demand for a product. A case in point is the tri-level auto rack. It brought back from the dead rail transportation of new automobiles and with it, a need for entirely different loading and unloading trackage and facilities.

Fig. 3 A view of a freight yard as seen today at Norfolk Southern's Debutts Yard in Chattanooga, TN. (Gregg Ames photo)

Freight Houses and Team Tracks

An example of the relatively sudden elimination of a classic structure is the demise of railroad freight and transfer houses following World War II. Essential for L.C.L. shipments, they became surplus once the general availability of regulated common-carrier trucking allowed railroads to phase out accepting this generally unprofitable traffic. Boxcar-loads of such shipments, consolidated by forwarders in their own facilities, continued to ride the rails.

Some team tracks, where cars could be spotted for shippers who did not have their own sidings, have had a longer life. With the advent of piggyback service though, such deliveries are more likely to take place at bulk transfer terminals, where the railroad, or contractor, provides trackage and facilities specifically for transferring particular classes of commodities from car to truck.

In the case of particularly sensitive commodities, such as plastic pellets which must be transported under controlled conditions, storing a producer's inventory in specialized tank hopper cars until sold may be more economical than providing equivalent warehouse capacity. Special rail yards that cram car-holding trackage into suitably-zoned, low-rent acreage are the answer.

Multi-car and Contract Rate Effects

From the earliest days of government regulation of railroad rates and services, public policy was designed to protect individual producers and shippers from their larger competitors. Regulations decreed that the single carload would be the largest rate-setting unit. Thus, the cost per ton for shipping one car, or a hundred cars, would be the same. Dozens, or even hundreds of carloads of coal, grain or ore headed for a power plant or ship, would obviously have to converge at a single point. The massive unloading or transfer facilities and supporting rail trackage that were required were well developed by the time of Droege's work. There was, however, little incentive for shippers and railroads to work out ways in which better terminal facilities, matched to trainload schedules and a sustained level of traffic, could improve car utilization and thereby save money for everybody.

During the 1970's, reduced multi-car rates became legal and the bulk-commodity specialized-car unit train was born. The result, terminal-wise, was virtually non-stop loading, or unloading, usually in a tightly-curved loop track.

Similarly, contract rates authorized by the Staggers Act in 1980, allowed shippers to negotiate lower rates and higher levels of service in return for such considerations as a long-term guaranteed volume of traffic. One important result was fewer, but longer, private sidings, served by trackmobiles or car-movers, capable of loading 25 or more cars at a time.

Classification Yards

Unit trains, now accounting for practically all of the coal traffic, as well as such seemingly unlikely commodities as orange juice and salt water, travel from origin to destination without classification. Similarly, the classification of intermodal traffic takes place primarily at loading, with the trailers or containers being loaded onto blocks of flatcar platforms headed for their individual destinations. Nevertheless, a large portion of today's rail traffic still moves in blocks of one, or a few cars, going, not from hub city to hub city, but from isolated plants to consumption or distribution points -- from nowhere to nowhere -- via, more often than not, more than one railroad. These loads must be classified at one or more points, even though they will travel most of their journey in freight trains that by-pass many intermediate yards.

In 1924, many yards were arranged for and did most of their classification by poling. Increasingly, the larger yards pushed cars over the hump, but in only a few were the ladder switches thrown mechanically from control towers. Most still relied on switch tenders dashing from one hand-throw to another, as the cars rolled toward them.

The first car retarders went into service in the Gibson Yard of the Indiana Harbor Belt in 1924. They eliminated 60 car riders while essentially substituting 15 retarder operators for an equal number of employees replaced by power-operated switches. Retarder yards soon proliferated, although the 1920s installations required a relatively large number of retarders — sometimes one retarder for each track — controlled from several towers. Latter-day hump yard design does the job with fewer retarders; master retarder at the foot of the hump and a retarder on the lead to each of the groups of 5 to 10 tracks that make up the yard.

Taking into account such factors as the weather, the rollability on straight and curved track of each car or cut, the curvature of the track to which it is headed and the distance to the cars already in that track, the computer target shoots by letting the group retarder release each cut with just the right exit velocity to couple up at a safe speed of less than 4 mph. Except for pulling the pin at the hump, the entire operation, including control of the locomotive during humping, is automatic and monitored by a single operator watching from above in the yard office (As one computer programmer remarked, most of the time the operator could just as well be in the basement, but nobody has had the nerve to let things run blind, so yard offices remain multi-story.)

The changes in traffic patterns have made it possible to concentrate classification at fewer -- but generally larger -- electronic yards. At other junction-point yards, where switching is now largely a matter of exchanging a few large blocks of cars previously assembled at the humps, flat switching becomes acceptably efficient. The arrangement of lead, ladder and body tracks hasn't changed much, but radio and talk-back loud-speakers throughout the yard make the operation smoother.

With these enhancements to flat and hump classification, routine poling dropped out of the picture. Although the last steam locomotives built in the 1940's and first-generation diesel road-switchers still had dimples on their bumper beams or end sills to accept a push pole in an emergency, yard poling was no longer a possibility when poling pockets on freight cars were phased out after World War II.

Fig. 4 Mechanized hump yard design rapidly developed a grouped-track configuration, allowing control with a minimum number of retarders. The Twin-hump Rice Yard in Waycross, Georgia with weigh-in-motion scales operates either as separate side-by-side yards humping simultaneous or as a single yard with twice as many classification tracks.

Intermodal Terminals

When piggyback traffic became significant in the early 1960s, railroads installed simple loading ramps for "circus" (endwise) loading trailers on one, or a string of, bridge-plate-equipped flatcars. Many sites loaded only a few trailers a day, so their loads would most likely be moved in ordinary freight trains, providing uncompetitively slow service. At busier terminals the circus loading process was too slow and not conducive to pre-classifying trailers by destination.

As a result, by 1980, top- or side-loading with gantry crane or "piggypacker" in mechanized terminals generally supplanted circus loading. Only hub terminals can provide the volume of lifts necessary to justify the expense of mechanization. The concentration of service at the terminals that are still active (fewer than 300) has fostered the scheduling of dedicated intermodal trains providing competitively fast service. Design of intermodal terminals, especially those handling marine containers arriving in shipload quantities, has evolved along with the double-stack railcars. The goal is to move the boxes more directly between ship or highway and railcar.

Engine Terminals

In the latter days of steam, the ability of locomotives to operate over longer runs between servicing was beginning to reduce significantly the number of active engine terminals. Dieselization, eliminating the need for supplying large quantities of water and solid fuel to the locomotives and disposing of ashes by the carload, further changed the design requirements for engine terminals. Trackage requirements dwindled to those needed to allow the largely interchangeable units to be rearranged into consists for their next assignments. Fueling could even be done on the main line. This left engine sand the major supply concern and periodic required inspections the main need for in-house work between overhauls. The result was the demolition of most, if not all, of the turntable-served roundhouses of yore.

With reliable, high-adhesion, wide-cab locomotives accommodating the entire two-person train crews and putting out up to 6,000 horsepower, a back-to-back, two-unit locomotive has become an overkill on many main-line assignments. Dispatching trains with a single unit again becomes feasible, thus bringing back the need for a way to point this definitely single-ended machine in the right direction. Perhaps some of those turntable pits should not have been filled in after all.

The Freight Train

What has happened to the design of freight trains in these years, and therefore to the trackage and train control systems needed to assemble, expedite and receive them? Since the late 1920s, train length has gone from an average of 47 to 67 cars, with most of the increase occurring before 1950. With the average length of haul approaching 700 miles, the proportion of train miles accumulated by the relatively short local freights that pick up and set out cars has decreased. However, with the weight of the average car in the train -- loaded or empty -- rising from 35 to 66 tons, average train tonnage has increased steadily from 1,600 to more than 5,000 tons. Average speed over the line -- which in recent years includes terminal delays -- rose from 13 to 19 mph by 1960 and has since leveled off in the 20 to 22 mph range.

The net result has been a six-fold increase in the amount of transportation a train produces for each hour it occupies a main track or passing siding. Thus, for a given level of business, there is correspondingly less need for double track, but increased pressure on the maintenance forces to keep that single track in shape within narrowing windows of allowable on-track work time.

The number of freight trains traversing the average mile of line per day near the start of this era (1929) was 7.5. It fell to less than 6 by 1960. With subsequent abandonment or downgrading of many parallel lines and with increased traffic, it has risen to about 12 a day. In some cases it has brought back the congestion problems that prompted much of Droege's concern. Don't let a train out onto the line until it has some place to go, and be sure there is receiving yard capacity to get it in the clear when it gets there, he admonished.

Recent practice has been to increase the track center spacing for double track and passing tracks beyond the 13 to 14 foot standards. Some yard trackage is now even more widely spaced to allow inspection vehicles to operate.

From a practical standpoint, freight cars can not get any wider and bulk commodity cars can not get much taller. As a result, today's 100-ton hopper is almost twice as long as the 50 ton car of the 1920's (55 vs. 32 feet). Intermodal, auto rack and high-cube boxcars are about 91 ft. long over the couplers, leaving the 40 ft. boxcar extinct.

Therefore, while the number of cars per train has stalled, train length continues to grow. Passing-track length has become a major factor affecting the traffic capacity on single-track routes, amplifying the value of double-stack equipment. Passing tracks are being lengthened, but because the existing sidings often were already as long as convenient, considering such impediments as grade crossings, high fills, bridges or deep cuts, this is often a slow and expensive proposition.

Today, the most visible change in the freight train has been the substitution of the end-of-train monitoring device for the caboose. This has provided only a minor reduction in train tonnage but a significant saving in yard switching hours and supporting trackage.

Few can predict the future with any precision. Let us simply hope, and assume, that freight trains will continue playing a vital role in our continent's commerce with interesting evolutionary changes that will spark the imagination of today's and future modelers everywhere.

John Armstrong
Silver Spring, Maryland
July 1998

FREIGHT TERMINALS
AND TRAINS

BY

JOHN A. DROEGE

General Manager, N. Y. N. H. and H. R R. Co.

SECOND EDITION
SECOND IMPRESSION

McGRAW-HILL BOOK COMPANY, INC.

NEW YORK: 370 SEVENTH AVENUE

LONDON: 6 & 8 BOUVERIE ST., E. C. 4

1925

THE MAPLE PRESS COMPANY, YORK, PA.

PREFACE

Since 1912, when "Freight Terminals and Trains" was published, replacing and enlarging its predecessor, "Yards and Terminals," the many interesting developments in the field of transportation have necessitated this revision. Some new ideas have been advanced which have stood the acid test of time and there has been development and refinement of earlier recognized methods. The basic principles heretofore recorded governing the design and operation of railroad facilities have generally remained unchanged. Where warranting more than passing mention, full descriptions and views of recently designed facilities, typifying new developments, have been included. Chapters on "Electrical Operation" and "Integration of Freight Transportation" have been added, reviewing the progress made in the use of electricity as a means of train propulsion, and treating of the widely discussed question—the use of adaptations of the motor truck to supplement rail transportation. The companion volume "Passenger Terminals and Trains" treats more particularly of passenger service and facilities which necessarily interlock to some extent with those described in this volume. The object is to produce two volumes covering the whole field of operation of freight and passenger train service, the design, construction and maintenance of terminals and accessories, with a discussion of the plans of organization and operating methods, while avoiding unnecessary duplication.

This book is essentially a treatise on freight transportation in all its ramifications. The subject is treated from the viewpoint of the engineers who plan, build and maintain, and the officers who operate the various plants which are cogs in the great machine. The importance of the freight station, where the freight is received or delivered and cared for prior or subsequent to road movement, as well as the responsibilities and methods of the agent are recognized. The viewpoint of the yardmaster and his subordinates is developed at length; as is that of the trainmaster and train forces, on whom devolve the safe, expeditious and economical movement of trains. The mechanical department is considered, and the important relation which the engine terminal and its operation bear to train and yard service is discussed in detail. The attitude and problemy of the management, responsible for favorable net returns, are constantsl kept in mind.

Because of the expressions of many readers of the former editions on the value of the many detailed descriptions of yards, terminals and equipment, it was deemed unwise to curtail them. No two terminals are alike in their physical and traffic characteristics.   Every illustration of successful design or description of good operating methods is of assistance to the railroad man who is seeking new ideas to help solve his problems.   This is particularly true where original and unique ideas and features occur.

In a field where there is such a diversity of opinion and practice and where "standard practice" is yet to be established, it seemed advisable to include all possible information and to quote freely from the views of experts, both those confirming and opposing the views of the author. For such quotations, references and acknowledgment has usually been made in the text.   The author's appreciation is due to the Railway Age, Railway Review, Engineering News-Record and other technical and railroad periodicals and to railroad officers and others who have rendered assistance.   Use has been made of committee reports, codes and manuals of the American Railway and American Railway Engineering Associations.

Assistance in the preparation of Chapters IV, XXI, XXII and XXIII, XXVI, and XXXI, respectively, as well as helpful suggestions on other parts of the book, were received from C. B. Breed, Professor of Railway and Highway Engineering, Massachusetts Institute of Technology; F. C. Horner of the General Motors Company; G. Marks, Assistant to General Manager of the New York, New Haven and Hartford Railroad Company, E. C. Calkins, Superintendent of Equipment, Fruit Dispatch Company, and S. Withington, Electrical Enginneer of the New York, New Haven and Hartford Railroad Company.   Helpful comments and criticisms were obtained from C. W. Foss, of the Railway Age, F. J. Brackett of the General Motors Company, George F. Hand, General Assistant Engineer and E. T. Hyland, Chief Transportation Clerk of the New York, New Haven and Hartford Railroad, J. E. Slater, Professor of Transportation, University of Illinois, Major E. C. Church of the Port of New York Authority and Colonel Charles DeLano Hine, consulting railroad expert.

J. A. D.

New York, N. Y.
October, 1925.

CONTENTS

FREIGHT TERMINALS AND TRAINS

CHAPTER I

THE TERMINAL PROBLEM

There were in the United States 249,231 miles of first track, 32,465 of second track, 3,002 of third track, 2,449 of fourth track and 113,839 of yard and side tracks—a total of 400,986 track-miles on Dec. 31, 1922. For every 3 miles of railroad there is in use today 1 mile of switching or terminal tracks. A glance at these figures indicates clearly that the terminal feature of railway operations is very important. The switching mileage of some of the larger roads reaches as high as 35 and 40 per cent. of the entire number of revenue train-miles. With the general increase in business handled and in density of traffic, and with the more insistent demands of the public for quicker movement and delivery, the difficulties of the problem will increase rather than decrease. The importance of terminals and terminal operation, therefore, justifies the most careful and comprehensive study.

The following statistics, based on 1922 figures of the Insterstate Commerce Commission are surprising to one who has not studied the results, indicating as they do: (1) that only 54 per cent. of the capacity of freight cars is utilized; and (2) that the average number of miles each freight car is moved per day is ridiculously low.

On Dec. 31, 1922, the railroads of the United States had in service 2,355,225 freight cars having an average capacity of 42.5 tons each. These cars carried 1,908,556,000 tons of freight an average distance of 178 miles. Altogether, the cars made 21,205,235,000 miles, of which approximately 70 per cent. were loaded, and the total ton-miles amounted to 341,018,361,000. Dividing the total ton-miles by the total freight car-miles, it will be seen that the average load per car was but 16.1 tons and per loaded car about 23 tons, or only 54 per cent. of the average car capacity.

The mileage of yard tracks and sidings in the United States in 1922 was 28.6 per cent. of the total mileage, while in the Eastern District it was 35.4 per cent. in the Southern District 26.9 per cent. and in the Western District 25.0 per cent. In the twenty two years 1900 to 1922 it increased as a whole from 20.1 to 28.6 per cent.; in the Eastern District from 25.6 to 34.4 per cent.; in the Southern District from 16.0 to 26.9

1

per cent. and in the Western from 17.1 to 25 per cent. These figures clearly show the importance of the terminal problem with relation to road movements. That the relative increase of the percentage of miles of yard tracks and sidings was 42.3 per cent. for the country as a whole in this period, while it ranged from 34.4 per cent. for the Eastern to 46.2 per cent. for the Western and 68.1 per cent. for the Southern tells a story of short-sightedness years ago, in not providing for necessary expansion where it was most needed and before industrial development and increased property values rendered it almost prohibitive.

The Interstate Commerce Commission's preliminary figures for 1923 indicates for larger railroads:

Mileage of 176 roads reporting....................	280,688
Revenue freight cars owned.....................	2,317,609
Freight car mileage............................	25,418,630,774
Average miles per car per day...................	27.8
Per cent. loaded car mileage....................	64.0
Average net ton-miles per car mile..............	16.2
Average net ton-miles per loaded car mile........	25.2
Average net ton-miles per car day...............	509
Average miles per hour for trains in freight service...	10.9

Note.—Net ton miles represent the number of tons of 2000 pounds of freight moved one mile.

Since the average speed of a freight train from terminal to terminal, including road delay, is only slightly better than 10 m.p.h., it is plain that two to three hours in a train will give a freight car the average mileage per day shown by the above statistics. This indicates that freight cars are in motion just about 10 per cent. of the time, and, since but 54 per cent. of their capacity is utilized, when loaded, irrespective of empty-car movement, a clear indication is given of the need for railroads to pay particular attention to methods and facilities which will on one hand increase the percentage of car capacity utilized and on the other hand reduce the delay to freight cars in loading, unloading and movement through yards and terminals.

The study of the question of consolidation of railroads should be primarily for its effect, favorable or adverse, on the terminal question. That is the big if not the whole question. This problem is increasing in importance and in difficulty of solution. It is a comparatively simple matter to build a railway from one point to another of sufficient capacity and with enough equipment to move all of the traffic which can possibly be offered, but it is a much more difficult problem to provide adequate terminals for the distribution of that traffic upon its arrival in large centers of industry and population. In other words, there is only one serious technical problem in the transportation industry of the United States, and that is the terminal problem.

The average gross freight revenue per ton-mile on all the railroads of the country in 1923 was 1.116, or a little over 1 ct., the handling at terminals absorbing a large part of the revenue. While there is no accurate separation of accounting, the terminal costs of car switching and the loading or unloading of l.c.l. freight at both origin and destination, and sometimes at one or more transfer points en route, are by far the most costly part of the transportation service. This is particularly true in the case of short-haul freight.

There are 12 railroads, exclusive of purely local enterprises, entering in the Port of New York. Nine of these have their railheads in New Jersey, including the B. & O. at Staten Island. There is only one all-rail freight connection to Manhattan Island. Exclusive of Hudson River and Long Island Sound vessels, some 9,000 vessels clear New York Port annually. There are, moreover, nearly one hundred transportation companies (rail and water) having freight stations in New York City. Some of these companies have as many as six or seven different stations. Figure 1 is a map of New York City and its harbor, showing the railroads entering it and their yards and terminals. A recent casual visit showed 35 loaded trucks in line in front of one dock on West Street, New York, and this is not uncommon. It is claimed that hundreds of these trucks are kept waiting in line, in this city, from two to six hours a day during seasons of heavy traffic movement. The loss due to congested and inadequate terminals from this item alone is enormous. This problem is discussed in detail in Chap. XXXII.

Handling freight traffic in and through New York is doubtless the most complicated terminal problem in the world, and from it alone many lessons may be learned. Since New York is the greatest port of entrance to this country, the increasing volume of traffic, together with the growing demands for quicker movement, would in themselves present endless operating and traffic problems. But added to this is the constant tendency on the part of industries and warehouses to crowd the water's edge to an extent which either necessitates the confinement of railroad lines to their present limits or compels enormous expenditures to secure more territory, as has been done by the Pennsylvania Railroad. The view shown in Fig. 2 is characteristic of the railroads' rapidly vanishing foothold in New York City.

The shore lines of this port measure about 800 miles and embrace the largest body of sheltered waters of any port in the world, and through it passes nearly one-half the foreign commerce of the United States. Recent figures show 125 million tons of freight arriving and leaving the port yearly, two-thirds by rail and one-third by water. The annual food requirements alone would, if loaded in freight cars, require 4,020 miles of freight cars, or one train extending from New York to San Francisco and another from New York to Chicago. One and one-quarter

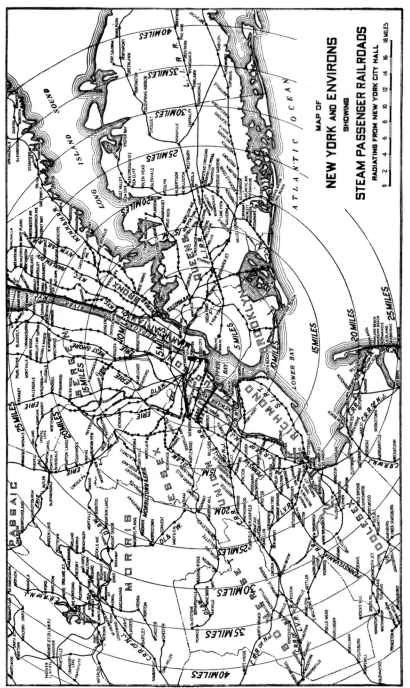

Fig. 1.

million tons of dairy products, 500,000 tons of meat and poultry, 100,000 tons of fish and 70,000 tons of coffee and tea are consumed in New York annually.

Handling New York's freight traffic requires an enormous water fleet of tugs, car floats, lighters and barges, with an extensive system of water-front piers and docks and float bridges with supporting freight yards for classifying, delivering and forwarding freight cars. The railroads and terminal companies alone operate some 1,873 vessels in New York Harbor, including 56 ferry boats, 158 tugs, 371 car floats, 38 steam lighters, 388

FIG. 2.—The only freight yard on Manhattan Island—West 69th Street.

derrick lighters and 862 covered lighters, grain barges, coal boats and miscellaneous craft. Including the tugs, lighters and barges operated by the steamship lines and the numerous outside companies, there are no doubt fully 10,000 boats engaged in transferring freight in New York Harbor. Within the harbor limits there are about 50 dry docks and plants for marine construction and repairing, representing an investment of $10,000,000 and, in connection with the movement of freight on car floats either interchanged between railroads or to and from the Manhattan pier stations, some 86 float bridges are operated.

To show what has been done and what may be expected in the way of future development, the following figures of the length of available wharf berths along the New York Harbor water front are given:

	Water-front miles	Length of wharves
Manhattan...........................	44	93
Brooklyn.............................	132	197
Queens..............................	116	132
Richmond............................	51	69
Bronx...............................	105	113
Total..............................	448	604
New Jersey Shore—Amboy to Fort Lee...	30	96
Total..............................	478	700

The Department of Docks and Ferries collects from leases and wharfage more than $5,500,000 annually. In addition to the thousands of tons of freight handled by lighters, there are some 2,000 cars handled on floats daily between Canal Street on the North River and Jackson Street on the East River. The usual charge for lighterage, as prorated, is 3.6 cts. per 100 lb., but in many instances the actual cost is greatly in excess of the revenue.

The railroads carry about 63,000,000 tons of freight into and out of New York annually, of which 11,000,000 is moved all-rail, 11,000,000 by car float and 41,000,000 by lighter in addition to 12,000,000 tons of freight interchanged between railroads and not included in the total.

About 45,000,000 tons of foreign commerce pass through New York annually, of which 75 per cent. requires drayage and the remainder lightering. Figure 3 is a typical New York water scene looking northward up West Street along the North River.

It is safe to predict that in time freight will be moved continuously into and through New York through river tunnels. Passenger tunnels are in operation and have demonstrated the feasibility of similarly handling freight. Serious consideration is being given to the possibility of motor truck handling from outlying railheads. Large, or larger, classification yards will be built on the Hackensack meadows, in New Jersey, a few miles from the Hudson River.

The plan of the Port of New York Authority contemplates a tunnel connection across New York Bay and there is also now under construction by the City of New York a freight and passenger tunnel connecting Staten Island with the Brooklyn shore. Both of these projects will provide a rail connection with the New York Connecting Route, which leads over the Hell Gate Bridge into New England.

The movement of perishable fruits and early vegetables from the South and West has increased rapidly from year to year, this freight requiring prompt and specialized handling to deliver it to its destination in good condition. This is made possible only by cheap and prompt transportation, and the extent to which this traffic may develop is difficult to overestimate.

Fig. 3.—North River water front—New York.

It is well stated by Wellington, in his "Economic Theory of Railway Location," that in planning a railroad there are three ends to be attained:

1. To sell all the transportation possible.
2. To dispense with all the train-miles possible.
3. To reduce the cost of running trains per mile.

As respects freight traffic, rates must in the long run be made equal not simply from station to station, but from the door of the consignor to the door of the consignee; in other words, all additional cost for cartage or switching service and something more as compensation for the trouble (usually a very considerable addition) must be borne by the railroad, before it is in a position to compete at all.

The terminal problems confronting railroad managers are usually those which involve the correction of errors previously made or, more accurately, the providing of facilities at an enormous cost which could have been furnished at a moderate cost had the terminals been properly designed when the roads were built. In some instances these conditions were due to lack of foresight. In many cases, however, they were due to the paramount desire of running a line to a large city and the failure to provide sufficient funds to carry the line well into the terminal city. Or, in the words of Wellington:

> Had it not so often happened that roads which have expended millions for the construction of long lines to a certain place have then begrudged or failed to raise the necessary additional money to carry their line into it, contenting themselves with hanging to the skirts of the town somewhere where they can be reached by horse cars or hacks and drays, it would seem incredible that business corporations could so frequently commit an act of folly which can fairly be paralleled with that of building a long bridge and erecting every span but one—assuming, on account of some difficulty with foundations, or what not, that a ferry would be good enough for that because it would be "such a little one."

There have been notable exceptions and these are the lines which are now successful in making money on freight traffic even at the prevailing low rates. As a result of this policy the railroads are now adding to, revising or remodeling existing yards and terminals and constructing new ones. For this reason the "ideal" or "model" yard is mainly interesting, in that it affords a guide for remodeling, adapting or extensively revising existing inadequate yards.

The relative importance of terminals and main line has been given, taking into account the cost of operating and the miles of track in use. Viewed from the standpoint of the amount of capital invested, the importance of terminals is even greater. The terminals alone represent a greater amount of money than all the remainder of the properties of the roads. This statement is true even when smaller or intermediate stations are omitted and only the great water terminals and general internal distributing centers, known as "division terminals" or "yards," are included. Their relative financial value in the countries of Europe is necessarily even greater than in the United States. In England alone hundreds of millions have been spent in remedying initial errors to enable successful transportation lines to reach the centers or interiors of great cities. Millions have been spent by the larger roads in improving their various terminal points, and, apparently, such additions will always have to be made.

One of two great railway systems in the Far Northwest, in competitive railway building, is said to have expended between $11,000,000 and $12,000,000 for terminals in a single coast city to care for an extension 180 miles long, which amounts to a charge of $64,000 per mile of line for terminals alone. Terminals for a new four-track trunk line in New York City would cost anywhere from $125,000,000 to $150,000,000. Even on the Jersey water front they would cost $75,000,000. This amounts to from $75,000 to $150,000 per mile for the tide-water terminal alone, for a line from Chicago to New York.

In Chicago, the problem is presented in a form more concentrated than in many other places. The business district comprises about 1½ square miles. It is almost completely surrounded by railway terminals, 25 trunk lines, having their freight and passenger stations ranged around this one point. Naturally, with these railroad terminals depositing their enormous volume of freight in so circumscribed an area, the conditions soon became unbearable. It was estimated that 112,000 tons of freight a day are handled at the terminals around the business section.

To relieve this congestion, the Chicago freight subway was begun in September, 1901. It is the only subway in the world designed especially to relieve the freight congestion of the streets. The tunnel is egg-shaped, with concrete walls 10 in. thick and a 14-in. bottom. The height of the tubes is 7.5 ft., width 6 ft., inside measurement, and their average depth below the street level is 40 ft. The work of the construction went ahead rapidly, the ground being of a character favorable to rapid progress. The first 5 miles were built in two months. However account of its limited capacity and lack of connections little car load business is handled.

Most of our larger freight terminals are examples of evolution from smaller to larger yards. Like Topsy, they "jus' growed." Additional tracks were hung on wherever there happened to be a vacant piece of land and where the least grading was required. In many cases it was necessary to get any additional track facilities that could be had and at any place available, to avoid congestion or blockade on the line. In other cases the situation was due to lack of foresight. The bill has been paid many times over.

To reduce the number of cars in service, a road must handle them promptly. They must be moved over the line at the economical speed which has been found suited to the characteristics of each part of a line. The penalty for detentions can now be figured down to a penny. It does not require much detention, due to congestion in terminals, or awkward or reverse movements, to run into large amounts in a month.

One railroad company took records on three separate occasions and found that from 81 to 84 per cent. of all the cars on the road, at the time the records were taken, were not in motion. In the ordinary course of business, cars in good order stand in yards from three to ten hours. This is about the time needed to haul them to the next division terminal. In busy periods, then, it would seem that cars in good order should be kept in motion about half the time; but they are not, and there is a field for an immense profit by working to approximate this ideal condition. For example, in a terminal handling 4,000 cars per day, an hour's reduction in standing, effected by improvement either in design or operation, makes a daily saving of the time of 166 cars, which, at the present per

diem rates, amounts to $166 per day. An expenditure of nearly
$600,000 to overcome this would be justified.

The detrimental effect of the yard aptly described as one where "all
tracks lead into it none run out of it," may readily be imagined and the
loss it occasions the operating road estimated.   In a meeting of the Association of Transportation and Car Accounting Officers, one of the largest
roads in the country testified that the average time of all freight cars in
terminals on its line had been 18 hours.   This it succeeded in reducing
to 13 and hoped eventually to get down to five.   The five hours' reduction
effected was remarkable and remunerative   It does not require an
exceptionally large yard, in these days of heavy freight movement, to
handle an average of 1,000 cars per day.   The five hours per day saved
would represent 5,000 car-hours, equivalent to 213 additional cars in
service, which, valued at $3,000 each, are worth to the railroad company
$639,000.   To figure on the earning capacity of these 213 cars, the rail-
road would secure an additional revenue, during times of brisk traffic, of
$400 to $500 per day.   To attain this end in half a dozen main and divisional terminals would justify the expenditure of considerable thought
and money.   Anywhere from 60 to 85 per cent. of the freight cars on a
line, at a given time, are not in motion.

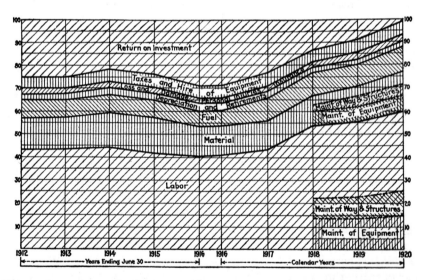

Fig. 4.—Proportionate distribution of railway operating revenues of class I railroads.

As already stated, a modern box car, with its air-brake and other equipment, costs about $3,000.   The annual cost of maintenance, barring
accidents, is somewhere between $200 to $300.   A cheaply constructed
warehouse will provide the same volume of storage space as a box car with
much less expense and its maintenance cost is about one-fifth that

of the box car. There are shippers, nevertheless, who deem it a great injustice not to be permitted to use freight equipment freely for storage or warehouse purposes.

The difficulties under which our railways work to meet the increasing cost of labor and of all material required in their construction, maintenace and operation, while freight rates do not increase, but in many instances decrease, is graphically shown in Fig. 4 for the class I railroads for the period 1912 to 1920.

The necessity for revising terminal facilities is made impressive by a study of those instances which increase the cost of a railway's living, as the terminals usually present the greatest opportunities for operating economies, not only in themselves but in their considerable effect in reducing the cost per train-mile on the road by furnishing easier movement into and out of yards and better train classifications.

A recognized authority[1] said:

It is safe to say that the expense or economy of any system of transportation, whether by water or by rail, depends almost solely upon the efficiency of its terminal operations. The big costs are the terminals. The voyage of a ship, the line haul of a railroad, are respectively the cheapest forms of transportation that exist. It may also be said that once cargo is stowed in the hold of a ship or loaded in a freight car the length of the trip is no great matter.

And further—some goods were shipped from San Francisco to Brooklyn; on arrival taken to a warehouse and shortly afterwards telegraphed for to fill a sudden demand on the Pacific coast, the cost of trucking to and from the warehouse, neglecting all storage charges—exceeded the water rate from New York back to San Francisco in the Panama Canal.

The broad-minded, liberal and competent engineer of today gets all the information to be had from practical operating men before he plans his yard and avoids making many of the blunders of the past which so seriously impede operation. It is not necessary to go a thousand miles from anywhere to find track scales erected by an engineer in the middle of a 50-car double-end connected track, obviously causing loss of track space, obstructing and delaying movements of engines and cars. The yard was one of the most awkward and extravagant to operate; the yardmaster asked for scales because he needed them—and he got them. This is merely typical of the many errors made because of a lack of cooperation. There is an improvement in cooperation between engineering and operating men today. An engineer is not permitted to arrange for the construction of a manufacturing plant or a steamship until he has the views of the men who are required to operate it afterward; neither should he construct a terminal or yard, the operating cost of which is usually dependent on proper design and in which errors are more difficult and costly to correct. A designer—be he the designer of a house, a yacht,

[1] Major Elihu Church, Transportation Engineer, Port of New York, authority.

a machine or a yard—needs all the practical knowledge and light to be had on the subject. "Sunlight kills germs."

Stopping, starting and detaining freight trains are extremely costly, and much of this waste is due to inadequate and inefficient terminals. The cost of stopping freight trains seems to have been given little study and is not fully understood. Many trainmasters, most train dispatchers, nearly all maintenance-of-way men and yardmen seem to labor under the impression that shutting off the engine throttle and again opening it is about all there is to the performance. In some cases they make an allowance for a few minutes of lost time. Exact figures covering the cost of stopping a freight train are not to be had. It depends on the characteristics of road, grades, weight of train and other operating conditions.

With the enormous strides that have been made in railway operations, costs have also increased and $5.00 may be accepted as a reasonably fair average cost of stopping a train.

At the meeting of the Signal Section of the American Railway Association, March, 1924, the results of a study were presented, showing that delays to freight trains cost $21.07 per hour, or, that is, for 20 freight trains the delays amounted to 1.25 hours per trip aggregating $526.75 per day, or $192,264 per year.

While operating officers may, from actual observation, appreciate the importance of, and the necessity for correcting yard designs or adapting them to meet increased or changed traffic conditions, it is usually desirable to place an actual money value on such changes or improvements. As this is largely guesswork and dependent on so many conditions, it is more difficult to estimate approximately than would be any other line of railroad improvement or betterment work. Some comparatively slight changes in tracks, connections or switches may be made by which, through reduced interference, cutting out lost motion or by more direct or fewer switching movements, a yard shift may be dispensed with. Estimating the expense of such an engine with its crew, fuel, supplies, etc. at $45 per day of eight hours, there is a saving of $16,425 per year, which, capitalized at 5 per cent. represents $328,500, from which it would appear that any lesser amount could profitably be expended to attain this result.

If, by correcting errors or improving the track layout a saving can be effected in the time of the crews of, say, five hours a day in the aggregate (and this, in a large yard, is ordinarily looked upon as a comparatively small matter), there would be saved $6,387.50 per year, assuming the time of the road crew to be worth $3.50 per hour and leaving out the value of the engine or the demand for it. This saving represents the interest at 5 per cent. on $127,750.

It should not be assumed that an amount for the corrections or additions may profitably be expended merely because it is known that a saving in operation may be effected representing the interest on this amount, unless it is probable that the saving will be continuous. In this character of work the greater part of the money spent is for labor and much of it for material of a nature tending to deteriorate. It is, therefore, impossible to recover the principal, should the earnings cease.

A study of what has been done and of what is being done is essential. It has been aptly said. "Our fundamental need is not the elucidation of the mysterious, but an appreciation of the significance of the obvious."

CHAPTER II

TERMS AND DEFINITIONS

For many years there was diversity among railroad men as to the usage and meaning of terms, and the names of certain parts of railroad equipment. The author recalls numerous instances when he was compelled to ask conductors or yardmasters whether, in telegraphing for a "pair of trucks," one truck was wanted or two. The Master Car Builders, Association helped out mankind generally, and the railroad world particularly, when it caused the "Car Builders' Dictionary" to be prepared and published. While there are still a few conductors and yardmasters who will ask for "a pair" of trucks when only one is wanted, it is possible to educate them, and there is now an authority for their enlightenment.

The American Railway Engineering Association, made the following list of terms, with accompanying definitions, relating to terminals or yards. The word "terminal" has been taken to include all the facilities provided for terminal work on a large or small scale, while the word "yard" relates only to the one set of tracks which were used for the switching or storage of cars. Following are the definitions given by that society:

TERMINALS

Terminal.—An assemblage of facilities provided by a railway at a terminus or at intermediate points on its line for the purpose of assembling, assorting, classifying and relaying trains.

Freight Terminal.—The arrangement of terminal facilities for the handling of freight traffic.

Passenger Terminal.—The arrangement of terminal facilities for the handling of passenger traffic.

YARDS

Yard.—A system of tracks within defined limits provided for making up trains, storing cars and other purposes, over which movements not authorized by time table or by train order may be made, subject to prescribed signals, rules or special instructions.

Receiving Yard.—A yard for receiving trains.

Separating Yard.—A yard adjoining a receiving yard, in which cars are separated according to district, commodity or other required order.

Classification Yard.—A yard in which cars are classified or grouped in accordance with requirements.

Departure or Forwarding Yard.—A yard in which cars are assembled in trains for forwarding.

Storage Yard.—A yard in which cars are held awaiting disposition.

Holding Yard.—A convenient relief yard for holding cars or trains for immediate use.

Gravity Yard.—A yard in which the classification of cars is accomplished by gravity.

Coach Yard.—A yard in which passenger-train cars are assembled, classified or prepared for service.

Assisting Grade.—The inclination given to tracks of a yard to facilitate the movement of cars.

Poling Yard.—A yard in which the movement of cars is accomplished by the use of a pole operated by an engine on an adjacent parallel track.

Summit or Hump Yard.—A yard in which the movement of cars is accomplished by pushing them over a summit, beyond which they run by gravity.

TRACKS

Body Track.—Each of the parallel tracks of a yard, upon which cars are switched or stored.

Ladder Track.—A track connecting successively the body tracks of a yard.

Lead Track.—An extended track connecting either end of a yard with the main track.

Interchange Track.—A designated track on which cars are delivered or received, as between railroads.

Drill Track.—A track connecting with the ladder track and used for movements in yard switching.

Running Track.—A track reserved for movement through a yard.

Cross-over Track.—A track connecting two adjacent tracks.

Relief Track.—An extended siding long enough to allow an inferior train to continue running.

Stub Track.—A track connected with another one at one end only.

Spur Track.—A stub track of indefinite length diverging from a main line or track.

House Track.—A track alongside of (or entering) a freight house, and used for cars receiving or delivering freight at the house.

Switching District.—That portion of a railway at a large terminal into which cars are moved, and from which they are distributed to the various side tracks and spurs to freight houses and manufacturing establishments served from this district by yard or switching engines.

Industrial Track.—A track serving one or more industries.

Team Track.—A track where freight is transferred directly between cars and wagons.

Note.—In a typical yard there will be several tracks, devoted to special purposes, varying with local conditions. These will include caboose tracks, scale tracks, coaling tracks, ashpit tracks, bad-order tracks, repair tracks, icing tracks, feed tracks, stock tracks, transfer tracks, sand tracks, depressed tracks, and so on.

Rail and Water Terminal.—A terminal where freight is transferred between railway cars and boats.

Wye.—A triangular arrangement of tracks used for turning engines, cars or trains.

Transfer Slip.—A protected landing place for transfer boats with adjustable apron or bridge for connecting tracks on the land with those on the transfer boats.

Incline.—An inclined track (or tracks) at a protected landing place, with adjustable apron and cable for connecting to the tracks on a transfer boat.

Siding.—A track auxiliary to the main track for meeting or passing trains, limited to the distance between two adjacent telegraph stations.

PIERS

Lighterage Pier.—An open or covered pier at which freight is transferred directly between cars and boats.

Export Pier.—A pier at which freight is unloaded and stored, mainly for shipment on ocean or coasting vessels.

Station Pier.—A pier having no rail connections, where freight is received and delivered by transfer boats.

Coal Pier.—An open pier where coal is transferred from cars to vessels' or barges.

The definitions prepared by the American Railway Association relating to main tracks and train movements also have bearing upon yard work, and some of them are given below:

Engine.—A machine propelled by any form of energy and used in train or yard service.

Motor.—A car propelled by any form of energy and used in train or yard service.

Train.—An engine or motor, or more than one engine or motor, coupled, with or without cars, displaying markers.

Regular Train.—A train authorized by a time-table schedule.

Section.—One of two or more trains running on the same schedule displaying signals or for which signals are displayed.

Extra Train.—A train not authorized by a time-table schedule. It may be designated as:

Extra, for any extra train, except work extra.

Work extra, for work extra.

Superior Train.—A train having precedence over another train.

Train of Superior Right.—A train given precedence by train order.

Train of Superior Class.—A train given precedence by time table.

Train of Superior Direction.[1]—A train given precedence in the direction specified by time table as between opposing trains of the same class.

---

[1] Superiority by direction is limited to single track. Some roads discard the "superiority by direction" and use what is commonly termed the "positive meet." Under this arrangement, trains of the same class wait at meeting points indefinitely, unless the "meet" is changed by train order. This method seems to make for safety and economy, requiring fewer train orders and reducing train dispatching. Most operating officers will concede the advantage, from almost every standpoint, of a "meet"

Time Table.—The authority for the movement of regular trains subject to the rules. It contains the classified schedules of trains, with special instructions relating thereto.

Schedule.—That part of a time table which prescribes class, direction, number and movement for a regular train.

Main Track.—A track extending through yards and between stations, upon which trains are operated by time table or train order, or both, or the use of which is governed by block signals.

Single Track.—A main track upon which trains are operated in both directions.

Double Track.—Two main tracks, upon one of which the current of traffic is in a specified direction, and upon the other in the opposite direction.

Three or More Tracks.—Three or more main tracks, upon any of which the current of traffic may be in either specified direction.

Current of Traffic.—The movement of trains on a main track, in one direction, specified by the rules.

Station.—A place designated on the time table by name, at which a train may stop for traffic, or to enter or leavé the main track, or from which fixed signals are operated.

Siding.—A track auxiliary to the main track for meeting or passing trains.

Fixed Signal.—A signal of fixed location indicating a condition affecting the movement of a train.[1]

Yard Engine.—An engine assigned to yard service and working within yard limits.

Pilot.—An employee assigned to a train when the engineman or conductor, or both, are not fully acquainted with the physical characteristics or rules of the railroad, or portion of the railroad, over which the train is to be moved.

Train Register.—A book or form which may be used at designated stations for registering signals displayed, the time of arrival and departure of trains and such other information as may be prescribed.

(The definition of "yard" as given by the American Railway Engineering Association, is taken from the definitions of the American Railway Association and is, therefore, not repeated.)

The American Railway Association's Codes of Car Service and Per Diem[2] Rules, contain the following definitions:

---

order as against a "time" or "wait" order. Superiority by direction establishes a series of permanent "time" orders. Unless it is admitted that trains are not, or cannot be, run on time as a general rule, there is no good argument for perpetuating an old-time makeshift originally used to overcome inadequacies in other directions. There would not seem to be any good foundation for the principle, on any road, that its passengers traveling west (or east) are to enjoy any privileges not accorded those going in the opposite direction; the points of the compass should not settle priority of train rights. A recent revision of the standard code recognizes this principle by permitting the use of the positive meet in a footnote to rules 71 and 72.

[1] The definition of a "fixed signal" covers such signals as slow boards, stop boards, yard limits, switch, train order, block, interlocking, semaphore, disc, ball or other means for displaying indications that govern the movement of a train.

[2] Per diem is compensation due to car owner for use of equipment while in possession of añother railroad, renumeration being on daily basis.

Home Car.—A car on the road to which it belongs.

Foreign Car.—A car on a road to which it does not belong.

Private Car.—A car having other than railroad ownership.

Home.—A location where a car is in the hands of its owner.

Home Road.—The road which owns a car, or upon which the home of a private car is located.

Home Junction.—A junction with the home road.

Switching Service.—The movement of a car to be loaded, unloaded, reconsigned or reshipped, or the movement of a car between railroads, the services performed being within designated switching limits, the road performing the service not participating in the freight rate.

CHAPTER III

GENERAL REQUIREMENTS OF TERMINAL DESIGN

The business of a freight carrier is to move freight from one point to another for a consideration, and the least and cheapest possible handling enables it, ordinarily, to do this at a profit. As rates are usually rigid or have a tendency to decrease, the only way to increase the margin of profit, and in many cases create it, is to reduce the cost of transportation. One of the best ways, if not the very best way, to accomplish this is to reduce the number of cars needed to handle the business. Under the existing method of reimbursing foreign roads at per diem rates for the use of their cars, this holds absolutely true. It was frequently possible under the former method of payment on a mileage basis to hold a number of cars on tracks without expense beyond the interest on land and tracks occupied, and doubtless this is the principal reason why so many yards were operated in an expensive and awkward manner. Tracks were built for storage purposes rather than for switching. Under present methods of per diem payments, cars standing around unnecessarily are a daily loss and a drain on the margin of profit. A reduction in the number of cars used means a reduction in the cost of handling. As already explained, this holds true whether a road uses its own or foreign cars. The desideratum is to handle the business with the fewest cars possible. All good operating methods and principles dovetail into this.

In the construction of new terminals or the revision or enlargement of those already in existence, the operation of the entire railroad should be carefully considered. It is not enough to keep close watch on the efficiency of each yard or terminal separately. It is just as important that the same attention be given to coordinating their work and having it fit in with other phases of operation. In many cases it may be desirable, if not essential, to go beyond the limits of the road itself and study the methods, yards and character of traffic of immediate connecting lines, also probable changes in character of traffic and methods of handling. The construction and operating departments should confer closely and freely. It is usually wise to include a representative of the traffic department also, in order to obtain his views as to the necessity now and hereafter for faster time and more prompt deliveries. The traffic department should be consulted more especially with reference to the probable future volume of business to be provided for, its character, direction and new routes to be opened up with a tendency to divert traffic from established routes to or from the lines carrying it through the terminal under consideration.

The author has in mind a case on a trunk line where a "yard" consisting of two long tracks, with a cross-over half way, sufficed for many years to enable changing of engines, inspection, and related work, to be done with reasonable promptness for a comparatively heavy business. In the course of a few years it proved entirely inadequate and had to be increased to something like ten times its original capacity, although the traffic of the road had not increased in anything like this proportion—certainly not to exceed 15 per cent. This was due to the fact that the road originally handled a traffic consisting of about 80 per cent. of bituminous coal, requiring little or no separating or classifying and only ordinary movement as to time. New connections and traffic arrangements, a thousand miles away, produced a condition by which the traffic percentage changed. The general merchandise freight, live stock, meat, and the like, which formerly was 20 per cent. of the road's traffic, increased to more than 50 per cent. This required different treatment.

Of late years, the tendency is to rectify the common error of leaving the matter of design—both for new and for revising old yards—entirely to the engineering department (usually with insufficient data as to existing conditions and probable future conditions), or letting the yardmaster decide the whole question. It is now the general practice to get the fullest possible cooperation between departments.

An excellent plan was adopted by one railroad company a few years ago, when confronted with the necessity for revising some of its most important yards. The general manager appointed a committee consisting of the chief engineer, the principal assistant engineer and the superintendents, engineers and assistant engineers of all the divisions entering the yard under consideration. The superintendent in immediate charge of the yard in question acted as chairman and the committee met once a week for two months to prepare plans and report. The entire committee, during the first part of the period of its existence, visited large yards on other roads. The subcommittees meanwhile prepared detailed information concerning the yard to be revised. The officers engaged in this were divided into:

1. A subcommittee to gather all the statistics of the operation and traffic of the yard.

2. A subcommittee to make various sketch plans to be discussed by the general committee.

3. A subcommittee to read and abstract a number of the important articles on yard design and operation in the technical journals and books for the preceding period of 10 or 15 years. These abstracts were accompanied by sketches of yards described and were in shape to be readily studied by the general committee.

After the preliminary work of obtaining statistics and preparing plans, the yardmasters and their assistants were requested to attend one or more meetings of the committee and were invited to criticize the plans. The committee also interrogated the yardmasters and men with a view to informing itself fully as to details.

The fewest possible number of division terminals should be built consistent with reasonable length of locomotive runs which have in recent practice been successfully extended and the physical characteristics of the road. The latter frequently determine the point at which engines are turned. Handling locomotives at terminals is expensive. Where from 100 to 150 engines are turned per day, the cost of handling ranges from $5 to $8 per engine. This does not include removing ashes from pits, handling coal, sand and water, or furnishing steam heat in firing up. The cost during severe winter weather, or where boilers are washed out more than once in two weeks, often exceeds these figures. The cost of turning an engine on the turntable depends on the power used to move the table. With hand power it is from 8 to 16 cts. per engine. Power-driven tables are ordinarily economical where more than 75 engines are turned per day, the cost per engine turned ranging from 5 to 10 cts. This is discussed more in detail in Chap. XXVII.

It is a mistake to suppose that, when facilities are inadequate, the only thing to do is supply more track room. Merely to "extend" yards or tracks is a practice which cannot too strongly be condemned. Design is more important than car space. It often happens that a terminal with limited track room, but well designed, will permit the movement of more cars in a given time than one having much greater track room. The taxes and interest on the real estate occupied and the material used in construction often form a substantial fixed charge, which should be carefully considered. The size of the yard or terminal should be kept to the smallest necessary number of lineal feet of track. It should be planned and constructed so that every foot of track may be used profitably and economically. A mistake in design, requiring unnecessary or expensive movement is a continuous handicap which is difficult afterward to overcome. Like Tennyson's brook, it "goes on forever."

The study should by no means be confined to the one terminal under discussion. Its relation to other terminals and to the operation of the entire line should be carefully considered and a well-defined and comprehensive policy mapped out. An exhaustive study may show that some yards may be abandoned entirely and others reduced.

Some roads believe that each division terminal should do its own switching—that is, that they should do only such work on trains as will carry them to the next division terminal without further switching. Others start their trains from the system terminals made up to go as far as practicable without rehandling. Each method has its good points, but there are cases where the switching is unnecessarily duplicated. Occasionally, these expensive methods cannot easily be avoided because of inadequate facilities at vital points. On the other hand, unfortunately, the practice is frequently due to officers in charge of general train movements not fully understanding the situation in detail, or failing to take time to study the problem closely enough to arrive at an intelligent solution. This subject is treated at length in Chap. VI.

It may, perhaps, be assumed that a road is working on a well-defined and carefully thought-out policy regarding its operating divisions. Many instances, however, have passed into history where certain track changes, grade or curve reductions, shop installations, acquirement of additional track mileage, and wage schedule changes have made it desirable or essential that an operating division be added or eliminated. A change of this kind has an important bearing on the terminals. An expression of opinion should be obtained from the management as to the likelihood of a general revision of division lines or traffic channels in so far as they may affect the terminal situation.

Some years ago an important railroad in this country was operating its main line in five operating divisions. As the physical characteristics and traffic conditions permitted, it was decided to operate in four divisions, with about 160 miles of line in each. One division disappeared and the operating expenses were materially reduced, but the troubles of the yardmaster began. None of the old terminal yards, except those at the two ends of the road, were of any further service. They represented so much dead track. New terminals were built, but the outlay required for roundhouses and the usual accompanying facilities was so heavy that these yards were curtailed. Ample track room was provided in the course of time, but until then the trainmasters and yardmasters spent many sleepless nights and the business of the company suffered.

The problem of providing and handling freight at great centers of population and industries is often perplexing. The general tendency is to provide large classification and train terminal yards outside of cities, purchasing land within city limits for commercial yards and houses only, handling cars between such houses (or team yards) and the classification yards by yard-transfer engines. Land costing $7 a square foot should not be used for the ordinary switching of trains, when suitable sites in suburban districts, usually susceptible to more advantageous development, can be purchased for a few cents per foot. The financial side of the question resolves itself, broadly, into whether the cost of the transfer service (minus the saving by less road train mileage) will be more or less than the interest, taxes, and other fixed charges on the excess cost of inside property. The engine houses and attendant facilities should be located near the classification yards, and consideration should be given to the probability of objection being raised by municipalities to the "smoke nuisance" and the noise of switching if within city limits.

It is hard to figure on the future, and ordinary foresight dictates a policy of preserving or providing the greatest possible amount of elasticity in the terminal. There are two general methods by which this can be done, if permitted by property limitations, physical characteristics and the size of the appropriation. The first plan is to design and construct the terminal so as to make possible the transfer of work during an abnormal rush of business or an emergency from an overcrowded part of the yard to another part that may not be worked to its capacity. Emergencies may include accidents on the line, a heavy run of business in one direction or of certain kinds of freight, a shortage of power on a certain division, a bunching of power due to various causes, and delayed passenger trains. The other plan, which perhaps is more in the nature of supplement than an alternative, is to design the terminal so as to enable any of the yards to be enlarged at any time. This is a wise course, too, because of the possibility of unforeseen changes in traffic conditions.

The enormous increase in freight traffic caused the Pennsylvania to reach the decision that yards may become too large for prompt and economical movement of traffic, and to arrange new yards for coal, coke and limestone, thereby confining others to general merchandise traffic.[1]

The question really resolves itself into: "What is the limit in size of a freight-yard unit?" A large number of units can be placed in proximity, provided the entrances and exits are so free that the movement to and from any one unit will not interfere with the others. Therefore, the ground available usually limits the size of a collection of units. A unit consists of a receiving, classification and departure yard, together with car-repair, caboose and engine tracks. One set of departure, car-repair, caboose and engine tracks often serves two or more sets of receiving and classification tracks. The number of receiving tracks will depend on the density of traffic and the liability to interruption from wrecks. After laying out one unit, care must be taken to avoid impairing its usefulness by placing another one so that the movements conflict.[2]

So far as practicable, cars should move continuously in one direction from loading point to unloading point. Reverse movements should be avoided, as they cause unnecessary mileage of cars and engines, loss of time to freight, interference with switching and road movements,

[1] The *Railway Age* reports a record-breaking west bound freight movement, over the Pittsburgh Division of the Pennsylvania July 3, 1923, of 5,091 cars passing Gallitzin, the previous heaviest day being 4,852 cars on Sept. 15, 1919. Twenty years ago the average demand annually for transportation in this country was 1,300 tons freight 1 mile for every man, woman and child. Today it is 4,000 tons, compared with 700 tons per capita by the most developed country in Europe.

[2] The subject of interlocking and approaches is covered in Chap. III of "Passenger Terminals and Trains."

and additional wear and tear on rolling stock in stopping and reversing the direction of its movement. The expenditure of considerable money to keep the movement continuously in one direction may be justified by the saving in operating expenses.

On double-track roads, the terminal should be located between two main tracks but this cannot always be done. This principle is shown in Fig. 7. Property limitations, topographical considerations, necessity for handling passenger business in the vicinity, errors in original design, making the cost of revision excessive, and the location of engine houses and coaling stations may prevent. Other things being equal, it is desirable at larger division and system terminals to divorce entirely the passenger and freight traffic. Where this can be done, it is to the benefit of both, while the consolidation, necessary at times, is detrimental. This applies only to larger points where a reasonably heavy business is being handled. Where traffic is light, it is usually economical to combine the freight and passenger business. At large system or line terminals it is of decided advantage to separate the passenger lines from the freight lines some distance in advance of the yards. When the passenger terminals are located near the center of a city, it is often advisable to run the freight tracks around, where yard room can be had cheaper. Better time can then be made with less liability of congestion. If tracks through the city are laid at street levels, the advantage of such an arrangement is apparent.

Fig. 5.—Main tracks through center of terminal—yards opposite each other.

Fig. 6.—Main tracks to one side of terminal.

Fig. 7.—Main tracks separating and outside of terminal.

The objection to separating main tracks around terminals, that enginemen cannot read signals carried by engines on trains in the opposite direction, is not a material one. Where such an arrangement of tracks exists, the entrances and outlets at either end of the terminal should be protected by operators in charge of interlocking plants, and outgoing trains should be governed by signals given them. By the separation of the tracks there is a minimum of interference through cross-over movements. Freight and passenger trains in the same direction use the same tracks, and no connection with passenger tracks need be made except at the two ends of the terminal or at the point where the four-track system converges into double track. But one side of the passenger train is exposed to the possibility of entanglement, with accidents occurring on the yard tracks next alongside. This is a safer arrangement than dividing the terminal by having the passenger or high-speed tracks run through the center, as shown in Fig. 5. In this plan, yard engines in charge of hostlers or going to or from their freight trains need not come in contact with or cross the high-speed tracks. Conversely, passenger trains cannot interfere with the movements of freight engines or detain them.

When the high-speed tracks, for any reason, cannot be run around the terminals, the next best plan is to run both on one side, as shown in Fig. 6. As compared with the preceding arrangement, this is open to the objection of compelling freight trains moving in one direction to cross the passenger tracks in the opposite direction when entering and leaving the terminal. It will be seen that this arrangement will frequently compel freight trains to be stopped for passenger trains in the opposite direction, causing some detention and considerable expense. But one side of passenger trains in one direction is alongside of a yard track. As in the previous plan, the advantage exists of enabling interior terminal movements to be made from any yard to another, to or from engine houses, and related facilities, without interference with high-speed trains. Both plans have the decided advantage of enabling a transfer of work from one yard to another when one part of the traffic runs abnormally heavy or when emergencies arise. These transfers can be made without encountering the high-speed track movements at any point. The advantage of this is that a class of enginemen can be employed who may not be permitted to go out on the open road because of lack of familiarity with train rules. Such men are always available, and in times of a heavy rush of business or abnormal conditions it is usually difficult to secure men who can run on the main line.

To run the two main tracks through the center of the terminal, dividing the east or southbound side from the other, is often the only alternative, and doubtless more terminals are operated on this plan than on the other two combined. The liability to accident is somewhat greater under this arrangement, and there are many objections which have been briefly reviewed. There are, nevertheless, many who favor this plan as against running the two passenger tracks on one side because of the necessity of crossing movements in the latter. These movements exist in one form or another, however, as the engine houses, coaling plants, repair tracks, and related accessories are usually located on one side and cross-over movements are made necessary for road engines to or from the engine house, cabooses to be returned from the direction in which they arrived and cars moving in one direction to be repaired.

Where a four-track road uses the two middle tracks for freight, these should be separated to permit of the location of the yards between them. The Pennsylvania remodeled its Conway yard near Pittsburgh to accomplish this. Interference with passenger traffic had become annoying. With the high-speed tracks in the middle, passenger trains are usually run through the center of the yard. To avoid interference with switching and cross-over movements, it would then be necessary to elevate the passenger tracks and establish yard connections beneath. "Jump-overs" are used to avoid interference, the passenger tracks crossing the eastbound freight track by a separation of grade levels.

It is important, before proceeding with the plans for a terminal, to make a study of traffic conditions as they exist and as they will probably exist years hence. After this has been made as accurately as may be, committees should be appointed and a study of all conditions made. An examination of available plans of yards already in operation or in course of construction will be valuable. With this information, a summary should be made of the number of cars moving to and from each of the divisions centering in the terminal and to and from the industries and other unloading points. These figures should show the number of loaded and empty cars and the number of trains, from which a tabulated statement may be worked up, including the average and maximum number of cars to a train in each direction. In some cases it may be well to go into greater detail as to the number of cars in a train, tabulating for each division and each direction the trains with fewer than 10 cars, those between 10 and 20, those between 20 and 30, and so on. Figures of movements during certain hours or periods of the day may be advantageous. From these data a fair estimate may be made of the capacity needed for each receiving, separating, classification and departure yard and the length and number of tracks required. Consideration should also be given to the possibility of adopting a different class of road locomotive on any of the divisions; or of a transfer or an exchange of power which may affect the length of trains hauled.

Notwithstanding the fact that no two terminals can satisfactorily be constructed on the same plans, and that local conditions govern largely, there are a few general principles which should be considered and which may be applied wholly or in part to the design of any terminal.

In many plans of typical terminals, the yards for each direction lie alongside each other. This arrangement is objectionable, in that the engine houses, coaling plants, ash tracks and repair tracks must be inconveniently located for one yard, or must be duplicated. An engine coming in from a westbound train must travel to the east end of the eastbound yard to get its return train; and a similar movement in the opposite direction must be made by the engine arriving on an eastbound train. By locating the yards so that they will "head in" on each other (see Fig. 8), *i.e.*, having the west end of the westbound yard terminate near the east end of the eastbound yard, the engine houses and attendant facilities can be located where they may be readily reached by incoming engines from either yard, and the facilities for caring for engines may be concentrated. This advantage applies also to the organization of the employees. It reduces the engine mileage and cuts out the running tracks needed for engines going to and from their trains. The caboose tracks

Fig. 8.—Main tracks through center of terminal yards on "lap" principle.

should be located where the cabooses will not be disturbed in switching, as the men frequently use them for sleeping quarters. As some crews are usually assigned to regular or preferred runs, such as fast freights, local or work trains, it is desirable to have two caboose tracks, and they should preferably be located near the outlet end of the terminal to enable the pooled or "first-in first-out" crews to drop their cabooses to the rear of outgoing trains. The author has, nevertheless, recommended the construction of classification yards for two directions on the opposite principle, *i.e.*, heading the yards away from each other. The topography thereby enabled the utilization of favorable grades to aid switching for both yards, while the principle explained in Fig. 8 would have caused these grades to oppose switching.

The location of terminal yards should be convenient to the business terminal of the railroad, the freight houses, team tracks and the points of interchange with other roads or divisions, and should be arranged so that trains can enter or leave the yard without crossing the path of other movements. When possible, advantage should be taken of natural grades to assist switching. In some locations, assisting grades cannot be had; in others, grades can be had in one direction; while in others—grades can be used to help in each direction. The assistance of grades is a great advantage.

In the foregoing, a yard with reference to the movement of traffic in one direction only has been considered. For movements in both directions, a duplication of yard facilities would, of course, be required. A segregation of the component parts of a terminal in logical sequence follows:

Receiving Yard.—Consider first a terminal at the actual end of the line. In the receiving yard, the road engines and cabooses are cut off and the work of assorting and distributing the cars is turned over to the switching engines and the crews. The proper length of tracks depends on the unit selected and is governed by the following factors:

1. Length of train of loaded cars.
2. Length of train of empty cars.
3. Average length of trains.
4. Number of trains of average length per day.
5. Number of trains of maximum length per day.

Consideration should also be given to prospective changes in grade and to a possible increase in the length of trains entering the yard. The length of train is the controlling factor and the logical unit. When the number of trains of maximum length is less than 20 per cent. of the total number of trains entering the yard daily, the average train length is the most practical basis for a receiving yard having tracks of equal length. The yard may, however, be made with a portion of the tracks of sufficient length for maximum trains and the remainder of the tracks of sufficient length for average trains. In this case the tracks of each group should be of equal length, whichever unit (the maximum or the average train) is taken. The tracks should be of such length as to accommodate a train with two engines and a caboose. If the average train length is taken as a unit, the length of track should be such that a train of the maximum length can be disposed of on not more than two tracks.

The proper size of a receiving yard depends on:

1. The frequency of the arrival of trains.

2. The rate at which cars can be received and disposed of in the separating yard. The receiving yard, however, should have a sufficient number of tracks to hold the trains arriving during one hour of maximum traffic and preferably additional capacity to care for delays, accidents and so on.

Separating Yard.—This yard occasionally included is the second in the series and here the first breaking up of a train and the distribution of its cars are effected. The cars entering the yard are usually distributed so that, according as the separations are to be by destination or commodities, the cars destined to assigned territory or containing the same commodities will be placed together on separate tracks. The yard should be located in advance of the receiving yard and in such a way that cars can readily be moved into it. The number of tracks in the separating yard should be governed by the number of separations to be made. The length of these tracks should be determined by the number of cars for each separation and there should be extra room allowed for emergencies.

Classification Yard.—When the separation in the preceding yard is by districts, the purpose of the classification yard is to put the cars of the different districts in regular order. The cars of each district (already placed on one of the tracks of the separating yard) are switched in the classification yard in the order required for delivery at destination. When the separation is by commodities, the cars of each commodity (already placed on one of the tracks of the separating yard) are further assorted by classes or grades. Thus, all the cars of grain placed indiscriminately on a track in the separating yard will be rearranged in the classification yard so that the cars of wheat, corn, oats, etc. are each grouped on separate tracks. The classification yards should be located in advance

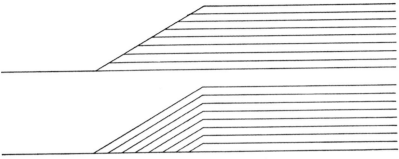

Fig. 9.—Types of grid-iron ladders.

of the separating yard, in such a way that cars may be readily moved into them from any of the tracks of the latter yard. The separating yard is usually in the form of a gridiron (see Fig. 9) and its capacity will be determined by the number of cars going to a district, with allowance for an excess number or for emergencies. As an example, with 36 cars going to a district, two gridirons of six tracks each with a capacity of six cars to a track will give such control to the entire set of cars that it can be turned end for end, or car for car. This type of yard may be made up of a series of parallel stub tracks instead of gridirons. Such an arrangement is sometimes termed a "lancing yard."

It is well to avoid unusual length of classification or assorting tracks, and where the classifications are numerous no attempt should be made to provide a track for each classification. In such cases a second classification yard beyond the first, reclassifying from one of the tracks of the first into the second yard, would be a wiser plan, unless a yard of enormous proportions is planned. With a V-ladder possibly 30 to 36 tracks may be economically used, one-half running from each ladder, but in practical working it may be desirable to reduce the number to about 20 tracks and reclassify into a second yard. The long ladder increases the distances cars must travel in switching (see Fig. 10).

Departure Yard.—Here the work of the yard engines and their crews ceases and that of the road or transfer engines and their crews is begun. It should be located in advance of the classification yard, so that cars from all tracks in the latter can be readily moved into the departure yard.

The number of tracks and the length of tracks in this yard are governed by the same requirements as the receiving yard.

Storage Yard.—The location is important and depends almost entirely upon the character of the cars to be stored or held.   Three distinct cases may be mentioned:

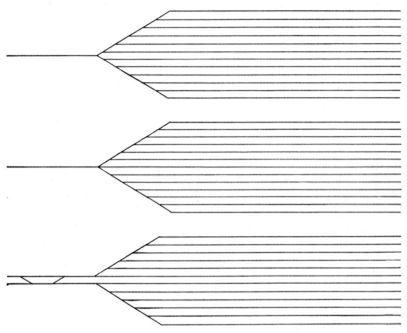

FIG. 10.—Types of V-ladders.

1. On some railroads it is known in advance that entire train loads arriving will have to be held.   In such cases the storage yard should be located with, or held in close relation to, the receiving and separating yards so as to permit of direct movement of trains to the storage yard and then to the separating yards as required.

2. The cars to be held may arrive mixed in with cars that are to go forward.   In such cases the storage yard should be located in relation to the separating yard so that the cars can be moved directly into the storage yard from the separating yard and then delivered to the classification yard as required.

3. The character of the freight to be held may be such that it can be put in district and station order at once.   In such cases the storage yard should be so located in relation to the classification and departure yards that cars can be moved directly into the storage yard from the classification yard and then delivered to the departure yard as required.

There are probably other cases, but the three principal ones mentioned indicate that the location of the storage yard cannot be determined arbitrarily or theoretically. It must be determined by the character of the business in each case. The size should be governed almost entirely by the number of cars to be held, and the length of the tracks should be such that a switching engine can readily handle all the cars stored on one track.

Transportation officers dislike the term "storage." It is often argued that yards and tracks should be built for movement, not storage. Because of conditions they cannot control (many due to traffic department requirements), they find storage tracks not only useful but necessary. To meet purely operating conditions, little storage room would be required.

Body Tracks.—These should be spaced 11 ft. 6 in. to 13 ft., or more center to center, and, while the minimum spacing is not recommended for general use, it is often necessary in city yards. Curves should be avoided. At intervals of five or six tracks an extra width of spacing should be given in order to allow space for drainage and for piling track material, etc. It is also advisable to allow a space of 15 ft. between the center of a main track and a yard track, to give ample space for water columns or standpipes, signal posts and other similar requirements.

Ladder Tracks.—Where there are two ladder tracks or where a yard track parallels a ladder track, these tracks should be spaced 15 ft. center to center. The extra room is required for the safety of trainmen in throwing switches, and moving in and out between the cars. The angle which the ladder track makes with the body tracks should be the greatest angle which the frog used will allow. A No. 7 (8 deg. 11 min.) should be the minumum number of frog for yard use and it is advisable to use no smaller numbered frog than No. 8.

By continuing the curve of the switch leading out 10 ft. beyond the frog, No. 8 frogs can be used on a No. 7 ladder or No. 7 frogs on about a No. 6.5 ladder, thereby saving track room and at the same time giving easy switch leads.

The arrangement of the ladder tracks demands careful study. The ordinary gridiron ladder is simple and satisfactory, but where more capacity is required the V-ladder (Fig. 10) may be used to advantage and gives a larger scope to be reached by one lead. Twenty tracks may be reached comfortably from a V-ladder; as a maximum, 30 to 36. Any increased length of ladder brings about much lost motion and increased distance to be traveled by riders.

The central ladder (Fig. 11) is advocated and has it advantages and disadvantages. On it are two curves to be turned by the car before reaching the deflecting switch on the ladder. The car that does not run freely is, therefore, retarded shortly after obtaining its start, which necessitates

a heavier descending grade.   The ladders are ordinarily higher than the
body tracks, to secure the essential gravity movement.   An advantage
in drainage is, consequently, had and the water is easily carried away from
the ladder tracks and the switches.   Since the ladders are in a direct line,
at all times in view of the cutter (the employee who parts the cars), he is
enabled to work to better advantage than when his view is occasionally
obscured, as with other ladder designs.   The compact location of switches
enables them to be handled more economically if thrown by hand and,
if handled mechanically from a tower, a much better view will be afforded.

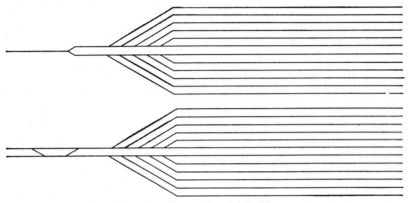

Fig. 11.—Types of central ladders.

The central ladder may reduce crew expense, as trainmen may be available for service on either side of the yard as soon as they reach the ladder,
while under the usual V-ladder they are not always in readiness for cars
going to the opposite side until they have reached the distributing
point at the head of the yard.   The open space between the ladders
permits locating electric light poles at a point where light is most needed
and where a minimum number of lights will suffice.   Where heavy snow
storms are encountered, this ladder possesses advantages on account of
its higher location and consequent freedom from drifting.

There is probably no large yard where the central ladder scheme has
been tried.   The flexibility by which the V-ladder capacity may readily
be extended to meet increasing traffic demands is lacking in the central
ladder.   With the V, two or more leads may be operated.   It is contended
that on the central-ladder arrangement cars run more freely because
they do not reach the curves until they have attained some headway;
but this is more than offset by the additional curvature introduced.

Lead Tracks.—The connections of these tracks with the main line
should be controlled by a telegraph or telephone office and interlocking
plant, both for safety and to facilitate train movements.   The most
efficient guardian is the interlocking plant.   Main-track movements

should not be permitted indiscriminately.   Yard engines should only be allowed on main tracks when properly protected by interlocking and other signaling.   Main tracks should be protected with derails.

The late Walter G. Berg said:

Another important point is that trains that are to go into the yard or leave it should make those movements quickly.   They should be got off the main tracks promptly when entering the yard.   It is important to have approach tracks leading to the yard.   The great mistake usually made is that the yard lead track turns out of the main-line track.   There should be an approach track or lead-in track approaching the yard switches proper, long enough to accommodate at least one train, so that if a freight train is just able to make the yard ahead of a passenger schedule it can turn into the lead-in track quickly without having to slow down, or the possibility of encountering a switching engine or some yard operation and having to block the main line for a considerable time.

Similarly, at the departing end of the yard it is very important, especially when there is not a system of yard tracks known as a departure yard or advance yard, to have a track leading away from the yard out along the main track for some distance.   There are cases where this lead-out track has been extended several miles advantageously.   It means that, when the train is boarded in the yard ready to leave, it is pulled out slowly into this lead-out track and goes out of the yard and away from it and then stops with the nose of the engine at the signal tower, at the head of the lead-out track, and when it gets the board it can rush out on the main line and make a quick run and get out of the way at the next passing siding.

Drill Tracks.—These tracks should be so located as to cause a minimum interference with other movements.

Open Tracks.—The track selected as the open track should be one that will enable movements to be made from one end of a yard to another with the greatest convenience.

Running Tracks.—Tracks of this class should be provided for movement in each direction, to enable yard engines to pass freely from one portion of the cluster to another, also for road and yard engines to get to and from the engine house and other points where facilities are located.

Caboose Tracks.—Cabooses arriving at a yard ordinarily return over the same division instead of going forward.   It is usually necessary, therefore, to locate caboose tracks between the receiving yard and the departure yard and to arrange them so that the cabooses can be readily pushed from a receiving track to the caboose track and then dropped by gravity to a train departing in the direction from which the caboose has arrived. There are various ways in which this can be accomplished, but in locating these tracks care should be taken that only a minimum amount of switching will be required.   The tracks should be so arranged that cabooses feed "first-in first-out."   Occasionally, special tracks must be provided for the cabooses of fast freight trains.

Scale Tracks.—These are usually located between the receiving and separating yards. This is undoubtedly the best location for automatic weighing, because no reverse movements will be required in taking the cars on and off the scale.

The scales should be located on the lead over which all cars are passed on their way to the ladder of the classification yard. They should in every case be provided with a "dead track" to avoid unnecessary strain on the scale bearings. If but a small proportion of the cars needs to be weighed, or if only cars for a few tracks in the classification yard are to be weighed, the scales may better be located on the ladder of the classification yard in advance of two, three or half a dozen of the body tracks, as circumstances may require. If but very little used, they may be placed on a short-body track well back from the working part of the yard. There is a disposition to make scales too long rather than too short. The long scale is objectionable, as it necessitates keeping cars far apart, which delays switching.

Coal, Ashpit, Sand and Engine Tracks.—The engine-coaling apparatus is usually located on the track leading to the engine house. Water and sand should also be taken at the same time as the coal, where this arrangement is possible. The facilities for supplying coal, water and sand are sometimes provided on the outgoing engine-house track, as well as on the incoming track. It will be of advantage to provide a run-around track, so that switch engines may clean fires, take coal and water and pass around waiting road engines.

Bad-order Tracks.—These are required so as to get the bad-order cars out of the way of the switching movements. They should be arranged for easy access at all times and be adjacent to the yard. From them the cars are taken to the repair shops.

Repair Tracks.—These should connect with the bad-order tracks where practicable. Their capacity should not ordinarily exceed 15 cars. These tracks should be located at points where cars can be run directly into them from the receiving yards, the same as other cars being classified. The usual method, and that prescribed by the rules of the American Railway Association, is to place an inspector's blue flag in advance of the cars being worked on. This is to prevent engines or cars from coming in contact with the cars on the repair track and possibly injuring the men under or about them, engaged in repair work. A better and safer plan is to put special locks on the switches of one-half the repair tracks, letting the foremen of the repairers alone have possession of the key. The yardmen will then put cars in one-half the tracks while the repairers are working on the other half. When the cars are ready to be taken out, the foreman removes the special locks and places them on the switches of the tracks last filled, enabling the yardmen to pull out the cars repaired and make room for placing other bad-order cars. Portable derails may also be used to an advantage. Repair tracks should hold 15 or 20 cars each, tracks longer than ordinarily designed for that number of cars are required because bad-order cars are usually separated several feet to give repairers an opportunity to get around them conveniently. They should be laid in pairs, about 16 ft. center to center, and with a clear space between each set or pair of about 25 to 30 ft., for placing and handling material. A narrow-gage track may be laid in the wide space and small trucks for handling material run thereon. Small turntables are used to connect them at one end of the repair yard to a cross-track leading to the material yard and supply house. The author has had two or three tracks set aside from the body tracks of a separating yard to be used for light repair work. These were planked over to enable wheels to be rolled and material handled. One track was cut out for material, including wheels. This arrangement worked very satisfactorily, as it saved time in movement of cars and switching and it relieved the regular repair yards of light work which interfered with making heavier repairs. In one yard a track alongside the repair track was reserved for repairs to cars in fast freight and stock trains and this prevented and reduced many delays. Wheels were put under stock cars in 20 minutes without any special exertion and cars were forwarded in the same train in which they arrived. Under the old method they were taken over to the regular repair yards and forwarded by a later train. This usually resulted in six or eight hours' detention and at times twice as long.

Icing Tracks.—These should be between the receiving and separating yards, so that the cars to be iced may be readily moved from the receiving yard to the icing track and thence to the separating yard.

Other Special Tracks.—The particular purpose for which such tracks are required should be considered and they should be so located that their use will involve a minimum amount of switching and the least possible interference with the regular yard movement.

Air Plants.—An air-testing plant is essential in the departure yards of each terminal. Here brakes may be tested, all leaks closed, repairs made and auxiliaries charged with full air pressure before the road engine arrives. Much valuable time of engines and crews may thus be saved. Such a plant is particularly desirable since the passage of the Safety Appliance Act with its requirements as to the control of trains by air brakes. Brake apparatus can be maintained better and trains will be started out in safer condition than when the repairs are made hurriedly after the engine has coupled to the train and pumped up the pressure in the main train line and auxiliaries. Usually the repairs are neglected when the men are hurried. The cars on which brakes are non-operative are either cut out and air worked through—a very bad practice—or the cars are switched out and put in the rear of the air-braked cars. As a result, the braking power of those cars is lost, and delay to road engines and crews occurs both while switching them out and in testing the air after switching. A testing plant is comparatively inexpensive, requiring usually only one line of pipe across the end of the yard with a connection between each pair of tracks, made by a hose coupling.

Engine Facilities.—Engine houses and the coaling plants, sand plants, ashpits, water stations and turntables should be located in such a position as to prevent movements of engines to or from them or from one part to another from being blocked by the movements of road trains or yard engines. In some yards it is necessary, unfortunately, to have these light engine movements cross the main tracks. Where this occurs, the engines should be in charge of regular road runners and the movements should, if practicable, be under the control of interlocking plants. Where the terminals for the two directions are on the "lap" plan, or head into each other, the engine houses, etc. can advantageously (at the lowest cost and with a minimum of delay) be concentrated at one point to serve engines from two or more divisions. The usual movement for an engine coming in from the road is to go to the ash track first and have its hoppers dumped and fire cleaned or drawn. A hostler has a better opportunity to work on the fire when the tender is empty because then he has more room in which to use the long-handled tools. Then, too, if the fire is to be drawn for washout of boiler, repairs or other reasons, the engine is not loaded up with a tank of coal which may not only be in the way and prevent repairs to the tender, but is objectionable in other respects if the engine is to be laid up. The author once saw several steel-tired wheels completely ruined after having stood under a tender loaded with bituminous coal for two or three months. Rain had run through the coal and caused a constant drip of water containing sulphuric acid, which cut considerable depressions into the steel tires and necessitated their removal. The ash track is usually slightly elevated, sometimes on columns, and has a depressed track alongside for empty cars into which the ashes are loaded.

The engine's next movement is from the ash track to the coaling plant and it should either take sand and water while taking coal, or at some convenient point close by. In some cases engines have their fires cleaned and ashes drawn while taking coal, a conveyor system being used for elevating coal as well as removing the ashes. The engine is then turned and, if necessary, run into the roundhouse. The movements from roundhouse to coal plant should not conflict with those in the opposite direction.

While the foregoing is an outline of the usual handling, it is the exception to the rule that is the disturbing element in handling engines and in all transportation work. An engine is needed for an assigned run; it may be a fast freight or live stock train. A passenger engine is required ahead of freight engines. Even the yard engine with its crew waiting in idleness may demand preferred attention. In such cases it becomes necessary to run an engine around others and out of its turn. This results in a corresponding or greater delay to other engines to be handled. The arrangement for handling cabooses in turn may be similarly broken up. The fast freight train takes precedence on the road over trains of more weight and frequently of greater value and earning power. It is necessary, therefore, to locate the ash tracks, and other engine facilities, in such a position as to enable one engine to be run in ahead of another. To this end the facilities for cleaning fires, coaling, taking water, sand, etc. may be advantageously located so they can be reached either from the outgoing track or the return track. A depressed track under a switching summit may be utilized to enable light road engines to cross from one side of a switching yard to the other without interfering or being interfered with. This idea may well be given consideration in connection with the design or revision of a busy terminal. Tracks used for engines exclusively require little overhead clearance, and comparatively steep grades may be introduced to attain the very desirable condition of free and uninterrupted movement of road power. Loss of use of road power during "rush" seasons is extremely costly. Its value at such times is many times greater than when lying on sidings "white-leaded" awaiting a freight movement and it is just at such times that terminal delays in the handling of power are most excessive and exasperating. Every facility should be provided to take care of engines promptly during heavy traffic periods and to prevent yards from choking up at such times. All calculations for terminal work and work elsewhere should be made to meet the requirements of the months of heaviest traffic movements. It may be wiser, in places, to base calculations on the *heaviest day's* movement. The remaining days will then have been provided for.

Telephone service connecting telegraph offices, interlocking stations, engine houses, crew dispatchers' and yardmasters' offices with each other is essential. A local exchange is convenient and a money saver.

Electric lighting should be carefully planned to give ample light and avoid throwing shadows, especially along ladder tracks and switching centers.

The yardmaster's offices should be located in the most central point available and preferably in a building two or three stories high, to enable him to get a fairly good view of his yards. Separately, or in connection with the yardmaster's building, a room should be provided for yardmen to eat their lunches. Another room should be provided with a sufficient number of lockers, with wire-screened doors for ventilation (one to each employee), so that the men may change clothes before reporting for duty and after finishing work. Buildings of a suitable character and at the most convenient points should also be provided for car inspectors and repairers and for their materials. It is desirable to have the yardmaster and engine house foreman located in adjacent or near by buildings.

Rest Rooms.—If there is no Railroad Y. M. C. A. or men's club room, one of the best investments to be made is a good and well-kept bunk house for road crews. This should be located at a point where men can be called quickly as needed, but where it is also sufficiently quiet for them to obtain rest. The cost of building and maintaining a house of this kind is comparatively small and affords substantial returns in better service from men who have actually rested and are in condition to perform their duties satisfactorily. It also keeps them away from their cabooses which, for many reasons, are not desirable bunk houses while lying around yards, and from the usual accompaniment of the cheap boarding house, with its erstwhile bar-room attachment. A day and night lunch room, near the bunk room , is desirable and can usually be made self-sustaining, but no attempt should be made to have it earn more than running expenses.

The following excerpt from a report made by a committee of the American Railway Engineering Association aptly summarizes the various phases of yard work and indicates its importance in relation to the railroad's main function—the economical production of transportation:

The actual practice in the methods of operating the switching traffic, or switching movements of such yards and terminals, varies at different yards, owing to the local conditions of yard plans and traffic. The proper handling of traffic is largely a matter of individual ability, and must be governed to a large extent by the peculiarities of the traffic and the physical characteristics of the yard. For these reasons, therefore, the operation of the switching traffic can only be dealt with in a general statement.

A terminal is composed of the facilities of a railroad in a city for handling its business and usually embraces all the tracks and facilities. The distance from the large general yard or cluster to the docks, wharves, freight houses, team tracks or other facilities is in some cases as much as 15 or 20 miles. This territory is divided into districts, for convenience in switching and for the assignment of switching crews. Each switching district is usually provided with a small switching yard, from which the various private side tracks, freight houses and manufacturing establishments in the district are supplied with their cars. The district yard is supplied and relieved by movements to and from the cluster to the general yard. These latter are made by what are termed "transfer crews."

The movement of a train after its arrival at the general yard or cluster where the engine and caboose are detached is as follows: At large terminals the cluster is usually several miles from the city and is the point at which all trains are received and dispatched. The manifest of the train is taken by the train conductor to the yard office immediately upon arrival; from this manifest a card is prepared for each car in the train, by the train-carding clerk. These cards are prepared and turned over to the car carder, who takes them to the yard and tacks the proper card on one or both sides of the car. The cards have various colors, shapes, letters, monograms, marks, etc., designating the various districts to which the cars are to be moved. While the cards are being prepared and attached to the cars, the cars are inspected by the car inspector, so that they are ready to be moved as soon as carded.

A yard engine and crew now take the cars in charge and classify them, either by drilling, poling or pushing them over a summit, thus putting the cars for each district on the track in the separating yard assigned to that particular district. After completing this work, the engine in question commences work on another train. The conductor doing this work keeps no record of the cars handled. The next engine to handle these cars is what is known as a "transfer engine" and makes what is termed the "interior and exterior" movement of cars, that is, movement from one yard or district to another (interior), or to the yards of various other railroads (exterior). When this engine takes a train to the district yard or to the yard of another railroad, it has nothing more to do with the train and may return light to the cluster. If there is a return load at the yard in question, or a load can be picked up on the way back, this engine handles the movement. It sometimes happens that one of these engines will have freight for two or more districts as it proceeds. After the freight arrives in the district in which it is to be unloaded, some of it is held for orders of consignee, while other freight of the same lot may be switched to consignee without waiting for orders. That lot for the freight house and team tracks, if there is room for it, is delivered immediately, or as soon as convenient after arrival. That part of the freight consigned to industries, for which there may be a number of other cars that have arrived previously, will be held and placed in the order of its age, or ahead of its turn, according to the wants of the consignee. These latter movements are all made by the district switch engine, that is, the engine working in that district and doing the local switching.

At nearly all clusters or general yards quite a large percentage of the business arriving consists of what are termed "hold cars," that is, cars which are to be held at the outer yard until final destination or switching directions are given. On arrival, these cars are switched to the "hold" yard and are daily reswitched in order to take from among them the cars for which direction for delivery have been received. When directions are received the cars are carded and treated just the same as cars which move directly to destination. The "hold" car is a great nuisance, as large roads will frequently have 500 or 600 "hold" cars and receive orders daily for 50 to 100 of them. These must be switched out from the entire lot, entailing a large amount of work.

The movement in the reverse direction is made in practically the same way as the movement from the general yard or cluster to the industrial districts, that is, the district engine gathers up the cars for movement, a transfer engine takes them to the general yard, where they are switched to the outbound or classification tracks. Here the trains are made up in station order, the bills are prepared by the yard clerk and the road engine finally couples on and the train is complete and ready to leave.

At larger terminals, in order that cars may be readily located and not get lost, a record is kept as follows: The conductor of the road engine brings the train into the general yard or cluster and fills out a card, giving number and initials, kind, lading and condition of seals of every car in the train. The conductor or foreman of the transfer engine fills out a card, stating whether loaded or empty and the point at which set off or picked up. The district switch-engine conductor makes a similar record for all cars moved to and from large industries. These cards are forwarded at once to the car-record office and entered in the car-record book, so that the record of any particular car may be found in the book by turning to the number of the car.   Thus it may be found that it arrived at the general yard or cluster on such a date and moved from the district yard to some industry on a certain date.   The record may also show that the car has been reloaded from this particular industry and again moved to the general yard; or, if it does not show movement from the industry, the car is still on its tracks.   Thus the location of any car at a large terminal may be ascertained in a few minutes.

Fig. 12.—A large gravity yard at Feltham, near London.

In the movement of outbound freight the cars are carded by the district or local yard clerk, who works under the direction of the local agent.   The agent prepares memorandum bills, which are sent by train mail or messenger to the general yard.   At this point the bills are taken in charge by the yard clerk, who checks the train and prepares the train list and bills for the conductor, a bill or manifest being furnished to each car in the train.

The movement of transfer engines, especially those working from the freight houses, is made on regular schedules.   This is done so that, immediately on closing the freight houses at night, cars are moved from them into the general yard, and cars for morning delivery are at the freight houses before they open for business.

CHAPTER IV

TRACK CONSTRUCTION AND MAINTENANCE DETAILS[1]

Passing Sidings.—Side tracks used for train service as distinguished from those used for storage or for switching movements are often termed "passing sidings," because their function is to permit trains to pass one another on single or double tracks, and thereby to relieve traffic. While it is necessary that passing tracks shall be connected with the main tracks and often by the introduction of facing point turnouts, still it is not good practice to connect many switching and industry tracks to the main track, but rather to connect them to a lead track, which, in turn, is connecting with the main track, preferably at both ends, thereby avoiding many switches on the main line.

In single-track operation passing sidings are frequently arranged as in Fig. 13. Design (a) places the outgoing turnouts directly before the eyes

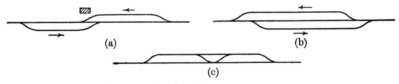

Fig. 13.—Passing sidings on single track.

of the towerman. In such an arrangement two trains headed in opposite directions on the two sidings may proceed after the main-line train has passed, without waiting for each other's movement. If the sidings are long enough to accommodate two freight trains, the second freight can follow the first one and wait at the tower for orders to proceed. Plan (b) shows another and less desirable arrangement for double siding. Design (c) is a single siding long enough for two trains, with cross-overs located near the middle of the siding connecting it with the main track, so that, if both are headed in the same direction, either train on the siding can pull out first onto the main track; or, if they are headed in opposite directions, then both trains can pull out onto the main track as soon as the main-line train has passed.

Similar designs for passing tracks adapted to double main-track operation are shown in Fig. 14. In design (d) the single passing track between the main tracks can be used for a train or trains in either direction; it is a convenient arrangement for approaching trains but awkward for departing trains when there are two trains on the siding.

41

Plan (*e*) is simple but not flexible.   Plans (*f*) and (*g*) are well adapted for handling traffic from a tower located near the cross-over.   Schemes (*h*) and (*i*) are similar in operation to (*f*) and (*g*), but have the disadvantage that curves have to be introduced into the main track.   In (*e*), (*f*) and (*g*) it will be noticed that both main tracks are straight, whereas

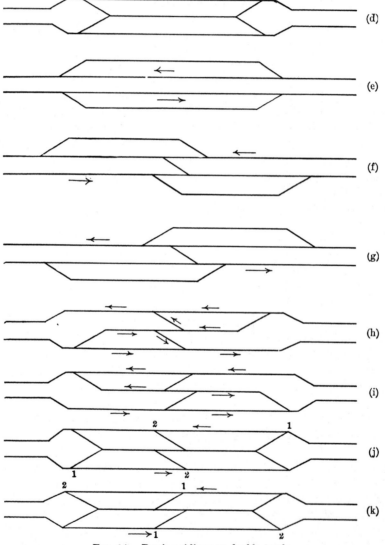

Fig. 14.—Passing sidings on double track.

in the rest of the designs they have been spread apart to admit constructing middle sidings.   Where the main tracks are thus spread apart, in some instances it is possible and good practice to preserve one of the main tracks straight and put all the curvature into the other one rather than to move both of them half of the total amount of spreading required.

Plans (*j*) and (*k*) present the most flexible arrangement of passing sidings; the tower should be located opposite the middle cross-overs. As a rule, trains will operate through this arrangement by pulling in at point 1 and out at point 2.

The turnouts of passing sidings should be equipped with interlocking switch and signal apparatus operated from a tower, which should be one of the block signal towers, where manual block signals are used. The tracks of passing sidings should be spaced 16 ft. on centers wherever possible.

Industry Side Tracks.—Industry tracks are, whenever possible, designed as trailing turnouts rather than facing-point turnouts. In fact, it is not uncommon for a railroad to refuse to construct industry side tracks requiring facing turnouts leading out from the main track. It is the growing practice in large cities to construct parallel to the main track an industry track connected at both ends to the main track, and to this lead track all the industry tracks are connected. Since the operation of cars over this lead track is in all cases slow and is freight service only, there is little necessity for concern as to whether or not a side track requires a facing or a trailing turnout. In many cases of industry tracks the physical limitations are such that the track must contain very sharp curves, unusual frog connections with the lead track, and in many instances special track construction is required. As a rule, a side track which has a down grade toward the main track should not be constructed, but, with proper derailing devices which are mechanically interlocked with the switch of the turnout, even such side tracks can be made substantially safe so far as main-line traffic is concerned. Grades of 3 per cent. are not common on industry side tracks where but few cars are to be handled at one time; it is common, for example, to have grades of 5 to 7 per cent. on coal chute tracks.

Care should be taken in establishing the alinement of side tracks to the obtaining of side clearances of 8 ft. from centers of track to any structure which is as high above the track as the car floor on tangent track, making allowances for curvature and superelevation on curves to obtain a net clearance of 8 ft.; the headroom should be at least 16 ft. above the top of rail. If the track runs inside a building the cars must be so handled that the locomotive, on account of fire risks, will not enter the building.

It is customary, in constructing side tracks, for the railroad to enter into a "side-track agreement" with the shipper, by which the railroad agrees to construct the side track and to operate cars over it for the shipper's benefit, provided he complies with the railroad's rules of operating and caring for freight cars on sidings and provided he pays for all the side track which lies beyond the clearance point. Siding should be designed, when practicable, to permit placing of cars by road engines so as not to compel the use of a switching engine for that purpose.

In cases where a side track must connect with a main track and where the logical connection is a facing-point turnout which is prohibited, the arrangement shown in Fig. 15 may be adopted. A trailing switch is installed in the main track running back as a gauntlet track along the main track and then a facing switch runs out of the gauntlet into the

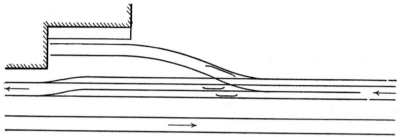

Fig. 15.—Gauntlet track arrangement to avoid facing point turnout.

industry. This arrangement, of course, has the objection of requiring two frogs and two sets of switches, although only one frog and switch is crossed by the main-line traffic, and the liability of a locomotive backing over the end of the gauntlet track causing a derailment on a traffic track.

Sharp Curves.—In many yards, and particularly on industry tracks, very sharp curves exist. On the Jessup Branch on the Erie Railroad, for example, is an 18-deg. main-line curve on a 2.3 per cent. grade. In the first location of many railroads sharp curves were installed which have since been reduced at great expense. In revision of railroad lines it is not infrequent that the maximum degree of curvature on main-line track is kept at a maximum of 4 deg. Road engines are, in practice, limited in the degree of curvature over which they will operate, depending upon the length of their wheel base and the number of wheels which have flanges. To meet special requirements of operation over sharper curves, special types of engines have been designed and used extensively. Some passenger coaches will not go around 20-deg. curves unless the truck-swivel chains are disconnected, which should never be done except in an extreme case where it becomes necessary to place a coach on a very sharply curved track for some special purpose.

A four-wheel switching engine will, as a rule, go safely around a curve of 75-ft. radius, and six-wheel switching engines around curves of 90- to 150-ft. radius, depending upon their design. A single box car can be pulled around a curve of 50-ft. radius by means of either a special switching engine equipped with a long connecting link or of some kind of tackle. In fact, two box cars can be pulled around curves of 80- to 100-ft. radius if a specially long link coupler is used between the cars and between the tender and the locomotive.   On a radius of about 140 ft. the corners of cars are liable to strike if the equipment is the ordinary M. C. B. coupler.   In the terminals about New York City are several cases of tracks of 80- to 100-ft. radius.

On all specially sharp curves the gage should be properly widened, rails braced, guard rails set and curvature maintained uniform.   It is advisable to lay guard rails on all curves sharper than 14 deg.

Following is a table of degrees of curves and their corresponding radii given to the nearest foot, tangent offsets and middle ordinates to the nearest tenth of a foot:

DEGREES AND RADII OF CURVES

Degree	Radius, feet	Tangent offsets for 100-ft. chords, feet[1]	Middle ordinate for 100-ft. chords, feet	Degree	Radius, feet	Tangent offsets for 100-ft. chords, feet[1]	Middle ordinate for 100-ft. chords, feet
1	5,730	0.9	0.2	22	262	19.1	4.8
2	2,865	1.7	0.4	24	240	20.8	5.3
3	1,910	2.6	0.7	26	222	22.5	5.7
4	1,433	3.5	0.9	28	207	24.2	6.1
5	1,146	4.4	1.1	30	193	25.9	6.6
6	955	5.2	1.3	35	166	30.1	7.7
7	819	6.1	1.5	40	146	34.2	8.8
8	717	7.0	1.7	45	131	38.3	9.9
9	637	7.8	2.0	50	118	42.3	11.1
10	574	8.7	2.2	55	108	46.2	11.6
11	522	9.6	2.4	60	100	50.0	12.5
12	478	10.5	2.6	65	93	53.7	13.4
13	442	11.3	2.8	70	87	57.4	14.4
14	410	12.2	3.1	75	82	60.9	15.2
15	383	13.1	3.3	80	78	64.3	16.0
16	359	13.9	3.5	85	74	67.6	16.9
17	338	14.8	3.7	90	71	70.7	17.6
18	320	15.6	3.9				
19	303	16.5	4.2				
20	288	17.4	4.4				

Yard Tracks.—The lead, body and other tracks running alongside main tracks, especially where passenger trains are operated, should be

[1] The tangent offset here given is the perpendicular distance from the tangent line produced to a point on the curve 100 ft. from its beginning.   The tangent offset, therefore, represents the amount in feet that the curve deflects from a straight line in a length of 100 ft.   In any curve the distance measured perpendicular to the 100-ft. chord from the middle point of the chord to the curve is called the "middle ordinate," and the middle ordinate is practically equal to tangent offset divided by 4.

spaced 16 ft., center to center, from the main track so as to give ample space for telegraph, telephone, electric-light and signal-line poles, and for signal posts, water standpipes, mile posts, section posts and whistle posts, without encroaching upon the prescribed clearance between them and cars on the adjoining tracks.

Tracks running parallel to ladder tracks should be at least 16 ft., center to center, from the ladder tracks, so as to enable switch lights to be readily seen and men to have room in which to move while throwing switches, for giving signals and cutting cars. When conditions permit it, ladder tracks should be straight and frogs on ladders should be all of the same angle.

Under usual conditions body tracks should be spaced 12 or 13 ft., center to center, and frogs of greater angles than No. 7 frogs (8 deg. 10 min.) should not be generally used. The spacing of 12 ft. for body tracks in a storage yard is satisfactory, but for receiving, departure and classification yards 13 ft. should be obtained where practicable. For a No. 7 frog the use of turnout curves of about 16 deg. is required, over which all the usual kinds of rolling stock can operate, whereas a No. 6 frog calls for a turnout curve of about 22 deg., which is about the limiting curve for road engines and is too sharp for some passenger coaches. It is advisable, where it can be readily obtained, to use no smaller numbered frog than a No. 8 frog in yard design and nothing with a smaller number than No. 10 for main-line connections. It is usual and practicable to equip yards with No. 8 turnouts.

When the body tracks make an angle with the ladder track equal to, or in some cases slightly greater than, the frog angle, then every body track can be connected with the ladder track without danger of the joint at the heel of the frog coming too close to the point of the following switch. If the body tracks make an angle with the ladder track of about twice the frog angle, then every other body track can be connected to the ladder track and the remaining body tracks will have to be joined to the next preceding track.

A common practice is to have every second, and occasionally every second and third, body track connected by a switch to a preceding body track instead of running directly out of the ladder. Property limitations, physical characteristics or urgent need for all space available sometimes compel this arrangement. It should be avoided, when possible, because the better arrangement and compactness of the switches, the unobstructed view from end to end of the ladder and the ease with which the engineman may select his track, read signals and know his route are advantages which may frequently justify a heavy expenditure to secure them. Then, too, if every body track joined the ladder, the movement in and through the body tracks is much safer and more simple, because a view alongside from end to end of the train may be had (provided the body tracks are straight), which permits signals to be transmitted more readily. In some cases it may be necessary to omit one or two switches from the ladder to make room for scales, a switchman's box, bridge pier or other structure, in which cases it is simply a question of whether or not the advantage of such location for the particular structure outweighs the disadvantage of breaking into the uniform alinement of switches on the ladder.

Repair tracks should have sufficient capacity to provide for the immediate needs and be so designed as to permit subsequent enlargement or extension as may be required, and should be spaced alternately 16 and 24 ft., center to center, and conveniently connected to bad-order tracks.

Team tracks should be stub tracks located in pairs 12 to 13 ft. on centers; a few railroads prefer to have them constructed in clusters of three tracks. A distance between the outside tracks of the clusters of at least 50 ft. from center to center of tracks should be provided to permit the efficient movement of vehicles loading or unloading at the cars. The width of the driveway required depends largely on the kind and number of vehicles using it. At delivery tracks where large-capacity motor trucks form a substantial percentage of the trucking vehicles, a wider driveway than 50 ft. would be found desirable. Where the freight house or team track is on one side and a wall or fence on the other, the minimum width of roadway should be 40 ft. As a rule, team tracks should not have a capacity exceeding 20 cars each, assuming 42 ft. as the overall length of the freight car, which is the usual practice. The lay-out should be so arranged as to render crossing of tracks by vehicles unnecessary. Two end team tracks are. desirable where inspection or reconsignment privileges are in effect.

Standard Turnouts.—It is universal custom to designate frogs by their number, ranging up to about No. 20. As a rule, standard frogs are used, but in special cases a frog of an odd number, such as No. 7.32, may be required to fit the needs of a particular situation.

The number of a frog is the ratio of its length divided by the spread between gage lines at the heel, the length being measured from the theoretical point of the frog where the gage lines cross each other. The actual point of the frog is blunt, and in some frogs is several inches from the theoretical point. A practical method of obtaining the number of a frog in place is to measure the distance between gage lines of the frog rail, using a rule or any piece of material. Then the number of the frog would be the number of times this unit would go into the distance between the point of measurement and the theoretical frog point, allowing a few inches past the actual frog point.

In constructing a turnout the switch ties are first installed. Then the main-track rail is thrown out in line with side track to serve as stock and side-track rail. Then the frog and switch are installed, and these, as a rule, are the only parts of the actual turnout defined by the engineer's stakes. The details of the portion from the frog toward the switch point are all given on standard turnout sheets which every railroad prepares and which vary as regards the distance from the frog point to the switch point (called the turnout *"lead"*), the length of switch rail, the spread at the heel of the switch, the tie spacing and many other minor details. The track foreman, however, follows the standard for that particular frog number and for that particular style of turnout.

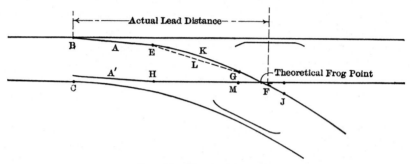

Fig. 16.—Standard turnout.

A No. 8 spring frog has the same angle as a No. 8 rigid frog, likewise a No. 8 frog on a standard-gage railroad has the same angle as a No. 8 on a narrow-gage or industrial track. The number, therefore, defines the angle that the outer rail will make with the inner one where they cross each other. But with a No. 8 frog the turnout lead will be different for different lengths of frog, of switch rail, spread at heel of switch, etc.; and the spread at the heel, for example, will depend upon the weight of rail used on different divisions of the railroad, for yard tracks, and for main-line tracks. So that a No. 8 turnout on any given railroad does not define the entire turnout from switch to frog; there may be three or four standard No. 8 turnouts on one railroad, each one suitable for a certain class of construction.

Every modern turnout is composed of a pair of split switch rails, AA' (Fig. 16), which in many instances are half a rail length 15 ft. or 16.5 ft. long. The switch rails are joined by splices to the rigidly spiked stock rails at E and H; both switch rails swing together about E and H as pivots; at B the switch rail forms a flat angle or wedge which forces the wheel to pass around the turnout; at C the stock rail is kinked so as to bring it parallel to BE and at the gage distance away from it. The portion EG of the turnout is a simple circular curve tangent to the switch rail at E and to the frog at G. The frog is usually straight from G (its toe) to J (its heel). The angle which the gage line of the switch

TABLE OF PRACTICAL TURNOUT LEADS

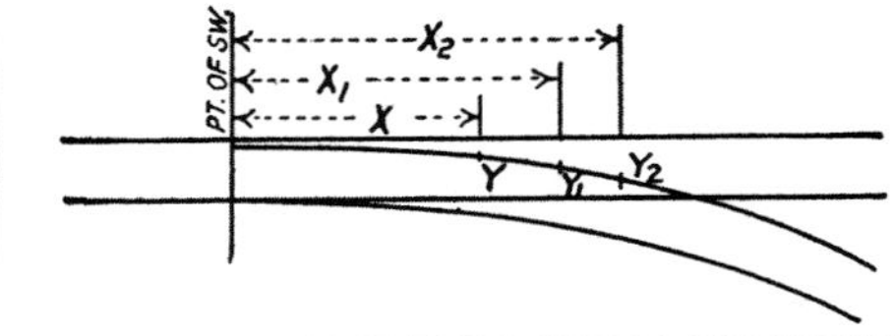

Frog number	Length of switch rail, Feet	Length of switch rail, Inches	Lead-distance actual point of switch rail to frog ½ in. point, Feet	Lead-distance, Inches	Closure rails (number of rails and lengths in feet and inches): Straight rail		Closure rails: Curved rail		Lead curve: Radius of center line, feet	Degree of curve: Degrees	Minutes	Seconds	X Feet	X Inches	X₁ Feet	X₁ Inches	X₂ Feet	X₂ Inches	Y Feet	Y Inches	Y₁ Feet	Y₁ Inches	Y₂ Feet	Y₂ Inches	Tangent adjacent to switch rail, Feet	Tangent adjacent to toe of frog, Feet
5	11	0	42	6½	....	1-28-0	1-28-3¾	....	175.40	33	07	28	17	11	24	10	31	9	0	11 5/8	1	8 5/16	2	8 5/16	0.00	0.97
6	11	0	47	6	....	1-32-9	1-33	....	254.00	22	42	20	19	2¼	27	4½	35	6¾	1	0 5/16	1	9 1/2	2	9 15/16	0.00	2.00
7	16	6	62	1	1-26	1-14-10½	1-26	1-15-1½	361.69	15	53	30	26	8½	36	11	47	1½	0	11 3/4	1	8 11/16	2	9 1/8	0.00	0.22
8	16	6	68	0	1-30	1-16-5	1-30	1-16-7	487.37	11	46	36	28	1¼	39	8½	51	3¾	1	0 1/16	1	9 3/16	2	9 5/8	0.32	0.00
9	16	6	72	3½	1-33	1-16-5	1-33	1-16-7	605.18	9	28	42	28	9	40	11¾	53	2¼	1	0 1/4	1	9 1/8	2	9	0.00	0.57
10	16	6	78	9	1-28	1-27-10	2-28	....	779.82	7	21	08	30	3⅜	44	0⅝	57	9¾	1	0 7/16	1	9 7/16	2	9 3/8	1.56	0.00
11	22	0	94	3¾	1-33	1-32-10¼	2-33	....	922.65	6	12	47	40	8⅞	56	5⅝	72	2¼	1	0 15/16	1	10 1/16	2	10 7/16	2.99	0.00
12	22	0	100	9⅝	2-24	1-23-10⅝	3-24	....	1,098.73	5	12	59	43	11⅞	60	7¾	77	3⅜	1	1 13/16	1	10 13/16	2	10 15/16	5.33	0.00
14	22	0	106	3¼	2-30	1-16-5¼	2-30	1-16-6¾	1,512.14	3	47	23	41	1¼	60	2½	79	3¾	1	0 15/16	1	10 1/2	2	10 15/16	0.00	2.84
15	30	0	126	2¼	2-30	1-27-10¾	2-30	1-28	1,748.29	3	16	40	52	0	74	0	96	0	1	0 5/16	1	9 11/16	2	10 3/8	0.00	0.51
16	30	0	131	6¾	2-30	1-32-10¾	2-30	1-33	2,019.18	2	50	16	53	2¾	76	5½	99	8¼	1	0 1/2	1	9 15/16	2	10 5/8	0.00	0.40
18	30	0	138	6	2-33	1-32-11	3-33	....	2,380.47	2	24	26	54	8¾	79	5½	104	2¼	1	0 3/4	1	10 5/16	2	10 15/16	0.00	6.38
20	30	0	151	5½	2-33 1-30	1-14-11½	2-33 1-30	1-15-0½	3,322.13	1	43	29	57	9	85	6	113	3	1	1 3/16	1	10 15/16	2	11 7/16	0.00	0.27

TURNOUTS AND CROSS-OVERS RECOMMENDED
For main-line high-speed movements, Nos. 16 or 20.
For main-line slow-speed movements, Nos. 12 or 10.
For yards and sidings, to meet general conditions, No. 8.

Note.—When conditions require a wider gage than 4 ft. 8½ in., the length lead as shown for 4-ft. 8½-in. gage shall be maintained and the gage widened on the inside rail back of the heel of switch.

rail *BE* makes at *B* with the gage line of the main rail is called the "switch angle." Neither the gage line of the switch nor of the frog are brought together to an actual point; both the switch and the frog have blunt ends, so that the theoretical lead distance and the actual lead distance are different in amount. The trackman is interested in the actual lead distance, which, together with the other usual dimensions, is given in the following turnout table. This table, it should be remembered, will be slightly different on different roads.

The American Railway Engineering Association, in an attempt to standardize turnouts of a given frog number, has assigned certain arbitrary values to the lead distances which shall correspond closely to the computed leads but which shall require little cutting and waste of rails. This is partially accomplished by using short standard lengths of rail which are always kept in stock, such as 18-, 24-, 27- and 30-ft. lengths. The American Railway Engineering Association's Table of Turnouts with Practical Leads is given on page 49.

In passing around a turnout from the switch toward the frog, as soon as the frog is reached, the connecting track may be run either straight by extending the side of the frog, or it can proceed by a curve of any degree, provided the curve is tangent to the frog.

If the body tracks of the yard are straight and the ladder is straight, then, with the ordinary track spacing used in yards, every body track can be connected to any ladder track which makes an angle with the body track equal to the frog angle. The following table gives distances between frog points measured along the ladder track in the case just mentioned. It will be seen by examining this table that with tracks 13 ft. on centers and No. 8 frog there is 104.40 ft. between the frog points. In the preceding table the lead distance of a No. 8 turnout is given as 68 ft.

DISTANCE BETWEEN FROG POINTS ON LADDER TRACKS WHEN BODY TRACKS MAKE AN ANGLE WITH THE LADDER TRACK EQUAL TO THE FROG ANGLE, IN FEET

Frog No.	Spacing of body tracks center to center, in feet							Frog No.
	12	12.5	13	13.5	14	14.5	15	
4	48.75	50.78	52.81	54.84	56.87	58.91	60.94	4
5	60.60	63.12	65.65	68.17	70.70	73.22	75.75	5
6	72.50	75.52	78.54	81.56	84.58	87.60	90.62	6
7	84.43	87.95	91.47	94.98	98.50	102.02	105.54	7
8	96.37	100.39	104.40	108.42	112.44	116.45	120.47	8
9	108.33	112.85	117.36	121.87	126.39	130.90	135.41	9
10	120.30	125.31	130.33	135.34	140.35	145.36	150.38	10
11	132.28	137.79	143.30	148.81	154.32	159.83	165.34	11
12	144.25	150.26	156.27	162.28	168.29	174.30	180.31	12

If the lead is assumed to be about 68 ft., this leaves 36 ft. between frog point and the following switch point, part of which is taken up by the distance from frog point to the heel of the frog and the rail splice at the frog heel (usually 7 to 8 ft. in all), and the remaining distance 28 or 29 ft. is clear distance between the end of the rail splice at the frog and the point of the next switch.

If the tracks in this example had been 12 ft. on center, the distance between frogs as given in the last table is 96.37; the lead distance plus

Fig. 17.—Typical easy-lead cross-overs.

proper clearance from frog point to the next switch point would be about 68 + 12 = 80 ft., which leaves only 16 ft. to be gained by swinging the ladder track to make a slightly greater angle with the body tracks. The advantage of laying the ladder track at the greatest possible angle with the body tracks is that body tracks can thereby be given the greatest possible length and still insure that every body track will join the ladder by its own turnout without having to join it through another body track, as is always required when the angle the ladder track makes with the body tracks is much in excess of the frog angle.

It will be observed from the Table of Standard Turnouts that the curved track of a No. 10 turnout is a 7-deg. 21-min. 08-sec. curve. This is the curve which the rails between the switch and the frog will have if the turnout joins a straight main-line track. If the main line, however, is a 3-deg. curve, then the turnout curve will be 3 deg. sharper (or a 10-deg. 21-min. 08-sec. curve), provided the turnout passes out on the inside of the main-line curve, and the turnout curve will be a 4-deg. 21-min. 08-sec. curve if it leaves the main line on the outside of the main-line curve. If the mainline curve happened to be a 7-deg. 21-min. 08-sec. curve, then a No. 10 turnout on the inside of the curve would require a 14-deg. 42-min. 16-sec. curve for the turnout, whereas, if the turnout is on the outside of the main track, it will be a straight track.

The total length of a cross-over between parallel tracks is dependent upon the track spacing, the numbers of the frogs and the lead distances. While all these vary with different railroads, the following general table gives some idea of the length of track required for cross-overs in which the same number of frogs is used at each end and where the track between the frogs is straight.

TOTAL LENGTH OF CROSS-OVERS (A.R.E.A. STANDARDS)

Frog. No.	Track centers							
	12 ft.		13 ft.		14 ft.		15 ft.	
	Feet	Inches	Feet	Inches	Feet	Inches	Feet	Inches
6	109	6	115	$5\frac{1}{2}$	121	5	127	$4\frac{1}{2}$
7	141	$2\frac{7}{8}$	148	$2\frac{3}{8}$	155	2	162	$1\frac{5}{8}$
8	155	$7\frac{1}{2}$	163	$7\frac{1}{8}$	171	$6\frac{3}{4}$	179	$6\frac{3}{8}$
9	166	9	175	$8\frac{5}{8}$	184	$8\frac{3}{8}$	193	8
10	182	$2\frac{3}{8}$	192	$2\frac{1}{8}$	202	$1\frac{7}{8}$	212	$1\frac{1}{2}$
11	215	$10\frac{1}{4}$	226	10	237	$9\frac{3}{4}$	248	$9\frac{3}{8}$
12	231	$4\frac{1}{4}$	243	4	255	$3\frac{3}{4}$	267	$3\frac{1}{2}$
14	247	4	261	$3\frac{3}{4}$	275	$3\frac{1}{2}$	289	$3\frac{1}{4}$
15	289	$8\frac{1}{8}$	304	$7\frac{7}{8}$	319	$7\frac{3}{4}$	334	$7\frac{1}{2}$
16	302	$11\frac{1}{4}$	318	$11\frac{1}{8}$	334	$10\frac{7}{8}$	350	$10\frac{3}{4}$
18	321	10	339	$9\frac{7}{8}$	357	$9\frac{5}{8}$	375	$9\frac{1}{2}$
20	352	$9\frac{1}{4}$	372	9	392	$8\frac{7}{8}$	412	$8\frac{3}{4}$

Even though these do require an increase in length of track, cross-overs and turnouts of large numbered frogs (small angles) are being used in main-line connections to permit their operation at medium and even at high speed. Figure 17 shows several small-angle track connections which will permit of rapid handling of traffic.

On some roads today No. 24 frogs and 33-ft. switch rails are used at points where a two-track and a four-track system join, and it is not uncommon to operate at the rate of 35 miles an hour through these turnouts.

Three-throw and Slip Switches.—Split switches of good pattern should be used in all yard work; slips should be avoided as far as possible. Three-throw switches should not be used with any work, where it is possible to avoid them. There are places where the only possible solution seems to be a three-throw switch, but it is difficult to conceive of any situation where a little mental energy will not enable the engineer to substitute a less objectionable arrangement. The saving in the operating expenses will soon overbalance the additional outlay of both energy and capital necessary to secure the result. The liability of three-throw switches to get out of order, with the close and constant supervision required, will increase the maintenance account considerably. There remains the cost of accidents resulting and interference to yard operations by such obstructions, and the vastly greater probability of derailment or other accident due to mistakes by switchmen.

There are conditions where a three-throw turnout or a tandem turnout are the only devices available. The tandem arrangement is one in which the second pair of switch points does not rest against the first pair of points, as in a three-throw switch, but rests against the stock lead rail; that is, the first pair of switch points is 20 to 30 ft. in advance of the second pair of points. The tandem turnout does not have many of the disadvantages which the three-throw turnout has, and there are conditions where entirely separate turnouts are not possible if a flexible operating layout is to be devised, but where a reasonably good operating design can be made by the introduction of a tandem turnout.

It is sometimes desirable to have a yard cut in two by running a ladder across the middle of it, and in such cases it is difficult to argue against the use of the very flexible but expensive slip switch, which is expensive both in construction and maintenance. Its use enables any movement from any track in the first yard to any track in the second half, lying in line or in advance. Figure 18 shows a track layout involving a double slip switch which gives great flexibility in operation. The only partial substitute for the slip-switch ladder is a double ladder, and that does not give the same flexibility of operation. On the other hand, it does enable two sets of operations to be conducted without fouling each other, which is an impossibility with one double slip-switch ladder. In the double ladder, for instance, a train may be pulled out of the first yard or may "double" its cars over in or out of two, three or any number of tracks, while an engine is using the second ladder to separate cars in the second yard. Much additional ground space is required for the double ladder, which results in a curtailment of the yard capacity. This may in itself prevent the use of the double ladder where the capacity is limited.

Fig. 18.—Typical use of double slips, permitting flexibility in movements.

Crossing Frog.—On the main line, and not infrequently in yards and on industry tracks, crossing frogs have to be used. When the angle of the frogs in a set of crossing frogs is less than 9 deg. (about a No. 6 frog) it is practically impossible to arrange the guard rails so as to prevent derailments, and it therefore requires that such frogs shall have movable points, which adds considerably to the maintenance cost. Rigid-center frogs are not recommended below 8 deg. 10 min. on tangent track. For curved track, the recommended limiting angle for rigid-center frogs is 9 deg. 30 min., for curves 6 deg. and under, increasing 1 deg. for each 2 deg. of greater curvature up to a maximum angle of 15 deg. 30 min. for 18-deg. curves and over. Movable-point crossings are recommended below these limits.

The practice is growing of making frog points of manganese steel and in many cases of providing for removable points. In fact, removable manganese-steel switch points are now being used to some extent; and recently manganese steel has been rolled into the standard rail sections, whereas only a few years ago all rails made of this steel had to be cast, requiring extra thick webs for the rails.

In yards, worn switch points, frogs, and rail ends are frequently built up in place with oxyacetylene welders.

Spring Switches.—A spring switch, through which a car can trail even though the switch is not set for the car, may be tolerated in some places, but not on a ladder in a yard, because of the liability to accident and the seriousness of tying up the whole or most of the traffic in a busy yard while making repairs to a switch on a ladder track. While it is a subject to be discussed under the head of organization, or discipline, running through a switch should be just as carefully and thoroughly investigated and the discipline applied should be just as rigid as though it were out on the open road at a point where more serious damage could happen. That it was "in the yard," and that the switch was built for just that kind of thing, should not be permitted to influence the case at all; otherwise, the disease will certainly spread and the results may be far reaching.

There are places where switches may regularly and intentionally be run through with good operating results. Where movements inside a yard or its adjuncts and away from the main tracks are normal, spring switches may be used in such a manner as to permit their being run through in one direction regularly. This statement refers to points where all movements are made over the same track and switches in the same direction. On electric roads this is usually done at passing sidings, where each car regularly turns to the right (or left) and avoids the delay of having someone throw the switch. For engine movements between engine houses and coaling plants or ash tracks, this method can frequently be applied with a saving of time for engines and men and a saving in wages for switch tenders. A set of switches was rearranged at a large locomotive-coaling plant and ash track, and by the introduction of four or five spring switches at points where they were usually kept in one position, at a cost of not exceeding $500, it was possible to dispense with four switch tenders, two during the day and two at night, which alone involved a saving in wages of $540 a month. Furthermore, there was a considerable economy due to the possibility of more rapid locomotive movements.

Only solidly coupled switches should be used in main-line work, because they are less liable to derangement and simpler to maintain than the spring switch. After being run through, they are usually rendered unfit for service and repairs must be made. This tells its own story; discipline accompanied by education does the rest. With the spring or joint connection, a switch, after being run through, may be slightly damaged and yet to the trainmen appear to be safe. If left in this condition, it may cause an accident later on. The greatest objection, however, is the possibility of a small obstruction, pebble, snow or ice, or a bolt or nut falling between the track rail and the switch rail and holding the points open while the switch lever is permitted to be seated and locked.

On ladders, there should be a good pattern of ground throw switch stand, which does not obstruct a man riding on the side step of a freight car or while running alongside to uncouple cars. The lever must lock itself automatically to prevent its flying over when it has been carelessly or hurriedly thrown by the switchman, and it should throw "fore and aft;" that is in the direction the track runs instead of crossways or at right angles to the track. Many stands are made that fill these requirements.

Switches in yards, and particularly on ladders and at other important points, should be maintained in good condition. The track numbers should be painted on the targets for the convenience of the switchmen. It is good practice to assign a set of numbers to each yard. Most roads have a system of numbering trains, tracks, signals, etc. with the odd numbers in one direction and the even numbers in the other. The general practice seems to be to use odd numbers on west and southbound trains. A certain set of numbers should be set aside for numbering main tracks and passing or additional running tracks in conformity with the general practice. In a cluster of yards it may be well to start the first series, assuming it to be eastbound on an east and west road, at 10, and on the westbound at 11. If the eastbound yard contains eight tracks, the numbers would be 10, 12, 14, 16, 18, 20, 22, and 24. The next yard should then start at 30 or possibly 40. This keeps the numbers in a certain series, and at the same time allows for the extension of any yard without disarranging all the numbers. It also corresponds with the practice of numbering trains with even numbers south and east, and odd numbers north and west. All switches on ladders should be located on the side opposite the frogs. The targets with lamps should be low enough to clear the pole of a poling engine.

Power-thrown vs. Hand-thrown Switches.—The use of power-thrown switches, or those thrown from a central interlocking point, in connection with freight terminals is not uncommon. Where passenger movements are involved, an interlocking of switches which connect the main-line tracks with the yard is not only desirable but essential.

Whether or not the ladder switches of a freight classification yard should be thrown by power is a question upon which there is much to be said on both sides. The hand-thrown switches on the ground seem to possess many advantages. From the standpoint of interference with operation due to labor troubles, the arguments are pretty evenly balanced. When introducing towers and interlocking, men of higher order of skill and intelligence are employed; and with men of this type, who naturally have some sense of responsibility and duty, a sudden, unnecessary or uncalled-for cessation of work with a view to embarrassing employers to the greatest possible extent is less likely to occur. On the other hand, switches are often manned by crippled men who have been injured in the railroad's service while in the discharge of their duties, for whom it is a matter of moral obligation and good policy to provide employment. The switch tender who is on the ground may read the chalked number on the rear end of cars of each "cut," in summit or pole switching, and know what to "line up" for the next "cut." Movements can be made closer together because the switch tender does not have to wait for a car to pass the clearance point before throwing the switch for the next movement. In this way much time is saved as compared with the electric systems which have to be designed so as to insure complete clearance before the next switch can be operated.

Switch tenders can do much toward keeping hand-thrown switches free of snow and ice and other obstructions. Their most important work is to keep the points open. When one switch is open, such switch may be used independently of all others, and one switch snowed up does not interfere with another. There is considerably less wear and tear on hand-thrown switches. Their first cost is low and maintenance charges are light. Repairs are readily and quickly made and in case of a derailment there is usually little interference with other switches and tracks.

At Perth Amboy the Lehigh Valley has for many years operated switches on its coal docks by direct hand-power lever machines, not interlocked. These have given satisfactory service. The switches are not far distant from the tower and the operator can readily follow the movements of cars with his eye. The system is simple and there is, therefore, little likelihood of its getting out of order. The electric lighting is ample for the men unloading coal, but work at night is done only in emergencies.

Many improvements are being made in the application of electric power to throwing switches and, doubtless, some improved system may appear which will meet entirely, or to a great extent, the objections cited. All things considered, the plan of throwing switches from a tower or central point, by direct lever movements, not interlocked, is the one that seems most practical and economical for classification-yard ladders. This view is taken with the knowledge that this method permits fouling of cars, and that special arrangements must be made for advising the switch thrower of the position of cars during night, foggy weather, snow and rain storms.

In some terminals complete systems of centrally operated switches are installed. The Altoona yard of the Pennsylvania was probably the first to install and operate power-thrown switches controlled from a central point. During many years of service this system has been operated with ease, reliability and rapidity. The power is compressed air actuated by electricity.   The operator in the tower controls the switches by push buttons and, when one is thrown, an indicator shows when the car sent to that particular track has cleared the switch so that it can be closed again.   An advance "cut report" is received from the conductor of each train to be classified.   Copies are made of this report and placed in the hands of each employee engaged in breaking up the trains, including the towerman, thus enabling the operator to set up the proper route for each car without receiving any verbal directions or consulting switching signals.   Loud speaking telephones connecting hump conductor and tower operator are of value and distant audible and visible signals are of service.

The admission of air by electrically controlled valves to the cylinder directly throws the points of the switch: It is the regular electropneumatic switch movement, without the lock cylinder and magnet.   There is no locking movement.   In the cabin are two rows of push buttons, an upper and a lower one, and there are two buttons for each switch.   Each button in the upper row closes its switch, and the button below it opens the switch.   The ladder and tracks leading from it are divided by insulated joints into blocks embracing each turnout, and one of the point rails of each switch is insulated from the main rail.   An indicator, in circuit with the insulated rails of the switch and turnout, is located on the operating board just above the set of buttons for throwing the switch.   When the track is clear, the indicator shows white, and when a car is in the limits of the circuit and in rear of the clearance point, or the switch has not completed its throw, the indicator shows red.   A record of 133 cars switched in an hour is claimed, and an average performance of 95 cars can readily be maintained.   The air pressure is about 40 lb., and the switch farthest distant from the tower is 1,500 ft. away.

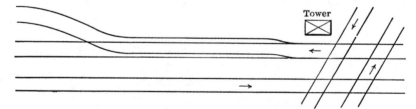

Fig. 19.—Gauntlet arrangement to shorten throw connections.

In the Clearing Yards near Chicago, out of a total of some 459 switches, 120 along the ladder of the classification tracks are operated by electropneumatic cylinders.   These are built on substantially the same plan as those at Altoona, the central or lock magnet being omitted.   The tower has 10 push-button machines, each machine controlling 12 switches. Indicators similar to those at Altoona are used.

In the case of small yards the only yard turnout operated by a towerman is the lead from the main track at one end of the yard, and it sometimes occurs that that lead is at a considerable distance from an existing tower which cannot be removed and the lead cannot for physical reasons, without great expense, be extended parallel to the main track so as to join it near the tower. A method which has been used in cases of this sort is shown in Fig. 19. The lead track to the yard is extended as a gauntlet track to a point near the tower where the switch can be directly under the control of the towerman. An electric lock is introduced which prevents the towerman from clearing the signals for the main track until a train has pulled onto the siding far enough to clear the main track.

Clearing Snow in Yards.—In places where there is much snow the hand switch has a decided advantage. It requires an army of men to keep an interlocking plant in operation during a driving sleet or snow storm, because there are so many parts of the switches, locks, rods, signals and their connections, and every part must be kept open for movement to enable any switch to be used.

An experiment was tried on the New York, New Haven and Hartford at Providence, R. I., which was successful in keeping switches and movable frogs clear during a snow storm. An engine was equipped with two 9.5-in. Westinghouse pumps, two reservoirs with a capacity of 52,000 cu. in. and a line of hose 75 ft. long and ⅜ in. inside diameter. The opening at the end of the hose was of the same size. An engine crew and four or five men with this apparatus could reach four or five tracks on either side of the engine. On one morning following a fall of 4 or 5 in. of snow, a test was made and a complete set of double slips was blown out in 4.5 min. The pressure fell from an initial pressure of about 90 lb. to 70 lb., but was readily maintained at from 70 to 75 lb. The engine was again tried in 4 or 5 in. of snow a few days later, with equally satisfactory results. It would make little difference if the depth of snow were four or five times as great. It is, of course, necessary to load up and haul away the snow, but the first and main object is to get the interlocking plant in operation quickly, and this it accomplishes, doing the work of from 100 to 150 men. It is difficult, if not impossible, to get that number of men out and to work during the night in less than four or five hours, while an engine and crew can be got out in a few minutes.

The use of hydrocarbon for fighting snow is also advocated where it is available. It was very thoroughly tried out at the South Terminal passenger station at Boston during severe snow storms, and its use has been continued. On one day there was a fall of 10 in.; on another 15 in. with 18 in. additional snowfall on the following day with several inches more added by snow blown from the roofs on the 13.5 acres of buildings comprising the terminal. The latter storm commenced at 10:30 p. m., continuing about 24 hours, the heaviest part of the snow falling between midnight and 6 a. m. of the following day, while a blizzard raged, the wind velocity reaching 40 m.p.h. and the thermometer dropping to 6° above zero. The snow drifted badly and packed in around the switch points, detector bars and other interlocking apparatus. Not a minute's delay occurred to traffic because of the storm, although a few of the switches could not be thrown promptly because water from engines or cars fell on detector bars and froze, causing them to stick for a few minutes at a time. The hydrocarbon was handled by the regular track gang of 33 men and the interlocking gang of six men, no extra men being employed. It was handled in safety distributing cans, capacity 2.5 gal. each, a lighted stream being sprayed to points where desired. Snow and ice in or about switches and interlocking apparatus are thus quickly melted. The height of the blaze is from 1 to 3 in. above the top of the rail. A switch can be thawed out in from 3 to 5 min. It does not injure ties, it is claimed that it acts as a preservative and the heat applied to rails is not injurious. This South Terminal interlocking plant covers about 15 acres and contains 29 double slips, 43 single slips and some 500 ordinary switches. The cost for hydrocarbon used in these two storms was between $50 and $75; the cost of extra labor used in previous storms would range from $800 to $1,000 and at least 150 additional men would have been required. Permission was given by the Underwriters to use the hydrocarbon.

One of the recent developments in equipment designed to enable the railways to keep their switches open and in operation during the heavy snows of the winter season with a minimum of manual labor, is an installation of nozzles along the switches, by means of which hydrocarbons and other low flash oils are ignited and discharged at and around the switch points. The operation is controlled by valves at the various switch installations, the oil being lighted by special ignitors. One man's attention is required for a fraction of a minute and approximately once an hour, thus permitting one man to care for a large number of switches.

The installation for a standard switch consists of two short lines of one-inch pipe mounted on brackets along the ends of the ties, each line carrying five or more plain nozzles according to conditions and two special ignitors with nozzles directed toward the outside of the running rails. These two lines of pipe are connected together and to a feeder line from the oil supply. The connection between the two lines is electrically insulated. The oil supply is generally in the form of a tank for a large number of installations but ordinary "drums" are often used at smaller installations. The required pressure is obtained by elevating the tank at a minimum of about 10 ft. above the level of the nozzles. The plain nozzles are directed toward the ball of the rail and are located between the ties. The special nozzles and ignitors are located at the ends of the installation and are arranged so that on each line, one ignitor is on the inside and one on the outside of the running rail, each pointing toward the other. This arrangement secures the ignition of the oil discharged from the plain nozzles independently of the direction or intensity of the winds.[1]

[1] *Railway Engineering and Maintenance*, Nov., 1924.

Electric snow melters have also proved their value in preventing accumulations of snow and ice at switches and other points. These snow melters consist of a heating coil contained in a brass case 18 inches by 6½ inches by 2 inches and are placed loosely in the ballast so that the top is about 1 inch below the base of the rail. While in service they use about one kilowat per hour and attain their maximum temperature 600 degrees fahrenheit in 45 minutes. An ordinary turnout will require about 14 units to protect it. These heaters are usually placed under the rails in the fall and removed in the spring and there is no operating expense involved until the current is turned on during a snow storm or when it is desired to melt ice or sleet which hinders switching operations.

Lighting Yards.—The proper lighting of yards facilitates switching and prevents pilfering from cars. Arc lights on poles not too high, set in such a position as to prevent, so far as practicable, the casting of shadows, are most satisfactory. It is particularly important that the summit of pole engine leads and the classification ladder tracks be well lighted. Care should be exercised to avoid placing arc lights in positions where they may obscure or confuse signal lights. When lights are badly located they cause patches of bright light and moving shadows of deep blackness, intensified by contrast. There is more liability of confusion and accident under such conditions than there would be in uniform darkness, to which the men's eyes become more or less accustomed. For lighting hump or ladder tracks the lamps should be spaced 140 to

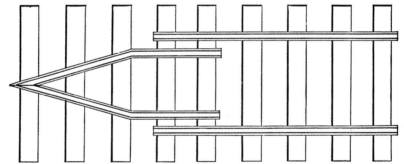

Fig. 20.—Re-railing device as substitute for bumper.

150 ft. apart and hung 28 ft. or higher above the tracks. For lighting body tracks the spacing should be such as to render cars clearly visible.

Bumping Posts.—For ordinary single-end tracks, bumpers are not necessary. It is usually better to let cars drop off ends of rails, where the ground is level and no damage can ensue. In many instances bumpers are abused because switchmen prefer to trust to them to stop cars instead of riding the cars and applying brakes. In passenger stations and in many passenger yards they are necessary to prevent serious accidents which may result from cars being pushed into or across spaces where persons may be injured; and because, in many instances, passenger cars cannot readily be coupled without bumpers to hold cars against the locomotive.   On coal or other trestles bumpers should be erected, as well as on the ends of tracks abutting against buildings, or where persons are employed who are liable to be injured by a car running off the end of a track.

On some roads, in lieu of bumpers, a very simple rerailing device is used, made something like the inside rail guard on bridges, except that the rail comes out closer to the track rail.   The diagram (Fig. 20) will convey an idea of its construction and method of operation.   In some cases, wedges, or inclines, are placed at the ends of the main rails to enable a car wheel to ascend to the top of the rail after having been pushed off the end of the track.   A car dropping off the end of a track so arranged will generally pull back on again.   The cost is perhaps less than half that of the best known bumpers.

In a modern development of bumping posts a metal post angled away from and supporting the upturned ends of the rails is used instead of the rigid upright post.   This construction has the advantage of giving a clear space below the bumping plate so that no part of the car can come in contact with the bumper except at the plate.   Sliding car stops have been employed successfully.   These devices are fastened to the head of the rail and are designed to allow the leading truck to mount the device, the sliding friction increased by the weight of the car gradually bringing the car to a stop.   Usually with these devices small stops are bolted to the ends of the rails, limiting the movement of the sliding stop.

Approximate Cost of Track.—The operating officer occasionally needs to determine approximately what it would cost to extend a track, put in an additional switch or make some slight track change, possibly for the purpose of deciding whether the cost warrants the improvement. For such use the following approximate costs are given.

In yard construction a No. 8 turnout with 80-lb. part-worn rail will cost about $400; with 100-lb. part-worn rail, about $450; and with 100-lb. new rail and manganese center frogs, $725.   A No. 10 turnout to a side track from the main line will cost about $600 with part-worn 100-lb. rail and $900 with new rail and manganese center frog.   A No. 10 main-line cross-over with new material will cost about $1,725.

CHAPTER V

CLASSIFICATION YARDS

A classification yard is essentially a machine for separating trains or drafts of cars, according to prearranged plans for distributing the cars in groups according to destinations, routes, commodities or traffic requirements, so as to accomplish their movement to tracks for these purposes. Classification or "shunting" yards may be operated under the old push-and-pull method (also called "link-and-pin" or "tail switching"); by poling; by using an artificially constructed summit or hump; and by gravity. The use of gravity alone is infrequent, but it is often taken advantage of to assist hump switching, poling and the ordinary push-and-pull.

Push-and-pull switching is neither efficient nor economical. It is slow, expensive in operation and damaging to cars, the disadvantage increasing with the use of heavier power. In many yards, and particularly in cities or other points where a crowded condition exists, it is the only practicable method of handling. Small yards, such as freight-house, transfer, local-delivery and coal yards, are invariably operated in this manner. In larger terminals the method should be done away with as rapidly as possible. Among other bad features is that of moving cars in the reverse direction. In most cases many reverse movements of a car are made before it reaches its proper track in the separation, classification or storage yard.

The poling method is so far in advance of tail switching, is so susceptible to expansion and has made such an exceptionally good record in passing cars through division, junction and tide-water terminals with a minimum of delay and of damage and was formerly considered to be one of the best methods of separating and grouping cars although now very generally superceded by the hump method described later on. It requires an additional track for the ram or poling engine along side the entrance leading to the yard. In some cases yards are arranged to enable the poling to be done directly from the receiving yard into the separating or classification yard. The yard engine has a pole attached to the breast beam, which is so manipulated as to come in contact with the poling pocket on the rear corner of the last car in the "cut" to be started. Usually a car is built, called a "poling car," equipped with four poles, two on each side, one of which works forward and the other to the rear. This car is also used for the men to ride on, and is probably a safer method of working than to use a pole directly from the engine's breast beam, by which the man guiding it can easily get caught if it should miss its mark or slip from its hold on the car. Frequently, two cuts (known as a "double cut") are started by placing the pole behind the last car in the first cut and then uncoupling between the two cuts after the cars are under fairly good headway, after which additional momentum is, of course, given the first cut in order to give sufficient room between that and the following cut to enable proper throwing of switches. On a level road the poling method is very hard on equipment. The cars require a heavy start and engines are rapidly worn out on account of heavy, quick starting and reversing. These conditions are aggravated during cold weather when cars run harder. In such yards it is desirable and usually necessary to continue the poling track along the ladder. In every switching yard, a descending grade running with the traffic movement is of great advantage, and it is especially desirable in a poling yard. Without an assisting grade, a poling yard handling a heavy business requires an engine to push trains being switched to the front, but when the grade is favorable the train may be started and, under regulation of brakes, continue to drop forward at a uniform speed as rapidly as the poling engine can work up the cuts. A descending grade of 0.4 per cent. is valuable, but as heavy as 0.8 or even 1.0 per cent. may be used to good advantage and during winter will be none too steep. In larger poling yards it is found economical to provide an additional track for an engine to work on in running down into the separating yard and bringing back the car riders, although usually the poling engine may be used to make an occasional run when car riders are not returning fast enough. In some yards a car propelled by electricity by an overhead trolley, running on a separate track, is used to return the car riders. In one yard, where the company has an electric plant for other purposes, the switch lamps are illuminated by small incandescent electric lights.

The hump or summit method consists of a natural or constructed hump, in the lead track or a part of the ladder, anywhere from 6 to 10 or 15 ft. in height, with a grade on either side, ranging all the way from 0.4 to 3.0 per cent. usually tapering off on the descending side. The body tracks may be level, but a light descending grade greatly facilitates the work of breaking up trains. By this method cars are pushed over the summit and after uncoupling are run down from the hump or summit by gravity. The plan has many points to commend it. Remarkable work has been done and excellent switching records made with it.

In gravity switching the grade must be sufficiently steep to start a car when the brakes are released. The yard engine is then only needed to start or feed the cars, and when low temperature or other weather conditions are such as to prevent a car from running. Gravity yards are somewhat uncommon, because it is difficult to find, at the proper place, a large tract of land of the proper shape and suitable to the economical construction of such a yard.

An interesting comparative record of the operation of yards using hump and flat switching was compiled by a committee of the American Railway Engineering Association.

A hump yard and two flat yards were compared. The hump yard is designated[1] "yard A," the flat yards as B and C. The figures were for the month of August, 1914, and represent the actual operating conditions and costs.

At yard A cars were counted only on entering yard. At B and C cars were counted entering and leaving. For this reason 211,760 cars are shown in A at a cost of 23.76 cts. per car, instead of 105,880 cars (actual) at 47.43 cts.

The cost of switching each cut of cars, as well as each car is shown. In making comparisons between two yards, one road might average two, and another five cars per cut.

The cost per car for salaries of yardmasters, assistants, engineers, firemen, switchmen, towermen, clerks, car riders, car inspectors, switch tenders, weighmasters and others was itemized, as well as the cost of supplies, power, air, light and heat, the total cost of each item per car equaling the total cost of switching per car. The cost of switching per cut of cars is shown for A.

It was suggested that the engine employed on the approach to the hump be of sufficient power to handle from a start the maximum train received in the yard.

There is much to be said, however, in favor of pole switching, and especially where it has the advantage of gravity assistance. The author had charge of a large coal yard where 1,428 loads were passed through in 10 hours and 20 min., or an average of 138 cars per hour. This was done with a ram and an assisting grade extending throughout the entire yard. All these cars were passed over scales and over half of them were weighed. The scales were not automatic. The record was a remarkable one, but it is only proper to add that the conditions of weather, character of lading (coal), heavy loads, good running cars, daylight hours and trained and reliable help all were favorable.

Diagrams of these yards are well worth careful study, not only by those interested in designing new yards or remodeling or revising existing yards, but also by those interested solely in the operation of yards. It is a mistaken idea that points in the operation of terminals may be obtained only by watching and studying actual movements; the author has, in his own experience, derived many good lessons in operating from the study of plans of terminals built on different lines from those of which he was in charge.

One of the strongest points in favor of the pole yard or pole system of switching is the facility with which cars may be started at varying speeds in entering the separation or classification yard. This feature is

[1] See table, p. 66.

STATEMENT SHOWING COMPARISON OF OPERATING CONDITIONS IN ONE HUMP YARD AND TWO FLAT YARDS

One month

Questions asked	Yard A (hump) eastbound hump, double track westbound hump, double track	Yard B (flat)	Yard C (flat)
1. Percentage of south or eastbound traffic	64½ per cent. loads 35½ per cent. empties	69 per cent. loads 31 per cent. empties	87 per cent. loads. 13 per cent. empties.
2. Percentage of north or westbound traffic	71 per cent. loaded 29 per cent. empties	55.8 per cent. loads 44.2 per cent. empties	65 per cent. loads. 35 per cent. empties.
3. Character of south or eastbound loads	Fresh meat, live stock, live poultry, fruit, dairy and other food products, machinery, merchandise, grain, mill products, raw and finished coal and coke	Fresh meat, perishable merchandise, grain, flour, stone, coal, coke, etc.	Fruit, potatoes, sugar, vegetables, asphalt, cement, coal, flour, grain, hay, lumber, live stock, etc.
4. Character of north or westbound loads	Live stock, fruit, vegetables, merchandise, mill products, raw and finished machinery, coal, coke, limestone and ore	Perishable groceries, merchandise, lumber, slag, etc.	Automobiles, b e e r , furniture, machinery, fresh meat, merchandise, cement, coal, etc.
5. Number of loaded cars handled during the month	102,734 loaded cars	96,903 loaded cars	43,341 loaded cars.
6. Number of empty cars handled during the month	53,692 empty cars	68,720 empty cars	13,037 empty cars.
7. Number of cars weighed during the month	10,852 cars weighed	2,696 cars weighed	6,275 cars weighed.
8. Maximum number of cars handled during 24 hours	4,998 cars (3,962 over humps) (a)	2,976 cars (a)	1,537 cars (a).
9. Maximum number of cars handled during any one hour	632 cars	450 cars	316 cars.
10. Number of cars classified	211,760 cars	79,081 cars	83,832 cars.
11. Cost per car	23.76 cts. per car	21.34 cts	63.01 cts. per car.
12. Rental of engines	$1.64 per hour (b)	$1.09 per hour (c)	$1.09 per hour (c).
13. Cost of air	$258.77	$4.51	$523.73.
14. Cost of lighting	$76.39	$97.08	$361.88.
15. Cost of supplies	$96	$33.45	$148.70.
16. Number of cars damaged	78 cars	60 cars	31 cars.
17. Cost of damage to cars	$1,854.50	$241.29	$359.50.
18. Are trains departing from yard made up in station order?	With exception of 2 divisions, set-off trains are not made up in station order—all trains are made up to embrace districts affording the longest haul to the break-up point	Yes	All trains are made up in station order, except drag trains, which handle dead freight exclusively, and empties.
19. Estimated cost of duplicating yard, exclusive of grading, bridges and buildings	$750,000	$329,200	$554,180.

particularly advantageous in colder climates where there is a greater range between the extremes of temperature. Some kinds of cars, or cars of certain construction, will run more readily than others. Those with well-supported, stiff body bolsters, preventing heavy riding on side bearings, will run more rapidly or with less start, particularly through curves, as in entering ladders and in leaving the ladders and entering the body tracks than others. Loaded cars will run better than empty cars and heavy loads better than light ones. As the temperature drops, cars run harder, and in the face of a head or, what is worse, a side wind, or on snow-covered tracks a harder push is needed, because the cars will slow down to a stop in a short distance. The pole method has its advantages in such cases because the start can be made sufficiently strong to meet the adverse conditions.

It is to be said, too, as one of the arguments in favor of the pole system, that the engine starting the cars works close to the front. The men in charge are, therefore, able to keep themselves informed as to the clearance distance of each body track and to start cars accordingly. They also have the advantage of receiving signals at short range. This advantage is particularly apparent during snow, rain or foggy weather preventing damage to cars and contents.

The ease with which a change in switching methods may be made in a yard arranged for poling is one of the arguments in favor of such a yard. The Dewitt hump yards of the New York Central near Syracuse were discontinued temporarily as hump yards during a business depression and were thereafter operated by tail switching, because there was not sufficient business moving to continue them economically.

(a) These cars counted but once.

(b) At yard A the cost of engine rental is made up as follows:

Cost per 100 locomotive miles run for repairs of locomotives, including replaced locomotives.. $18.29

Cost per 100 locomotive miles run for fuel yard locomotives...................... 5.26

Cost per 100 locomotive miles run for lubricants for locomotives (yard and road).... .29

Cost per 100 locomotive miles run for other supplies for locomotives (yard and road).. .40

Cost per 100 locomotive miles run for engine-house expenses (yard and road)....... 3.07

Total cost per 100 locomotive-miles run.................................. $27.31

Average per mile... .2731

Average per hour, based on 6 m.p.h. for yard engines....................... 1.64

(c) Cost of engine rental at yard B was figured at $5 per day, and at yard C $24 per 24 hours. For comparison purposes committee figured it as follows:

Cost per 100 locomotive miles run for repairs to locomotives including replaced locomotives.. $18.29

Average per mile... .1829

Figuring 6 m.p.h. for yard engines makes the cost $1.09 per hour as shown.

Fuel, lubricants, other supplies and engine-house expenses are not included in engine rental, as they have been included in general expense.

The comparatively high cost of handling cars in yard C is accounted for by the fact that wages paid in yard C are higher than in yard B and because extra expense was incurred in yard C handling cars to and from other railways and the stock yards.

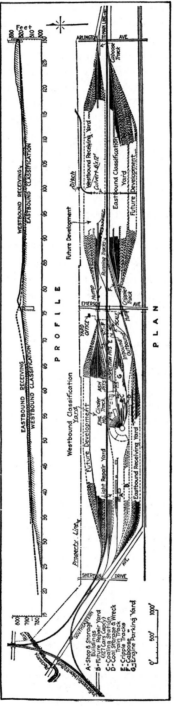

Fig. 21.—Plan and profile of Hawthorne yard of the Pennsylvania system, near Indianapolis, Ind.

The hump, or summit, yard has become the standard with most railroads. Many yards built within the last few years have been planned to be operated by gravity switching, aided by the summit, to give the cars their initial start after separation from the train. So important is the assistance of gravity in switching now regarded, that traffic is even reversed in direction and a cardinal principle in yard design violated in order to take advantage of a natural grade in the wrong direction.

The yards of the Pennsylvania at Hawthorne (near Indianapolis— see Fig. 21) provide a capacity of 3,500; ultimately, 10,000 cars. There are two double-track humps for gravity classification of traffic in opposite directions. These units comprise the general layout—a receiving yard, a switching hump and a classification yard for each direction, and parallel to each other. The third unit includes engine house, car-repair yard, and accessory facilities. Two thoroughfare tracks separate the eastward and westward units. Capacities are: westward receiving yard, 680 cars on 80 tracks—75 to 100 cars each; classification yard, 1,195 on 20 tracks, 45 to 85 each. Eastward: receiving yard, 360 cars on 5 tracks—70 to 80 cars each; classification yard, 1,160 cars on 17 tracks for 55 to 90 cars each —all figured on 45 ft. for each car. The arrangement of grades, according to profile on plan, is:

GRADES THROUGH HAWTHORNE YARD

	Eastbound	Westbound
Receiving yard..........	−0.22 per cent. for 2,000 ft. Level for 2,515 ft.	+1 per cent. for 715 ft. +0.4 per cent. for 3,235 ft.
Hump approach.........	+1 per cent. for 585 ft. +3 per cent. for 125 ft. 50-ft. vertical curve	+1½ per cent. for 800 ft. +3 per cent. for 180 ft. 50-ft. vertical curve
Hump starting..........	−5 per cent. for 100 ft. −3 per cent. for 100 ft.	−3 per cent. for 160 ft.
Hump ladders..........	−1.25 per cent. for 650 ft. −1 per cent. for 530 ft.	−1.25 per cent. for 750 ft.
Classification yard.......	−0.3 per cent. for 2,865 ft. −0.8 per cent. for 1,050 ft.	−0.3 per cent. for 1,100 ft. Level 1,400 ft. +0.5 per cent. for 1,500 ft. +0.7 per cent. for 300 ft.

So far as can be learned, the first summit yard in this country was constructed by the Pennsylvania road in 1882 at Huffs Station, 2 miles south of Greenbush, Va. Before then, the idea had been applied in European yard design. Germany had a summit yard at Speldorf in 1876, and in 1888 France had one in service on the Paris, Lyons & Mediterranean Railway. There is record of a gravity yard in Dresden in 1846; in St. Étienne, France, in 1863; and one in 1873 (see Fig. 22) in Edge Hill, near Liverpool, England.

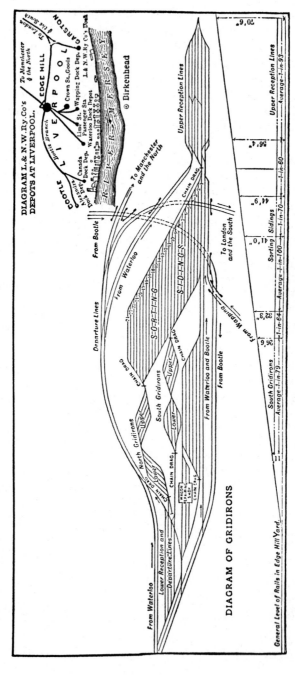

FIG. 22.—Diagrams of grid-irons, Edge Hill yards, England—London Midland and Scottish.

Statistics relating to the performance of the early summit yards in this country are rare, but there is a record of tests made by the Pennsylvania road in its yard at Honey Pot, Pa., on the Sunbury division. On Nov. 2, 1899, they handled 176 cars in six drafts, one car to each cut, each car being weighed as it passed over the scale, and the work was done in 63 min., almost three cars a minute—a remarkable performance.

In the *Railway Gazette* (London) the editor, W. H. Boardman, discussed the theory of summit yards as follows:

When a train of cars, uncoupled either singly or in groups, or "cuts," is pushed over the summit, the leading car or cut plunges down the sharp grade at a greatly increased speed. This acceleration produces a time and space interval between each cut. It is desirable to know what conditions increase or decrease these intervals. The space interval may be disregarded if the speed at the last switching point from the lead, or ladder, is twice the speed at the summit. It is plain that if two equally easy running cars were instantaneously set free on a uniform down grade, they would keep together—there would be no interval between them; but the change from level, or up grade to down grade allows the front car to get away at higher speed during the time that the following car moves its length on the level, and this time becomes the time interval between them.

This time interval between car centers is a constant all the way down the incline and through the yard, as will appear quite clearly when the reader recalls that all the cars would run their distance from the summit to the same stopping point in the same amount of time; and that the leading car has just a car length advantage over the following car in beginning its acceleration. The length of wheel base has nothing to do with the case. Sir George Findlay, in his valuable book, "The Working and Management of an English Railway," seems to have been in error on this point. If two cannon balls were sent in a guiding trough over a summit, the time interval between their centers as they rolled down the incline would vary only with their diameters, and bear no relation to positions of the points of support.

It makes no difference (assuming equal ease in running) whether the car is poised on a pony truck, or supported by 8 wheels with either a long or short wheel base. The elements controlling the time interval between car centers are: overall car length, speed in approaching the summit and increased speed after passing over the summit. Therefore, if a train of uncoupled cars, each one 40 ft. long, approaches the summit at 1 mile per hour, each car is moving its length in 27.27 sec., and, theoretically, this will be the time interval between the centers of the cars as they rush down the incline to the yard, where the switch points are moved to turn each car to its proper siding. (In this discussion we are considering cuts of one car each.) But it is not sufficient to compute the intervals between the centers of the cars, for the buffers will come in collision long before the centers touch each other, and meantime undesirable things are happening.

There needs to be deducted from the interval between the centers the time taken to run a car length in the yard. For example, if the initial speed at the summit is 1 m.p.h., and if the grade from the summit is adjusted to produce a speed of 3 m.p.h. in the yard, where the car would then be moving its length in 9.69 sec., the interval between the buffers would be 27.27 sec. − 9.09 sec.

= 18.18 sec. The time interval between the buffers of any two adjoining cars is, therefore, not a constant; it is a variable on the incline and in the yard It decreases in proportion as the cars slow down in the yard. The derived formula, which is true for any point on the incline or in the yard, is:

Time interval between buffers = Time of car moving its length at the summit − Time of car moving its length on the ladder.

Reversing this formula, in order to find at what speed cars can be fed to the summit.

Car-length time on the summit = Car-length time on ladder + Time interval needed for moving the points.

If the train is to be broken up in sections of more than one car each, the same formula is applicable if the length of each section is substituted for the car length.

The ease with which the summit can be utilized to facilitate separation in large and small yards and the advantage of operating yards under this system economically, with light traffic, commend it for general use. There are many sizes of humps, or gravity mounds, with varying rates of grade, both on the ascending as well as on the descending side, and the distances differ through which the latter grade continues. The gravity-assisting grade for a summit yard may be too long or too great. A study of various profiles and tables in this section indicates the trend of modern practice. Local conditions govern, and climate is an important factor.

The capacity of hump yards may be increased by improved methods of returning riders to the humps. Consideration must be given to the direction and velocity of prevailing winds and to temperatures and the length of time incoming trains may stand, in winter, before being humped. Incidentally, float-yard-switching capacity has been increased as much as 25 per cent. by the simple expedient of substituting the poling method. Even the best yards retard car movement. Therefore, cars should pass through—overhead, to the utmost.[1] A study of yard operations in 29 hump yards showed an average cost per car of 21.2 cts., and in 11 float yards of 22.91 cts.; 22 hump yards give an average of 72 cars over hump an hour, and 24 yards an average capacity of 1,973 cars each 24-hour day; they also decide that the hump operation is not warranted for less than 800 cars a day. Twenty yards use switch lists as an aid in cutting, eight chalk track numbers on the ends of cars and one uses the telephone.

Yard studies today are becoming somewhat conventional. It is the out of the ordinary, the unique situation which creates an interest and contributes in an educational manner, in meeting the unusual condition. Of this type is the freight-yard layout of the New Haven, recently constructed at Cedar Hill, Conn., near New Haven, plans of which are shown in Figs. 23, 24 and 25. Instead of the usual two, or possibly three, continuous or parallel routes, there are in this instance, no less than eight traffic directions, besides the local yards and transfers—a

[1] See reference to "Main-trackers," Chapter XI, page 185.

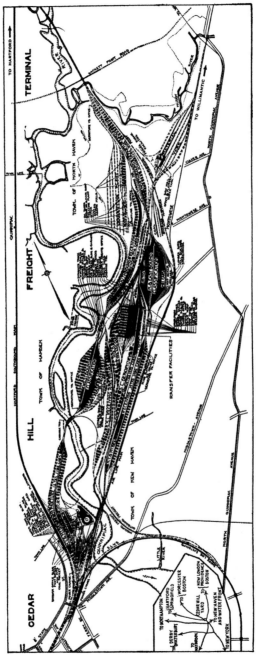

Fig. 23.—N. Y., N. H. & H. yards at Cedar Hill near New Haven, Conn.

typical New England condition, and one which justifies the type and capacity car and overnight methods of England, but is rendered impracticable here because of "west-of-the Hudson" interchange. The directions

FIG. 24.—The North and Eastbound classification yard, speeder tracks and tunnel portals on the right, of the N. Y., N. H. & H. Cedar Hill yards, near New Haven, Conn.

of train routes are about as varied and numerous as the points of the compass and are shown on the outline sketch of the general plan. The location was selected because of many dominatin reasons, some of which

FIG. 25.—Views of operations at the Cedar Hill yards of the N. Y., N. H. & H. R. R. near New Haven, Conn.

are the converging (and diverging) traffic routes, combining classification opportunities and assembling for the two major western gateways;[1]

[1] Over 70 per cent. of New England's population and industries are within 50 miles of the seacoast. About 90 per cent. of its interchange business comes in by four western gateways—which, in the order of importance, are Harlem River, West Albany, Mechanicsville and Maybrook.

practical prohibitive values of property west of New Haven for large development; length of engine runs from the two heavy western gateways, as a basis for eastward runs; center of a heavy industrial distributing territory, and existing facilities in the vicinity; ownership of 1,160 acres of land, and the limit of its electrical operation to the westward. The yard is 6 miles long and ½ mile wide and furnishes standing capacity for 11,000 cars. There are 95 miles of tracks and 460 switches. There is a northbound connection to Hartford, a loop connection to the New York and Maybrook departure yard for westbound movements from the Shore Line to that yard; two l.c.l. transfer platforms, each 1,200 ft. long and 20 ft. wide with eight complementary tracks, a material storage yard and a 100,000-ton coal storage yard.

The hump facilities consist of a summer and a winter hump track, each with scales, speeder tracks leading to the north and south units of the classification yard, a garage for riders' cars, an office for the hump conductor, a car riders' building, a signal tower and auxiliary air supply facilities; electropneumatic switches at the hump and the head end of the classification yard. The signaling apparatus is of the electropneumatic type. Three air whistles in the New York receiving yard and one at the hump may be operated either by the towerman or the conductor of the hump, to warn in case of trouble at the head end of the train.

The principal objective in design was to pass 180 cars an hour over the humps. Different profiles were developed over the winter and summer humps and one of the problems was to harmonize the grades from one hump track to the other to secure efficient operation of the diamond crossovers placed between these tracks for flexibility.

The profiles have worked out for a speed of from 4 to 5 m.p.h. when leaving the last switch to run the cars to the end of the yard. With wind resistance varying from 8 to 20 lb., the speeds are 4 and 5 m.p.h. at the scales, accelerating to 12.5 to 15 m.p.h. entering the switches and to 12.5 and 18 m.p.h. leaving the last switch. Over the summer hump, the grades established were 1.0 per cent. over the scales, then 1.25 per cent. for 125 ft., and 3.0 per cent. for 897 ft. to the end of switches. Over the winter hump, the grades are 1 per cent. over the scales, then 2 per cent. for 80 ft., followed by 5 per cent. for 48.5 ft., 1.25 per cent. for 40 ft., 3 per cent. for 100 ft. and 1 per cent. for 897 ft.

With the speed predetermined, the switches were located with reference to the summit of the hump, so that the desired number of cars per hour could be classified over the hump, with ample time to clear cars following.

There are two speeder tracks, one for each unit of the classification yard, standard gage and extending from the car riders' building to the throat of the classification yard, where they pass under the railway tracks through concrete tunnels and thence into the yard between the leads.

These cars are of the Kalamazoo type, and make the round trip in 3½ min. which with the short distance the car riders walk, has reduced the number of men ordinarily required.

A separating yard with a rather heavy grade throughout would tend to increase, rather than to decrease, the expense of operation, as it would necessitate car riders accompanying each cut until stopped, thereby making a greater force of car riders necessary. A uniform, moderately heavy descending grade part way, bringing up on nearly level track, is a very good arrangement, provided the length and rate of grade can be nicely adjusted to balance the kind of cars and commodities handled, together with the temperature and wind resistance during the greater part of the year. In the Honey Pot yard of the Pennsylvania the author has seen classifying done over the summit without car riders accompanying the cars. The freight handled, however, consisted wholly of coal. It may be remarked that the ground was well covered with coal. In a yard with a continuous descending grade of considerable fall, say 0.6 or 0.8 per cent. or greater, throughout, difficulty is experienced by outgoing road engines, when they find it necessary to back up their trains, or part them, to make couplings.

The tabulated summary of summit inclines on pages 77 and 78 gives the principal characteristics bearing upon a study of proper grades. Columns 5 and 8 may be used to assist in the comparison; the velocity at the foot of the grade is the important factor. Nothing has been added thereto for the initial velocity of the cars as they are pushed over the hump. Owing to the difference in the running of cars, as between loads and empties, gondolas loaded with coal or ore and box cars lightly loaded, and extremes of temperature, the velocities are of necessity only approximate and the effect of switches, frogs and curves cannot be considered.

Assuming a rolling friction of 8 lb. per ton, which is too high for heavy cars but not excessive for empty and very light cars, a grade of 0.4 per cent. is required to overcome this resistance and keep the car moving. The 0.4 per cent. grade is desirable for the classification yard, or at least a minimum of 0.3 per cent. In some cases, however, 0.2 or 0.25 per cent. have been satisfactorily used. For heavy lading, such as ore and coal, 0.5 to 1.3 per cent. grades seem preferable, while 0.9 to 1.5 per cent. may be necessary where many empty cars are moved. The first grade from the summit down is important, as it starts the cut quickly, and separates it from the following car a sufficient distance to allow the switches to be thrown between. It depends on the length of average cuts and the vertical fall required to impart the initial velocity. It is generally assumed, with short cuts and no scales to be run over, that a short grade of 60 to 150 ft. in length with a 3.0 to 4.0 per cent. grade is required; with a slope of 100 ft., a 3.5 per cent. grade. With a length of from 200 to 600 ft., a grade of from 1.2 to 3.0 per cent. will probably produce the desired velocity.

TABULATED SUMMARY OF HUMP OR SUMMIT GRADES

Yard	First grade from summit				Average remaining grade from 1st grade to bottom of ladders			Grade of ladders, per cent.	Grade of classified yard, per cent.	First grade from scales when any, per cent.	Distance from summit to center of scales, ft.	Standing car capacity of all yards	Character of traffic
	Grade per cent.	Fall, ft.	Horizontal length, ft.	Velocity at foot, m. p. hr.	Fall, ft.	Horizontal length, ft.	Velocity at foot of ladders, m. p. hr.						
1	2	3	4	5	6	7	8	9	10	11	12	13	
Enola............E.	3.5	4.2	120	10.2	5	500	19.4	1.0	0.1	None.		10,705	Coal.
Enola............W.	3.5	3.5	100	9.3	10	700	23.3	1.4	0.3	None.		10,500	Empties.
Altoona..........W.	3.9	5.8	150	12.2	13.8	1,500	27	0.92	0.29	None.		10,015	Empties and mdse.
Harrisburg.......W.	3.6	5.4	150	11.6	14.6	1,100	25	1.5 & 1.2	0.0	None.			Empties and mdse.
Conway ....E.	2.5	5.5	220	11.4	15	2,800	21.9	0.5 & 0.3	0.3	0.83	250	8,967	Ore, grain and mdse.
Conway ....E.	3.0	6.3	210	12.4	13	2,000	24.3	1.0 & 0.3	0.0	1.80	350		Ore, grain and mdse.
Conway ....W.	1.8	8.6	480	13.7	8.4	1,800	19.7	0.6	0.14	1.80	220		Coal, coke and mdse.
Gr'nville (mdse)...E.	2.5	1.3	50	5.4				1.0	1.0	None.		7,842	Merchandise.
Gr'nville (coal)...E.	2.0	1.0	50	5.5				1.0	1.0	2.0	100		Coal.
Columbus ....E.	2.0	4.8	240	10.4	9	1,000	22.2	1.0	0.8	2.5	280	3,402	Mdse., grain and empties.
Columbus ....W.	2.5	9.8	350	14.4	7.5	750	25.6	1.0	1.0	2.5	190		Coal, coke and mdse
Alexandria.......N.	2.5	2.5	100	7.7	11.5	900	22.6	1.0	0.35	2.0	170	3,127	Mdse. and produce.
Alexandria.......S.	2.5	2.5	100	7.7	13.5	1,100	23.7	1.0	0.30	2.0	170		
Edgemoor ....N.	1.54	0.8	50	4.0	5.25	300	14.6	1.5		1.5	80	2,819	
Edgemoor ....S.	1.0	0.7	70	4.0	7	800	18.7	1.75	0.0	1.75	80		
Logansport ....E.	2.4	3.0	125	8.4	2	450	10.7	0.5	0.04	On sum't		2,124	Mdse, grain and empties.
Logansport.......W.	1.45	3.6	250	8.4	2	400	16.8	0.43	0.4	On sum't			Mdse, coke and coal.
Crestline.........W.	3.0	7.5	250	13.5	12	1,000	27.4	0.75	0.3	None.		1,784	Mdse, coke and coal.
Marysville........E.	2.5	6.5	260	12.4	8.4	700	22.7	1.2	0.0	2.5	110	1,756	Mdse, coke and coal.
Marysville........W.	2.0	4.6	230	10.2				1.2	0.36	None.			

TABULATED SUMMARY OF HUMP OR SUMMIT GRADES.—Continued

Yard	First grade from summit				Average remaining grade from 1st grade to bottom of ladders			Grade of ladders, per cent.	Grade of classified yard, per cent.	First grade from scales when any, per cent.	Distance from summit to center of scales, ft.	Standing car capacity of all yards	Character of traffic
	Grade per cent.	Fall, ft.	Horizontal length, ft.	Velocity at foot, m. p. hr.	Fall, ft.	Horizontal length, ft.	Velocity at foot of ladders, m. p. hr.						
1	2	3	4	5	6	7	8	9	10	11	12	13	
Scully..........E.	2.5	2.5	100	7.7	13	1,000	20.5	1.3	0.5	2.5	150	1,740	Coal.
Bradford..........W.	3.0	2.4	80	7.6	3.2	700	10.6	0.45	0.45	None.	....	1,715	Coal, mdse. and empties.
Ebenezer..........N.	1.75	14.9	850	18	0.0	0	18	1.75	0.57	1.75	120	1,620	Mdse., grain & empties.
Chicago, 55th St....E.	3.0	4.5	150	10.5	3.5	700	14.9	0.5	0.17	0.5	330	1,278	Merchandise and coal.
Chicago, 55th St....W.	3.0	4.5	150	10.5	3.5	700	14.9	0.5	0.5 & 0.05	0.5	400	}	Merchandise and coal.
Honey Pot..........W.	2.0	0.8	40	4.2	5	500	13.4	1.0	0.12	1.2	90	1,194	Coal.
Sheridan..........E.	1.67	2.5	150	7.3	6	700	16.8	0.74	1.0	1.55	170	1,103	Coal.
Richmond..........W.	2.5	2.5	100	7.7	2	400	11.0	0.25	0.25	None.	....	745	Merchandise.
Linwood..........W.	3.0	3	100	8.5	4	400	16.8	1.0	0.0	On sum't	0	656	Merchandise.
Mansfield..........E.	2.5	3.2	130	8.7	4	600	15.3	0.2	0.2	1.0	250	630	Merchandise & empties
Mansfield..........W.	2.5	5	200	10.9	2.5	400	15.9	0.2	0.2	None.	}	....	Merchandise and coal
Chgo. Clear'g...N. & S.	2.5	5	200	10.9	19.8	2,200	28.5	0.9	0.0	None.	....	14,000	Not in use.
Youngwood..........W.	1.74	1.4	80	5.4	....	....	....	1.3	0.3	2.0	120	....	Coal and coke.
Hollidaysburg..........	2.0	1.0	50	5	....	....	....	2.0	0.9	2.0	100	....	Coal.
Waverly..........	1.5	9	600	13.6	....	....	....	1.5	0.5	None.	....	....	
DeWitt.......E & W.	1.0	2.5	250	6.5	....	....	....			None.	....	....	
Winnipeg.....E. & W.	3.7	11.1	300	16.7	....	....	....	2.0	0.0	On sum't	0	....	
Elkhart..........E.	4.3	12.9	300	18.1	....	....	....		0.16	....	....	....	
Elkhart..........W.	5.0	15	300	19.7	....	....	....	1.5	0.18	....	....	....	

In calculating columns 5 and 8, the following data were used: A single loaded car weighing 150,000 lb. = 75 tons; rolling friction = 8 lb. per ton; grade acceleration = f = 20 × rate of grade per cent. (Wellington, p. 340); grade of repose, or grade to balance resistance to motion = 0.4 per cent. (Wellington's "Railway Location," (p. 335, Table 118.) No initial velocity included in column 5.

With scales on the slope, the speed over the scales must be moderate, say, from 3 to 6 m.p.h. The skill of the weigher is a factor in regulating the speed over the scales. If the hump is any higher than is necessary to produce this speed, the car must be checked by the brakes. A 46-ft. scale will weigh six cars per minute at a speed of 4 m.p.h. It is possible

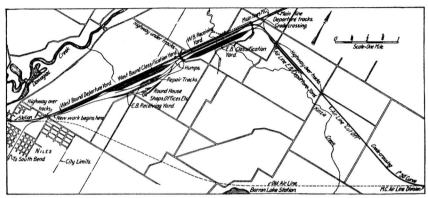

FIG. 26.—Yards of Michigan Central at Niles, Mich.

to attain a maximum of ten cars per minute, but this speed cannot long be maintained. Unless a large number of cars in each train is weighed, the summit does not appear to be a good location, because the weighing is probably done with the car at rest, which would materially delay the rest of the switching. The scale grade should not exceed 2.5 per cent. for a distance of 100 ft. and perhaps 2 per cent. for a distance of 50 ft.

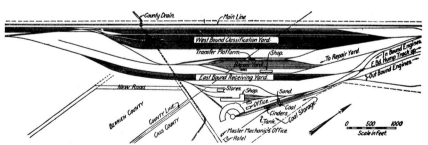

FIG. 27.—Engine terminal layout and west end of yards of Michigan Central at Niles, Mich.

would be better, locating the center of the scales between 90 and 150 ft. from the summit. The top of the hump should be level for about 100 ft., or the curve of the top should at least have a pretty long radius.

The hump may frequently be introduced in an existing yard, with comparatively light business, and effect a considerable saving in operating expense, and secure as well greater rapidity of car movement. This has been done in a number of instances at a cost of $2,000, or $3,000 and without eliminating any tracks. The saving in the enormous distance traveled by an engine with the old method of "tail-switching," and the reduction in damage to equipment and contents of cars, usually make the introduction of the hump a profitable investment.

Of interest, because of its size, cost and conditions to be met, are the Michigan Central's large classification yards, built during government control, at Niles, Mich. (see Figs. 26, 27 and 28). It involved the handling of over 2,000,000 cu. yd. of dirt, the laying of 75 miles of track and completed costs over $4,000,000. An east and westward receiving, classification and departure yard, a car-repair yard, a 30-stall engine house, a locomotive shop, office buildings, oil houses, a 600-ton coaling station, a $50,000 hotel and a double-track cut-off, having four departure tracks, to connect with the Air line are included.

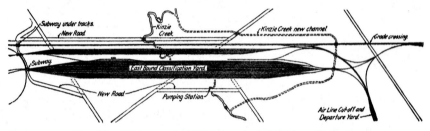

Fig. 28.—Eastern end of Niles terminal, Michigan Central.

The yards are parallel to the main line and are about 4 miles long, requiring the purchase of 1,100 acres of cultivated land.

Freight trains from the west division leave the main line at the city limits entering the east receiving yard, which consists of eight tracks —13-ft. centers and 4,200 ft. long in the clear. Cars are then pushed over the hump into the eastward classification yard—24 tracks with a minimum length of 4,000 ft. on alternate 13- and 15-ft. centers. East-bound trains are made up on two 4,200-ft. departure-yard tracks which parallel the main line. The westward arrangement is similar. The classification yard having 28 tracks of 4,000 ft. length and laid on alternate 13- and 15-ft. centers. The westward departure yard consists of four tracks paralleling the main line a minimum length of 4,200 ft. The car-repair yard has eight repair tracks, 1,400 to 1,900 ft. in the clear, laid on alternate 20- and 22-ft. centers, four transfer and "cripple" tracks, two depressed wheel tracks, an unloading and transfer platform, and a large independent car-repair shop.

The tracks of the receiving and classification yard are connected by ladders at each end laid on an angle of 9 deg. 26 min., with the center line of the yards. No. 9 frogs are used throughout. Switching will be done over two humps which follow closely the A.R.E.A.[1] standard profile, with grades 0.5 per cent. ascending to the ladders, increasing to 1 per cent. through the ladders of the receiving yard, then to 1.67 per cent. leading to the crest of the hump. Beyond the summit a short 2 per cent. run-off changes to 1 per cent., decending through the ladders of the classification yard, reducing to 0.5 per cent. for two-thirds the length of the yards and from there level to the end of the yard.

The engine-house layout has six tracks, two inbound, one outbound, one cinder-pit track, a coal-receiving track and a coal-unloading track which passes over the receiving hopper of a 600-ton link-belt coaling station, having four discharge chutes, only three of which are used, the fourth being over the coal-receiving track. The two inbound tracks and the cinder-pit track pass under the coaling station. The inbound tracks also pass over 125-ft. concrete cinder pit, where the cinders are dumped, wet down and shoveled into cars standing on the lower center track. Water is delivered to engines through three standpipes from a 100,000-gal. steel tank, which is kept filled by a pumping station delivering water at the rate of 1,200 gal. per minute through approximately 9,000 ft. of 12-in. main.

The movement of the engines in and out of the yards and through these tracks has been carefully worked out to follow the one-way feature. Inbound Middle division engines leave their trains in the westward receiving yard and pass over the hump to an inbound engine track leading through a subway under the eastbound track to the roundhouse; inbound Western division engines leave the trains at the receiving yard, run about 300 ft. east and then switch back on the second inbound track to the engine house. Outbound engines leave the roundhouse by the single outbound engine track, the Middle division engines passing directly out and over the eastbound hump to a thoroughfare leading to the extreme west end of the departure yard, while Western division engines make a 10-deg. loop under all tracks in the vicinity of the hump through two subways and then move west over a thoroughfare track between the main line and the classification yard. An interesting feature at this point is the carrying of this engine track and one of the road diversions through the same subway, the highway conforming to the curve of the track until it clears the second structure.

Hump profiles, as recommended by the American Railway Engineering Association, are shown in Fig. 29. Numbers 1, 2 and 3 are for use in cold climates, in moderate climates and in warm climates, respectively. They require the use of track scales and the operation of a mixed traffic of merchandise and empty cars. Various suggestions accompany the recommendations, namely, a higher hump during winter, if traffic or climatic conditions demand; if needed, a track scale not

[1] Shown in Fig. 29.

exceeding 60 ft. in length at such a distance from the summit of the hump that, when cars to be weighed reach the scale, they will be properly spaced from following cars and will move slowly enough readily to enable correct weighing; nothing sharper than a No. 8 frog for average classification-yard conditions; for tracks holding empty cars a sufficiently increased gradient to cause these cars to move with the same velocity as loaded cars to adjoining tracks. The Association uses 42 ft. in rating tracking capacity, 50 ft. for repair tracks, air and water pipes and air outlets, with air hose, at 50-ft. intervals on repair tracks and, where heavy repairs are made, tracks under cover and provided with

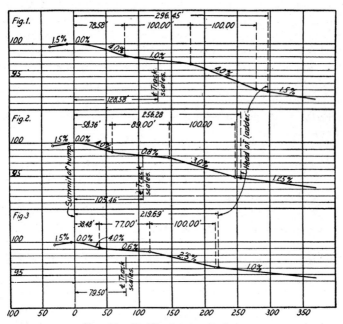

Fig. 29.—Profiles for gravity humps.

cranes for heavy lifting. Classification tracks should be long enough to hold a full train and, when conditions permit, there should be as many of them as can be used to advantage to avoid subsequent classification and consequent delay. Departure tracks should be of full-train length and of sufficient number to provide ample standing room for trains being tested for air and awaiting engines. The hump should be so constructed that the greatest possible number of cuts of cars may be classified over it, the steepest part of the grade may be reached in the least available distance after passing the summit and the grade or fall may provide sufficient momentum to carry all cars to the lower ends of the classification tracks.

For yard lighting the Association recommends nitrogen lights of 1,500-watt capacity, equivalent to 2,200 candlepower, a spacing of 140 to 150 ft., 28 ft. or more elevation for hump and ladder tracks and such spacing on body tracks as to render cars clearly visible.

A plan and two views of the Potomac Yards of the Richmond, Fredericksburg and Potomac, near Alexandria, Va., are shown, Figs. 30, 31 and 32. Electropneumatic non-interlocked switches are installed, to be operated from two towers; one on the apex of each hump. The tower for the southbound classification yard cares for 34 switches; the other

Fig. 30.—Transfer and southbound classification tracks in the Potomac yards of the Richmond, Fredericksburg & Potomac Railroad near Alexandria, Va.

for 38, displacing 14 ground switchmen. An average of 2,200 cars per day is handled and separated into 27 "undisturbed" classifications, northbound and 26 southbound. One engine works continuously on each hump. The crew for an engine consists of a conductor, a cutter, six riders and four switchmen.

A plan of the B. & O. eastbound yard at Brunswick, Md., is shown in Fig. 33. The objectionable but unavoidable curvature stands out prominently. The splendid main-track separation arrangement is apparent.

The New York Central's new Selkirk yard is shown in Fig. 34. The ultimate capacity of the yard as planned will be 20,000 cars. The present grading has been completed in such manner that tracks with a total capacity of 11,000 cars can be laid, although the initial capacity will be 8,500 cars. Eastward trains arriving at Unionville will move directly into the eastward receiving yard, the engine will cut off and move to the engine terminal at the east end, and the train will pass over the hump to the classification yard where separations will be made for the three lines to the east.   After being made up trains are transferred to the departure yard and eventually routed over the eastward thoroughfare track to the east end of the yard where in passing through the interlocker they are diverted to either of the three destinations as required.

What are known as "inside classifications," that is, classifications for specific destinations at terminals, to eliminate as much switching as possible at these terminals, are being made for New York, Boston, and Weehawken.   In addition, because through the New England territory there are a large number of diverging

Fig. 31.—Entrance from the south to the Potomac yards of the Richmond, Fredericksburg & Potomac Railroad near Alexandria, Va.

routes "short" classifications are required for New Haven, and for Boston and Albany points such as Springfield, Pittsfield and others.   Short classifications are also made for the Hudson division and the West Shore.   All told there are now 20 classifications made for eastward cars, and after the operation of the yard is fully organized it is expected this number will be increased.

At each classification yard is a re-classification yard where shorts and cars for local freight are switched into station order.   These tracks are short, and when a train is switched up the engine doubles over onto the necessary tracks to assemble the cars for the train and transfers it to the departure yard.

The fast freight trains also enter the yard at Unionville, but instead of pulling into the receiving yard diverge to the eastward freight track and pull into the fast freight yard.   Normally there is little switching on these trains as they come into the yard made up for destination.   Bad orders and cars reconsigned in

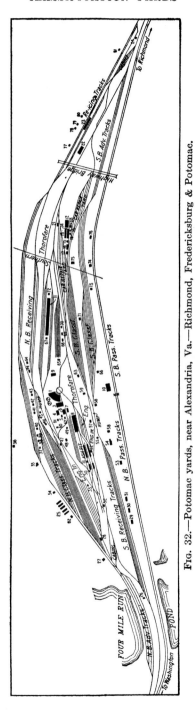

FIG. 32.—Potomac yards, near Alexandria, Va.—Richmond, Fredericksburg & Potomac.

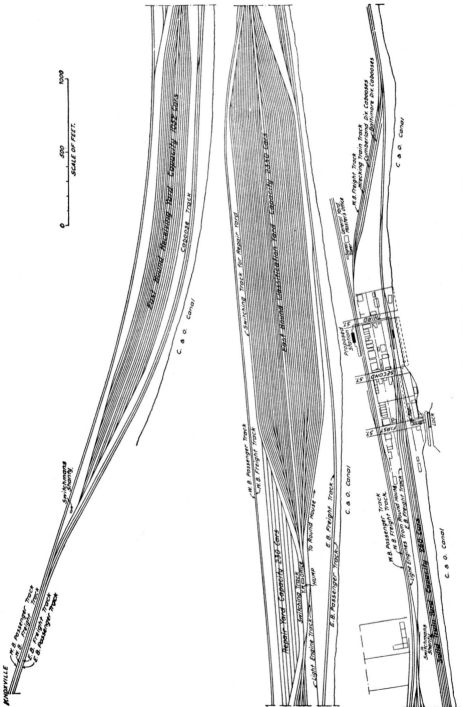

FIG. 33.—Eastbound yard system at Brunswick, Maryland—Baltimore & Ohio.

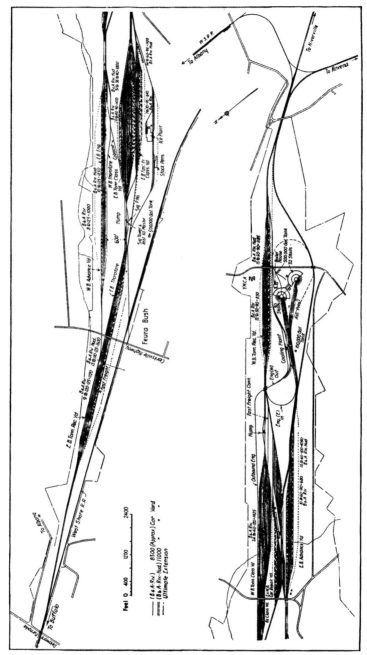

Fig. 34.—Selkirk yard—New York Central.

transit must be set out, and such switching as may be necessary for icing is done. Flat switching only is done in this yard.

At each hump there is an air compressor and lines are run to the departure yards for the purpose of testing brakes and charging the train lines. All of the switches at the hump ends of the classification yards are remote controlled from a tower at the hump. Switching is by list and the operator, or signalman, controls all switch movements without signals, save the usual switch light indications. The train movements are controlled by signals operated by the hump master from a control station on the ground near the corner of the tower. The signal indication are given to the trimmer engine as well as to the train which is being switched.[1]

The proposed Proviso hump yard of the C. & N. W. Railway lies at the junction of the Chicago-Omaha main line (Galena Division) and a low grade double track line leading north to a connection with the Chicago-Winona and the Chicago-Milwaukee lines (Wisconsin Division). The Indiana Harbor Belt Railway, giving access to all line haul carriers entering Chicago, lies just to the East; it is physically possible also to reach the Clearing Yard of the Belt Railway of Chicago and the tracks of the Baltimore & Ohio's Chicago Terminal Railway, the other principal mediums of Chicago interline interchange.

The Galena Division tracks are directly connected with the Eastbound receiving yards, the Westbound departure yard the L.C.L. yard the car repair and storekeepers yard, various grain, hold the storage yards and, without yard interference, with the mains leading north to Winona, Milwaukee and points north and northwest. Main line trains can, and will be run around the yard without in any way affecting yard operations. The Wisconsin Division tracks, are similarly connected.

To the North a double track line is available for exclusive freight service, to the East some construction is planned to afford two exclusive freight tracks, to the West two tracks for freight use are contemplated with connection to the passenger mains by means of a "jump over" some miles west. Temporarily this connection is made about one mile west by means of cross-overs under interlocking control.

Construction work has been done and the necessary land secured but it is not expected that all will be completed for some years. Construction will proceed as money is available and traffic conditions warrant. When complete the yard will have a standing capacity of 24,000 cars and a maximum handling capacity of 10,000 cars per day.

The Markham Yard[2] of the Illinois Central, near Chicago, when fully developed will contain 175 miles of track with a standing capacity of 12,000 cars and a working capacity of 6,000 cars per day. Nearly all of

[1] *Railway Review,* Dec. 27, 1924.
[2] *Railway Age,* Feb. 23, 1924.

the grading for Markham yard, amounting to approximately 4,000,000 cu. yd. will be embankment. A light cut will be necessary in the south-bound section at the Homewood end.

It consists of receiving, classifying and departing units for both north and south-bound movements. In addition, an l.c.l. transfer yard with five 700-ft. transfer platforms, a 1,000-car repair yard, complete modern icing facilities, and a 60-stall engine terminal. The north-bound receiving unit consists of twenty 100-car tracks, divided into groups of 10 tracks spaced 13.5 ft. center to center, with a 19-ft. space between groups. Twelve of these tracks have been built. The remaining eight will be built as the necessity arises. In conjunction with the north-bound receiving yard five additional 50-car tracks have been provided for cars requiring reclassification.

The hump end of the north-bound receiving yard is arranged with two parallel ladder tracks leading directly to the hump. Movement to the secondary ladder track is accomplished by means of slip switches in the main ladder. In all cases the train being moved over the hump uses the secondary ladder, thus leaving the main ladder clear for the release of road engines after pulling their trains into the yard.

The hump in the north-bound unit is located just north of 171st street. It has been designed for the use of a mechanical hump at the apex and a 60-ft., 150-ton, automatic recording scale located beyond it. The distance from the center of the mechanical hump to the center of the scales is 101.5 ft., with 35 ft. of 3.25 per cent. gradient between. This affords a maximum weighing speed of 7 miles per hour. It is approximately 3,000 ft. from the scales to the lower end of the classification yard and the gradients have been fixed to give a velocity of 11.7 miles per hour at the end. The scale is laid on a 1 per cent. descending gradient, beyond this is a 3 per cent. grade for 95 ft., next there is a 2 per cent. grade for 158 ft., which connects with the 1 per cent. grade through the yard.

The north-bound classification yard has 62 tracks, not including a grid of 13 tracks for commercial coal and the necessary tracks for light repair and bad order cars. The tracks vary from 20 to 60 cars in length, the short tracks being used for industrial classifications. The total capacity of this unit is 2,600 cars. Tracks are divided into groups of 10, with a ladder for each group at the hump end and a separate ladder for each 5 tracks at the lower end. Tracks are spaced 13.5 ft. center to center with 19 ft. between groups. Each two groups are separated by a space of 34 ft., giving three routes into the yard for the electric rider cars.

The north-bound departure unit consists of twenty 80-car tracks, spaced 13.5 ft. center to center. A space of 17 ft. has been left between each five tracks to permit the erection of trolley poles at the time that the freight tracks are electrified into the city. Ten tracks are now laid; the other 10 will be built as the need arises. At the north end of the departure yard a complete air testing plant will be installed to test and charge the trains before they are forwarded. A plant similar to this will be located at the south end of the south-bound departure yard.

The south-bound units are similar in arrangement to the north-bound. The south-bound receiving unit will consist of twenty 80-car tracks, 12 of which will be built at the present time. The classification unit will consist of 42 tracks with capacities ranging from 20 to 50 cars, and a total capacity of 1,500 cars. Two rider return tracks will be provided through the yard. The departure unit will consist of twenty 110-car tracks to accommodate trains of empty coal cars moving south to the mines.

The less-than-car-load transfer yard plans provide for placing 150 cars at the transfer platforms, and arrangements have been made for tracks leading directly from the classification yards into the l.c.l. yard. Switching of cars, when necessary, will be done in the l.c.l. yard, so no sorting will be necessary at the classification yards, other than the ordinary segregation of cars containing less than carload freight.

There are so many conditions governing terminal switching that an actual case of switching by continued gravity alone is not in use where winter weather is severe. There are many yards in which cars are dropped into the tracks of a separating or classification yard during many months of the year by gravity, without the assistance of poling, a summit, or "kicking." Except in the mild climates, however, where extremes of temperature are infrequent, it is probably not practicable to construct a gravity yard that can be successfully operated as such with all kinds of cars and loads during 12 months of the year. If the grade is sufficiently heavy to start a car during very cold weather, the speed attained on such a grade during warm weather will be excessive, and, on the other hand, if the grade is right to permit of safe handling during summer, there will be times during winter when cars will not start and the assistance of an engine becomes necessary.

A terminal worked by gravity solely during the greater part of the year may, for all practical purposes, be properly termed a "gravity yard," that is, one wherein a car, or a number of cars coupled together will start on releasing the brakes. To accomplish this, grades from 0.8 to 1.0 per cent. are necessary. In many instances even a 1.0 per cent. grade will not be sufficient to start a car, as, for instance, when the journals and packing in the boxes have become thoroughly chilled or when the opposite extreme, an excessively hot box exists, or has recently existed.

The result to be achieved must be carefully worked out in each instance by design, based on theoretical knowledge backed up by developed facts, and then preferably tested out in the particular locality before final construction.

A combination[1] of gravity and tail switching has advantages using a low grade hump which assists the switch engine in starting a cut of cars towards the ladder. From the ladder each classification track is on grade sufficient to enable each car to hold its speed without acceleration. As cars accumulate, a locomotive is used to couple them and "trim" them into shape for departure.

With the use of much lighter and smaller cars, and an arrangement whereby brakemen can apply brakes from the side, gravity switching is in more general and satisfactory use in Europe than in America. There they also use "shoes" to assist in stopping cars. These are chocks made to fit over the rails in such a manner as to force the car wheels to run up the inclined upper side of the shoe, from which they roll back again, releasing the shoe. "Chain drags" are used, too, to catch run-away cars. This is a large, heavy chain located in the track in such a way that a switchman by throwing a lever causes the hook at one end of the chain to engage with an axle under the car and the dragging of the chain gradually brings the car to a standstill.

A unique, interesting and progressive hump-yard accessory has been installed and is in operation in the New York Central Yard at Gibson, Ind., near Chicago, on the Indiana Harbor Belt which eliminates the use of car riders, reduces car damage and speeds up operation. This is the use of so-called retarders, first used in Europe, which consist of a number of cast iron shoes placed along both sides of each rail in such a manner as to grip the car wheels and reduce speed when air pressure is applied from a centrally controlled plant. There are five 32-ft. and two 40-ft. sections on the hump and three 56-ft. units on each lead proper, spaced about 225 feet apart. In future installation a 32-ft. unit will probably be adopted putting in one or more units as the conditions may require. This yard handles about 1,800 cars a day over the hump and before the installation of retarders employed 15 switch tenders and 60 hump brakemen, or riders. With the use of retarders, 15 retarder operators replaced the 15 switch tenders and 9 switch tenders will handle certain switches not yet centrally controlled, but no riders will be required, making a total reduction of 51 employes. Car damage has been materially reduced and hazard to employes practically eliminated. Later units are controlled by electro-pneumatic valves, eliminating return piping and resulting in quicker response to the control. Under observation a train of 38 cars, with 30 cuts, was classified in 13 minutes. An air device has also been developed for placing a track skate on the track in case the car is out of control. This device operates very efficiently and quickly, placing a skate on the track between the trucks of a rapidly moving car

[1] *Railway Review*, Jan. 24, 1925.

thereby eliminating the hazard to employes when the skate is placed on the track close ahead of the car. These skates quickly stop the car. The successful operation of retarders will, as a matter of course, eliminate speeder or trolley cars and similar methods of returning car riders, which is a heavy expense, costly to install, occupies valuable property and cumbersome at best.

While this development is subject to further alteration and refinement, its success is amply demonstrated by the results already accomplished. These results may be summarized as follows: (1) Car riders are dispensed with saving labor; (2) cars are spaced more uniformly and closely with a consequent potential increase in yard capacity; (3) complete control of cars on the grades prevents rough handling and damage claims; (4) the use of an outside braking medium obviates the necessity of preliminary train brake tests; (5) the elimination of car riders promotes safety, particularly in winter when the cars, ladders, hand holds and hand brake wheels are often covered with snow and ice; (6) the provision of a mechanical device for placing skid shoes or skates on the rails at the will of the tower operators removes the danger from this operation.

The function of the car retarders in saving labor will perhaps be better appreciated from an examination of figures showing the cars handled and men employed in October of the present year as compared with October a year ago. There are two humps in the Gibson yard and on October 23, 1923, a total of 2,665 cars were handled over both humps with 105 car riders and switch tenders, or an average of practically 25 cars per man. On October 23, 1924, after installation of the car retarders, 1,667 cars were handled over the north hump with a total of 39 men including 24 switch tenders and 15 car retarder operators. In other words practically 43 cars were handled per man, an increase of 84 per cent. It is expected that a still further reduction in force of 12 men will be made following the installation of power switch-throwing machines in place of the hand-operated switches now used. The best performance on the north hump to date, using the car retarders instead of individual car riders is 1,042 cars in eight hours. In one case 220 cars in three long trains were handled over the hump in 80 minutes, but this represents a performance above the average.[1]

It is apparent that the first cost of a gravity yard is prohibitive unless the lay of the land happens to be quite nearly adapted to it naturally. In 1873 the Edge Hill yard at Liverpool, England (Fig. 22), was designed and the work of construction begun. Its design is still considered one of the best for the prompt and economical distribution of cars. It is commonly believed to be the first yard of any importance constructed on the so-called "gridiron" plan for classifying cars by gravity. It is also generally assumed that it was the first to use an advanced method of switching on a large scale and to abandon the old push-and-pull, or "link-and-pin" process, for classifying cars. It was not unduly costly, for nature had shaped its topography in a wonderful way at the precise spot where the yard was needed.

[1] *Railway Review*, Nov. 15, 1924.

A gravity yard was put in operation in 1846 at Dresden, Germany, and is remarkable for its high cost of construction. At the upper end a fill 70 ft. high was necessary. From an operating standpoint this proved very satisfactory. It is about 1½ miles long and ½ mile wide. This Dresden yard is probably the one in which the first gravity switching was done in Germany.

Fig. 35.—Goods switching yards, Crewe, England—London Midland & Scottish.

The conditions in England are different, principally because of the small car and predominating fast freight service. The view of the Crewe (London Midland & Scottish) "goods-switching siding" (Fig. 35)

Fig. 36.—Switching horses, England—London & North Eastern.

shows an interesting and pretty bit of railroad scenery. The "shunting" horses at work on the London & North Eastern (Fig. 36) are perhaps novel to many, although horses were used to shunt cars in many places in this country years ago, before our cars grew in weight and capacity.

CHAPTER VI

OPERATION OF YARDS

Yard or terminal operation differs from most other administrative work, in that the actual arrangement and execution constitute only its beginning. The vastly greater and more important duty of the executive head consists of constant vigilance and alertness in estimating the flow and nature of traffic, and in providing an easy channel for it. He must know what the situation is every hour and minute of the day and night, not only as to local conditions, but also as to approaching train and car movements, and must know what is required to dispose of the traffic promptly and certainly, while at the same time arranging for outward movements and interior exchanges.

The yardmaster who handles a small yard with two or three yard engines (the so-called "switchman yardmaster," who graduated from the ranks and knows the work of "following an engine" from center to circumference) and the yardmaster who handles a large terminal covering many miles of territory and many combinations of yards, and who works twenty or more engines, may both be men of ability, but of very different caliber. Both must be men of the hour, men of initiative and resourcefulness. As one prominent leader puts it, what is needed is "action—consistent, insistent, persistent."

The position of yardmaster calls for administrative and executive capacity. He should be thoroughly familiar with all the details of the work of his subordinates, but he can better devote his time in supervising than in falling into the common errors of attempting to do the work of a switchman or clerk. The late E. H. Harriman's remarks about a general manager aptly apply: "I want to see him with his feet on his desk—thinking, thinking!" It is easy to fall into and follow a rut. Constant agitation is necessary to prevent it. Things jar one's nerves today; tomorrow the edges have been rounded off, and the day after nothing out of the ordinary is observed. Constant study and investigation are beneficial to determine whether:

New cross-overs are needed.

Existing cross-overs can be relocated or turned around to advantage.

Leads can be extended to keep engines off main tracks.

Ladders should be rearranged.

Scales may be more advantageously located.

Switches can be taken into interlocking systems.

Signals should be changed or relocated.

94

Additional water cranes should be erected or existing ones located to better advantage.

Engines turned around may work better.

Train make-up may be improved to save switching somewhere.

Handling of cars may be reduced.

Too many cars are being handled in switching—in some cases unnecessarily fouling main tracks or leads.

Unnecessary switching or "spotting" is being done at freight houses, transfers and similar points.

Too many cars are handled in transfer movements, causing loss of time to transfers and other trains or engines.

Houses and transfers are disturbed oftener than necessary.

Industry track schedules enable work to be done at times when there is a minimum of main-track interference or conflict with other yard engines.

Local freights arrive and leave at hours when they can be handled to best advantage.

Local freights can be run nights to relieve other conditions.

Delays are due to slow furnishing of supplies or inconvenient method of getting them.

Time engines are coaled or watered is the most advantageous.

Hours for relieving engines are suitable.

Time is lost nights, or day or night in winter, by crew not getting in motion promptly after engine's absence for any purpose.

There are other loose ends to be gathered up. Constant watching, eternal vigilance, leads to prompt and economical service.

The operation of yards in relation to train service covers, broadly, the handling of in and out car movements with all the accessories connected with the care of engines and cabooses, such as engine houses, coaling plants, ashpits, sand plants, water stations, repair shops and supply depots. A general analysis of the features of receiving and forwarding trains and handling of cars disposes of the units of which an inbound train is composed in one or more of the following movements:

1. Engine to engine house for return or continuance of trip.
2. Caboose to track provided, or to an outbound train.
3. Cars to be held for orders:
    (a) Diversion (loads).
    (b) Orders of car distributor (empties).
    (c) For anticipated traffic (empties).
4. Cars to be forwarded in other trains.
5. Cars for connections.
6. Cars for industrial sidings.
7. Cars containing package or l.c.l. (less than car-load) freight for freight houses.

8. Cars containing bulk or c.l. (car-load) freight for team delivery tracks.

9. Empty cars to be held until needed.

10. Cars containing company material taking various points of delivery.

Many of these cars, before being placed as indicated above, must be weighed, repaired or transferred, and frequently go through two or all of these processes.

In assembling cars for outward movement the divisions, commonly termed "classifications," are more varied and complicated because of the large number of diverging routes and destinations to be considered. These are governed largely by the capacity of the terminal to arrange the trains without impeding the movement of traffic, and the capacity of terminals (in advance or following) to care for their tributary territories. The following are some of the features entering into the assembling of outward trains:

1. Destination of cars.

2. Character of contents (*e.g.*, live stock, perishable freight, time freight, export freight, etc.).

3. Character of trains (*e.g.*, fast or symbol freight, through ordinary freight, drop or switching locals, local or package freight trains).

4. The general policy of train classification.

Much can be said regarding the general policy of a railroad in reference to classification of trains. In making up local freights, the work is usually done according to methods best adapted to the division. The common method is to place cars in station order. The first cars to be set off are put next to the engine, next the cars for the second station and so on, to enable them to be set out with the least possible switching. In many cases, the merchandise cars (also known as platform, peddler, break-bulk, l.c.l. or package cars) are kept on the rear for the twofold purpose of enabling the engine crew and part of the train crew to set off or take on the station cars, while the remainder of the train crew loads or unloads the package freight from or to the freight house opposite the rear end of the train. The conductor, with his waybills, and a part of the train crew, can then reach the platform cars quickly from the caboose. Unfortunately, it is more often the practice to make up the local freights with no attention whatever to car arrangement, usually because the yard is inadequate and hardly able to classify the through freights properly, thus causing the most important trains (the divisions locals) to be neglected.

If the cars picked up on the road are kept together in the train according to destinations, it increases the road work and decreases the yard work. On the other hand, if they are picked up indiscriminately, the reverse is true. The classifications to be made at the initial point of a through train and maintained at each successive "breaking-up" point are governed by the road's general policy and are, or should be, dependent on the ability of each general or divisional terminal to do its part of the work, or care for a part of the work a weaker terminal is unable to perform; on the necessity for fast time; on the character of the traffic; and on the number of diverging routes and connecting lines.

In very general terms, the policy may consist of one of two methods:

1. No classification is to be attempted until the last yard of the road or division is reached, where cars going beyond are separated.

2. Originating and all subsequent yards to arrange cars in groups for final and intermediate deliveries.

If the railroad serves a few large cities, toward which traffic naturally gravitates, the second method will entail more work than the first. If the larger terminals are inadequate, the first method will reduce the work in them, and correspondingly prevent delay or congestion therein. At the same time it will undoubtedly add to the expense and detention in the terminals in advance. In practice, a compromise between the two methods will usually be found most economical and expeditious. A fast or important freight train should be made up at its originating point classified to final destination on the home road, and it is not infrequently desirable to classify to a considerable distance beyond on the line participating in the fast freight service. It is a very good general proposition to make up as many straight trains (fast and ordinary freight) to distant points as can be assembled within a reasonable period of time, if the switching facilities at such originating points are ample and sufficiently well balanced for this purpose. These trains should be made up solid for points as far distant as practicable. A general rule under which cars are held for a solid train for any point to which there are sufficient cars to make such a train every 24 hours has worked out successfully on one road. In many instances freight would be more expeditiously handled by holding 48 hours, or even longer, as compared with the "potpourri" method. Holding the cars at the originating terminal for this purpose keeps them out of many intermediate yards and saves extra handling. The remaining freight may then be more advantageously moved by following out a line of final classification under the first method. Actual mathematical analysis will prove that, when trains can be made up solid to final destinations, the first method will actually reduce the switching of cars.[1]

It is the purpose of this work to avoid expressing the views of one individual alone and preferably to present both (all) sides of every discussion and the various opinions of those who have given them thought. An interesting dissenter to the second method of classification is the *Railway Age*, as follows:

[1] This is exemplified on the B. & O. (see page 185).

The matter of switching can easily be overdone. It sounds very well to talk of lining up a train at a hump near Chicago so that it can run through solid to New York. There are so many other terminals to be encountered en route that this admirable theory seldom works out in practice. To begin several hundred miles back to get cars in a certain order at A or B to save switching at Z, the final terminal, is misleading. It is like sitting up all night to avoid oversleeping in the morning. Perchance at B there is a car for E between two cars for Z. Why, then, switch out at B, when by the set-out at E the switch has made itself? Again, a car becoming bad order and switched out along the road may save a switch at the terminal.

This view voices the opinion of a very respectable minority of practical operating men, who claim that true economy delays the making of a switch to the last terminal possible. They would require each division to do its own switching, except in the case of certain fast trains handling special high-class freight. They claim that the ideal conditions justifying initial classification for distant terminals are almost never realized in practice. The ruling grades on various intermediate divisions are so different that it is seldom possible to balance the motive power so as to maintain a train of uniform tonnage over all divisions. Some of the officials go even further and claim that, as a rule, switching in station order for the next division is a fallacy born of the trainmen's disinclination to extra exertion. The irresistible conclusion of their reasoning is a minimum number of classification tracks at intermediate terminals.

In another chapter[1] the yardmaster and his territorial possessions, duties, responsibilities and authority are discussed. It is unfortunate that too often the yardmaster of an important terminal and the agent in charge of a heavy station are expected to perform miracles, but are not delegated with real authority to act, unless an actual emergency arises, when it is usually immediately recognized that, of the several scores of bosses, inquisitors, investigators and specialists, who ordinarily spend their time prodding, and conducting inquests, few, if any, are competent to handle the plant. It may be a case of departmental operation gone mad. The terminal is a very difficult kingdom in itself.

Among the numerous minor salves and lotions are budgets, controls, profit-sharing, bonuses, vocational guidance, phrenology, payroll inserts, and the committee form of management.

One reads with pleasure, and with benefit, what was said by a recognized authority[2] on an important occasion:

Strength and weakness are best shown in emergencies, and an actual emergency will best show how division and department organization work. On a certain occasion it became necessary to rebuild certain trestles near each other on parallel roads organized differently. The superintendent of the railroad with a division organization got his carpenters together at once, bridge carpenters, shop carpenters and all, and ran them by special train to the scene of the accident, with

[1] Chapter VII, "The Yardmaster."

[2] Arthur Hale, in address to the New York University students.

all the heavy timber he could get together, and simply reported the facts to his general manager. The superintendent of the road with a department organization could do nothing but report the facts to his general manager. The superintendent had no control of the bridge carpenters or the shop carpenters in his vicinity. It was a Sunday, and, to tell the truth, he did not know where they were to be found. The general manager was not in much better plight, but he managed to organize a force composed of his general superintendent, his superintendent of floating equipment and his engineer of bridges, and he made very good time with his trestle. It would have been better on a week day, but the organization went to pieces on Sunday.

From the side of economy and efficiency, the division organization also has advantages. When a superintendent can be held responsible for everything on his division, he will see that he has enough men, and no more, to keep his engines and tracks in condition. Under the department system all the work will be authorized and done on order from headquarters without so intimate a knowledge of local needs.

An eminent writer,[1] with splendid practical experience, goes into the qualifications of a terminal superintendent as follows:

Since a terminal-yard organization is composed of individuals, many of whom must perform similar duties and have had similar .experience and training,. logical reasoning seems to justify the belief that the successful operation of a terminal yard must follow the adoption and application of a plan, the underlying principle of which is represented by continuous active interest on the part of individual members of the organization, because interest is the unmistakable evidence of properly utilized education (mind development), and the latter is indicative of progress.

Mind training of the individual member of a department of whatever nature may of itself be classified correctly as the elementary step of the series of steps essential to the various stages of development in connection with the formation of an organization or working plan. The molding or crystallization of this available mental energy of any number of members into a compact and powerful mental force capable of effectively resisting opposition to desirable or necessary methods and practices is the result which the head of a department must be able to accomplish. These two factors, namely, continuous active interest on the part of individual members of an organization in their respective positions and duties, and proper utilization of the available energies of all members, form the true basis of a terminal-yard operation plan.

The executive head of a railway, who is responsible, morally at least, to its stockholders, for the satisfactory management of their affairs, should possess qualifications that will enable him to perfect an organization arrangement efficient not only when applied to one detail, but when subjected to tests involving maximum demands and extreme conditions. The assumption that this reasoning rests on the right principle appears to be ample ground for the conclusion that the head of a terminal-yard organization must be as capable an executive in his limited sphere as is the president of a railway whose responsibility extends to the

[1] S. W. Roberts, General Superintendent of Passenger Transportation, Pennsylvania Lines—*Railway Age.*

operation of a complete system. Hence, the standard of a terminal-yard organization, be it good, bad, or average, as indicated by its acts, must thus reflect directly the ability of its head and, perhaps, indirectly the strength or weakness, as the case may be, of the entire organization scheme of which it is a component part.

Having indicated that the true basis of a terminal-yard organization plan is, first, a maximum degree of continuous active interest on the part of each unit (member) in his particular service assignment, and the general results; and, second, a proper utilization of the maximum degree of combined energies of all units (members); and having placed the head of a department or organization, irrespective of what his title may be, in the same relation to each of his assistants as is the president of a railway company to each member of his staff, the foundation is thus laid for the question, "What should be the qualifications of a man capable of perfecting an efficient yard organization and obtaining the maximum service from it?" The answer to this question must deal with the standards of many attributes, the more prominent being morality (including temperance), honor, integrity, perseverance, patience, knowledge (including experience) and the innate desire and ability to grow along the right line and influence others to do so.

While a high standard as applied to each of the attributes specified, and each of numerous others of lesser prominence, but of a distinctly kindred nature, has always been recognized as a desirable and valuable asset of a representative of a railroad, particularly one vested with a considerable measure of governing or supervisory authority, too often those qualities which cannot be absent from the life of that type of man whose services are exemplary, and, therefore, educational and inspiring to his associates (assistants and others), have been disregarded in the interest of greatly overestimated ability based upon practical experience only. This statement is not made with the view of depreciating the value of experience to the head of an organization, but to emphasize the fact that, since "like produces like," the development of members of a terminal-yard organization in accordance with instructions and examples of a head deficient with respect to qualifications other than knowledge acquired by experience could not possibly conform to the standard of efficiency demanded by conditions of the present age.

The general prevailing tendency in almost all branches and departments of the business world is to employ, as far as practicable, methods which have back of them principles harmonizing with the results of scientific study and research; and that policy, indicating as it does, the growing need of earnest and persistent, but fair, competition among individuals, to the end that reforms in the direction of development may be assured regularly, removes completely the basis for arguments favorable to the assumption that a man whose mind is not clear and active and whose moral character is not clean could meet so much as the preliminary requirements of a successful terminal yard organization head.

This conclusion is not expressed either for the purpose of thus conveying the impression that a man with a ripe experience to his credit is incompetent because his moral character is clouded; but in defense of the theory that the highest standard of usefulness and service of any man to his family, his friends, his employer, his community or his country must involve the highest standards of development in the attributes heretofore mentioned. Since serious, unprejudiced study, observations and discussions do not disclose many, if any, permanent benefits which accrue from lax morals and all they embrace, but do disclose divers substantial benefits attributable to the reverse condition, we are reasonable in declaring that the dominating influence for good in a terminal-yard organization will not emanate from a head with lax morals as a qualification, regardless of the extent of his experience and educational training; the fact that he may possess a pleasing personality, or be able to boast of an enviable physical development, or justly claim credit for recognized social leadership among certain classes in a community.

The duties of the head of a terminal yard organization are executive and supervisory in character. The limitations of the former are, in general, so clearly defined that unauthorized deviations therefrom would be the outgrowth (barring exceptions on account of emergencies) of wilful disobedience or ignorance only, the first of which is a true indicator of disloyalty and the second of incompetency.

The supervisory duties of a terminal-yard organization head, however, are practically without limitations, other than his capacity as measured by the standards heretofore described, and his ability to create among his assistants that degree of personal interest in their respective service assignments which will insure not alone the transmission of a corresponding degree of interest to their subordinates or fellow members, but the proper utilization of the energy thus developed.

The supervisory duties are both comprehensive and important, involving, as they do, results dependent on services contributed by many employees and bearing a direct relationship to transportation expenses and net earnings. The member of an organization who is interested in his work and who knows the purpose of his existence and appreciates the opportunity to employ his faculties toward the accomplishment of something worth while combines knowledge with theory and practice and gages his progress by comparative results. The application of the principle supporting that method or system to all members of a department or division thereof suggests immediately, as the foundation of supervisory duties, systematic education of employees and accurate measurement of member, branch and department efficiency.

The term "systematic education" implies training regularly in accordance with a stated course, embracing those features of terminal-yard operation which must undergo changes frequently to keep pace with progress, reference being made especially to new or improved methods, improved facilities including equipment and reforms affecting working regulations or the policies of a company.

It is true that different methods of training may be successfully employed by different men, and likewise true that the same methods will not produce the same results when applied to different organizations (qualifications of individual members representing one of the most common factors responsible for variations in training methods and practices); but that a head fully conversant currently with conditions under his jurisdiction may intelligently analyze his forces and their obligations, and prescribe instructions required for their development, is certain.

To be of the greatest possible value to an individual, a branch, a department or a system as a whole, this training must extend from the unit of service in all cases to the final conclusion, with the relationship of each to each direct and indirect kindred detail clearly established; and the object of efforts and energy expenditures in that direction made manifest through deserved promotions and recognitions otherwise, and statistics disclosing the grades of unit efficiency determined by the employment of accurate measures.

The oft-repeated statement that a certain terminal yard is operated as economically as possible, consistent with the character of demands on it, because the head, a man of long experience, is in close contact constantly with the services of each of the members of the organization no longer has any weight or standing among progressive railroad men, it having been rightfully superseded by the principle that, no matter how insignificant may be a position, the services involved by it should be performed under the supervision of someone who is able to judge, using as his guide a reliable measure, whether the services are or are not satisfactory.

Details, knowledge concerning which should be contemplated by a system of education adapted to the needs of terminal-yard employees under the direction of the head, are numerous, a few of the more prominent being:

The direct and indirect functions of a terminal yard, the relation of the yard to other parts of a railway system and the relation of its organization to other departments and the public.

The value of loyalty and efficiency to the individual employee and an organization, and their probable rewards.

The meaning of the word "discipline"; the necessity for discipline, and the method of administration which is most effective.

The value of harmony among members of an organization.

Effect of dissensions and discord among members of an organization on operations.

The purpose and value of accurate reports relative to service; extraordinary conditions affecting operations; prospective traffic movements (passenger and freight); personal injury and other accidents; classified cars on hand, cars damaged and cars repaired or relieved of lading by transfer; prospective new or enlarged industries and any other matters bearing upon some feature of terminal yard operation with which a head should be familiar.

Courteous treatment of passengers, shippers and receivers of freight and other patrons of the company contrasted with the reverse policy.

The connection of originality of the individual employee with success.

Punctuality, system and self-control; their value to the individual employee and an organization.

Team work contrasted with the reverse organization arrangement.

Patience and sympathy; when necessary, and why.

Economy contrasted with extravagance or near extravagance.

Service measures; the necessity therefor and their value to the individual, branch (or subdepartment) and an organization.

Harsh, rough language, and its effect on loyalty and efficiency.

Train and personal injury accidents; the common causes therefor and precautions necessary to prevent them.

The light loading of cars and the light rating of locomotives; the adverse effect of such practices on yard and train operations.

Rough handling of cars in yards, and the results as applied to freight claims and car maintenance expenses.

Detentions to foreign cars within yard limits; the common causes therefor and the character of reports and records, and individual employee interests, necessary to reduce detentions to the minimum.

The result of improper or late assignment of work to branch (or subdepartment) heads of an organization, reduced to an efficiency loss representing abnormal operating expenses.

While each of these details, as well as each of various others, has a definite place to fill in the educational program of the head of a terminal-yard organization, they are of unequal utility, of which fact through study and practice an individual employee will learn in the same manner as his knowledge concerning the function of each of the parts of his body, their service value to him and the relationship to life is acquired.

Summarizing briefly the substance of the foregoing, the head of a terminal-yard organization must himself be a real man, which type cultivates interest and harmony, inspires confidence, encourages ambition, influences loyalty and capability and condemns vice in every form, by acts founded upon honor, equity, fairness and frankness, the enforcement of intelligent and reasonable instructions and the exhibition of results of precise unit service measurements.

During the World War activities, when we were reminded that the Bible itself says that, in an emergency, it becomes a duty to set aside its command, if one's ox is in the ditch, get him out, intensive study was made by a committee of practical railroad engineering and operating officers, which asked certain questions, well worth repeating here:

Are you now handling the maximum number of cars by the most economical or direct route, either existing or reasonably attainable?

Can the number of interchange movements be reduced advantageously by combining movements from various origins to various destinations?

Can you extend the practice of reciprocal interchange now working . so advantageously at many points?

Are you interchanging directly between yards instead of on assigned interchange tracks?   Could not delay and rehandling be reduced by so doing?

Are you, as far as practicable, making interchange with regular crews who are familiar with the routes and the work to be done?

Can the volume of direct interchange be increased by minor track changes or changes in practice?

Are interchange facilities at any point inadequate for periods of heavy traffic under new conditions, and, if so, is it practicable at reasonable cost to make the necessary increase of capacity, or is it better by rerouting interchange to relieve the situation?

Have you any separate route of interchange that could be discontinued to advantage by consolidation with another route?

Can you have cars grouped, either in cuts or solid trains, before they reach the terminal, so as to reduce terminal switching?

Can interchange in any terminal be reduced to advantage by rerouting through outside junctions?

Have all industrial plants sufficient track capacity and other facilities so that cars may be promptly placed, loaded or unloaded to the full capacity of the plant during each working shift without unduly frequent switching or interference with plant operation?

Can you arrange for "one-line" switching of individual or grouped industries or team tracks?

Can greater efficiency in yard operation be obtained through the consolidation of the yards of one or more railroads:

By dividing large terminals into zones and assigning as great a number .of receiving yards to as small a number of classifying yards as possible, thereby assembling the maximum number of cars into the minimum number of classifications?

By pooling similar yards of neighboring railroads so as to conserve yard room, avoiding both the duplication of switching and interchange between yards?

By consolidating existing facilities, adapting such combined facilities to a new program of operations which disregards prior uses, with or without minor physical changes; or by pooling the same in the sense that one line's facilities are used to serve the overflow of traffic confronting a neighboring line's facilities?

By combining the use of two or more yards to adapt them to the segregation of freight with respect to commodities or destinations?

Can you reassign or coordinate the use of engine terminal facilities so as to avoid or reduce delay and congestion, reduce expense and engine-miles or improve supervision?

To what extent can neighboring engine-terminal facilities be adapted to the economical housing and handling of engines grouped according to the nature or location of their service or their size without regard to road ownership?

Has "single inspection" been instituted wherever cars are interchanged?

Can greater efficiency be obtained by consolidating the car-inspection forces at adjacent yards, junctions or stations?

Are car inspections and repairs so made as to insure safety and prevent further damage to equipment and lading?

Is such inspection made so as fully to detect violations of loading rules and are these rules effectively enforced in every case of such violation?

Has the force of inspectors been *educated* to the making of effective inspection and is the inspection followed unremittingly by the making of adequate repairs?

Can you obtain greater efficiency through extending consolidation of car-repair forces and facilities:

(*a*) By combining in one repair yard the work of one or more roads?

(*b*) By combining the forces and facilities in a given zone?

Do you require car inspectors at outlying points to repair cars as far as possible and to make light repairs to cars in industrial districts where cars are "made empty" or placed empty for loading?

Are you keeping the maximum number of cars in service by giving preferred attention to those needing light repairs?

Can the number of records, and incidentally the amount of clerical work, be reduced:

(*a*) By the consolidation of car-record departments?

(*b*) By the consolidation of car-record forces in yards reasonably near, one to the other, whether these yards are combined or not?

(c) By the elimination of certain intermediate car records on each road through a more comprehensive and manifold use of train and yard reports so as to supply the greatest amount of information from each report?

In connection with this subject, E. H. Lee, Vice-President, Chicago & Western Indiana, commented as follows:

Congestion is defined as a condition of undue pressure, a state of unnatural crowding; and congestion on the railroads, like congestion in the body, is a disease which interferes with the normal functions, and is to be reduced by the use of various devices and means adapted to remove the undue pressure in the parts affected. Two of the principal causes of congestion in terminals, which, in turn, act in a vicious circle with congestion itself, each to cause the growth of the other, are dead time and the rehandling of cars. It is safe to say that any method or practice which secures the maximum reduction in dead time, and in the rehandling of cars, will also secure maximum reduction in the congestion of terminals, and therefore maximum increase in the efficiency of the railroads of the country as a whole.

For the purpose of this discussion, dead time is limited to and may be defined as time spent by the train crew after an engine has been manned in getting out of the roundhouse, pulling up to and coupling onto the train, testing the air, etc. at the outgoing end of the trip; time lost in setting out and picking up; and time spent in putting away the train, with the various similar attendant operations at the incoming end. This so-called dead time thus defined is to be distinguishable from time spent in actually passing over the road. Its serious effect in terminal operation is not generally appreciated, being of much less relative importance in open-country operation than in terminal operation. This is true because dead time remains more or less constant, while running time tends to vary directly with the length of the run. As an illustration: Assume an open-country division 100 miles long, average freight running time over the division 8 hours as compared with a transfer run in a terminal 12 miles long, average running time 1 hour. If the dead time is in each case 2 hours, the dead-time loss on the country division is only 20 per cent., whereas on the transfer run it is $66\frac{2}{3}$ per cent. This comparison may seem exaggerated, but an investigation made by the writer some years ago, which is believed to have been reasonably accurate, disclosed that, in an actual case under ordinary conditions and where no undue congestion existed, dead time as above defined consumed 65 per cent. of the total service time of all transfer trains. . . .

At most minor terminals and junction points, direct deliveries are made between the railroads, and at some points the chief improvement possible is doubtless to be secured by a coordination of facilities when practicable, and an improvement in methods, as, for instance, by the reciprocal delivery of cars, thereby eliminating light running. In the case of industries served by more than one line, it has been the general practice in the past for each road to handle its own business into and out of the same, although in one case familiar to the writer all such industrial deliveries have been handled by a terminal railroad for the tenant companies using its line for a period of over thirty years, and with results entirely satisfactory in the way of a reduction of both engine time and cost.

With flat switching ordinarily eight or ten classifications are made without rehandling, a greater number being bunched and reclassified. An analysis will show that in very many cases only few classifications are required to straighten out a large proportion of the business. In one case in Chicago about 50 per cent. of the through transfer business in one direction goes to only two railroads. If all cars for these lines were delivered to the belt line in straight cuts, approximately 50 per cent. of the classification in that direction would disappear and much of this 50 per cent. could be run in straight trains from terminal to terminal, thus eliminating dead time and helping to keep yards clear. Moreover, this preliminary classification could be made with little or no additional expense by the through line, because it must in any event switch out many cars, such as bad orders, holds and those for other deliveries. Also, a considerable amount of this preliminary classification could be done to advantage at the division yards of the through line beyond the large terminals.

The place to control congestion is at or near the various points where business originates. By proper measures the through line may, in a degree, control congestion in its own important terminal yards, by holding back business, something impossible to the belt line, without the help of the through lines.

Business moving even in heavy volume is not congestion, and, where they exist, belt lines, if kept reasonably open and uncongested, are the best means of keeping cars moving in terminals, thus avoiding congestion and blockades.

Preliminary or advance classification as above described is not a theoretical measure, but has been used with success to prevent and to lift blockades in terminals, many times.

Where transfer or belt roads are of considerable length and where equipped with motive power to handle transfer trains, it is the better practice to keep foreign engines off the belt line, performing the transfer service with belt crews. Better supervision can be secured where train crews are kept at home. It is difficult, if not impossible, to enforce discipline over crews while operating on a foreign road (particularly against loafing on the job), even though in theory they become the employees of that road while so engaged. Moreover, discipline and standards of performance differ on different railroads, being better on some and worse on others. Where foreign trains and engines operate over a transfer road, it ordinarily happens that the general movement is regulated by the slowest and most indifferently operated train. There is also a difference in the standard of power maintenance as between railroads. A stalled train, caused by the engine breaking down, not steaming or being overloaded, delays all following trains, and, if a foreign crew, the railroad officers who should apply discipline have no direct stake in the failure, and find excuses ready. The practice of using foreign crews on the transfer road is not sufficiently elastic. The crew may have a full train in one direction and a light train in the other, because it runs between two points only. The belt crew may be ordered to any one of several different points, as the business may indicate.

The conditions and problems to be met, and combated by the terminal organizations of today are as varied as the colors of the coat Joseph wore, some time after the first authentic case of abuse of the storage in transit privilege, in connection with the apple traffic in the Garden of Eden. The terminal must receive the 201 cars or the 16,000 tons—plus—freight trains. In troublous times—often covering 12 months of every year—

most extraordinary methods have to be followed to "dig out" the car of unusual importance. Picking out a car from the middle of a long string, by lifting it over with a derrick, to an adjacent track, while not a routine move, is by no means infrequent. Cars containing perishable freight were so specialized on by the Pennsylvania during the winter of 1915–16, when such cars were stored on the main running track, where they could not be reached by a locomotive in the ordinary way.[1]

In one congested terminal a new superintendent took charge who was an organizer, and had executive ability. He was pushed into his job—told to "go to it"—and let alone. His experience for the first few weeks was that of many another—every move he made was watched, scrutinized, criticized, discussed. Knowing the value of cooperation, of a thorough *esprit de corps*, he called a staff meeting of his yardmasters, engine and car foremen, agents and heads of the different branches. After reassuring all, expressing confidence in their loyalty and ability, he outlined his plan of campaign and explained briefly his reasons for each step to be taken. His men were impressed with the absolute necessity of supporting the plan in every detail, after a thorough discussion of it, although honest differences of opinion might be held. All latent prejudice and opposition were thereby eliminated. Meetings were held at frequent intervals; each subject was freely and fully discussed, and definite conclusions reached. In this manner, unity of action and understanding was secured and, through an exchange of views and opinions, beneficial results were secured.

In one case, in a large and disjointed terminal,[2] necessitating many main-line movements, delays to yard engines proved onerous. The scheduling of transfer engines and efforts to keep scheduled trains on time developed a weakness in the method of handling train movements within the terminal. Movements were handled principally by signalmen and switch tenders, using telephone communication with adjacent offices and the yards. Interference of movements, often with heavy delays, to systematize the handling of trains, a three-trick dispatcher's office was arranged at terminal headquarters; telephone dispatching circuit provided with connections at interchange and heavy industrial points and with the yard and freight offices by commercial service through a private exchange. Yard engines were given advantage of delays to passenger trains in making main-track movements and still kept out of the way; yardmasters could quickly locate any transfer or industrial yard engine with which they desired to communicate; all movements were made to the best advantage.

The switching of freight houses and team tracks was done by engines from yards most conveniently located, and the general method was good.

---

[1] Vice-President George D. Dixon, Pennsylvania, addressing National Wholesale Lumber Dealers' Association, Philadelphia, Mar. 16, 1916.

[2] G. D. Brooke, Division Superintendent, B. & O.

Definite work had been assigned to each engine to be done on an approximate schedule. Cars for placing were switched in order in one cut by crews in the working yard, moved to the freight house and team yard by the engine assigned to that work and spotted after outbound cars had been moved. The switching of merchandise and quick-dispatch cars required particular attention.

At a certain freight house the receipt of freight stopped at 5 p. m.; at 5:45 p. m. the cars were sealed and the night engine was standing on the lead ready to move the cars for points beyond the adjoining divisions. They were taken to the working yard and switched into eight classifications—five east and three west. In the meantime another engine had worked the team tracks and arrived with the quick-dispatch loads, which it classified in turn while the first engine returned to the freight house to resume work there, taking with it cars from industries which had been collected by a day engine. It assisted in completing the classification, switching the cars into one cut, and proceeding in turn to the east and west terminal yards where the fast freights were being made up to start at 10 p. m.

A terminal yardmaster[1] who accomplished much towards reducing the rough handling of cars in a yard which had achieved an unenviable reputation in that direction first secured the hearty support and cooperation of his engine foreman, and then made frequent visits to his engine crews during the night, but not on regular schedule. If he saw a crew handling cars roughly, he would call them together at once and talk to them impressively, pointing out the bad effects of their work—in direct expense, inconvenience to customers whose goods were damaged and danger to employees and others because of weakened equipment, often almost invisible. Much of his time was spent around the freight houses and industrial tracks where most of the damage was known to occur. It was seldom necessary to talk to the same crew a second time.

Economic and intensive utilization of freight cars involves high average car mileage and car loading. Either without the other misses the mark. But there must be a minimum of unproductive mileage—both in car-miles and in ton (contents)-miles. There cannot always be a return, or "balancing" load, and there is ever present the "ferry," or "trap car," with its short mileage and the incompatibility of loading l.c.l. freight to meet all the conditions, at once, of producing "working" car-miles, productive ton-miles, heavy car loading, avoidance (absence) of transfer stations and expeditious movement of freight.

In March, 1920, the railroads established a record in reducing empty-car-mileage to 27.7 per cent. of the total, but those were abnormal times and there is little probability that the traffic conditions and the temper of the shipping public will again enable this record to be made. It was

[1] J. Farley, Yardmaster, Michigan Central.

then, as to the shipping public, a case of "When the devil was sick the devil a monk would be" but he got well and his point of view changed. To attain heavy car loading—and, correspondingly, a low percentage of empty-car-miles—it is fundamentally desirable to utilize all suitable cars for loading in the direction of light movement; and traffic should be intensively solicited to that end. Freedom from congestion in road movement, prompt handling in yards and at stations and quick loading and unloading by shippers' and company's forces are essential desiderata. Car distributors should endeavor to adapt the size and capacity cars supplied to fit the character of the load. Shippers should cooperate in an endeavor to load cars to either weight or volume capacity. At freight houses, transfer stations, warehouses and storehouses operated by the company's forces, the heaviest possible loading should be practiced.

Worn-out or light engines are sometimes used for yardwork. Light engines are suitable for certain kinds of yard work, and in such cases there can be no possible objection to them, but in many instances their use in yard service is uneconomical. An engine in a classification yard should be sufficiently powerful to handle as many cars as a road engine brings in, and to start them quickly. It requires just as many men to man and follow a small worn-out engine as a larger engine designed for this class of service, and it usually burns as much coal, while the larger engine will perform much more work. Two engines in a yard will usually interfere with each other and, of course, also interfere more with road engines than will one. It is questionable economy to use in yard service road engines not adapted for quick starting and stopping and from which signals cannot readily be seen, fore and aft, and from either side.

One of the first desiderata in a yard is the delivery of incoming trains with regularity, and another of nearly equal importance is to have outgoing trains start as soon as they are ready. These desirable practices are almost wholly within the province of the chief train dispatcher and, barring shortage or bad condition of locomotives, he may substantially carry out the yardmaster's wishes; or, in edging over, one way or the other, he may materially embarrass him. Thorough harmony and frequent conference are necessary. A yardmaster dreads having a number of ordinary freight trains coming in just ahead of a stock or other fast-freight train demanding preferred attention. In such matters the chief train dispatcher can greatly assist the yardmaster by keeping the yard informed as to the road conditions, and, in turn, informing himself as to yard conditions. The holding back of freight trains may, on the other hand, be carried to excess and result in greater embarrassment if they finally come in "bunched" faster than they can be comfortably handled. There is a line to hew to in this as in many other things, and it is the intelligent chief train dispatcher with a good supply of common sense and discretion who finds it.   When freight is heavy and weather conditions are unfavorable, the chief dispatcher, in figuring ahead, may keep the terminal well supplied with power for outward movements by adjusting the tonnage rating of locomotives to weather changes and by insisting on good dispatching.   These practices will also do much toward getting trains over the road promptly.   If the locomotives are overloaded or if the trains are neglected on the road—remaining too long on sidings— neither the locomotives nor the men will be available for early use when they get into the terminal.   Unless there is an abundance of motive power and men, a congestion may result because of inability to start trains out when they are ready.   The situation becomes aggravated by the necessity for holding out approaching trains because of such congestion.   This, in turn, renders more locomotives and more men unfit for service.

The chief dispatcher should watch the tonnage rating and make readjustments as frequently as conditions make them necessary.   The government weather report should be had from the nearest signal station, both the full detailed daily mail reports and the more frequent brief telegraphic advices.   Weather reports by wire must also be had from designated railroad telegraph stations along the line at stated times, and during threatened or existing storms at additional times.   Close watching of these reports and other data will often keep a road open and going where a little neglect would cause a blockade.   A train must never be permitted to become stalled in a snow storm if there is any possible way to prevent it.   The temperature reports sent at regular intervals from the different stations are of great value.

Much may be accomplished by having everything in readiness at all points—the decks should always be cleared for action.   Enormous delays occur in many yards made up, in the aggregate, of very small and almost unnoticeable items.   The failure or neglect to have switching lists, instructions and other clerical matter in readiness for assistant yardmasters or conductors going on duty is more expensive than would be supposed, because it holds up the work of an entire crew while the conductor is getting instructions.   It may be but 10 or 15 min., but at an approximate cost of 6 cts. a minute it means a loss of 60 or 90 cts. The composition of approaching trains should be known in ample time to communicate the information to yard conductors and others requiring it, so that they may be ready to take hold quickly after these trains pull in.   Time may be saved by arranging fixed signals to tell enginemen of yard engines what moves are wanted, instead of having them depend entirely on the hand signals of trainmen.   The enginemen then need look only in one direction for signals.   This plan is especially adaptable to engines employed in hump switching.

Delays often ensue because car inspectors do not inspect trains and couple up hose early enough to enable the trains to start on time.   After snow storms there may be delay in cleaning out yard switches, thus preventing full use of the power and men. If repair tracks are awkwardly located, the time of switching the crippled cars may sometimes be changed to reduce the interference with the forwarding of loaded cars. Signal lights may be relocated or added to facilitate transmission of signals and reduce liability of confusing them. Every added facility in the way of office conveniences, filing systems, record books, bill racks, telephone and telegraph connections assists in securing economical results.

On the arrival of a freight train, the yard clerk (sometimes called a "checker" or "chalker") goes along one side of the cars with a switch list showing car numbers, initials, contents and destinations, checks off the seals and notes their numbers and condition in the proper columns. In some yards the clerk takes the card bills handed to him in a package by the conductor. The card for the first car is on top and the others are arranged to follow in regular order. The cards are checked against the train and the seal records noted and afterward copied in a permanent record. In his inspection, going down one side of the train and returning on the other side, the clerk also notes the condition of the doors. The cars are marked on the switching side, so as to indicate to the yard conductor where the cuts should be made and the tracks to which they should be switched. The marking is done by carding or chalking. When a card is used, it is usually of a distinctive color and has a large plain letter or number representing the final destination within the terminal, or the train and division for outward movement. The card is tacked on the side of the car near one end. When chalk is used, the number or letter or abbreviation for destination, and the date, are noted, thus: "B 3/20," meaning the destination or route for which "B" stands, and Mar. 20. Chalk is cheaper than talcum, is easier to mark with and more readily effaced by rubbing or by rain. The permanence of marking is objectionable because a number of marks on a car would be confusing.

The disposition of the power to the best advantage, with a system for checking it; the knowledge that it is kept moving without making false or unnecessary moves; that it is kept properly balanced; and that it reaches the point where cars require movement are the prime essentials of successful and satisfactory operation. Regular engine schedules should be maintained so far as practicable; but, while every effort should be made to maintain them, there should not be the slightest hesitancy in discontinuing or readjusting them as conditions change and seem to warrant. In many large terminals, a system of train dispatching by the use of telegraph or telephone lines is in effect. A dispatcher may be assigned to keep records of engine movements at the various reporting stations and perform additional duties. He should follow up and demand an explanation of apparent detentions. In one terminal a record board is used instead of the ordinary train sheet. The board is ruled in squares, with a peg hole in each square. Each yard engine is represented by a peg with the engine number on it. Horizontal lines represent reporting stations; vertical lines half-hour divisions progressing from left to right, there being 48 to represent a 24-hour period. The arrangement is on the general plan of a time chart. As the engines are reported, they are moved to the corresponding peg hole, at the intersection of the horizontal line representing the reporting station and the vertical line representing the nearest half-hour division to the time at which the report is received. The peg remains in the hole until the next report of the engine's movement is received. The movements may be copied on a train sheet for permanent record and subsequent study by the yardmaster.

To work up a perfect set of yard-engine schedules in a heavy and complicated terminal is a task of no mean dimensions. The road movements, both in and out, must be met on one side, and on the other the interior movements, which include the freight-house and transfer work and the placing of cars on private-industry tracks, in engine-house, coal-trestle and team yards, all of which must be dovetailed smoothly and accurately. Each private-industry track should be visited once in 24 hours on working days, and at about the same hour each day. If the plant is working, it should not be omitted. On the other hand, visits should not be attempted oftener, as other industrial plants may claim discrimination unless similar service is given them, and this is usually impracticable. In some instances more frequent switching is given for operating convenience; it may be necessary to bring about a more prompt release of cars at a time when cars are in demand

The use of relief engines is advocated. This enables regular yard shifts to continue work while the relief engine substitutes for those requiring coal, sand, water, fires cleaned or light repairs. In this country the 8-hour yard, with penalty overtime, is in vogue. Overtime is not usually permitted in these yards, it being the theory that the three shifts cover a 24-hour period without intermission, except for meal periods, a theory which may work out satisfactorily in a classification yard, operated day and night every day in the year. It is uneconomical and awkward in commercial yards where the work may be done by an engine in 10 hours one day and where 12 hours or 14 hours are required the next. The 8-hour arrangement as usually applied permits economical work only in multiples of 8—that is, 8, 16 or 24 hours, because of the prohibited overtime.

To get the best results, the power should be very carefully assigned after the schedules have been mapped out. Light engines, with short wheel base, should be used on curves of short radii or where structures are weak. Freight cars, coupled, may be moved around curves of 150-ft. radius (38 deg.), but engines of ordinary design will not go around such curves. An ordinary road engine will go around a curve of 318-ft. radius (18 deg.). By cutting away between engine and tender to permit short turning, and separating cars by bar couplings, curves of 100-ft. radius (57.6 deg.) may be operated. The heavier power should be placed where tracks, bridges and curves will permit and where heavy tractive power can be utilized to advantage.

The Edge Hill yard of the London & North-Western,[1] Liverpool, England (built in 1873), was one of the first to use gravity, abandoning the push-and-pull method and working on the gridiron plan. It is today one of the most interesting and instructive car-handling machines—2,000 to 2,500 cars ("wagons") come in every afternoon and evening from the various docks, quays and depots around Liverpool. From the "reception lines," near the summit, where the road engines leave the cars, they are sorted by gravity into the "upper group" of storage sidings, consisting of 24 parallel lines, each taking the cars for a particular train. Just before a train is ready to leave, its cars are dropped into one of the "departure lines" through two groups of short tracks called "gridirons." In these short tracks the positions of the cars are changed to station order. The entire work is done by gravity, no power being applied at any point, the grade being sufficient to start a car when its brakes are released. At the neck of each group of lines, a "sand drag" is arranged to stop run-away cars. The Edge Hill yard is described in another chapter.

The plans of the Brunswick, Md., yards of the B. & O. (Fig. 33, page 86) have been discussed. They have a capacity of 6,500 cars and handle upward of 2,000 cars daily in each direction when business runs heavy. The eastbound classification yards have 36 tracks, 18 in each, using a central-ladder scheme on each side, with nine tracks to a ladder. An electropneumatic push-button machine operates the switches. A brakeman tags the cars as they come from the receiving yard to the hump. For example, if a train pulls into the receiving yard with the first 10 cars for Washington and the next 20 for Baltimore, a tag reading "10-4" is put on the front of the first 10 cars, indicating that the first 10 cars in the shift are to go on the Washington track in the classification yard. The next 20 are tagged in a similar way for Baltimore. The outlet from the classification yard is by double ladders through the center of the yard and a single ladder on each side, each ladder having nine switches. Trains from the northern half of the classification yard pull directly out on the eastbound freight track.

The Potomac yard of the Richmond, Fredericksburg & Potomac, at Alexandria, Va., is a large, two-direction hump, in which about 1,100 cars are received and the same number forwarded daily under normal conditions. A plan and description appears on pages 83, 84 and 85, Figs. 30, 31, and 32. There are 27 "undisturbed" classifications made north-

[1] Now part of London, Midland and Scottish.

ward, 26 southward; one track is used for "mixed" classifications. The cars on the latter track must be reclassified, as the tracks in the south-bound yard are insufficient to enable the necessary 29 classifications to be made. Six engines are worked nights and five during the day. Two engines work continuously on the humps, with six car riders, a cutter, a conductor and four switchers for each engine. About 20 per cent. of northbound and 50 per cent. of southbound cars are weighed.

The yard forces employed in the Chicago terminal district of the Chicago & Northwestern include about 700 men. On a basis of 10 hours' service as an "equivalent engine day," 105 engines are worked daily in the terminal territory. Of these, 60 work days and 45 nights. This service requires about 70 *actual* engines, including those in the shops at any one time. The engine crew consists of an engineman, a fireman, with three or sometimes four switchmen to each engine. There are 24 yardmasters employed (including general yardmasters, yardmasters and assistant yardmasters), 40 switch tenders and 80 yard clerks or markers. In the 40th Avenue yard there are 34 engine crews, 17 working days and 17 working nights. Eight of the 16 transfer crews work out of 40th Avenue. The Wisconsin division yard force is composed of 1 general yardmaster, 11 yardmasters and assistant yardmasters, 24 yard clerks, 4 train clerks and 8 switch tenders. This number includes both day and night forces, but does not include the office force (5 men) of the train-master of freight terminals, whose office is in the former 40th Street depot.

The tables[1] on pages 116 and 117, compiled from the various details of operation of yards, gathered by the Committee of the American Railway Engineering Association, give some interesting features.

In the New York Central's Elkhart and Collinwood yards, the number of riders employed is dependent upon advices as to composition and number of approaching trains. In other yards it is based upon the number of cars passing over the hump during the working period of the day. In the Altoona yard of the Pennsylvania a record was kept to determine the number of cars and cuts each rider was capable of riding for the entire day, it being placed at about 28 cuts in 12 hours. The number of riders to be assigned to each hump is then arrived at. In the Reading

[1] While these tables are old, they are presented because, with the exception of the column, "Cost per car"—now wholly out of step—the actual operating results are both interesting and instructive. They may be well used for purposes of comparison—and may indicate the extent to which there has been a "slowing up" if any. Costs of yards and work done are not comparable, in the light of relative operating efficiency; they are useful for planning yards, or in the revision or extension of existing yards. For operating results, a yard may be compared with its own previous best, or average, record. The higher operating costs may indicate economy in rendering a close-up service and, again may be due to a close and conscientious analysis of the situation and establishment of a basis which includes every possible item of expense entering into yard operations, and a scrupulously exact count of the number of cars handled.

yard at Rutherford, Pa., 16 or 17 cuts are classified in from 5 to 7 min. If there are more cuts in a train, the work has to await the return of the riders. In some instances, therefore, trains are classified at upward of 400 cars an hour, for very short periods. The East St. Louis yards assign the riders from a forecast of business given to the general yardmaster.

In weighing cars the general practice is to uncouple them, whether they are weighed while running over the scales on the descending side of a hump or on a separate track for that purpose. In a few cases they are weighed without uncoupling. Riders usually walk back to the humps, an engine being run down to meet them if there is likely to be a wait. In a few cases provision is made for returning them more quickly. At Altoona, a pick-up car, handled by a small engine, operates on a track for that purpose, running alongside the extreme north side of the eastbound yard. It would be preferable if this track ran in the center of the yard, but it would probably interfere with the switching work. In the Conway (Pennsylvania road) yard, a pusher engine is used to shove out tracks in the classification yard and to carry riders back. In a few other yards electric trolley cars are used to return the riders. Current is obtained from a near-by company power house.

Ladder-track switches leading into the body tracks of classification yards are usually thrown by hand and it will be seen from the table that one man usually covers from eight to ten switches. In the Altoona yards the switches are operated by direct-move electropneumatic power controlled from the tower by a push-button machine. In the Enola yards (Pennsylvania road), one man at each hump operates the switches by compressed air.

The New York Central uses a heavy type of locomotive (135 tons) to push cars over the humps at Collinwood   Some roads use two engines. At Gibson, Ind., the New York Central uses an engine weighing 270,000 lb. on drivers. The Norfolk & Western at Bluefield, W. Va., uses a 90-ton engine—two engines in emergencies.

In switching over a hump, a uniform speed of about 2 m.p.h. should be maintained without a stop, until all the riders are taken up. If cars do not run freely, a second engine, equipped for poling, may be placed alongside the ladder and used to good advantage in starting stopped cars and keeping switches and entrances to body tracks open. With low temperature or during a heavy snow storm, this will greatly aid the movement.

A record in a number of hump yards shows that the time consumed in switching is from one-fourth to one-third of the total time; and the time in disposing of one car ranges from 54 to 111 sec., depending largely on the distance of the classification yard switches from the hump, the rate of grade, the kind of cars, lading and weather conditions.

OPERATING RESULTS IN LEADING YARDS

Yard	Max. number trains rec'd in an hour	Av'ge cars per train	Av'ge No. trains rec'd in 24 hr.	Train one engine can push over hump — Cars	Train one engine can push over hump — Tons	Av'ge cuts per train	Per cent. cars w'gh'd over hump	Un-couple to weigh	Scales on hump	Dist. from summit (feet)	Avg. classifying capacity 1 hr.	5 hr.	10 hr.	24 hr.	No. car riders	Switches to each switchman	Cost per car
Brunswick, Md......E.	6	45	30	40	3350	23	2	Yes	No		50	250	500		11	Electric	10.0
Newcastle, Pa.	4	50	12		2500	28	30	Yes	Yes	50	25–75	125–375	250–750	600–1700	5	14	8.5
Holloway, O.	4	34	15	34	1913	15	70	Yes	Yes	127	20–70	100–350	200–700	400–1400	7	9	11.0
Winnipeg, Can.	5	50	40		2500	25	0				100		500		8	12	5.0
Haney, Ills......N.	4	51	18	51		35	20	Yes	Yes	110	85	425	850		14	8	10.0
Galesburg, Ills.	8	51	50	51	1559	31	25	Yes	Yes	50	100	500	1000	3000	10	7	11.9
Gibson, Ind.	6	40	7	60	3840		0				100	500	1000	2000	20	7	
Oneonta, N. Y.	9	43	30	43	2300	28	1	Yes	No		32–50	160–250	320–520	640–1000	7	4	10.9
Pen Horn, N. J.	8	25	40	25		20	0	Yes	No		50–75	250	500	1003	12	10	9.0
Elkhart, Ind......E.	6	75	15	75		35	4	Yes	No					2500	8	6	9.0
Collinwood, O......W.	6	75	20	75		40	4		No		100	500	1000	2000	10	6	9.0
Oak Island, N. J.	6	35	15	20	900	20	0	No	No					2400	4	6	6.5
River Rouge, Mich.	3	65	10	65		30	3		No		80	400	800	800	4	10	
East Bottom, Mo.	10	40	36		1500	25	15	Yes	Yes	50	30–50	150–250	300–500	600–1000	8	10	27.0
Avis, Pa.	8	60	20			42	98	Yes	Yes	80	38–70		500–620	850–1100	4	8	8.9

Where one set of figures are shown, under "classifying capacity of hump" they represent the average. Where two sets, the small number represents the average and the large the maximum.

Cost per car is supposed to cover the expense of handling from the time the road engine cuts off on receiving track until the road engine is coupled to the train on departure track.

OPERATING RESULTS IN LEADING YARDS—*Continued*

Yard	Max. No. trains rec'd in an hour	Av'ge cars per train	Av'ge No. trains rec'd in 24 hr.	Train one engine can push over hump (Cars)	Train one engine can push over hump (Tons)	Av'ge cu's per train	Per cent. cars w'gh'd over hump	Un-couple to weigh	Scales on hump	Dist. from summit (feet)	Avg. classifying capacity of hump 1 hr.	5 hr.	10 hr.	24 hr.	No. car riders	Switches to each switchman	Cost per car
West Albany, N. Y........E.	7	50	29			40	2	Yes	No		95–160	400–500	800–1123	1600–2000	6	6	28.0
West Albany, N. Y........W	7	35	35			28	2	Yes	No		95–160	400–500	800–1125	1600–2000	6	7	28.0
Dewitt, N. Y..............E.	5	75	50		3300	35	1	Yes	No		200–300		2000–2783		12	6	10.2
Dewitt, N. Y..............W.	5	80	35		3300	42	1	Yes	No		200–300		2000–2783		12	6	10.2
Williamston, W. Va.......	11	60	24			60	95	Yes	Yes	75	40	180	300	350	10	10	11.0
Bluefield, W. Va..........	7	30	24			30	80				30–110	150–265	300–500	720–1240	16	4	20.0
Altoona, Pa..............	10	38	90		4800	30	90	Yes	Yes	30	100–120	500–600	1000–1030	2000–2240	18	Elec.	
Enola, Pa...............E.	7	50	33	68	3800	25		Yes	No				1318	2151	7		10.0
Enola, Pa...............W.	9	45	38	68	3800	29		Yes	No				1396	2488	7		10.0
Conway, Pa..............E.	12	45	25	55	3500	20	5	Yes	Yes	300	63–90	295–425	550–810	1060–1450	20	8	18.0
Rutherford, Pa..........	5	44	30	44	2500	29	0.5	No			150	600	900	1500	17	7	
Hazleton, Pa............	5	65	22	45	3350	25		Yes			70–100	350–500	700–1000	1400–2000	7	16	9.0
Asheville, N. C.........	4	30	20	30	1200	15	10	Yes	Yes	50	80	400	800	1000	5	5	5.0
E. St. Louis, Mo........	3	40	25	25	500	12		Yes	Yes	30	100	500	1000		7	5	10.0
Terre Haute, Ind........	12	19	30	30	1000	12	10	Yes	Yes	30					8		8.0
Alexandria, Va.........N.	5	22	32	20	840	15	20	Yes	No						7		32.0
Alexandria, Va.........S.	7	21	29	20	520	14	0.5	Yes	No						6		32.0

The yards at Alexandria, Va., are commonly known as the Potomac yard.

One road operating many hump yards has a rule that the speed at impact between cars must not exceed 2 miles an hour, and that, in classifying, cars must be ridden home when necessary to obtain this result.

The Pennsylvania has installed two electric search lights in its Harrisburg classification yards, to facilitate the distribution of cars in incoming trains. The westbound classification yard at Altoona has one very powerful electric search light which affords adequate illumination at the extreme end of the longest classification track. The light is operated from the tower and its rays are directed with the movement of traffic, and, therefore, on the backs of the car riders.

CHAPTER VII

THE YARDMASTER

The yardmaster leads an eventful life. Receiving, sorting and dispatching large numbers of small parcels without error require alertness and accuracy. The yardmaster must have these qualities, but when, for parcels, there are substituted huge, complicated vehicles, occasionally broken and always breakable, coming in irregular flow and numbered by thousands, the yardmaster needs to be something more than a parcel handler. Every unusual incident hinders him—nothing helps him—for his work is movement, his danger is blockade. His work is quite unlike the engineman's, because the yardmaster cannot make the movement approximate uniformity, nor can he personally perform the work— he must depend upon fallible mankind. Cars come to him in bunches to be unloaded, or sorted into new trains, or to be repaired and sent forward—for his bailiwick is simply a part of the main-line movement, slightly expanded for his purposes of breaking up and marshaling trains.

A good yard is as nothing if not kept in condition to perform properly the service required of it. A blockaded yard means a blocked road, an absolutely useless, expensive tool; and this can be brought about in a day, not necessarily by doing the wrong thing, but by the yardmaster not doing enough. In times of emergency, to err on the side of safety does not mean, as in many other kinds of work, to watch and wait. Delay is often fatal. The yardmaster must do something vigorously, even if it be far from the best thing, and he must keep on going without admitting, for a moment, an impossibility. The ideal man for this work should have an aptitude and ingenuity for meeting small and great emergencies, quite beyond the ability to follow rules. He must be resourceful. In a big terminal the difference in value between a good yardmaster and a poor one may amount to a president's salary.

Many yardmasters are retained because they are not well watched. Their highly expensive operations may be lower than those of other yards, although the other yards may be handled more successfully. Apparent success in one yard may be due to congestion existing in other more difficult or crowded yards which are attracting attention, or to the erroneous assumption that yards not complained of are well handled.

The yardmaster who is competent to handle a difficult situation is not always estimated at his full value. This may be due to superficial criticism by chief clerks and others in the offices of the superintendent or general superintendent who may be without practical experience. Their superiors are busy and the yardmaster may lack the time or training necessary to convince. An awkward location, want of facilities, unadaptable motive power, insufficient wages paid to secure competent or reliable help, bad make-up of trains approaching the yard and requirements as to make-up of outgoing trains—these are some of the conditions that occasionally give the good yardmaster a bad name.

The question was asked a well-known transportation officer: "What kind of a man does it require to run a big yard satisfactorily?" The reply was: "The kind of a man who can run this United States Government." The ability to do things can hardly be overestimated. It is better to risk censure for doing something than for doing nothing. When a washout, snow blockade or other obstruction closes the line and cuts off communication, it is gratifying to discover afterward that somebody took the responsibility to start relief trains and get things moving—that somebody did something. There are men of the other stamp who do nothing unless directed and who have to be told everything and then do but a part of what they are required to do. They are comparable with the engineman who wires the dispatcher that his engine is disabled and asks what he shall do about it. Let it not be forgotten that ingenuity begins where rules end.

The greatest difficulty in securing competent help and in honest, capable workers securing positions of trust, exists in the very limited number of persons who may be known intimately by anyone employing others in positions of responsibility. Many are in need of faithful and efficient help; many deserving workers need employment.

Officers accepting responsibilities must assume them: for they go with authority and cannot be evaded. They should clearly understand their duties, and the results expected. A superior officer should deal only with the subordinate in charge; he should never go around or ignore any officer, be he lower or higher in rank. An organization of men of an ordinary type will accomplish more, if responsibility is definitely fixed all along the line and a definite policy is outlined, than will the same number of brilliant men, working along individual lines and their own ideas. Someone has to fix the standard; only one person can do it—the chief executive. It is impossible to realize a high standard unless it is known what constitutes a high standard.

A man without an accurate sense of justice is disqualified for an executive position. A superior should never frighten or threaten a subordinate. If he makes no impression, there is little heed paid to what he says; if he makes an impression, it will be passed on to the rank and file. There are officers whose ideas of justice and of methods are good, so long as they are calm, but who become unjust when disturbed. A calm, courteous and definite officer is usually just and efficient. It requires but a short time to disorganize an undertaking which may have required years and much effort to build up. Men are usually what they are expected to be. Much should be expected of them, but nothing that is unreasonable, impracticable or impossible. Orders impossible of fulfilment have been responsible for many failures in organizations.

To gain and hold the support of his men the yardmaster must have their confidence and respect. This will be given him if he is a man of good character and knows his business. Respect is not accorded a man who is incompetent. In manner he should be quiet and unassuming, but in conduct just and firm. He is assumed to have been one of the men with whom he works. He should continue to associate with them sufficiently to know them thoroughly, while preserving the necessary amount of dignity to prevent even an intimation of favoritism.

A successful yardmaster in a difficult yard had been advanced from the position of freight conductor. Once, in the train of which he was in charge, the draft timbers were pulled out of the front end of a refrigerator car loaded with fresh meat. It was impossible to chain up or replace the drawhead. Trains were not frequent, it was a long distance to the terminal and shops and business was highly competitive. The conductor made his plans and immediate action followed. He pushed the car and part of his train back to the next spur track in the rear. The brake rigging was disconnected, one truck of the car was run down the main track and the other truck on the spur. The trucks were worked back in this way until the car body stood at right angles to the main track. The truck on the main track was then worked forward. This turned the car, end for end, after which it was coupled to the rear of the train and moved to its destination. That this man was selected from a large number of employees to fill the responsible position of yardmaster in a heavy terminal does not seem surprising. The way in which the trouble was met and overcome is characteristic of the man who is full of resourcefulness and prepared to meet any emergency.

Because yard- and roadmen are usually kept in separate classes by wage schedules and seniority lists, and because they perform a different character of work, a road brakeman seldom makes a good switchman and, as a rule, a road conductor makes a poor yardmaster. Yardmen, by reason of their training, fill the position better. A road engineman is usually of little use on a yard engine. Road- and yardmen are sometimes used interchangeably, and the work is done, yet few managers know the ultimate cost of this method.

When the position of yardmaster has been satisfactorily filled, things move smoothly. When or how this is done is not apparent to the casual observer. Good yardmasters do things. They do not usually tell much about what was done or the manner in which it was done. This is unfortunate because many of their "shop kinks" are valuable and they would make interesting and instructive reading. In numerous details they make themselves felt and only their close associates know how it was done. There was a case not long ago where a yardmaster who knew his business supplanted another who was supposed to be a first-class yardmaster and whose yard was being handled without criticism. It was not so badly congested nor as expensively handled as some others. The new yardmaster decided there were more men accompanying the engines than seemed necessary. It was explained to him that curves and certain obstructions made it necessary to have one man to pass or repeat signals. He had several of the engines turned around, enabling the engineman to take signals direct. In this manner, without detriment to service, he was able to take one brakeman off each of five engines. As these men were paid $4.80 per day, this resulted in a saving of $24 per day or $8,760 per year. The reader will probably ask why it did not occur to someone to make this slight and insignificant change by which the new yardmaster saved double his salary. These little things which should be apparent to everyone are the ones which often pass unnoticed.

In another case an engine was compelled to work headed toward a coal-storage plant on the approach grade, placing the engineman on the outside of a curve and on the side opposite that from which the switching was done. It was necessary to repeat signals through the fireman, and, as a result, detentions and accidents occurred. At an expense of a few dollars the engine was made left-handed, that is to say, the throttle, reverse lever and air-brake valve were placed on the left, or the fireman's side. The engineman, thereafter, rode on the left side and took the signals direct. The saving of one brakeman's wages was effected and the amount lost in accidents materially reduced—a simple move and one anybody could have made, yet nobody thought of it.

In many instances money may be saved by connecting near-by switches to distant levers through the use of pipe lines, enabling one switch tender to cover the work of two or more. The use of spring switches on inside tracks where movements are normally in one direction has already been referred to (Chap. IV) and is among the many devices that may be utilized to increase efficiency and reduce operating costs.

A superintendent whose engines ran into and were turned in the terminal at one end of the adjoining superintendent's division complained bitterly of the detention to his engines in the terminal. The yardmaster spent much time in explaining why the engines could not be returned more promptly and in this way the stereotyped complaints and explanations mechanically followed each other. The superintendent in charge of the terminal, tired of this unproductive work, made an investigation in person. After a careful analysis he found that about one-half of the cars in the trains coming in with engines to be turned were destined to the next division terminal beyond, while about the same number of engines that were not to be turned had about half their cars for the first terminal. In other words, the through and "turnback" trains and their engines were being badly delayed because of the switching work made necessary by the neglect of the yardmaster at the last division terminal back, and for which the complaining superintendent was responsible. There is nothing to be said in defense of the yardmaster who had not the intelligence or interest in his work to inform himself as to existing conditions instead of writing letters explaining his own shortcomings. This incident may serve to illustrate the difference between two types of yardmasters —the broad-gage and the narrow-gage. This yardmaster worked in a rut and seemed unable to lift himself out of it without assistance.

While in charge of a busy terminal yard where 12 or 14 switching engines were working at one time, the author devised a plan to avoid the loss of time by each engine and crew of from five to seven men while the engine was run to and from the engine house to have fires cleaned and take coal, water and sand, or to have minor repairs made. Delays on these accounts usually occur when the engine is most needed, and they are a source of annoyance to the yardmaster and expense to the company. A relief engine was put in service, manned by a hostler and a helper. It started out in the morning following a regular schedule in going to one engine, taking it back to the ashpit while leaving the relief engine for the regular crew to work with, returning the yard engine to its crew and then moving on to relieve the next engine. One engine and crew were dispensed with in this way and the remaining engines and crews were kept moving continuously at the cost of one hostler and helper. This plan is still carried out in the yard referred to.

The author was once told by a yardmaster in a busy switching yard, where much placing of cars had to be done for local industries on crooked and steep-grade tracks, that in the face of enormous opposition he reduced the number of men in each switching crew by one man. It was claimed that the work could not possibly be done and that accidents would increase in number and extent. After a test of a year, his accident account was found to have been reduced 30 per cent., while an increased amount of business was handled without additional engines. The accuracy of these figures is not vouched for, although there is no reason to question his statement. One can readily see how such a result might be attained. In a measure, it reflects on the discipline of the yard under the previous management. This is in line with the reasons given by the roads operating wide fire-box engines as to why an additional man should not be placed on engines to take the engineman's place in case he dies of heart disease. They argued that, instead of securing additional safety, the opposite would probably result, as the two men would spend much of the time "visiting" and nobody would be on the lookout.

In a certain yard an engine was required to take care of one of the freight houses and do certain yard work in a large city and at the nearby coal pockets. During the fall and winter months when general freight required much attention the coal would run heavier and it required several hours' work of the engine each morning to push the loaded coal cars to the foot of the approach to the coal trestle. They were then hauled to the top by a cable on a drum, operated by a stationary engine. From the top of the incline the loaded cars were dropped by gravity over the various pockets and then by gravity over a switchback arrangement to the empty-car track, on which they were returned to a track alongside the starting track. This method had been followed for years, in fact, since the coal pier was built. It had never occurred to anyone that an improvement could be made. The yard engine's inability to do all its work and the fact that the freight platform was being neglected, notwithstanding the men worked overtime, did not start a train of thought anywhere. But when an old hoisting engine, found in one of the scrap piles, was connected to the stationary engine boiler at the foot of the incline, at a total expense of not exceeding $100, thirty or more loaded coal cars, or enough for the heaviest day's work, were placed on the approach tracks at one operation, and from thence were reached by a cable and drawn, by the stationary engine, to the foot of the incline. No additional men were needed at the coal pier and several hours' time was saved each day for the busy yard engine, a saving amounting to more than $200 a month.

Close scrutiny of the work at a transfer station, a manufacturing plant, a shop yard or other "side issue" may develop a feasible and advantageous change in the manner of doing it. A consolidation with other work will sometimes make possible a saving of half a day's work for an engine. A slight change in the track layout or the addition of a switch or two in the yard of some private industry may make possible a reduction in engine service. Because a reliable conductor has been following up the work in a district for years, it must not be assumed that he would see all the possibilities for improvement. He may be conscientious enough to tell about it if he saw it; he is nevertheless liable to fall into and remain in a rut. Men are creatures of habit. A condition may today be noted in yard operation that seems, and is, entirely irregular or improper. For some reason it cannot be got at immediately and is permitted to exist for a time. After seeing it day by day for some weeks, it begins to grate less harshly on the nerves and after awhile does not attract one's attention. This situation is something to be avoided. It becomes a habit or custom to do yard switching at outlying points at a certain time of day. It may be done more advantageously at some other time. A different hour may benefit the work at another point.

Frequent interviews with the managers of manufacturing plants and other industries requiring special switching service will often suggest a plan whereby work may be cut out to the mutual benefit of both corporations. Aside from this, however, such interviews usually do good by enabling the yardmaster to keep in close touch with the road's patrons and learn of objections to, or irregularities in, the method of doing switching before they assume the proportions of a formal complaint. The manager of an industry is encouraged to state his wants direct to the yardmaster, thereby securing the quickest and most satisfactory result, and he may give the yardmaster valuable suggestions.

The congested or blocked yard will happen occasionally. No general plan of action can be formulated to cope with this trouble successfully. Attention should first be directed to the inward movement with a view to stopping or reducing it. The demands and threats of shippers and the traffic officers should not be permitted to influence other action; they themselves will be the greatest sufferers if heroic measures are not adopted and faithfully executed. Switching room is as essential in a yard as is an open main track for train movements. The incoming freight may be stopped by placing a general embargo, by sidetracking on the home road or in such other manner as may be determined under the conditions existing. After the disease has been diagnosed, its cause should be removed. If this is lack of power or improper handling of power on a connecting division, that difficulty needs attention. A foreign connecting road may not be moving its cars because of indifference or inability; a large industry may not be unloading promptly, or may be receiving more material than it can handle. Be that as it may, the cause of the blockade should be quickly eliminated. Sufficient forces may not be provided to take out as many cars as are brought in. This can result in but one thing, and it is only a question of time when the blockade is on.

The blockade troubles may be aggravated by the action of a weak yardmaster who is overawed by a chief train dispatcher and permits one of his main tracks to be blocked. After this track is filled—whether a single track or one of two double tracks—the yard is in worse condition than it was before. It has the additional handicap of reduced switching room and increased attention necessary on the part of the organization to care for main-line trains, while it is in no better shape in the matter of moving cars. When confronted with a blocked yard, no attempt should be made to single out preferred or special-delivery cars on urgent requests from anybody. As this stand is taken solely in the company's interest and for the benefit of its patrons, it should be indorsed by everybody from the trainmaster to the president. If the congestion is serious, the efforts of the yardmaster to single out a few cars scattered here and there, instead of taking all in their turn, may cause the condition to continue for months, or until relieved by a gradual reduction in business handled. If, on the other hand, he ignores the special or preferred-car orders, he may succeed in relieving the blockade in a comparatively short time. It requires some nerve on the part of a freight agent to decline to order a car placed immediately for a consignee who presents a bill of lading showing that it is already some two weeks overdue, and who can point to his car standing on a certain track in the yard, accompanying his request with harrowing tales of suffering, loss of business, and prospective damage claims. It requires even more nerve for the higher traffic or operating officers to maintain the same position. The point which is not usually explained and which cannot always be accurately demonstrated is that in all probability 99 cars are delayed as a result of giving, or attempting to give, preferred attention to one car.

The evil of the "hold car" is another obstacle in the way of opening a blocked yard. Where few hold cars are handled, or where ample facilities are provided to care for them, the evil may not be a serious one; other things being equal, the annoyance becomes more far reaching as the number of hold cars increases and the average time of enforced detention lengthens. While it is generally assumed that the term "hold cars" embraces only such as are detained for traffic reasons, cars held for any purpose, as awaiting entrance to shops, empties held for loads or orders for distribution, embargoed cars, and so on, will produce the same effect.

The usual move made, when a blockade threatens, is to put away trains or cars in any tracks that may be convenient in order to tide over the difficulty temporarily without regard to the hereafter. These tracks may be convenient to get into but are usually difficult to get out of. The cars are then overlooked and lost; in any event, they cause more trouble afterward by reason of their getting into the wrong place. These and other temporary makeshifts should be avoided. A well-regulated yard, like a well-ordered house, has a place for everything, and everything should be kept in its place. To vary from this practice is sure to cause trouble. The car that finds its way into the wrong and unusual track is a trouble breeder, and will probably cause enough loss of the time of engines and men to handle several hundred cars that were run into the right tracks.

The yardmaster who, in person or through his assistants, keeps a close check on the cars standing last on single-end tracks—that is to say, the cars farthest from the switch or connected end of the track—and does not permit them to stagnate will ordinarily keep things moving. Double-end tracks seldom have "ancient" cars on them. When they do, it is an indication of the extreme indifference of employees or inadequacy of facilities.

No detail in handling is more exasperating than the attempt to locate responsibility for accidents when engines back or push cars and permit them to strike too hard. The engineman usually sees no stop signal; the trainmen gave it in ample time, but it was not obeyed. An excellent rule is one requiring an engineman to consider the disappearance of hand signals when pushing cars ahead of the engine as a stop signal. This practice will avoid many controversies.

The yardmaster, like the general in command of an army, must, above all things, retain his composure and control his temper. The worst effect of his failure to do this is in its result in the work of his subordinates. "Like master like man." Little can be expected of men during disturbing times when they see their leader become "rattled" and going about in an excited manner talking and gesticulating wildly. The habit of suppressing any visible signs of emotion or chagrin may be difficult to acquire, but it is one that should be cultivated.

The yardmaster in charge of a terminal should have the authority to make minor changes and not be compelled to go to someone higher in authority for approval of them. If he is not competent to exercise this authority, he is not the man for the position, but, if he is capable, he may be so handicapped by instructions regarding details as to render his administration a failure. The nature of the work often requires quick, intelligent and positive action. If more engines are needed, or additional men with certain engines, he should put them on and not be required to waste emergency time in asking authority to do so and in making explanations. Conditions frequently arise where a delay of a few hours or even a few minutes may cost much more than the expense of preventing it. A sluggish road movement may be followed suddenly by a heavy run into the terminal. A derailment in the terminal may create a condition necessitating help in a certain district, to enable other parts of the machinery of the terminal to keep up speed. Failure to supply the necessary assistance may tend to cause a complete cessation of work by plugging up an important part of the terminal. In such emergencies, the yardmaster should be permitted to act and make his explanations later on. If he lacks the capacity to do this, he is not the right man in the right place.

A certain terminal was badly congested in the early winter, through a penny-wise, pound-foolish policy. On account of the constant heavy run of freight, this terminal was not cleared until the following spring, when there was a considerable decrease in the freight movement. In this case the yardmaster and the trainmaster were wide-awake but lacked authority to act—and were unable to get the necessary support. They had fully appreciated the situation and anticipated the condition approaching them, but were not empowered to act. For every dollar they wanted to spend to keep things moving, the company afterward spent $500. In this amount were included heavy claims paid for freight damaged by detention.

The reader doubtless knows of similar instances; in any event, he has read of many cases in the newspapers during the last few years of congestions in big terminals that seem to indicate incompetent terminal managers. It is convenient to charge it up, in the newspapers, to "abnormally heavy traffic." Somebody should have seen it coming and received it with guns loaded.

The manager of the terminal, the yardmaster, must have his organization in such shape that it will be necessary for him to spend but a small portion of his time indoors. He should have a free hand to come and go at will, and occupy his mind with the larger and broader proposition while not overlooking the smaller. It is his duty, and during the season when his yard is heavily taxed, his salvation to know all he can possibly learn in advance of heavy and unusual train movements, to prevent his being caught in a state of unpreparedness. As to how far ahead he should look for heavy traffic movements—he should look as far as he can see, and farther. This Hibernicism means that he should get information from those who have the means of knowing more than he does of the probable amount of freight traffic to be handled. The men at the head of the traffic department are always well informed on these matters. Their representatives are scattered over all parts of the country and are required to make reports to the general officers, in whose offices they are conveniently tabulated. Frequent conferences with the traffic officers should secure much information as to amount, kind and direction of anticipated traffic. While something of this kind is usually done, the author knows of no road where it is gone into as thoroughly as it should be. The theory of forecasting the probable trend of business has been developed to some extent and is of value, also, in anticipating the peaks and sags of traffic.

The yardmaster should know when his organization is perfectly balanced and keep it so by making the necessary adjustments as needed. The terminal system or "cluster" is usually divided into subyards or districts. It is the practice to put one or more engines into each district. Satisfactory service follows when an engine, with its crew, is kept in the same work. Because of the comfortable, easy working of this method, an engine is often continued in its district, although the business may have decreased one-half, or the engine in the classification yard may be unable to keep up with its work, while the engine in the shop yard or at the transfer platform may have enough spare time to assist the former. Sometimes the work may be facilitated and the necessity for additional engines obviated by adding one or more car checkers, brakemen, switch tenders or car riders. It can be readily figured out how many men may be added before reaching the cost of an engine and its crew.

Through the follies of red tape or the employment of men in whom no confidence is felt, it is occasionally left to the yardmaster to add engines and crews, as he deems necessary, while, to get an additional car checker, he is compelled to go to Rome and back again. He has to make out an application, which passes through the hands and requires the approval, in turn, of the trainmaster, the superintendent, the superintendent of transportation, the general superintendent, the general manager and in some cases, finally—after passing one or more vice-presidents or assistants or assistants *to*—reaches the president. After all approvals have been regularly affixed, the return trip is made through the same channels. This because the car checker comes under the head of "fixed force." By the time the yardmaster gets his authority for the employment of the car checker the necessity for the additional help may have passed. It is, therefore, no cause for wonder if, instead of asking for the assistance of the man to tide him over the impending crisis of a heavy run of freight, or of bad weather tomorrow or possibly tonight, or even today, he calls for the engine with its five or six men. He adds an expense of something like $45 instead of $4 or $5.

This preponderance of machinery works loss in another direction: A yardmaster knows he can dispense with the service of one or more clerks, checkers, switch tenders or others of the "fixed force" as the business eases off, in the spring presumably, but that he will again require this help in the autumn, and probably on short notice. He has also learned from experience that it will take a long time to get his applications through. It is not surprising, then, that he makes up his mind that "a bird in the hand is worth two in the bush," and keeps the useless men on the payroll all summer. He may recall the famous "Liberty or Death" speech of Patrick Henry in 1775 in which he said: "I have but one lamp by which my feet are guided and that is the lamp of experience. I know of no way of judging the future but by the past."

Much interest was manifested in a recent discussion on "team work in railroading." Team work is nowhere more needed than in a railroad terminal. The most capable yardmaster cannot succeed without the cooperation of his fellow workers. The spirit of "the company for all, all for the company" is as essential to the success of a railroad as the rails upon which its traffic moves. Organization, coordination and system are indispensable to efficient terminal operation.

Abraham Lincoln said:

When people saw Stephen and Franklin and Roger and James, each working independently, as they proclaimed, turning out mortised timbers which fitted perfectly together to complete the framework of a house, with not a stick wanting and not a stick superfluous, it was natural to conclude that Stephen and Franklin and Roger and James were operating according to a common plan.

CHAPTER VIII

MANAGEMENT AND DISCIPLINE

Among the many perplexing problems of railroad management, none are more important or more difficult to solve satisfactorily than those of organization and discipline. One has but to note the many forms of organization and methods of discipline on American and foreign railroads to see how authorities differ in their estimate of the essential or desirable. On one point, however, there is little difference of opinion. All agree that the *sine qua non* of discipline is constant and unremitting vigilance on the part of those charged with the duty of supervision. No system will take the place of it; no system will succeed without it. Such action alone will justify hereafter the statement that "These railroads[1] are officered and manned by as high a type of manhood as there is in any industry in the country: that without the power of exercising military discipline there is maintained a degree of discipline and obedience to orders within this organization that is only paralleled by that in the armed forces of the country."

It is not the purpose here to deal with the moot questions of organization, that by going into the arguments for and against the divisional type or the departmental type of organization. The Pennsylvania road is the best example of the divisional plan; the New York Central is a good example of the departmental plan. On the Pennsylvania the operating unit is the division, and the division superintendent is in complete charge of all its operating activities. Not only does he control station operation and train movement, but to him report the division officers of the maintenance-of-way and maintenance-of-equipment departments, except in technical questions of design and standard practice, which are decided by staff officers reporting to the higher operating officers. Thus, the superintendent is supreme on his division. Under the departmental plan, the operating unit is the department. The division superintendent has direct control only over the transportation department—the operation of stations, yards and trains—and has no jurisdiction over the maintenance of roadways and the maintenance of equipment. The division engineer in charge of the roadway, reports to a chief engineer instead of to the superintendent; the division master mechanic in charge of motive power and car maintenance, reports direct to the superintendent of motive power. The lines of authority and

[1] Samuel M. Felton.

130

responsibility under the departmental plan do not converge short of the general manager; under the divisional plan, they converge in the division superintendent.

The departmental form of organization has its highest development in England, and it may be said to be the general plan for all railways outside of the United States. Yet it can hardly be said that American railroads are typically of the divisional type. Many cling to the departmental form, but the tendency is strongly toward the divisional. Several roads have a type of organization which is neither one nor the other. The Santa Fé, for instance, gives its superintendents jurisdiction over track, but leaves the maintenance of equipment to the master mechanics and the higher officers of the motive-power department. The Frisco lines changed over from an organization of that type to the straight divisional plan. On the New York Central, the tendency is to strengthen the superintendent by giving him more voice in affairs of maintenance, but his authority is not definite nor indicated by the organization chart.

Some years ago the "unit" system was in effect on the Union Pacific and Southern Pacific comprising 18,600 miles, with some 80,000 employees. The system is a high development of the divisional plan and the "unit" of authority is the division superintendent. It can best be described by quoting from Colonel Charles Delano Hine's writings on the subject. Touching first on some of the defects in the common form of organization he says:

The most difficult task in any organization of human endeavor is to correlate the activities of the workers on the outside with the necessary requirements of correspondence, records and accounting on the inside. The artisan in the shop, the traveling salesman on the road, the soldier in the field, the sailor at sea, the railway man on the line, all have their troubles with the man in the office. When the inside man knows the outside game at first hand, such differences in points of view are minimized, friction avoided and therefore money saved. Railway operation is the most exacting of human tasks. Like the conduct of a household, a farm, a hotel or ship, it is a continuous performance. Unlike those exacting occupations, it must maintain its own communications over hundreds or thousands of miles of territory. So complex is its administration that chances should not be taken of losing money through half-baked decisions of partially trained office occupants. Most railway officials flatter themselves that when on the line they maintain a grasp on the office, yet every hour in their absence action must be taken on matters which, apparently trivial in themselves, have far-reaching results. This statement is not a reflection upon the splendid ability and earnestness of railway officers; it is merely a recognition of the fact that a man can be in only one place at a time; that there are only 24 hours in the day and only 365 days in the year. The salary of one officer is negligible as a percentage of the operating cost of the average unit. Accordingly, the system insists that the second best man of the unit, with practical outside training, shall stay at headquarters and sit on the lid. In some cases it has been found necessary to appoint another officer to perform the previous outside duties of the senior assistant. In other cases it has been found that the outside work could be divided up among other members of the staff . . . A railway harnesses the forces of nature, including its divinely human elements, for one purpose—the manufacture and sale of an intangible commodity—transportation. The more closely interwoven the constituent parts of production, the more efficient and economical should be the output. When weaknesses develop, when education is needed as to the increased importance of a given element, the remedy is not necessarily the creation of a separate department.

Colonel Hine then explains his remedy. Briefly, it is to consolidate all the subordinate offices on the division with that of the superintendent; substitute an experienced outside man for the chief clerk to represent the superintendent when the latter is on the road; and breakdown departmental lines by abolishing the titles of the trainmaster, master mechanic, division engineer, road foreman of engines, chief train dispatcher and division storekeeper, in each case substituting the indistinctive title of "assistant superintendent," giving each officer equal authority in all departments but assigning each to his former specialized work as his prime duty. The underlying principle is to broaden these men out beyond their departmental limitations and afford them a training which will fit them better for promotion to positions of greater responsibility. The system forces men to assume responsibility and, as Colonel Hine tersely puts it, by so much increases the protection to the company's interests. More is heard about "this division" and "the company" and less and less about "my department."

Formerly, office work was grouped around officials. This resulted in petty principalities and bureaucratic administration. By tearing down some office partitions there were razed those figurative department walls which so often operate to keep in the man who is trying to keep the other fellow out. Under the new conception the work is grouped by classes. The technical term among business experts is "the concentration and coordination of routine and related processes."

The methods of discipline in effect on American railways may be summarized under three headings:
  1. Discipline by suspension from duty with loss of pay.
  2. Discipline by record—the Brown system.
  3. Discipline by both actual and record suspension—a combination of (1) and (2).
Under all three plans, certain capital offenses call for summary dismissal from the service.
George R. Brown, while General Superintendent of the Fall Brook Railroad, nearly forty years ago, formulated and applied what is known as the "Brown system of discipline without suspension," or punishment

without loss of pay. *Actual suspension* means laying an employee off for a period of from 5 to 60 or even 90 days, for which he receives no compensation. A *record suspension* is an entry of a certain number of days (or demerit counts) on the employee's record, while he continues work and receives compensation. The *record* suspension in days or demerits counts is ordinarily the same as would be the number of days *actual* suspension under the old system. When an employee's record days, or demerit counts, reach a certain number—usually 100—he is dismissed.

The Brown system was new in detail only, for some of its important features had previously been tried on the Pennsylvania. The essential features of this system are keeping a record of an employee's irregularities in the performance of his service as well as of acts of special merit, and posting bulletins containing brief accounts of the incidents, causes and lessons connected with each record entry.

Many roads use the Brown system in a modified form. Some use the "record suspension" for every offense, except for cases meriting dismissal; others use record or actual suspension according to the merits of the case or the general character of the offending employee; while others, again, use only the bulletin feature. There are varying opinions as to the real benefits to be derived from the record-suspension feature, and the effect depends largely on the class of men employed. There is, however, a general belief in the beneficial effects of bulletining a history of each offense. It is especially desirable in unusual cases and in instances where ordinary rules are being violated. This system has the effect of warning employees without resorting to the objectionable practice of issuing a notice calling attention to the necessity of observing a certain rule, thereby implying that other rules are of less importance.

Take the case of a flagman who is disciplined for not going back a sufficient distance to protect the rear end of his train. Under the old system, when the facts in the case were not officially promulgated, his disposition would be to misrepresent to his fellow workers the actual cause of his suspension and he would make the case look as favorable to himself as possible while correspondingly reflecting on the judgment or ability of the officer directly responsible for inflicting the discipline. The impression is naturally created that the officer is despotic, or unfair, and that the employee has been imposed upon. Such impressions have the effect of creating bad feeling, particularly among the lower classes of employees. The bulletining with the Brown system changes this and is the strongest point in its favor.

One modification of the Brown system embraces a record book in which two pages are devoted to each employee, one for the debit and the other for the credit side. The usual entries, covering the employee's age, height, color of hair, eyes, weight, dates of service and of various changes or promotions, are made at the top of the page in blank spaces provided for that purpose. For each offense requiring disciplinary action the employee is charged with a certain number of demerit marks, or nominal days of suspension, and for acts of special merit he is credited with merit marks, or days, which in some cases are allowed to cancel a like number of demerits or days of suspension on the opposite page. A bad record is followed by dismissal, while a clear record for a given length of time, say, three months, six months or a year, usually entitles the employee to a certain number of merit marks, or cancels a certain number of demerit marks. All roads continue to apply the penalty of dismissal to cover cases of intoxication, insubordination and other extreme offenses.

When a record is entered, on either the debit or credit side of the book, a bulletin is issued containing a brief history of the case and is posted on the bulletin boards at designated points. Locations, names of men, dates and train numbers are omitted for the purpose of avoiding attack by agitators and to prevent undue embarrassment to sensitive employees. For similar reasons, and to avoid controversy or comparisons, the extent of discipline is sometimes omitted. It is customary, too, on some lines to give the actual or estimated amount of damage done where damage results.

The following is an example of a bulletin taken from actual practice:

A freight conductor and flagman have been disciplined for failure to protect their train properly while it was stopped at a point on the main track. The explanation made by these men was that, since it was daylight, with a good view to the rear, it was deemed unnecessary for the flagman to go back farther than he did. A flagman employed for the purpose and out the required distance will doubtless succeed in attracting the attention of an engineman who may be working on the injectors or watching the water gages, and may also arouse him if he has for the moment dropped off to sleep. Leaving out the question of the engineman's neglect of duty in the case, the flagman's attention to duty may prevent a serious accident and possible loss of life.

Another example from a bulletin is the following:

By throwing the wrong switch in a divisional yard, a switch tender caused cars to "corner" on a frog, resulting in damage to the extent of $1,690, and for his negligence has been disciplined. The investigation developed that he was engaged in conversation with a car rider, and as a result started for the switch too late and became confused because of the short time he had to clear the car. Yard employees, and particularly switch tenders, need to have their wits about them and their minds on their work while on duty. They cannot properly perform their work when engaged in outside occupation, or "visiting," or when they come on duty without good, clear heads due to insufficient sleep or use of intoxicants during the hours they have been off duty.

It is the usual custom, where book records of employees are kept, to permit an employee to look at his own record at any time, but he may not look at the record of any other employee.

One of the strongest arguments in favor of discipline without loss of pay is the prevention of suffering to the family of the employee. During an actual suspension, the loss of pay entails undue hardship upon innocent women and children. To an employee with a conscience the thought of pangs of hunger which are causing suffering to his wife and children, due, possibly, to a miscalculation or error in judgment on his part during a brief moment while working, perhaps, with the best intentions, may permanently cloud his efficiency; it certainly does not tend to make him a better man or to engender in him any strong feeling of loyalty or regard for his superior officers or the company.

Every railroad has its busy and dull season during each calendar year. There is a time each year when it is unable to give its men sufficient employment, and another season when it is unable to secure a sufficient number of competent men to perform its work. During this season of heavy traffic, in many sections accompanied by unfavorable weather, trainmasters, yardmasters and others are inclined to overwork their men rather than employ a number of "green" men. The strain due to density of train movement and overloading of cars develops all weaknesses in locomotive power. The liability of men to make mistakes and cause accidents is correspondingly increased. Under the older systems of discipline, the suspension of the trained and experienced employees would then begin, followed necessarily by the employment of inexperienced men. The number of accidents and failures of various kinds then further increases. Under the system of nominal suspension this difficulty is done away with, while the record kept still enables the value of the employee to be ascertained and the educational features are not lost.

On the general subject of discipline, Mr. Brown said:

It often occurs that the disgrace and injury occasioned by a strict enforcement of a sentence does more to ruin the guilty than anything else, and a wise provision has been made allowing courts to use their judgment as to carrying out punishments; this is known as "suspending sentence." If the sometime offender does better, and is not guilty of the same or other offenses, the judge conveniently forgets the indictment hanging over him, but, should he go on committing one misdemeanor after another, his record rises up to condemn him. I believe in the practice of "suspending sentence" with railroad employees.

With this system the good men are retained, developed, benefited and encouraged, and the culls are got rid of to the betterment of the service all around. Every wreck, every accident, every mistake, every loss has taught its lesson, and these are of no less value to the railroads and to the railroad men than the successes. I practice making every mishap a lesson to every man on the road. It often happens that an accident, or a close shave for one, is the best kind of a lesson to the man who could be blamed; and, if he is retained in the service, he is a more valuable man than he would otherwise be or one who could be hired to take his place.

The Brown system of discipline is incomplete without the accompaniment of the credit or merit feature, but this is dangerous unless cautiously handled. Shall every meritorious act be bulletined or rewarded, or where shall the line be drawn? The author recalls an instance where a passenger-train flagman went back and remained out several hours in a rain storm, damaging his new uniform. The trainmaster secured the approval of his superintendent for the purchase of a new uniform. A generous act, certainly, but with disturbing results. Why should an employee be specially rewarded for doing his duty? Why should not the passenger-train or freight-train flagman provide himself with a rain coat and rubber shoes, and have them at hand during rainy weather? For a time other passenger flagmen, who had to go back during a drizzling rain, or while the dew fell heavily, asked for new uniforms. They were highly indignant when their requests were not granted. It is difficult to draw the line accurately between special merit and duty. The danger does not exist in rewarding one employee, but in the fact that always there are many who are not rewarded though equally entitled to special recognition.

A flagman hanging out of a caboose cupola saw a broken rail on the opposite track and signaled a fast passenger train, preventing it, by quick work, from running over the broken rail and possibly from being derailed. He received a number of credit marks. It was his duty, after he discovered the break, to notify the passenger train; he had done just what any employee should have done. It was not his duty to look at the rails on the opposite track; he was evidently doing it in a dreamy indifferent way. While looking at the rails of the other track he was not watching his own train, to detect heating journals, break-in-twos, loose car doors, and it was his duty to do this. Incidentally it may be added that this flagman was dismissed some six months later for being intoxicated while on duty.

An engine ran away from a hostler, and got out on the main track, running the wrong track, *i.e.*, against the current of traffic. A switch tender promptly notified a yard engineman, who got his engine out and overtook the runaway. He climbed over the pilot of his engine, reached the cab of the runaway, shut off the steam and stopped it. This engineman took some risk, but he received no credit marks. The speed was low, the actual risk taken was probably no greater there than he incurred every night in his regular yard work and his action was considered as being in line with duty.

One of the commonest errors, if not the most common one made in disciplining employees is that of considering the result or effects of a violation of rules or instructions instead of the actual offense. Trainmasters often inflict comparatively light discipline on a flagman who does not go back a sufficient distance to protect his train, provided no damage has resulted, but few trainmasters would let a flagman off short of dismissal if his failure to go back the prescribed distance resulted in several thousand dollars' damage, loss of life and a badly blocked railroad. Is this not because the reports in the case with disastrous results will be carefully read and considered by those high in authority? But is the effect on the service desirable?

Of the large number of men in positions of authority, who fully understand what is to be done and how it should be done, but a small proportion are successful in their dealings with subordinates. These dealings require a special tact which is seldom acquired. Men cannot be regarded as so many machines. The human and the humane side of the question must be considered. An interest taken in the general welfare of employees, consideration for their families and an occasional "heart-to-heart" talk with one or more of them will go a long way toward securing their earnest and hearty cooperation.

Nevertheless, a distinguished railroad president of wide and varied practical experience in subordinate service comments as follows:

The arguments for Brown's system are very attractive, but I do not believe the method is adaptable to this wicked world. You may catch flies with molasses, but our lives, our fortunes, our civilization we owe to our jails, penitentiaries and gallows. Next to the influence of the labor unions, I think the greatest element in the general deterioration of discipline, so manifest in late years, is the general use of Brown's method. The records should, of course, be kept. They were kept by the Pennsylvania lines before Brown's system was heard of. My experience leads me to believe that the bulletins soon fail to be read by the men. If the investigations are properly conducted, with all the men of the crews present when the finding is announced, and pains are then taken to draw and enforce the lesson, I believe in the long run much better results are obtained. As to punishment, I do not see how we can safely eliminate it, and in any event the gap is wide between chiding and dismissal.

Roy V. Wright, managing editor of the *Railway Age*, performed a good service in giving publicity to the Golden Rule Pledge, as indorsed by the Chamber of Commerce of Philadelphia and other similar bodies:

As Americans, we recognize that we face a crucial condition in our social, political and industrial life, which, if not corrected, can lead only to individual and national disaster.

We Recognize that the trend of combining interests of individuals and groups will continue.

But We Likewise Recognize that such interests in the creation of their relationships to the many must be controlled by the spirit of equity and reason if they are to endure.

Unjust Exploitation of the many by the few, regardless of its position or field of activity, must be discontinued, for self-preservation would force all citizens into hostile groups.

The Remedy of our present malady lies in approaching the interests of others, be they employer or employee, buyer or seller, producer or distributor, individual or group, in a spirit of fairness actuated by the *Golden Rule.*

We are all workers; The United States is our union; Our membership is over 100,000,000 in good standing; Our allegiance is first to God and then to that union; Our nation is a living expression of belief in our Creator; and Liberty is our human right by divine right.

The Declaration of Independence acknowledges American liberty to be a gift of God: "All men are endowed by their Creator with certain inalienable rights . . . With a firm reliance on the protection of Divine Providence."—(*Declaration of Independence.*)   The Declaration of Independence establishes, without discrimination: Independence of person, property and contract.

The Declaration of Independence is maintained by the Constitution of the United States which is administered by a representative government controlled by public opinion which is based on ignorance, illusion, prejudice—or knowledge, truth, judgment.   The Declaration of Independence—the Constitution of the United States—and representative government will be maintained or destroyed by public opinion!   Public opinion is what men think.   Our problem is not to change habits, laws or men, but to make facts the basis of thinking.

We, as Americans, recognizing the fundamental nature of the above facts, do hereby declare that we will in all ways urge upon our associates, and those with whom we come in contact, the importance of making *facts the basis of their thinking,* and

We Pledge our loyalty and renew our allegiance to *God* and *Country* to the end "That this nation under God shall have a new birth of freedom and that the government of the people, by the people and for the people" (*Lincoln*) shall be sustained.

The value of frank expression of opinions should be borne in mind or as expressed by Voltaire to Helveticus, "I wholly disapprove of what you say and will defend to the death your right to say it."

We are passing through just one more period—there have been many others—when we hear much about radicalism, anarchism, socialism and much profound deep counter-argument—a great deal of which passes over the heads of those for whom it is intended because of the profundity of thought expressed in verbose and abstruse language.   Under these circumstances a simple story illustrating the underlying principles man be of interest.   In the woodlands of France in the eighteenth century, James and John were hewers of wood and with their axes and by diligent labor, each turned out two pieces of timber a day.   James had an idea and worked on its development late into the night, while John smoked, strolled about or slept.   After a time James constructed a plane, with which he was enabled to get out six pieces of timber a day. John demanded the plane, to enable him to increase his output, claiming it should be common property.   James disagreed, maintaining the plane to be the product of his own mind and effort.   He permitted John to use the plane, and required him to give up two of the additional pieces of timber as compensation for its use. While not satisfied John accepted the plan as a better arrangement because by it his output was doubled.

The conference method of settling disputes with employees—and disputes will always arise—is an old one; it has its origin in biblical history.[1]

An excellent general dissertation on discipline by a well-known operating officer[2] describes four kinds of discipline to be recognized, namely, reprimands, suspended sentences, actual suspensions and dismissals:

The amount of discipline should be decided at a staff meeting held once each week by the superintendent, he having present the assistant superintendent, chief train dispatcher, trainmasters, master mechanic, foreman of car department and all others to whom the men report. The head of the department should make his recommendation in writing, giving full details of each case, with the service record of the man; and, after being reviewed by the superintendent and the staff meeting, if he or any other member of the staff believes that the recommendation is wrong, it should be modified or increased in accordance with the judgment of all the members of the staff; the superintendent, however, reserving the right to apply the discipline, if he is satisfied the recommendations of the others are wrong.

After these meetings a written record is made and given to the head of the department concerned, who personally delivers it to the employee disciplined, having the proper understanding with him as to the reasons therefor; and a copy is placed in his envelope record.

All discipline should be applied:

To get better service.

To avoid taking men out of service, resulting in loss of money to them, and, if they are competent men, loss of efficiency to the company.

To keep the men out of debt, making them of greater benefit to their families.

When a man is first suspended a certain number of days, the sentence should be suspended pending good behavior, and on the stipulation that he keep out of any further trouble.

After the expiration of one year, the man should not be required to serve any actual suspension; but it will still remain a part of his record.

If within one year he offends to the extent that a suspension is necessary, he will be called upon to serve the suspended sentence, and a new suspension will be

[1] Matthew XVIII, 15–17: "Moreover, if thy brother shall trespass against thee, go and tell him his fault between thee and him alone; if he shall hear thee, thou hast gained thy brother. But if he will not hear thee, then take with thee one or two more, that in the mouth of two or three witnesses, every word may be established. And if he shall neglect to hear them, tell it unto the Church. But if he neglect to hear the Church, let him be unto thee as an heathen man, and a Publican."

There are other biblical references to the problems engendered by the eternal triangle of "public-employer-employee:"

Six days shalt thou labor and do all thy work (Ex. 20:29).

Come to Me all ye that labor (Matthew 11:28).

The laborer is worthy of his hire (Luke 10:7).

The laborer is worthy of reward (1 Timothy 5:8).

[2] G. H Wilson, Superintendent, Hudson Division, New York Central, addressing American Association of Railroad Superintendents, Memphis, Aug. 16, 1916.

placed against him for another period of one year.   Slight infractions which call for reprimands only should not cause a man to serve a suspended sentence.

The system does not involve the elimination of anything from the man's record, the items being cumulative.   It is inadvisable to eliminate entirely from a man's record gross carelessness, personal bad habits and so on, and for that reason it is pretty hard to draw a line whereby any system of discipline should take anything from a man's record.

Meritorious service is that which is performed by an employee when going out of his regular line of duty, and not the prompt and proper application of good judgment in his regular line of duty, which is expected of everyone at all times.

An employee who is not on duty and sees a dangerous condition and takes action which prevents an accident, or an employee while on duty, who takes action of this kind to prevent an employee in another grade of the service from causing an accident, is termed meritorious, and the facts entered upon his record.

Where two or more roads operate in contiguous territory and pay their employees on different wage scales, the effect on discipline is marked; the roads paying the higher rates being enabled to maintain a correspondingly higher standard of discipline.

The influence on discipline of wages paid was noted in the following incident in the experience of the author: There were two railroads in the same section of the country, operating under quite similar conditions, except that one road was financially and physically stronger than the other.   The stronger line had the better track, equipment, and signaling, and, in addition to its ability, in consequence, to get its trains over the line with certainty, punctuality, safety and comfort, paid slightly higher wages than its competitor.   In its terminals the same relatively superior conditions existed.   Better facilities and regular road movements kept its terminals open for free movements and this, in turn, made employment in the yards and in train service more desirable and more sought after.   The result in the way of discipline may be readily guessed. The strong road had more applicants for positions than it could accommodate; the other line was, at times, hard pressed for sufficient help. The men who were discharged on the former line because of violations of rules or decreasing traffic were usually employed by the weaker road. On the other hand, when men were needed on the stronger line they were generally recruited from among the most desirable employees of the weaker, the latter being, in effect, a preparatory training school for the former.   This was, in itself a system of discipline which worked to the benefit of the stronger road.   On the other line, the effect was, of course, the opposite, and constantly tended to harass and embarrass its operating officers.

An instance is recalled where a trainmaster undertook to work a rapid and radical reform on his division by secreting himself at unexpected places about the terminals and along the line to watch the performance of his men.   It worked for a few days.   The men inaugurated a very complete and successful method of checking the trainmaster. By a system of hand and telegraphic signals they kept themselves thoroughly informed as to his whereabouts. The watcher was watched. The result was the opposite from that desired by the trainmaster and the lack of confidence shown in the men did not increase their respect for their superior officer.

By proper and discreet handling any division or terminal officer should secure the confidence of his men, at least of the better element among them, so as to enable him to keep reasonably well informed of any general violation of rules or serious defects in judgment. This knowledge will enable him to keep the whole machine pretty well keyed up. The men will do this, usually, for their own protection and the general good if it is carefully explained to them so that they will see it in the right light and understand the advantage to themselves.

The following is from the *Railway Age:*

A high corps spirit is one of the valuable assets of a railroad company. Perhaps in times of close competition it is one of the most valuable. Money cannot make this; general orders cannot make it; it is a plant of slow growth. A year of arrogance, stupidity or coarse sense of justice may destroy the growth of years. We have all seen, time and again, examples of the truth of this statement; and here we suggest a matter for the serious meditation of the gentlemen who have suddenly taken on such importance in the railroad world. The prosperity of a great undertaking depends ultimately on the skill, zeal and devotion of its servants. That fact we cannot get away from, although we are sometimes tempted to forget it. No ability in combination of ownerships, no lavish expenditure in physical improvement, no headquarters orders for economy all along the line, can command prosperity without the devoted cooperation of the working staff.

The notions which underlie . . . the modern theory of railroad organization are careful selection with regard to physical, intellectual and moral qualities; steady promotion by merit, with decent regard to seniority, other things being equal; constant watch of the corps and prompt removal of vitiating elements; fixity of tenure.

Hard-and-fast rules of discipline cannot be made. The question revolves itself into getting as much for your money as you can. The law of supply and demand largely governs the labor situation and operating officers must adapt themselves to the condition. The labor question is one of the primary factors in building up discipline. The rate of wages has an important bearing on discipline. A traffic officer has said that freight rates were regulated by "comparison, competition and compromise." This holds true of the adjustment of wages.

A disciplinarian must never be an extremist; he should preferably be an educator. He should be neither too exacting nor extremely indifferent; he should endeavor to strike a happy medium adaptable to the particular temperament and disposition of the individual. The story is told of a German prisoner who was caught during the World War and sentenced to be shot at sunrise.   Because of inability to understand the language spoken, he did not realize his predicament until he was told to back up against the stone wall and he then remonstrated.   The Sergeant in charge of the shooting squad told him that he had his orders to carry out, whereupon the prisoner responded: "Oh vell if it's orders of course I have nodding to say."   This and the story of the Charge of the Six Hundred—"Their's not to reason why; their's but to do and die"— are but perhaps the rigid end of disciplinary methods while the other end may be in line with that described by Kipling:

"The 'eathen in 'is blindness bows down to wood and stone,
"'e don't obey no orders unless they is 'is own."

In all matters of discipline or education, first principles and fundamentals may best be kept in mind by considering the intelligent handling of children by their parents.   No real progress was made when the father asked his boy why he had been whipped and received in reply: "Because you are bigger than I am."

With the enormous growth of railroad traffic and the consequent necessity of closer attention to details, with the introduction of intricate machinery, as in automatic and mechanical signaling, the age of the specialist in railroad work has been reached.   Special training is necessary to care for special branches of railroad work.   The specialist in his legitimate field, with correct methods and under a proper system of organization, is of great value to the railroad as a whole and indispensable to the special work in which he is engaged.   By placing these expert observers in position to ignore or harass the local or division officers, however, and having them report direct to general officers, the effect on the organization may in some instances be bad.   A feeling may be created among subordinate officers that, no matter what they do, whether good railroad practice or not, they are liable to be criticized by one of the specialists.   Under certain methods of organization, these men may occupy the position of being able to claim what glory there may be for good results, while not being responsible for any poor showing that is made.   As a rule, the specialist is a theorist, strong in his convictions.   He is invariably closely in touch with the head of the company. It is dangerous to oppose him, except in a diplomatic way, which takes time and taxes the mind and patience of the operating officer.   It annoys and worries him and takes his mind from more important work.   Nothing is more distasteful to the subordinate officer than the demand for letter-writing.   It causes him to neglect his work and consequently lose touch with the actual details.   It is distasteful to the subordinate because he sees nothing gained by it, while the time he is frittering away is largely lost for the work he is anxious to accomplish and which he knows is more important. These remarks apply only where the specialist is but partially equipped for his position of authority.

The working officer whose time is largely taken up with office correspondence is in the same difficulty as the engineman who fritters away his air pressure on a long descending grade by making a number of light applications without giving time to recharge his reservoirs. In both cases the operating officer and the engineman are traveling downhill at an increasing rate of speed and both may hit the bottom very hard.

A so-called expert was recently appointed on a trunk line. His duty, so far as could be determined, consisted in making recommendations to increase the safety of train movements and following them up to see that they were faithfully carried out. On the face of it, this seemed commendable and desirable. The expert was an extremist and was in no way responsible for congestion to traffic or increased cost of handling. A rapid-fire gun was directed against the division officers; impracticable propositions were advanced along with a few good ones to prevent accidents. Some of them would have put the road out of business during the months of heavy traffic; most of them involved increased cost; while many of the recommendations could not be entertained. They kept the division officers on the defensive, glued to their desks explaining why the recommendations should not be acted upon. The experiment did not have the effect of improving the service, because the officers could not give the work the close personal attention they did before the advent of the specialist. This is merely one illustration where the specialist retarded the work of the machine instead of aiding it.

Men who are trained in special work only, and not on broad lines, can only hope to advance in narrow lines. A road foreman of engines, for example, who only interests himself sufficiently to know that engines are being properly handled and fired, is hardly competent to fill the position he holds. Any engineman could or should know and do as much. The road foreman's position is one above the capabilities of the ordinary engineman. If he does not interest himself in matters outside of the management of an engine, he is of little use. It is safe to say he will not be considered good timber for advancement to a higher position. The extent to which he interests himself in all operating problems is the measure of his ability to fit himself to assume increased responsibility. It is not to be expected that any employee will be considered for a position with increased responsibilities and compensation, until he has demonstrated that he not only is capable of, but actually is, earning more than he receives in his present position.

The men employed by a railroad are usually widely scattered and most of them are not under the direct supervision of an officer. Even the conductor of a train cannot always keep the members of his crew in sight. It is essential, therefore, that every man from the lowest to the highest be impressed with the necessity of doing everything that he should do and nothing that he should not do. Every employee should be made to feel that implicit confidence is reposed in him, that the fact of his retention in the service in itself indicates confidence in his loyalty, honesty, ability and application. The author is convinced after many years of experimenting with different systems of discipline that the so-called "spotting" method does not always produce the best results. Men may be browbeaten into doing their work, possibly, with threats of dismissal or the knowledge that they are being watched and spied upon; but this work will be sluggish. It will lack that snap so noticeable on well-managed roads.

Having and showing confidence does not imply absence of supervision. Of honest, open, intelligent and constant supervision, too much cannot be had; when railroad officers try to carry out false ideas of economy, there is usually too little. This right kind of supervision carries with it the constant and untiring education of employees, the value of which is not generally recognized and which is occasionally underrated because of the incompetency of the officers entrusted with educating the men.

CHAPTER IX

LOADING CARS

The president of a trunk line said: "First load your cars; then load your trains." The car loading is the more important and vastly more difficult to check and control. The train load is apparent, either to the eye of an experienced officer passing over the road, or by casual glance at the train sheets which tell the story of trains run, light engine mileage, engines underloaded, train tonnage, direction of movement and all the other ills of train service. Not so with the car loading. If the doors on empty box cars are closed, the loads and empties look alike, as the seals may not be detected. The loading of carload freight is under the control of the shipper and the railroad can exercise little control except by moral suasion. This chapter is largely devoted to the handling of less than car load freight.

Only the closest and most constant supervision and checking will determine whether the agent and the house foreman are intelligently doing their full duty. There are the vital questions; (1) whether the cars are utilized to the fullest extent by securing the heaviest practicable load consistent with despatch in movement of freight and avoidance of damage; (2) whether the contents are properly packed and distributed to withstand shocks in transit; (3) whether heavy articles are being placed on top of fragile ones; and (4) whether oil or other freight of that character is loaded alongside of flour. There are also questions of (5) loading l.c.l. freight into the cars that will take it to the proper destination or transfer point; (6) of securing proper weight and kind of cars; and (7) of using foreign cars that would otherwise travel home empty.

Full cars may not always be obtained because:

1. Of insufficient freight for the destination.

2. Commodities fill up in volume but run light in weight.

3. Of difficulty in loading cars fully and consequent tendency to start new cars.

The universal use of automatic couplers, and the remarkable increase in the size and weight of locomotives and cars, increased the liability of damage to freight and made necessary greater care in loading and switching because more care was needed in bringing cars together when an employee had to guide the link to the drawhead. Freight-house men must be taught to so load large cars with package freight as to prevent shifting. After part of such a car is unloaded, the remainder must be arranged to avoid shifting. When the old link-and-pin couplings were in use, the brakeman had to go between the cars as they were approaching each other to couple and they had to guide the links with their hands. Sticks were used only in the rule books and while within the range of the superintendent's or trainmaster's vision. The brakemen in those days were, in a sense, law makers. Their rules had more weight. and were more respected by the enginemen than those issued by the company. This was natural. The brakemen knew the safe speed for hand coupling and they did not hesitate, when narrowly missing the loss of fingers or a hand, to bring powerful arguments to bear on the engineman, backed by a coupling pin or link. These weapons have since disappeared. Urging the yardmen to get our trains faster, to do more work in a given length of time, usually results in more damage to contents of cars. Many serious breaks-in-two on the road are caused by damage done to couplers or draw gear while trains are being made up in the yard. Most yardmasters and their assistants dislike to reprimand or discipline employees for doing rough work, so long as there is no visible damage, because they fear a slowing down in the movements of the men. Possibly, too, the nightmare of a congested terminal may have something to do with it.

Employees are liable to become careless in the handling of freight unless closely followed up. After unloading a half car, they will often leave the remainder four or five tiers high instead of breaking it down and arranging it so it will not become damaged when the car is moved. Freight conductors have been known to unload freight in the rain at some small station instead of taking it by and returning it the next day. Failure to remove seals, after unloading a car, may cause error or confusion, when the car is again loaded or started empty. Old side cards, too, should be carefully removed after they have served their purpose.

The day may come when American railroads will overcome that prolific source of trouble, the car arriving at its destination without the waybill, or the waybill reaching its destination without the car. This trouble will be overcome by arranging a receptacle inside each box car, into which the waybills for that car may be placed. The waybill should be a triplicate copy of the shipping receipt. A car reaching the freight house or team delivery yard will have its freight delivered immediately and, if the waybill at originating point is properly made out, it may also be used for freight-delivery bill and receipt. The saving in clerical work would be enormous, the loss of time in delivery greatly reduced and vast economies effected in switching service and freight handling in the freight houses. Until this millenium is attained, the necessity for having waybills reach destination with the freight is great. Much complaint results because of the failure to get waybills to destination on time. Claims for lost and damaged freight, opportunity for theft and delays, expensive handling and unnecessary clerical work are some of the difficulties resulting. In cases of cars loaded on distant sidings and less car load cars it may be best to forward the bills by railway or U. S. Mail.

Increased service from equipment may be brought about largely by a proper loading system, which insures the placing of freight in the right cars. Proper points should be designated at which freight from each individual station for all other stations may be transferred. This requires an intimate knowledge of conditions and a carefully worked out schedule subject to occasional revision as conditions change. At each transfer station a loading program must be worked out, dovetailing into the larger general plan for the road as a whole. Another is needed for smaller stations, and, finally, one for the conductors of local freight trains. Much loss and damage to freight, loss of use of freight equipment, slow time and improper deliveries may result from lack of intelligent handling or improper or insufficient instructions to the local freight conductors.

Instructions requiring freight to be loaded direct to certain large stations or to certain substations or piers in controlled territory, with a specified minimum per car, should be issued to all concerned, including agents at stations and transfer points and local freight conductors. When the minimum load is not available, the instructions should specify the transfer point to which the freight should be sent to be consolidated, or state how long such freight may be held at originating point to secure the required minimum for a straight car for any destination. Freight for certain districts, including a number of smaller stations, is usually loaded to the transfer station just in advance of the territory, although in many cases it may make better time or be more economically handled by loading it beyond its destination and arranging for its return. The general object is, of course, to get the greatest possible service out of cars with the least expense, and this involves consideration, primarily, of time and mileage. While maximum load is the goal, it is not always in the interest of economy and good service to seek this blindly to the exclusion of other features. Foreign cars, when not in demand, may be started homeward with a light load. In this practice the judgment of the individual must finally determine how long it will be permissible to hold the car for a certain lading. He must figure on the amount of per diem charges involved, the distance the commodity and the car move, the supply of cars at hand and the demand therefor, and the train service. In the handling of system cars the officer in charge of car service may, for the guidance of his subordinates, lay down the general proposition that in the predominating traffic direction cars should be loaded to their full capacity and worked to necessary transfer points to avoid as far as possible any movement without full tonnage. When the predominating traffic direction changes, his instructions necessarily require revision. The traffic in both directions may nearly balance for a while, when heavy loading is desirable. In the direction of light traffic, cars may usually be loaded light and cars forwarded to stations with comparatively light loads, to save time and reduce handling. Time is an important element, as there is naturally keen competition for traffic in the direction in which light cars move, while the condition in the opposite direction may be such that no great effort is made to secure additional tonnage. Power or facilities may be taxed to their utmost and cars in which to move the business offered may be difficult to obtain. The last contingency may again affect the methods of loading in the direction of the empty-car movement.

It is instructive and impressive to know the value of an ordinary box car, which is composed of 18,500 parts, embracing upwards of 400 kinds of units. Of these units, not over 25 per cent. are standardized. At this time (1923) a car probably costs about $500 a year, of which amount maintenance, about $200, is the greatest item; interest at 5 per cent., about $150; depreciation $105; the remainder being made up of incidentals and taxes. Its average trip has been computed at 14.9 days. Of this time 5.74 days are chargeable to movement for loading and unloading; 2.48 to movement to, and delay on, interchange tracks; 1.55 to movement through intermediate yards; 1.49 to road movement; 1.34 to time on repair tracks; 0.90 to Sundays and holidays; 0.75 to time on storage tracks; 0.50 to reconsigning and 0.15 to delay in road movement. Out of every 24 hours of its existence, it spends 10.1 hours in shifting and interchange movement. It is in the railroad's control 66.4 per cent. of the time and is used by shipper 33.6 per cent. of the time.

It may seem good practice to load cars light, or to load below the prescribed minimum to certain stations, in order to save time and eliminate additional handling. If this tends to delay the movement of empty cars at a time when such cars are in demand for return loading, it becomes objectionable. To illustrate: A station of some importance on a branch line, perhaps 100 miles away from the main line, necessitates, for every car going there, a haul of 200 miles from the time it leaves the main-line junction until it returns. If the contents of ten or twelve cars may be transferred into four or five cars at the junction, or the regularly designated transfer in advance, it will be economy to go to the additional expense of transferring and incur the risk due to handling in order to save the mileage and get perhaps two or three days' additional service out of the seven or eight cars. This is an extreme case and the saving of the mileage may justify the transfer at any time, although this is dependent largely on the characteristics of the line, the distance, amount of business, fixed-train service and car supply.

Take the case of a station on the main line, to which a number of cars may be moving in the light-car direction, and which is located midway between division terminals and transfer points. The object is to utilize empty-car movement to the utmost by taking advantage of the light engine mileage made necessary in balancing power. The traffic conditions may be such as to necessitate cutting these cars out at the first division terminal, awaiting the local freight of the following day, and the movement of the empties from the point where released will be by local freight, one, two and probably three days later. On arrival at the next division terminal they again await their turn on the classification lead and move out on some following train. In such cases the unloading, consolidation and reduction of the number of cars at the first transfer point reached may be justified by the additional number of days' service to be gotten out of some of the cars. The saving in per diem charges is another argument in favor of the additional handling. The whole question is one requiring constant watching and changes in the program without hesitation when conditions require.

The points to be studied in trying to effect economies in loading cars may be summarized as follows:

1. Loading to avoid all transfer if possible.

2. Loading to transfer farthest from originating point.

3. The avoidance of too light loading from transfers to other transfers, as it is many times more economical and time saving to hold freight over one day and secure consolidated tonnage.

4. Consideration and action on the fact that short distances should not always govern the handling of short-line traffic, as loading to a transfer which receives and distributes from a large number of stations often warrants longer mileage to secure prompt movement of cars and freight.

5. The loading of proper cars, especially with a view to quick handling of foreign equipment.

6. Checking arrival and departure of all cars for transfers and seeing that they are promptly placed at platforms and forwarded.

7. Reporting to the freight accounting department delays to freight by non-arrival of waybills.

8. Careful consideration of freight-train schedules in connection with proposed transfer movements.

9. Consideration, in connection with actual experience, of the best method of forwarding in both directions l.c.l. freight to and from eastern and western divisions, laying particular stress upon improving transfers within home territory.

10. The proper storing of freight to withstand transportation.

The manager of the transfer station and the freight house has the opportunity to contribute largely to good service and to reduce the cost of handling materially. The one great difficulty at these points is that of inducing those in charge to take a broad view of the general conditions on the line instead of confining their vision entirely to their own transfer or freight house to the exclusion of the remainder of the line. In their

efforts to reduce the cost of handling at the platforms under their immediate charge they may abnormally increase the cost at other points or
along the line generally. A car to be handled by a local freight may be
badly loaded, and such hurried loading at the transfer may save a few
cents at that point. The rehandling or return of freight to the house
and the reloading or holding for another car, instead of loading beyond
the point of delivery and requiring its return, may cost the railroad many
dollars in consuming the time of an engine and entire freight crew.
The time taken in hunting for the freight wanted, unloading and reloading, damage claims resulting from exposure or additional handling at
points where facilities provided are meager, and the occupation of the
main track to the exasperation of the train dispatcher and the crews of
other freight trains, are costly. This slovenly work at transfer stations
and at other loading points is one of the difficult things to check. One
of the best remedies is a wide-awake, intelligent trainmaster, who unex-

Fig. 37.—A 12,000 ton shipment carried on a single car.

pectedly starts out with a local freight, takes possession of all the conductors' waybills, and notes the condition of the interior of each car
as the various stations are reached. He will not stop at the questions
of loading in station order; method of loading; putting flour in proximity to oils or syrup barrels; safes or stoves on top of bric-a-brac;
freight for points on other divisions or districts having to be rehandled and
returned; but will also note the manner in which freight is being loaded
at transfers on divisions over which he has no jurisdiction. Such
information and any suggestions occurring to him he should convey to
the officers in charge of car service.

It is more expensive to haul an empty car of 80,000-lb. capacity than
one of 40,000-lb. Therefore, if a shipment can be handled in a lighter
car, it should be done, and cars ordered accordingly. At the same time,
a heavier car or a number of heavier cars should be used if thereby the
shipment can be forwarded in fewer cars. The heavy load is most desirable for economical operation. Assume an 80,000-lb. capacity car loaded

with grain to 10 per cent. above the marked capacity. At a freight rate of 15 cts. per 100 lb., this load would earn $132. A 60,000-lb. car similarly loaded would earn $99 and a 40,000-lb. car, $66.

The transporting of extremely heavy shipments has developed specially designed cars for this purpose. In Fig. 37 is shown such a special car loaded with part of a 12,000-ton hydraulic forging press manufactured by the Bethlehem Steel Co., which moved from Bethlehem, Pa., over the Lehigh Valley and Pennsylvania railroads to the Carnegie Steel Co., of Homestead, Pa. The shipment including blocking weighed 287,000 pounds, which, together with the car, which weighed 196,420 pounds, makes a total weight above the rails of 483,420 pounds. The shipment was loaded on a specially constructed bridge car of 300,000 pounds capacity, having two trucks of 16 wheels each.

The rules for handling explosives and inflammables should be carefully studied and followed. Copies of these regulations are easily obtainable.

The relative increase in freight revenue, revenue ton-miles and loss and damage claims are shown in Fig. 38 for the period 1900 to 1923, taking 1900 as 100 per cent.

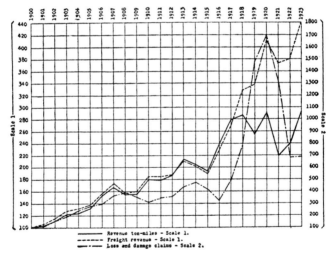

Fig. 38.—Relative increase in freight revenue, revenue ton-miles and loss and damage claims each year compared with 1900 (1900 = 100 per cent.).

In 1923 the amount charged to loss and damage was $49,540,377, or 1.05 per cent. of the gross freight revenue on an average, the rates ranging from 0.006 to 3.5 per cent. for individual carriers. On analyzing the principal causes for damage payments, it is shown that rough handling and unlocated damage account for 33.5 per cent. of the total payments; delays, 13.5; defective equipment, 11.2; loss of entire package, 8.1; and robbery of and from package, 6.3 per cent. Car-load damage was 71.6 per cent. of the total damages and car-load losses were 54.2 per cent.

of the total losses. Fresh fruits and vegetables amount to 20.4 per cent. of the total payments; coal and coke, 6.6; grain, 5.6; live stock, 5.6; and new furniture, 4.2 per cent.

The principal causes of the increase in loss and damage claims are:

1. Lack of interest by employees.
2. Lack of knowledge of the rules.
3. Failure to comply with the rules when known.
4. Failure to check property before receipting for it.
5. Receipting for more than is actually delivered.
6. Receipting for property as in good order when it is in bad condition.
7. Giving clean receipts for property loaded by shipper and not checked.
8. Failure to check freight properly when delivered to consignee.
9. Failure to report shortages, damages and overs promptly and properly.
10. Failure to notify consignees promptly and properly of the arrival of freight and to keep a record of such notice.
11. Making greater advances on property than its value warrants.
12. Delivering property to persons other than the consignee without the proper order.
13. Mistakes in billing caused by failure to compare waybills with shipping instructions.
14. Forwarding freight not marked with name of consignee and destination.
15. Improper loading, stowing and bracing freight.
16. Loading freight in dirty or leaky or otherwise unfit cars.
17. Carelessness in taking and transmitting verbal shipping instruction (especially on the telephone).
18. Improper use of airbrakes.
19. Failure to give prompt notice of refused and unclaimed freight.
20. Failure to ice cars properly in warm and heat them in cold weather.

After all, personal, intelligent supervision and actual observation, at the point where the work is being done (or is not being done), constitute the best remedy, and the elimination of many of the typewriter contests will permit this. In an address to the New York Railroad Club, December, 1921, Howard Elliott, assistant to the president, Union Pacific system, called the typewriter "a vehicle for red tape and shifting responsibility." He described it as "a small manually operated machine which repeats parrot-like anything it is told." They move as freight, yet there are on some roads as many typewriters as locomotives. The typewriter is the buck passer's chief ally . . . Many reports which are started to meet a real need are continued after the need disappears and many statements over which the men on the road sweat blood are perused in a perfunctory way at headquarters or not perused at all.

White-leading of typewriters should be considered along with or ahead of white-leading locomotives. Letter writing and report making are expensive. A prominent paper manufacturer gives the cost of producing an average business letter at 18.42 cts., of which 7.27 cts. go for stenographic service, 7.27 for office overhead, 2 for postage, 1.26 for paper and envelopes and 0.62 for printing or lithographing. An analysis of the first 100 letters written one day in an operating office showed that 40 were plain letters of transmittal, referring matters to others for attention; 20 asked or answered simple routine questions; 20 enclosed agreements to heads of departments (in the same building) for approval; 10 approved train-service and other details which had been arranged by subordinate officers and 10 contained definite rulings on sundry matters. The effect of this on railway operations is probably more responsible for slowing up the car wheels than any one thing that can be mentioned. With few exceptions the letters refer to post mortem studies.

CHAPTER X

MAKE UP AND MOVEMENT OF TRAINS

General Principles.—The first destination of a car is governed by its contents and the loading program. The general practice of getting trains out of terminals as a matter of convenience to that particular terminal alone, and without regard to the safe movement over the line to the next terminal, cannot be condemned too severely, unless extreme conditions compel it. It means duplication of work at the following terminals and the loss of time along the line. Lack of system is pernicious and unbusiness-like. There are cases, however, where the facilities at one terminal are so inadequate that a part of its work must be shifted to another.

Make-up Policy.—Trains should be made up to go to single destinations as far as practicable; but this frequently entails too much delay in waiting for the necessary number of cars at the starting terminal to get a solid train. Where it is impracticable to make up a train with all its cars for one destination, the cars should be assembled with a view to running the train without further switching, to the most distant breaking-up point possible. The only limitations to carrying out this method are the time cars may be held to get enough together for one destination or breaking-up point (for reclassifying) and the ability with the facilities provided, at the starting point, to hold cars for that purpose without causing congestion or interference to an extent that will increase the cost of switching. The subsequent saving in time and work will justify a considerable detention at the originating terminal. The limitation is apt to be the needs of the consignees.

Following out this general plan, it is to be expected that a few of the cars in such through trains will "fall by the wayside" because of hot journals, broken trucks and other car disabilities. Where these cars cannot be made ready to go forward in the same train without undue detention, arrangements should be made to forward other cars for the same destination in their places. In the absence of such cars, those for a divisional terminal may be added, to enable the full tonnage rating to be maintained, unless the direction is that of light traffic, but they should be placed so as to permit of their removal without delay or unnecessary switching. The distributing trains for the division and the local freights are supposed to be made up in station order, with first cars to be set off next to engine, and so on.

Position of Platform Cars.—The cars containing the "break-bulk" or platform (l.c.l.) freight are usually placed next to the caboose, although practice varies considerably in this respect. On a heavy local run, in districts where the track occupation is dense, this plan possesses considerable merit. The front part of the train may be engaged in doing the switching for the station and industries, while the platform cars are placed alongside the freight house and are worked at the same time. Where the conditions alluded to warrant it, many trains may, in this manner, be worked to advantage.

Live Stock.—It is considered good practice to handle live stock at or near the front end of the train, to reduce the shock and to facilitate the quick delivery on arrival at destination.

Explosives.—Cars containing explosives must not be hauled in a passenger train, nor in a mixed train, when it can be avoided. The cars must be at least 15 cars from the engine and 10 cars from the caboose in through-road freight trains, when the length of train will permit. In local-freight and shifting trains, these cars must be coupled with others, in which air brakes are operative and placed as near the center of the train as possible. They must be placed between box cars not loaded with inflammable articles, charcoal, cotton, acid, lumber, iron, pipe or other articles liable to break through end of car from rough handling. When explosives are loaded in stell-underframe cars, such cars may be placed between steel-hopper cars. All cars containing explosives must have air and hand brakes in service.

When handled in yards or on sidings, cars containing explosives must be coupled to an engine with a car between, unless it is practically impossible to do this, and they must not be cut off while in motion. Couplings must be made carefully and unnecessary shocks avoided, nor must other cars be permitted to strike such cars. They must be so placed in yards or on sidings that they will be subject to as little handling as possible, removed from all danger of fire, and, when avoidable, engines on parallel tracks must not be allowed to stand opposite or near them.

Explosives include black or brown powder, dynamite and other high explosives, smokeless powder for small arms, fulminates, blasting caps, electric blasting caps, ammunition for cannon, explosive projectiles and detonating fuses. A square placard on each side with the name "Explosive" designates a car containing explosives.

Inflammables.—Tank cars containing inflammables must be placed at least five cars from the engine and five cars from the caboose, if possible; if the length of train does not permit this, they must be placed as near the middle of the train as practicable. In switching, a car containing inflammables must not be started down a ladder track, incline or hump until the preceding car has cleared the ladder. Such a car must also clear the ladder before another car is allowed to follow. A car containing inflammables is designated by a diagonal placard placed thereon.

When cars containing inflammables are involved in wrecks, the instructions of the Interstate Commerce Commission should be carefully carried out. These rules follow:

1. Action in any particular case will depend upon existing conditions, and good judgment will be necessary to avoid disastrous fires on the one hand, and useless sacrifice of valuable property on the other.

Volatile, inflammable and combustible liquids, such as gasoline, naphtha, petroleum oils, etc., in large quantity and spread over a large surface will form vapors that will ignite at a considerable distance, depending on the kind and quantity of liquid and the direction and force of the wind. Many of the liquids, regarded as safe to carry under ordinary conditions and transported in tank cars without the inflammable placard, should still be treated as dangerous in handling a wreck.

2. When oil cars are leaking, all lights or fires near them that can possibly be dispensed with should be extinguished or removed. Incandescent electric lights or portable electric flash lights should be used when available. Whenever practicable, the work of handling a wrecked oil car should be done during daylight.

3. Lanterns necessarily used for signaling should be kept on the side from which the wind is blowing and at as high an elevation as can be obtained. The vapors will go with the wind but not against it. The ash pan and fire box of a locomotive or steam derrick, especially on the side of a wrecked or leaking tank car toward which the wind is blowing, are sources of danger. Wrecks involving oil cars should in no case be approached with lighted pipes, cigars or cigarettes, and all spectators should be kept away from the vicinity.

4. Effort should be made to prevent the spread of oil over a large surface by collecting it in any available vessels or draining it into a hole or depression at a safe distance from the track. When necessary, trenches should be dug for this purpose.

It is not safe to drain inflammable oil in large quantities into a sewer, since vapors may thus be carried to distant points and there ignited. Care should be exercised also not to permit oil to drain into streams of water which may be used by irrigation plants or for watering stock. Dry earth over spilled oil will decrease the rate of evaporation and the danger. A stream of oil on the ground should be dammed and dry earth be thrown on the liquid as it collects.

5. Sudden shocks or jars that might produce sparks or friction should be avoided. When possible, the wrecked cars should be jacked carefully into position after removing other cars and freight that might be injured by fire. Only as a last resort, to meet an emergency, should a wrecked car be moved by dragging, and when this is done all persons should be kept at a safe distance.

6. (*a*) No unnecessary attempt should be made to transport a damaged tank car from which inflammable liquid is leaking. Safety in short movements may be secured by attaching a vessel under small leaks to prevent spread of inflammable liquid over tracks. Tracks at intervals in rear of a moving car should be covered with fresh earth to prevent fire overtaking the car. Engines should be kept away; also spectators who may be smoking. If wrecked or derailed, and

not in a position to obstruct or endanger traffic, leak should be stopped as far as possible, and the car should be left under guard until another tank car or sufficient vessels can be provided for the transfer of the liquid, which should be transferred by pumping when practicable.

(b) Highly volatile products, such as casinghead gasoline, cannot be transferred in the usual way by a vacuum pump. The pump can only be used when placed so that liquid flows to it from the tank by gravity.

(c) Whenever the leaking condition of a tank car is such that transfer of lading is necessary, the car must have stenciled on it, in letters 3 in. in size, adjacent to the car number, the words, "Leaky tank. Do not load until repaired," and the owner must be immediately notified. This stenciling must not be removed until the tank is repaired.

Even a tank that is not leaking is liable to be ruptured by the use of slings, and slipping of chain slings may produce sparks. Saving of the contents of the tank is not as important as the prevention of fire.

(d) An empty or partially empty tank car, with or without placards, is very liable to contain explosive gases, and lights must not be brought near it.

7. All wrecking outfits should be equipped with portable electric lights.

8. *Water will not quench an oil fire.* If the fire cannot be smothered by use of earth, steam, or wet blankets, effort should be concentrated on confining it and saving other property.

9. Should a leak occur by the breakage or displacement of the unloading valve and pipe at the bottom of the tank car, it may be stopped by removing the dome cap on the top of the tank and dropping the plunger into the plunger seat, as a shock sufficient to damage the outlet valve and pipes may have unseated also the plunger.

The dome cover should be unscrewed by placing a bar between the dome-cover lug and knob. The dome cover should not be hammered, and should not be unscrewed until the absence of vapor pressure in the tank is verified by lifting the safety valve.

To ascertain whether the valve is properly seated, the valve-rod handle in the dome should be moved back and forth a few times. The following drawing indicates the general plan covering valve rod and unloading or discharge valve:

Empty or loaded flat cars, empty oil tanks, and, at times, empty or loaded gondolas, with low sides, are required to be kept at the rear end to minimize the liability of such cars having their bodies broken in two, especially when handled in long trains partially air-braked. This precaution is hardly necessary with the modern heavy-capacity, steel flat and gondola cars, as they will withstand a more severe shock than wooden box cars. Passenger cars on freight trains should be kept at the rear end to avoid damaging platforms and straining their longitudinal framing.

Loads and Empties.—An old and good rule is to keep the loads ahead and empties in the rear. There is some difference of opinion as to the merits of the claim that trains so made up pull easier. In some dynasmometer tests no difference was observed. Trains made up with load-ahead are less likely to part on hilly or "choppy" roads, and there is reduced liability of damage to equipment and contents where the slack runs in and out in making stops.   This shock is more severe on partially air-braked trains than on fully equipped trains.   The requirement of the Interstate Commerce Commission, that at least 85 per cent. of the cars in a freight train shall be equipped with working air brakes, makes more difficult what was already a difficult and complicated question in train make-up, but the problem is now becoming easier on account of the almost universal use of air brakes on freight equipment. The courts have decided that if a train is equipped with an air brakes, all must be operative.

Doors to Be Kept Closed.—It is difficult to keep car doors closed on empty cars. Aside from the physical effort required to close many doors, the conductor generally thinks that the open door is the natural symbol for an empty car.   When men are disciplined for moving empties as loads, and *vice versa*, it is perhaps not surprising that this view is taken.   This appeals more forcibly when a conductor and one brakeman are handed cards for 90 or 100 cars and told to clear the yard in 10 minutes.   Tramps will more readily board trains containing cars with open doors and there is greater liability of losing doors along the road when the doors are open than when they are closed and latched or hasped. A door partly open, in falling off, may cause considerable damage to property, and serious personal injuries have been inflicted on double-track roads and along passing tracks where freight-car doors scraped the sides of passenger trains.   There is more resistance in a train of empty box cars with open doors, due to the wind or air resistance, and sparks from the engine may lodge inside the car and set it on fire.   Perhaps 90 per cent. of freight cars have doors which open by moving to the left, in the car-door runway, as the car is faced from the outside.   In a moving train, therefore, the doors on the left side are more liable to open because the stops tend to move the doors forward.   The doors on the left side are, consequently, more likely to spread out or fall off than those on the right side.

Rating Locomotives by Cars.—Some roads, as a matter of convenience, or because of peculiar local conditions, continue to load their road engines according to the number of loaded cars for which the rating is made. Two empties are then rated as one load.   The best results are obtained where the tonnage rating is used and, with this, a uniformity of loading is secured that at once increases the average train load and improves the general train movement.   A record kept by one trunk line of a large number of freight trains showed that 2,000-ton trains ran all the way from 27 to 65 loads, the lesser number being a train consisting entirely of steel coal cars of 100,000-lb. capacity, loaded to 10 per cent. in excess of marked capacity.   This statement, in itself, will indicate the unfairness of the method of rating engines on a car-load basis, and the unsatisfactory results to be obtained therefrom.

Rating by Tonnage.—A satisfactory tonnage rating system must make allowance for lightly loaded cars, for empty cars and for weather conditions. The rating should, in the first instance, be made to fit average conditions. Actual service tests form the best basis, but the mistake is frequently made of selecting an engine in the best order, a picked crew, good weather and daylight runs, and giving special attention to dispatching. When it is attempted to haul this maximum tonnage under adverse conditions, such as bad track, heavy head or side winds or low steam pressure due to poorer coal than usual, the train is stalled. The yardmaster is the controlling factor and he must combat the temptation to overload engines merely to open or clear his yard for the time being. The inability of the engines to move and to return promptly for another load is too far in the distance for him to figure on, and he therefore loses sight of the fact that, in the end, he has only added to his troubles. Trains move with more difficulty during the night. Hand signals cannot be interpreted as easily as in the daytime, telegraph offices are more infrequent and men are not as active, mentally or physically.

Train Resistance and Tractive Power.—Those having the supervision of making up trains should know how to determine what an engine is capable of drawing over a road of known grade and curvature under certain weather and atmospheric conditions. The tractive power of the engine, that is, the pull in pounds exerted on the drawbar in the rear of the tender, must be known, and then the resistance of the train to be moved.

The theoretical drawbar pull in pounds may be found by the formulas[1] arranged in the following table:

Simple engine
$$T = \frac{0.85P \times C^2 \times S}{D}$$

Vauclain balanced and tandem compound
$$T = \frac{S \times P}{D} \left(\tfrac{2}{3} C_h^2 \times \tfrac{1}{4} C_1^2 \right)$$

Two cylinder or cross compound high pressure cylinder
$$T = \frac{C_h^2 \times S \times 0.6P}{D}$$

Two cylinder or cross compound low pressure cylinder
$$T = \frac{C_L^2 \times S \times 0.25P}{D}$$

Mallet compound high pressure cylinder
$$T = \frac{C_h^2 \times S \times 1.2P}{D}$$

Mallet compound low pressure cylinder
$$T = \frac{C_L^2 \times S \times 0.50P}{D}$$

Where T = tractive effort in pounds.

C = diameter of cylinder in inches.

C_h = diameter of high presure cylinder in inches.

C_L = diameter of low pressure cylinder in inches.

S = Stroke of piston in inches.

[1] Locomotive encyclopedia.

P = boiler pressure in pounds per square inch.

D = diameter of driving wheels in inches.

For two cylinder and Mallet compound engines assume a cylinder ratio of 2.35 to 2.40.

An engine with 20- by 26-in. cylinders, 60-in. drivers and 200-lb. steam pressure on pistons would, according to the formula for simple engines $(0.85 \times 200 \times 20^2 \times 26 \div 60 = 29{,}400)$, have a 29,400-lb. tractive power at the rim of the drivers. All of this is not available at the rear drawbar of the tender because part of it is used in overcoming the friction of engine machinery and the rolling resistance of the engine and tender. The American Locomotive Company estimates the machinery resistance as 22.2 lb. per ton of engine on drivers, and considers the rolling resistance of engine and tender to equal the rolling resistance of a heavy car—say, 4 lb. per ton. If this engine has a weight of 115,000 lb. on drivers, 43,000 lb. on forward truck (total 158,000 lb.) and the tender when loaded weighs 97,000 lb., the resistance of the machinery would be 57.5 × 22.2 = 1,276 lb. The rolling resistance of engine and tender would be $(79 + 48.5) \times 4 = 510$ lb., or a total resistance of $1{,}276 + 510 = 1{,}786$ lb. to be deducted from the tractive force available at the rim of drivers. The net drawbar pull, therefore, would be $29{,}400 - 1{,}786 = 27{,}614$. Taking again the American Locomotive Company's figures for resistance of 40-ton cars at 10 m.p.h. (4.65 lb. per ton), it will be found that this engine should haul 27,614 ÷ 4.65 or 5,938 tons on a straight and level track. Such an ideal condition, however, rarely exists. If the road is fortunate enough to have a limiting grade as low as 0.4 per cent., the resistance of the grade would be (at 20 lb. per 1 per cent. grade) 8 lb. per ton, or, plus rolling resistance (4.65 lb.), 12.65 lb. per ton. The rating for the engine, then, would be 27,614 ÷ 12.65 or 2,183 tons, which is equivalent to 55 cars averaging 40 tons each.

Computations of the hauling capacity of locomotives are based on the assumption that engines have ample grate area and boiler capacity to supply cylinders with steam at maximum pressure, and that the weight on drivers is sufficient to prevent slipping before the maximum tractive power has been exhausted. The Committee of the Master Mechanics' Association which investigated the proportioning of locomotive cylinders arbitrarily assumed the proportion of weight on half-worn driving wheels available for adhesion as follows:

Passenger engines,	25. per cent.
Freight engines,	23.5 per cent.
Yard engines,	22. per cent.

The train resistance may be divided into the following three parts:

1. Resistance on a level straight track.
2. Resistance due to grade.
3. Resistance due to curves.

Resistance on Level Straight Track.—This resistance is composed of:

1. Rolling resistance, due to deflection of rail and roadbed under the loaded train.

2. Journal friction between the journals and bearings of axles.

3. Atmospheric resistance on the front of the train, the sides and rear.

4. Oscillation and concussion.

Very little is known about the amount of resistance due to rolling friction, and practically nothing about that due to oscillation and concussion, but more or less information has been determined by experiments with reference to journal friction and atmospheric resistances.

These four resistances are usually classed as one and termed "level straight-track resistances," and are, as a rule, given in the form of pounds of resistance per ton of weight of train. This quantity is determined experimentally by various methods, and from these experiments a great many formulas have been derived applicable to the special cases with values ranging from 3 to 8 lb. per ton. All these fail when applied to practical tests and the results of dynamometer car tests must, therefore, be relied upon.

Resistance Due to Grade.—It is customary in America to express grades as a certain per cent.; that is, a certain number of feet vertical rise in 100 ft. horizontal. This on a 1 per cent. grade means 1-ft. rise in 100 ft. horizontal.

When a train is hauled up a grade the resistance due to friction is increased by that due to lifting the train against gravity. The amount of this increased resistance is determined as follows: One mile equals 5,280 ft. and if the grade be one foot per mile the pull necessary to lift a ton of 2,000 lb. will be 2,000 ÷ 5,280 or .3788 lb.

If the grade is expressed in feet per hundred or per cent. the resistance will be 2,000 ÷ 100 or 20 lb. for each per cent. of grade. Therefore the grade resistance in pounds will be 20 × per cent. of grade.

By examining the formula and experiments for level straight-track resistances, it will be seen that, for freight trains running at ordinary freight-train speed, the resistance in pounds per ton is in the vicinity of from 4 to 8 lb., which, when compared with 20 lb. per ton resistance due to a 1 per cent. grade, gives a very practical appreciation of the relative importance of lower grades on freight-train lines.

Resistance Due to Curves.—It is usual to express the resistance due to curves in the form of a grade, and the best practice appears to be to consider that the resistance due to a 1-deg. curve is practically the same as a 0.04 per cent. grade; for a 2-deg. curve it is twice as much; and so on.

Since the resistance due to grade is 20 lb. per ton for a 1 per cent. grade, for a 0.04 per cent. grade it will amount to 0.8 lb. per ton, so that the resistance due to a 1-deg. curve could just as readily be represented as 0.8 lb. per ton of train.

For example: If a 6-deg. curve occurs on a 0.4 per cent. grade, the resistance due to the curvature would be 6 $\times$ 0.8 = 4.8 lb., and the resistance due to the grade would be 0.4 $\times$ 20 = 8; or the total resistance due to grade and curve would be 12.8 lb. per ton.

If to this is added the level straight-track resistance obtained from one of the above formulas (depending upon whether the train is a passenger or a freight train), the total resistance in pounds per ton for any given train at any given place on the road, such as on the ruling grade, can be computed.

Limitations in Practice.—Knowing the actual tractive power of a locomotive, its working limit, due to the track and other conditions, can be determined. An engine will draw a heavier train over heavy, well-supported rail than on a light-rail section, with ties spaced at considerable length, and no ballast, or ballast of such a nature as to permit the ties to move or sink. On such inferior or light track there would be a succession of depressions as the engine passes over it, although to the eye it may appear to be fairly well-surfaced track. The difference in movement might be compared to the difference in that of a ball running down a well-constructed bowling alley and the same ball rolled over a piece of lawn, both stretches being perfectly level. On the smaller rail section the point of contact between the rail and driving-wheel tread is less, reducing the adhesion. When the rail or tire, or both, are worn, the results are less satisfactory. The design of the rail head also affects the adhesion somewhat. Engines regularly running over a light-rail section were found to have greatly reduced adhesion on heavier rail sections afterward, because of the grooves worn in tires.

Locomotive Capacity.—After the working tractive power has been determined, the number of tons the locomotive can haul at a given speed over the maximum grade can be readily determined by dividing the working tractive power of the locomotive by the total pounds per ton resistance as determined by the method given above.

Use of Sand.—Sand for increasing the adhesion between the locomotive drivers and the rail is, at best, a necessary evil. On a good clean rail the train will roll easier, but, if slightly wet or greasy, the engine drivers will slip for want of adhesion. Sand, judiciously used, will tend to prevent the slipping by increasing the adhesion, but it will also cause the train to draw harder. It may be used too freely, thereby increasing the troubles instead of diminishing them. The ideal condition would be a sandy rail for the locomotive drivers to pass over and a wet, clean rail for all the following wheels of the train. This condition would be approximated by a pneumatic blast or a sweeper behind the last driver to blow the sand off the rail. Inexperienced enginemen stall their trains on sand about as often as they prevent stalling through slipping. Over interlocking points, sand must not be used on account of movable point frogs, slips and switch rails, although often needed badly at those particular points because of the lack of surface of a full rail. The size and contour of the rail section greatly affect adhesion, as does the condition of the driving wheel tires.

Engines are loaded at terminals from three entirely distinct viewpoints, *viz.:*

1. To move the maximum tonnage consistent with speed requirements on the line.

2. To move the maximum tonnage per day, for a long period of time including all engines both in or out of service.

3. To move the tonnage at a minimum cost per ton-mile.

These methods are affected by such helping or assisting engine service, doubling on hills, setting off or picking up of cars between terminals where grades change, and double heading as may be required. The tonnage per engine depends on:

1. Rate and length of maximum or "ruling" grade.
2. Average grade.
3. Amount and degree of curvature.
4. Density and character of traffic.
5. Running time allowed.
6. Average gross weight per car.
7. Location and extent of passing track facilities.
8. Weather conditions and temperature.
9. Wind velocity and direction.
10. Condition of rails.
11. Car-journal lubrication and condition of journals.

An economical tonnage rating is estimated by one authority to be 80 per cent. of the maximum available drawbar pull, under favorable circumstances. This may be determined by the use of a dynamometer car and should be confirmed by service tests. On one division of a large road it was claimed that, by dropping from the full maximum rating of 100 per cent. to an 80 per cent. rating for comparative months in two consecutive years, the tonnage per engine-mile was increased 13 per cent., and per train-mile 16 per cent., with a decrease of 9.3 per cent. in coal consumed per ton-mile. If these figures are correct, they can only be explained by the large number of cars set off with the higher rating by stalled trains.

An exhaustive series of experiments conducted by Prof. Edward C. Schmidt, in charge of railway engineering at the Experimental Station of the University of Illinois, resulted in the preparation of the following table of the "values of resistance at various speeds and for trains of different average weights per car" applying to trains running at uniform speed on tangent and level track of good construction during weather when the temperature is not lower than 30° F. and when the wind velocity does not exceed about 20 miles per hour.

TRAIN RESISTANCE—POUNDS PER TON

Speed m. p. hr.	Average weights per car, in tons													Speed m. p. hr.
	15	20	25	30	35	40	45	50	55	60	65	70	75	
5	7.6	6.8	6.0	5.4	4.8	4.4	4.0	3.7	3.5	3.3	3.2	3.1	3.0	5
6	7.7	6.9	6.1	5.5	4.9	4.4	4.1	3.8	3.5	3.3	3.2	3.1	3.0	6
7	7.8	7.0	6.2	5.5	5.0	4.5	4.1	3.8	3.6	3.4	3.2	3.1	3.1	7
8	8.0	7.1	6.3	5.6	5.0	4.6	4.2	3.9	3.6	3.4	3.3	3.2	3.1	8
9	8.1	7.2	6.4	5.7	5.1	4.6	4.2	3.9	3.6	3.4	3.3	3.2	3.1	9
10	8.2	7.3	6.5	5.8	5.2	4.7	4.3	4.0	3.7	3.5	3.3	3.2	3.2	10

From the foregoing it will be seen that the resistance on straight, level track ranges from 3 to 8.2 lb. per ton, under varying conditions of car weights and speeds.

The results are primarily applicable to trains which have been in motion for some time. When trains are first started from yards, or after stops on the road of more than about a 20-min. duration, their resistance is likely to be appreciably greater than is indicated by the results here presented. In rating locomotives, no consideration need be given this matter except in determining "dead" ratings for low speeds, and then only when the ruling grade is located within 6 or 7 miles of the starting point or of a regular road stop.

In a series of tests, under the auspices of the American Railway Engineering Association, upon a variety of trains in regular freight service, upon well-constructed and maintained main-line track, some interesting results were produced, and the diagram showing the relation between freight-train resistance and speed is shown in Fig. 39.

It is to be expected that some trains to be met with in service will have a resistance about 9 per cent. in excess of that indicated by Fig. 39, due to variations in make-up or in external conditions within the limits to which the tests apply. If operating conditions make it essential to reduce to a minimum the risk of failure to haul the allotted tonnage, then this 9 per cent. allowance should be made. This consideration, like the one preceding, is important only in rating locomotives for speeds under 15 miles per hour. At higher speeds, the occasional excess in the resistance of individual trains will result in nothing more serious than a slight increase in running time. It should be understood that this allowance, if made, is to be added to the resistance on level track, not to the gross resistance on grades.

The effect of train loading and train speed on cost per 1,000 gross ton-miles is very clearly brought out in a series of tests on the Illinois Central.[1] The following table shows the comparative results of operating full-and reduced-tonnage trains of that road:

COMPARATIVE COSTS PER 1,000 GROSS TON-MILES OF FULL- AND REDUCED-TONNAGE TRAINS

	Champaign district, tons	Fulton district, tons	McComb district, tons	Talla-hatchie district, tons
Train load—full tonnage..........	3,750	3,308	3,192	3,547
Train load—reduced tonnage.......	3,271	3,091	2,389	2,948
Per cent. reduction...............	12.7	6.5	25.1	16.9
Cost per 1,000 gross ton-miles: (prorata overtime)				
Full-tonnage trains..............	$.165	$.156	$.202	$.161
Reduced-tonnage trains..........	$.150	$.162	$.228	$.174
Reduced-tonnage trains including cost of engines and crews returning light and additional engine-house expense................	$.173	$.174	$.300	$.209
Cost per 1,000 gross ton-miles: (time and one-half overtime)				
Full-tonnage trains..............	$.173	$.156	$.207	$.167
Reduced-tonnage trains..........	$.151	$.162	$.229	$.180
Reduced-tonnage trains including cost of engines and crews returning light, and additional engine-house expense................	$.174	$.174	$.301	$.215
Per cent. of increase in cost of reduced-tonnage trains:				
Prorata overtime..........Decr.	9.1	3.8	12.8	8.0
Prorata overtime includes cost in light direction and increased engine-house expense............	4.8	11.5	48.5	29.8
One and one-half overtime Decrease	12.7	3.8	10.6	7.7
One and one-half overtime, including cost in light direction and increased engine-house expense.	0.5	11.5	45.4	28.7

In each case the lower average ton-mile costs were obtained with the higher average gross ton-miles per train hour. The relationship of

[1] Conducted for the U. S. Railroad Administration.

train load to ton-miles per hour, however, is not at all clear and it is evident that under the test conditions the speed between terminals is not generally affected in a sufficiently marked degree by the tonnage reductions to increase the ton-miles per train-hour. The road delays, which in the main are unaffected by reductions in the train load or by the average running speed, appear to be the controlling factor. In this connection it is pertinent to note that the test trains were run during a period when the gross ton-miles handled were from 15 to 34 per cent. below normal on the districts where the comparisons were made and that, in the opinion

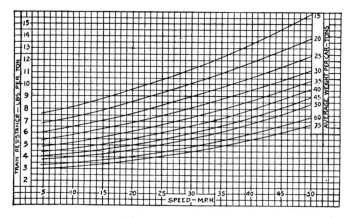

Fig. 39.—The relation between freight train resistance and speed.

of the officers in charge, greater reductions would have been necessary under heavy traffic conditions in order to have secured the same effect on the average time between terminals.

The following are the conclusions, based on the results of these tests:

1. There is no general agreement as to the percentage of tonnage rating which will bring the lowest cost. In the majority of cases this is effected by a load of 100 per cent., but in others the most economical load (considering the cost in one direction only) is about 85 per cent. Each division is governed by its own operating characteristics and no general law appears in the results in this study.

2. The cost per ton-mile decreases as the gross car load increases, due probably to the lower train resistance per gross ton.

3. The cost per ton-mile increases with the delay on the road. This is well illustrated, by the results of the Memphis division. With 2 hours' delay, the cost per 1,000 gross ton-miles was 14.2 cts.; at 3 hours it was 15.8 cts.; at 4 hours it was 17.4 cts., and at 5 hours it was 19 cts.

4. Up to a certain critical point the cost per ton-mile decreases as the ton-miles per train-hour increases. The cost is stationary or rises slightly, as the ton-miles per train-hour increase beyond that point. The critical point is reached only by trains running so far above the normal average speeds for trains of their weight that the increased fuel consumption offsets the saving in wages.

COMPARATIVE RESULTS OF OPERATING FULL- AND REDUCED-TONNAGE TRAINS ON FIVE DISTRICTS OF THE ILLINOIS CENTRAL SYSTEM

	Champaign		Paducah	Fulton		McComb		Tallahatchie	
District	130		99	128		96		{So. 145, No. 144}	
Length, miles	North		North	North and south		One direction		North and south	
Direction of tests									
Ruling grade, feet per mile	31 and 26		66 and 26	26		21		{So. 13, No. 17}	
Line	Double track		Single	Double track		Double track		Single track	
	Full load	Reduced load	Full load	Full load	Reduced load	Full load	Reduced load	Full load	Reduced load
Number of trains	30	9	25	9	32	7	9	32	20
Ratings, gross ton-miles	526,600	....	236,700	457,832	....	364,800	....	{So. 551,000, No. 547,200}	....
Ratings, gross ton-miles per train-mile	4,051		2,401	3,577		3,800		3,800	
Average actual gross ton-miles	487,453	425,280	228,908	423,452	395,721	306,435	229,397	513,188	425,915
Average train load, tons	3,750	3,271	2,314	3,308	3,091	3,192	2,389	3,547	2,948
Per cent. of rating hauled	92.5	80.8	96.6	92.5	84.1	84.0	62.9	93.3	77.5
Gross ton-miles per train-hour	39,202	43,468	27,299	48,364	45,419	34,102	30,361	40,144	35,075
Average number of cars per train: Loads	69	65	50	55	59	62	33	67	51
Empties	3	5	5	5	9	24	55	11	19
Average time between terminals, hours, minutes	12–26	9–47	8–23	8–45	8–43	8–59	7–33	12–47	12–08
Average delays, hours, minutes	4–01	2–41	2–32	1–26	1–47	1–56	1–37	3–05	3–18
Average speed in motion, miles per hour	15.8	18.4	16.9	17.6	18.3	13.6	16.2	15.0	16.5
Average speed between terminals, miles per hour	10.8	13.4	11.8	14.6	14.8	10.6	12.7	11.4	12.0
Costs per trip: Wages	$41.77	$33.41	$26.80	$31.13	$31.03	$27.73	$25.09	$43.41	$41.57
Fuel	$38.95	$30.25	$24.83	$34.95	$33.09	$34.32	$27.29	$39.32	$33.17
Total	$80.73	$63.66	$51.63	$66.08	$64.12	$62.05	$52.38	$82.73	$74.74
Pound coal per 1,000 gross ton-miles	68.59	61.02	93.1	70.8	71.8	96.1	102.1	65.8	66.9
Pound coal per train-hour	2,689	2,659	2,544	3,426	3,260	3,281	3,102	2,640	2,345
Cost per 1,000 gross ton-miles: Wages	$.0857	$.0785	$.1170	$.0735	$.0784	$.0905	$.1090	$.0846	$.0970
Fuel	$.0799	$.0715	$.1084	$.0825	$.0836	$.1120	$.1190	$.0766	$.0770
Total	$.1656	$.1500	$.2254	$.1560	$.1620	$.2025	$.2280	$.1612	$.1740
Cost per train-hour: Wages	$3.36	$3.42	$3.20	$3.56	$3.56	$3.09	$3.32	$3.395	$3.42
Fuel	$3.13	$3.09	$2.96	$3.99	$3.79	$3.82	$3.61	$3.076	$2.73
Total	$6.49	$6.51	$6.16	$7.55	$7.35	$6.91	$6.93	$6.471	$6.15
Total cost with 1½ time overtime: Per 1,000 gross ton-miles	$.1735	$.151	$.231	$.156	$.162	$.207	$.229	$.167	$.18
Per train-hour	$6.80	$6.58	$6.315	$7.55	$7.36	$7.14	$6.98	$6.73	$6.34

5. There appears to be no distinct relation between the train load and the hours of delay on the road.

6. The delay on the road apparently has more effect on the gross ton-miles per train-hour than variations in speed while in motion. The element of road delay is probably the most important single factor in the equation.

The practical application to that road of the facts developed by the tests is summarized by the following general conclusions in the report of the manager of the Illinois Central:

1. It is not practicable to reduce the train load to avoid overtime because of the increased cost incident to the operation of the necessary additional trains in the direction of heavy traffic to handle the same tonnage and in the direction of light traffic to balance power.

2. To a large extent the cost of handling the most economical train load includes considerable overtime.

3. Increased cost resulting from overtime, like any other wage increase, must be met by increasing facilities instead of by reducing train load. This reduction, on a good many districts, would add train units in excess of present capacity.

As another angle relative to proper loading of trains, the following from a paper by J. E. Davenport, engineer of Dynamometer tests, New York Central,[1] indicates how fuel consumption may be increased 10 per cent. by careless adjustment:

Many errors are made by the yard forces in computing the size of the individual train, this condition existing whether the load is by adjusted tonnage or actual tonnage, and occurring in the make-up in both fast and slow freight trains. These errors in numerous cases on the slow-freight side amount to as high as 20 per cent. in the tonnage ordered and on the fast-freight side running at times to 15 per cent. When errors of this nature produce a train heavier than is ordered, the resultant will produce a more economical coal consumption, since the operating speed in this service is from 14 to 20 m.p.h. However, when the error results in an underload of from 10 to 15 per cent., the increase in the operating speed of this particular unit will result in an increased coal consumption as high as 10 or 12 per cent. These errors in train load, which result in underloaded trains, increase the fuel consumption in the fast-freight service, since the operating speeds are higher than the speeds which would produce the minimum fuel consumption for these trains.

In conclusion, the method outlined herein for ascertaining the relation between train load, speed and fuel consumption is suggested as possible for practical application for use during that portion of freight-train movement that the locomotive is using steam. The fuel consumption during that portion of the run that the locomotive is drifting and during the delay periods must be computed in a different manner, and from the locomotive test plant results will amount to a figure from 300 to 900 lb. per hour, depending upon the class of locomotive and method of firing. It is evident that local operating conditions will in each case

[1] *Railway Review*, June 3, 1922.

govern the ratio of the portions of the run during which the locomotive is using steam and hauling the train and during which the locomotive will be consuming coal at this lesser figure; or, in other words, the relation between train load, speed and fuel consumption varies in each territory and each direction and can best be solved by local studies. Assuming the foregoing proposed method as containing a fair amount of merit, the conclusion is reached that for each weight train in each direction there will be a definite speed at which the minimum coal consumption will result, and with speeds either higher or lower than this definite speed there will be an increase in coal consumption. Generally speaking, the handling of heavier cars and heavier trains and the elimination of excessive speeds will greatly assist in reducing the fuel bills.

The economical operation of trains depends largely on accuracy in loading on proper train make-up, on the avoidance of stops and on the length of engine and crew runs.

It is highly expensive to stop and start a freight train. Nothing is more open to conjecture than the cost of train stops. Necessarily, this figure must vary with conditions. A writer in the *Railway Age* (March

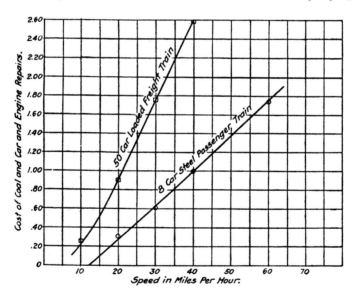

Fig. 40.—Approximate cost of stopping freight and passenger trains from different speeds.

22, 1918) presents this diagram (Fig. 40), for a 50-car freight train: Mikado engine, 130 tons; on drivers, 100 tons; tender two-thirds loaded, 63 tons; 50 cars loaded, 3,750 tons; freight-car resistance (4.4 lb. per ton), 16,500 lb.; tender and engine resistance (4.4 lb.), 409 lb.; engine-friction and head air resistance, 2,715 lb. Cost of coal per freight car-mile, 40 cts.; cost of freight-car repairs per car-mile, 0.87 cts.; engine repairs per mile, 9.49 cts.

The passenger train sh own was made up as follows:

Total weight of Pacific type engine......................	120 tons
Weight on driving wheels...............................	75 tons
Weight of tender (two-third load)....................	63 tons
Weight of eight coaches at 110,000 lb..................	440 tons
Total car resistance at 6.0 lb. per ton....................	2,640 lb.
Tender and engine-truck resistance at 6.0 lb. per ton.......	648 lb.
Engine-friction and head air resistance.................	2,090 lb.
Cost of coal per car-mile............................	2.63 cts.
Cost of engine repairs per mile.........................	9.49 cts.
Cost of car repairs per mile per car..................,......	1.75 cts.

Another writer reminds us that the Interstate Commerce Commission operating statistics of large steam roads, for February, 1921, places an average cost of freight-train operation by selected amounts at \$2.11 per mile—and deduces from this that a cost of \$5.06 is met for each unnecessary freight-train stop. The B. & O. conducted tests to show that a train running an average speed of 7½ m.p.h. consumed 238 lb. coal more than if no stop were made, or 21 per cent. in excess of a non-stop run.

In striving for the best possible performance consistent with common-sense limitations, to get heavier car loading and train loading, a note of warning should be sounded against that type of statistical "economist" who "rushes in where angels fear to tread" and makes comparisons between different roads on the basis of their various achievements in train loading, car loading, car-miles per day and other operating units, instead of confining his efforts to comparisons of a road, or a part of a road, with itself. The futility of a comparison on any other basis is obvious. It is not necessary to go further than to point out that some roads are averaging as little as 5 miles, and others upwards of 60, and divisions of one and the same road vary from 12 miles a day to as high as 100.

Impact registers are being used to determine how roughly—or smoothly—a train or car is handled. This machine is placed in a car and records the exact time and the force of the shock sustained in each case of rough handling. A ten-day clock mechanism propels a chart from a feeder roller to a receiving roller, passing over a third roller, above which a pencil, held by a movable weight, is suspended, the point of the pencil resting on the chart. The weight is kept in position by two specially calibrated springs, one on each side. When the car receives a shock, the pencil responds, moving to one side a distance depending upon the intensity of the shock, and then rebounding to the center, the point of the pencil making a line on the chart. As the chart is graduated into 24-hour periods and each hour period into 15-min. subdivisions, the exact time the shock was received is thus obtained. Lines are also placed on the chart running lengthwise, dividing it so that the impacts are indicated at certain speeds in miles per hour. Figure 41 shows one of these machines.

Dispatching and moving freight trains has been satisfactorily accomplished by the use of the "peg" system, on the Buffalo, Rochester & Pittsburgh since 1916. A "peg" is a non-time-table schedule for a freight train. The peg system[1] is the provision of pegs for all-freight trains. On the line mentioned the system has resulted in savings of from one to two hours in moving trains over engine districts approximately 100 miles in length.

Register being removed from car.   Time 10:15 A. M.
Car being spotted at freight house.   Time 8:28 A. M.
Car receiving violent impact. Hours switching crew rough handling. Time 8:05 A. M.
Car moving to freight house from terminal yards. Time 6:40—7:05. A. M.
Train being broken up.   5:45 A. M.   Rough handled 5:50 A. M.
Train standing in yard.   5:15—42 A. M.
Train arriving at terminal.   5:15 A. M.
Station stop.   4:50 A. M.
Impacts caused by slack in train.   3:20—30 A. M.

FIG. 41.—Typical record of impact register.   (Start at bottom and read up.)

This is primarily a bituminous-coal carrier; most of whose freight originates in the territory north of Pittsburgh and moves northward to connections with eastward lines and the Lakes at Buffalo and Rochester, especially the latter. Mallet locomotives are used extensively and more have been ordered, 2-6-6-2's for road service and 2-8-8-2's for pushers. The absolute-permissive block system

[1] *Railway Age*, March 17, 1923.

is in operation on the more important single-track lines and has greatly facilitated train operation. No "31" train orders are used on sections so signaled. The "A.-P. B.," however, was installed before the adoption of the peg system and the accomplishments ascribed to the latter are in addition to those already attained by the former.

The Buffalo, Rochester & Pittsburgh has a considerable mileage of single track and the system is in operation on both single- and double-track sections with equal success. Before the peg system was installed, the officers of the company made schedules, or pegs, sufficient to handle maximum business. These pegs contemplated the best probable performance, barring accident, if all employees and all departments entering into train movement exerted their best efforts in this direction. For example, officers were stationed at water towers to time engines taking water. Under their surveillance the employees speeded up the operation as much as possible and it was this performance which was allowed for

FIG. 42.—Conductor's delay report.

in the peg. If any crew uses more time in taking water than experience has shown to be necessary, a satisfactory explanation must be made. In making observations before installing the peg system, the officers found that switching movements at one point were holding up practically all their freight trains. With the publication of the pegs, however, these delays were reduced to a minimum, since it was the duty of the switching crew to clear the time of these pegs almost the same as of regularly scheduled movements.

The peg system has greatly simplified the work of the roundhouse forces because they know when they are going to be called upon to deliver locomotives. Dispatchers are able to arrange meeting and passing points on a definite basis and are required to keep watch on irregularities only, instead of on every movement of every freight train on the road, as is necessary under the system of running all freight trains as extras whenever tonnage, power and crews are available. Yardmasters cannot send freight trains out in bunches whenever tonnage, power and crews are available, thus making the trains assume their correct space interval

FORM 314 | 25 M 5-17

BUFFALO, ROCHESTER & PITTSBURGH RAILWAY CO

FREIGHT TRAIN DELAY REPORT ______________ 191

TRAIN ______
ENGINE ______
ENGINEER ______
CONDUCTOR ______

Initial Point ______ Ordered to Leave ______ M. Destination ______ Arrived ______ M. Time Tied up ______ M.

DELAYS IN MINUTES BY

STATIONS AT OR BETWEEN	Engine Late	Train not Switched	Trainmen Late	Train Orders	Way Bills	Car Inspection	Coal, Water or Sand	Enginemen Late	Meeting or Passing No.	Meeting or Passing Mins. Delay	Passenger Train Late	Hot Boxes No.	Hot Boxes Mins. Delay	Engine Failures	Other Equip't Failures	Derailments	Trackmen
	D1	D2	D3	D4	D5	D6	D7	D8	D9	D10	D11	D12	D13	D14	D15	D16	D17

STATIONS AT OR BETWEEN	Bridgemen	Set-off or Pick-up	Stalled	Overloaded	Pusher	Defective Brakes	Yard Engine	Freight Trains Ahead	Work Trains	Local Freights	Operators Failures							REMARKS
	D18	D19	D20	D21	D22	D23	D24	D25	D26	D27	D28	D29	D30	D31	D32	D33	D34	

FIG. 43.—Dispatchers fill out one of these forms for every freight train moving over their district.

Train No.	Class of Service	Road Engines		From	To	Engineer	Conductor	Time Consumed Between: E. Sala – Ashford		Ashford – Foolle		Foolle – Bless		Bless – Goolle		Goolle – D.L.W. Jct.		D.L.&W. Jct. – L. Park		&		&		&		Time Ordered to Depart			Time Tied up at Destination			Time of Trip To Time Tied up		Overtime of Trip		Peg Time of Trip	
		Class	No.					Hrs.	Mins.	Hrs.	Mins.	Hrs.	Mins.	Hrs.	Mins.	Hrs.	Mins.	Hrs.	Mins.	Hrs.	Mins.	Hrs.	Mins.	Hrs.	Mins.	Hrs.	Mins.	A.M. P.M.	Hrs.	Mins.	A.M. P.M.	Hrs.	Mins.	Hrs.	Mins.	Hrs.	Mins.
A	B	C	D	E	F																																
32		Z	418	E. Sala	L. Pk.	McNalley	Tappy	1	40		54		37		42	1	46	1	31							10	45	p	6	25	a	7	40	—	—	7	10
1/22		Z	407	—	—	Harsla	McTamegler	1	00	1	34		54	1	24	1	25	2	08							8	05	a	5	00	p	8	55		55	8	30
2/22		Z	425	—	—	E. Mooney	Dungels	1	08	1	13		45	1	01	1	18	2	10							9	35	a	5	15	p	7	40	—	—	8	40
1/34		X	389	—	—	Jusbely	Moonl	1	04	1	33	1	00	2	05	2	13	2	50							12	25	a	11	40	p	11	15	3	15	8	15
2/34		Z	400	—	—	Strohm	Burnters		45	1	14		39	1	27	1	51	2	03							2	15	p	10	23	p	8	08		08	8	45
28		Z	432	—	—	Foote	Simpson		52	2	44		52	1	18	1	36	2	05							7	35	p	5	11	a	9	36	1	36	8	35
30		Z	412	—	—	Wells	Smith	1	25	1	02		58	1	18	1	45	2	31							2	35	a	12	14	p	9	39	1	39	8	20
						Total	Time	7	54	10	14	5	45	9	15	11	54	15	18													62	53	7	33	58	15
						Average		1	08	1	28		49	1	19	1	42	2	11													8	59	1	05	8	19
						Peg		1	14	1	13		58	1	01	1	31	2	11																		

DELAYS IN MINUTES BY

Train No.	Engine Late	Trains not Delivered	Trainmen Late	Train Orders	Way-bills	Car Inspection	Coal, Water or Sand	Enginemen Late	Meeting or Passing: No.	Meeting or Passing: Mins. Delay	Passenger Train Late	Hot Boxes: No.	Hot Boxes: Mins. Delay	Engine Failures	Other Equip't Failures	Derailments	Trainmen	Bridgemen	Set-off or Pick-up	Stalled	Over-loaded	Pusher	Defective Brakes	Yard Engine	Freight Trains Ahead	Work Trains	Local Freights	Operators' Failures	Yard Blocked	Signal Failures	Held by Foreign Road Trains	Cut Pushers in and out							Train No.	Assisting Engine: Class	Assisting Engine: No.	From	To
	D1	D2	D3	D4	D5	D6	D7	D8	D9	D10	D11	D12	D13	D14	D15	D16	D17	D18	D19	D20	D21	D22	D23	D24	D25	D26	D27	D28	D29	D30	D31	D32	D33	D34	D35	D36	D37	D38					
32																																							32				
1/22	20								2	22					10																			10					1/22	X	332	E. Sala	L. P. k.
2/22																																							2/22				
1/34	30								5	45									125																				1/34	Z	404	E. Sala	L. P. k.
2/34																			10																				2/34				
28									2	20		2	25						30													10	15						28	X	324	E. Sala	Warsa
30		40										1	15						63																				30				
	50	40							9	87		3	40		10				228													10	15	10									

FIG. 44a.—Report of freight train performance.

out on the line and consuming more road time than necessary. Train crews, also, know from the pegs assigned to their runs just what is expected of them. No delay reports are required even where delays are met with unless the peg time is exceeded. On the other hand, if the peg time is exceeded, the train crew must account satisfactorily for all time lost.

In the table, on p. 180 pegs in use on the Rochester division (most of which is single track) are shown. The distance covered is 107 miles. It will be noted that the peg time on the southward trains is somewhat less than on northward trains. This is due to the fact that the northward trains are, as a rule, heavily loaded and the southward trains are largely made up of empties. The variation in time as between trains in the same direction is largely due to the exigencies of single-track operation—*e.g.*, the number of meeting points—and to the fact that one or two of the trains are fast-freight runs.

Train No.	E Sala ... Ashford				Ashford ... G.dlle				BETWEEN G.dlle ... Warsaw				Warsaw ... P&L Jct				P&L Jct ... L Park			
	CARS		TONNAGE		CARS		TONNAGE		CARS		TONNAGE		CARS		TONNAGE		CARS		TONNAGE	
	Loads	Emp-ties	Actual	Rating	Loads	Emp-ties	Actual	Rating	Loads	Emp-ties	Actual	Rating	Loads	Emp-ties	Actual	Rating	Loads	Emp-ties	Actual	Rating
	T1	T2	T3	T4	T5	T6	T7	T8	T9	T10	T11	T12	T13	T14	T15	T16	T17	T18	T19	T20
32	22	3	1135	1625	34	3	1695		29	3-	1525		27	3	1445		26	3	1415	1625
1/22	46	0	2765	2750													—	—	—	2750
2/22	27	1.	1620	1625					23	0	1335						23	0	1325	1625
1/34	45	10	2730	2750					36	10	2138		11	10	859		—	—	—	2750
2/34	26	0	1622	1625									29	0	1742		3	0	120	1625
28	50	2	2768	2750	48	2	2634										48	2	2634	2750
30	22	18	1629	1625					21	11	1408						21	0	1166	1625
	238	34	1426	4750													121	5	6670	4750
	34	5	2038	2107													17	1	953	2107

FIG. 44b.—Report of freight train performance.

Some freight trains on single track have time-table schedules in addition to the pegs. These schedules, however, are, as a rule, considerably ahead of a peg time and they are used primarily for northward trains to give the heavily loaded movement precedence by class, as well as by direction, over the southbound movement, which is largely empty. Emphasis should be laid upon the fact that, while these pegs are published in the time table, they are, nevertheless, not a part of it and the fact that a train is running on a certain peg gives it no rights not bestowed by the time table proper or by train order.

The pegs are for information only and can be varied from without the issuance of train orders. On double track the peg time between the same points does not vary with the different trains. It will be noted that the peg time shown in the accompanying schedule for a number of trains calls for the payment of a small amount of overtime. The company feels, however, that it is impossible to operate heavy coal trains without some overtime.

So much for the pegs. The really important part is the check which is made to see that these schedules are lived up to. In the first place, conductors report delays by wire at several designated points on each division, using the blank shown in Fig. 42 for this purpose.   As has been noted above, no delay is reported unless the train is running behind its peg.   Each dispatcher keeps a record on a separate blank for every freight train in his district and on this blank he records every delay reported by the conductor as it is wired to him, classifying each

BUFFALO, ROCHESTER AND PITTSBURGH RAILWAY CO.
DAILY REPORT OF OVERTIME
DuBois, Pa., January 31st. 192..

DIVISION	ROCHESTER	BUFFALO	MIDDLE	CLEARFIELD	A. & W.	INDIANA	TOTAL	COST
Number of Trips	14	9	25	5	15	8	-70	
CAUSED BY:	MINUTES	MINUTES	MINUTES	MINUTES	MINUTES	MINUTES	MINUTES	$
Trainmen late	-40					50	90	14 50
Coal or water		25	194	20	10	60	299	46 06
Train orders				30			30	4 50
Yard failures	85	230	115		65	125	600	93 80
Yard blocked	55	75	25			150	305	45 75
Number of trains / meeting or passing	55 / 557	40 / 576	30 / 879	11 / 370	58 / 1490	42 / 948	230 / 4420	741 76
Passenger trains late								
Pusher				65			65	9 75
Set-off or pick-up	552	10	701	400	515	495	2773	434 15
Operator failures								
Trains ahead		53	239		60		352	51 00
Local freights			65				65	9 75
Derailments					85		85	14 45
Stalled								
Other transportation delay	115	19	230	60	70	20	494	75 90
Slow orders								
Work trains								
Bridgemen or Trackmen		10	25		47		82	13 24
Signals or telephone			5		60		65	10 95
Track failures								
Car Inspectors		40					40	6 00
Equipment failures	132	100	495	75	15	110	927	141 55
Engine failures	47	85	803				935	140 25
Hot boxes	40	50	315	15	35		435	65 95
Engine late	50	60	108	95	119	25	477	74 45

ACTUAL OVERTIME MADE

DIVISION	ROCHESTER		BUFFALO		MIDDLE		CLEARFIELD		A. & W.		INDIANA		TOTAL		COST
	Hrs.	Min.	Hrs.	Min.	Hrs.	Min.	Hrs.	Min.	Hrs.	Min.	Hrs.	Min.	Hrs.	Min.	
Through freights	23	25	16	52	71	39	22	52	70	45	49	47	254	58	$1616 52
Local freights	6	47	1	40	16	00	11	55	11	12	14	12	62	44	514 57
Pushers	3	40		52	56	54	3	47	16	56	6	13	66	02	160 05
TOTAL															$2291 15

Fig. 45.—Overtime shown on this report is all time in excess of regular time.

delay by cause in blanks provided for that purpose.   A copy of this report is illustrated in Fig. 43.   The totals of these reports governing the movements of each train are entered on a large sheet, such as is shown in Fig. 44*a*, and *b*, where the average time per train and the peg time per train are made easily comparable for the benefit of operating officers.

This report is made on a ruled sheet 15 by 42 in. The illustrations making up Fig. 44*a* and *b* do not portray the whole report but only the upper part of it. For purposes of adequate reproduction, the portion of this report which is shown has been divided into three parts, all of which are shown in the illustrations in Fig. 44*a* and *b*. To get a true picture of the appearance of the report, these three illustrations would have to be placed side by side to be read straight across.

The portion of this report which is shown here covers the movement of all northward freight trains, except locals, over the Rochester division on Jan. 31, 1923. Portions *not* shown describe the movement southbound and local freight trains. In addition, *also not shown*, are notes explaining delays, remarks with reference to tonnage and a weather report.

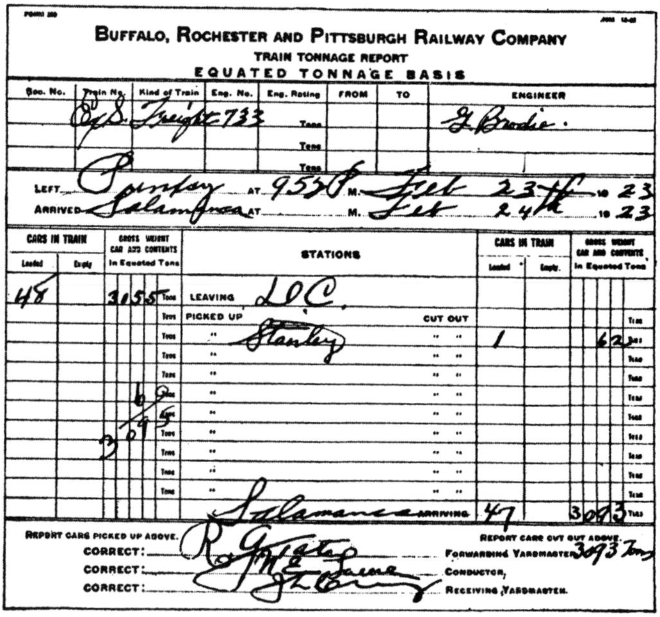

BUFFALO, ROCHESTER AND PITTSBURGH RAILWAY COMPANY
TRAIN TONNAGE REPORT
EQUATED TONNAGE BASIS

Sec. No.	Train No.	Kind of Train	Eng. No.	Eng. Rating	FROM	TO	ENGINEER
	Ex S.	Freight	733	Tons			G. Brodie.
				Tons			
				Tons			

LEFT Punxy AT 9.55 P. M. Feb 23th 19 23
ARRIVED Salamanca AT .... M. Feb 24th 19 23

CARS IN TRAIN Loaded	CARS IN TRAIN Empty	GROSS WEIGHT CAR AND CONTENTS In Equated Tons	STATIONS		CARS IN TRAIN Loaded	CARS IN TRAIN Empty	GROSS WEIGHT CAR AND CONTENTS In Equated Tons
48		3155 Tons	LEAVING LOC.				
		Tons	PICKED UP	CUT OUT			Tons
		Tons	" Stanley	" "	1		62 Tons
		Tons	"	" "			Tons
		Tons	"	" "			Tons
		Tons	"	" "			Tons
		Tons	"	" "			Tons
		Tons	"	" "			Tons
		Tons	"	" "			Tons
		Tons	"	" "			Tons
		Tons	"	" "			Tons
			Salamanca ARRIVING		47		3093 Tons

REPORT CARS PICKED UP ABOVE. REPORT CARS CUT OUT ABOVE.
CORRECT: R. G. Yates FORWARDING YARDMASTER. 3093 Tons
CORRECT: W. E. Fuena CONDUCTOR,
CORRECT: J. L. Berry RECEIVING YARDMASTER.

FIG. 46.—Tonnage report.

It will be noted in Fig. 44*a* and *b* that all northbound trains run on this particular day had time-table schedules As has been noted above, however, these schedules are used solely for convenience in dispatching, *i.e.*, restricting the number of train orders issued, and for no other purpose. Delay reports and other records of performance are based on the peg and not on the time-table schedule. Most of the southbound trains run on the same day were extras.

The peg time between stations shown in Fig. 44*a* and *b* is *average* peg time. The actual peg time between the stations varies with each train. The peg time for the entire trip, however, is shown in the last column of the first illustration for the individual trains. On double-track, the peg time of all trains is the same between the same stations.

From this general report on freight-train operation, separate reports are made to the mechanical department and to the transportation and maintenance-of-way departments, showing in detail the delays chargeable to these departments. Specimens of the reports to these departments are shown below. In addition, daily reports are made showing the average time of all trains between all points divided between local trains and through-tonnage trains. The company, moreover, prepares a special overtime report which gives all overtime classified by divisions and by causes together with costs. An illustration of a typical overtime report is shown in Fig. 45. These overtime reports are made up directly from the general report shown in Fig. 44a and b and do not include the small amount of overtime which is contemplated in the various pegs. The company expects to pay a certain amount of overtime even with the very best of operation as outlined by the pegs, and, consequently, does not include this overtime in its overtime report. In addition, a daily report is made giving the average time of freight trains on all divisions.

In Fig. 44a and b, in addition to the information concerning delays, will be seen data regarding the tonnage of all trains run. The company has tonnage-computing machines in all its yard offices for obtaining the equated tonnage of every train. With his bills, each conductor is given a slip (Fig. 46) showing the tonnage of his train, which is certified as correct by the forwarding yardmaster. The conductor must check this slip and certify it, as also must the receiving yardmaster, and all cases of light tonnage must be explained on the back of the slip.

STATEMENT OF IRREGULARITIES—ROCHESTER & BUFFALO DIVISIONS MECHANICAL
DEPARTMENT. JANUARY 31, 1923

1/22 eng. 407.......E. Salamanca 10 mins. engine late.
1/34 eng. 389.......E. Salamanca 30 mins. engine late.
No. 28 eng. 432.....Bird 25 mins. hot box NYC 403657-CGN 27864.
No. 30 eng. 412.....Gainesville 15 mins. hot box GT 75684.
No. 21 eng. 414.....SL Jct. 47 mins. low steam and stoker trouble.
Ex. 403............Warsaw 72 mins. truck broken under BR&P 44237.
No. 33 eng. 435.....WS Jct. 45 mins. switch out NYC 412411 tight brake connection
                    and make four couplings on train.
Ex. 429............WS Jct. 30 mins. PRR 350813 leaky train line; Mile Post
                    102–20 mins. brake beam down NYC 414441.
No. 27 eng. 406.....Buffalo Creek 10 mins. engine late, 20 mins. air men.
1/26 eng. 406.......F. Salamanca 20 mins. air men.
2/45 eng. 417.......Riceville 30 mins. train parted acct. low draw head DII 100215.
2/50 eng. 377.......E. Salamanca 15 mins. engine late; E. Salamanca to Ashford
                    20 mins. low steam engine 377.
1/52 eng. 401.......Great Valley to Ashford 30 mins. No. 132 ahead with low steam
                    engine 603; Mile Post 33–25 mins. stoker trouble engine 401.
No. 22 eng. 401.....Buffalo Creek 35 mins. engine late; Glenwood 50 mins. draw
                    head out C of Ga. 51159.
2/54 eng. 402.......Beaver 20 mins. hot box SVE 22856; E. Salamanca 20 mins.
                    repairs to caboose.
No. 27 eng. 402.....Buffalo Creek 20 mins. engine late.

STATEMENT OF IRREGULARITIES—ROCHESTER & BUFFALO DIVISIONS. TRANS. &
M. OF W. DEPARTMENTS. JANUARY 31, 1923

1/34...............P&L Jct. 40 mins. setting off.

No. 28.............Brooks Ave. 30 mins. setting off.

No. 30.............E. Salamanca 40 mins. train not switched; P&L Jct. 30 mins.
setting off.

No. 21.............Lincoln Park 40 mins. engineer called late; LeRoy 35 mins.
picking up; DL&W Jct. 30 mins. picking up and setting off.

Ex. 403............WS Jct. 80 mins. picking up; DL&W Jct. 80 mins. cut and went
to Warsaw for water acct. no water at DL&W. Jct.

No. 33.............WS Jct. 45 mins. switch out NYC 412411 tight brake connection
and make four couplings on train.

No. 25.............P&L Jct. 35 mins. picking up and setting off.

Ex. 429............WS Jct. 50 mins. picking up; E. Salamanca 20 mins. yard
blocked.

No. 29.............Brooks Ave. 30 mins. picking up; E. Salamanca 15 mins. yard
blocked.

No. 27.............Buffalo Creek 20 mins. train not switched.

1/26...............Kellogg 10 mins. trackmen.

1/45..............Buffalo Creek 35 mins. train not switched, 10 mins. pick up head
end; E. Salamanca 50 mins. yard blocked.

2/33..............Buffalo Creek 90 mins. train not switched.

No. 47.............Tifft. St. 20 mins. train not switched; E. Salamanca 25 mins.
yard blocked.

1/52..............E. Salamanca 20 mins. blocked by yard engine 279-526.

No. 23.............Buffalo Creek 15 mins. train not switched.

THEORETICAL MOVEMENT OF TONNAGE TRAINS BASED ON PROPER OBSERVANCE OF SPEED RESTRICTIONS AND THE ELIMINATION OF AVOIDABLE DELAYS

Northward trains.

	A. M.	A. M.	P. M.	P. M.	P. M.	P. M.	P. M.	P. M.	P. M.	P. M.	A. M.	A. M.	A. M.	A. M.	A. M.
Tied up	8.50	10.55	1.25	4.40	6.15	6.55	8.10	8.50	10.40	11.40	12.50	2.10	4.00	5.05	5.55
Lincoln Park	8.40	10.45	1.15	4.30	6.05	6.45	8.00	8.40	10.30	11.30	12.40	2.00	3.50	4.55	5.45
D. L. & W. Jct.	6.25	8.36	11.04	1.58	3.35	4.24	5.50	6.25	8.21	9.06	10.28	11.47	1.44	2.43	3.58
Gainesville { Lv.	5.10	6.54	9.28	12.39	2.07	3.10	4.27	4.50	6.45	7.42	8.47	10.13	12.30	1.20	2.27
Gainesville { Ar.	4.48	6.32	8.41	12.14	1.45	2.47	4.05	4.27	6.23	7.21	8.25	9.36	11.38	12.57	2.10
Bliss	4.17	6.00	8.06	11.39	1.10	2.12	3.17	3.55	5.24	6.48	7.50	9.08	11.01	12.19	1.47
Farmersville	3.20	5.00	7.10	10.46	12.05	1.12	2.20	3.00	4.20	5.47	6.48	8.10	9.50	11.19	1.08
Ashford	2.05	3.45	5.50	9.20	10.50	11.45	1.05	1.50	3.05	4.32	5.45	6.45	8.35	9.55	12.15
East Salamanca	12.55	2.35	4.40	8.10	9.35	10.35	11.55	12.45	1.55	3.20	4.45	5.35	7.25	8.45	10.45
Ordered	12.55	2.35	4.40	8.10	9.35	10.35	11.55	12.45	1.55	3.20	4.45	5.35	7.25	8.45	10.45
	A. M.	A. M.	A. M.	A. M.	A. M.	A. M.	A. M.	P. M.	P. M.	P. M.	P. M.	P. M.	P. M.	P. M.	P. M.
Time of trip { Hr	7	8	8	8	8	8	8	8	8	8	8	8	8	8	7
{ Min	55	20	45	30	40	20	15	05	45	20	05	35	35	20	10

Southward trains.

	A. M.	A. M.	A. M.	A. M.	A. M.	A. M.	A. M.	A. M.	P. M.	P. M.	P. M.	P. M.	P. M.	P. M.	P. M.
Ordered	12.15	1.15	2.40	4.00	6.15	7.45	9.00	11.35	1.15	2.55	4.15	6.25	8.05	9.20	10.35
Lincoln Park	12.15	1.15	2.40	4.00	6.15	7.45	9.00	11.35	1.15	2.55	4.15	6.34	8.05	9.20	10.35
D. L. & W. Jct.	2.20	3.23	5.00	6.05	9.13	10.23	11.40	1.44	3.35	5.14	6.36	8.21	10.28	11.47	12.55
Gainesville { Ar.	3.53	5.10	6.54	7.35	11.08	11.52	1.25	4.05	5.37	7.42	8.47	9.27	12.13	1.20	3.19
Gainesville { Lv.	4.13	5.29	7.30	8.00	11.25	12.14	1.45	4.27	6.00	8.01	9.06	9.36	12.20	1.39	3.42
Bliss	4.39	6.00	8.06	9.27	12.05	12.42	2.12	4.54	6.48	8.40	9.45	9.58	1.15	2.29	4.17
Farmersville	5.24	7.10	8.52	10.12	12.48	1.45	3.00	6.11	7.28	9.25	10.40	10.27	2.15	3.20	5.00
Ashford	6.30	8.05	9.50	11.55	1.50	2.45	3.45	7.25	8.15	10.30	11.25	11.35	3.05	4.10	5.45
East Salamanca	7.00	8.35	10.20	11.55	2.20	3.15	4.15	7.55	8.45	11.00	11.55	11.35	3.35	4.40	6.15
Tied up	7.10	8.45	10.30	12.05	2.30	3.25	4.25	8.05	8.55	11.10	12.05	11.45	3.45	4.50	6.25
	A. M.	A. M.	A. M.	P. M.	P. M.	P. M.	P. M.	P. M.	P. M.	P. M.	A. M.	P. M.	A. M.	A. M.	A. M.
Time of trip { Hr	6	7	7	8	8	7	7	8	7	8	7	5	7	7	7
{ Min	55	30	50	05	15	40	25	30	40	15	50	20	40	30	50

Time consumed at or between designated stations in excess of time shown will be considered delay, and must be explained on delay reports.

AVERAGE TIME TONNAGE FREIGHT TRAINS—ALL DIVISIONS, JANUARY 31, 1923

From	To	Trains	Hours	Minutes
East Salamanca	Lincoln Park	7	8	59
Lincoln Park	East Salamanca	7	9	51
East Salamanca	Buffalo Creek and return	9	10	36
Punxsutawney	East Salamanca	11	15	45
Du Bois	East Salamanca	1	10	23
Punxsutawney	Clarion Junction and return	0	0	0
East Salamanca	Punxsutawney	10	10	04
East Salamanca	Du Bois	1	11	51
New Castle	Punxsutawney	2	12	16
Punxsutawney	New Castle	2	12	27
Allegheny	Punxsutawney	1	12	05
Punxsutawney	Allegheny	1	13	05
Glenwood	Punxsutawney	2	15	29
Punxsutawney	Glenwood	2	12	39
Punxsutawney	Echo and return	2	13	31
Punxsutawney	Clearfield and return	3	15	13
Punxsutawney	Vintondale	2	12	42
Vintondale	Punxsutawney	1	13	45
Punxsutawney	Lucerne and return	0	0	0
Punxsutawney	Josephine and return	1	13	17
Punxsutawney	Coy-Snyder and return	0	0	0
Punxsutawney	Iselin and return	2	14	38
Punxsutawney	Cummings and return	1	14	10
Punxsutawney	Jacksonville District and return	1	14	32

TIME OF LOCAL FREIGHT TRAINS—ALL DIVISIONS. JANUARY 31, 1923

From	To	Hours	Minutes
East Salamanca	Lincoln Park	10	00
Lincoln Park	East Salamanca	13	10
Lincoln Park	Gainesville	14	30
Gainesville	Lincoln Park	8	10
Perry	Perry	8	05
East Salamanca	Buffalo Creek	7	55
Buffalo Creek	East Salamanca	9	01
East Salamanca	Du Bois	10	14
Du Bois	East Salamanca	13	15
Du Bois	Clarion Junction and return	14	25
Du Bois	Clearfield	12	29
Clearfield	Du Bois	14	40
Punxsutawney	Indiana and return	12	03
Punxsutawney	Marion Center and return	11	13
Cummings	Aultman-Iselin-Cummings	14	10
Butler Junction	Punxsutawney	11	23
Punxsutawney	Butler Junction	10	04
Butler Junction	Craigsville and return	8	18

CHAPTER XI

TIME-FREIGHT SERVICE

The railways of Great Britain lead in prompt and certain handling of high-class freight; their methods are described elsewhere. In point of speed for long distances, however, they have nothing to compare with the movement of perishable freight from the South to New York and Chicago, or with the package and perishable-freight trains between Boston and New York and between New York and Washington; or with the movement of package and perishable freight between New York, New England and the West.

As distinguished from ordinary slow freight, the fast-freight service handles commodities, usually made up of package freight of an important or perishable nature, generally moving through freight houses or piers for receipt or delivery and solid carloads of high-class freight usually perishable, although under certain conditions commodities such as cement, lumber, and petroleum require and are given fast freight movement. It is usually handled at higher rates and classified to have preference in this over common through and local freight. Among the reasons for the existence of this service are the necessity for quick marketing of high-class goods, which are manufactured on very close margins of profit to avoid the loss of the use of capital invested, and desirability of the jobber's carrying the smallest stock, with which he can meet the demand. It is not unusual for the merchant in New York City to telephone or telegraph the New England manufacturer 200 or 300 miles away for goods he expects to have on his counter the following morning, or for dealers in Buffalo, 400 miles away, at noon to order goods from New York which they expect to receive the following afternoon.

To operate fast-freight service successfully on the time allowed for transit and with reasonable certainty, it is essential that the prescribed speed be such as can be maintained with regularity. The capacity of the engine should be such as to enable it to make approximately the average speed, on the maximum grades. Careful inspections should be made to prevent other than the authorized commodities going in fast-freight trains. Cars traveling as fast freight should be readily distinguished by a card or mark on the side of the car and on the card bill.

Authorized fast-freight cars should be kept out of trains of ordinary freight. There should be a clearly understood arrangement with connecting lines for prompt and complete delivery of fast freight from or to such lines. Full information must be given as to the necessary icing or ventilating when needed. Notice of time live stock is to be loaded, fed and watered must be furnished and shown. Proper service at division yards should be arranged for gathering and distributing fast-freight cars so as to avoid stops of regular fast-freight trains, and the necessary preference should be given through terminals and in switching and changing of engines and cabooses. Full reports and records should be made of cars set out short of destination for any reason and prompt action should be taken to have them moved again. A full schedule for loading and moving fast freight from points between terminals should be planned and placed in the hands of all interested in the handling.

It is advisable to arrange for the smallest number of regular trains to be run, and add sections as required in preference to annuling schedules not wanted, to permit flexibility in train and yard operation.

The time freight originating at Boston is handled by the Boston & Maine and New Haven roads, in trains made up in proper order; and the cars are so placed at the houses as to enable an immediate start, avoid switching and accompanying detentions. The Boston & Maine places 120 cars at its No. 10 house at one setting. Freight is loaded up to within 10 to 30 min. of leaving time, allowing time for closing doors, sealing cars and testing air brakes. Transfer cars from near-by manufacturing towns are also handled in these trains. A running slip is made for each car and accompanies it to destination. Waybills are made up and forwarded by train mail, U. S. mail or express. Boston and Maine train 9051 leaves Boston at 6:30 p. m. and arrives at Mechanicsville at 4:15 a. m., a run of 187 miles in 9 hr., 45 min.; and train 9053 leaves at 7:20 p. m. and arrives at Rotterdam at 7:00 a. m., a run of 212 miles in 11 hr., 40 min. New Haven symbol train B.H.-1—commonly known as the "fish train"—leaves Boston at 6:05 p. m. and arrives at Harlem River at 3:00 a. m., making the run of 227 miles in 8 hr., 55 min.

The Boston and Albany runs two fast trains with freight destined beyond Buffalo. L.S.-3, with cars for Chicago and points on the Lake Shore and Big Four, leaves Boston at 8:45 p. m., passes Selkirk Yard (near Albany) at 7:00 a. m. and arrives at Chicago (1,036 miles) 2:30 a. m. of the fourth day. M.C.-3 with cars for Chicago via Suspension Bridge and for points on the Michigan Central leaves Boston 9:15 p. m., passes Selkirk 9:00 a. m., and arrives Chicago 2:30 a. m. of the fourth day.

A good example of modern railroad service in swift transportation of perishable commodities is the Southern Railway's handling of the Georgia peach crop. At Atlanta, in the heart of Dixie, trainloads of fruit are assembled for the northern journey. Through the Carolinas and Virginia the long trains rush, finally rolling into the Nation's Capitol, a distance of 637 miles, only 22 hr. from terminal to terminal.

It is customary on some lines to designate fast-freight trains as "symbol trains." This is known as the symbol method. A combination of letters and numbers is used to indicate, in a general manner, the origin and destination of the train. The object is to preserve its identity among other trains. Where a schedule number is used over the entire line, the use of such numbers seems to answer all purposes and a number of large railroad companies follow this plan. Where the symbol method is used, the first letter of the symbol indicates the starting point, where most of the freight is taken on. The second letter indicates the destination or the point where the train ends its run. The numbers indicate direction as in conformity with practice of American railroads; west or southbound symbol trains·or tracks have odd numbers, and east or northbound ones have even numbers. On the Pennsylvania, as an illustration, assuming J to stand for Jersey City and P for Pittsburgh, J P 1 would indicate a westbound train originating at Jersey City and destined for Pittsburgh. P J 2 would indicate an eastbound train originating at Pittsburgh and destined for Jersey City.

The symbol freight service, to be successful, must be handled very much like passenger service. The outgoing cars should be placed at piers or houses in such positions that practically the train is made up in book order when loading is completed. In some instances it may be necessary to "double" over onto two or more tracks because one track is not long enough to hold all the cars. At intermediate points and division terminals, these trains are not usually run into the regular classification yards, because, being made up for final destination, it is only necessary at most to drop the cars for these points and take on those to be added. The cars to be dropped are probably at the head end and, if engines are changed, the incoming engine holds onto these cars and sets them off. Cars to go from the station must be placed in the proper position in the train and if this would cause detention they are usually held for a later and slower train. When the final or system destination is reached, the train may be pulled directly to and alongside the house into which the freight is unloaded, or, if stopped in the outlying or auxiliary yard, it is promptly moved to the unloading point by a yard engine.

First-class locomotives, adapted to high speed and in good condition, with picked crews, should be assigned to fast-freight runs when practicable. The symbol or working book should be placed in the hands of dispatchers, yardmasters, agents, conductors and others interested, and should give information in detail as to starting time of train, time at intermediate points, how cars are to be taken into trains along the line and how cars for various points are to be disposed of; it should also give movements to and from branch and connecting lines and arrangements for advance notice to divisions ahead.

The tonnage of the fast-freight trains should be closely watched to avoid overloading and consequent inability to make the necesssary time.

Schedules should be worked out to arrange for picking up high-class freight along the division and for delivering freight at the intermediate points with the quickest possible dispatch and without requiring stops by the through fast-freight trains.

It is good practice to use a card bill of a distinctive color for cars to be moved on fast-freight trains. Some roads use a red card; others have a red stripe across the face of the card, while others again use an ordinary card with a large red or black cross on its face. This quickly attracts the attention of the yardmaster, conductor or agent, and there is less likelihood of the car going astray or becoming indefinitely side-tracked in some "pocket."

Yardmasters should have advance information of the make-up of an approaching fast-freight train and the number and location of cars to be taken out of the train, to enable prompt handling and to have cars to fill out in readiness.[1] Fast freights should be made up in proper order and all cars added should be placed in their proper positions to avoid delay along the line in switching. Something has already been said about making up trains as far along as "the traffic will bear." This is essential in fast- or expedited-freight service. A new word has been coined to designate the train that passes through switching yards intact—"main trackers."

This class of service has been extensively developed on the Baltimore and Ohio, both as to expedited- and slow-freight service, and a full description of that system may be of interest.[2] The primary object was to reduce switching and yard delays. The result is indicated by the fact that on its eastern lines there were 553,991 cars handled in June, 1921, and 522,113 cars in June, 1920. Cars per engine-hour in June, 1920, were 6.7, and 8.5 in June, 1921, an increase of 27 per cent.

The divisional and through classification comprises an outline in book form giving minute instructions as to the correct make-up of freight trains dispatched from the principal yards on the system. This book is indexed for quick reference to the composition of any train and is divided into two sections, the forward section on tan-colored paper applying only to westward movements, while the back part of this book, which is printed on blue paper, is devoted to eastward freight-train movements. Pages from this book showing the classification symbols as listed and maps of the system showing distances between freight terminals and territories of the district supervisors of terminals are reproduced in Figs. 47 to 54 inclusive.

---

[1] Building up time tables—is covered in Passenger Terminals and Trains, Chap. XVIII, Timetables and Train Schedules and Chap. XX, Accidents and Their Prevention.

[2] Developed by E. T. Horn, General Supervisor of Terminals of Baltimore and Ohio.

The principle on which this classification is based is the movement of trains with a minimum of break-up between origin and destination, such switching as is necessary being concentrated at the point where this can be most economically and effectively performed.   This classification is based on a thorough study of the physical characteristics of the railroad and a careful analysis of yard conditions and costs at all points.   The aim has been to classify trains completely as near their origin as possible so they may be run solid through the succeeding terminals to destination without subsequent break-up.   This is illustrated in the accompanying specimen pages from the classification book showing the proper consist for time

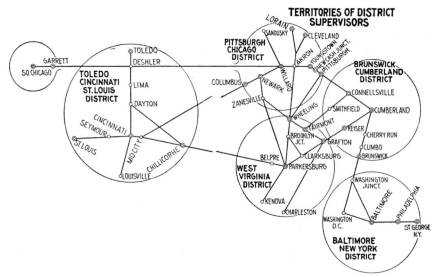

FIG. 47.—Territories of district supervisors—Baltimore & Ohio.

freight, number 94, dispatched from Chicago to Willard and from Willard eastward.   Willard is the concentration terminal for freight eastward from Chicago, the cars being there assembled in trains that run intact to Brunswick.   At Brunswick westward trains are made up solid for Pittsburgh, Chicago, Cincinnati, St. Louis, etc.   Through freight to the principal eastern and western cities is only delayed at one terminal for classification.   The same system applies to slow freights handling the maximum tonnage, the plan being to confine the classification work for each train to as few points as possible.

The benefits are increased car-miles per car-day, decreased locomotive-miles per car-mile, and decreases in per diem, overtime, and yard delays and reduction of thefts, which tend to increase as the time consumed in yards increases.

The success of this and any other unusual undertaking depends on the men employed.   Nowhere is this more necessary than in trans-

CHICAGO TO NEW YORK   FOR ROUTES—JUNCTIONS
.NO. 94   DIVISIONAL POINTS
Refer to SYSTEM DISTANCE CHART
LAST SHEET

CHICAGO TERMINAL
BUNCHING, GROUPING
and DISPATCHMENT

NEW YORK
94

CHICAGO
SOUTH CHICAGO } TO WILLARD

Classifi-
cation
Symbol

X-2   Classify station order for
Indiana Harbor—McCools, } —
and Walkerton

X-4   Bunch for all points East
of Willard—with live stock } —For Garrett to maintain and Willard
on hind end   to classify and dispatch

Note 1: This train enroute between South Chicago and Willard
will pick up regular 94s freight at Indiana Harbor—
McCools—Walkerton—Garrett—Defiance—Deshler and
Fostoria, keeping stock on hind end.

Note 2: Chicago Section handles the Quick Dispatch merchandise.
South Chicago Section handles meat and stock from
U. S. Yards and Wolf Lake Yards.

Note 3: Chicago–New York 94
St. Louis–New York 94 } —Consolidate at Cumberland
Pittsburgh–New York 94

FIG. 48.—Baltimore & Ohio classification of time freight No. 94 Chicago to Willard.

CHICAGO TO NEW YORK   FOR ROUTES—JUNCTIONS
NO. 94   DIVISIONAL POINTS
Refer to SYSTEM DISTANCE CHART
LAST SHEET

WILLARD TERMINAL
CLASSIFICATION
BUNCHING,
GROUPING and
DISPATCHMENT

NEW YORK
1st SECTION 94

WILLARD TO CUMBERLAND

Classifi-
cation
Symbol

X-8	Bunch C. V. R. R. and W. Md. R. R. with Cumberland Division	For New Castle Junction and Connells——ville to maintain and Cumberland to classify and dispatch
X-10	Bunch Brunswick and beyond with i c e r s ahead, stock on hind end	For New Castle Junction–Connellsville —and Cumberland to maintain and Bruns——wick to classify and dispatch

Note 1: When short of regular 94 tonnage, Willard will fill out with expedite loading Symbol X-8–X-10.

Note 2: This train enroute between Willare and Brunswick will pick up at Connellsville 94s regular freight Symbol X-8–X-10.

Note 3: Chicago–New York 94
St. Louis–New York 94   —Consolidate at Cumberland
Pittsburgh–New York 94

FIG. 49.—Baltimore & Ohio classification of time freight No. 94 Willard to Cumberland.

CHICAGO TO NEW YORK   FOR ROUTES—JUNCTIONS
NO. 94   DIVISIONAL POINTS
Refer to SYSTEM DISTANCE CHART
LAST SHEET

CUMBERLAND TERMINAL
CLASSIFICATION
BUNCHING, GROUPING
and DISPATCHMENT

NEW YORK
1st Section 94

CUMBERLAND TO BRUNSWICK

Classifi-
cation
Symbol

X-10   Bunch Brunswick and beyond with } —For Brunswick to classify and
       icers ahead—stock on hind end   dispatch

C. S. D.
94

CUMBERLAND TO CUMBO

X-22   Classify W. Md. R. R.   } —To be backed off enroute

X-24   Classify C. V. R. R.   } —To be backed off enroute

     Note 1: When short of regular 94 tonnage for C. S. D. Section,
             Cumberland may fill out with C. V. R. R. slow freight.

     Note 2: Chicago–New York 94
              St. Louis–New York 94   } —Consolidate at Cumberland
              Pittsburgh–New York 94

     Note 3: C. S. D. 94   } —Connects with all 94s at
                         Cumberland.

FIG. 50.—Baltimore & Ohio classification of time freight No. 94 Cumberland to Brunswick.

CHICAGO–PITTSBURGH–ST. LOUIS
TO
BALTIMORE–PHILADELPHIA
AND NEW YORK
NO. 94

FOR ROUTES—JUNCTIONS
DIVISIONAL POINTS
Refer to SYSTEM DISTANCE CHART
LAST SHEET

BRUNSWICK TERMINAL
CLASSIFICATION
BUNCHING, GROUPING
AND DISPATCHMENT

JERSEY CITY SECTION
ST. GEORGE SECTION   }—NO. 94
PHILADELPHIA SECTION
BALTIMORE SECTION

BRUNSWICK TO CRANFORD JUNCTION

Classifi-
cation
Symbol

BALTIMORE SECTION

X-42   Classify Camden   }—For immediate delivery from Mt. Clare
                                   to Camden by road crews.

X-44   Bunch Mt. Clare and   }—For Mt. Clare to classify and Terminal
        Locust Point Districts   Transfer crews to deliver the Locust
                                     Point District loading

PHILADELPHIA SECTION

X-46   Bunch all freight for Park
        Junction and Philadelphia }—For East Side Yards to classify and
        proper   deliver

JERSEY CITY SECTION

X-48   Bunch entire P. & R. R.
        R.-C. R. R. of N. J. with }—To be handled in accordance with P. &
        locals on head end   R. R. R. instructions

ST. GEORGE SECTION

X-50   Bunch entire St. George
        loading with Staten Island }—To be backed off by road crews at Cran-
        Railroad   ford Junction.

Note 1: East Side Yard will handle Philadelphia Section in
        regular way.

Note 2: The locals on Jersey City Section will be handled in accordance
        with instructions of P. & R. R. R.

Note 3: St. George Section will be backed off at Cranford Jct. and will be
        handled by B. & O. R. R. crews to St. George.

Note 4: Chicago–New York 94
        Pittsburgh–New York 94   }—Consolidate at Cumberland and
        St. Louis–New York 94   Brunswick

FIG. 51.—Baltimore & Ohio classification of time freight No. 94 Brunswick to Baltimore,
Philadelphia and New York.

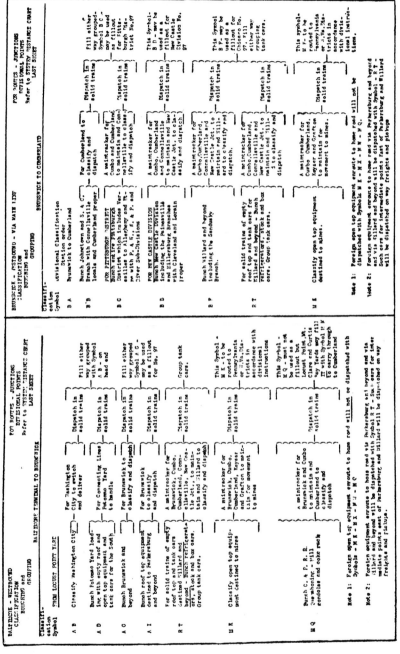

Fig. 52.—Baltimore & Ohio westbound classification at the Baltimore & Brunswick Terminals.

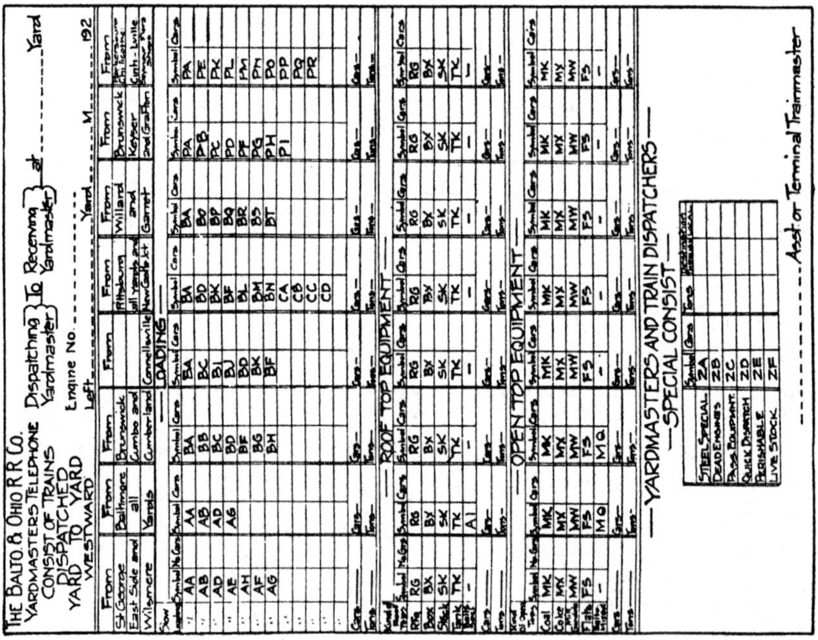

FIG. 53.

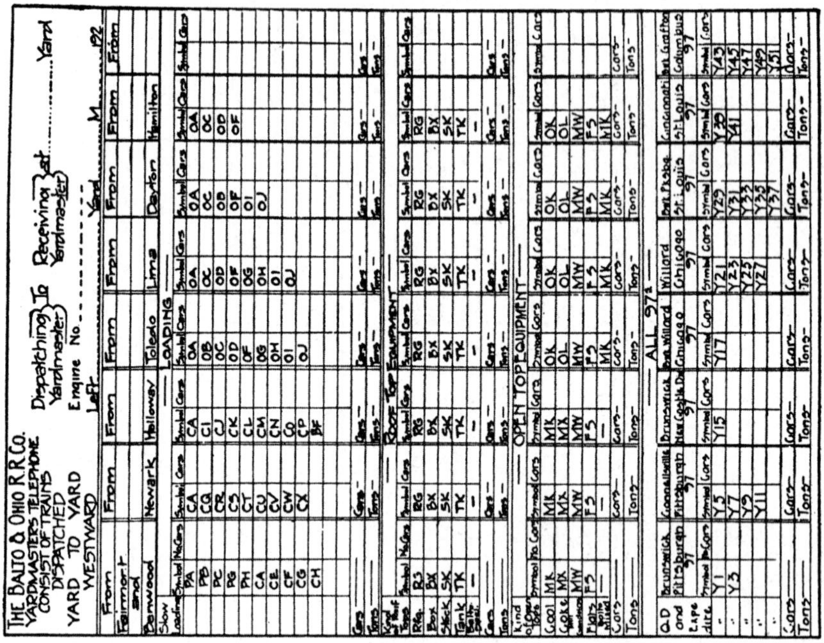

Consist symbol indication employed by the Baltimore & Ohio in classifying westbound freight train movements.

FIG. 54.

portation work. The selection of the right kind of men and the execution of the movement by such men as are selected, without interference by others *is important*.

The runs of through-freight engines were extended to conform to the movement of "main trackers" until now freight locomotives are operating successfully in both directions without change between:

	Miles
New York terminals and Baltimore, Md.	180
Philadelphia, Pa. and Brunswick, Md.	182
Baltimore, Md. and Cumberland, Md.	189
Brunswick, Md. and Connelsville, Pa.	195
Cumberland, Md. and Pittsburgh, Pa.	150
Cumberland, Md. and Parkersburg, W. Va.	205
Parkersburg, W. Va. and Cincinnati, O.	195
Cincinnati, O. and Washington, Ind.	169
Washington, Ind. and East St. Louis, Ill.	165
Cincinnati, O. and Toledo, O.	203
Connellsville, Pa. and Willard, O.	264
Pittsburgh, Pa. and Willard, O.	200
Pittsburgh, Pa. and Fairport, O.	135
Willard, O. and Chicago, Ill.	278

From the reports covering these operations it is possible to supervise closely the movement of "main trackers" and other details involved in the strict observance of divisional and through-classification regulations which have been arranged and from a study of these reports it became evident that certain delays were occurring from time to time to these through trains because of the method of freight-car inspection in vogue. A further study led to the changing of the method of inspection, as a result of which a system was established at originating points and at points en route, conforming to the make-up and routing of "main-tracker" trains in both directions. This system involved the separation of the inspection into what is termed "A" inspection, given at originating and breaking-up points, and "B" inspection, at intermediate points. The A inspection is designed to disclose all defects existing on equipment that can be detected without dissecting the car, while the B inspection is an intermediate passing inspection for safety made at points where the train stands a sufficient length of time, while changing engines or train crews and is for the purpose of detecting such defects as may have developed after the A inspection was made.

When A inspection has been applied and it is impracticable, by reason of lack of men or of material, to make the needed repairs at that point they are side-carded, billed and forwarded to a large car-repair point. To avoid the breaking up of "main trackers" en route, the cars so forwarded are placed in classification order for repair points rather than for final destination.

This system of inspection has been productive of good results.   It has practically eliminated the necessity for cutting cars out of "main trackers" because of defects; has reduced the number of loaded cars waiting repairs; has expedited the repair of freight equipment; permits of greater regularity in, and more economical distribution of, the car-repair forces, inasmuch as the bad-order repairs are now concentrated at originating or breaking-up points; and has made possible a material saving in the cost of inspection, by employing a much smaller force of inspectors than formerly.

CHAPTER XII

TEAM-DELIVERY YARDS

The general location of team yards should be as near to the industrial center of the city as practicable. If there is water competition, a central location is particularly desirable, as an additional team haul of a few city blocks will often be the deciding factor in routing the freight. The competition of other railroads in a smaller degree is more readily met by a central location. Those responsible for securing railroad traffic usually favor the location most convenient to the shippers.

On the other hand, consideration should be given to the higher taxes and interest charges on the more valuable real estate occupied by the central location. The problem is to ascertain whether the central location will bring sufficient additional traffic to justify the higher fixed terminal charges; or, to put it in another way, how much business the road can afford to lose while availing itself of the lower fixed charges of a terminal in a less central and less expensive location. This feature is discussed somewhat in detail in Chap. III.

The location of team yards with reference to the facilities is of more direct interest to those having to do with the operation of the road. Obviously, they should be as convenient to the freight houses as practicable. This arrangement will enable the freight agent's force to supervise the loading and unloading of freight and arrange the car supply more readily, as cars made empty in the team yards and not required for immediate outward loading may readily be transferred to the houses, or *vice versa*. If the team yard is near the freight house, it is satisfactory to the patron, because a teamster taking a load to the freight house may get a return load from the team yard, or, in going to the team yard, return by way of the inbound house.

The contour and track spacing of a team yard depends upon the size of the property available and such property, because ordinarily so close to the city's business center, is rarely adapted to an ideal layout. A number of tracks, each holding 10 to 15 cars, are preferable to fewer tracks of greater length, but property restrictions usually determine which shall be used. The shorter tracks tend to quick handling and permit cars to be placed with the least interference to draymen. A capacity of 12 to 15 cars per track may be considered the maximum economical length. To save space, they may be laid in pairs, similar to repair tracks, and as a matter of safety in working around teams and draymen they should be single-end connected. This plan gives more available track space than where ladders are put in at each end of the yard. An acute angle—as abrupt as 60 deg.—between the ladder tracks and the body (team delivery) tracks may be permitted to increase the length of the team track alongside of which there may be sufficient width of roadway for unloading and loading purposes. Close spacing between each pair of tracks—11 ft. 6 in. or 12 ft., center to center of track—is advisable. For the roadway, a space of as much as 48 ft., center to center of track, giving about 40-ft. clear width for team use, is advantageous. This gives a full width of roadway for teams, when both tracks are filled with cars, and, as the width of the ordinary wagon does not exceed 6 ft., although some motor trucks are more than 8 ft. wide, the space is ample to enable teams to stand backed up to cars in each track with wagon poles turned at right angles to the body of the wagon. With the increasing of motors for trucking, it is found that less roadway is needed than with teams, although the motor trucks are built considerably larger than the drays. Crossing of tracks by drays should be avoided.

To determine the proper width of driveways and to ascertain the effect of the increasing number of motor trucks, actual measurements were taken at Providence, R. I., of trucks and drays as they arrived, during a 24-hr. period, with the result indicating a maximum width of 8 ft. 6 in.; average width, 7 ft. 2 in.; maximum length of 33 ft. 9 in. and average length of 23 ft. 5 in.

In each case the length was measured to cover the space the truck would occupy if standing at right angle to a house or car.

In establishing a width of driveway for team yards, some designers figure on using multiples of the adopted track center. Assuming 12-ft. centers to be used, the width of driveway would, under this method, be made 36 or 48 ft., center to center of track. If a 48-ft. center to center driveway is used and tracks are laid in groups of two paralleling, as is customary, it would be practicable afterward to put in a third track, establishing groups of three—one center or "dead" track not accessible to teams—and still leave a 36-ft. center to center driveway. This system of using groups of three tracks is in effect in yard 17, at Providence (see Fig. 55). Should it be desired for any reason to abandon the yard for team-delivery purposes and use it as a storage or classifying yard, additional tracks—to the extent of two on a 36-ft. center, three on a 48-ft. center—may be laid without disturbing those already in use. This is discussed in Chap. IV.

Track scales should be provided and located where convenient for switching, preferably on the principal lead track to avoid reverse or additional movements in weighing cars going to or coming from the loading and unloading points. Unless all cars are weighed, the scales should be provided with "dead tracks" to avoid the necessity of running

Fig. 55.—Gaspee Street team delivery yard, Providence, R. I.—New York, New Haven & Hartford.

over the scale machinery unnecessarily. This subject is more fully discussed elsewhere.

Wagon scales should be located where teams may readily reach them without obstructing the driveways, and where the greater part of the freight to be weighed on teams is handled, if cars for such freight are separately placed.

Transfer cranes are ordinarily located at the entrance of the yard and at the point most accessible to teams with heavy pieces of freight. A crane operated by power is desirable in large yards. If much bulky or heavy freight is handled, it may be well to have both a heavy-capacity crane and a lighter one. These appliances greatly facilitate the release

Fig. 56.—Typical freight transfer crane.

of cars. A good arrangement is a bridge crane, with a trolley on top, covering one track and the adjacent roadway. The crane may be operated by hand or electric power. The one shown in Fig. 56 is typical of a crane in general use.

The gantry type of crane is arranged not only to transfer a piece of freight from wagon to car or car to wagon but may also move freight from one car or team to another car or team. A typical gantry is shown in Fig. 57, with which the B. & O. unloads 40 cars without making a switch or moving a car.

In its 12th Street yard, Chicago, the B. & O. has a heavy gantry crane. The main hoist has a capacity of 23 tons, the auxiliary, 5 tons. Its motors are operated by 500-volt current. The gantry has a width of 42 ft., center to center of ground rails, and spans a wide team driveway with a track on each side. Twenty-four cars may be covered without moving them.

The type of crane shown in Fig. 58 is built for sturdy work and possesses great flexibility. The one shown in the cut is located at 12th

Fig. 57.—Electric power crane—Baltimore & Ohio.

Street, Chicago—New York Central—and covers four tracks and three driveways, accommodating 25 cars at one placing. It is electrically operated and has a lifting capacity of 25 tons.

Fig. 58.—Electric traveling crane, Chicago—Lake Shore & Michigan Southern.

The Lake Shore also has a gantry at Cleveland, Ohio, with two hoists, one of 30 tons capacity and the other—an auxiliary—of 5 tons. Two side tracks and a driveway are covered. Electric power is used, and thirteen gantry loads have been handled in 20 min. One operator is employed, the hoist being attached to the load by the teamers.

Inclines running from the roadway to the car-floor level at the end of a track are advantageous, especially where heavy machinery on wheels, agricultural harvesters, threshers, mowers, traction engines, fire engines and the like are to be handled. The same result has been obtained by depressing the end of a track so that the floor level of a car on the depressed track will be on a level with the roadway.

Ramps or inclined driveways crossing team yards or tracks should be avoided, but in securing locations near centers of cities, particularly where these yards are contiguous to streets where grade crossings have been abolished, ramps become unavoidable. Grades on driveways exceeding 2.5 to 3.5 per cent. should not be used. Where turns are necessary, they should be made level if possible, or, at most, not to exceed 2 per cent. By building the yard on a grade of from 0.5 to 1.0 per cent., ramps can sometimes be avoided or decreased in length. The grade of tracks in a team yard should not exceed 1.0 per cent., and even this grade may be deemed excessive because of the opportunity for accident, through rough switching.

Bumping posts are expensive to install and maintain. Where the failure to stop a car at the end of the track is not liable to result in serious consequences, a piece of timber or a mound of dirt may serve the purpose. Occasionally, these are objected to because their appearance does not conform to surroundings. Where the ends of tracks abut on streets or sidewalks with considerable travel, or where they end close to buildings which might be seriously damaged, the risk of such damage and personal injury to pedestrians and others justifies the installation of some approved type of bumping or buffer post.

The roadway should be well paved and ample drainage provided to permit and encourage unloading during wet and stormy weather. This is particularly desirable under the demurrage rules, which do not permit the assessment of demurrage during inclement weather. It is advisable to plank or pave the tracks or the ladder if the yard is so located as to make it necessary to drive across the tracks.

The kind of paving to be used depends upon the character of the principal commodities handled and the character of the subsoil and is based on the average weight of the truck with its load. Stone flagging will cost about 50 cts. a square foot; asphalt 2 in. thick 17 cts. a sq. ft., if on a 6 in. concrete base 23 cts. additional; stone paving of Belgian blocks without grouting or concrete base about 55 cts. a square foot. A good gravel with a heavy top dressing of crushed trap rock makes a good driveway, much cheaper and equally durable where the traffic is not heavy. The average two-horse truck is supposed to be able to haul, on a level on good roads, a load of 9,500 lb., including the weight of the wagon. One of the New York ferry companies weighed about 200 trucks some time ago, and found the average weight 16,000—and at times as high as 20,000 lb. gross each. It is difficult to keep driveways in good shape under such loads unless the pavement is well drained and has a good foundation.

Typical team-delivery yards in actual use are always interesting, and it is noteworthy that extensive ones recently constructed show no material change from existing ones. This is due more to the necessity for conforming to physical and property limitations than the usual acquirement of knowledge as to the needs. A good freight-delivery yard getting the most out of a very valuable piece of property is that of the Lehigh Valley at West 27th Street, New York, shown in Fig. 59.

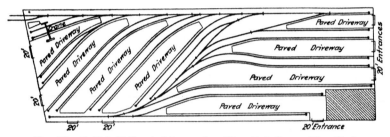

Fɪɢ. 59.—Lehigh Valley freight yard at West 27th Street, New York.

Figure 55 shows the team-delivery yard of the New Haven at Gaspee Street, Providence, R. I., which has a capacity of 675 cars, of which 458 can be placed accessible to teams and the remaining 217 on so-called "center" or dead tracks. The yard occupies 21.8 acres of land and consists of 26 tracks ranging in length from 400 to 1,600 ft. In some cases groups of three tracks parallel are laid instead of two. The center track is then not accessible to teams, but cars thereon may be unloaded through the doors of cars on outside tracks. Ordinarily, these "center" tracks are used to hold empties, to be placed for loading or on which to make up drafts of cars to go out—loaded cars or empties which were unloaded. In the Gaspee Street yard, driveways are 48 ft. wide, center to center, and tracks are laid to 12-ft. centers.

In the sketch of a yard by F. H. McGuigan (Fig. 60), presented to the American Railway Engineering Association, a car may be put on or taken from one point or any track without disturbing any considerable number of teams loading or unloading cars on the same track. The yard also utilizes a short, square piece of ground available for only two or three short, parallel tracks.

The St. Louis Terminal Association has team tracks at 13 places, with room for 1,123 cars, and anticipates immediate need for double this

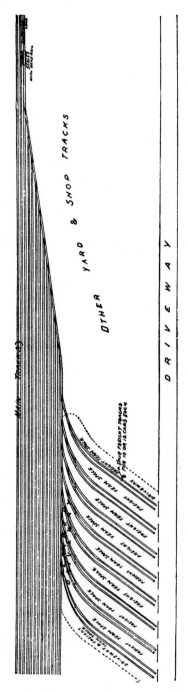

Fig. 60.—Plan of team yard suggested by Mr. F. H. McGuigan.

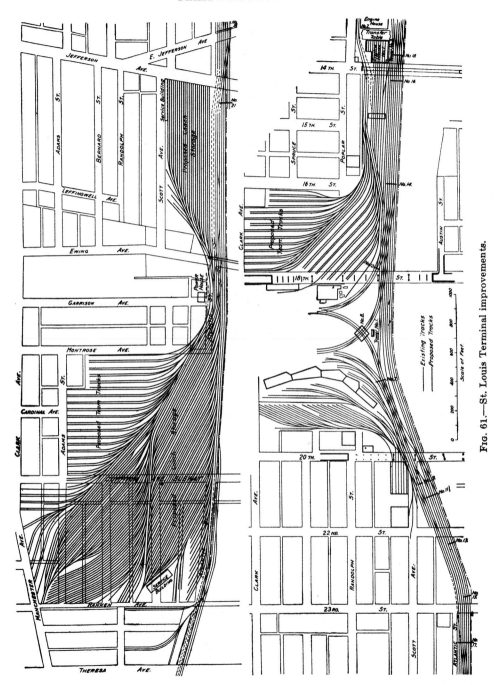

Fig. 61.—St. Louis Terminal improvements.

Fig. 62.—Perishable freight delivery yard, Providence, R. I.—New York, New Haven & Hartford.

capacity. An acre of land will enable placing 25 cars for team delivery. Estimating the cost of the land at $200,000, with interest at 6 per cent., and the prevailing rate of taxes on one-half the cost of the land, the charge on each car for land interest and taxes would be $5.40, assuming that the car occupied the track three days, not counting Sundays and holidays. The plan shown in Fig. 61 shows the proposed team yards of the Association in St. Louis.

Figure 62 shows the New Haven's Stillman Street yard at Providence, R. I., with a capacity of 440 cars, of which, 311 can be placed accessible to trains. A large power crane may be seen on the left. This yard is used for handling fruits, meats, vegetables and other perishable freight. Driveways are 43 ft., center to center; tracks are spaced to 12-ft. centers. Ten acres of land are covered; there are 33 tracks, in groups of three parallel, each being from 400 to 600 ft. long.

The American Railway Engineering Association advocates team tracks located convenient to freight houses, to enable the freight agent's force to control the work; stub-end track construction arranged in pairs spaced 12-ft. centers, and, if permissible, the pairs spaced not less than 52 ft., center to center of pairs—30 ft. in clear—capacity of tracks not to exceed 20 cars each, for convenience in handling; if necessary, crane for heavy freight; ingress and egress for teams at each end of each teamway, if possible; and wagon scales conveniently located near entrance to driveway.

The team- or bulk-delivery car is becoming increasingly important. Like the industrial or private-siding car, it is virtually beyond the railroad's control while in the process of being unloaded or loaded. The seriousness of this fact is, as already pointed out, that this period of non-control amounts to considerably more than half the car's existence. It is essential, therefore, that the team-delivery yards be conveniently and suitably located; that they be well arranged, to encourage prompt loading and unloading, and that the service of placing cars for the shipper and of promptly moving them out when released be as nearly perfect as may be. Unless this is done, the moral effect on the shipper is lost. It is difficult to make him see that the failure to move the car promptly is in itself the railroad's penalty. The usual attitude is to take it for granted that if the railroad is slow in its work the shipper can consistently be correspondingly slow. The situation is rendered difficult because the terminals having much of this kind of business are usually those to feel the first and most severe pinch of congestion in freight movement.

CHAPTER XIII

LIVE-STOCK HANDLING

In 1827, there passed through a turnpike gate on the Cumberland River 105,517 hogs on the way to the South Atlantic states. During the five years 1847–1852, one man drove 13,000 sheep from Vermont to Virginia. In 1884, about 416,000 head of cattle were driven from the Southeast to northern ranges. With the opening of the railways, the driving was reduced and the time in transit reduced to days instead of months. One of the first rail cattle shipments, consisting of 100 head, from Cincinnati to New York, occurred in 1852, having first been driven

Fig. 63.—Cattle pens at Kansas City stockyards.

from Lexington. They were carried in cars from Cincinnati to Cleveland, thence by steam boat to Buffalo; then driven to Canandaigua; moved in cars to Albany; and from there taken by boat to New York. The freight charge was $120 per car, Cincinnati to Buffalo; the total expense, Lexington to New York, $14 per head.

From this small beginning the handling of live stock by rail has increased until there are now received at the ten foremost markets in the country some 38,000,000 cattle, 49,000,000 hogs and 30,000,000 sheep each year. The Union Stock Yards, Chicago, cover 500 acres and have 13,000 enclosures; they will hold 75,000 cattle, 125,000 sheep, 300,000 hogs and 6,000 horses at one time. There are facilities for unloading 60 cars per hour.

The cattle pens at Kansas City stock yards are shown in Fig. 63. Kansas City is the second largest livestock and meat packing center in the country. More than seven million head of livestock were handled at the stock yards in a single year. At Chicago, the largest, some fifteen million head are handled annually.

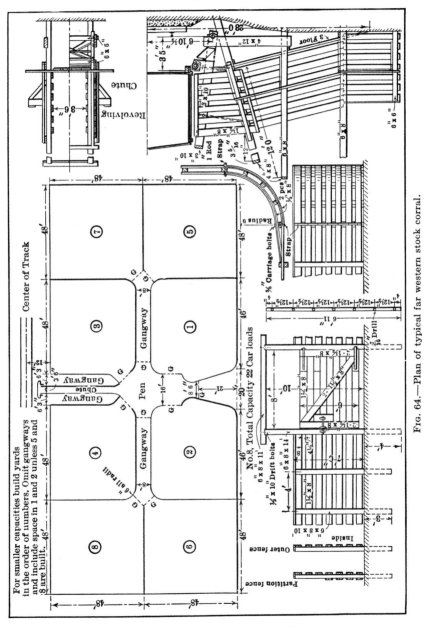

Fig. 64.—Plan of typical far western stock corral.

With the increasing use of refrigerated dressed meats, the movement of live stock to other points than packing house centers tends to decrease.

Between southern Idaho and Omaha, cattle have ordinarily to be let out of cars three or four times, to be fed and rested; while in shorter trips such as between Omaha and Chicago, or between Chicago and Boston or New York, once is usually enough.

About 25 head of cattle are loaded into a car; 75 hogs into a single-deck and 240 sheep into a double-deck car. Cattle weigh 950 to 975 lb. each.

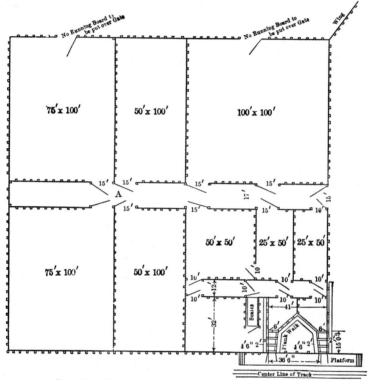

Fig. 65.—Plan of stock pen, chute, platform and scales.

Intelligent location and construction of terminal and way pens will enable much time to be saved in the handling of live stock. Stock may have been in transit approaching the 28- or the 36-hour limit and it becomes necessary to reach unloading pens quickly. The location should be convenient to the receiving yard and at a point where cars may be run in with a minimum of interference. Proximity to the source of feed and water supplies is also essential.

Where the business runs heavy, tracks fronting the yards, long enough to hold an average train without cutting it in two, are preferable, as it is objectionable to couple or uncouple cars in stock trains, because of the added liability for injury to stock. For smaller business, fewer pens would be provided and correspondingly shorter unloading tracks. The unloading platforms run alongside the track, with fences on the track side containing gates and runways to the pen side, with adjustable chutes to reach the upper decks of double-deck cars. Swinging gates are ordinarily arranged to be thrown across the long unloading platform, acting as movable runways from the pens to the car, or *vice versa*. A system of continuous gates alongside the cars, to enable an opening to be made opposite any car door, is desirable and usually planned in all larger layouts. This makes it unnecessary to "spot" cars and avoids coupling and recoupling for that purpose.

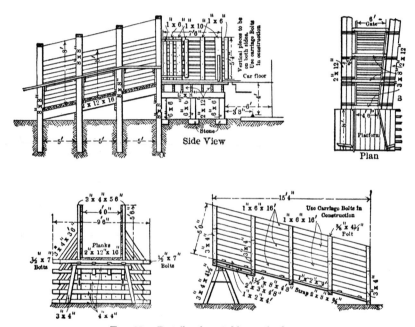

Fig. 66.—Details of portable stock chute.

The plan shown in Fig. 64 is that of a typical far western stock "corral" illustrating the general layout and some details of construction. This "corral" is arranged for any number of pens and readily permits additional pens to be attached.

The drawing in Fig. 65 is of a stock yard 200 by 225 ft., nine pens, two alleys, two chutes, with platform and stock scales. In Fig. 66 a portable chute and a chute with a swinging gate to match with car doors and platform are shown with full detail of typical dimensions.

The railways pay from 50 cts. to $1 per car for loading live stock, and a similar amount for cleaning cars. During hot weather they have to arrange for spraying with cold water at different points, entailing another expense of perhaps 25 cts. per car. An attendant is carried free with each two car loads and is returned free. One stock-carrying road estimates its damage claims at an average of $1.61 on each car handled. This road puts the average cost for construction of stock pens for loading at $1,422 each—and, when paved, $1,000 additional.

The federal law relating to feeding, watering and resting cattle, approved June 29, 1906, provides that:

Cattle, sheep, swine or other animals shall not be confined in cars, boats or vessels of any description for a period longer than 28 consecutive hours without unloading the same in a humane manner into properly equipped pens for rest, water and feeding, for a period of at least 5 consecutive hours, unless prevented by storm or by other accidental or unavoidable causes which cannot be anticipated or avoided by the exercise of due diligence and foresight; provided, that upon the written request of the owner or person in custody of that particular shipment, which written request shall be separate and apart from any bill of lading, or other railroad form, the time of confinement may be extended to 36 hours.

It also stipulates that the time consumed in loading and unloading shall not be considered in estimating the confinement and it does not require the unloading of sheep during the night; and when the time expires during the night, in case of sheep, they may be continued in transit to a suitable place for unloading, subject to the limitation of 36 hours. Animals so unloaded shall be properly fed and watered during such rest either by the owner or person having custody thereof; and in case of his default, by the transportation company at the owner's expense. "When animals are carried in cars, boats or other vessels in which they can and do have proper food, water, space and opportunity to rest, the provisions in regard to their being unloaded shall not apply." The penalty is $100 to $500 "for every such failure"—which is interpreted to apply to "each carload" rather than to each train load or each separate shipment.

Hogs are liable to suffer during warm weather and should be sprayed ("slushed") with cold water on the appearance of the first warm weather, and troughs should be kept filled. Shippers usually ask that hogs be sprayed as soon as the train stops and that the train be kept moving when practicable. They should never be sprayed after they have been allowed to stand in the hot sun for any length of time and have become heated, as water sprayed on heads of hogs under such conditions is liable to kill them. Neither should they be sprayed during the night, as this abruptly awakens them from a quiet sleep and is detrimental.

No class of freight handled by railways is more susceptible to heavy losses, real or imposed, than live stock. It is a debatable question whether the profits thereon justify the movement at the rates in effect. The so-called professional stock trader usually accompanies the shipment and carefully notes every case of air-brake application; and, if the market is not all to his liking, he makes his claims against the transportation company for loss in value. Reparation is then asked on grounds of rough handling, detentions and other alleged irregularities to compensate the owner for loss or shrinkage due to bad condition of stock, diseases or improper or insufficient food.

Special yards must be provided; high-speed trains run, with their accompaniment of low train load and interference to other traffic; specially constructed cars, which can be used for but little beside stock, consequently running empty in one direction; special facilities for loading and unloading; and preferred handling in yards. The various agents of the Society for the Prevention of Cruelty to Animals are usually well meaning

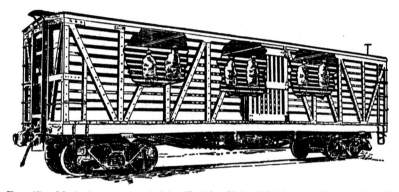

Fig. 67.—Method, recommended by Freight Claim Division, of the American Railway Association, of suspending six bags of ice to prevent hogs becoming overheated in transit in hot weather.

and sincere, but in many instances, actuated by political motives or moved by heart-rending stories of disgruntled railway employees or live-stock attendants, entail unnecessary cost and actual injustice on the railways.

The Freight Claim division of the American Railway Association suggests suspending from the car ceiling, as shown in Fig. 67, six burlap bags, each containing 50 to 75 lb. of ice, to keep hogs from becoming overheated when in transit in hot weather. This quantity of ice will keep the air of a car cool during an ordinary trip. The swaying motion of the bags causes the drip from the melted ice to be distributed throughout the car and keeps the floor damp and cool. In cars not so equipped, records show the loss of about one hog to every four cars, while in cars provided with ice bags, 184 shipments during summer of 1920 lost 12 hogs, or one to every 11 cars; during 1921 but 66 hogs died in 1,127 cars—one to every 17 cars.

The instructions require hogs to be brought to the shipping station in ample time to permit them to become rested and cooled off before being loaded; cars to be cleaned, preferably bedded with sand and the bedding and interior of car to be wetted down before being loaded. A light grain feeding should be given before loading as heavy feed generates more body heat; no corn should be placed in cars. Loading should be done slowing and carefully, to avoid excitement, and without beating or bruising of animals, and entirely completed at least one hour before train departing time. Good judgment will tell when a car is loaded safely and it must not be overloaded.

The Western Weighing and Inspection Bureau, in one pear handled 949,556 cars of live stock received, forwarded 205,715 cars and passed upon 154,293 dead and crippled animals. There were 18,745 dead animals received, a loss of approximately $560,000, at the then market prices. The death loss is greater with hogs than with other live stock and much of this loss can be avoided if shipments are properly handled, especially at the time of and immediately before loading them into the cars.

The great loss in live stock can be traced to two causes, disease and injury. More than half of the losses involved while the animals are in the carriers' hands are due to the character and condition of hogs at the time of loading, since a checking of cars in the same train shows that some hogs hauled a much greater distance than others arrive without loss when proper treatment is afforded before loading, while other cars traveling a shorter distance arrive with heavy loss, due to mistreatment prior to shipment. This is due to feeders often placing their hogs in small enclosures for a period prior to shipment to markets, and feeding them with fattening foods, of which corn in some form is the most common.

If the weather is hot and sultry when hogs are moved to the loading chutes for shipment, the animals inhale and exhale very rapidly because of the necessity for getting oxygen into the air cells of the lungs to purify the blood. In this condition they are placed in the stock pens, where the breeze is shut off, or they are crowded into a stock car, where the close contact of heated bodies gives them no chance to cool. The heart is exhausted from its exertion, and the lungs, being the only organs through which the surplus heat of the body can be removed, are engorged with blood, and death from suffocation is the result.

Hot and tired animals are especially susceptible to diseases of any kind. It is the history of swine plague that animals so attacked will seldom develop fatal cases unless their vitality is weakened, or their resisting power lessened, by some predisposing cause or some other disease. Since this is the case, the animals in a congested and weakened condition are excellent subjects for bacillus to work on and fatal cases of swine plague may develop in a few hours, with the result that hogs will frequently develop this disease and die before they reach market, while a portion of the herd left at home will not be affected.

Hogs should never be loaded into cars when hot or panting. The carrier is often at fault in furnishing an inadequate supply of water at the loading pens of the average country station. Especially is this true of non-agency stations, at most of which the water supply comes from a pump, and according to shippers' reports these pumps are always in a questionable state of repair, and the pail which should be there is missing. At stations where the water supply is drawn from a supply tank or from the city pressure, a pipe connected with this, and so placed on or near the loading dock that water from it could be thrown directly into the car, would make it so accessible that a shipper would use it. If the train is late, the water may be easily sprayed on the floor of the car under the hogs, and in this way they will not be allowed to get hot.

If the hogs are not overheated when picked up for shipment, they will not suffer severely during any ordinary summer weather while the train is in motion. When a division or terminal point is reached, the hogs should immediately be drenched with cold water, because they are in a cool condition from riding, and the cold water applied to their heads and back will not likely injure them. However, the practice of drenching hogs with cold water after allowing the load to stand until they are ready for the road and are hot is very bad, as many hogs are instantly killed by having cold water sprayed over them while hot. When it becomes necessary to cool off hot hogs, the water should be allowed to run on the floor of the car so they will have a cool place to lay; it should never be applied to the heads and backs of hot hogs.

Cars should always be cleaned before stock is placed in them; especially for hog shipments in spring and summer, as a heavy collection of straw and manure left in the car will develop heat which, with the gases that arise, will cause the hogs to become restless and nervous and undo all other good care that may have been given them. Sand makes the best floor covering for all shipments of live stock during the summer months. In winter the cars may be matted with straw, but too much should never be used, as it is likely to heat when it becomes damp.

The minimum of 17,000 lb. that is applied to a 36-ft. car seems to be taken by a great many shippers to mean that a car will transport that many pounds of hogs regardless of their size, while in reality the smallest hogs that can be loaded to this minimum are those averaging 240 to 250 pounds. Overloading causes great losses.

It is especially necessary when cattle are moved in mixed shipments that they be always partitioned or tied, as, owing to their unusual viciousness, they are almost sure to cause a great amount of damage unless so protected.

Improperly fastened doors cause injuries and deaths to cattle. Shipments should not be accepted with doors wired; wires will slip enough to let a foot through and a broken leg is the result. Shippers should not be allowed to build a double deck in the car, as in one instance one of these broke down and 16 head of sheep, 4 head of cattle and 3 hogs were found dead in the car, while in another case a hay rack broke loose from its fastenings, causing serious injuries to the live stock in the car.

A pneumatic apparatus which shortens the time of feeding a carload of hogs is in use on the Chicago, Milwaukee and St. Paul and is shown in Fig. 68.

A car carrying a supply of corn with which the hogs are to be fed is pushed along a track adjacent to a standing stock train, and compressed air, for blowing the grain into the hog cars, is conveyed from a locomotive through the hose shown at the extreme right in the picture. The larger hose, with a flat nozzle which can be pushed between the slats of a stock car, is held by a man standing on a removable shelf or platform attached to the doorway of the grain car. The hopper, from which the grain falls to the large hose by gravity, is placed in the center of the grain car and is filled, by shovelers inside the car. Admission of air pressure is regulated by a valve beneath the hopper.

The feed is scattered uniformly through the car of hogs, giving each animal the needed supply—a task which, with double-deck cars, is neither pleasant nor expeditious when done by hand.

The hopper serves as a measure, and effects a decided saving in the amount of feed used. The grain car, pushed slowly along, is stopped, when at the right place, not by motioning or shouting to the engineman, but by starting the grain blower, which exhausts enough air from the train pipe to stop the locomotive—and the car.

Fig. 68.—Hog feeder used on the Chicago, Milwaukee & St. Paul.

This feeder has also been found useful for transfering a load of grain from a defective car, consuming about one hour. A train load of hogs is fed in about one-third of the time required under ordinary methods and the stock-car doors are not opened at all.[1]

At times, too, great stress is laid on high speed and heavy train tonnage in the transportation of live stock, without weighing with sufficient care, the loss resulting through claims for injury. Fast, heavy freight trains are incompatible with smooth handling. Trains of live stock should be made up solid—that is, wholly of live stock—when practicable, and only sufficient tonnage to enable the engine to maintain a nearly average schedule speed on ascending grade sections to permit of an approximately uniform speed. The train dispatcher should endeavor to keep this train on the main track, avoiding stops and arranging for such stops as must be made, at points where the train may be comfortably started, and without taking the slack. More than ordinary care should be given air brakes on stock cars, to keep triple valves particularly

[1] *Railway Age,* July 11, 1919, Nov. 25, 1922.

well cleaned and oiled, to prevent so-called "kickers" from throwing the brakes into emergency when not intended and to keep piston travel of brake cylinders adjusted, so each car will do its part, and only its part, in retarding the movement of the train. When it is necessary to fill out a train of live stock with other freight, such freight should be put in the rear, to reduce the liability of shock in brake applications when stopping. Engines and enginemen should be selected for this service to give the smoothest possible handling consistent with speed requirements. It has seemed to the author that the speed question is frequently overdone in live-stock handling, and that is perhaps due more to overzealousness of the traffic departments in securing a "talking point" than to any actual necessity for fast service. A train load of live stock has been rushed from Chicago or Buffalo to tidewater at breakneck speed and then has remained in stock yards for a week or 10 days awaiting space in a steamer for export.

Much can be done to protect live stock in transit and add to its comfort by intelligent loading and caring for it afterward. Horses need room, and can balance themselves fairly well on a moving train or a boat. Preferably, they should be handled in specially arranged cars with stalls, as is invariably done with race horses and frequently with horses of smaller value. Cattle are jolted backward and forward and travel more comfortably if packed reasonably close in cars and on boats, as they then support one another. It is nothing short of cruelty to put hogs in the same car with cows. This was formerly a common practice, but is seldom done nowadays. The hogs will bite and otherwise constantly annoy the cows.

The provision of an adequate supply of water at stock yards and the maintenance of this supply under all conditions is as essential to the operation of railroads as the furnishing of cars for transporting live stock.

The water is usually taken from existing mains supplying other facilities. At the smaller yards a driven or dug well will furnish an adequate supply. Where water is close to the surface, a $1\frac{1}{4}$-in. pipe with a drive point and a 3- by 10-in. cylinder with a hand pump will answer. Where these cannot be used, a 2- or 3-in. tubular well is used with a windmill or other power for pumping.

Because the need of water at stock yards is intermittent, the use of gas or oil engines for pumping is not practicable except at large feeding-in-transit yards, and at these water can usually be secured from city mains or railway pumping plant.

Storage tanks vary in size from 1,000-gal. capacity up, according to the needs of the yards. At the smaller yards, where it is not necessary to protect the water supply from freezing, galvanized iron tanks of 1,000- to 2,000-gal. capacity are preferable, because they can be drained in the fall.

Pipe lines should be of a size consistent with the need of the yard, ranging from 1-in. for small yards to 6-in. for large feeding yards. However, 1¼- to 2-in. mains will be sufficient for the average yard with branch lines to hydrants of corresponding size. Wherever practicable, water mains should be located outside the yards.

While watering troughs are constructed of galvanized iron, wood and concrete, and are of various lengths and sizes, wood is most commonly used. For stock, these are made 16 ft. long with flaring sides 10 in. deep, being 10 in. wide inside at the bottom and 12 in. wide at the top with one ⅜-in. bolt at each end and two struts at the center. While these troughs are of low first cost, they are not always satisfactory, because when not used they dry out and leak.

Troughs for hogs are constructed of 2- by 10-in. by 16-ft. and of 2- by 12-in. by 16-ft. plank spiked together V-shaped with ends and three struts between. These troughs are favored in many places, as freezing does not damage them to any great extent and, unless decayed, cracks can easily be repaired with a little thick paint and battens. Metal troughs are from 12 ft. to 16 ft. long and 20 in. wide at the top with half-circle bottom. Concrete watering troughs are used with success by many railroads, even in the colder climates. Showers should be located at all stock-yard chutes for wetting down cars for hogs before loading, as previously explained. They are also provided by many railroads at roadside tanks or water penstocks. For use at stock chutes, a 1-in. hydrant with hose connection is suitable. Showers for wetting down hogs in transit are usually located at or near water stations, are constructed of 2- or 3-in. pipe and are provided for both double- and single-deck cars. A gate valve is provided in the main to control the flow of water. For single-deck showers the riser pipe extends about 6 ft. above the rail, where a spray nozzle is attached with elbow and tee with loose joint and handle on the side opposite the nozzle. A rope is attached to the end of the handle for convenience in pulling up the nozzle. The nozzle is constructed by flattening out the end of the pipe to leave a ⅜-in. opening. Stock in cars can be wet down thoroughly with this type of shower while moving by slowly.

CHAPTER XIV

WEIGHING FREIGHT

In theory, every pound of freight transported should be accurately weighed, and this condition is being rapidly approached. The object is to insure the receipt of the revenue to which the road is entitled and to protect the shipper against overcharge.

Car-load freight is occasionally weighed by passing each team load to or from the car over wagon scales, but, ordinarily, the car with its load is weighed on the track scales most convenienty located for that purpose. The tare weight (that is the weight of the car itself, as stenciled on the side of the body) is subtracted from the gross weight to obtain the net weight. Many shippers insist on having cars weighed light as well as loaded, objecting to the use of the stenciled weight. For this service a small charge is made. Coal and a few other coarse commodities use the long ton—2,240 lb.—which complicates the calculation. Many anthracite-coal roads show the car weight in long tons and hundredweight, to aid the weigher in determining the net weight. The general practice is to have some definite rule whereby each loaded car is to be weighed on a certain scale in the direction of its movement, and the card bill on which car travels also indicates the point where the car shall be weighed. It is the usual practice to require car-load freight to be weighed at originating point, if there are track scales. If there are none, then the freight is weighed at destination. If there are no scales at either the originating or the terminating point, the car is weighed on the first track scale passed en route. Light and bulky commodities, billed at a minimum weight under the tariff (where it is usually impossible to secure the weight by reason of limitations of car volume), are not usually weighed, neither is freight that is transported by measurement, estimated weight, rate per car, cord or thousand.

When shippers request weighing of loaded or empty cars for reasons of their own, no charge is usually made where the cars move over private scales when being placed for delivery or when taken from sidings. Where an extra move has to be made, it is customary to collect at the rate of $1.35 per car for general merchandise, if weighed on company scales; and 63 cts. if on privately owned scales; and cars containing coal, on either company or private scales, 1½ ct. per ton. Occasionally, the rules provide that for coal, if the scale weight varies not to exceed 1,000 lb. from the weight shown on the waybills, or stenciled weight, no charge is made for the discrepancy. On coarse freight, such as sand, clay or kaolin, discharged from vessels to cars, the usual charge is 1 ct. per gross ton for weighing on railroad scales. For general merchandise, the charge is generally 3 cts. per ton. The rate for weighing empty cars is generally $1.35 per car, except on private scales where no additional switching is necessary.

Package freight, or l.c.l. freight, also commonly termed "house-freight," should be weighed at the point where it is received by the railroad from the shipper, in order to have the lowest freight charges entered on billing and to enable quick delivery to be made when it reaches final destination. An exception is sometimes made on freight that is handled in standard packages, such as flour in barrels, each weghing 196 lb., where a count of the barrels is sufficient.

The railroad is interested in track scales for weighing car-load shipments; house or platform scales for l.c.l. freight; team or wagon scales, usually for the accommodation of its customers; and special types of scales, such as large-frame beam scales for weighing cotton, and permanently arranged scales for weighing coal or sand in pockets for supplying locomotive tenders.

Scales for weighing l.c.l. freight should be located along the side of the freight-house interior, where delivery is made from teams. They should be provided at frequent intervals—about 50 to 100 ft. apart—with the beams parallel with and adjacent to the side walls, to reduce chance of interference to trucking. They should be far enough away from the walls to permit storing freight against the walls.

Platform or freight-house scales—movable or stationary—are made in almost any size or style desired. The manufacturers make types suitable for special purposes. Some excellent multiweighing scales were planned by the operating officers of the Merchants' and Miners' Transportation Company and installed in its Baltimore piers. With a number of beams and several weights on each beam, running up weights progressively, 16 articles may be placed on a scale and each weighed separately, without removing any of them. This is a great advantage at that and similar points, because frequently a number of consignments will be taken from teams before a trucker gets around, and rehandling is thereby avoided.

Another company has something similar to the Merchants' and Miners' scales, in a platform scale with a self-locking poise beam on which different commodities may be weighed and kept separate; for instance, cotton may be weighed on the upper bar, sugar on the second bar, salt on the next and so on.

A type-registering beam scale is furnished, with which the operator, at the end of each day, is enabled to have a certain number of checks showing the number of loads that have passed over the scale. The recapitulation of these slips gives the total weight of the loads for the day.

The slip is placed in the type-registering device and, when the bar is secured, it is clamped together and the weight is imprinted on the slip.

Team or wagon scales are ordinarily best located at the entrance to the team yard, where they will not obstruct the movement of teams going to or from the yards with no freight to be weighed. They should be located in that part of the yard where commodities which are ordinarily weighed on teams are generally handled.

Track scales for freight service range in capacity from 100 to 150 tons, with a platform length of 36 to 60 ft. On longer scales cars may be weighed without stopping, as they move by gravity. The long scales (80 to 100 ft.) are not found reliable because of their great length, and are not being used except in extraordinary cases.

The location of track scales has been fully considered in other chapters. There is much variance of opinion among operating and constructing officers as to the proportionate number of cars to be weighed to cause scales to be located just beyond the hump of a classification yard rather than on the hump. Views expressed place the proportion anywhere from 5 to 25 per cent. of the total number passing through the yard. The American Railway Engineering Association assumes "that the greatest economy would be secured by locating the scale on the hump, if it is assured that from 5 to 10 per cent. of the cars must be weighed." Mr. North, when Engineer of Construction of the Lake Shore & Michigan Southern, now part of the New York Central Lines said:

There is no possible scheme of grades for a hump where a scale is placed within the hump limit, which will enable traffic to be handled within 50 per cent. of the speed that can be secured at the same point if the scale is not placed on the hump.

The Association's committee differed with Mr. North and cited instances where 300 cars an hour had been classified and weighed over a hump and scale, for a limited time. It was suggested that scales of higher capacity than ordinarily required be used, with correspondingly greater length of bearings. This plan would enable operation without the usual dead track; and, by placing the scale very close to the hump's summit, the retardation due to scales would be greatly reduced. This can only be done to advantage where a large proportion of cars passing over hump have to be weighed, and it would be necessary to keep a stock of spare scale parts on hand to replace parts with worn bearings as often as required. Cars not to be weighed, in running rapidly over scales, wear the knife edges, and when these become dull the friction is increased, requiring more weight to overcome the inertia of the parts. The accuracy of scale weights depends largely upon the sharpness of the bearings.

The Pennsylvania standard track scale is 52 ft. long and of 300,000-lb. capacity. Some of the original and unique features are: suspension bearings supporting the platform, mechanical relieving gear, which eliminates the dead rail, and a mechanical hump, which provides the proper control of the movement of cars over the scale.

The B. & O. standard track scale (shown in Figs. 69, 70, 71, 72, 73, and 74) is 50 ft. long, of 300,000-lb. capacity, "pit-suspension-bearing" and consists of four sections.

The bridge is made up of two 24-in. 80-lb. I-beams under each scale rail to provide rigidity and better to distribute load over the bearings. The ties crossing I-beams provide a cushion and protection to the scale and serve to brace it. The grade on hump scales is made with them and adjusted to 0.75 per cent. grade.

The scale parts are 54 ft. long, while the scale rails are but 50 ft., causing the load to be applied to the scale inside of the first bearing, distributing a part of

Fig. 69.—Standard track scale—Baltimore & Ohio.

the load to the second bearing and preventing a reflex action of the bridge. Further to relieve impact on the scale, a buffer or transfer rail, made of manganese steel, is used to transfer the load from the approach to the scale rail. This is bolted to the approach rail and the box beams, and carries the outside tread of the car wheel. The buffer is in no way connected with the scale. Ample clearance is provided by cutting it out underneath and planing off the outside head of the scale rail. All levers and other parts are designed to carry a load of 75,000 lb. per section—allowing for dead weight, and 100 per cent. for impact. The main and the fifth levers, the cross-bars and the rocker are made of cast steel; other levers of cast iron. Locomotives may pass over scales of such capacity without damaging them. When a lever is deflected, its two arms are liable to have different relative positions under different loads, and this condition interferes with its proper adjustment, making the scale inaccurate; it is, therefore, aimed to keep the deflections of the levers at a minimum. The stands are rigidly supported by concrete foundations, and the load is supported at eight points on the middle pivots—commonly called the knife edges—of the main levers.

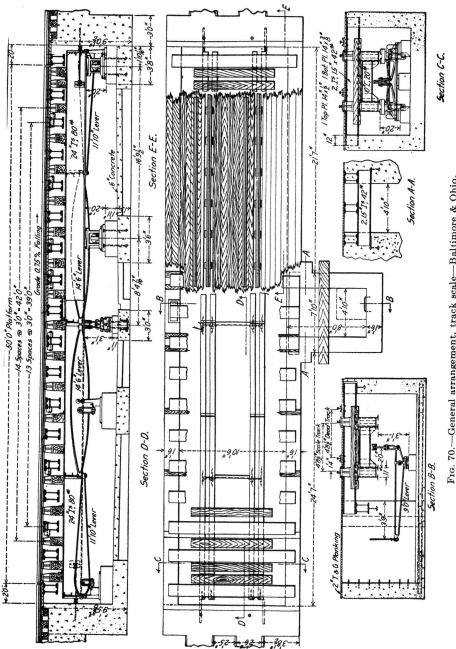

Fig. 70.—General arrangement, track scale—Baltimore & Ohio.

From these the load is transmitted and reduced through the extension, fifth and shelf levers, to the beam, at which point a force of 1 lb. balances a weight of 800 lb. on the scale.

The construction of the suspension bearing is shown in detail (Fig. 73) and, as shown in the section *CC* of the general arrangement of the scale (Fig. 70), the load is transmitted from the rail through the scale stands, the ties, I-beams, or bridge, to the bearing yoke and then to the cross-bar and rocker. The rocker is suspended by two 1.5-in. links hung from a bearing block, which rests in the knife edge of the main lever. The arc of suspension from the base of the rail to the bottom of the rocker is 79 in., which gives the platform a freedom of action with sliding friction, longitudinally, between links, rockers and bearing blocks and a transverse pendulum motion in the main lever pivot. The rocker compen-

Fig. 71.—I-beams for bridge, track scale—   Fig. 72.—Lever arrangement, track scale—
        Baltimore & Ohio.   Baltimore & Ohio.

sates for any deflection there may be in the bridge, and a uniform bearing on the knife edge is always secured. The wedges, as shown on the top of the bearing yoke, provide the means of securing a uniform distribution of the load on each section, which might otherwise be prevented through the unevenness of the I-beam, the installation or the wear of the scale parts. The extension lever parts are provided with compensating steels. The accessibility of the nose-iron pivots, and the means provided for the proper alinement of these levers, are notable. Leveling tabs are fitted on the top of levers. All pivots are accessible for inspection and cleaning. The pit is 54 ft. long, 10 ft. 6 in. wide, 7 ft. 3 in. deep and equipped with electric lights. On the theory that more scales rust out than wear out, the inaccuracy and short life of many of them may be traced to lack of attention in the way of cleaning, inspection and testing.

The main lever stands rest on 2-in. bed-plate castings, which are anchored to a concrete pier through slotted holes. The slotted holes in the stands are at right angles, permitting some adjustment lengthwise or crosswise, which may be found necessary. No loops or links are permitted to vary more than $\frac{1}{16}$ in.

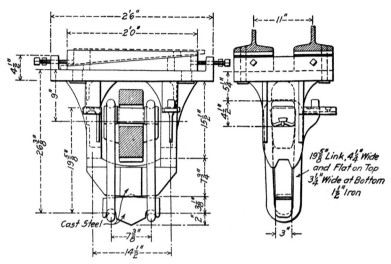

Fig. 73.—Detail of suspension bearing, track scale—Baltimore & Ohio.

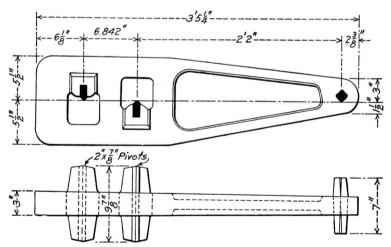

Fig. 74.—Detail of transverse lever, track scale—Baltimore & Ohio.

To handle freight properly, as to weight, charges and loading, correct weights should be used, as stated in the foregoing. The methods of obtaining weights are:

1. Weighing at initial point.
2. Accepting shipper's weight under proper weight agreements.

3. Standard weights.
4. Estimated weights.
5. Connecting line weights.

The weighing of l.c.l. freight was facilitated in a large outbound freight house by adjusting all hand trucks, by adding leaden weights to them, thereby bringing them up to a predetermined uniform weight. The platform scales were then adjusted to balance, with the empty truck on the scale. A support was also placed on the scale and included in the adjustment, to enable the truckers to rest the handles of the truck at the normal trucking height, avoiding the necessity of stooping down to deposit the loaded truck on the scale, and again to move it, thereby saving much time. This is one of the practical applications of "scientific management."

The rate of speed for weighing cars has been investigated and it developed that the right speed for accurate weighing is somewhere between 3 and 6 m.p.h., according to the skill of the weighman. At 4 m.p.h. over a 46-ft. scale, the rate is equal to about six cars a minute, and at 5 m.p.h., to about eight cars a minute. As many as ten per minute have been weighed by a skilled weighman. Ore trains coming on the unloading dock are nearly always weighed without uncoupling, the speed being about 4 miles an hour and as uniform as possible.

The accuracy of weighing, when cars are not uncoupled, has often been questioned. The Railway Accounting Officers Association decided that: "Based on practical experience, proper care being exercised, correct weights can be determined on track scales by weighing cars coupled at both ends, coupled at one end or uncoupled at both ends."

Variations in tare weights of cars was gone into in a hearing before the Interstate Commerce Commission in Chicago. Testimony was introduced tending to show that during one winter month, out of 384 cars weighed by one industrial concern, on 132 a variation of 500 lb. each from stenciled weights was found; 97 of them weighed 141,350 lb. over stenciled weights and 35 weighed 37,690 lb. under. During a summer month, of 317 cars, 95 shows variations of 500 lb. or over, 21 of them weighed 47,300 lb. over 74 weighed 83,420 lb. under stenciled weights. It was explained that the variations were probably due to the effect of snow and ice in the cars in January, and that débris and other foreign substances frequently affected car weights. Of the cars weighed during one year by the weighmasters of the Western Railway Weighing Association and Inspection Bureau, 73 per cent. had a stenciled tare exceeding the actual weight. On the Santa Fe it is the practice to weigh all cars uncoupled while not in motion, excepting only those containing live stock.

Coal-weight shrinkage was discussed by the International Railway Fuel Association in Chicago, in connection with the subject of correct weighing of coal at mines and on railway track scales, including legitimate shrinkage allowable on car lots. The false impression prevailing regarding the effect of weather on the weight of loaded coal cars was referred to. It was asserted that a full inch of rain, falling on and retained by the coal loaded in a 36-ft. car, would increase the weight 1,600 lb.; but, as drainage occurs almost as fast as the rain falls and as evaporation is rapid, the effect is only temporary. In the discussion of this report the secretary submitted an interesting statement of a test made by the St. Louis & San Francisco, of coal from Pittsburg, Kan., fields, to determine the shrinkage or gain due to weather conditions. The test was made in the latter part of May and extended over 13 days. There were 25 cars, 10 box or stock, and the remainder open cars. The average moisture content of coal from this district is 2.85 per cent. During the first 7 days there were light rains on three different days; but with one exception the loads showed a shrinkage in weight averaging 0.24 per cent. for the closed cars and 0.64 per cent. for the open cars. Following the seventh weighing a heavy rain set in which continued through the following day and until 4 a. m. of the second day, the weather clearing at noon and continuing clear throughout the rest of the test. Weights on these days were taken at 1:30 p. m. Although weighings of the closed cars were discontinued after the tenth day, the weight showed an average shrinkage of 0.05 per cent. The open cars showed a net gain in weight of 22,360 lb. in the first weighing after the heavy rains, which shrank to 4,150 by the end of the test, an average of 188 lb., or 0.14 per cent. per car; and, while the extreme gain and shrinkage for individual open cars were 1,080 and 450 lb., respectively, the average result well bears out the committee's statement that the weather effect, on the whole, is relatively unimportant.

The benefits to be derived by weighing less than car-load freight at point of origin, as well as promptly upon its receipt, may be enumerated as follows:

As shipments at point of origin are necessarily complete as receipted for, weights then taken afford a substantial basis on which to determine the merits of claims for alleged subsequent loss from whatever source.

Weighing at point of origin insures a more detailed check as to the number of packages constituting the entire shipment, the handling of which in the course of weighing should materially assist in bringing to light cases of illegible or duplicate marking, improperly prepared or improperly described packages, and the like.

It precludes the possibility of failure to weigh promptly packages subject to natural shrinkage.

It provides for actual rather than estimated weights for original insertion in revenue billing, eliminating the necessity for extension corrections at destination based on weight variation.

It permits of more expeditious delivery at destination.

It provides for more prompt and effective accomplishment of supervision.

In case weights are not taken at point of origin, and the physical movement of a shipment is followed by a claim for loss, the carrier is thrown into a state of perplexity, neither knowing nor being in a position to determine the authenticity of the claim; whereas, had the shipment been weighed when originally tendered, such weight would immediately establish the extent of the carrier's liability for loss, and enable the carrier to more quickly and satisfactorily dispose of the claim.

The American Railway Association's specifications for track scales require that they:

... be divided into two classes, namely, heavy-service scales and light-service scales; and, except when otherwise specifically provided, these specifications are to apply to both classes of scales. Heavy-service scales are those over which a large number of cars are to be weighed; and they shall have sectional capacities of 75 or 100 tons, except for special cases. Light-service scales are those over which only relatively few cars are to be weighed; and they shall have sectional capacities of 60 to 75 tons, except for special cases.

The capacity of a scale should be the weight of the heaviest car it will weigh, provided that the scale will support a train of such cars passing over the scale without stresses being developed in the members of the scale which are in excess of those hereinafter specified. The sectional capacity is the greatest weight which, if applied on the load knife edges of each pair of main levers, will produce stresses in the scale parts not exceeding those given in the table of working stresses.

The Association decided that:

The most essential features of a good track scale are its design, capacity and length, and in the selection and installation of such a scale the following must be given careful consideration:

1. Maximum loads to be moved over the scale for weighing or otherwise, considering the spacing of and concentration of weight on axles.

2. Length of wheel base of cars or other equipment to be weighed.

3. Whether cars are to be weighed spotted or in motion.

4. Location with respect to yard work and grade.

5. Character of foundations.

6. Method of installation.

7. Drainage, lighting, heating and ventilation.

The length of the scale is the distance between the ends of the available live or weighing rail.

When cars are to be weighed spotted, the scale should be of sufficient length to place the entire car on the scale, and preferably longer, to facilitate spotting. A length of 50 ft. is recommended.

When cars are to be weighed in motion, the length of scale shall be such that, at a maximum speed of 4 m.p.h., each car will be entirely and alone on the scale a minimum of 4 sec.

The length of pit inside of the end walls should be not less than 2 ft. longer than the extreme length of scale parts.

The ends of scale rails should not project beyond the knife edges of the end main levers.

The proper location of a track scale depends principally on:

The volume of traffic to be weighed in comparison with that switched over the scales and not to be weighed.

Whether the scale is to be equipped with a dead rail or relieving gear.

Whether a run-around track will be installed for switching and a separate track for weighing.

Whether cars are to be weighed spotted or in motion.

The cost of extra switching when the scales are not located on a lead to a classification track.

Cost of maintenance when the scale is located on a lead to classification tracks and only a small proportion of the cars are to be weighed.

The necessity for quick dispatch of cars that are weighed. So much depends on local conditions that it would be difficult to give exact rules in connection with the above suggestions. It is recommended, however, that there be not less than 50 ft. of tangent track at both ends of the scale rail. When only a small proportion of the cars handled are to be weighed, the rails leaving the scale in the direction of weighing may be curved and the dead rails straight, or the curvature may be equalized between them.

When scales are located on a lead to classification tracks in a hump yard, they should be at such an elevation that cars will run by gravity as far as desired into the classification yard, considering a maximum speed of 4 m.p.h. over the scale.

When not located on the hump, they should be at sufficient elevation to provide the necessary grade on the track leaving the scale in the direction of weighing, and such that the usual cut of cars to be weighed will run away from the scale by gravity in order to prevent impacts on the scale, and also for protection against surface water. They must be built level, and supports used to fix the weighing rails at the desired incline. The distance and grade from the top of the hump to the scale should be such that free running cars will pass over the scales at a speed not to exceed 4 m.p.h. without brake application, and cars be so spaced that the minimum weighing period of 4 sec. shall not be reduced. Scales to be used for motion weighing should be constructed with scale rails on a grade not greater than 1 per cent. Where it is the practice for one car rider to take several cars into the classification track, the grade over the scale should be maintained for at least 100 ft. (and preferably 200 ft.) beyond the scale in the direction of weighing. This provides that cars may be stopped easily by the car rider, and that succeeding cars will not cause excessive impact when striking the car ahead, which should occur not less than one car length from the scale.

On the subject of maintenance and operation, the following is for the guidance of those in charge:

All track scales should be numbered and referred to by number and location.

Extensive repairs to scales, such as the renewal or sharpening of pivots, should be made in a properly appointed shop.

When scales are in service regularly, the scale parts, substructures and foundations should be cleaned at stated intervals, and at such other times as may be necessary.

The application of rust preventatives to bearings is desirable, but they should be so applied as not to interfere with the proper working of the scale.

If ice obstructs the levers, salt should not be used to melt it; artificial heat should be used.

Equipment should not be allowed to stand on the scales except when being weighed.

Engines or other equipment not to be weighed should not be passed over the live rail, except on authority of the weighing department.

Cars should not be bumped off the scales by an engine or another car on a dead rail, nor be pulled across the scales coupled to another car moving over the dead rail.

Enginemen should not apply sand on the scale or dead rail, nor should the injector on the engine be applied when the engine is standing on or passing over the scale.

The weighing beam should be balanced before the scale is used, and, when not in use, it should be locked with the beam catch.

Cars should not be stopped violently on the scale by impact, by the sudden application of brakes or by throwing obstructions under the wheels. When pushing off the scale cars which have been stopped for weighing or otherwise, the impact must not occur at a greater speed than 2 m.p.h. When necessary for any reason to run cars over the scale rails, the speed must not exceed 4 m.p.h.

The weighmaster should familiarize himself with the construction of the scale and make such inspections at such intervals as are necessary to determine if the scale is in proper working condition.

Parties appointed to inspect and maintain scales should be properly instructed and duly authorized. It is desirable that they be present with the scale inspector when scales are tested.

The metal work in the scale and the structural steel must be maintained in a well-painted condition.

The Bureau of Standards, United States Department of Commerce employs three special testing equipments which travel over all the country testing railroad track scales. As these scales will weigh loads up to 150 tons and as the prescribed tolerance calls for an accuracy of 0.2 per cent. of the applied load or 200 lb. in each 50 tons, the testing must be well done. In 1924, there were 56.9 per cent. of the track scales tested within the limit prescribed, compared to 51.6 per cent. in the preceding year. In the first year of this testing service, only 38.2 per cent. were rated as satisfactory.

In the report of the Committee on Yards and Terminals of the American Railway Engineering Association, Feburary, 1925, the following list of tolerances was presented, which had been adopted by the Sixteenth

Annual Conference on Weights and Measures held in May, 1923. These tolerances are applicable to heavy-duty automatic indicating scales other than track scales.

Load in pounds	Tolerance, Class A		Tolerance, Class B	
	On ratio	On dial or beam	On ratio	On dial or beam
	Ounces	Ounces	Ounces	Pounds
50	½	1	. . . .	. . . .
100	1	2	. . . .	. . . .
200	2	4	. . . .	. . . .
300	3	6	. . . .	. . . .
400	4	8	. . . .	. . . .
500	5	10	10	1¼
600	6	12	12	1½
		Pounds	Pounds	
800	8	1	1	2
1,000	8	1	1	2
1,200	10	1¼	1¼	2½
1,500	12	1½	1½	3
1,800	14	1¾	1¾	3½
	Pounds			
2,000	1	2	2	4
2,500	1¼	2½	2½	5
4,000	2	4	4	8
6,000	3	6	6	12
8,000	4	8	8	16
10,000	5	10	10	20
12,000	6	12	12	24
16,000	8	16	16	32
20,000	10	20	20	40
24,000	12	24	24	48
30,000	15	30	30	60
40,000	20	40	40	80
50,000	25	50	50	100

Class A scales include the following: Scales of the portable platform type; and also scales of the self-contained or dormant and built-in types which are installed inside of a building having side walls and roof, which protect the scale from weather effects and from sudden changes of temperature.

Class B scales include the following: Scales of the motor truck and wagon types; and also scales of the self-contained or dormant and built-in types which are not installed inside of a building having side walls and roof and which are exposed to weather effects and sudden changes of temperature.

CHAPTER XV

RECORDS AND STATISTICS

For yard and terminal work and road handling in its relation to the terminals, it is necessary to keep certain records to enable the supervising officers to know that cars are properly moved, placed or delivered and to direct such work, and it is necessary also to arrange certain statistics with these records as a basis, whereby those in charge of and responsible for operations may know that the work is being handled in a satisfactory manner as to time of movement (service) and expense of work performed (cost). An eminent authority said:

If this be a fair statement of the innocuous desuetude of such statistics, in what respect are they lacking in practical value? Evidently, in so far as they are unfitted for the uses to which they should be applied; and this because they are largely based upon unpractical methods, upon methods devised by men without experience in the occupation or enterprise from which the facts have been obtained. Furthermore, because their classification has been overburdened by the enumeration of irrelevant details. No busy man has the time to wade through hundreds of pages of columns of figures which cannot be directly applied to his own affairs. He wants that information predigested and made available for immediate assimilation. Therefore, let all irrelevant facts be excluded from such publications, as also the innumerable details with which they are frequently overloaded. Then, too, the statistics should not be so delayed in publication as to have become stale and useless under current conditions. To have practical value, they should relate to the immediate past, not to that past which is so remote as to savor of antiquity. We do not want to compare the performance of the steam turbine with that of Watt's pumping engine, but with that of compound reciprocating engines.[1]

In all yard handling the line of demarcation between service and cost must be fixed, and the general policy very largely determined therefrom. It is not exactly a case of "all the traffic will bear"—but, to a great extent, the commercial yard and freight-house work is performed at the lowest cost permissible and for which the shippers will stand, commensurate with the demand for cars in revenue service. When cars are a drug on the market, their quick release and prompt handling are ordinarily deemed of less importance than when a car famine exists but the per diem charges go on for-ever. Records and statistics are helpful in watching the line.

[1] HAINES, "Efficient Railway Operation."

The record and report business is essential, but may be readily over-done and become an actual obstruction instead of an aid to the real result-producing work. Any general office clerk may have or may assume the authority to call for reports of all kinds, while it may be nobody's business to know they are discontinued when they have served their purpose.

An unfortunate condition exists in the transportation department of some railroads on which the operating head has not the time necessary to watch such details as yard or train reports and is dependent largely, if not wholly, on a chief clerk or other subordinate officer. The chief clerk is what is termed in railroad parlance an "office man;" that is to say, one who has gained his railroad knowledge in an office and has, therefore, had little practical or actual outside experience. As a natural result, when he wants anything he asks "somebody" for it. Had he in times past worked as or with a switchman, yard conductor or a yardmaster, he probably would know that the information desired was already being received in some form. It may be, too, that the chief clerk is a "six o'clock man."

The author knows of instances where reports requiring many hours' work were sent in daily by yardmasters, trainmasters and superinten-dents, which had not been needed or used in years. When the discovery was accidently made, the explanation followed that there had been a time once when the information was required.

A system of reports or blanks is usually prepared by a clerk who is expert in that kind of work. He makes an estimate as to how long it will take him to make out each report. He may not take into considera-tion the fact that what he with his special training can accomplish in 8 or 10 min. in his office at a desk with ample light, ventilation and heat may take a yardmaster or other outside employee, not so skilful with a pen, five or ten times as long.

In one office, the author was shown an elaborate report of engine movements at terminals. It required records to be kept by eight different persons, and these were consolidated on one blank before being sent in. It was a fine production. A superintendent could easily put in two or three hours daily in getting unnecessary lessons from it. Many reports are made and pigeonholed because they may be needed "some day." Somebody is paying for them in the meantime.

In a large terminal, a yard engine was assigned to a district and its work was usually behind. The work done was analyzed and it did not seem sufficient to jusify the use of more than one engine. The conductor spent about two hours a day working on "reports" and, while he was an exceptionally good yard conductor, he had neither the ability to plan work successfully for others, or to take a prize as a rapid recorder and report maker. Moreover, the greater part of his reporting was of cars moving from one point in his district to another, the car-service office having at some time in the past asked for this information. As, apparently, no use was being made of this information, he was told to discontinue sending in this report. There were no further complaints of work not being done in that district, and years passed without anyone in the car-service office discovering the discontinuance of the "interior" car-movement report.

The author has frequently watched a freight conductor making out his switch list while riding in the cupola of a four-wheel caboose, rounding the curves, and bracing for the running in and out of the slack in the 80 or 90 cars ahead. A lantern, tucked under the conductor's arm, gave all the light to be had and further embarrassed him in endeavoring to comply with the printed instructions, "Write figures legibly." To put down 80 numbers of five figures each, 400 in all, under such conditions, in a space so small that they could hardly be inserted by one of the "Lord's Prayer on a dime" experts, and adding the initials of the cars, the designation for "loaded" or "empty," giving the contents, kind of car, originating point, road's destination, final destination and, in many cases, the record of seals on each side of each car and on end door must of necessity take much of the conductor's time. Clerks should do as much of this work as possible. Road and yardmen are not chosen for their bookkeeping ability. Committees of road employees have been known to defend negligence in the physical handling of their trains by claiming that the individual conductor or trainman was engaged in "making out his reports."

To operate a terminal satisfactorily it is essential that records of all movements be kept. These reports and records are not altogether for the purpose of answering questions asked by those at a distance relative to movement or location of certain cars. They are primarily to enable the yardmaster or other operating officer in charge of the terminal to inform himself at any time as to the general situation. It is apparent on many roads that the report and record business—especially the report—is overdone. This seems to be due to an increasing demand for information and the closer tracing of freight by shippers and traffic officers. The easy abuse follows, by which department heads and officers ask for more and more reports by wire, or mail, or both, weekly, daily and ofttimes at several specified times daily. The result is to demoralize and confuse the organization and overload the local forces with a mass of detail apparently serving no good end. It prevents the local operating head from receiving the information he needs in the conduct of his business. As he cannot secure a considerable increase in clerical and other forces, without being able to show a corresponding increase in traffic to justify it, the business of the terminal suffers. All the information asked for in the special and additional reports is usually already made up and sent in, in some form or other, but is perhaps not readily and conveniently abstracted, or is not known to be at hand by the clerk in charge. In any event, it seems easier to wire the superintendent or yard-master for it. When such additional demands for information are made, a general revision of the entire system of reports, cutting out five or six that are going in and substituting one or two simplified forms, will in many cases accomplish the desired result and enable a reduction of clerical work at the terminal, instead of necessitating an increased force. It will also enable the superintendent to get more result-producing work out of his subordinates. When that ideal condition is reached in a terminal, where no questions need be asked, special reports will not be needed.

Records vary on different roads, and in the different terminals of the same road, to meet the different and varying conditions. It is customary to have a record of the cars contained in each train arriving at the terminal; occasionally, this is telegraphed to the yardmaster in advance, sometimes it is made up by the conductor and handed to a yard clerk on arrival and again it may be made up after the train has arrived. The card bills are delivered and checked with this list, and usually the train is marked up for switching or is switched by it. The list should show the car numbers, with the names or initials of owning roads; whether empty or loaded; kind of car; kind and condition of seals on each side door and on end doors, if any; contents and final destination. The heading should give the number of the train and of the engine, direction of movement, total number of loads, empties and gross tons, also the names of engine-man and conductor. The cars are entered from this list into a car-record book, from which all cars are checked and traced. This is an important record and will be described in detail later. Records of transfer or interyard movements and cars to and from shops and repair yards and other points are similarly reported by the conductors of the yard transfer or road engines moving them. Each yard keeps a record of its handling of cars made up in a more or less complicated manner, depending on the extent of the yard and the number of movements required.

One of the first essentials, and doubtless the most important, is to keep records by which one can intelligently and with reasonable accuracy determine the cost of handling a terminal, adopting some unit as a basis, for comparison with other terminals and for comparison with itself during a previous period. That both comparisons are beset with difficulties is apparent. Many factors enter into the computation, and allowances have to be made for weather conditions, changes in character and volume of traffic, increased or decreased number of cars or tons for private sidings or warehouses (where work is attended with extraordinary difficulties), change in power used, kind of fuel, amount of passenger work, revision of loading and transfers, regulations imposed by the Interstate Commerce Commission, State Boards of Railroad Commissioners, Public Utilities Commissions, Boards of Trade and similar bodies.

One railroad operating man said[1]

Operating statistics, like most railroad statistics, published or available, are largely historical. An operating officer is generally a poor statistician and a statistician is not, as a rule, a good operating man. At least, this seems to be the opinion each has of the other. The operating man, whose job it is to keep things moving, is more vitally interested in what there is for him to do and what there is ahead of him than what was done a couple of months ago. This is perfectly natural, for, if he does not move the business currently, the whole works are mussed up. After all, his job, for at least most of the time, is to move the largest amount of business in the shortest possible time and in time of peak loads the cost of doing this becomes incidental to the main object, which is keeping free from expensive congestions and a lot of incidental troubles. The job of the statistician seems to be to ascertain what has been done. This is dull stuff for an active operating man, who generally puzzles his brain over a mass of figures and tries to prove an alibi.

Another practical railroad man puts it this way:

Statistics are not a cure-all, but a pointer or index to those who can read and interpret. They should not be used as a cause of action, but as an aid to the judgment in reaching a decision. The cost of producing the essential data is small. They may usually be assembled upon forms and reports currently made, and on an operating division will not employ the time of more than one clerk, while summarizing and working out the averages in the general office will not take over one hour per day. As a means of checking the shifting of blame from one department to another, and for reducing the friction between departments, statistical work is very valuable. The knowledge that the "head office" is in possession of all the essential facts with which to measure the efficiency of the work performed has a most stimulating influence, both upon the sluggard and upon the ambitious.[2]

The railway world is passing through the age of the specialist and the statistician—both are useful in their respective fields; both necessary but, like prohibition and other more or less desirable theories, may be carried too far; may be overdone. The realization that 16 out of every 100 railway employes are engaged in clerical or related lines of at times a non-productive nature, causes reflection as to the possibility of another side to the many stories told of marvelous economies effected. This reflection becomes more acute and interesting when roads heavily supplied with efficiency experts of various varieties making good showings are, nevertheless, not much out of step with other roads obtaining the same results with little beyond the ordinary field or working organizations. Nowadays—with all kinds of governmental standards prescribed—the general operating efficiency of roads becomes somewhat general in scope and hinges largely on business prosperity, weather con-

[1] CHARLES E. LEE, in *Railway Age*, May 10, 1924.
[2] LOREE, L. F., "Railroad Freight Transportation."

ditions and, by no means least, governmental regulations and restrictions. A popular novelist[1] caused one of his characters—a typical Connecticut country lawyer—to remark dejectedly: "Education is responsible for a lot of ignorance," after much hard effort as guardian to straighten out the affairs of his college graduate ward—a girl of decidedly erratic and impracticable ideas. The temptation becomes strong, at times, to paraphrase this with: "Economies are responsible for a lot of extravagance."

Besides the irrelevancy and voluminousness of much of the information[2] compiled by statisticians, the terms in common use in statistical literature are also open to criticism. Those most frequently to be met with are the Maximum, the Minimum and the Average, as the economic factors deduced from the array of numerical facts. The importance is readily perceived of the Maximum, as being the highest attainable, and of the Minimum, as being the lowest; but the Average is a term of which the importance is often overestimated in considering an actual business environment or the efficiency of an organization. There are many possible gradations, in either of these cases, between the Maximum and the Minimum; but the Average, as an actual fact, can occur but once. If figures may be made to prove anything, this is true of "the deadly parallel," and of the equally deadly average. The one may be used to compare things essentially dissimilar, and the other is but the arithmetical mean between perhaps widely different conditions, and actually represents but one of them.

The term Average, as employed in statistics, is capable of four different meanings, according as it refers to the arithmetical mean, the "weighted" arithmetical mean, the "median" or the "mode"; and statisticians admit that, in the application of the average to any individual case, the result may vary accordingly. An average may, therefore, be considered as an arithmetical abstraction, of value in the application of a widely extended series of data to some general proposition, but leading to incorrect conclusions when applied to individual cases. The wider the range of observation, the more numerous the number of individual instances observed, the fewer and simpler the characteristic data, the more reliable will be the average thus obtained.

Such averages may be of value in the construction of mortality tables for a life insurance company, but not in determining the relative efficiency of railroad managements. In applying the principle of the average to such a case, it should include a consideration of all relevant data and exclude all that are irrelevant. In whatever terms it may be expressed, its practical value lies in its illumination or coordination of many individual cases of a similar character, for averages may be based upon data too limited as to number, or in groups affected by dissimilar characteristics.

An average may be based upon too small a number of individual cases to be of value or, as is sometimes done where the number of cases is very great, resort is had to an "estimated" value. It is not possible to deduce, from the bare statement of the figure of an average, the number of individual instances considered in its computation, or whether one may be dealing with a mere estimate. Those who make the estimates, as a rule, know only a small part of the individual cases,

[1] IRVING BATCHELOR.
[2] HAINES, "Efficient Railway Operation."

and perhaps give a judgment from limited observation. Estimated values occur sometimes without being evident. In such cases there is danger of ascribing to the value in any question greater reliability than it actually possesses. Relative numbers having the character of averages are also often estimated when there are not sufficient data for their computation. Every estimate must be regarded as simply an approximate value. It may be quite accurate in some cases, but there is no certainty. Modern statisticians endeavor, therefore, to secure data sufficient to enable them to dispense with estimates.

After all, again and always, success depends to a very great extent on the organization, its methods and the morale or *esprit de corps*. One of the most capable operating officers, a deep student of all railway problems, said:[1]

The service in railway transportation is a complexity of mental and physical activities, exerted through the intervention of appliances and devices which are controlled by agencies in separate places and at different times. This complexity of activities must be so coordinated as to work harmoniously for a special purpose —the transmission of persons and things. Upon first thought, it seems impracticable to condense within reasonable limits an adequate description of that which may be termed the art of railway operation. For it should comprise a reference to every fact essential to a comprehension of the present state of that art, if it is to be of value to those who are associated in its practice or who desire to obtain a theoretical acquaintance with it. It is given to but few men to acquire an adequate conception of efficient railway operation entirely from personal experience, and such opportunities are confined to those only who have attained the higher offices in railway service.

The art of railway operation is like a maze of many-colored threads from which each independent operator is disentangling here and there a strand for a web of his own weaving; but for the entire mass to be utilized in a fabric of orderly design, some clew must be found to the labyrinthine web. "Order is Heaven's first law," and organization is the prime essential in efficient service of a multifarious nature.

The aim and intent of the organization of industrial activities are their coordination to a common purpose. Any combination of individuals may be readily coordinated under a single executive official, so long as their field of action is under his personal observation; but when that field extends beyond his personal purview, it becomes necessary to depute some part of his authority to subordinates. Here is the parting of the ways between two methods of organization, the departmental method, or the delegation of power in specific lines of authority to deputies who remain under the direct supervision of the central executive, and the divisional method, or the delegation of full authority over these several lines of activity to separate deputies in specific fields of action. Contention as to the relative advantages of these methods has existed since warfare became a recognized profession. The officer on the staff favors the departmental method, while the line officer prefers the divisional method; and this contention has accompanied the development of isolated railways into connected systems covering thousands of miles of line.

[1] HAINES, "Efficient Railway Operation."

The increased use of the so-called "main tracker" has possibilities where the facilities and character of business permit. A "main tracker" is defined as "a train dispatched from a terminal for continuous movement to destination or to a breaking-up yard, passing through one or more intermediate yards or terminals."[1] This is the "overhead" movement of the greatest number of trains possible through terminals. It is, in other words, a newly coined word for the old-fashioned and well-known transportation axiom to make up straight trains to as many and as far distant points as practicable—and to keep them moving. It may be expressed in the equation of having cars held to make up straight trains to a destination so long as the terminal delay will equal or not greatly exceed the delays eliminated in switching or reswitching at the several terminals along the route.[2]

Endeavors to compare one division with another or one yard with another are ordinarily of little value. Weather conditions, fuel, grades and water have each a share in producing differences in cost which it is difficult to estimate, but, apart from this, there is an even more serious difficulty in making comparisons between two or more railroads. The data used in compiling results are rarely available, and, when available, are still more rarely harmonious. By comparing one division or district with itself for a corresponding period, the difficulties of weather and grades are largely eliminated or, at all events, any change is on record; and fairly reliable conclusions may be drawn from such comparisons. Most roads divide their statistics as between east- and westward or north- and southward. Such division may be useful as denoting the general trend of traffic, but it seems more than probable that a further subdivision setting forth such traffic as is in the direction of the balance of traffic, as distinct from that in the direction of turning power, would be a truer basis from which to criticize locomotive or train performance. With the present system, assuming the balance of tonnage for an entire month is eastward, it is possible that, during a large portion of the month, the balance was in the opposite direction and, as a consequence, eastward results as shown are misleading and the good actually attained by careful loading, proper handling of empty cars and economical fuel performance is lost sight of.

The unit of cars handled is probably the only practical one. In this, however, the figures may be manipulated so that they are misleading. Every movement of a car may be counted, in one case, and only arrival at and departure from terminal in another. In the former it may count as ten, or even more, and in the latter as two. What constitutes a car movement, or a car handled must first be determined.

[1] E. T. HORN, Chief of Yard and Terminal Operations, B. & O.
[2] The author in *Tech Engineering News*, for Dec., 1923.

For the reasons outlined, the basis of computation, cars handled, is about as unsatisfactory for the purpose intended as it is possible to make it. It is, nevertheless, the basis used more often than any other. The yardmaster's desire to make a good showing for himself and his yard by reducing the cost per car handled will induce him to run up the number of cars handled to the highest figure.

The author at one time had charge of a large marine terminal yard, and had reduced the cost of handling to what he considered a fair figure, and included every car movement that he conscientiously considered right and fair, in the number of cars handled. An interior yard of very much smaller size and lighter business showed a decidedly lower cost, to the suprise of everyone. Inquiry developed the fact that the smaller yard showed a much greater number of cars handled than did the larger yard. Knowing that this was not the actual condition, the author spent several days in the interior yard and analyzed its methods. The business actually done did not compare with that of the marine terminal, but every movement or apology for a movement was recorded and reported. A record was kept of a car moving from the general yard to the transfer platform; from the transfer to the freight house; from freight house back to transfer and again back to the outgoing yard. Aside from the manifest unfairness of the method, the amount of time spent on these reports should be considered. The work was done by men not trained nor intended for that kind of work, and all of it was absolutely useless. This instance will illustrate the futility of using the present general methods of accounting in yard work, for the purpose of making comparisons between yards, unless an understanding is first arrived at as to a common and uniform basis.

An excellent plan has been advanced—and it was many years ahead of the times when actually tried—in the determination of units in yard work and basing thereon a standard for comparison, every item of work and cost being analyzed and separated. It was then commonly known as the "standard-unit" method. The actual performance for a period of months or years back was taken and from it a statement was made dividing up all the principal items of work done, and the cost. This basis was used as the standard with which comparisons of following months were made and increases or decreases explained. Some of the items to be enumerated are:

1. Cars received and forwarded in trains.
2. Cars delivered to and received from connecting lines.
3. Cars delivered to and received from private industries.
4. Cars to and from freight-house and team tracks.
5. Cars to and from coal-chute tracks.
6. Cars to and from transfer tracks.
7. Cars weighed.

The total of these items would represent the number of "cars handled," and it is necessarily many times greater than the actual number of cars involved in the computation.

For illustration, let it be assumed that there were handled, the first month, a total of 7,000 cars, and the same number the second month, with the exception that during the second month there were fewer cars handled in certain movements and more in others. Using the item numbers in the list of movements just given:

Items	First month	Second month
1	1,000	500
2	1,000	500
3	1,000	1,000
4	1,000	1,000
5	1,000	1,000
6	1,000	1,500
7	1,000	1,500
Total	7,000	7,000

To apply the standard-unit method, it is first necessary to fix a value for each item. A movement may become more difficult and expensive. An industry may change its track connections or may change the method of loading or routing of cars requiring less "spotting" of such cars when being placed. The movement may be made less difficult and expensive. Approaches to a coal chute may have reduced grade or improved track connections enabling a locomotive to put up more cars than formerly. It is, therefore, desirable from time to time to revise the standard.

Assuming item No. 1 to be the simplest, the value may be placed at 1. Item No. 2 may be no more difficult than item No. 1 and would be given the same value. Items Nos. 3, 4 and 5 each require three times the work of item No. 1 and would be placed at 3. Items Nos. 6 and 7 may each require twice the work of item No. 1, and their values would be placed at 2. If 1,000 movements were made in the first month under each head, the number of units would be:

Items	Cars handled	Value of each	Total units
1	1,000	1	1,000
2	1,000	1	1,000
3	1,000	3	3,000
4	1,000	3	3,000
5	1,000	3	3,000
6	1,000	2	2,000
7	1,000	2	2,000
Total	7,000		15,000

Dividing the 15,000 units into the total cost of handling the terminal for the month gives the cost per unit for purposes of comparison.

Applying the unit basis to the month following in which the total number of cars handled was the same but varies as between the items:

Items	Cars handled	Standard values	Total units
1	500	1	500
2	500	1	500
3	1,000	3	3,000
4	1,000	3	3,000
5	1,000	3	3,000
6	1,500	2	3,000
7	1,500	2	3,000
Totals	7,000		16,000

While the number of cars handled is the same in each month, there were 1,000 more units of work performed and, with an increased total cost of handling of 6.7 per cent. the cost per unit would be the same. If the standard of values has been correctly assessed, this would approximate actual conditions. The author used this system very successfully and satisfactorily in a large and busy terminal.

In some terminals the whole computation has been made on the basis of the number of cars received and forwarded in trains and cars delivered to and received from connecting lines. This is not worth while. In other terminals the calculations of cost are based on the number of cars in and out in trains, and cars switched for revenue. Aside from the futility of so comparing the yard work done on one road with another, there is probably little use in endeavoring to bring about a satisfactory comparison between any two yards on the same road. There is no good reason why the standard-unit system cannot be satisfactorily used for several or all yards, and the general officers of the transportation department could have figures showing the operating cost of the different yards that would mean something.

Under the system of assessing values to units of yard work in each yard, it is necessary, if comparisons between two or more terminals are to be made, that the value of the units be established on some uniform basis. To secure uniformity of values, a committee might be appointed to fix the value of each unit in the different terminals. It would be well to have a representative from each important terminal on this committee, and three or more general transportation officers to act as arbitrators. After the values are once fixed, they need not be disturbed until some change in conditions necessitates a local adjustment.

This method is not intended to apply to the figures given and records kept of the cost of classifying cars in terminals by summit, poling or gravity methods, because there are no great complications in the kinds and costs of train movements in such yards, and so the figures usually kept of such operations are full of meaning and of the greatest value.

The contract, or so-called "piece-work" system, would seem a most satisfactory one to use in classifying yards worked by either summit, stake or gravity methods, and its use here, as well as in freight houses, would tend to simplify greatly the record problem. It is not difficult to estimate the cost per car, and the men under their foreman, as a sub-contractor, could be paid on that basis at the end of the month or week. This plan would tend to do away with the necessity for supervision and paying overtime, and would, under the law of the "survival of the fittest," weed out the sloth and drone. Damage to cars might be expected to be reduced, because a derailment or accident obstructing the work would cause the men to be idle and lose pay.

A simple, intelligent, accurate, reliable and closely followed-up car record is essential in any yard of even moderate proportions. The usual error made in adopting a record in yards that have been operated without any records is to record more than is absolutely essential. The record should give just such information as is needed in the particular terminal in which it is installed, and no more. The per diem method of paying for the use of cars has made records necessary where they were not needed before and has extended those already in use. Records of the movement of cars in and out, on each of the various divisions and connecting lines involved, whether loaded or empty, of cars to and from shops, freight houses, etc. are necessary in a car record at the average division terminal.

One of the simplest and most economical records is that using the ending or terminal figure of the car and, where nothing more is required, it is decidedly the best. This is usually kept on large loose sheets divided into ten squares each, the last figures across the sheet and the second and third figures up and down making it necessary to write only the figures in advance of the three last ones in each number. As men become accustomed to the record they can fill in the numbers very rapidly. One man should easily enter 2,500 car numbers a day besides replying to telegraphic and telephonic inquiries as to cars. The date is entered, abbreviations for divisions, connections, etc., by using A, B, C, etc., and the symbols X for loaded and — for empty. The X or — is placed ahead of the number when it indicates "arrival"; and after the number when it indicates "departure."

A simple form of report is one on which each sheet is divided into ten squares, numbered 0, 1, etc. to 9, inclusive. The car numbers are entered in full, and all those ending in the figure 1 in the space headed 1, etc.; in this record it is only necessary to look up one-tenth of the entire lot of numbers when one is wanted.

Another simple form of record, useful only in small terminals, requires each conductor, on arrival, to bring in a list of cars. A yard clerk notes the departure opposite the numbers of the cars as they move out.   These lists are deposited in a pigeonhole in a large case having a compartment for every day in the month

An elaborate record is sometimes kept in which no part of the car number itself needs to be written.   A book of 100 double pages with 10 horizontal divisions to the page and 100 vertical lines is used.   Car 18,945, for instance, is entered on page 45 in horizontal division 9 and in column 18.   The owning road's initials or its customary abbreviations are entered with the indications for load, empty, date (occasionally time) of arrival or departure, and other essential data.

Sometimes one colored ink is used to indicate cars arriving between midnight and 8 a. m., another for those between 8 a. m. and 4 p. m. and another between 4 p. m. and midnight, in order to estimate the time of arrival more closely.   One of the objections to this form of record is the large amount of leafing of the books, making it difficult to bind them substantially enough to last through their ordinary period of service.

A brief description of a system of checking car movements by the use of especially prepared cards is interesting, and, while it is in no sense a substitute for a regular car record, is worth some study because of its good features.   A case is used containing 100 pigeonholes labeled 0, 1, 2, etc. to and including 9 across, and the same vertically.   After a train has been entered a card is made for each car, giving initial, number, date received, reference to page of entry, date outbound, engine, train, time, contents and destination.   The ticket for each car is then placed in its proper pigeonhole.   Car 43,228, for instance, would be placed in pigeonhole in row 2 (from top) and across in vertical row 8; that is to say, in box 28. Any ticket may be found readily by looking over those in the box corresponding in number to the last figures of the car number.   When the car has been forwarded, the ticket is removed from the case and filed in a box containing six drawers, two compartments in each drawer, to provide a separate compartment for each month.   Each compartment is provided with 100 pockets numbered in conformity with the original case to enable the tickets to be found more readily when it is necessary to refer to them.

For the special purpose of checking car movements for per diem charges, one road uses a case divided into 310 pigeonholes, numbered from left to right, 1 to 31, indicating the days of the month.   On the sides of the case are the numerals from 0 to 9 inclusive, reading from the top down.   A blank ticket, of suitable size, is made for each car, giving car number, initial and date of arrival and such other information as may be deemed desirable.   Car 27,342 arriving Oct. 10, would be placed in column 10 on line 2.   The yardmaster can tell at a glance what cars are being delayed.

A bill rack may be so arranged as to enable a closer check to be kept than the last described plan. To accomplish this, a "rack" should be made for each division, connection, branch or other forwarding destination. The case contains 10 boxes from left to right (horizontally) with five compartments in each or five boxes deep. The original or accompanying card tickets for the cars are placed in the boxes according to the last figure; those for cars arriving between midnight and 8 a. m. in the upper; those between 8 a. m. and 4 p. m. in the second tier and those between 4 p. m. and midnight in the third. Cars remaining over a day are then placed in the next tier, "Yesterday," and those two days or more old in the lower tier, "Day before yesterday." The bill rack is made on the following plan:

New York Division

	0	1	2	3	4	5	6	7	8	9
12 midnight to 8 a. m...........										
8 a. m. to 4 p. m..............										
4 p. m. to midnight............										
Yesterday....................										
Day before yesterday...........										

At midnight the bill clerk moves all bills or cards remaining in tier "Yesterday" to the one just below, and those from the three tiers above to "Yesterday." Additional tiers may be added if deemed desirable. A glance will show any cars remaining in the yards more than eight hours.

In connection with the last described system, or with any system, a dating and timing stamp is valuable. A simple, cheap stamp has a time dial, which is set by hand just before the bills for an incoming train are distributed and with which each card ticket or bill is stamped. This records the yard, date and time and answers many questions. The clock time stamp is more expensive and also more likely to get out of order. It does not serve the purpose any better than the hand-set machine.

As the practice of rating locomotives on a tonnage basis is nearly universal, a considerable portion of the time of the yardmaster's force is taken up in computing the weight of trains, by taking the weight of each car plus contents when loaded, and adding them together. Much of the time of the bill clerks and train crews can be saved if tonnage-computing machines are furnished for this purpose. These machines have been in use at some heavy forwarding points and, while they will get out or order occasionally, are on the whole very satisfactory. In addition to saving time, they insure accuracy and eliminate controversies between the train conductor and the yard clerk or yardmaster, in which the conductor always thinks he has too much load while the yardmen think another car or two should be added. The yard clerk is frequently interrupted by questions while adding up the weight of his car tickets. The tonnage-computing machine holds his place for him; that is to say, he may go to some other work and, as soon as he returns, continue on the machine just where he left off, provided he keeps the tickets counted separated from those not counted.

With a properly designed and operated terminal, where "hold" cars and "diversions" do not exist, where the conditions are ideal, the records may be dispensed with altogether. This necessitates a yard with double-end tracks, continuous in and out movements and ample road power. The conductor of the incoming train hands or telegraphs the list of cars making up his train as they stand from the engine back. The ram or summit-engine crews "cut" from this list and the signalman arranges the ladder switches from the same list. Cars for certain destinations are run into designated tracks and the signalman keeps a list of cars in each track by which the outgoing road power is ordered. The cars moved by an outgoing train are checked off, the date and time of that movement being added. Cars are always moved in rotation, that is to say, the oldest cars go out first.

Every yardmaster should personally keep a log record. In this all incidents out of the ordinary are recorded. Accidents of all kinds, unusual weather, inability to obtain necessary road or yard power, injuries to employees, obstructions on the main line and, in fact, anything that interferes with the smooth working of his yard should be noted. Questions will come up months afterward which, by reference to his log, may be readily answered. Log records kept by train masters and chief dispatchers are invaluable.

CHAPTER XVI

WATER-FRONT TERMINALS

The transfer of ordinary freight between rail and water and from rail to rail lines over intervening water is accomplished by:

1. Car and load straight, by car floats or ferries, using float bridges to adjust for varying depths of water.

2. Lightering, transferring between car and vessel or pier, by using a barge or self-propelling vessel as an intermediary.

Fig. 75.—Loaded car float, in tow—New York Harbor.

3. Car and vessel direct, avoiding a second handling; either trucking freight to vessel or *vice versa*, or into and through a pier.

The bulk of the freight business in and about New York is handled on car floats. Some of these are of 12-car capacity, six on either side, with a center-loading platform. The larger ones, used by the New Haven, New York Central and Pennsylvania roads, will carry 20 to 22 cars each. The float bridge must be constructed to accommodate itself to the varying levels of the car float, due to tides, which range from 4 to 12 ft., and the difference in the depth of water drawn by the float itself, when fully loaded and when light. The older type of float bridge is supported at one end by pontoons, which keep it afloat and raise or lower the bridge with the tide but the more modern bridges are supported mechanically and raised and lowered by electric winches. Figure 75 shows a car float loaded, and being towed by a tug alongside.

The float is brought up to the transfer bridge and made fast by ropes or chains drawn taut by winches. There is one rope or chain at each side, and these draw the float up snug, so that the tracks on the float and on the transfer bridge are in approximate horizontal alinement. The final adjustment is made by a ratchet working a screw, by which the tracks on the bridge can be slid over a few inches. The bridge is raised or lowered before the float comes in, until the tracks are in approximate vertical alinement with those on the float. If the alinement is not accurate enough to slide the toggle bars on the bridge into the toggle caps on the float, time can be saved in adjustment by running the yard engine onto one of the bridge tracks, until its weight depresses that side far enough to let the toggle bar engage the cap. The locomotive is then moved to the other track and that toggle bar is made fast. A difference in height of several inches can be adjusted by this means in less time than if the float were lowered in the ordinary way. After the bridge has been used for some time, the toggle bars may have some play, so that the difference in the height of the rails on the bridge and on the float may be as much as 2 in. As this is too much of a drop for the trucks of the tender to take safely, a flat car is coupled to the locomotive and backed up to the end of the string of cars on the float. Transfer bridges are usually double-tracked. When the float has three or more tracks, the tracks bend together with a crossing frog a few feet from the bow of the boat. The switch points are on the bridge. Many recently built bridges are operated by electric power, saving much time in raising or lowering bridges to make the float fast.

It is comparatively rare for cars to be lost from the floats while in transit; most of the accidents occur while at the dock. The engineman of the yard locomotive sometimes misunderstands or fails to obey the trainman's stop signal, if given, and backs a string of cars up against the bumper. If this holds, the force is usually enough to break the ropes which make the float fast and the float is driven out from the dock and the cars may be dropped between the bridge and the boat. Low bumpers are preferable, as the trucks of the last car will go over a low bumper and the car will come down on its body on the end of the boat. This is evident at once to the engineman, who stops the train before serious results ensue. Steel floats are flat on top; wooden ones are sometimes cambered to give them greater strength. For this reason, in case the float breaks loose from the dock while the cars are unsecured and the brakes off, the cars are more liable to move downgrade from the middle of a wooden than from a steel float. Another advantage of the steel float is that the bow is not so bluff as a wooden boat; it has a long overhang and, when there is ice at the pier it rides over it, instead of packing it up in front. The pontoon is weighted with rocks inside and kept as free from water as possible, so that its lifting power may be near the maximum, it being easier to let the float down than to raise it. When the pontoon is damaged, a rope is passed under the bridge at high tide and made fast to a gallows overhead. When the tide falls, the pontoon drops with it and can be floated out from under the bridge and the necessary repairs made. The bridges are made very strong. They are hinged at the shore end so rigidly as to allow no torsion at that point. When heavy cars are run on one of the tracks, their weight warps the bridge, throwing an exceedingly heavy strain on the material of which it is made.

The steel barge "Mastodon"—of Morgan's Louisiana & Texas Company, now part of the Southern Pacific Lines, for use in transferring passenger and freight trains across the Mississippi River, at New Orleans, shown in detailed drawings in Fig. 76—is said to be the largest steel barge in America. It handles 16 passenger trains and more than 100 freight cars daily. It is constructed entirely of steel and carries three parallel tracks with 12-ft. centers. The length is 368 ft. overall; depth of hull is 50 ft., and depth at center 11 ft. 4 in. The principal construction figures are shown in the drawings.

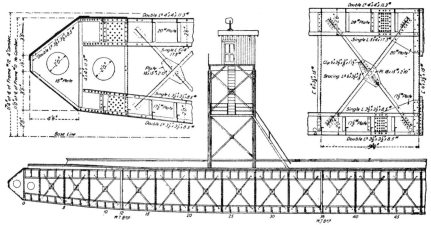

Fig. 76.—Framing of steel barge, "Mastodon"—Southern Pacific Lines.

The New Haven floats its cars between its terminals at Harlem River and Oak Point and its connections on the New Jersey side of the Hudson River, a distance of about 12 miles, and between Bay Ridge and the Pennsylvania terminal at Greenville. The movement between Oak Point and Bay Ridge is by way of the New York Connecting railroad which spans Hell Gate with a steel arch bridge, 1,017 ft. long. In New York harbor besides the interchange service the railroads float cars to and from Manhattan pier stations using car floats from 8 to 14-car capacity with a covered trucking platform in the middle.

In addition extensive lighterage operations are conducted. Including the four Brooklyn Terminal Companies, the railroads at New York operate 1,873 units of floating equipment divided as follows; 56 ferryboats, 158 tugs, 372 floats, 38 steam self-propelled lighters, 388 hoisting lighters, and 861 barges, grain boats, coal boats and miscellaneous craft.

A considerable amount of interesting information on the subject of piers for handling freight at water-front terminals is contained in the report of the Committee on Yards and Terminals of the American Railway Engineering Association, from which the following is quoted:

At large marine terminals, whether ocean or lake ports, the railroad facilities for handling business differ very materially from those of inland terminals. At such terminals it is advantageous to unload into warehouses all classes of freight which can be placed on platforms, and only retain in the cars such classes of property as cannot be provided with housing accommodations. The great bulk of export and import freight is moved by lighterage service of the terminal railroad company. Where it is the practice to bring the ocean vessel to the dock of the terminal company, the agent has preliminary advice and is guided accordingly in making provision for the method he will adopt in furnishing service. The maintenance of special warehouses for export freight is not always essential, but the general warehouses employed for the unloading of lighterage freight can often be used also for export freight which is delivered direct to the vessel.

It will facilitate matters if these warehouses are skirted with tracks on the outside, which, in turn, may be used to unload to or from the car, in addition to securing freight from the warehouse or discharging thereon. Greater economy in labor necessarily results if loading directly to and from the car can be brought about, and in a greater measure this suggestion permits either process to be employed in serving a vessel. A series of open docks is also essential for the handling of coarse freight, and also to extend the hoisting facilities operated by the terminal company in the interest of such vessels as have no means of taking on or discharging a cargo with their own power. In fact, open docks can be employed successfully for general cargoes usually loaded in box cars and the general trade transacted with small vessels and barges.

The facilities provided at large seaport terminals are generally as follows:

(1) A cluster or general yard, into which trains are moved; (2) lighterage piers, either open or covered, from which cars are unloaded or loaded to and from vessels; (3) export piers, from which freight for export is unloaded and transferred from vessels, or *vice versa;* (4) storage piers, in which is held (preparatory to being loaded on vessels) such freight as flour, machinery, lumber, provisions, canned goods, etc., the traffic rules allowing quite an amount of free time on this class of commodities; (5) inbound and outbound freight-station piers, located at points where they are only reached by water, and cars are moved to and from them on car floats. These are used for the city delivery or receipt of freight, and team-track delivery yards are provided in connection with them; (6) coal piers, upon which cars are run and unloaded into coal barges or vessels; (7) grain elevators; (8) warehouses; (9) stock yards.

The general yard or cluster at a rail and water terminal is the large yard into which all business is moved. It should be so arranged that cars as they come in can be readily switched into the necessary classifications, which are usually as follows: cars going to the export piers, storage piers, in- and outbound freight-station piers, team tracks, elevators, stock pens, etc., or to the yard from which the car floats are moved for making deliveries to other railroads in the harbor. This yard should be so arranged that the cars, after they are separated or classified as above, can be readily moved to the proper point (either the coal pier or the freight pier) without interfering with the other movements. The yard is not often so well developed as receiving yards at inland terminals because of the high value of terminal property at such points. As a rule, the area or track room at a terminal does not increase in proportion to the growth of the other facilities. It should have a receiving yard, in which the trains on arrival are held previous to being classified. It should have a departure yard, in which the trains ready for movement are held. There should be caboose tracks so arranged that the caboose from an inbound train can be readily placed upon the rear of an outbound train. The movement of engines from the engine house to the receiving or outbound tracks should be arranged to give a minimum amount of interference.

Covered lighterage piers should be about 600 ft. long and about 125 ft. wide, with two tracks in the center, built at such an elevation that the floors of the cars will be level with the deck or floor of the pier. It is sometimes recommended that the sides of the pier should be composed of iron rolling or folding doors, but this feature does not seem to be desirable. It cuts down the storage space and very frequently it will be found that the post between two doors will obstruct one gangway to a lighter. Most lighters have but two gangways, and, where a railroad company handles the bulk of its lighterage business, the lighters are usually built with a standard spacing for the gangways, so that the doors of the pier can be spaced to accommodate the gangways. There should be a platform 4 ft. wide outside the walls, on the three water sides of the shed, the platform being provided with mooring piles or posts for securing vessels. Many of the older piers were built with sides having an inward slope or batter of about 1 in. to the foot, or usually about 3 ft. in the height. This was done so that in loading or unloading lighters the packages would not strike the sides of the building. This contingency is better provided against, however, by having a wider platform outside of the building, and, in fact, practically all modern pier sheds are built with vertical sides.

The shed or superstructure of the pier should be of steel-frame construction or slow-burning mill-timber construction. If wood is used, it should be white washed, to prevent sparks from setting fire to it. In large cities the law usually requires steel construction. The roof should be designed to give as much light as possible during the day. This is preferably effected by means of windows on the sides of a monitor roof, and these may be supplemented by raised skylights or small monitors running transversely across the side slopes of the roof, parallel with (and between) the roof and trusses. Flat skylights are objectionable, as being liable to leak and to be damaged by storms or heavy snow. The monitor roof should have pivoted sashes to provide for ventilation, the sashes being handled by suitable mechanism. The shed should be lighted by electricity at night. It is important to provide good, smooth floors, and the lamp room should be thoroughly fireproof. The height of the floor above mean tide will vary with the kind of vessels to be handled and with the daily tide changes. These must all be carefully studied in order to arrive at the proper height above mean tide at any given location. Usually such height as will make the deck of the pier and boat at the same elevation at mean tide will be the most satisfactory. Between piers there should be a water space of about 200 ft. The tracks running into the piers should be so arranged that they will feed directly to and from the proper part of the general yard without interference. This type of pier will be often used for export business, and will then take on the features of an export pier and be built accordingly. In weighing freight, automatic scales are being used, and should result in a reduction of expense.

Where heavy tides must be provided for, adjustable ramps or inclines should be introduced in the floor, the outer edge of the ramps being in line with the edge of the pier. By this means freight may be trucked to and from lighters at any stage of the tide without serious interference. The ramps are usually 15 to 20 ft. long, fitted with counterweights and worked by a worm gear. Fixed ramps are sometimes used for convenient access to the lower decks of vessels.

Open lighterage piers should be about 35 ft. wide and 600 ft. long, with a 6-ft. platform along each side. In many cases only two tracks are used, but long piers or piers which have more than two berths along each side should, however, have a third track, connected with the others by cross-overs. This facilitates the shifting of cars and enables the berths at the outer end of the pier to be served without disturbing the work that is being done at the other berths. A pier with three tracks should be 45 to 50 ft. wide, and with tracks at least 11 ft. 6 in., center to center. The floor of the pier may be depressed so as to bring the car floors level with the 6-ft. platforms on each side. This, however, is not usually done.

For most freight as handled by derricks, the boom derricks on the lighters are used, but the pier should have a power crane or derrick of greater capacity for handling freight that is too heavy for the lighter derricks. This crane may either be stationary (in which case the lighter must be moved to the crane) or it may travel by power along the platform to any desired point. Traveling cranes of this type are extensively used at water terminals in Europe. Heavy freight, however, is usually handled by special lighters with powerful derricks, as the freight may have to be discharged at places where pier derricks are not provided. Stationary cranes for handling heavy loads, cases of glass, machinery, etc. are also of advantage. There is undoubtedly much room for the improvement of freight-handling facilities at piers, largely by the introduction of machinery for the purpose of effecting greater rapidity and economy than are possible under the common method of employing men with trucks or slow hand winches and derricks. At European water terminals, traveling power cranes are extensively used along the sides of piers and docks.

The piers should be built at such a height above water that cars to be unloaded can be most conveniently handled. A study of the tides and the freeboard of boats is necessary to arrive at this height. Owing to storms and specially high tides, it is necessary to build the piers at a height above mean tide slightly greater than that at which work can be done to the best advantage. There should be an open water space of at least 150 ft. between the sides of these piers. This space should prevent boats from being blocked in, and would give space for a tug with a lighter alongside to pass through two lines of boats and bring a barge from the bulkhead or land end of the pier to the stream (or *vice versa*), without interfering with the loading of boats alongside the piers. Ample space will be found advantageous when the ice is running free.

The piers should be so located that cars will feed directly to and from the proper part of the cluster or general yard with the minimum amount of interference. The pier is principally used for the handling of coarser products moving in gondola or flat cars. It is frequently built wider than described where stone, pig iron or other freight requiring storage on the dock is to be handled. These conditions, however, will vary with the conditions of each road. The pier above described is the type best adapted for the handling of such business as will not have to be unloaded and held or stored on the pier.

Export and storage piers are constructed for ample storage, as well as for the economical working or handling of export freight. Under the traffic rules export freight must be held free of storage for 60 days. This is done to provide time for the arrival of steamers, or to make arrangements for the shipments. An export pier should be about 600 ft. long and about 125 ft. wide. On account of the great height of ocean steamers, it should usually be double-decked, the first-story deck having 20 ft. head room; second story, 18 ft.; height at eaves about 43 ft. The pier should be surrounded with a 6-ft. platform, arranged with the proper number of mooring piles for tying up vessels. The pier should be provided with a proper number of fire hydrants and a general system of fire protection, included in which a chemical engine is desirable. There should be two tracks running down the center of the pier, arranged at such an elevation that the floor of cars will be level with the deck of the pier. The house should be furnished with roof lights and electric lights, as already noted for lighterage piers. In fact, the general features and requirements for storage piers are similar to those of covered lighterage piers, already described.

If possible, at least one track should be provided on the upper floor. In any case there should be a proper number of elevators for moving freight from floor to floor, and more elevators will be required if the second story is not provided with a track. In case flour is to be handled, and there is no track to the second floor, it will be found desirable to supplement the elevators by an endless barrel conveyor, such as is used in flour warehouses. The use of this type of conveyor is recommended for any special kind of commodity of which a great quantity is to be handled. Inclined chutes leading from a trap in the upper floor to the side of the pier may also be used for sending bagged flour direct to boat by gravity. The chute is hinged at the upper end, and its lower end has a telescopic portion which may be adjusted to deliver the bags where required. If bonded goods are to be handled, it will be necessary to divide off part of the house as a bonded warehouse.

The double-deck pier has a number of advantages over a single-deck pier. The foundations are little, if any, more expensive, and it has approximately double the floor space, while, comparing floor space with roof, the cost is only one-half that of a single deck. The amount of real estate required is only about one-half. These advantages are great when the enormous value of terminal real estate is considered. Very frequently the second story of these piers is so arranged that immigrants can be handled in it.

It is frequently desirable to have an open track alongside export piers, as the character of goods to be handled is often such that they can be unloaded directy to or from the steamer and the car. This applies where the commodity is bulky and can be loaded in open cars, and in such cases it is frequently desirable to have this track. It saves the handling of the goods to the floor and from the floor to the car, or one handling. At certain European ports various types of traveling gantry cranes are used, which greatly facilitate the handling of freight.

The storage pier has many features of the covered lighterage pier, but it is designed primarily to accommodate the large ocean-going steamers, while the other pier is built to store only goods for harbor lighters. The export pier is for the handling of general export business. It often happens, however, that the business of one road will be very largely made up of flour, paper, tobacco or some other special commodity. In such cases the description above will hardly answer, and the design is made to meet the special requirements of the traffic. In the case of flour, which usually has to be held a long time, the pier should be several stories high, and the stories should be only about 10 ft. high in clearance. Cutting down the height of the stories saves in the cost of the building, and also in the labor of tiering up freight to a great height. In the flour storage warehouses all floors are reached by elevators, usually hydraulic or electric, and by endless-chain conveyors. Each warehouse should have platform elevators to facilitate the handling of trucks, etc., from floor to floor. With these arrangements, goods can be handled to and from any floor at very little cost.

Where a pier is built in this manner, it is usually called a storage pier, but it should have all the other features of an export pier. Export piers should be so located that tracks will lead directly to and from the proper part of the general yard with the least amount of interference.

Freight Station Pier and Team Track Delivery.—In many harbors there are freight stations having no rail connections, and at which freight is received and delivered by car floats. The piers at these stations should be about 600 ft. long and 125 ft. wide. This width will allow for a 35-ft. driveway in the center, and 45-ft. storage space on each side. Where the tides will allow it, the driveway should be located at a level about 2.5 ft. below the storage floor. In working out the height of the deck pier, the height of car floats, the fall and rise of the tide and mean tide must be carefully considered. Ramps should be provided, as noted for open lighterage piers. The height of the abutting city street must not be overlooked, and the height that will require the least amount of work in handling freight under all conditions should be chosen. The pier should be surrounded on its three water sides with a 3-ft. platform, arranged with a proper number of cleats and mooring piles for tying up car floats. Along the water street should be built a bulkhead in connection with each pier 325 ft. long, to permit the tying up of two rows of car floats on each side of the pier.

The pier will be used for inbound or city delivery freight, which in the morning will be moved from the cluster or general yard on car floats and placed alongside the pier. The cars are at once unloaded. Outbound freight will be received alongside the bulkhead and moved by trucks over the ends of car floats and on the platform between the lines of cars on each float. In this way none of the outbound freight will pass through the pier proper, and all interference will be done away with. Inconveniences will only be had when the inbound freight is arriving so late in the day that the outbound must be loaded at the same time. During the morning hours it is customary to store the outbound freight on the floor of the bulkhead until some of the cars containing inbound freight have been unloaded. It is then moved directly from the wagon as it is received over the scales and into the proper car.

In the design of these piers the same principles and requirements must be considered as in the case of covered lighterage piers. It is especially important to provide them with fire hydrants and possibly a chemical engine. Adequate roof lights should be arranged for, the lighting at night to be by electricity. It is usually not best to double-deck the pier, but the bulkhead should be two stories high, the second story to be occupied by offices for the agent and his staff, and for the storage of records. Where much fruit is handled, it will also be necessary to provide an auction room on this floor for the sale of fruit. It will often be found necessary to provide a water tank at the extreme end of the pier for supplying tugs with water. Alongside the roadway, leading into the pier at the front end of the bulkhead, should be provided a small office for the use of the cashier in issuing freight bills. This will do away with the necessity of teamsters going to and from the office on the second floor to pay their freight and leaving their teams unprotected and blocking the driveway. It will be found to expedite the movement greatly. Scales for weighing freight should be provided at proper intervals along the bulkhead, with small houses in connection with each for the receiving clerks and the weighmasters. These piers are frequently divided alphabetically, so that the goods for any person can be easily found. At some other points this classification is made by commodities, eggs being unloaded at one location and glass at another. Water closets should be provided both on the office and on the lower floor. A lamp room is usually necessary, as it is difficult to reach the cars on car floats with electric lights, so that lanterns are generally used. This room should be as fireproof as it is possible to make it.

Similar accommodations can be had by buying a block of property and building upon it the usual inbound and outbound freight stations, arranging the tracks from them to lead to a transfer bridge, so that cars can be moved between the freight houses and car floats. For operating the yard, it will then be necessary to provide a small dummy engine, or to handle the cars by electric power. The team tracks at such points are usually arranged in pairs, with the proper space for roadways. These tracks connect with ladder tracks leading to the transfer bridge. The arrangement will depend largely upon the shape and size of the property acquired.

As water-front space increases in value, particularly at harbors on tide-water coasts, the practice of building two- and three-story freight piers is becoming general. With the use of elevators, freight can be moved readily and quickly to or from any story, and, considering the value of ground space, the cost of elevating, with the improved machinery in use and the application of electric power, is often less than the interest on additional ground space needed.

The Lehigh Valley, at its Jersey City terminals, has had two-story freight piers in use for many years and during more recent years it has built two three-story piers. The dimensions are 130 by 570 ft. and freight is moved to and from the upper floors by electric elevators. Electric power is obtained from a city plant and, while the prices are rather high, the cost for current during the average month was 13 cts. per car handled, some of the freight going to the second and some to the third floor. Most of this freight was flour, in sacks and barrels. The truck haul is shorter than if the same area was contained in a single floor. For handling

general freight, a system of inclined endless-chain moving platforms—
something like the escalators in large department stores—might be adhan-

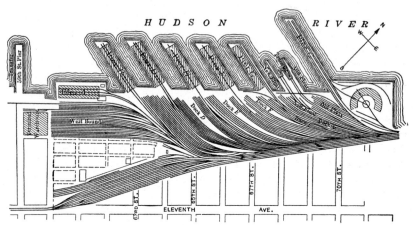

Fig. 77.—Plan of yards and piers, West 69th Street, New York City—New York Central.

tageously adopted. Platforms of this kind are in use in some freight piers
for unloading and loading vessels, and are arranged so as to permit their
removal or adjustment to different positions or elevations.

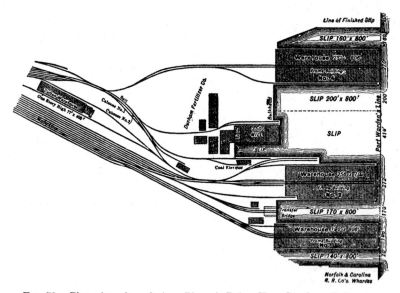

Fig. 78.—Plan of yards and piers, Pinner's Point, Va.—Southern Railway.

Figure 77 shows a modern type of freight delivery, water-front pier
and float-bridge arrangement, at a point where property values are high,
that of the New York Central yard at 69th Street, New York, extending

from 60th to 72nd Streets along the North (Hudson) River. It includes an elevator, six piers, a transfer dock and an engine house, with the usual minor structures, and has a large storage capacity for freight cars.

The plan shows the freedom with which all tracks on the piers and transfer docks may be approached from the main track, and how the remaining space has been ingeniously used for storage tracks. A general view is shown in Fig. 2, page 5.

The Pinner's Point terminal of the Southern Railway near Norfolk, Va. (Fig. 78), represents a fair development of a tide-water frontage where ample space was available and where land values were moderate. A large proportion of the freight handled through this terminal is cotton.

Fig. 79.—Covered pier of Bush Terminal.

The Bush Terminal in Brooklyn is also a tide-water front delivery yard where every available foot of space had to be utilized to its utmost because of the high values of property.

Figure 79 shows one of the large piers of the Bush Terminals in Brooklyn. A general plan, a view of a typical water scene, an end view of warehouses and a bird's-eye view of yards are shown in Figs. 80, 81 and 82.

Figure 83 shows the dock at Tampico Mexico and Figure 84 the Cunard dock, New York, with one of its newest and largest ships alongside. New York City collects upward of $5,500,000 a year in rent for municipally owned docks.

An interesting and extensive water-front development (shown in Fig. 85) is that of the Louisville & Nashville at Pensacola, Fla., consisting of several modern and well-built wharves, of which the Muskogee

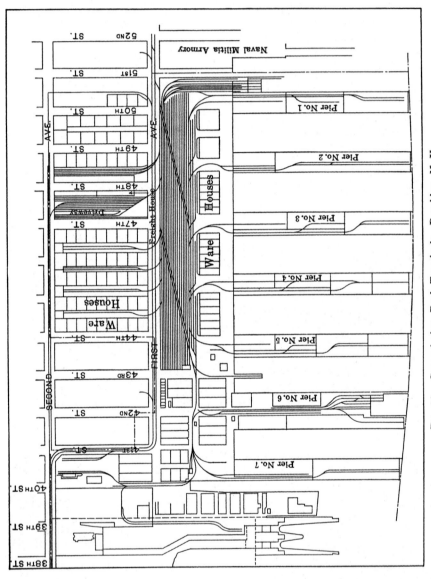

Fig. 80.—General plan, Bush Terminals—Brooklyn, N. Y.

FIG. 81.—Typical water-front scene—Bush Terminal.

FIG. 82.—Warehouses of Bush Terminal.

FIG. 83.—A modernized railway dock at Tampico, Mexico.

is used mostly for coal, phosphate, rock and lumber. It is 2,440 ft. long, 120 ft. wide at the sea end and 46 ft. wide at the shore end. On the lower level are five tracks and on the coal trestle above, two. The trestle

Fig. 84.—Cunard dock, New York City, with one of the large Cunarders alongside.

has 13 coal chutes and 4 grain chutes. These are hinged so that they may be drawn up out of the way when not in use. They have extension aprons to accommodate the hatches of vessels of any size. Coal cars

Fig. 85.—Coal, grain and lumber dock, Pensacola, Fla.—Louisville & Nashville.

are run out on the outer of the two elevated tracks, unloaded through the chutes and then moved to a transfer table at the end of the trestle, going back on the inner track to the railroad yards north of the wharf.

Phosphate rock is loaded in the same way. Vessels may be loaded from cars on the upper and lower tracks at the same time, taking on bunker coal while loading cargo, or taking coal or phosphate rock through the

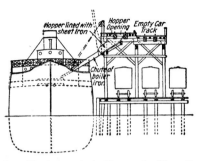

Fig. 86.—Sectional view, Muskogee dock, Pensacola, Fla.—Louisville & Nashville.

chutes and miscellaneous freight from other cars on the lower tracks. Lumber is also loaded direct from the cars. Timber is usually unloaded into the water from skids near the shore end of the wharf and held in booms until needed. The sectional view in Fig. 86 clearly shows the construction plan and operating methods.

Fig. 87.—Land-end view of Commandacia and Tarragona docks, Pensacola, Fla.—Louisville & Nashville.

The Tarragona and the Commandancia Street wharves (Figs. 87 and 88) are about a mile west of Muskogee dock. They are parallel to each other, with a slip about 160 ft. wide between. The Tarragona

Street wharf is 1,950 ft. long. At the shore end is a grain elevator of 500,000-bu. capacity. A belt conveyor runs from the elevator to the outer end of the wharf through a conveyor gallery. There are two belts, each designed to deliver 10,000 bu. of grain per hour. Along the west side of the wharf are 27 grain spouts, through which grain is delivered to the holds of the vessels. Grain can thus be loaded from both belts to one hold or separate holds of the same or different steamers. There are two warehouses on the dock; the outer one is 50 ft. wide and 404 ft. long, divided into 11 compartments, and is served by a Hunt elevated automatic railway. The other is 50 by 140 ft. On the west side are two tracks.

Fig. 88.—Water end view of Commandacia and Tarragona docks, Pensacola, Fla.—
Louisville & Nashville.

The Commandancia Street wharf is the newest—110 by 2,075 ft. The warehouse is a two-story building, 50 by 1,200 ft. Alongside of it, on the upper story, there are two railroad tracks, one on each side, and on the lower story there are three. As at the Tarragona Street wharf, vessels can be loaded from either the upper or lower floors or from both at once, and at the same time take on bunker coal. The warehouse has 400 doors—each 8 ft. wide, opening vertically. Both floors are designed to carry 600 lb. per square foot.

A bird's-eye view of the East Boston, Mass., water-front terminals of the Boston & Albany is shown in Fig. 89. In July, 1908, the plant, with the exception of one dock and two warehouses, was destroyed by fire. The present terminals cost $4,000,000, and cover about 50 acres of land.

The new piers are 780 ft. long, 240 ft. wide; the slips between are from 200 to 250 ft. wide with sufficient water to berth the largest steamships at low tide. Ships of the Cunard and Leyland lines, operating between Boston and London,

Boston and Liverpool, and Boston and Manchester dock here. The new grain elevator and dryer—the largest in New England—has a capacity of 1,000,000 bu. and cost $1,000,000. The elevator is fireproof and electrically operated. Conveyors run directly along the sides of the piers, insuring quick and easy delivery to the ships. The building is 269 ft. long, 73 ft. wide and 185 ft. high, and rests on foundations of reinforced concrete, under which are 2,600 piles. There are 192 steel bins. On the water side of the elevator are the bins from which the conveyors, which are on belt system, distribute the grain to the ships. The piers at East Boston are the largest used for commercial purposes on the Atlantic Coast except the new docks at Brooklyn and Staten Island. They are accessible for the largest ships, there being from 36 to 40 ft. of water in the slips

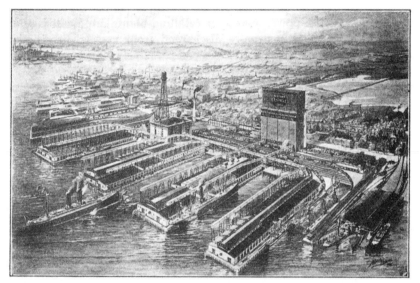

Fig. 89.—Water-front terminals, East Boston, Mass.—Boston & Albany.

and the berthing and warping in of a large ship is easily accomplished. On Pier 3, there are large rooms where incoming passengers of all classes can be easily handled, and here the United States Custom House inspectors, quarantine officers and immigration officials have their quarters.

At Superior, Wis., the double-deck flour pier of the Great Northern, 127 by 1,800 ft., handles from "house to boat" between 650,000 and 750,000 tons annually. About 80 per cent. of its business is eastbound and 60 per cent. of that is flour. Tracks are laid on both floors.

The Northern Pacific pier at Duluth is single-deck, measuring 80 by 1,700 ft.

An interesting water-front terminal is shown in Fig. 139, on the insert opposite page 330, that of the New Haven at South Boston, Mass. While it is a very important water-front development, its freight-house features are of greater importance and it is, therefore, treated under that head.

CHAPTER XVII

COAL PIERS AND STORAGE PLANTS

Piers at which coal is transferred from cars to boats or from boats to cars are located at many tide-water and fresh-water points and are equipped with mechanical appliances to facilitate rapid and economical movement. Where power plants or retailing plants are located on the water front, the coal is usually discharged from vessels directly into storage bins or coal bunkers. It is a comparatively simple undertaking to unload coal from cars to vessels and, with proper facilities, the cost need not exceed a fraction of a cent per ton. For economical and rapid handling, the highest development is in the air-dumped car, by which the engineman can in a few minutes dump his whole train load through chutes into vessels. With the machinery in use on the Great Lakes, and at many other places, an entire loaded coal car is picked up, elevated and its contents dumped bodily into the vessel alongside.

Discharging from vessels to cars is more complicated and costly. Usually a charge of from 35 to 45 cts. per ton is exacted for this service. The actual cost with the best equipped plants will vary greatly, being influenced by the character of vessels used, unloading machinery, reliability and kind of labor, and so on. The usual method of wearing out old vessels or barges in the coal-carrying trade increases the discharging expense by reason of the "between decks," small hatches, and deep keels with cross-bracing, as in such cases a very large proportion of the coal cannot be reached by the clam-shell or orange-peel grab buckets and has to be gotten out by "trimmers"—that is, shovelers who fill tubs, which are afterward hoisted. Frequently the tubs have to be wheeled some distance to reach the hatches.

The annual output of coal in this country is approximately 590,000,000 tons of 2,000 lb., of which over 15 per cent. is anthracite. Pennsylvania produces nearly all the anthracite, about 84,000,000 tons, and nearly 139,000,000 tons of bituminous coal. Illinois produces about 730,000,000 tons, and West Virginia over 92,000,000 tons of bituminous.

The Virginia Railway's coal piers (Fig. 90) at Sewalls Point, Virginia, are operated electrically throughout. Power is purchased from the Virginia Railway & Power Company, the service being 11,000 volt, 3 phase, 60 cycle, at the Railway Company's substation. This power is converted in the substation to direct current, 550 volts, for operating all the machinery, and is transformed to alternating current, 110 volts, for lighting the piers and yards.

The dumping capacity for Pier No. 1 is 5,400 tons per hour and for Pier No. 2—7,200 tons per hour, or a total of 12,600 tons per hour for both piers.

Coal Pier No. 1 is 1,045 ft. long beyond the bulkhead, 70 ft. wide, 69 ft. high at inshore end, and 76 ft. high at outshore end. The Pier consists of a steel superstructure on concrete foundations with 62 pockets, each of 60 tons capacity, and 62 adjustable chutes, 31 on each side; one car dumper and haulage for handling up to 70 ton capacity coal cars; one car dumper and haulage for handling one 120 ton or two 60 ton capacity coal cars; one incline haulage for handling 60 ton, elec-

Fig. 90.—Coal pier at Sewall's Point—Virginian Railway.

trically operated, conveyor cars; one elevator for handling 120 ton, electrically operated, conveyor cars; six 60 ton conveyor cars; six 120 ton conveyor cars; one 300 ton track scale, and yard tracks for loaded and empty coal cars.

The loaded coal cars are pushed over the hump at Maryland Avenue with a switch engine into the loaded receiving yard. They are then dropped by gravity over the scales to a barney of the disappearing type, which hauls either two small cars or one large car up on the cradle of car dumper, where they are dumped into electrically operated conveyor cars. The empty coal cars run by gravity from car dumper to kickback and thence to the empty car yard. The loaded conveyor cars are raised to the top of pier, either by incline haulage or by elevator and are dumped into the pockets on either side of pier, from which the coal flows by gravity through adjustable chutes into the holds of vessels, where it is trimmed by hand labor.

Coal Pier No. 2 is located on the south side of Coal Pier No. 1, with a slip of 319 ft. between the two Piers. It is approximately 1,074 ft. long beyond the bulkhead, 86 ft. wide, and 74½ ft. high above mean sea level.

The pier consists of a steel superstructure supported on cylindrical concrete foundations; 2 elevating car dumpers with haulages, each to handle one 130 ton or two 65 ton coal cars; one elevator for taking empty conveyor cars to and from top of pier; 4 traveling loading towers with mechanical trimmers, two on each side of pier; 4—130 ton electrically operated conveyor cars; 1—300 ton track scale, and yard tracks for loaded and empty coal cars.

Coal cars are dropped by gravity over the scales to a barney of the disappearing type, which pushes either two small cars or one large car up on the cradle of car dumper. The car dumper then dumps the coal into a steel container, which is elevated and discharges the coal into 130 ton electrically operated conveyor cars on top of pier. The empty coal cars are then pushed off the cradle by loaded coal cars, and run by gravity to a kickback and thence to the empty car yard.

The loaded conveyor cars operate on top of pier only and dump into the pockets of the traveling loading towers on either side of pier, after which they return on a middle track to the car dumpers for reloading with coal.

The coal from the pocket of the traveling loading tower is fed on a steel apron conveyor operating in the boom of the tower and is conveyed to a telescopic chute at end of boom, through which it flows by gravity to a mechanical trimmer and thence either by gravity over a curved surface of the trimmer or is distributed by a high speed belt of the trimmer into the hold of the vessel.

Two large ships or three smaller ones may be loaded on each side of each pier at the same time. The minimum depth of water in the slips and approach to the pier is about 35 ft. below mean low tide.

The Curtis Bay coal pier of the Baltimore & Ohio has a capacity of 12,000,000 tons a year and was constructed at a cost of more than $2,500,000. It was designed to overcome breakage while at the same time increasing the speed at which vessels may be unloaded. The coal-handling plant consists of two car dumpers located at the land end of the reinforced concrete pier, reinforced concrete balancing or storage hoppers located between the dumpers and the pier, and four loading and two trimming towers built of structural steel. The car dumpers and the barneys that deliver the cars to them are steam operated. Beyond the car dumpers the operation is all electrical. The coal at the dumper is dumped into an elevatingp an of 120-ton capacity which after receiving a load is lowered to an angle of 50 deg. with the horizontal, depositing the coal into the receiving hopper which feed the conveyors leading to the pier or balancing bin. Views of the plant are shown in Figs. 91, 92 and 93.

The mechanical coal trimmers, four in number, which by means of high-speed belts distribute the coal at a rate of 0.25 ton per minute up to distances of 50 ft. from the device make this plant a very complete

Fig. 91.—Two trimmers working in hold of vessel at Curtis Bay, Md.—Baltimore & Ohio.

and efficient unit. An example of fast loading is the transfer of 7,222 tons bituminous coal from 151 cars to the ship *Malden* in 1 hr. and 58 min.[1]

In discharging coal from cars to vessels, directly or indirectly, it is necessary to build piers to a considerable height above the water. There

Fig. 92.—A view of the pier, with three of the six belts in operation, Curtis Bay, Md.—Baltimore & Ohio.

is much variation in the height of vessels to be loaded. The coal may be dumped directly from a car into a chute, which, in turn, dumps into the hold of the vessel, or it may be dumped into pockets and later on be drawn from the pockets into the vessel's hold, when the vessel arrives which is to take that particular kind of coal. Usually chutes are made

[1] *Railway Age*, June 15, 1917 and June 24, 1921.

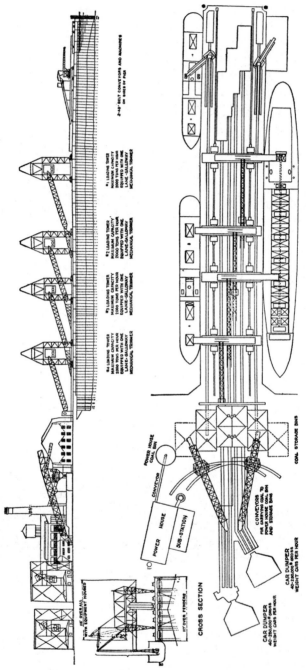

Fig. 93.—General plan Curtis Bay coal pier—Baltimore & Ohio.

to be raised or lowered to reach the proper part of the vessel. In handling anthracite coal, screens are added to separate the dust from the coal.

Ordinarily, coal piers are made up of three tracks, the two outside ones for loaded cars, which, after being unloaded, are moved ahead and switched to the middle track, dropping back by gravity to the empty car yard. The grade of the loaded car tracks should descend sufficiently toward the outer or water end of the pier to enable the cars to be moved easily and the grade of the middle or empty car track should drop in the opposite direction so the empty cars, after being transferred thereto, will return to the land end of the pier by gravity. This enables rapid and economical handling. On exceedingly long piers five tracks are used, with suitable cross-overs, so cars can be moved around those unloading at any particular berth.

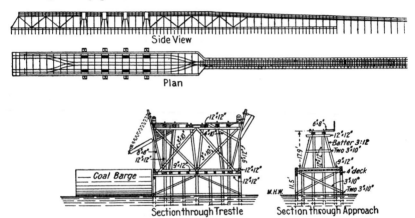

FIG. 94.—Standard tide-water coal pier—Am. Ry. Engineering Ass'n.

A number of coal pockets can be provided, spaced the proper distance, so that each of a string of cars may be unloaded. To allow for unequal lengths of cars, the distances between centers of pockets should be that of the longest car, or, preferably, a little greater.

The water space on each side of a pier or between piers should be about 150 ft., so that vessels may be docked with a tug, turned or run by others already docked. Platforms or walks should be built around the pier so that men may walk from car to car, without using tracks; suitable railing should be provided for their safety. Mooring piles are necessary at intervals alongside the piers for tying up coal barges. The plan, side view, longitudinal and transverse sections, shown in Fig. 94, are those of a standard tide-water coal pier recommended by the American Railway Engineering Association.

The Reading Company has recently completed and placed in operation at its Port Richmond Terminal, on the Delaware River, Philadelphia, Pa., one of the largest car dumping plants on the Atlantic Seaboard engaged in the shipment of tidewater coal, a view of which is shown in Fig. 95.

The car dumping machine is of the lift-turn-over type designed for the direct handling of coal from the railroad cars to vessels. It is capable of handling the different sizes and types of open top cars engaged in the coal trade, not exceeding 120 tons contents and a total weight for car and coal of 165 tons at the approximate rate of forty (40) cars per hour. Vessels with a beam of 60 ft., a height from the water line to top of hatch of 36 ft., and a draft of 35 ft. at mean low water may be handled. The structural frame of the car dumper consists of two columns at the front and three in the rear. The rear columns are built of laced channels, while the front columns are constructed of plates and angles. The front columns are provided with suitable guides for guiding the cardle as it is raised and lowered and for guiding the girder supporting the chute up and down these columns. On account of the movement of the chute and cradle no bracing could be provided between the front columns and in the erection of the machine this feature was taken care of by specially designed columns.

Track girders are provided at each end of the dumper over which the loaded and empty cars are run as they enter and leave the dumping machine. A track consisting of rails mounted on steel girders braced and supported by cross girders and the frame of the dumper is provided through the rear of the dumper frame for returning empty cars. This feature is an innovation made necessary by the limited width of the existing pier structure and required a wider structural frame than necessary in the type of dumper in which the eight car track is run around the rear of the dumper. The platform or cradle of the dumper is arranged to elevate the car to the height of the receiving pan or chute and rotate the car through an angle of 160 degrees. Upon the lower part of the cradle is mounted a movable platform provided with rails for receiving the loaded car. The mechanism for moving this platform consists of four ¼ in. cables, which run from the side of the platform around sheaves up the side of the cradle to the top of the dumper frame and across the frame down the rear of the dumper to the counterweights. This mechanism serves a double purpose—for moving the car against the cradle, and presses the four clamps against the car to prevent it from leaving the cradle as it is elevated and revolved.

The coal is dumped from the car into a concentrating pan or chute made of steel plates supported by channels and beams. A covering is placed over the pan extending from its lower end about one-half the distance to the upper end. The object of this pan is to collect the coal for delivery into the telescopic chute placed at the end of the pan. This chute is made in sections so that it may be lengthened or shortened under the control of the operator to extend or withdraw the point of delivery of the coal in the hold of the vessel.

On the lower end of the telescopic chute is a mechanical trimmer consisting of an endless belt 4 ft. wide and 4 ft. center to center of rollers driven by an electric motor placed immediately in the rear of the driving pulley of the belt at high speed to deliver the coal under the decks of the vessel, at 1,500 tons per hour with practically no breakage.

The car dumping machine has a repair crane mounted on a runway extending the entire length of the dumper and located on the top members of the dumper frame, capable of lifting a five (5) ton load from the ground to the top of the dumper and to travel the length of the dumper.

For pulling cars from the foot of the incline onto the cradle there is a haulage machine or barney car made of structural steel mounted on four railroad car wheels. This car has a swinging arm, which lies flat when running down the incline and rises up to engage the coupler of the loaded car when moving it up to the cradle of the dumper.

An electric boat haulage machine is provided for moving vessels along the dock consisting of two drums driven by an electric motor with two ropes, one extending each way along the dock from the machine.

Connecting with the approach and run-off track girders at each end of the dumper and extending the entire length of the pier are reinforced concrete trestles over which loaded cars are run up the incline by the barney car to the cardle of the dumper, and returned by gravity to switchback at the outer end of the pier and thence to the light car storage yard.

Track facilities for yard classification and storage are provided with a capacity of 915 cars.

The thawing house is constructed of cinder concrete blocks, with brick veneer, structural steel frame, poured in place gypsum with roof properly water-proofed and reinforced concrete foundations. The building is 448 ft. long, divided into four stalls, with railroad tracks the entire length. Forty-four cars may be placed in the building for thawing at one time.

Figure 96 shows four hoisting or unloading towers of the New Haven at Providence, arranged to take coal from vessels to cars or storage pockets. Upward of a million tons of coal are discharged at the dock each year. Each tower is provided with two hoppers with a capacity of 10 tons each, from which the coal is delivered into cars through gates.

Figure 97 shows a steam revolving locomotive crane unloading coal with a 2.5-yd. clam-shell bucket and delivering into cars. The plant shown in Fig. 98 is a fast unloader, with tramway working independently, used by the Milwaukee Gas Company for discharging and storing coal. Each is typical of its kind.

The problem of storing anthracite coal through the dull season is an important one with the coal-mining and coal-carrying companies. The rush orders during the fall and winter tax the mines beyond their capacities and the falling off during the summer reverses conditions so that only the storage of enormous quantities of coal permits the continuous operation of the mines from one end of the year to the other. When trade is dull, the coal goes to the piles and when a rush of orders comes, the piles are drawn upon to meet the demands. They also permit a policy of encouraging mining operations during summer months when coal cars would otherwise be idle. The location of a storage plant is governed by the cost of the site, conformation of the ground for the trackage necessary to the switching and disposal of cars and accessibility to the mines, tide-water and railroad shipping facilities.

One system of storing anthracite consists of two stationary trimmers, which are conveyors supported by shear trusses, for piling the coal; and

FIG. 95.—Car dumper, Port Richmond Terminal, Philadelphia-Reading Company.

FIG. 96.—Coal discharging plant at Providence, R. I.—New York, New Haven & Hartford.

a conveyor working in a tunnel between the trimmings for transferring the coal back from the piles to the cars. A series of such groups consti-

tutes the plant of the Philadelphia & Reading at Abrams, Pa., which
has a capacity of 500,000 tons. A modification of this system is that

FIG. 97.—Revolving locomotive crane unloader.

FIG. 98.—Fast unloader—Milwaukee Coal Co.

of the Lehigh Valley, at Ransom, Pa., shown in Fig. 99, in which a
single trimmer does all the work. The lower end is supported on a

truck traveling on a track of 10-ft. gage and the upper end on a mono-rail runway which is carried on a structure supported by 16 steel columns, 83 ft. high.   A 50-hp. motor furnishes the power and may be seen in the view of the trimmer (Fig. 100).   It takes current from a third rail, on the side of the trestle in which are the necessary bins.   The flight con-

FIG. 99.—Coal storage plant, Ransom, Pa.—Lehigh Valley.

veyor carried on the trimmer is operated by a 90-hp. motor mounted at the upper end.   For unloading there are two tunnels—a longitudinal one under the trimmer and a transverse tunnel from the middle of the runway on the side away from the trimmer.   Two reloaders, one on the trimmer side and one on the other side, move on longitudinal tracks and

FIG. 100.—Coal storage plant, Ransom, Pa.—Lehigh Valley.

carry coal in conveyors from the edge of the pile to the longitudinal tunnel in which the flight conveyors carry the coal to the center, whence it is discharged in chutes leading to a bucket conveyor running in the trans-verse tunnel, by which the coal is carried to the edge of the pile and then elevated to the screen tower over the unloading tracks.   The two sets of shaking screens have a capacity of 300 tons an hour. This rate is so rapid that it is found economical to store all sizes of coal indiscriminately, instead of separating it into piles of different sizes. The power house, supplying electricity, can be seen at the right of the photograph. The manufacturers estimate the cost of installing the system at $1 per ton of storage capacity and the cost of handling coal, both ways, from 3 to 6 cts. per ton. The Ransom plant forms a pile 83 ft. high, 342 ft. wide and 1,244 ft. long, with a capacity of 400,000 tons, which may readily be increased.

For storing coal, to hold for market requirements and to unload and reload it mechanically, the New York Central erected a plant at DeWitt, which consists of a revolving steel truss 210 ft. long between supports. The inner end is carried on an elevated turntable and the outer end upon a steel frame, resting upon four-wheel steel trucks, traveling on a circular track 420 ft. in diameter, concentric with the elevated turntable. Under the turntable is a coal pit, on two sides of which coal can be discharged from hopper-bottom cars. The coal is elevated from the pit by means of a 2.5-ton clam-shell bucket, conveyed along the truss by wire-rope trolley and deposited at any desired point in the storage area. The storage area has a capacity of 25,000 tons on each side of the coal-delivery tracks. Coal may be delivered in and out of storage at the rate of 60 tons per hour, although on a test 120 tons per hour were handled.

The British Admiralty conducted extended research into the effect of salt-water storage on coal. In 1903 there were 2-ton crates of coal submerged in sea water, and samples burned at various times since have shown that the treatment improved the coal. Later several cargoes of coal submerged in Long Island Sound since the Civil War were salvaged, and the combustion was found to be excellent, with little ash.

In the storage of coal, particularly in large quantities, the question of the fire risk or the danger of the so-called spontaneous combustion is important. Many disasters have occurred through this combustion without the action of any outside agency. This action results from the oxidation or the chemical union of oxygen with some part of the substance. Oxidation may take years or minutes. Combustion in substances susceptible to oxidation occurs when the air supply is sufficient to support oxidation, but does not occur when the air supply is sufficient in volume not only to support the oxidation of the material, but to carry away all the heat generated.

The primary cause of spontaneous combustion in soft coal is oxidation by the atmosphere, as described, aided by impurities, such as sulpur, to the degree that they are present. The oxidation process is more rapid with finer or powdered coal, and less rapid with large lump coal. Coal piled against wooden beams is apparently more susceptible to oxidation than coal in the remainder of the pile.

The source and kind of the coal are important in considering methods of piling and fire risk.   For example, anthracite is practically immune from danger of fire.   This is also true of some of the high-grade coals from West Virginia—such as Splint, Pocahontas, New River and Gas. These are all good storage coals.   Coal from Kentucky, Pennsylvania, Ohio, Illinois and Indiana are generally susceptible to spontaneous combustion in varying degrees.   Coal from some particular localities in these fields is far more susceptible than that from others; and, even when it is from a district generally producing poor-stocking coal, successful storage has been accomplished when the fine coal has been removed.   The size of the coal in itself greatly affects the combustion hazard.   Fine coal particles have more surface exposed to the action of the oxygen in the air than larger lumps.   It should be remembered that air must reach the fine-sized coal to make it dangerous, and screenings sometimes may be stored more successfully than mine-run coal, because it can be packed tighter and thus exclude the air.   The presence of iron pyrites in coal, that heavy yellow or white metallic substance, through its tendency to disintegrate when exposed to the air, assists materially in causing the coal to break into finer pieces and enhances the fire hazard.

The method of placing coal upon the ground is probably one of the most important factors to be considered in relation to its successful storage.   It should be unloaded in such a manner as to avoid the separation of the different sizes.   Lump coal naturally rolls to the outside when the pile is of any height.   This should be avoided, as it permits the accumulation of fine coal in spots, and the larger pieces of coal may form a chimney for the admission of air to the smaller pieces in the interior of the pile. When dumping continuously in one spot from railroad cars, by grab buckets, wheelbarrows or similar means, the coal will follow its natural tendency to pyramid, resulting in the separation of the fine from the lump.   The effect of this tendency can be overcome, by building the pile up flat or in layers, and an ever distribution of the fine coal throughout the pile will result.

The proper depth of the pile is important.   Generally, it should be as shallow as the amount of coal to be stored and the area available will permit.   Screenings should not be piled higher than 8 to 10 ft., the lower pile giving the greater opportunity for the escape of gases or heat.   Lump coal or sized coal, from which the fine coal has been separated, may be piled to greater depths without danger, but too great a depth renders the taking of temperatures more difficult.   When space is available, separation of a coal into several medium-sized piles instead of into one large one is advisable in order to localize trouble.

Other factors are the avoidance of placing wood or other easily combustible materials in contact with the coal, avoiding contact with steam pipes, manholes, brick furnace walls or other possible sources of heat, without ventilation of the pile. This may do more harm than good, as it more often admits just enough air to encourage combustion without furnishing enough ventilation to carry off the heat and gases from the pile.

With proper temperature readings it is easy to determine whether trouble is brewing in the pile or not. A temperature of 150° or over indicates danger, and, as the coal will not burst into flame until it reaches 600 to 700°, there is ample time to devise means to combat the fire—either by using water or its equivalent, or by moving the coal. Water, to be effective, must be gotten to the seat of trouble in sufficient quantities to put out the fire. To spray the top of the pile is the worst thing possible. Water should be introduced into the pile through a long pipe to the trouble. In moving the coal, it is preferable to move it dry, using water anywhere it is too hot to handle.

Summarizing, the following recommendations should be followed in storing coal:

1. Coal to be placed in storage should be piled as shallow as possible in the space available.

2. When lump, egg or nut, coal is unloaded it must not be broken by allowing it to drop a great distance, forming smaller particles, which may be the source of trouble later on.

3. When it is unloaded, it should be piled flat—in other words, not allowed to pyramid so the lumps will segregate from the fine coal and form a chimney for the admission of air to the fine coal.

4. Coal should be packed tight rather than an attempt made to ventilate it. This will prevent the easy admission of air to the inside of the pile.

5. No oily waste, pieces of paper, straw, wood or anything that is of an easily combustible nature must be permitted to get in the pile.

6. Wet coal must not be placed in storage.

7. Coal must not be piled over the top of hot pipes, manholes or against the hot outside walls of furnaces.

8. If a fire has started in a coal pile it is bad policy to wet the pile with water unless the fire had gone so far that it is impossible to work, due to the heat and gases being given off.

9. If a fire had started, the source of trouble should be found by taking the coal out and spreading it over the ground, piling it not more than 2 ft. deep, if possible. It will naturally cool down, if it is not blazing, and the coal coked until it is a glowing red. If very hot, it should be cooled with water.

CHAPTER XVIII

ORE AND LUMBER DOCKS

Methods of loading and unloading coal, ore, sand, cement and other coarse ordinary freight and of discharging vessels containing it necessarily differ as does also the machinery used to assist in such work. They vary particularly because the character and quantity of freight handled at each dock usually is of many kinds. Coal handling is described elsewhere.

Lumber is usually handled by cranes such as are described hereinafter.

Fig. 101.—Ore handling machine, Stockton, Ind.—Illinois Steel Co.

As water transportation is vastly more economical than rail for coarse, bulky commodities, on which time is not essential, much freight is transferred from cars to vessels, or *vice versa*, to utilize the water transportation afforded by the rivers and lakes of the United States. A vast amount is handled on the Great Lakes. In many instances the handling includes storage in addition to the transfer. Ore, coal, coke and lumber freight may be accumulated on the water front, and stored until needed, because of opportunities to purchase in favorable markets, necessity for storing quantities in advance, to care for anticipated orders for finished product and, in the case of coal, because it may be mined, screened, etc., to better advantage during summer months, and at the time when railroads have a surplus of coal cars on hand. In addition to the machinery for transferring a cargo from cars to vessels or *vice versa*, it then becomes necessary to supply additional machinery and track arrangements for unloading into storage pockets or onto piles, and again reloading it.

A view of a successful and rapid machine for handling coke and coal in the storage yards of the Illinois Steel Company at Stockton, Ind., is shown in Fig. 101. The machine consists of a system of conveyors which handle coal and coke both into and from the storage yards. All operations are performed by one self-contained unit, instead of by entirely

FIG. 102.—Union Sand Material Co.'s Plant, St. Louis.

separate systems. The machine operates on its own track. To increase the storage capacity of a yard, the only expense necessary is the cost of lengthening the machine track and the trestles from which the cars are dumped. In the Stockton yard, the machine handles material from any part of the present yard, which is 100 ft. wide and over a quarter of a mile long. There is room to extend the siding on which the machine runs three-quarters of a mile further if necessary. About 100,000 tons of coke are ordinarily stored. The machine is operated by three men and delivers the coke to the car at the rate of 3 tons per minute. The first cost is small and the operating expenses are comparatively low.

This machine has numerous applications. Different sizes are built, ranging from the mine-car loader, having a capacity of 30 to 40 cu. ft.

per minute, to machines running as high as 300 cu. ft. per minute. It is adapted for the use of contractors in tunnel work, as well as in mines in general. The storage machine in its different sizes will handle coal, coke, loose rock, tailings, fire clay, gravel, sand and other loose materials, at a cost claimed to be surprisingly low.

A machine for handling sand from barges to bins, with a capacity of 90 cu. yd. per hour, running on four wheels on an independent track, with grab-bucket crane, is in use in St. Louis, by the Union Sand and Material Company, and is shown in Fig. 102.

Figures 103 and 104 are views of the Hulett ore unloader of the Buffalo, Rochester & Pittsburgh at Buffalo; Fig. 103 showing a steamship alongside the unloaders, giving a good idea of the rugged construction of these unloaders and Fig. 104 showing the leg of the

Fig. 103.—Mechanical (Hulett) unloaders at Buffalo.

unloader in the hold of the boat and also bringing out the advantages of the modern construction of vessels, enabling them to discharge their cargoes rapidly and economically, as compared with the adapted "between decks" with numerous small hatches of the older ships.

Formerly all ships at the Buffalo terminus were unloaded by hand, making the cost high. Later on improvements were completed, consisting chiefly of the installation of a complete Hulett unloader plant, which has been in satisfactory operation and greatly decreased the cost of unloading iron ore.

The dock upon which the machine is located is comparatively short, making it necessary to use four stub tracks beneath it, as shown in the

general elevation. Ore can thus be unloaded into cars on either one of
these tracks, the normal capacity being about 2,000 tons per day of 10
hours.

The unloader consists essentially of two parallel girders at right
angles to the length of the dock, mounted on trucks. These support
the trolley or carriage which, in turn, carries the walking beam, the outer
end of which supports a vertical leg provided at the lower end with a
bucket. The bucket leg is suspended in a vertical position and the
operator rides in it just over the bucket, and therefore goes into the
boat at each trip. From his position he can see its working and control

Fig. 104.—Leg of Hulett unloader in boat.

its movements. By means of hoisting mechanism, the beam is made to
oscillate up and down, carrying the bucket up over the hatch or to the
bottom of the hold. When the bucket reaches the pile of ore in the
boat, it is closed and filled, after which the leg is raised and trolleyed
back over the hopper on the dock into which the contents of the bucket
are discharged. From the hopper, the ore is dumped into an auxiliary
"bucket car," which, in turn, transfers the ore to the cars, while the
bucket is returning to the hold for another load. The bucket leg is
mounted on rotating trunnions in the walking beam so that the bucket
can revolve and reach out in all directions beneath the hatch.

The bucket has a capacity of about 10 gross tons, and a speed of 60
buckets in 40 min. has been obtained. The usual speed is about one
trip per minute and is easily maintained. The bucket has a spread
of 18 ft. 3 in., with an additional scraping motion of 2 ft. 11 in., thus
making it possible to reach more than halfway from the center of one

hatch to the center of the next, considering 24-ft. centers of hatches.   The
bucket leg also travels lengthwise of the hatch so as to reach both sides
of the boat.   In an ordinary ore-carrying boat no difficulty is experienced
in reaching 90 per cent. of the cargo, and in some of the modern boats
97 per cent. has been unloaded without the help of shovelers.   The
bucket operator controls all the movements of the machine except
the travel from hatch to hatch and the operation of the "bucket car,"
which are controlled by another man.

An hydraulic pump and a steam boiler, each of 175-hp. capacity,
furnish the necessary power.   Hydraulic cylinders furnish the power
for hoisting, for lowering, for trolleying and for rotating the bucket.
Excessive pressure on the water bottom of the boat is prevented by the
use of a counter-balance cylinder.   Each hydraulic cylinder has automatic plugging valves which stop its motion at the end of the stroke.
An auxiliary steam engine is used for moving the machine along the
dock and for operating the "bucket car."

Steamers arriving at Lorain, Ohio (B. & O.), with ore are unloaded
by Brown hoist machines, driven by electricity, equipped with three grab
buckets, having a total capacity of 1,000 tons of ore per hour.   These
buckets scoop up from 7 to 10 tons of ore each trip.   The ore is dumped
into hoppers for storage or directly into cars.

In loading and unloading lumber, machinery plays an inconspicuous
part, because the long pieces cannot ordinarily be handled by anything
but ordinary derricks, after chaining around as many sticks of timber
or pieces of board as may be kept together.   Lumber-handling vessels
usually have fore and aft hatchways through which lumber is passed,
but in many cases it has to be lifted vertically through deck hatchways.
At some water-front docks handling large amounts of lumber, conveyors
are provided to carry it to the storage points in yards or alongside tracks
for transfer to open cars and reshipment by rail.   These conveyors
are usually a series of rollers, similar to those in use at the large sawmills.

Figure 105 shows a plant consisting of 12 ore-handling towers, each
equipped with 2-ton clam-shell ore buckets for taking coal or ore out of
vessels and delivering it into storage and later taking it out of storage and
delivering into cars.

On the Great Lakes much progress has been made of later years in
improving the type of vessels used in ore- and coal-carrying trade and
this made it possible to use faster working loading and discharging
machinery and thereby greatly to reduce the handling cost.   On the
Atlantic seaboard little has been done in this direction.

Steamers "James E. Davidson," 524 ft. long; "James P. Walsh,"
500 ft.; and "James C. Wallace," 552 ft., operating on the Great Lakes,
have a carrying capacity of 8,000, 9,000 and 10,000 gross tons respectively
and are unloaded by clam-shell machines.   They are of the lake type.

The "E. H. Gary," built for the Steel Corporation, carries 10,000 gross tons—has carried 10,887—and is of low power. Its economy lies in the fact that it carries its load on the same fuel consumption as the "Manola," which has but 3,000-tons capacity. The ore carrier has undergone many changes of design and construction. Hatches were formerly spaced 24 ft., center to center. All hatches are now spaced 12 ft. center; that is to say, it is 12 ft. from the center of one hatch the center of the other. This leaves a deck strip of only 18 in. between hatches, and the deck is, therefore, almost a continuously open hole from pilot house to engine,

FIG. 105.—Twelve ore-handling towers in one plant.

the space between hatches being only that necessary for the transverse girders. The engines of the lake freighters are far aft. By this system vessel hatches have been practically doubled in number, thus affording greater convenience in loading and greater dispatch in unloading.

Longitudinal rigidity was once secured by stringers and stanchions extending from the sides of the vessel. These projections interfered with the unloading machines and it became necessary to obviate them in some manner if the utmost dispatch was to be secured in unloading. Their place was afterward taken by a girder, straight in some ships and curved in others, extending from side to side of the ship directly between the hatches. This system leaves the hold absolutely unobstructed and is the accepted design of the lake freighter today The system has marvelously facilitated the great unloading machines the steamer "Geo. W.

Perkins," with a cargo of 10,514 tons, having been unloaded in 4 hours and 10 min. The great unloading machines, with automatic clam-shell buckets, grab from 10 to 12 tons of ore at a time and make a trip a minute. This cargo was unloaded directly into the cars, the car moving very slowly under the machines and receiving the contents of the buckets as it went along. Four of these buckets will fill a car. The "Perkins" took on this cargo in 89 min., 9,000 tons of it being the work of the first 35 min. She was in port altogether 180 min., which included shifting. Ships of special design, docks of special design and unloading machines

Fig. 106.—Ore dock of Duluth, Missabe and Northern on Duluth-Superior harbor. Double room traveler erecting the steel work.

of special design, all working in unison, have brought this about. At its Ashtabula Harbor facilities the New York Central established a high mark by unloading 83,086 tons of iron ore from 10 steamers into 1,386 freight cars in one day.

The largest ore-shipping dock in the world is that of the Duluth, Missabe & Northern on Duluth-Superior Harbor (Figs. 106, 107 and 108). As a record structure of its kind, the quantity of the more important material items used during its three-year construction period are of interest, such as, 1,067,971 lin. ft. of timber piling 50 to 85 ft. in length, 174,230 lin. ft. of 12-in., 43-lb. U. S. Steel sheet piling, 162,570 sq. ft. of triangular mesh reinforcement, 59,846 cu. yd. of concrete and 29,609 tons of steel. The removal of the old dock involved the pulling of 8,255 piles and the removal of three rock-filled timber cribs.

The entire dock foundation, being surrounded by sheet steel piling, has been pumped full of sand (182,000 cu. yd.) and this leveled off for a support for the concrete foundation slab 2,438 ft. long, 69 ft. wide and 6 ft. thick, the piles projecting 9 in. into the concrete.

The superstructure has a structural steel frame with concrete partition walls, pocket walls and sidewalk slabs. The entire pocket structure is

Fig. 107.—Ore docks of the Duluth, Missabe and Northern on Duluth-Superior harbor. View of the approach viaduct.

carried by two lines of steel columns (each designed to carry 1,500,000 lb.) spaced 12 ft. apart, arranged in pairs to form bents under each transverse wall. There are 384 pockets with 6,540-cu. ft. capacity each. Eight standard 50-ton ore cars can be dumped into each pocket without trim-

Fig. 108.—Ore docks of the Duluth, Missabe and Northern on Duluth-Superior harbor. View of completed dock.

ming, thus providing a storage capacity of 3,072 cars, or 153,600 tons.

The top of the dock is 76 ft. 5 in. wide and carries four tracks the entire length and is designed to carry the heaviest engines of the Duluth, Missabe and Northern, a 304-ton Mallet and a 266-ton santa Fe with 55,000-lb. axle loads.

The dock has a two-track approach trestle, 3,087 ft., with 400 ft. of elevated embankment carried between parallel concrete retaining walls 24 ft. apart.

The old methods of loading and unloading vessels by the handful have passed into antiquity in all up-to-date ports.   Anywhere from 15 to 100 tons at a time are now handled on the big docks.   The improved machinery for bulk cargo handling, makes the old methods look like stoking a furnace with a teaspoon.   In the past six years several factors have caused interest among shippers in a cheaper and more rapid scheme of handling heavy commodities.   The manufacturers of apparatus started a movement in this direction 24 years ago, and succeeded in getting a limited number of plants installed as early as 1902.   The development of plants for handling large tonnages of coal and iron ore was the most obvious necessity and it was the first attacked on a large scale.

"The necessity for such development centered around the Great Lakes region and the pioneer installations were put in in this vicinity . . .   The coal supply of the states bordering on the iron-ore region was largely taken from the lower lakes on the return trip of the ore boats.   In order to perform this task with the minimum of equipment and operating costs per ton, it was plainly necessary to provide machinery for cheap and rapid discharge of cargo from ship to dock or railroad and *vice versa*, the length of time the ship was tied up to the dock being a vital factor in costs.   The result has been a high state of development and concentration of bulk cargo-handling plants in the Lakes region.

"In the late nineties the Wellman-Seaver-Morgan Company brought out its ore unloader, each machine capable of handling ore at from 500 tons per hour upward.   At about the same time the car dumper, for overturning standard railroad cars and dumping their contents, was developed.   The latter have been evolved until at present they will handle 30 dumps per hour and upward, some installations handling as much as 3,000 tons per hour of net material, two cars in tandem.   A car dumper is shown in Fig. 109.

"Conditions due largely to the European War caused a more general interest to be developed along our coast line in these methods.   Prior to our participation in the war a few installations had been made on the Atlantic Coast, especially in the line of loading cargo and bunker coal.   Rising labor costs and necessity of rapid 'turn around' on the comparatively few vessels available brought the issue of improved dock facilities to the forefront . . .   In this connection two contracts . . . may be noted.   One is with the Lehigh Valley Railroad Company and covers an automatic ore unloader carrying a 15-ton clam-shell bucket on the unloader leg and designed to make a complete cycle or round trip in 50 sec.   The machine is electrically operated throughout and is similar to that shown in an accompanying illustration.

"This unloader consists of a main framework mounted on trucks which travel along runway rails . . .   The girders of the main framework form a support for runway rails on which a trolley travels.   This trolley supports a balanced walking beam, from the outer end of which a stiff bucket leg depends.   At the lower end of this leg is the bucket, which is operated by machinery located on the walking beam

"In addition to the vertical movement, which is given to the bucket leg by the walking beam, it also has a motion of rotation around its vertical axis. This motion is introduced to enable the machine to reach along the keel of the boat and clean up ore between hatches. The distance from point to point of bucket shells when open is approximately 21 ft. About 97 per cent. of the ore is removed from the boat without hand labor.

"Records of 50 machines in operation indicate that this type of machine will handle ore at 2½ to 4½ cts. per ton, including all fixed charges, and records of as high as 783 tons of ore per hour per machine from tie-up to cast-off of boat have been made.

Fig. 109.—A device for "dumping" railroad cars.

"The other contract is with the Western Maryland Railroad Company, covering a Wellman car dumper to handle 100-ton road cars at Port Covington, Baltimore. It is the first electrically operated lifting dumper for seaboard coal loading to be negotiated. The lifting feature is designed to raise the road car high enough before overturning to cause the coal to run down the apron and chute into the ship's hold as illustrated. Dumping directly into the ship eliminates breakage and waste due to rehandling. The entire cargo is trimmed without the use of hand labor.

"The machine consists essentially of a rectangular frame work supporting a rotating cradle in which the loaded railroad car is held while discharging. An entirely automatic counter-weight device clamps the car to cradle which is inverted by the revolving mechanism, carrying the car with it."[1]

[1] *Literary Digest*, Sept. 18, 1920.

CHAPTER XIX

GRAIN ELEVATORS

From the first preparation of the soil for wheat growing until the wheat is turned into flour, machinery plays an all-important part in the process, beginning with the plow and reaching its highest development in the modern grain elevator.

Dr. Dodlinger, in his "The Story of Wheat," divides the transportation of wheat into four aspects: (1) transportation from the farm to the local market; (2) from the local market to the primary market; (3) from the primary market to the seaboard; and (4) from the seaboard to the foreign market.

From the farm to the local market the wheat is usually hauled in wagon loads. Except on the Pacific slope, where it is sacked, wheat is transported from the farm to its ultimate destination in bulk and its flowing quality is used to assist in its economical handling. Direct from the field or from the storage granaries on the farm the wheat is carted to the local market, and from there shipped to the primary market. To take care of the wheat at the local market and facilitate its transfer from wagon to car, the grain elevator performs the useful functions of storage, cleaning and drying. The wheat flows from the wagon into receptacles at the elevator, from whence it is lifted by power-driven buckets to the storage bins. From these bins it flows into the cars or into the drying and cleaning apartments, as may be desired, or is held indefinitely, up to the capacity of the elevator. At the local markets are many small elevators, ranging from a capacity of 10,000 to 40,000 bu. Most of them are owned by elevator companies; others belong to local grain dealers; the remainder belong to farmers. On the Northern Pacific a few years ago there were upward of 800 elevators, of which 58 per cent. belonged to the line elevator companies, 39 per cent. to the local grain dealers and 3 per cent. to the farmers.

The grain elevator assumes its greatest importance at the primary market.

The table[1] following shows the number and estimated capacity of elevators at leading United States and Canadian grain storage centers, Jan. 1, 1923.

[1] Miller's Almanac, 1924.

UNITED STATES

	Number	Capacity, in bushels
Minneapolis, Minn.	64	55,285,000
Chicago, Ill.	63	54,235,000
Duluth, Minn.	29	38,825,000
New York, N. Y.	12	8,650,000
Buffalo, New York	28	31,950,000
Kansas City, Mo.	41	29,930,000
Detroit, Mich.	7	2,625,000
Indianapolis, Md.	13	2,635,000
Toledo, Ohio	14	5,670,000
Cleveland, Ohio	11	1,840,000
Cincinnati, Ohio	17	2,995,000
St. Louis, Mo.	42	10,554,000
New Orleans, La.	8	7,670,000
San Francisco, Cal.	10	147,000*
Port Costa, Cal.	2	100,000*
Stockton, Cal.	5	103,000*
Seattle, Wash.	9	2,490,000 / 45,200*
Portland, Ore.	20	253,100*
Tacoma, Wash.	16	232,100*
Baltimore, Md.	8	8,800,000
Boston, Mass.	3	2,500,000
Council Bluffs, Iowa; Omaha, Neb.	20	11,100,000
St. Joseph, Mo.	13	3,592,000
Milwaukee, Wis.	14	8,45,000
Philadelphia, Pa.	4	4,100,000
Galveston, Texas	4	3,750,000
Louisville, Ky.	7	2,945,000
Nashville, Tenn.	9	2,325,000
Memphis, Tenn.	13	1,225,000
Norfolk, Va.	3	1,325,000
Newport News, Va.; Fort Worth, Texas	16	5,871,000
Evansville, Ind.	5	1,410,000
Portland, Me.	2	2,500,000

CANADA

	Number	Capacity, in bushels
Fort Williams & Port Arthur	35	63,310,000
Montreal, Que.	6	10,150,000
Port Colbourne, Ont.	2	3,500,000
Port McNicoll, Ont	1	4,200,000
Vancouver, B. C.	7	1,633,000
West St. John, N. B.	2	1,700,000
Tiffin, Ont.	2	3,250,000
Depot Harbor, Ont.	2	1,750,000
Goderich, Ont.	2	1,600,000
Kingston, Ont.	2	1,030,000
Halifax, N. S.	1	500,000
Midland, Ont.	1	3,000,000
Prescott, Ont.	1	1,000,000
Quebec, Que.	1	2,000,000

* Capacity in tons for sacked grain.

In these great storehouses the grain is gathered and loaded into cars or vessels for shipment to the seaboard. Some of the storehouses hold a million and a half bushels. Again, at the seaboard, the elevators play their important part in transferring the grain from car to ocean steamer.

It may be of interest to sketch briefly the successive steps taken by the grain in its movement from car to ocean steamer at a seaboard grain elevator. When unloaded from the cars into the receiving hoppers of the elevator, the grain is carried upward to one of the series of weighing bins. Here the weight of each car is ascertained and recorded. The bin itself is a, scale and is carefully adjusted before the contents of the car begin to flow into it. From the weighing bin the grain flows to storage bins, where it is held subject to the orders of the owner. Possibly it may need cleaning or drying, or the agents may desire to mix it with a better or poorer grade. In either case, the grain flows from the storage bin to the dryer, the cleaner, or is mixed with other grain as desired, and again elevated to a storage bin to be held until orders are given to load it into a steamer. Then from the storage bin it flows either directly through spouts to the open hatch of the vessel or is transferred by belts through galleries along the pier until it reaches a loading spout through which it finds its way into the hold of the boat.

As already stated, the farmers on the Pacific Coast adhere to the older European practice of loading the grain in sacks instead of taking advantage of the flowing properties of the grain, which allow it to be so readily handled in bulk. One reason is that the well-defined limits of the rainy season on the Pacific slope make it unnecessary to provide protection against rain in the dry season, and the wheat may be stored in sacks on platforms, a practice which could not be followed east of the Rockies. Thus, the problem of storage capacity is made easier, but, on the other hand, the sacking method is plainly uneconomical.

The loading of a 1,000-bu. car of sacked grain at the country warehouse takes two men two hours, while it can be loaded in bulk by one man in 5 min. The railway freight on bulk grain is the same as on sacked grain; in other words, the transportation of the sack has to be paid for at the same rate as the transportation of the grain. At tide water it takes 12 men, including the weigher, one hour to unload and pile a car of 1,000 bu. in sacks. In bulk, three men can sweep out a car, unload the grain and bin it in from 5 to 10 min. It takes 15 men 4.5 days of eight hours each to load a vessel with 125,000 bu. of sacked grain. In bulk, the same quantity of grain can be loaded in three or four hours by one-half as many men.

It is advantageous to a railway to have elevators on its lines. Grain can be accumulated in the elevator until there are several carloads of it, and then poured rapidly into the cars. Thus, the delay to rolling stock is less than when the grain is shoveled from the farmers' wagons into cars or is transferred direct from the farmers' wagons to the cars in sacks. There was a time when there were a number of little flat warehouses along the railways in the Middle West, some of them having a capacity as small as 1,000 bu. It took two to four days to scoop enough grain from one of these to load a car. On the other hand, the ordinary country elevator had a capacity of several thousand bushels—a modern one usually has a capacity of not less than 25,000 bu., and 10 to 15 cars can be loaded from it daily. Where sack grain is accumulated in flat warehouses before being loaded on cars, the delay to railway equipment in loading is less than the delay that would be caused by shoveling it from a wagon into a car, but it is substantially greater than the time taken to load cars from an elevator. In seasons of heavy railway traffic the elevators afford a place where large quantities of grain can be stored awaiting cars. The elevator system, therefore, tends at such times to reduce the congestion of traffic.

The foregoing relates mainly to the country elevators. The advantages to the farmer, the shipper and the railway, of terminal elevators at large markets were early recognized to be equally great. The grain, as it came from the farmer, often needed to be dried, cleaned or graded, to render it fit for export or for milling. In Illinois, for example, during a wet season, there is occasionally a soft corn crop. In this condition it cannot be transported far without spoiling, and it is necessary to get it to a point where it can be properly treated. This usually can only be done in a large terminal elevator, as the country elevators are seldom equipped with machinery for any purpose but the elevation and loading of grain. The existence of facilities for treating the grain so as to keep it from spoiling inures, in the long run, to the advantage of producer, carrier, grain dealer and consumer.

Usually, when grain is bought, its ultimate destination is unknown; it may be ground into flour in Minneapolis, St. Louis or Chicago, or it may be shipped to the Atlantic seaboard or sent to Europe. The merchant, therefore, needs a place to store it while seeking a buyer. The terminal elevator serves this purpose. It is often advantageous to mix a lower grade of grain with a higher grade in order to increase the value of the former, and the elevator usually is equipped with machinery for this purpose also.

The establishment of terminal elevators at the large markets on its lines is extremely desirable for the railway. When a terminal elevator is built on the lines of one road, the grain moving to that elevator is pretty sure to move over that road, thus insuring the traffic to that road. Much of the grain begins movement before its ultimate destination is known, and it is pretty sure to be held in storage somewhere. If not held in storage in a terminal warehouse, it must be held in cars, with consequent misuse of such cars, since their function is to move, not to store grain or other commodities. A great deal of grain has to be transferred at terminals from cars of one railway to cars of another, or to boats on rivers, canals, the Great Lakes and the ocean. These transfers, of course, may be accomplished through an elevator with the least delay to the cars. Both the country elevator and the terminal elevator enable

Fig. 110.—Grain elevator at Chicago—Santa Fe Road.

the railroads to load their cars to their cubic capacity with the lighter grains, such as oats, which cannot be done when grain is shoveled into the car or stored in it in bags.

The Sante Fe elevator in Chicago, operated by the C. R. & I., H. B. is a typical modern and capacious elevator. A general view is shown in Fig. 110, a plan in Fig. 111 and a section of working house in Fig. 112.

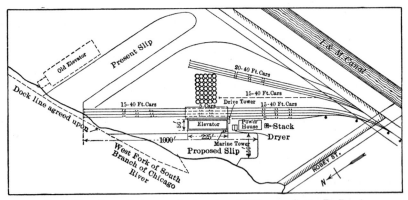

Fig. 111.—General plan, grain elevator at Chicago—Santa Fe Road.

The elevator comprises a frame working house of 400,000-bu. capacity, with car shed and marine tower; a reinforced concrete storage annex of 1,000,000-bu. capacity; drying and bleaching equipment and a 1,500-hp. plant. The working house is 225 ft. long and 56 ft. wide, of timber and cribbed construction, covered on the outside up to the top of the bins with brick and above that point with corrugated steel. The receiving and shipping legs are of unusually large capacity, namely, 15,000 bu. per hour each. There are five shipping legs and five receiving legs and, in addition, 15 smaller legs for serving the cleaning, scouring, drying and bleaching plants, also one leg for disposal of screenings.

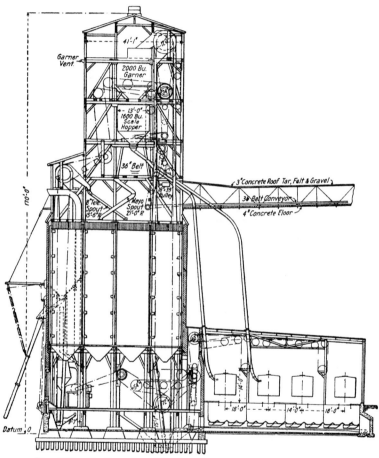

Fig. 112.—Section of working house, elevator, Chicago—Santa Fe.

In the cupola are 10 hopper scales, each of 1,600-bu. capacity. A dust-collecting system, a large car puller, a longitudinal conveyor in the cupola for conveying grain lengthwise of the house, a passenger elevator, etc. are essential portions of the equipment. A marine tower constructed of steel, with a 6,000-bu. marine leg, is at one end of the building and eight vessel-loading spouts above the dock. The storage annex consists of 35 cylindrical concrete bins, each 23 ft. inside diameter; and 24 interspace bins, with 15,000-bu. conveyors for filling and emptying. The drying plant has an hourly capacity of 1,000 to 1,500 bu.

The facilities provided for unloading cars form the distinctive operating feature of the working house. A steel shed extends over four tracks between the working house and the storage annex. On each track are five unloading places, located 45 ft. centers, in order to accommodate the longest cars. By this arrangement 20 cars can be set for unloading at one time. Beneath each unloading place is a steel track hopper with a capacity of a full car load. Each hopper discharges through four open-

Fig. 113.—Grain elevator in Baltimore—Baltimore & Ohio.

ings to a 15,000-bu. conveyor running below a line of four hoppers, across the basement under the track shed, to one of the receiving legs. The valves in the bottoms of each line of four track hoppers are controlled by an interlocking device under the control of the operator near the corresponding receiving leg.

The tracks are elevated to allow sufficient capacity in the hoppers and are carried on an embankment to a point 600 ft. beyond the elevator, making room for 15 40-ft. cars on each track outside of the track shed; and five cars on each track inside. This is a total of 80 cars which can be set at one time; 20 can be unloaded and pulled out of the track shed by the car puller and the next 20 pulled in, repeating for lots of 20 cars each, before further switching is required. After being pulled out by the car puller, empty cars will run down a gravity track to the place desired.

An elevator, of reinforced concrete construction, built for the B. & O. in Baltimore, is shown in Fig. 113. No wood was used in its construction. Its capacity is 250,000 bu., divided into 130 bins, varying in size from 1,000 to 3,000 bu. Most of the bins are of the smaller capacity. They are rectangular in shape, the reinforced concrete walls varying in thickness from 6 to 8 in.

The B. & O. unloads the cars, elevates the grain, weighs it and deposits it in bins. These bins are leased to numerous local dealers in Baltimore,

Fig. 114.—An aeroplane view of the Baltimore & Ohio grain elevators and freight terminals at Locust Point, Baltimore, Md.

and when the grain is in the bins it may be taken therefrom at the will of the lessee dealers.

For receiving, there are two tracks, each having two unloading pits of car-load size. The grain is unloaded by power shovels and then the operator pulls a lever opening a gate, which allows the grain to be discharged onto a 30-in. rubber-belt conveyor, below the car pits, and the conveyor belts transfer the grain to the bottom of the elevator legs, which lift it to the top of the cupola. From the head of the legs it is discharged into the garner and held until the weighman is ready. At the proper time he pulls a slide and allows the grain to drop into the scales from the garner. There are two hopper scales, each of 1,000-bu. capacity, with printing attachment on recording beams.

After the grain is weighed it is discharged into any one of the bins directly from the scales, through spouts. Underneath the bins are two stories, the upper one being the sacking floor, where the grain is drawn off from the bins and sacked by eight 3-bu. Richardson automatic bagging scales, arranged in a row on steel tracks which run under the bins.

The automatic scales enable the operator to bag seven bags, of 3 bu. each, every minute.

On the sacking floor are three 24-in.-belt bag conveyors for carrying the sacks across the building and discharging to the teams underneath. There are three driveways under the elevator and one alongside under an awning, to accommodate teams.

The readiness with which grain (a low-class commodity permitting slow movement) adapts itself to water transportation may be comprehended by the statement that the steamer "L. S. De Graff" has taken from Chicago in one trip 421,000 bu. of wheat, weighing 12,661 tons.

In Fig. 114 a view of the Baltimore and Ohio's grain elevators and freight terminals at Locust Point, Baltimore, Md., is shown. These elevators in one 13-hr. day loaded 285,000 bu. of grain into vessels.

Western Canada is today the wheat-producing section of the North American continent. In 1910 it produced 120,477,310 bu.; in 1923 this climbed to 452,260,000 bu. To handle this enormous crop successfully, in its movement from the farm to a milling point, or into the hold of an ocean freighter, demands extensive facilities. Practically all grain on the North American continent is moved by railroads—the primary move is by wagons or trucks to the railroad at a point where a country elevator is located; thence to a terminal elevator, where the box car is unloaded and the grain placed in storage until ordered on to its further destination. Much of it is handled by combined rail and water routes, necessitating handling through several elevators.

The elevator[1] of Canadian National at Port Arthur, Ont., is one of the largest grain handling plants in the world, having a storage capacity of over 8,500,000 bu. of grain. The plant formerly consisted of three fireproof tile storage annexes and two large capacity timber work houses. The deterioration of the timber structures made necessary the reconstruction of at least one of the timber work houses, and a single fireproof work house of reinforced concrete construction to do the work of both timber work houses was built.

The unloading device adopted consists of a tilting platform with auxiliary mechanisms for opening the grain door and introducing deflecting baffles into the car so that as the car is tipped endwise the grain content is discharged by gravity through the side door into the elevator receiving hopper. The introduction of this device into a grain elevator eliminates the inefficient process of car shoveling from the otherwise highly efficient methods of handling grain in bulk. All necessity for manual labor in the grain-handling process is removed, and the employes of an elevator thus equipped are operators, not laborers.

The fireproof portion of the elevator is known as elevator "B" and consists of the fireproof work house, having a storage capacity of 750,000 bu., and three tile storage annexes of a capacity of 2,250,000 bu. each. The timber work house, known as elevator "A," with a capacity of 1,250,000 bu. is cut off from the fireproof portion of the elevator and operated as a separate unit. This elevator holds

[1] *Railway Review*, Nov. 8, 1924.

the record for shipping grain to boats at the head of the lakes, having shipped out 1,110,000 bu. to three boats in 11 hr. working time.

While the business handled by this elevator is principally receiving grain from box cars and loading out to lake boats, during the season of closed navigation a maximum loading out capacity to cars of 100 cars per day is required. This is provided by five car-loading spouts having Sandmeyer ends, serving the loading-out track. For the loading-out process the use of the corresponding loaded-car track and empty-car track is reversed.

Grain from the receiving hopper at the unloader is delivered by multiple valves to a conveyor belt and lofter leg discharging to a 2,000-bu. capacity garner over the receiving scale. Conveyor belts and lofter legs serving the unloaders have a capacity of 20,000 bu. of grain per hour. The scales are specially designed for rapid weighing, the 2,000-bu. capacity scale hopper having a 28-in. diameter outlet valve at the bottom.

Distribution from the scale is controlled by a turnhead operated from the scale floor; separate spouts are provided direct from each scale turnhead to a shipping bin, car-loading spout, storage conveyor belt, transfer belt and to a Mayo spout serving a number of work-house bins. This rapid system of distribution not only permits economy of operation, but is necessary to permit distribution of the grain as rapidly as it is delivered from the car unloaders.

The cleaning capacity of the elevator is adequate to serve its receiving capacity. Grain is shipped to boats on five lofter legs with a total average capacity of 75,000 bu. per hour. The construction is of reinforced concrete throughout except the storage annexes, which are of tile construction; it is electrically driven, with a separate motor for each machine and its vacuum cleaning system is as complete as can be devised and unusual precautions are taken to prevent dust explosions.

The box car unloader apparatus installed in the new work house at the Port Arthur elevator "B" of the Canadian National Railways consists of a bridge made up of two built-up plate girders rigidly braced together. The lower part of the girders is formed into a circular tread which rests on steel tracks supported on a heavy concrete foundation. Lugs on the tracks mesh with slots in the girders, to insure proper alinement at all times, and a roller at each end of the bridge operates in a steel guide set in the concrete structure of the unloader foundation as a further aid to keeping the bridge alinement.

The tipping machinery consists of a 75-hp. motor connected through a worm gear and differential to a ram at each end of the bridge, by means of which the bridge can be rocked to an angle of 45 deg. in either direction. End locks are provided for locking the four corners of the bridge platform to the foundation. These locks consist of a heavy pin which slides into a cast-iron shoe set in the foundations, the pins being all operated simultaneously by one 5-hp. motor with suitable screw and link mechanism.

Bumpers for centering the car on the bridge platform and holding the car in position during the tipping operation are of the collapsible type and consist of heavy steel castings, hinged and supported on a crosshead in a guideway, and operated by large diameter screws driven from one motor located near the center of the bridge. These bumpers hold the car in position by clamping it over the draw bars.

The door opener consists of two steel levers cast into gear segments. The operation is effected by a motor connected by a worm transmission to a counter-shaft having a steel pinion at each end. These pinions are geared into the rack-segments of the arms before mentioned. Automatic means are provided for adjusting the door-opening mechanism to all varying heights of car floor. The operation of the door opener forces in the grain door without injuring it, and by a continuous motion carries the grain door inward and upward to the roof of the car, where it remains during the unloading operation. As the door opener is withdrawn the grain door is dropped on the car floor, and is not manually handled at any stage of the unloading operation.

Two deflecting baffles are provided, one at each side of the car door, each oper-ated by a motor connected to a drum shaft with a worm transmission gear. These baffles can be placed across the full width of car at a 45-deg. angle at the will of the operator, and are used for deflecting the grain out through the side door of the car. The steel baffles are connected by steel cables to the drums before mentioned, and are guided by upper and lower guide castings. In order to pro-vide for the variation in heights of car floor the forward end of the baffle is raised by means of a large nut supported in a casting under the baffle guideway. As the baffle moves into the car it is lowered until it rests on the car floor, fitting tightly to the car floor and to the far side wall of the car.

Deflecting plates are arranged under the car door to insure all grain being carried well to the center of the receiving hopper. Flexible deflectors are arranged to prevent any leakage of grain along the side of the car. Steel gratings are pro-vided to protect the fixed hopper and to cover all open spaces around the unloaders.

The fixed receiving hopper is part of the grain elevator structure. It is impor-tant that this hopper has a capacity of 2,000 bu. of grain, in order that the dump-ing operation may not be delayed while the hopper is being cleared. The end travel of the car door incidental to the rocking motion of this unloader insures an even distribution of grain in the receiving hopper, and makes it possible to obtain necessary capacity with a comparatively shallow hopper.

The operator's cab is located directly opposite the car door, and is provided with glass windows so that the operator has an unobstructed view into the car at all times during the dumping operation. The electrical control board is in convenient position before the operator and all operations of the unloader are under his direct control.

The complete operation of unloading a car has been made in 237sec.—approximately 4 min. With no delays and smooth operation it is found that a complete cycle, in unloading can be made in 7 min. or eight cars an hour; a bit longer time is required for oats, which usually require at least one extra tipping of the cradle. In ordinary operation, it is found at Port Arthur that about 250 cars can be unloaded on four unloaders in a 10-hr. day. This compares with one car per pit per hour at an ordin-ary hand pit with power shovels. There are four men required at each unloader—with twelve men for six hand pits, producing substantially same unloading results. The unloaders can ordinarily be installed in existing elevators. Their use is fully approved by local government weighing and inspection staffs.

CHAPTER XX

FREIGHT HOUSES

Aside from the terminal proper, there is no better opportunity for saving time than at the loading, unloading and transferring points. Freight houses and dray yards should be so designed as not only to enable quick movement between them and the classification yards, but to permit of prompt shifting and placing. The arrangement must provide for shifting, with a minimum of interference with freight handlers and truck men.

Handling package—l.c.l.—freight at terminals is a complicated problem. After the work of transporting it from one point to another has been performed, the heaviest part of the expense still remains. The house freight often has to be trucked 500 to 1,500 ft. The cost per ton-mile to truck freight and do the additional handling at the freight house have been given intensive study.

The cost of gathering and distributing freight in a large city is enormous. Economic conditions in this country have carried wages to higher and higher levels, and at the same time human efficiency to perform physical work without the aid of machinery has diminished. The cost of all work largely dependent on manual labor has increased in the last twenty years so much that every business man is constantly seeking some kind of labor-saving device or other means of economy to stem the tide.

Charles Whiting Baker, in the *Engineering News*, made an interesting analysis of the relations of terminal cost[1] to road movement and sets up two startling propositions:

1. That the total cost of moving freight from its origin in one city to its destination in another is *the same* for all distances less than 100 miles.

2. That the cost of terminal handling in cities is so great compared with the cost of moving a train or a vessel, when started on its journey, that the latter can be ignored.

While acknowledging at the outset that his propositions are exaggerations, he goes on to prove that they are not so greatly exaggerated as one might think at first thought. He follows a ton of freight from Philadelphia to New York. At the originating end it is loaded onto a wagon; the labor cost is 25 cts., to which is added the drayage to the freight

[1] These cost figures shown are low for present day conditions but are interesting in their relative values, and, of course, illustrate an extreme condition.

station and unloading, 50 cts. He estimates the cost of getting it onto the car and storing it at 40 cts.—including the placing on a hand truck, a long truck haul on the platform, loading into car, weighing, billing and other clerical labor. The yard engine pulls the car out of the freight house and, after many and devious movements, it finally lands in the road train for New York. Adding the cost and the value of land occupied by switching yards and freight houses and the value of buildings and other improvements, the company expends from $2 to $5 per car, or 10 to 50 cts. per ton—say 25 cts. on the average—from the time the car is loaded until it starts on its journey. Passing to the other (the New York) end, he takes the figures published by William J. Wilgus, formerly vice-president of the New York Central, of $2.25 per ton, divided as follows: Jersey City terminal costs, 15 cts; lighterage, 80 cts.; water-front terminal costs, Manhattan Island, 50 cts.; New York City cartage expense, 80 cts. This makes the terminal cost, for both ends, $3.65 per ton. Assuming the open-road cost at 3 mills per ton-mile, the total for a 90-mile haul is 27 cts.; therefore, Mr. Baker sums up:

> The cost of getting a ton of freight started on its journey at one end—Philadelphia—and handling it from the Jersey City terminal to the consignee's store at the other end—New York—is *nearly fourteen times* as much as it costs to haul the goods all the way from Philadelphia to New York.

In the location of freight houses and team yards, careful consideration should be given to the condition and gradient of the highway or street approaches. The necessity for keeping the shipper's side in mind is apparent. The term "shipper" here and elsewhere is used in a broad sense, including both consignor and consignee. It may be found necessary or advantageous, later on, for the railway to undertake the cartage, for reasons given elsewhere.

Where the amount of freight handled is sufficient to justify it, separate houses for inbound and outbound freight are desirable. When these are provided the outbound house should be narrow, 25 or 30 ft. in width, to shorten the truck haul from the team delivery to the car door. To increase the car capacity, it will be wiser to put in more tracks alongside, and these should be spaced to permit trucking platforms 12 to 15 ft. wide to be built between each two tracks, the wide platforms being required to permit tractor and trailer operation. These trucking platforms render "spotting" of doors unnecessary and obviate the straight line trucking through several rows of cars, by which the truckers are at all times liable to meet, causing confusion and delay. In the process of spotting cars exactly opposite the doors, a large amount of expensive switching is done, at the same time holding up the work of transferring and causing a force of men to be idle for a time. When the cars are taken out, the same process is repeated, as the cars must be recoupled. There is also more liability of injuring freight handlers than with the "island" platforms. A platform used for transfer purposes solely should be from 14 to 16 ft. wide, roofed and with a track on each side.

The Committee on Yards and Terminals of the American Railway Engineering Association reported, in March 1925, the results of an analysis of various types of freight houses.

Depending on the class of business handled, l.c.l. freight houses may be classified as outbound houses, inbound houses, transfer houses, and combination houses.

The outbound house is a freight station in which freight is received from the consignor generally by team or truck and is forwarded by rail.

The inbound house is a freight station in which freight is received by rail and is held for the consignee who generally calls for it with team or truck.

The transfer house is a freight station in which freight is received by rail and is forwarded by rail, the freight being transferred from the car in which it is received to another car going to the proper destination. Transfer houses are usually located at railroad centers or strategic points for the assembling of freight into through cars.

The combination house may consist of a combination of any two, or of all three, of the above types in one house. In nearly all inbound and outbound houses some transfer freight is handled. Frequently, for the purpose of obtaining a compact layout or easier supervision by one general foreman, an inbound and an outbound house will be combined in one layout, but usually such a terminal is readily divisible into units representing respectively the inbound house and the outbound house.

Until recent years all freight houses were, in substance, one-story buildings with tracks and driveways on the same level. Recently, however, several freight houses have been built consisting of two or more levels, and this leads to another classification.

A one-level freight house consists of a building with tracks and driveways at the same level.

A two-level freight house consists of a two-story building with driveway and freight house proper on one level and track and platforms on another level, either above or below, the freight being conveyed from one level to the other by mechanical means.

A two-track-level freight house consists of a two-story building with tracks on each level. Each level may be operated as an independent unit, or the two levels may be operated one in conjunction with the other as in the ordinary type of two-level house. So far as known, no house of this type has been constructed in this country, but at least two have been projected.

A one-level house with auxiliary floors is essentially a one-level house, having tracks and driveway at the same level, but having additional floors above or below the track level floor for inbound storage or warehouse purposes. Likewise a two-level house may have auxiliary floors for storage or warehouse use.

The estimated costs of typical one and two level houses are shown in table on page 300.

ESTIMATED COST OF L.C.L. FREIGHT HOUSE FACILITIES

Estimated cost—dollars

Item	Unit price—dollars	One-level house			Two-level house				
		Outbound, 50' × 596'	Inbound, 100' × 528'	Transfer platform, 18' × 594'	Outbound 2nd level, 40' × 596'	Outbound 1st level, 1-30' × 596', platform	Viaduct, 1-46' × 528', roadway	Inbound 2nd level, 112' × 528'	Inbound 1st level, 2-26' × 528', platforms
Excavation	3.00 per cu. yd.								3,280
Excavation	2.00 per cu. yd.	1,700	2,200	1,350	1,520	2,010	1,200	4,050	
Piles, creosoted	1.10 per lin. ft.								
Foundation concrete	15.00 per cu. yd.	12,750	15,840		16,632	14,490	16,500	42,900	24,600
Concrete platform slab	14.00 per cu. yd.	6,440	11,480	3,360	3,600	3,500	3,750	9,750	5,740
Concrete floor slab	24.00 per cu. yd.		1,760		12,336		19,200	30,720	
Encasement concrete	40.00 per cu. yd.		168		22,400		26,000	56,280	
Expanded metal	.21 per lb.								
Reinforcing bars	.06 per lb.		60		2,856		3,360	7,560	
Structural steel	.08 per lb.	25,600	45,760	720	6,900	840	10,200	15,660	
Structural steel	.07 per lb.				81,100		60,900	201,600	
Fill	1.00 per cu. yd.	3,500	8,000						1,400
Floor lumber	80.00 per M. B. M.	6,560	12,000	8,000	5,700	2,400		12,800	3,750
Maple flooring	120.00 per M. B. M.	5,400	10,500	2,100	4,500	4,800		11,400	6,720
Roof lumber	150.00 per M. B. M.	7,700	14,200	5,400	6,300	3,600		16,000	5,250
Composition roofing	10.00 per Square	2,850	5,200	1,080	2,300			5,900	
Brickwork	40.00 per M.	8,160	11,480		11,040	1,360		13,600	1,760
Coping	.45 per lin. ft.	630	612		600			665	
Windows	2.00 per sq. ft.	7,600	8,400		12,840			13,600	
Lighting	25.00 per outlet	2,700	4,100		1,350			3,000	
Doors	3.00 per sq. ft.	26,280	24,300		13,260	2,700	1,800	12,000	2,400
Paving	3.50 per sq. yd.					480	9,310		480
Drainage		2,400	5,000	3,000	3,000	2,500	1,350	5,000	5,000
Fire protection		4,000	6,000		4,000	6,000		10,000	10,000
Miscellaneous items		16,000	36,000		15,000		8,000	30,000	
Engineering	5 per cent.	7,030	11,140	1,290	11,306	2,320	8,030	25,480	3,620
Total cost		147,300	234,200	26,300	237,700	47,000	169,600	528,000	74,000
Area—sq. ft.		29,800	52,800	10,692	23,840	17,800	24,288	59,136	27,456
Price—dollars per sq. ft.		4.94	4.44	2.46	9.95	2.63	6.97	8.94	2.69
Price used in report		5.00	4.50	2.50	10.00	2.75	7.00	9.00	2.75

INVESTMENT COST AND OPERATING COST OF A 500-TON CAPACITY, TWO-LEVEL OUTBOUND HOUSE WITHOUT PLATFORMS

(Land Value $6.00 per Sq. Ft.)

Length of house, ft.	Number of tracks	Number of elevators	Total area occupied, sq. ft.	Cost—thousand dollars			Annual investment cost, dollars per ton	Operating cost—dollars per ton						Total combined investment cost and operating cost, dollars per ton
				Land	Improvements	Combined land and improvements		Spotting cars	Trucking		Stowing	Elevating	Combined spotting, trucking, stowing and elevating	
									Tractor	Hand				
1,260	3	4	125,900	755	1,080	1,835	1.068	.047	.217	.177	.230	.08	.751	1.819
945	4	4	112,485	675	882	1,557	.869	.047	.198	.165	.267	.08	.757	1.626
765	5	4	127,910	767	767	1,534	.854	.047	.187	.159	.244	.08	.717	1.571
630	6	4	127,060	762	645	1,407	.779	.047	.179	.153	.242	.08	.701	1.480
540	7	4	122,905	737	563	1,300	.721	.047	.173	.150	.251	.08	.701	1.422
*495	8	4	124,610	748	521	1,269	.702	.047	.170	.149	.267	.08	.713	1.415
*405	9	4	117,915	707	450	1,157	.635	.047	.165	.145	.287	.08	.724	1.359
*360	10	4	118,740	712	400	1,112	.612	.047	.162	.143	.310	.08	.742	1.354

Loading per car....................................... 6.0 tons
Tonnage per annum.................................... 130,500
Width of driveway..................................... 45 ft.
Width of house.. 40 ft.

* Too short for adequate team frontage facilities.

INVESTMENT COST AND OPERATING COST OF A 500-TON CAPACITY TWO-LEVEL INBOUND HOUSE WITH PLATFORMS
(Land Value $6.00 per Sq. Ft.)

Length of house, ft.	Width of house ft.	Number of tracks	Number of elevators	Total area occupied, sq. ft.	Cost—thousand dollars			Annual investment cost, dollars per ton	Operating cost—dollars per ton				Total combined investment cost and operating cost, dollars per ton
					Land	Improvements	Combined land and improvements		Trucking		Elevator	Combined trucking and elevator	
									Tractor	Hand			
756	86	2	4	112,870	677	973	1,650	.959	.185	.197	.08	.462	1.421
378	172	4	4	107,970	648	852	1,500	.869	.162	.223	.08	.465	1.334
*252	258	6	6	117,300	704	847	1,551	.896	.154	.270	.08	.504	1.400

Loading per car........................ 7.0 tons
Tonnage per annum................... 130,500
Width of driveway...................... 45 ft.
Settings per day....................... 2

* Too short for adequate team frontage facilities.

INVESTMENT COST AND OPERATING COST OF A 500-TON CAPACITY ONE-LEVEL INBOUND HOUSE WITH PLATFORMS

(Land Value $6 00 per Sq. Ft.)

Length of house, ft.	Width of house, ft.	Number of tracks	Total area occupied, sq. ft.	Cost—thousand dollars			Annual investment cost, dollars per ton	Operating cost, dollars per ton		Total combined investment cost and operating cost, dollars per ton
				Land	Improvements	Combined land and improvements		Trucking		
								Tractor	Hand	
1,620	40	1	168,480	1,011	360	1,371	.763	.229	.154	1.146
572	113.5	3	140,472	843	344	1,187	.663	.196	.198	1.057
*347	187.5	5	138,448	831	343	1,174	.656	.192	.242	1.090

Loading per car............................. 7.0 tons
Tonnage per annum........................... 130,500
Width of driveway........................... 45 ft.
Settings per day............................ 2

* Too short for adequate team frontage facilities.

INVESTMENT COST AND OPERATING COST OF A 500-TON CAPACITY ONE-LEVEL OUTBOUND HOUSE WITH PLATFORMS BETWEEN EACH PAIR OF TRACKS

(Land Value $6.00 per Sq. Ft.)

Length of house, ft.	Number of tracks	Total area occupied, sq. ft.	Cost—thousand dollars			Annual investment cost, dollars per ton	Operating cost—dollars per ton			Total combined investment cost and operating cost, dollars per ton
			Land	Improvements	Combined land and improvements		Trucking — Tractor	Stowing	Combined trucking and stowing	
2,002	2	328,276	1,920	682	2,652	1.475	.268	.157	.425	1.900
1,009	4	222,586	1,336	390	1,726	.955	.236	.157	.393	1.348
678	6	206,010	1,236	302	1,538	.847	.209	.157	.366	1.213
*527	8	204,346	1,226	264	1,490	.818	.204	.157	.361	1.179
*437	10	212,176	1,273	236	1,509	.828	.207	.157	.364	1.192

Loading per car................ 6.0 tons
Tonnage per annum............. 130,500
Width of house................ 50 ft.
Width of driveway............. 45 ft.

* Too short for adequate team frontage facilities.

INVESTMENT COST AND OPERATING COST OF A 500-TON CAPACITY, ONE-LEVEL OUTBOUND HOUSE WITHOUT PLATFORMS

(Land Value $6.00 per Sq. Ft.)

Length of house, ft.	Number of tracks	Total area occupied, sq. ft.	Cost—thousand dollars			Annual investment cost, dollars per ton	Operating cost—dollars per ton				Total combined investment cost and operating cost, dollars per ton
			Land	Improvements	Combined land and improvements		Spotting cars	Trucking Tractor	Stowing	Combined spotting, trucking, and stowing	
1,260	3	218,185	1,309	406	1,715	.950	.047	.209	.230	.486	1.436
945	4	179,660	1,078	304	1,382	.766	.047	.192	.267	.506	1.272
765	5	162,165	973	246	1,219	.674	.047	.182	.303	.532	1.206
630	6	149,170	895	203	1,098	.604	.047	.175	.340	.562	1.166
540	7	142,250	854	174	1,028	.564	.047	.170	.377	.594	1.158
495	8	143,330	860	159	1,019	.559	.047	.167	.414	.628	1.187
*405	9	132,235	793	130	923	.505	.047	.161	.450	.658	1.163
*360	10	130,325	782	116	898	.491	.047	.160	.487	.694	1.185

Loading per car.................. 6.0 tons
Tonnage per annum................ 130,500
Width of house.................. 50 ft.
Width of driveway................ 45 ft.

* Too short for adequate team frontage facilities.

INVESTMENT COST AND OPERATING COST OF A 500-TON CAPACITY ONE-LEVEL INBOUND HOUSE WITHOUT PLATFORMS

(Land Value $6.00 per Sq. Ft.)

Length of house, ft.	Width of house, ft.	Number of tracks	Total area occupied, sq. ft.	Cost—thousand dollars			Annual investment cost, dollars per ton	Operating cost—dollars per ton				Total combined investment cost and operating cost, dollars per ton
				Land	Improvements	Combined land and improvements		Spotting cars	Trucking		Combined spotting and trucking costs	
									Tractor	Hand		
1,620	40.0	1	158,760	953	336	1,289	.716	.040	.229	.158	.427	1.143
810	80.0	2	125,930	756	314	1,070	.597	.040	.184	.186	.410	1.007
540	120.5	3	116,500	696	308	1,004	.564	.040	.170	.214	.424	.988
*405	160.5	4	111,518	669	304	973	.545	.040	.162	.242	.444	.989
*315	206.0	5	111,370	668	302	970	.543	.040	.157	.273	.470	1.013

Loading per car.................................. 7.0 tons
Tonnage per annum.......................... 130,500
Width of driveway.......................... 45 ft.
Settings per day............................ 2

* Too short for adequate team frontage facilities.

INVESTMENT COST AND OPERATING COST OF A 1,000-TON CAPACITY, TWO-LEVEL COMBINED INBOUND AND OUTBOUND HOUSE
(Land Value $20.00 per Sq. Ft.)

Length of house, ft.	Number of tracks		No. of elevators	Total area occupied, sq. ft.	Cost—thousand dollars			Annual investment cost, dollars per ton	Operating cost—dollars per ton						Total combined investment cost and, operating cost dollars per ton
	Inbound	Outbound			Land	Improvements	Combined land and improvements		Spotting cars	Trucking		Stowing	Elevating	Combined spotting, trucking, stowing and elevating	
										Tractor	Hand				
756	2	5	8	194,616	3,892	1,620	5,512	1,541	.023	.185	.178	.151	.08	.617	2.158
504	3	8	8	195,400	3,908	1,421	5,329	1,484	.023	.168	.182	.138	.08	.591	2.075
*378	4	10	8	194,616	3,892	1,238	5,130	1,424	.023	.162	.183	.166	.08	.614	1.038

Loading per car............................ %Inbound, 7.0 tons %Outbound, 6.0 tons

Tonnage per annum.......................... %Inbound, 130,500 %Outbound, 130,500

* Too short for adequate team frontage facilities.

Width of driveway.......................... 75 ft.

Settings per day........................... %Inbound, 2 %Outbound, 1

A study of 6 houses using tractors and 8 using hand trucks, developed for the former an average trucking distance of 370.5 feet with costs ranging between 12 to 26 cents per ton and for the latter an average trucking distance of 162.7 feet and costs ranging from 12.9 to 52.1 cents per ton.

The tables on pages 301 to 307 show investment and theoretical operating costs of various types of freight houses assuming a fixed tonnage capacity and showing the comparison of investment and operating costs with different lengths of house and number of tracks.

Freight houses should be provided with scales at frequent intervals, say 50 or 100 ft. apart, arranged along the side where freight delivery is made. With the increasing interest in the weighing question, it will not be amiss to locate scales, in busy outbound houses, at each receiving door. The beams should be parallel with and against the wall, leaving no obstruction to trucking.

If a separate house is built for inbound business it should be wider than the outbound freight house so as to unload cars, release them and hold the freight for delivery. The inbound and outbound freight houses should be located with reference to each other, so that the empty cars may be quickly moved to the outbound houses for reloading. In some instances the two houses may be adjoining, and cars emptied at the one may be reloaded at the other without movement.

Freight houses usually have a track along one side and a driveway on the other, although more tracks are sometimes worked. The Illinois Central at Chicago, loads to cars on seven tracks, and the Wabash at Detroit and the North Western at Chicago loads to six tracks. The cars have to be "spotted," however, to bring the doors opposite each other.

There are many desiderata in the construction of freight houses, in the matter of general plan as well as details. The size and shape of the available property and the land values usually influence the results. The in-and-out house layout requires more track space and less storage area, but greatly facilitates prompt handling. For a heavy city business, the separate houses with a transfer between form the ideal plant. When the business outgrows this arrangement and additional houses are needed, the operating man's real troubles begin. It then becomes necessary to establish a transfer service between each inbound and each outbound house to get freight destined for points beyond the station to the proper outbound house for reloading. Ordinarily, a car is placed at each inbound house, to move this freight daily or oftener, but in some cases teams or motor cars perform this service. This condition is met in the exceptionally large and complicated freight layouts of the New Haven and Boston & Maine roads in Boston, described elsewhere.

Tracks should not be run inside buildings where it is possible to avoid it, as they cut up the floor space and necessitate higher roof trusses. Houses too wide entail unnecessary trucking; and, again, if too long, require too great a train length, which either stops house work while the set-up is changed, or detains cars. Freight houses have been built 2,000 ft. long, but they are usually failures in practical working, unless the track layout is so planned as to enable part of it to be worked without disturbing the remainder.

The arrangement of continuous doors on the track side of each house is essential to avoid "spotting" cars, and supporting posts should be set back from 4 to 8 ft. to prevent obstructing car doors. The receiving side of the outbound house should also have continuous doors. The standardization of freight cars, bringing about a car of uniform length, simplifies the work of "setting up" houses and platforms. To enable refrigerator car doors to be opened, track centers should not be less than 12 ft., because these doors open outward and measure from 2 ft. 2 in. to 2 ft. 10 in. in width. A slight incline of the floor in the outbound house descending from team to track side, and in the inbound house from track to team side, greatly facilitates trucking. A drop of 1 ft. in 60, adopted for some houses, has been found satisfactory.

Jambs of doors should be protected for 3 or 4 ft. above the floor by oak boards, or metal, to prevent damage by truckers. Cast-iron plates or angle irons are used at corners. Conductors for rain water should also be protected. Platforms, if used, should have angle irons facing on the team side, especially opposite doors. Wheel guards, to prevent wagons jamming against platforms, are desirable.

The chapter on freight-house operation contains frequent references to other details of freight-house design as they relate to operation. They will not be duplicated in this chapter, which is devoted mainly to descriptions of typical freight terminals.

The Pennsylvania has in Pittsburgh, nine freight houses, one of which handles l.c.l. freight only and one delivers c.l. and receives l.c.l. In Philadelphia it has 28 houses, three handling c.l. only, two l.c.l. only and one receiving c.l. and l.c.l. but only delivering c.l. In New York, the Pennsylvania has five freight houses in Manhattan and two in Brooklyn; New York Central has ten freight stations in Manhattan, one in Brooklyn and nine mostly small local stations in the Bronx. Both railroads also receive and deliver freight at the four contract terminal companies in Brooklyn. In Boston the New Haven has 12 and the Boston & Maine 50 freight houses.

The Pennsylvania has two-story houses in Pittsburgh, Chicago and Detroit. The Pittsburgh & Lake Erie, has a two-story house in Pittsburgh, with a driveway to each floor, and the Wabash house has four stories with tracks on the fourth floor and hydraulic elevators connecting all floors with the street. The Soo Line and Burlington at Chicago and the Great Western at Minneapolis have modern two-level houses. The

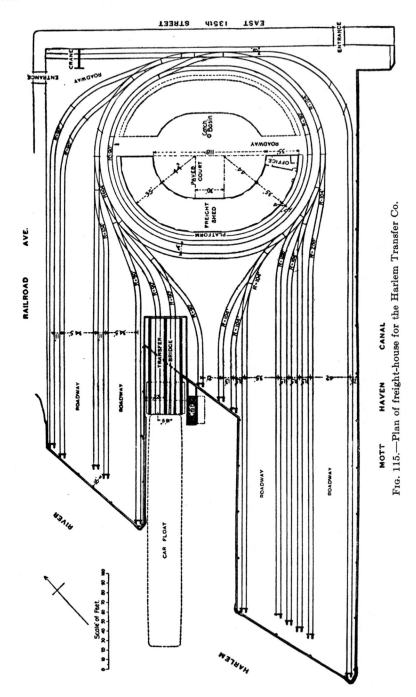

FIG. 115.—Plan of freight-house for the Harlem Transfer Co.

Louisville & Nashville's Atlanta, Ga., house is five stories, with eight elevators and has large areas for rent to merchants.

An interesting, novel and ingenious scheme for utilizing a small and valuable piece of land on 135th Street, New York, for a combination team yard, freight house and platform and float bridge, was designed by the late Walter G. Berg for the Harlem Transfer Company and is shown in Fig. 115. At this house all cars are taken in and out by floats and pass over the float bridge. The freight house is a hollow oval 158 by 188 ft., the building being 35 ft. wide. The court in the center is paved and used for teams, which deliver their freight at doors 20 ft. apart in the inner wall of the building. The doors on the track wall are 40 ft. apart and the building gives a total frontage for 16 cars. A 4-ft. platform extends around the outer side and the center of the circular house track is 7 ft.

Fig. 116.—Inbound freight-house, Chicago—Baltimore & Ohio.

from the platform. This track has end curves of 90-ft. radius. Concentric with it is the main switching track, with end curves of 104-ft. radius and having a single-switch connection with the house track. These are laid to 14-ft. centers. Other curves of 90- and 104- ft. radius connect the outer track with the transfer bridge and storage tracks.

Because of the sharp curves, a four-wheel "dummy" switch engine is used; cylinders 17 by 24 in., wheels 3 ft. 8 in. in diameter, wheel base 6 ft. 6 in., total length 27 ft., weight 45 tons. Long links are provided for coupling cars on the sharp curves and no difficulty is found in handling them. This engine hauled 11 cars, some loaded, around the curve of 104- ft. radius. The work has been satisfactorily handled.

The B. & O. inbound freight house in Chicago, as shown in Fig. 116, while not the largest freight house in the city, is in many respects one of the most convenient. It is on Polk Street, close to the Chicago River, and extends parallel to the river. For 400 ft. of its length this building is 51 ft. wide.   The southerly end of the building for a distance of 170 ft. tapers in as the west wall is carried easterly in conformity with the river bank, the width at the south end being 24 ft. 2 in.   The north end for 200 ft. is two stories high, the second story being for the offices of the freight department.   The building is 570 ft. long with an additional 100 ft. of platform on the south end.   Detailed sectional views, elevations and plans are shown in Figs. 117, 118, 119 and 120.

The general freight room is divided into two parts by the south wall of the two-story part.   One of the conveniences of the house is the location of the offices at the north end of the general freight room, making it unnecessary to go to the general office upstairs to transact detail business. At one of these offices teamsters may pay their freight charges and receive their delivery tickets, while at another, bills for transfer freight are handled.   The dead room at the northwest corner has slat walls, so that its contents can be readily seen at any time.   The vault is 11 ft. 6 in. by 15 ft. 6 in. with a cement floor, and it extends into the second story.   At the south end of the house is the bonded warehouse with office for the government officer.   This office is elevated so as to allow the use of all of the floor space.   The room is enclosed with brick walls and is nearly fireproof.   The distribution of the freight on the floor of the general freight room is such as to leave an aisle on each side, instead of through the center.   This arrangement avoids any chance of the freight piling up against the walls and hiding pieces, causing loss of time in looking for them.   The general offices occupy all of the second floor except 52 ft. at the south end, which is used for a record room.   These offices are light and have room for double the force that will occupy them at the outset.   They are entered directly from the Polk Street viaduct, which crosses the railroad yards, and also by stairways from the first floor. The agent's office at the northeast corner has a bay window from which he can see at any time the condition of business along the team side of the building.   A complete desk telephone system is installed for every clerk needing one.   Roomy, ventilated lockers are provided for the office force.   They are ranged along the walls of the toilet and stationery rooms in the southwest corner of the office.   The record room has storage for 5 years' records.   Additional space is available above the offices under the roof.   Shelving built in conformity with the road's record system is placed in the room as shown in the plan.   The two sets along the north wall are for current records, there being room for 8 months' daily records.   The compartments are each made just the size of a daily record book and are numbered for the days of the month.   Any clerk wanting the records for a particular day can put his hand on the book at once.   By this system as many clerks as there are books for the month can be looking up back records for that month without delaying one another.   As the current shelves fill up, their contents are moved over. a month at a time, to the storage shelves.

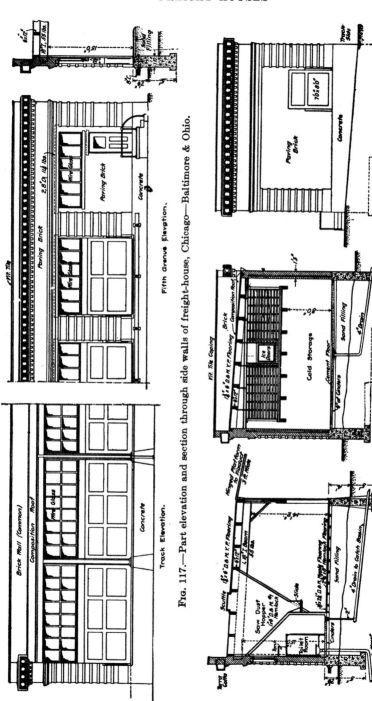

Fifth Avenue Elevation.

Track Elevation.

Fig. 117.—Part elevation and section through side walls of freight-house, Chicago—Baltimore & Ohio.

North End Elevation.

Section Through Cooling Room C–D.

Cross Section A–B.

Fig. 118.—End elevation and cross-sections of freight-house, Chicago—Baltimore & Ohio.

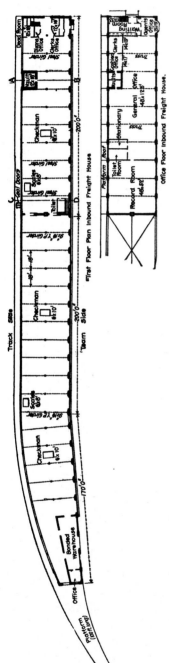

Fig. 119.—Plan of inbound freight-house, Chicago—Baltimore & Ohio.

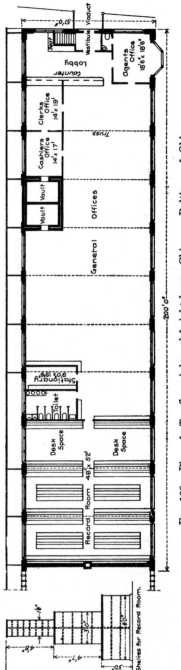

Fig. 120.—Plan of office floor, inbound freight-house, Chicago—Baltimore & Ohio.

The plans for an outbound freight house near this inbound house have been completed. The distance between the two houses is about 300 ft. The outbound house will be 780 ft. long and 30 ft. wide.

The inward freight house of the New York, New Haven & Hartford at Worcester, Mass., as shown in Fig. 121, stands on an awkwardly shaped property which was utilized in a unique manner. There was not sufficient room to continue the second track to the end of the house alongside the first track. The inside track was, therefore, cut off in such a manner as to extend the second track alongside a platform five car lengths beyond. This enables five cars to be handled while the other two tracks are being switched, and avoids cessation of freight-handlers' work while the house is being worked or "set" by the yard engine.

Fig. 121.—Inbound freight-house, Worcester, Mass.—New York, New Haven & Hartford.

There is difference of opinion as to the advisability of putting a narrow platform on the receiving side of outward freight houses. That it is an advantage to teamsters in getting rid of their loads cannot be questioned. On the other hand, it requires close checking and usually a larger force of receiving clerks than where the freight must be unloaded directly into the house. With the continuous or overlapping-door system, the absence of a platform is not so noticeable to the teamster.

Some roads build freight houses with one side entirely open and without posts. The doors are so arranged as to slide by each other, enabling an opening to be made wherever the car door stops. This arrangement renders the platform between the outside wall of the freight house and the first track unnecessary. Where the side of the house is close to the track there is, naturally, some difficulty in spotting cars opposite the doors. The posts may also interfere where the platform is enclosed. The Boston & Maine has wooden freight houses with side posts set 6 to 8 ft. in from the side of the building. The roof trusses overhang these posts and carry the side walls and doors. The doors are hung on two parallel tracks, to be run by each other, and also to be run apart to provide larger openings. At water terminals where freight sheds must accommodate vessels, teams and cars, the door problem is complicated. On the water side the doors must be 16 to 20 ft. high and continuous. It is best to hang them outside of the posts, though there must be a fender platform outside, not over 2 ft. wide. Doors for admitting teams to the shed must be large, 14 ft. high by 16 ft. wide. In an inexpensive and fairly convenient system of doors they are made in halves and are strongly hinged at the top. The lower half, which is counterweighted, slides up inside the upper half and is held by a crotch hitch to the lower corners of the upper half. The whole is then drawn up to a horizontal position. For sliding door hangers the essential features are strength, simplicity and impossibility of getting off the track.

Where the house abuts on the street, at least 20 ft. of good paved roadway, without obstructing the street, should be provided. Where the country is level, trucks will haul heavier loads, and in building roadways and approaches, this fact should be kept in mind. While the width of from 14 to 16 ft. has been given for transfer platforms, the class of commodity to be handled should be considered. Cotton, for instance, and other heavy baled goods may be handled to better advantage over a platform from 10 to 12 ft. wide. The height of the transfer platform should be that of a car floor, when standing on a track alongside, which is about 4 ft.

To transfer an occasional car of coal or grain, two tracks alongside each other, spaced 10 ft. 6 in., and with a difference in elevation between the two of 5 ft. 6 in., are used. The commodity to be transferred from the car placed on the high track is shoveled into chutes running into the lower car.

Another example of modern practice in freight-house design is the house erected by the Pennsylvania system in Indianapolis. A general plan, elevation and cross-sections are shown in Figs. 122 and 123. The property available was L-shaped, with the main stem 50 by 335 ft. on Georgia Street, and a lateral wing on Delaware Street 40 by 180 ft., with a two-story and basement office building 30 by 65 ft. on the corner. Entering from the south are 16 tracks, having a total capacity of 88 cars, spaced in pairs on 11-ft. centers and between pairs on 24-ft. centers to allow for a 12-ft. platform between. At the south end all tracks are laid out on a curve of 100-ft. radius, to keep them within the limits of the property owned. The floor slopes toward the driveways with a 6-in. fall in the width of the building.

The new freight houses of the C. B. & Q. at Chicago consist of a two-story and track level inbound house between Harrison and Polk Street averaging 70 ft. in width by 796 ft. long and a two-story and track level outbound house 112 ft. in width by 796 ft. long with the west wall at the street level set back 50 ft. from the street for a driveway and a driveway 56 ft. wide, located between the two buildings at street level with connections at the ends with Harrison Street and Polk Street

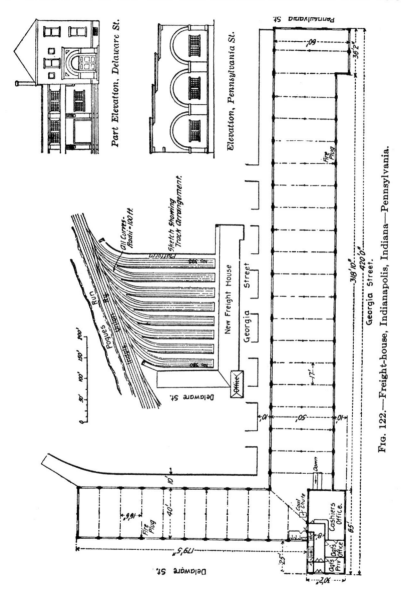

Fig. 122.—Freight-house, Indianapolis, Indiana—Pennsylvania.

viaducts. The two houses are connected above the street level with four connecting bridges 44 ft. wide, thus increasing the floor area of the upper floor and allowing for movement of merchandise from one building to the other.

In order to provide additional room for car setting and for the handling of tunnel freight, a one-story extension at track level 62 ft. wide by 475 ft. long is provided for both the inbound and outbound houses south of Polk Street. The full development of the structures between Harrison and Polk Streets contemplates a five-story and track level inbound house and outbound house.

The buildings between Harrison and Polk Streets are of fireproof construction of composite design. The foundations are of concrete caissons extending to solid rock. Track level and first floor framing are of structural steel encased in concrete and concrete floor slabs. Above the first floor these structures are of reinforced concrete flat slab construction and reinforced concrete columns. The exterior walls are of brick, cut stone coping, and steel sash throughout. The freight house floors are of asphalt block wearing surface. The upper floors are of concrete.

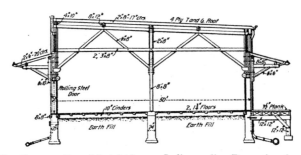

Fig. 123.—Cross-section of freight-house, Indianapolis—Pennsylvania.

Driveway doors on street level for receiving and delivering of freight by teams and trucks are of the cross-folding type 16 ft. wide, which permits two trucks at each door. All freight received and delivered at driveway doors is under shelter. The one-story extension on track level is of reinforced concrete, walls and columns, and concrete floor, with asphalt block wearing surface. The roof is supported by steel trusses with 60 ft. spans. Steel sash and steel rolling doors are used throughout.

All l.c.l. freight is delivered to and from wagons and trucks at street level and the freight lowered from or elevated to track level floor with highly improved automatic electric elevator equipment with microleveling device for bringing the elevator platform to the exact level of the freight house floor irrespective of the loads. These elevators are of 10,000 lb. capacity, platforms 9 ft. by 17 ft. 6 in. and are capable of handling five 4-wheel freight house trucks. There are six elevators in the inbound house and twelve in the outbound house with provisions for an addition of three elevators in the inbound and six in the outbound house. The elevator doors are tin-clad truckable doors equipped with electric door operating device which automatically opens the door when elevator reaches the landing. Elevators and doors are operated by push-button control and are so interlocked that the elevators cannot be operated until the door is closed nor door opened until elevator is at landing.

Both inbound and outbound houses are provided with improved type platform scales 10,000-lb. capacity with 6 by 8 ft. platforms. All scales for the outbound house are equipped with automatic dial attachments which are located in a heated check office.

In addition to the freight handled by teams and trucks, a large portion of l.c.l. freight in Chicago is handled between freight stations and business houses through tunnels and the one-story portion of the inbound and outbound houses are designed especially to take care of this business by providing suitable elevator shafts connecting with the tunnel with narrow gauge tracks for tunnel cars.

For handling heavy materials, electric cranes are provided at the south end of the uncovered platform at both the inbound and outbound houses. The outbound house crane is so located that material may be loaded directly from trucks to cars or from delivery trucks to freight house trucks. The truck capacity for the inbound and outbound houses will accommodate 325 cars. Team track facilities which are located between Harrison Street and Roosevelt Road have wide and spacious driveways, improved type auto scales of 20-ton capacity and automobile platform 20 ft. wide by 400 ft. long, also electrically operated gantry crane of 20-ton capacity. The team tracks are accessible by driveway approaches from Canal and Clinton Streets. The capacity of these team tracks is 170 cars.

In Philadelphia, the Philadelphia & Reading depressed its tracks to eliminate grade crossings and built a brick freight house 33 by 308 ft., with an upper floor for the delivery of freight from teams at the street level. Six elevators with platforms 10 by 4 ft. carry the freight to the lower floor, where it is transferred to cars standing on the house track. For the transfer of heavy freight direct from wagons to cars, there is a traveling crane, spanning the track nearest the foot of the retaining wall and extending over the side of the parallel street above.

Where the cost of land is greater than that of the additional building and equipment required to install tracks on two floors, such action would seem wise. It is roughly estimated that $2 per square foot, extra, above the cost of a one-story house, gives a good mill-construction, slow-burning type of building two stories high. This arrangement could be easily established on a side-hill location, but could also be established in flat localities with comparatively little additional expense, and prove a profitable and economical investment. Such freight houses are frequently a necessity where grade crossings are eliminated in large cities.

Mention should be made of storage warehouses in connection with freight houses. That of the B. & O. Southwestern in Cincinnati, Ohio, is a good example (see Figs. 124 and 125).

Fig. 124.—Track side of warehouse, showing transfer platform, Cincinnati—Baltimore & Ohio-Southwestern.

Fig. 125.—Interior of storage warehouse at Cincinnati—Baltimore & Ohio-Southwestern.

A development of the new in-and-out freight-house system of the Rock Island, in St. Louis is interesting. The property lines require all of the tracks to enter the house on a curve, which made it necessary to swing the north end of the outbound house around to parallel adjacent tracks. The plan and side elevations (Figs. 126 and 127) show the details.

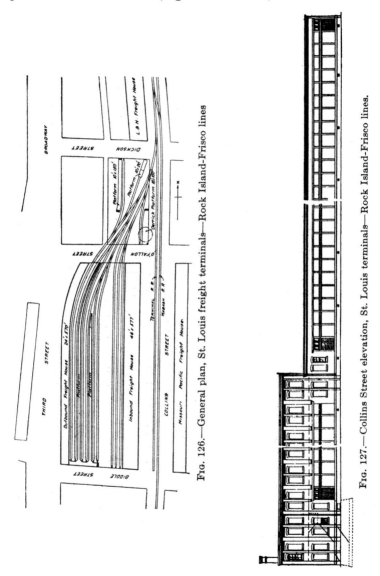

FIG. 126.—General plan, St. Louis freight terminals—Rock Island-Frisco lines

FIG. 127.—Collins Street elevation, St. Louis terminals—Rock Island-Frisco lines.

The outbound house is 24 by 570 ft. and the inbound house 46 ft. by 577 ft. The inbound house is two stories high for 208 ft. at the south end, for offices. The outline of a future six-story warehouse for the storage of inbound freight is indicated, including the one-story portion of this house, with a total height of 84 ft. The foundations, wall, columns, etc. of the present structure are designed to sustain the load which the additional five stories will impose. This explains the unusual dimensions of these parts of this one-story building. A primary object in the design of the houses was to obtain the most economical construction

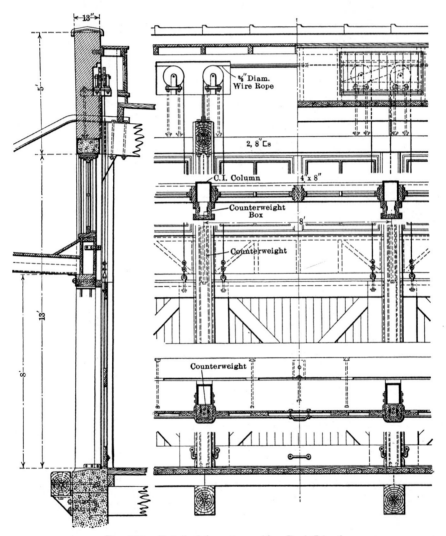

FIG. 128.—Detail of door, team side—Rock Island.

consistent with the requirements of the situation. High-pitched roofs, steel framework, etc. were omitted and such use made of iron, brick, etc. as compliance with the fire ordinance required. The typical cross-sections included in the illustrations show the character of construction, divided on the track sides and counterweighted sliding doors on the team sides. This type of door is cheaper and more satisfactory in many ways than other types intended for similar service. A detail of the door and framing is shown in Fig. 128.

The space of 152 ft. between the parallel portions of the houses contains nine tracks and two 8-ft. transfer platforms, which are joined at the south end to a 10-ft. platform fronting on Biddle Street, thus providing a good arrangement for handling agricultural implements, vehicles, etc. There is an unoccupied space 40 ft. wide in this area which will be graded for a driveway, converting the adjacent track on each side into a team track.

The local freight office is located on the second floor of the inbound house. The outer office contains a hundred clerks and special attention was given to the provision of suitable ventilation for their quarters. Ventilating fans of ample capacity are used, so that windows need not be opened for this purpose. Ample toilet facilities and all other necessary conveniences for the comfort and accommodation of the employees are provided. The buildings are steam heated and electrically lighted. The offices have combination gas and electric fixtures. On the first floor of the inbound house is a room 14.5 by 21 ft. to be used as a cooper shop for repairing damaged boxes, barrels, crates, etc. The cost is approximately $2,500,000, the greater part being for the site.

The general plan, transverse section, north elevation, east elevation and details of the front and side walls at the office of the Wabash freight houses in Pittsburgh, are shown in Figs. 129, 130, 131 and 132. The total width of the freight house is 145 ft.—length 572 ft. or, including an extension toward the Duquesne wye, 831 ft. The track level is elevated to correspond with the entrance of the line to the city from the Monongahela River bridge. The main buildings of the station are of steel and concrete construction, including total floor space of 124,000 sq. ft. The freight terminals are provided with five tracks of 10 cars capacity each, into which loading may be carried on simultaneously; and also with additional tracks for storage and shifting. All told, track room is provided for 125 cars.

Five exceptionally large, high-power elevators are provided. The building is four stories high. The ground floor is used for receiving and delivering merchandise, the two intermediate floors for storage and the upper floor for loading and unloading the cars. Forty doors of extra large size on the ground floor insure the quick handling of freight to and from teams.

On the intermediate floors large doors open into 14 warerooms which are rented to various tenants. The arrangement throughout, from the bottom to the top, is such that the station can be operated with the utmost economy. All incoming freight is handled from the cars directly upon trucks, which are then run up on the elevators and lowered to the

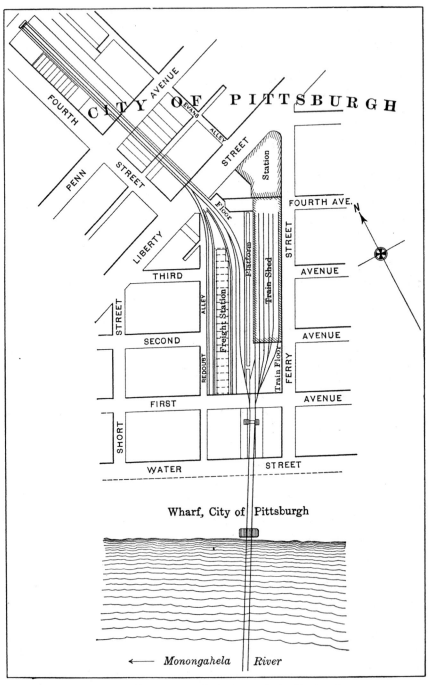

Fig. 129.—General plan, Wabash terminals, Pittsburgh.

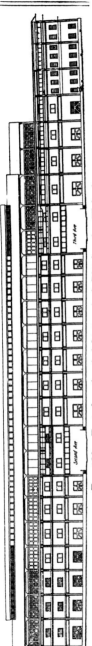

Fig. 130 —East elevation freight terminal, Pittsburgh—Wabash.

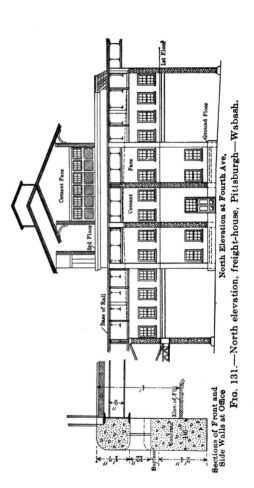

Fig. 131.—North elevation, freight-house, Pittsburgh—Wabash.

wagons or into the warerooms supplied for commission houses or other purposes. This scheme reduces the storage and rehandling of freight to the minimum.

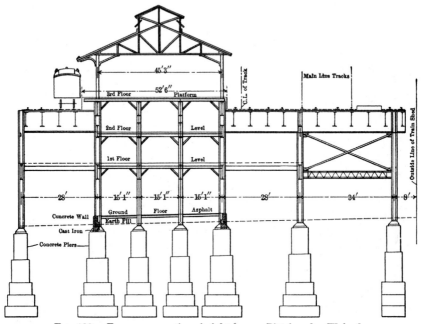

FIG. 132.—Transverse section, freight-house, Pittsburgh—Wabash.

Another above-the-ground-floor layout is the freight station and storage warehouse of the Minneapolis, St. Paul, and Sault Ste Marie in Minneapolis, shown in the general plan and first-floor plan in Figs. 133 and 134.

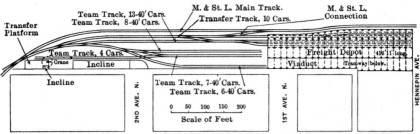

FIG. 133.—General plan, freight-house, Minneapolis—Minneapolis, St. Paul and Sault Ste. Marie.

The building is 417 ft. long, 79 ft. 7 in. wide on Hennepin Avenue, 66 ft. 1 in. wide at the rear and four stories high. It will be observed that the tracks are below the street grade, which leaves 18 ft. clear head room under the second-story floor beams. The freight is worked

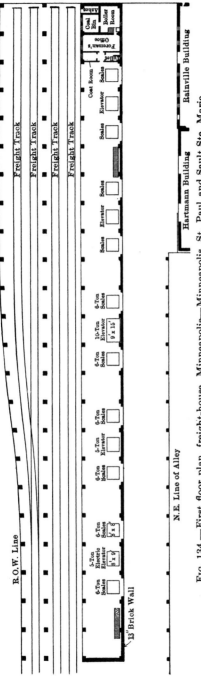

Fig. 134.—First floor plan, freight-house, Minneapolis—Minneapolis, St. Paul and Sault Ste. Marie.

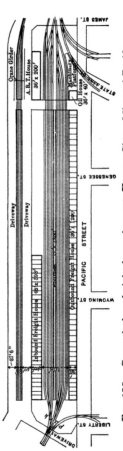

Fig. 135.—General plan, freight-house lay-out, Kansas City—Missouri Pacific.

in this substory on a platform 24 ft. wide and 415 ft. long and is hoisted to
the storage by five electric elevators.   Four of these are of 5 tons and one
of 10 tons capacity.   Scales are located in front of every door ·on this
floor.   On the other side of this platform, or subfloor, is a substreet for
incoming freight.   Above this is a 34 ft. roadway from Hennepin
Avenue to First Avenue north, which is intended primarily for transfer
and storage vehicles.   The front part of the second story, which is only

Fɪɢ. 136.—End and side elevation, freight-houses, Kansas City—Missouri Pacific.

a little above the street level, contains the offices and vaults, and the
remainder of this floor and the two floors above are for storage, there
being about 100,000 sq. ft. for this purpose.

The slab for the driveway is the Turner "mushroom" system.   There
are no beams and the flat ceiling thus secured allows a good distribution
of light and accomplishes a very necessary object—the saving of head
room in the substory.   This slab is 11.5 in. thick and spans 30 ft.   It is

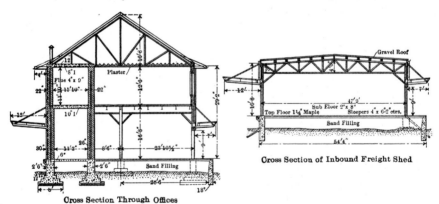

Fɪɢ. 137.—Cross-sections, freight-houses, Kansas City—Missouri Pacific.

reinforced in four directions, directly and diagonally from column to
column.   A great many advantages are claimed for this system in the
matter of speed of construction and cost.   The centering for the slab in
this, as well as the beam construction, was corrugated iron.

The Kansas City freight houses of the Missouri Pacific are large and
well arranged on the standard plan of (see Fig. 135) parallel in-and-out
houses, seven tracks between and a transfer platform midway.   End
and side elevations and cross-sections through offices and of the inbound

freight sheds are shown in Figs. 136 and 137. The outbound house is 36 by 1,200 ft.; the inbound house, 48 by 600 ft. A space of 96 ft. intervenes between the platforms of the two houses, midway of which is an island platform 12 wide and 1,200 ft. long, covered by an umbrella shed. The design and construction of the two houses are similar, each having concrete foundation and superstructure of brick and steel, with terra-cotta trimmings. The front end of each building is two stories high for a length of 200 ft. These portions have a tile-roof covering, the remainder of the roof being tar- and gravel-covered. Each house has an elevated platform on the track side 6 ft. wide, protected by a canopy 7 ft. wide; on the team side the canopy is 12 ft. wide. The character of construction is well shown by the typical elevations and sections exhibited herewith. The division offices are located in the outbound house. The local freight offices, with lockers and rest rooms, are located in the second story of the inbound house. The outbound house contains 22 sets of scales; there are 7 in the inbound house.

South of the inbound house are two driveways, one 42 ft. wide and the other 37.5 ft., with two tracks between. These driveways have 6-in. concrete as a foundation, overlaid with vitrified brick on edge, on a cushion of 1.5 in. of sand. At the west, or right-hand, end of these driveways is a gantry crane of 25 tons capacity with a 200-ft. runway electrically operated, for transferring heavy freight between cars, or from cars to wagons, and *vice versa*.

The Canadian National's in-and-out freight houses in Toronto are typical. The buildings are substantial and handsome. They include an office building fronting on Simcoe Street, 44 ft. wide, 180 ft. long and two stories high; an inbound freight house 50 ft. wide and 955 ft. long; an outbound house, 40 ft. by 910 ft. and a covered transfer platform between, 16 by 910 ft. The office building is a solid brick structure on concrete foundations, with stone trimmings and interior finish of southern pine. It is steam heated, has its own electric lighting plant and is fully equipped with vaults and all other necessary facilities.

The two freight houses are of similar construction. The concrete piers, resting on concrete foundations, are spaced 15 ft. on centers and carry Phoenix columns with bottom and top castings, which support steel-latticed roof trusses. The roof is formed of 2- by 8-in. rafters, 2-ft. centers, overlaid with 1-in. hemlock boards covered with four-ply felt and gravel roofing. Nine feet above the floor, between columns, is a 6- by 8-in. girder supported at the ends by brackets riveted to the columns, and at the middle by a 3.75-in. bolt running up through the beams. This girder supports the door track. Above each door, on both sides of the building, are two sashes, 6 ft. long by 4 ft. high. Above these windows are riveted beams carrying 5 ft. of brickwork with a stone coping. The doors are continuous, hung alternately outside and inside, enabling cars

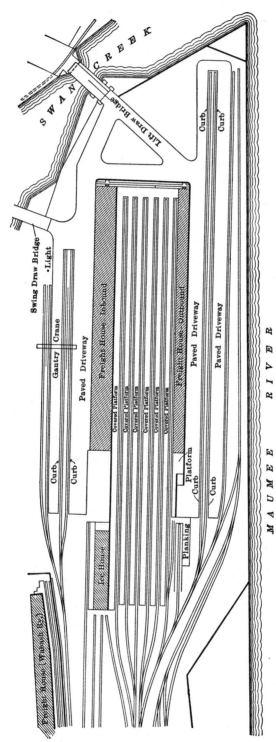

Fig. 138.—Plan of freight-houses, Toledo—N. Y. Central.

and wagons to be unloaded at any point. The floor consists of ⅞-in. maple laid diagonally over 1-in. hemlock resting on 2- by 12-in. joists 2 ft. on centers.

The transfer platform has a row of concrete piers on 15-ft. centers supporting an umbrella roof. The posts are Phoenix columns, and angle-bar braces carry the roof, formed of 15-ft. purlins covered with corrugated iron. The platform floor is 2-in. plank nailed to 2-in. by 12-in. joists. There are three tracks in the space for inbound cars and five tracks for outbound cars. The terminal occupies an entire block of 425 ft. in width. The freight houses fill 200 ft. of this and the remainder is used for team tracks, of which there are five pairs, with the necessary roadways between. The entrance to the terminal is over a single track, which crosses Front Street diagonally and then joins the converging sidings which run across John Street into the terminal.

The plan shown in Fig. 138 is of the New York Central freight houses in Toledo, Ohio. This arrangement is startling. The claim is made that in the house it superseded 29 gangs, of six men each, handled 200 cars in 24 hours at a cost of about 45 cts. a ton, while this layout enabled the same amount of work to be done with 17 gangs of six men each, for about 35 cts. a ton.

A general plan of the South Boston freight terminal of the New Haven is shown in Fig. 139. This is said to be the largest freight terminal in the country operated by one company in one location. There are 12 houses and 8 piers a total of twenty besides hay sheds, grain elevators, flour houses, etc. The combined floor area of the freight houses is 595,855 sq. ft. and of the miscellaneous houses 234,899 sq. ft. a grand total of 830,754 sq. ft. approximately 20 acres. Through the installation of modern mechanical equipment and prompter delivery methods including the advent of the motor truck, seven houses two outbound and five inbound are sufficient to meet the present requirements and the other five houses are not now in use. Fluctuations in business are met by opening or closing additional houses based on tonnage offered. One of the piers built during the war as an army base is now sub-leased for use by an independent terminal company.

Each house has a series of numbers for its doors, starting with 01, 02, etc. These numbers are affixed to the house number; house No. 9 would have doors numbered 901, 902, etc. Only two figures are painted over the door on the inside; on the outside, for teamers' guidance, the whole number is shown.

CHAPTER XXI

BRITISH FREIGHT SERVICE

Any treatise on the operation of the railways of this country would be incomplete without some reference to the transportation methods of foreign countries. One such country will suffice for the purposes of comparison, and England is selected because its railways are the most interesting to Americans, and because the roads are privately owned and operated, like those in this country, in distinction to the railways of the Continent, some of which are owned or operated by the government. In many respect, therefore, the railway situation in the British Isles is comparable to that of America.

In view of the present consolidation program of the railroads in the United States, the consolidation of English Railways effected under the provisions of the Railways Act of 1921, is of interest. This Act made amalgamation mandatory by July 1, 1923, except as the Amalgamation Tribunal, a commission of three, appointed by the King, might direct. A Railways Rates Tribunal of three members is also set up, consisting of a lawyer, railroad man, and a man experienced in commercial affairs. This latter tribunal has jurisdiction over a complete revision of all classifications and rates, the old rates remaining in effect until this is complete.

The standard net revenue is defined as the net revenue earned by the constituent companies in 1913 and the Commission is required to ascertain at the end of each year, after the appointed day, if this revenue plus such allowance as appears to the tribunal necessary to remunerate adequately any additional capital invested since the standard charges were fixed, has been secured. If, in their opinion, the management has been efficient and economic and such net revenue has not been secured it becomes the duty of the tribunal to increase the rates as a whole or in part to an extent which will permit the earning of such net revenue. On the other hand should the net revenue exceed such standard net revenue it becomes their duty to reduce rates by any amount equal to 80 per cent. of the excess.

The cartage section of the Act, in view of the interest in store door delivery is quoted in full:

The Act provides that on and after the "appointed day" (which has not yet arrived), a railroad company may collect and deliver by road any merchandise which is to be, or has been, carried by railway, and may make reasonable charges therefor, in addition to charges for carriage by railway. These charges must be published in the station rate book. Any company may, upon payment of the proper charges, perform these services of collection and delivery; but need not make delivery to any person who is unwilling to enter into an agreement, terminable at reasonable notice, for the delivery by the company of the whole of his traffic from the station at which the charges apply. Where any person does not so agree the Act provides that the company shall not be required to deliver any of his merchandise; but if such persons fails to take delivery within a reasonable time, the company may deliver such merchandise and make reasonable charges therefor. Disputes under this head are to be determined by the Rate Tribunal.

The following tabulation shows the results of the amalgamation.

	Number of companies consolidated	Route, miles	Track miles including siding
Southern Railway......................	18	2,194	5,410
Great Western Railway...............	13	3,793	8,689
London Midland and Scottish Railway...	30	7,204	19,738
London and North Eastern Railway......	30	6,732	17,291

There are in addition to the four roads herein mentioned 53 small industrial and switching lines; a part of these are owned jointly by the four larger systems. Their total route mileage of all gages barely exceeds 1,000.

At the outset it is well to notice the difference in trackage facilities and traffic density. From the following table it is evident that the British trackage capacity per mile of road is much greater than in the United States. They have but 37.3 per cent. of single-track mileage, whereas in this country the single-track mileage is 85.9 per cent. of the total road mileage. In Great Britain the total track mileage, including yards and sidings, is $2\frac{1}{2}$ times its road mileage; in this country the track mileage is but $1\frac{2}{3}$ times the road mileage, taking the United States as a whole. If, however, the comparison is made with the Eastern District, the territory of the most intensive American railway development, the comparison is not so unfavorable. Yet it must also be remembered that the figures for Great Britain include Scotland with relatively small railway mileage and thin traffic, tending to reduce the averages.

TRAFFIC DENSITY OF GREAT BRITAIN AND UNITED STATES[1] (1923)

	Great Britain		United States		Eastern District	
	Miles	Per cent. of road, miles	Miles	Per cent. of road, miles	Miles	Per cent. of road, miles
Miles of road..............	20,314	100.	235,563	100.	59,292	100.
Miles of second track......	12,728	62.7	33,125	14.1	17,806	30.
Miles of third track........	1,709	8.4	3,030	1.3	2,645	4.5
Miles of four or more tracks.	2,098	10.3	2,414	1.	1,953	3.3
Miles yards and sidings....	14,969	73.7	111,681	47.4	44,819	75.6
Total track miles........	51,818	255.1	385,813	163.8	126,515	213.4

[1] Class I Railroads.

As an indication of the use to which the tracks are put in moving trains, a second table is presented which shows the comparative train-mile density—that is, the yearly train-miles divided by the miles of road. It will be noted that the train mile density of Great Britain is four times that of the United States and twice that of the Eastern District.

TRAIN MILE DENSITY OF GREAT BRITAIN AND UNITED STATES (1923)

Train miles per mile of road	Great Britain	United States	Eastern District
Passenger trains................	12,389	2,438	3,933
Freight trains.................	7,045	2,689	4,201
All trains.....................	19,434	5,127	8,134

Having called attention to these marked differences in facilities and traffic density, a comparison of a more general nature will now be made with the British freight ("goods") service. On first view, the most striking dissimilarity is seen in the character of the freight itself and in the design and capacity of their freight cars ("goods wagons"). The freight traffic of England is said to be decidedly *retail* in character, while that of America is *wholesale*. The British merchant, because of his nearness to sources of supply, and the expeditious service of the railways, is not accustomed to carrying large stocks of goods. The service of the railways is such that goods ordered one day from the wholesale dealer are delivered at the merchant's door early the next day. American merchants, who are situated farther from the wholesale markets, must allow more time to replenish stocks. The English retailers find that they can rely upon the railways for good service, which equals the service of the express companies of this country, and it has had the effect of forcing the railways to handle a large volume of small packages and a relatively small number of car-load shipments.

The difference may be readily seen from the following tabulations which compare the weight of the shipments handled through typical freight houses of England and the United States in one day. The figures for England are taken from "Railways and Their Rates," by Edwin E. Pratt.

Item	Broad Street, London, Eng.	Providence, R. I.	Worcester, Mass.
Consignments........................	985	1,622	805
Packages............................	4,427	12,831	10,652
Destinations........................	53	342	312
Total weight (pounds).................	246,000	1,642,000	2,156,000
Average weight per consignment (pounds)	250	1,013	2,678
Average weight per package (pounds).....	62	128	202
Average weight to each destination (pounds).	641	4,801	6,910
Cars used............................	72	170	109
Average load per car (pounds)..........	3,400	9,658	19,760

It will be seen from these figures that the average weight of each shipment from the Providence freight house (128 lb.) is twice that of the average shipment through Broad Street, London (62 lb.), and in the case of Worcester (202 lb.) it is more than three times that of Broad Street. In average car load, Providence (4.8 tons) is nearly three times, and Worcester (9.9 tons) nearly six times, greater than London (1.7 tons).

The British shipper of small packages has a choice of other methods of transport. If the package does not exceed 11 lb. in weight, he may forward it by parcel post. The parcel post rates for this service, as for similar service in the United States, are moderate.

To illustrate further the distinctly retail character of British house freight. the following additional statistics are quoted from Mr. Pratt's book. They show one day's business at four of the principal goods depots of the London, Midland & Scottish.

From	Tons of 2,240 lb.	Consignments		Packages	
		No. of	Weight (lb.) (average)	No. of	Weight (lb.) (average)
Curzon St., Birmingham.......	1,615	6,110	592	51,114	70
Liverpool Station.............	3,895	5,049	1,728	79,513	110
London Road, Manchester.....	1,341	5,522	544	28,277	106
Broad St., London...........	906	5,201	327	23,067	88

The second important difference between the British and American freight service lies in the British practice of collecting and delivering freight. In Great Britain there are no express companies, as they are known here, but, instead, the horse-driven or motor vans of the railway companies call at the consignor's warehouse for the freight to be shipped,

FIG. 140.—Freight dray, Broad Street Station—London, Midland & Scottish.

and at destination deliver it at the door of the consignee. The freight rates include the cartage service at both points, but the shipper has the option of doing his own carting and paying a lower freight rate. For instance, between London and Manchester, 188 miles, the rate on a certain class of goods is 32.7 cts. per 100 lb., when the railroad performs the cartage; and 20.8 cts. if the shipper elects to do it himself. Generally speaking, however, the railways do practically all of the cartage except in the case of certain bulky or dead freight, such as bricks, coal, creosote, gravel, hay and straw, iron ore, lime and salts in bulk, manure, peat, scrap iron or steel, sand, slates, turf, wood blocks, etc.

Until quite recently, a large part of the cartage of freight for the railroads was done by large cartage or forwarding concerns, but now the railways do nearly all of this work themselves. The "horse department" is an important unit in the British railway organization. The London, Midland & Scottish for instance, has upward of 6,000 horses, and employs nearly 5,000 drivers, carmen and cart boys, 250 stablemen and nearly 300 cartage supervisors, the latter being provided with light carriages or motor cars so as to be able to move around rapidly from place to place. On the principal railways, the aggregate number of horses in this service is close to 18,000 with a corresponding number of drays, vans, automobiles and steam lorries, the number of horses exceeding the number of locomotives. A typical dray is seen in Fig. 140.

Competition between railways in England has taken the form of improved service and facilities rather than of lower rates. It is so keen, and such has been its effect on the expedition of the service, that a merchant in Liverpool, Manchester, Newcastle or Plymouth, all 200 miles or more from London, may rely with certainty on receiving at his door by the time he is open for business in the morning the goods he ordered by telegraph or telephone from his London dealer the previous afternoon. The same service is afforded the more distant points, such as Edinburgh (393 miles) and Glasgow (401 miles), as well as the principal cities of Ireland, but delivery at these farther distant points is later in the day.

The question naturally suggests itself, "What does the Englishman pay for his express freight service?" It is to be expected, of course, that the charges will be higher than those in force here, where the railways perform no cartage service, where the character of the freight is different in weight, bulk and consignment, and where the regularity and celerity of the freight service is hardly as excellent as in Great Britain. To make an exact comparison of rates is out of the question because of the dissimilarities in conditions (particularly in the collection and delivery feature) but the statement on page 338 shows a comparison as of Nov., 1923 between rates in effect in Great Britain and the United States.

In the collection of freight to be dispatched in trains, the British roads follow methods quite similar to those of the express companies of this country.

Many are perhaps unfamiliar with English transportation terms, such as "miscellaneous goods" for less-than-carload (l.c.l.) freight; "cartage" for trucking, "trader" for both shipper and merchant, "van" for horse-

COMPARISON OF RATES IN EFFECT IN GREAT BRITAIN FOR THE CONVEYANCE OF (1) PARCEL TRAFFIC BY PASSENGER TRAIN (INCLUDING COLLECTION AND DELIVERY) AND ALSO OF (2) SMALL PARCELS AND GOODS BY MERCHANDISE TRAINS (INCLUDING COLLECTION AND DELIVERY) WITH (3) RATES OF AMERICAN RAILWAY EXPRESS COMPANY AND (4) RATES OF U. S. RAILROADS ON L.C.L. FREIGHT AND SIMILAR CLASSIFICATION BETWEEN POINTS OF SIMILAR DISTANCE—ALL RATES CALCULATED ON 100-LB. BASIS

Between London and	Distance (miles)	Between New York and	Distance (miles)	Great Britain — By passenger train, First class	Great Britain — By merchandise train, First class	Great Britain — By merchandise train, Second class	United States A. R. E. Co. First class	United States A. R. E. Co. Second class	United States L.C.L. freight rates—U. S. railroads, First class	United States L.C.L. freight rates—U. S. railroads, Second class	United States — Allowing 30¢ per 100 lb. for cartage, both ends, First class	United States — Allowing 30¢ per 100 lb. for cartage, both ends, Second class
Cambridge	57½	Beacon, N. Y.	58	$2.18	[1]0.54 / [2]0.48	[1]0.40 / [2]0.35	1.03	0.77	0.40½	0.32	0.70½	0.62
Ipswich	55 as 70½	Bridgeport, Conn. / New Haven	55 / 72	2.18	0.60 / 0.53	0.33 / 0.29	1.25 / 1.25	0.94 / 0.94	0.50½ / 0.53½	0.43 / 0.45½	0.80½ / 0.83½	0.73 / 0.75½
Newmarket	72¾	Poughkeepsie	73	2.18	0.60 / 0.52	0.44 / 0.39	1.03	0.77	0.41½	0.34	0.71½	0.64
Leiston	94¾	Allentown, Pa	93	2.18	0.67 / 0.61	0.49 / 0.44	1.45	1.09	0.53½	0.44	0.85½	0.74
Swaffham	112	Hudson, N. Y.	113	2.42	0.74 / 0.66	0.53 / 0.48	1.45	1.09	0.47½	0.40½	0.77½	0.70½
Holt	134	Scranton, Pa.	134	2.42	0.84 / 0.76	0.62 / 0.56	1.59	1.19	0.66½	0.56½	0.96½	0.86½
Cromer	137½	Albany, N. Y.	142	2.42	0.81 / 0.74	0.59 / 0.53	1.45	1.09	0.51	0.41½	0.81	0.71½
Doncaster	183 as 156	Schenectady	159	2.65	0.87 / 0.80	0.65 / 0.58	1.45	1.09	0.51	0.41½	0.81	0.71½
Leeds	185	Baltimore, Md.	187	2.65	1.00 / 0.91	0.71 / 0.65	1.59	1.19	0.65	0.53½	0.95	0.85½
Leyburn	234	Utica, N. Y.	237	3.10	1.22 / 1.13	0.85 / 0.78	1.86	1.40	0.63	0.53½	0.93	0.83½
Guisboro	247	Rome N. Y.	251	3.10	1.27 / 1.17	0.74 / 0.66	1.86	1.40	0.65	0.55½	0.95	0.85½
Chevington	292	Syracuse, N. Y.	290	3.10	1.44 / 1.32	0.76 / 0.68	1.86	1.40	0.66½	0.56½	0.96½	0.86½
Tweedmouth	335	Lyons, N. Y.	335	3.28	1.49 / 1.39	0.86 / 0.79	1.86	1.40	0.66½	0.56½	0.96½	0.86½
Jedburgh	369	Roohester, N. Y.	370	3.28	1.57 / 1.47	0.96 / 0.88	2.00	1.50	0.66½	0.56½	0.96½	0.86½
Bridge of Earn	440	Buffalo, N. Y.	439	3.28	1.82 / 1.69	0.96 / 0.88	2.14	1.61	0.79½	0.69½	1.09½	0.99½

[1] Rates on "Smalls" up to 3 Cwt. (336 lb.). [2] Rates on "Goods" weighing in excess of 3 Cwt.

Note.—British rates have been converted to United States money on gold basis. Existing British tariffs are stated on a basis of 112 lb. to the cwt. and 2,240 lb. to the ton. In this exhibit they have been recalculated on a 100-lb. basis.

As is the case with express, the British system includes a graduate for shipments weighing less than one hundred weight.

drawn vehicle, "lorry" for motor truck and "carman" for driver or chauffeur. The English terms will be used in describing their methods, as, in most cases, they make for both brevity and expressiveness.

The term "miscellaneous goods" covers the class of freight that we usually term l.c.l.; in other words, the freight composed of small consignments, not the carload or large shipments, the so-called "store-door delivery" variety which, in England, is composed of consignments of about 300 lb. or less each. The details of the cartage and station workings constitute such a complex subject that it is only possible to give an outline of the system at this time, under the two main headings of delivery and collection. The delivery of goods begins at the time the car door is opened, and ends at the time the cartage vehicle leaves the trader's door. The major steps between those two points are best divided as follows:

1. Unloading and checking of goods from cars to vans or platform.

2. Barrowing (trucking) of goods to van-loading sections or warehouse.

3. Loading and checking of goods onto cartage vehicles in district and street order.

4. Loaded vehicles removed from sheds, and either parked by van setters or removed by carmen; accompanied by a pass, over scales and out into town for delivery.

The first step in item (1) is controlled by the checker, and his guide is the invoice of the contents of the car. The work of marking the invoices is a big subject, and one that cannot be thoroughly covered at this time. It is sufficient to explain that when the invoice reaches the checker at the car door it contains the following information pertaining to the cartage side of each consignment: (a) whether traffic is "delivered" or on a "wait order"; (b) the name of the street; (c) the postal area, including the area number; (d) the locality; and (e) the district number or mark. Regarding the information shown on each invoice, it should be noted that the "district markers," the men who mark the invoices, must be accurate. Local knowledge and experience gained by constant repetition of company and street names enable the marking to proceed like clockwork; in fact, in course of time, the staff becomes independent of the street lists for the most part.

The checker, furnished with the invoices duly marked, instructs the "barrower" to what point he is to take the packages, whether to a "delivered" berth or to a "wait-order" berth. The "barrower" in time becomes so familiar with this work of item (2) that he has only to be given the name of the consignee to know where the goods should be placed. Many of these men have been with the same railway all their lives, and a large part of the time on one particular job.

Item (3) constitutes one of the most important steps of all. The van loader has a "delivery sheet" for each consignment of goods. The delivery sheet is made out from the invoice, and is practically an exact copy of the entries on the invoice. The "single-entry delivery sheet" is used very generally by all English railways now and, as the name signifies, it deals with one consignment only. This document eventually becomes the railway company's receipt for the goods, and is the "Bible" of the carman, because his delivery sheets cover all of the goods on his van and each sheet is charged to him when he leaves the station and must be accounted for before he checks off at night.

The van is now loaded and ready for the carman. The vans that are parked after being loaded need not be described at this time. The carman must first get his delivery sheets, and from them find out the number of his van. Carmen usually have the same horse or horses every day or the same motor truck, but may have any one of several hundred vans. As soon as the carman obtains his delivery sheets from the cartage office, he is off to his district to deliver the goods, after presenting his gate pass to the policeman at the gate.

The subject of districts is covered more in detail in describing the cartage-control system of the London Midland and Scottish Railway. It should be explained, however, that there can be no hard-and-fast rule as to the size and shape of the districts. Thus, where the traffic ordinarily is sufficient for one vehicle per day only, a district carman will take a fairly large radius; on the other hand, where there are many firms in close proximity to one another, several districts may be comprised within a small compass. This means that exhaustive tests will be necessary to determine the most suitable divisions, and here is where the English postal-area map is so valuable in laying out the districts. In most cases, the districts are based on collection stops, and the carman is given a load into his particular collection district.

In following the carman through, we find that he makes his deliveries in the order in which he can save the most time and travel the shortest distance, but all the time bearing in mind his collections that are to be made that day. He usually finishes one or more loads of deliveries by 12 noon and starts on his regular collection rounds after lunch.

It should be noted here that the bulk of the miscellaneous-goods traffic on English railways is delivered to the consignees before 12 noon every day, and it is common practice to give 24-hour service for this traffic to places 200 miles distant, and often farther than that on certain classes of traffic. For instance—the "Bradford traffic," woolen goods largely, is picked up, say, before 5 p. m. today and is invariably delivered in the "Wood Street Zone" in London by 9:30 a. m. tomorrow; and Bradford is 230 odd miles from London. This is not a special performance. The English trader expects and demands this kind of service, and the railway-goods agent has a complaint to deal with very quickly if the goods are late in arriving at the trader's store door. One may ask, "How it is possible to give such service?" It all hinges on the "eye-of-the-needle" link in the chain of transporting the goods; that is, the freight-station handling-and-cartage system. It is generally felt that the traffic could not be handled expeditiously if the traders did their own cartage and the stations would have to be double their present size.

The collection of the goods from the trader's or consignor's door can be divided into four operations, and are practically just the reverse of the delivery workings; (1) traffic carted into the station, accompanied by "consignment notes"; (2) van loads backed to shed platforms or cars; (3) the unloading of the van loads and the weighing of consignments; and (4) the barrowing of goods to the car side. The districts assigned to the regular "district carman," or "roundsman," as he is sometimes called, are based on the collection stops in a given area or district. Each district carman has a list of the regular stops in his district; some are daily, some every other day and the like. In addition, he may have several special calls to make within his district. Special or extra deliveries and collections are usually taken care of by "unattached" or "odd" carmen. Here is where the "cartage controller" comes into the picture.

The London Midland and Scottish has, in London, a system as follows: St. Pancras and Somers Town are the two main London goods stations of the Midland Railway. In addition, they also have several substations with rail connections and some depots and receiving offices, none of which have rail connections and are used largely to receive traffic from the traders located in their vicinity. This traffic is consolidated into loads for the main outwards goods station, there to be loaded in cars and dispatched to the consignee. London is divided into what are known as "postal areas," such as N. W. 1, E. C. 4, S. W. 1 and so on. This was done by the Post Office Department to expedite the delivery of mail, and this postal area or zone map is used by every railway and road-transport firm engaged in collection and delivery service in London. Using the postal-area map as a basis, the Midland Railway has divided London into ½-mile squares based on the collection stops required. Each carman is allotted a district covering one or more of these ½-mile squares; he receives a district number by which he is known, and all the various documents, delivery sheets and the like that he deals with bear his district number.

Apart from the station working, it may be of interest to refer generally to the organization of the London goods traffic working,, which has been set up by the London Midland and Scottish Company with local headquarters at Somers Town. A new arrangement was established in 1916, whereby all its goods depots in the London area were linked up with the London Goods Operating Superintendent's Office at Somers Town by private telephones. The series of telephone circuits enables the responsible officers to keep in close and constant touch with the stations without the annoyance of the delays which are ordinarily experienced in "getting through."

All the important stations can be brought together on one circuit, and daily telephonic conferences take place at which the Goods Agents at St. Pancras, Somers Town, City (Royal Mint Street), Whitecross Street, High Street Borough, Bow, Poplar, Victoria Docks, and Commercial Road Depots are enabled to ascertain the traffic position at each of the other places, and arrangements can be made with facility for coordinating the workings of the different stations in the course of a few minutes' conversation, and for cartage equipment to be transferred from place to place, according to the exigencies of the traffic.

The telephone circuits referred to are also utilized throughout the day for the purpose of controlling the Midland cartage workings in London. The Cartage Control scheme has been in operation for nearly six years, and its operation is briefly as described in the following:

In normal times approximately 1,000 to 1,200 horses, or their equivalents in motors, are employed by the London, Midland and Scottish Company for the collection and delivery of merchandise traffic at the London stations. From each of these stations details are telephoned at regular times to the Cartage Control Office, particulars being given of those carmen and motor drivers for whom loads have not been arranged for the return journey, i.e., if a return load is not available when a carman or motor driver leaves the station, an intimation to that effect is given to the Cartage Control Office. The information is summarized hour by hour, and the Cartage Controller is in a position to anticipate the number of carmen who have been instructed to call at any particular station and provide loads for the men in the direction of their home station with a minimum of empty running, or alternatively to transfer them to points at which the traffic is in excess of the strength immediately available at such places.

A schedule of "calling points" has been arranged so that a carman will report at a fixed place or station when his deliveries are completed, and he is instructed at which point to call when leaving the stations.

In addition to the information as to the carmen's movements, each station telephones to the Cartage Control Office at frequent intervals particulars of the traffic on hand awaiting delivery, or orders received for the collection of traffic.

The operations of collection and delivery are thus coordinated, and the Controller is able to transfer equipment from point to point with facility, and the waste and overlapping, which would exist if each of the many depots was conducted without regard to the undertaking as a whole, is avoided.

Taking the delivery of the goods from the goods station to the trader's door first, the written instructions to the loading staff are to follow the lists prepared for them showing the principal streets in each postal area, and giving the number of the district carman responsible for the collection of traffic in each street. So far as possible, the same carman performs both delivery and collection work in his particular area, but, where this is not possible to arrange, he delivers in some closely adjacent area, and the loaders must load the vans accordingly. It is a rule that the arrange- ments made must not be such as will prevent the district carmen from gerting onto their collection work at the scheduled time. All the regu- lar collection stops are made on a schedule-time plan. When a carman leaves with his first load of deliveries in the morning, he knows whether he is to return for another load, to report to the controller's office or to perform either his regular or some special work. In most cases, the dis- trict carmen report to their call office after finishing their deliveries. Each call office is supplied with schedules of the district carmen working in the vicinity. These schedules show all details of the carmen's work, together with the streets and the houses covered by each. The follow- ing rules explain the method by which the cartage controller is kept informed as to the movements of all carmen:

1. Any orders of a miscellaneous character received at a call office, either through post or by telephone, must be numbered with the district number and handed to the carman when he calls.

2. Full-load collection orders received by the receiving offices and depots must be telephoned to the control office at Somers Town.

3. Orders received by the receiving offices and depots, subsequent to departure of the district carman, must be telephoned to the control office at Somers Town.

4. No alteration may be made in a district carman's scheduled work without obtaining sanction from the control office at Somers Town.

5. Any odd men arriving at a receiving office may be used for clearing the office, but for no other purpose without first communicating with the control office, which will anticipate the arrival of odd men, and endeavor to give instructions so as not to occasion delay.

6. Clerks in charge of call offices will be responsible for calling the attention of the controller to any district carman who fails to call at the office for instructions if he is scheduled to do so.

From the foregoing it should be plain what a thorough knowledge the cartage controller has at all times of the movements of every vehicle under his control. It is through this system that an efficient and econom- ical cartage service is maintained, giving better service to the public and better loading of trucks.

As soon as the district carman finishes his collection, he returns to his home station. When he enters the station, his van is weighed and he is given a ticket on which the weight of his van and its load are shown separately. The next step is at the "scrutinizer's" box, where the "consignment notes" are gone over and from them the "scrutinizer" knows where to send that particular load, so that the van will be berthed close to the car into which the bulk of the goods must be loaded, and so make the barrower's trip as short as possible. The carman then backs his van into the berth indicated by the "scrutinizer." The berth number is marked on the top sheet of the consignment notes. He turns his weight ticket and consignment notes over to the shed foreman, and this finishes his collection work, provided his consignment notes check with the goods on the van. To explain the nature of a "consignment note," the single-entry type is the best. They are handed to the railway company with each consignment tendered for forwarding by rail, and should accompany the goods from the van to the car; immediately the goods are checked and loaded, they are passed to the invoicing office. The carman's next duty is to turn over his delivery sheets and any money he has collected from consignees to the cashier's office and obtain a receipt or clearance for both. Then, after putting his horse away, that day's work is over for him.

Following the van load of collected goods, the third operation is the unloading of the goods from the van and the weighing of the consignments. At each unloading berth, a staff is stationed, usually two, but sometimes three, gangs. Each gang consists of a checker and "caller-off," or unloader, with two or three barrow men. The van is now ready for unloading and the checker has been supplied with the consignment notes for the load.

The packages are placed on a hand truck by the unloader and the barrow man is instructed where to take the goods. He also is given the consignment note covering these goods, usually quite near by. The loading staff take the consignment notes, pack the packages in the car and insert the number of the vehicle in which loaded, on the consignment note. The goods are now in the car, and the fourth and last operation is complete.

A "demountable flat" is being used with considerable success by English railways. Figure 141 shows this flat on a "stand lorry" ready for load and Fig. 142 shows a loaded flat being transferred from the "stand lorry" to the motor lorry.

On account of the density of the passenger traffic during the daytime and the relative infrequency of night passenger trains (night trains are not needed in the country of such relatively short distances and few are run except between London and Liverpool and London and Scotland), nearly all freight trains, particularly merchandise trains, are run during the night hours. From the large stations in London, trains are dispatched at all hours after noon. Trains, however, are sent in the early afternoon only to points where the volume of business necessitates two trains; the later one will carry all the late arriving goods.

Fig. 141.—"Demountable flat" in position on "stand lorry" ready for another load

Fig. 142.—Transferring loaded "flat" from "stand lorry" to motor lorry.

The loading of merchandise is largely completed by 6:30 or 7:00 p. m.; collections stops at 5 p. m. and only vans working far distant territory would come in later than 6 p. m.   It is the intention to dispatch during the night all the freight collected during the day, and to deliver during the day all the freight received in trains during the night or early morning hours.   In London the freight-house labor problem is easy of solution because of the large supply of what is termed "casual" labor, that is, men out of employment who are glad to have employment for one, two or any number of hours, without any guarantee as to the number of hours' employment to be given.   The agent can, therefore, increase or diminish his force of laborers to the need of the hour, and the rate paid is very low compared with wages of American freight handlers. Casual laborers may be engaged at 20 to 25 cts. per hour, plus a certain bonus when the tonnage handled exceeds a certain minimum.   The bonus

FIG. 143.—"Goods" train—London, Midland and Scottish.

system of paying for freight handled works satisfactorily and apparently is not objectionable to the men.   Including the bonus, it is a safe generalization to say that the earnings of the British freight-house laborer are about one-third of those paid to similar employees in this country.   With certain of the fixed forces, the proportion will run slightly higher— approaching one-half of the American rates.

Every night of the week the London, Midland and Scottish dispatches 30 trains from St. Pancras Station in London and about the same number in trains averaging 30 cars each from Broad Street Station. The cars are all equipped with air brakes and the trains are run at passenger-train speed, averaging 40 m.p.h.   Of course, this service is given only to the merchandise trains.   Trains of dead weight are run at lower speed, say 20 to 25 m.p.h.   Because of the very small cars, a merchandise train of 30 cars will weigh in the neighborhood of 300 tons—less than an ordinary passenger train in this country.   An ordinary "goods" train is shown in Fig. 143.   A train with bulk freight weighs considerably more—say 400 to 600 tons, and in some cases, with mineral trains, an extreme train load of 1,000 tons is obtained. Trains of this weight, however, are exceptional. Yet even this maximum load is but one-fifth to one-seventh the tonnage of an American 75 to 100 car coal train made up of 50 ton capacity cars.

The freight "wagon" of Great Britain runs on four wheels (two axles) and the great majority have a capacity of about 12 tons. Larger cars are used—many of 20-ton capacity, a few with a capacity of 30 tons. The visitor is inclined to joke about the diminutive British car when compared with the American car designed to carry four or five times as much, and often concludes off hand, without a thorough knowledge of conditions, that the adoption of large-capacity cars in Great Britain would revolutionize the freight service and substantially reduce operating expenses.

But this is not altogether true, at least under the present conditions. The small car is the result, and not the cause, of the retail character of the freight service. Even if larger cars were available and would clear their structures, it would be a long time before their capacity could be utilized, and the road, to begin the campaign of educating shippers to the economic necessity of holding cars for full loads, would suffer in competition whether filled or not. The average car load in 1923 was 5.65 tons for all cars and 2.88 tons for merchandise cars. Efforts to obtain more lading of merchandise cars would adversely affect the regularity and speed of the trains, the two factors in which competition is keenest. Such efforts would also reduce the number of through cars to small branch-line points, or junctions, increase the percentage of shipments transferred and otherwise tend to curtail privileges of long standing brought about by competition in service. A large part of the merchandise freight carried is handled in open-top cars with heavy tarpaulins which are fastened to the cars in a standard manner, and so effectively that relatively little damage from the elements occurs.

It may be argued that, while the reason just mentioned applies to merchandise freight, it has not the same force in its application to the transportation of dead freight, such as coal. But here again there are retail influences which restrict the car load. According to an official statement made a few years ago by the chairman of the London, Midland & Scottish the average *consignment* of coal is 17.5 tons. Eighty per cent. of the coal shipments are less than 20 tons and many are as small as 2 tons. These instances will show that, in order to make the larger car profitable, it will be necessary first to revolutionize the British system of sales and distribution, and unless and until something of that nature is accomplished the 12-ton car will continue in use. Some of the companies are experimenting with larger cars, but in using them another practical difficulty is encountered, in adapting the scales, chutes and other loading facilities, as well as trestles and unloading arrangements at destination.   These were all designed for the smaller car, and will not permit the use of the larger car, without extensive alteration. The cost of the necessary changes would reach large sums in the aggregate and the expense would not all fall upon the railways.   The general view of the Camden "goods" station of the London, Midland & Scottish (Fig. 144) gives a fair idea of the station and yard equipment and the character of cars used.   One of the household-goods moving vans is seen in the foreground.

It is easy to understand, therefore, the disinclination to disturb the present goods- and mineral-wagon standards.   But there is still another complication.   America is not unique in having its private-freight-car

Fig. 144.—Camden goods station and yards—London, Midland and Scottish.

problem.   A large percentage of the mineral traffic of England is moved in privately owned cars, and this fact adds to the difficulty of securing a better car and train load.   The Board of Trade is implicated as well, since its rules in the interest of uniformity in design of equipment restrict the dimensions of privately owned freight cars to certain standards. As will be seen from the illustrations, many of the freight cars are open. To protect the freight from rain, snow or dust, tarpaulin covers are used.

In some ways the British railways, by reason of their small cars, can afford facilities which would be appreciated in this country if conditions would permit.   For instance, the problem of loss and damage to shipments of household goods is solved by an ingenious design of moving van. There are two kinds of vans used; both are interchangeable between rail and road transport, viz: the "tunnel van" and the "lift van" or demoutable body.   The tunnel van consists of a long body mounted on a running gear with very low wheels which is drawn by horses and used for removals over both long and short distances. The goods are loaded at the residence, hauled either to another residence direct over the road, or to a railroad station to be transported to some distant point. If the latter, the van on its own wheels after unhitching the horses is hauled up a ramp onto a platform and from thence onto a flat car upon which it is securely fastented. At destination station the operation is reversed and the van is hauled by horses to the residence to which the goods are consigned and there unloaded. The vans are returned home either loaded or unloaded and the railways have a regular tariff for this class of traffic.

This type of van, while used for years as a convenient and economical accessory for the handling of furniture and household goods, has, since the advent of the motor truck been largely superseded by the demountable body. By use of these vans the shipment is handled but twice— once at the house where the goods are loaded and once at the house into which the effects are to be placed. The handling through two freight houses, and the consequent damage which usually occurs in the process, are eliminated. The same principle is applied in the transportation of fresh fish from wharf to inland market.

In another way, too, the operation of stations and shunting yards is simplified by the smaller car. Being so light, they may be switched by horsepower, or may be easily and rapidly moved by ropes attached to capstans operated electrically or hydraulically. Reference is made to this method in the description of the Broad Street Station, London.

The facility with which the cars may be loaded, unloaded and switched, and the expedition with which freight is handled through the stations, permit a large volume of traffic to be moved in a relatively small space. If the English roads were operated under American methods of freight handling, the longer period during which the freight remains in the house would call for much more space than is now occupied by the terminal in London, and the high value of property in congested centers of population make this an extremely important factor for consideration. Many of the London freight stations have several floors and the cars are elevated and lowered by lifts. The London and North Eastern has a station with five floors and a basement 16 ft. below the street level. One of the most interesting examples is the London, Midland & Scottish station at Broad Street, and it is believed that the reader will be interested in the following description, which is condensed from Findlay's "The Working and Management of an English Railway."

The Broad Street Station is the city depot and is right in the heart of London. Land being extremely valuable, the line is carried during part of its course by means of bridges and viaducts at high elevation, and in some cases over the tops of houses, and thus reaches its terminus at a point considerably above the level of surrounding thoroughfares. The passenger station having been built on arches, the London & North-Western[1], taking advantage of the situation, provided

[1] Now part of the London, Midland and Scottish.

themselves with an extensive freight station without the enormous expense of taking land for that purpose in the busiest part of the city, and the freight traffic is handled in the arches under the passenger station, the freight cars being moved on elevators from one level to the other. All along the front of these arches, 14 in number, and including some space beyond them which has been covered in, a roomy stage or unloading bank has been erected. Each arch measures 340 ft. in length and 32 ft. in width. The length of the stage is 430 ft. and its width 45 ft. From the main unloading stage, at right angles, are erected narrow stages, 12 ft. by 240 ft., with a track on each side, extending through each arch, these tracks being connected with a cross-line by means of which cars can be turned upon small turntables and taken to one of the hydraulic lifts.

On the further side of the arches some additional space has been acquired on the street level to form an open freight yard, on one portion of which a lofty warehouse has been erected for the storage of goods awaiting delivery or to be held in transit.

Traffic arriving from the country for delivery in London is called "up traffic." That sent from London is known as "down traffic." The "up traffic" consists largely of provisions for supplying the early markets with fish, meat, poultry, butter, eggs and other perishable commodities which have to be delivered as early as 4 a. m.; also general merchandise purchased from manufacturers in the Provinces the previous day and expected to be in the city warehouses by 9 a. m.

This part of the business is conducted in the warehouse, the ground floor of which is staged so as to form a platform upon which the goods can be sorted and transferred from the cars to the street vans. This platform is open on both sides, so that vans may be backed up to it on one side and the freight cars run in on the track on the other side. The invoices (waybills) are passed through the delivery office where each is entered in a book, stamped with a progressive number, timed as to arrival, checked as to the correctness of rates and extensions and is then passed to a marking clerk who marks against each entry on the invoice the position of the freight on the platform. The whole of London is mapped out into districts, each of which is designated by a letter and number, and the platform is divided into sections to correspond with these divisions. When the invoice is marked by the marking clerk, it is passed to other clerks who extract from it and enter on the carman's delivery sheets such of the entries as refer to the particular section of the city with which he is appointed to deal, and by this process the whole of the entries for delivery to a particular district are brought to a focus, although the goods may have arrived from hundreds of different stations and entered upon as many different invoices.

When the invoice reaches the platform from the delivery office, the goods are unloaded from the cars, checked with the invoice, and trucked to their positions on the platform according to the marks on the invoice. When the goods are taken from the platform to the vans, they are checked against the carmen's delivery sheets and finally taken in the vans to their destinations.

The "down" or outward traffic is handled in the arches. During the day the tracks alongside the platforms are filled with empty cars, into which the goods are loaded as they come in during the afternoon and evening. As fast as the "up" goods are unloaded at the warehouse platform, the empty cars are transferred to the "down" arches. As the loaded vans come in at the gates, they are placed in position for unloading on the platform. The consignment notes (shipping orders) relating to each load are checked against the freight as it is unloaded, and the freight is weighed on weighing machines stationed at regular intervals along the platform. Each arch is reserved for goods for certain stations or districts, and as the freight is unloaded from the van the checker directs the trucker where the freight should be trucked. From the platform the goods, when deposited in the proper location by the trucker, are placed in the cars by the loading gang, which consists of a checker, a loader, a caller-off and two porters. When the goods are in the cars, the consignment notes are taken to the shipping office and from them the invoices are prepared. The freight cars, when loaded, sheeted (with tarpaulin covers) and marked, are run out at the further end of the arches by means of ropes attached to hydraulic capstans, turned on turntables and elevated on hydraulic lifts to the upper level, where in a group of ten long sidings, and still by the aid of hydraulic capstans, they are marshaled into trains and dispatched. The process of marshaling is facilitated by arranging the cars in the arches in train order. In some cases the vans are driven alongside the cars and the freight unloaded directly from van to car.

The station embraces an area of 17 acres, including 3.5 acres on the high level. It has a capacity of 820 cars, of which 487 can be placed in position for forward loading on the low level at one time. On the average, 456 loaded cars are received daily and 508 are forwarded. Altogether, the station is equipped with 183 cranes—one of 10 tons capacity, one 5 tons and the remainder of 0.5 tons or less. These are distributed to assist (1) in loading from vans to cars, and *vice versa;* (2) from vans to platforms, and *vice versa;* and (3) from cars to platforms, and *vice versa.* The two high-power cranes are located in the yard to unload exceptionally heavy articles.

In order to give the reader some idea of the details of design, the following description of the North British freight station and warehouse in Glasgow is quoted from *The Engineer* of London:

The special feature of this warehouse is its equipment for the handling of traffic and the unusually large electrical plant which is provided, with a view to a rapid and easy disposal of a heavy volume of goods. The tracks inside the building are arranged in sets of three, the two outside tracks of each set being used for loading purposes, while the center track is used for removing empty cars from or feeding loaded cars to the outer tracks. As no locomotives are permitted inside the warehouse, on account of fire risks, special means had to be adopted for the handling of cars. Thirty electric capstans, each capable of exerting a pull of 1 ton, or hauling about 100 tons on the level at a speed of 250 ft. per minute, have been laid down. Each is worked by a 26-hp. motor running at 400 r.p.m. and driving the capstan head through a worm gear reduction.

The movement of the cars from the outer track to the center track and *vice versa* is effected by means of electric traversers running on rails laid at right angles to the wagon rails. The cars are pulled on to the traversers by means of the electric capstans, one at a time, and traversed across to the required track, where they are then run off, the traverser then being removed back out of the way. There are eleven of these machines, of the surface type, 12 ft. long exclusive of the ramps and arranged to travel on three lines of rails.   They are capable of carrying loads of 20 tons at a speed of 100 ft. per minute and are driven by 10-hp. motors.   There are 15 overhead revolving cranes—13 of 1.5 tons and two of 3 tons capacity, which are arranged to work over the ground floor and are used for loading and discharging both cars and wagons and for general lifting and transport purposes about the various loading platforms.   All the crane runways are parallel to each other and at right angles to the railway tracks, so that whenever the necessity arises a number of cranes may be concentrated on one row of cars, insuring rapid discharge with a minimum number of cranes.   Each crane consists of a traveling gantry 21-ft. 10-in. span, from which is suspended the balanced revolving jib, having a radius of 23 ft.

Facilities are provided on the upper floors for the rapid handling of goods by means of electric transporters traveling on runway girders suspended from the roof girders.   The loads are lifted from the railway trucks in the loading way through wells in the floors and are distributed by the transporters over the area of the floor covered by the respective tracks.   There are four of these transporters for each floor, each capable of lifting 1.5 tons.   The hoisting speed under full load is 100 ft. per minute, accelerating to about double this speed for light loads; and the traveling speed is 350 ft. per minute.   The height of lift for the transporters on the first floor is 34 ft. and for those on the second floor 50 ft.

Six jiggers, or short-travel transporters of 1.5 tons capacity, are provided on the uppermost floor, so placed as to command the roadway on the floor below along the north side of the warehouse through trap doors in the floor.   The three remaining are placed in outside walls on the south side of the building and may be used for raising goods from the yard to either floor and conversely.   The general design of the jigger is similar to that of the transporters, with the exception that the controllers are fixed on the warehouse floor near each track and the operator's cage is dispensed with.   The travel of each jigger is only 10 ft. and the height of lift is 50 ft.   The hoisting speed for the full load of 1.5 tons is 100 ft. per minute and the traveling speed 200 ft. per minute.

In addition to these appliances, nine electric hoists, each 1.5 tons capacity, have been provided—four at the west and five at the east end of the building—which are available for use on all the floors, communicating direct with the loading tables on the track floor.   There are two other hoists of the same capacity for the use of the portion of the basement lying to the east of the building proper, under the yard, and they communicate direct with two loading tables provided with special siding accommodation, apart altogether from the warehouse tables and sidings.

All these elevators are arranged to carry the maximum load at a speed of 150 ft. per minute and they are each driven by 26-E.-hp. motors running at 400 r.p.m.   The cages are steel-framed, lined with timber and kept in position by suitable guides fixed to the sides of the shaft.

To the south of the warehouse lies the general loading platform, which can accommodate more than 60 cars.   A considerable portion of this is roofed over, so that it forms to all intents and purposes a useful extension of the warehouse proper.   Close by there is a 40-ton electric traveling gantry crane for handling heavy machinery and special loads.   Small loads requiring the use of crane power are handled by means of hand cranes in the yard, the capacity of which varies from 5 tons downward.

In concluding this chapter on the British freight service, the question may be put, "In what particulars can any of their practices or ideas be applied to problems in this country?" The answer is difficult. A direct answer may be avoided by stating that English methods are adapted to English conditions and not to American. Dissimilarities in conditions make comparisons of doubtful value. There is, however, a feeling among a few railroad men that the railroads of New England might profitably take a leaf from the note book of Old England and experiment: (1) in the collection and delivery of freight; (2) in the use of the small-capacity car; and (3) in the running of express freight trains. In another chapter reference is made to the Baltimore and Canadian experiments in collecting and delivering, but it has not been tried in New England where conditions are perhaps more favorable. New England merchants would appreciate the advantages of additional overnight express freight service and the use of small cars would make such service more feasible. The preponderance of l.c.l. freight in New England might justify the small car and something approaching the British express freight service, but such service would cost more and call for higher rates, and it is a question whether the shippers would stand for higher rates then if the increased value of the service (which would be equivalent to shipping by express) would justify the English scale of charges.

Considerable study has been given to the use of the motor truck[1] as an adjunct to rail transportation in the United States, and by use of motor truck distribution from zone stations to which cars are loaded, a much better loading of freight cars would result.

[1] Discussion in detail in Chapter XXXII.

CHAPTER XXII

MECHANICAL HANDLING OF MERCHANDISE FREIGHT

The problem of handling freight today arouses the interest of all. It is a vital factor in prompt dispatch and in low transportation cost. Much has been learned in the past few years and there is much yet to be learned, and, beyond doubt, the results obtained in the coming years will be a surprise, even to those who closely follow the subject.

Freight may be handled at houses and piers by:

1. Conveyors—roller, chain, belt, platform.
2. Overhead traveling cranes.
3. Carrier systems.
4. Tractors and trailers.
5. Motor trucks.

Among the difficulties in the way of the satisfactory handling of freight in ordinary houses are: the great variety in shape, size and weight of packages; the necessity for receiving outbound packages from teams at various points or doors; and the necessity for moving inbound freight from various cars to many points in the house.

In discussing the mechanical handling of freight, consideration must, therefore, be given to: the utilization of all possible floor space for storage purposes; the transportation of freight from any point in the house to any other point in the house; and the handling of packages of various sizes, shapes and weights.

The ordinary two-wheel hand truck has been, and still is, one of the most useful implements on railways. It has been used in some form since railways were first built; yet that it will be displaced by other methods, where conditions are favorable, is just as certain as it is that the truck will be retained where it is better adapted to the purpose than any other method of moving package freight. Its existence is analogous to that of the horse, when the efficiency and adaptability of the latter is compared with the motor truck.

Two marked and important innovations have been the deciding factors in securing greater efficiency and economy in the handling of package freight through freight houses:

1. The introduction of the four-wheeled "drop truck," manually operated.

2. The installation of mechanical equipment through the substitution of electric tractors and trailers for hand-powered trucks.

The drop-truck system superseded the time-honored "gang" system, wherein it was the practice for gangs, consisting of a checker, loader-on, and four truckers, using two-wheeled hand trucks, to load the freight into the designated cars, picking the freight from the house floor, where it had been dropped by teamsters.

Under the drop-truck plan, a supply of four-wheeled trucks is placed adjacent to receiving doorways, enabling teamsters to unload their outbound freight direct to the truck, thus keeping the freight, except packages too large and bulky, entirely off the freight-house floor and on wheels.

The receiver or tallyman counts the number of packages, compares markings and then chalks the freight with the block number of the outbound car; the bill of lading is signed and returned to the teamster, while the shipping order, except in rush hours, passes immediately to the billing department.

Loaded trucks, after the completion of the tallyman's check, are pushed away from the doorways, thus keeping the doorways clear. The trucks can then be taken, either mechanically or manually, to the designated car.

Use of manually operated, four-wheeled trucks, under the drop-truck system, effected the first partial improvement toward speedier operation as compared with the gang system, but it was still impossible during the rush hours to move the freight as rapidly as offered, since laborers were unable to handle loaded trucks to the cars and return empties with sufficient promptness, resulting in freight being dropped on the house floor by teamsters, thus obstructing doorways and causing congestion. Further, a considerable amount of freight had to be held over until the following day. Extra care and double handling were required and the operation was necessarily slowed up during the late afternoon, because late-arrival freight could not be blocked or shipping orders passed to the billing department until it was definitely determined that sufficient time was available to load all shipments that had been previously checked, blocked and billed.

The replacement of the manually operated four-wheeled trucks by trailer trucks, hauled by electric tractors, has definitely demonstrated that rush hours can be taken care of and the actual loading kept abreast of the receipts, as well as eliminating consideration of the "distance to be traversed" feature, which must always be considered when man power is involved.

With electric tractors, after trailers have been loaded, it is possible to haul trailers to cars, in series, or train line, where freight can be unloaded and stowed by stevedores assigned for that purpose, and subsequently the empty trailers can be returned to the receiving platform for new loads.

The tractor principally used is of the three-wheel type, operated by a motor, power for which is furnished by a storage battery and is applied to the two rear wheels, usually by means of a worm-gear drive. Three speeds forward and reverse are used, the control being obtained from a lever connected with the controller. The brake is of the band type, applied by foot pressure, with an automatic cut-off of power established when the operator is off of seat. A battery charging outfit is required, consisting of one or more single or double panels, so that batteries can be charged at the proper amperage and voltage, either singly or in series.

Numerous types of trailers manufactured by various concerns have been used by the different railroads which have installed tractor-trailer operation. It can be said that each type of trailer has certain good features The type of trailer truck strengthened to resist tractor operation, which has been in service on the New Haven since 1917, has given very efficient and economical service under exacting conditions.

These trailers have wooden platforms 40 by 76 in. and are of three heights, 11, 16½ and 19¾ in. The platform has two stake pockets on each end and each side, so that racks can be used on either sides or ends, or both, if it is desired to obtain a closed-rack truck. Ends and corners are bound with steel to protect trucks when striking against each other or against sides of buildings, cars or platform posts and the corners are rounded off. Wheels are of wide tread, equipped with roller bearings, with caster wheels on the coupler end, to enable the trailer to be hauled in series and swivel around corners.

The coupler, which is attached to two rigg truss rods placed in the center of the trailer, to give a direct pull, as the coupling ring is attached to the opposite end of these truss rods, may be of various types. Again, experience with couplers has developed a special casting, equipped with a ball on the end of a hook, to bind and prevent jumping out when conditions might cause uncoupling. This type of coupler is especially valuable when trailers are hauled up or down grades incident to tidal conditions existent at water-front piers.

A three-wheeled trailer has been lately devised and placed in service, which is especially adapted to the handling of heavy-package freight. This three-wheeled trailer is a large-type, two-wheeled stevedore truck equipped with a swiveling third wheel and coupler, and will trail in series not only with others of its own type, but also with four-wheeled trailers.

With the various types of trailers indicated, the hand truck can be practically eliminated and an approximately 100 per cent. tractor-trailer operation obtained.

The height of trailers is important, and can be varied according to local conditions; for instance, it is necessary to consider the level of the present-day motor truck, which is much higher than the horse-drawn dray. If the trailer can be placed at the rear of the dray or truck, either at the same height or slightly lower than the dray floor, it is very easy for the driver to carry or roll his freight and place it on the trailer with a minimum of effort, thus releasing his dray promptly and still keeping the freight off the floor, which is highly desirable from the standpoint of the transporting carrier.

Trailer trains should be operated in units of from three to eight trailers depending upon block classification, floor conditions, grades to be overcome, and related conditions, and on return trips it is important that the tractor bring back to the receiving platform approximately the same number of empty trailers, to keep the supply available adjacent to the point most needed.

Among other mechanical equipment successfully used for handling freight are the "load-carrying truck" the "elevating lift truck," the "hand-operated lift truck" and the "elevating or tiering truck."

The load-carrying truck is operated by electric power like the tractor, but has less potential power. Platforms are a part of this truck and average approximately the same flooring space as the trailer described above; 40 by 76 in. Freight is loaded onto this platform, the truck moved to the desired car or house destination, the freight removed and the truck returned for another load. Load-carrying trucks are specially adaptable for handling baggage at terminal stations, or for shop work, but they are not economical for freight-house operation because of the time lost while the truck is standing still for loading or unloading. With a tractor and trailer system, the trailers stand idle until the transporting vehicle (tractor) is ready, and, upon arrival at destination, the trailer is dropped and can await the stevedore without delaying the tractor.

The electric lift truck is designed to work in connection with stationary platforms or skids, as the "lift" of the truck can be run underneath the skid and, by raising the lift, the platform is hoisted clear of the floor, and the lift truck with its two units becomes a load carrier. Upon arrival at its destination, the lift is dropped and the skid placed on the floor, there to remain until unloaded. The skids can be equipped with wheels, thus becoming "live" and capable of being pushed or pulled about by hand, a most desirable feature around freight houses or wharves. The lift truck of greater power than the ordinary tractor affords a valuable asset of operation at piers or freight houses, where the floor of the pier is at the same level as the tracks, with the grade between that level and the car floor to be overcome. Experience at the Army base, Boston, has developed the efficiency of lift trucks in making the grade of moving "live" skids from the lower to the upper level.

Use of dead skids, preferably, should be confined to warehouses where the freight placed on such skids is to be stored for a time before being forwarded. In such instances, it is possible at any time to pick up the skid and transport it, and the space occupied by dead skid is much less than would be taken up by skid on wheels.

The hand lift truck is designed for service similar to the elevating truck, but is much lighter and is operated by hand power.

The elevating or tiering truck is a combined load carrier and lift truck, which can elevate freight and place it onto piles at varying heights.

Experience teaches that the best results from tractor-trailer or any other mechanical form of operation are obtainable only through as nearly 100 per cent. use of both as possible. The trial of a single unit, when the tonnage handled warrants several such units, may not show up advantageously, as the slower procession of the hand trucks, still retained, will necessarily have to dodge the faster machine. The double operation results in the absorption by the slower of practically all the resultant gain and leaves the net economy very slight, so that, in making the change from hand to mechanical operation, sufficient equipment should be provided to protect 100 per cent. of the business, or as close thereto as local conditions permit.

While the foregoing covers the present-day handling of package freight mechanically, it is, nevertheless, true that the means and methods of handling merchandise and car-load freight are so rapidly developing that anything said on the subject today may be antiquated tomorrow.

Freight of one general class, such as flour in barrels, ordinarily moving from one point to another, may be handled satisfactorily and economically on conveyors. For heavy moving on usual paths, as on water fronts, the overhead cranes or gantrys may be more advantageously used, although the most expensive to install, because of the necessity for heavy wall construction of houses and ample overhead clearance.

Where the size shape and weight of packages vary, the overhead monorail, or carrier, system, with independent motors for lifting and propelling, is best adapted, but is also expensive, and heavy wall construction and overhead clearance are required.

The conditions to be met may be more clearly understood and accurately represented by following the investigations and results of practical and experienced men. E. H. Lee, Vice-President and Chief Engiseer of the Chicago and Western Indiana Railroad, gives the result of nome interesting investigations.

The handling of l.c.l. freight through freight and transfer houses, excluding inbound houses, involves a sequence of operations, which may be divided into:

	Average distribution of house costs at six outbound houses, per cent.
1. Unloading or checking...........................	32.5
2. Trucking..	43.7
3. Stowing...	13.1
4. Supervision and miscellaneous......................	10.7
	100.0

In searching for means for increasing economy, the reduction of trucking cost is the item in which the great saving is to be expected, and, in order to secure maximum economy, the cooperation of the management with the agent and foreman is required. The reduction of trucking cost may seem an insignificant matter to one not closely in touch with freight-house work. Allowing for the double handling required under present practice, about 24,000 tons of l.c.l. freight is handled per day through freight and transfer houses in Chicago alone, and, taking the country as a whole, the l.c.l. tonnage going through freight houses and transfer stations probably approximates 400,000 tons per day. Therefore, it is apparent that, if the conclusions reached herein are sound, the possible saving amounts to a large sum.

Almost without exception, the handling of material of any kind is based on a few broad principles, although in a given case their application is sometimes difficult to recognize. Ton-mile cost is frequently a useful standard for measuring efficiency in handling materials transported by other means than railroad cars. The means and methods involved in the economical handling of cars that, in turn, influence ton-mile cost, nearly all have a counterpart in the proper handling of trucks through a freight house. In either case it is essential to the best results that a smooth track or running surface be provided; that adverse grades be reduced or eliminated; that fouling points and causes of interference be avoided; that rehandling be reduced to the lowest terms; that full loading be provided for each carrying unit, and that these be transported over the shortest and most direct line or path at the highest safe speed, so far as is practicable in each item. In either case suitable appliances and equipment are required. Finally, if by good management and proper classification in the one case a larger loading on each carrying unit or car can be assembled with other units into larger trains to be hauled the greatest practicable distance before breaking up, with a favorable effect upon cost, it is fair to presume that the same general practice may have a like favorable effect in the other.

That the four-wheel truck should be generally substituted for the two-wheel truck in all except the smaller houses, and that in outbound freight and transfer houses having sufficient size and business the use of motor trucks and trailers will save money, are thought to be the general conclusions reached by almost everyone who will analyze the facts. Man power is one of the most expensive forms of power. One authority maintains that its cost per unit of power developed is from 10 to 12 times that of the next less expensive form. Evidently, therefore, where conditions warrant, the substitution of mechanical power offers an effective means of reducing cost.

The two-wheel truck has been standard for freight-house use for years, and it is still almost universally used. It is suited for economical hauling over short distances, and is convenient and well adapted for use in cramped and narrow runways; but a careful examination shows many defects in its use. Its average load varies from about 200 to approximately 400 lb., a rack being required in the latter case. Roughly, therefore, from five to ten trips are required in transporting a ton of freight through the house. The length of the trucking distance under load probably averages 200 ft. and upward in city freight houses, and thus the two-wheel truck travels from 1,000 to 3,000 ft. per ton   If the gang system of trucking is used, under which from 40 to 50 per cent. of the movement is with empty trucks, the distance traveled per ton handled is nearly doubled.

The four-wheel truck has now been so far perfected that one man can handle from three to six times the tonnage per trip as compared with the average load on a two-wheel truck, and with no greater fatigue, because the trucker is relieved from carrying any portion of the load on the four-wheel truck, and simply applies the horizontal force required for traction. With the use of the truck carrying the heavier load, a smooth trucking surface is of importance, and commodious truckways greatly facilitate the work. The four-wheel truck has already been adopted in some existing freight houses to the exclusion of the two-wheel truck, except for use in the shortest hauls; and the average loading is at least three times the loading of the two-wheel truck. For special purposes six-wheel trucks and dollies are found convenient.

Some of the objections offered to the use of the four-wheel truck are as follows:

"Their loading involves extra expense." The observer will note a partial answer to this objection in the fact that two men are often required in loading a two-wheel truck. He will also note that in any trip of a trucker there is a certain amount of lost time at the terminals or ends of each trip. The number of trips made by the four-wheel truck in handling a ton of freight being much less than with the two-wheel truck, the time lost at the terminals per ton handled is also reduced in proportion.

"It is necessary to mix freight on the truck to procure full loading." This, while true, is not a vital objection. The freight on a "peddler" truck can be classified for the cars in a certain rank or for ranks opposite a certain section of the house, the freight being loaded on the truck in proper sequence so that it may be convenient for unloading. To make such a classification most advantageously, an ample number of trucks is needed.

In loading cars for the way-freight train on the road, many are given a mixed loading. During the time such mixed freight is being handled at the way station, the expense for locomotive and crew is a dead loss, and in most cases the main track is blocked. Moreover, at most way stations the facilities for handling l.c.l. freight are so poor that the actual expense of handling is excessive. For these reasons some relatively light set-out cars are run, yet it would not be considered good practice to run cars with only 25 to 30 per cent of their average loading merely to avoid mixing freight in them. With a proper system of classification, mixing freight on the four-wheel truck is free from the objections that apply to the practice with the freight car on the road; therefore, all the greater are the disadvantage and loss caused by multiplying the distance required to handle the truck by three or four, merely to avoid a relatively small loss required by the classification described.

"The use of the four-wheel truck increases the cost of stowing." This may well be doubted. The use of stowers is required by the "drop-truck," or "no-gang" system, and this system probably saves money, although in this respect some difference of opinion may exist. The use of the four-wheel truck is particularly well adapted to the drop-truck system. Actual practice with the use of the four-wheel truck has shown that mixing freight on the "peddler" truck has actually made a substantial reduction instead of tending to increase the overs and shorts in the freight car. Moreover, it cannot be doubted that any extra expense involved in careful and proper stowing of l.c.l. freight in cars reduces the damage in transit and the placing of freight in the wrong car sufficiently to more than offset the extra stowing expense.

"Four-wheel trucks are not adapted for passing into and through cars." This objection, so far as it applies to the improved trucks now manufactured, is without foundation.

If the loading on the four-wheel truck is three times that on a two-wheel truck, it might seem that, by the use of the former trucking, cost should be reduced 66 per cent., but this is somewhat too much to expect. In the opinion of the writer, some additional labor is to be expected in sorting the freight onto trucks, as several shipments are required to make a truck load, the average shipment being only about 400 lb., to the best of our information. In certain cases additional expense for stowers is involved, but this is a positive advantage for the reasons already given.

The trucker can hardly be expected to travel so rapidly with the larger load, although an improvement in the floor or trucking surface will frequently offset this difference. It may be said here that a smooth trucking surface is a profitable investment in almost any house. Officers who would promptly authorize the repair of rough main tracks sometimes fail to appreciate that a rough trucking surface, although not involving the same elements of danger as a rough track, probably has a relatively greater effect upon the cost of transportation over it.

A typical performance of three tractors shows each one handling an average of 172 tons over an average distance of 393 ft. Each, therefore, carried 12.8 tons 1 mile. The average time per loaded trip was 5 min. 18 sec. An average of 3,070 lb. was carried per loaded trip on 2.71 trailers, or 1,130 lb. per trailer. The three tractors moved 515 tons, or 65.1 per cent. of the total tonnage. The average weight per shipment on that day was 398 lb., and, as the average trailer load was 1,130 lb., it was evidently necessary to mix the loading on a considerable percentage of the trailer trucks. These "peddler" trucks were hauled by the tractor to the proper section of the house, and there distributed into cars, as previously described. Two truck switchmen made up trailers into trains for the motor trucks, one working in each half of the house. Trailers were made up into station order, the last in the train being the first dropped. Hand trucking was used for distances of about 100 ft. or less. Tractors and trailers are considered to be better adapted for handling long pipe, sheet iron, lumber, machinery, pianos and other awkward and bulky freight than two-wheel trucks.

When the motor truck is used for carrying freight, instead of a tractor to haul it, a large part of the motor's time is lost in loading and unloading, and the average load is relatively smaller. For the same reason, automobile trucks for general road and street use have proved economical for the handling of miscellaneous material only when their running time is largely in excess of their standing time, and therefore their use for handling materials whose loading requires too much time has been limited, and in some cases entirely abandoned.

In designing plans for new house and track layouts, changes from present standards are required if motor trucks are to be used, in order to secure maximum efficiency. In substituting four-wheel trucks for two-wheel trucks, and in determining where motor trucks are warranted, how large the installation shall be, and what changes, if any, shall be made in existing houses and track layouts, a careful investigation is needed.

General Conclusions.—1. Motor trucks, when used without trailers, tend to decrease the cost of trucking freight, because they form single units of higher capacity and greater speed than do men with two-wheel trucks; but as their cost of operation per day is greater than the cost of a man and a two-wheel truck, the saving is not large, and, unless conditions are favorable (long haul, heavy packages, etc.), no saving is made. When compared with a man and a four-wheel (platform) truck, there is no saving, for the two have about the same carrying capacity, and the higher speed of the motor is more than offset by its greater cost of operation.

2. Motor trucks, when used as power for hauling loaded four-wheel trucks as trailers, show favorable results and greatly decrease the costs per ton. They can pull six times the load at twice the speed of a man with a four-wheel truck, at about twice the expense. Motor trucks, should therefore, be used to haul, and not to carry, freight. Under such a system they form an efficient, reliable and economical means of trucking freight.

3. To insure full train loads, an ample supply of four-wheel or six-wheel trucks and dollies is necessary.

4. Motor trucks, when used as tractors, can handle practically all kinds of l.c.l. freight.

5. Motor trucks need wide station platforms, and open runways wide enough to permit two motor-truck trains to pass each other, in order to secure the best results.

6. "Fouling points" or "interferences" should be reduced or eliminated entirely.

7. In motor-truck operation, distance is a relatively unimportant factor, for, once a train is made up and in motion, the cost per ton per 100 ft. is low.

8. Under fair conditions, on an ordinary freight platform, where the motor must operate largely as a way-freight, it can handle from 150 to 200 tons per day per motor, and do from 10 to 15 ton-miles of trucking.

9. Under ideal conditions, where the motor can operate as a "through freight," *i.e.*, pull a solid train of five or more trailers from origin to destination without stop and with few or no delays, a motor can probably be expected to handle from 250 to 500 tons per day, or do from 30 to 60 ton-miles of trucking.

10. Finally, while the substitution of the four-wheel truck for the two-wheel truck saves money, if conditions warrant, its use is particularly valuable because it may be a preliminary step to the use of one or more motor trucks, if the volume of tonnage and the local conditions indicate the need of a tractor. This method of procedure also eliminates the danger of installing motor trucks at a heavy investment expense, to perform work which the four-wheel truck used as a trailer will do more economically.

The conveyor system is the simplest mechanical method, but it is not adaptable to changing conditions. At a transfer station it may be necessary to take the contents of one car, often in small loads, into any of 200 cars or from any of the 200 cars into one car. There would be nearly 20,000 separate paths or courses for the trucks, and yet this problem can be easily solved by the use of the electric carrier and movable by-path track. Although the action of these electric carriers and trailers is almost continuous, yet each train being independent, an accident to one does not stop operation for a minute.

There is still another type of machinery for handling freight between variable points, the movable platform, which is used in two ways: (1) to move the freight itself when loaded on the movable platform, and (2) to move the trucks on which the freight is loaded. Both methods reduce the time and labor involved in moving the freight by hand over long distances. A traveling platform level with the floor has been devised, moving at slow speed, so that men, trucks and teams can cross it. As proposed for an inbound freight house of the B. & O., the moving platform would form a belt line; one side would be near the track side and the other near the team-delivery side. Packages, or trucks, from the cars would be dropped on the moving platform. The house would be

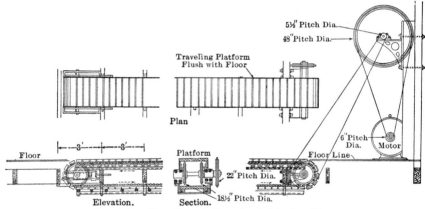

Fig. 145.—Traveling platform for freight handling.

divided into sections, with a man to each, and each man would pull from the platform the freight for his section as it passed him. In another system, the platform would be a single line only, the return side being underground. This was designed more particularly for steamship piers, where freight delivered at the end or from a ship has to be transferred for a considerable part of the length of the pier.

A system of handling freight trucks by a traveling chain has been patented by a firm of conveyor manufacturers, and is intended to reduce the labor of the trucking in a longitudinal direction. The idea was to devise a system that would provide for taking freight from any car along the platform and delivering it to any other car, as conditions required. In order to accomplish this, it was found desirable to use the ordinary hand truck, with slight modifications, so that it can readily be wheeled around from one place to another by manual labor when desired. The truck travels upon a narrow-gage track, and is provided with special attachments to engage an endless chain set underneath the track. This driving chain lies entirely beneath the floor, and is out of the way. As there is only a groove 1 in. wide in the floor, there is no danger of accidents and the floor is left entirely free to truck across or walk upon at any time. An elevation plan and other details of a moving platform are shown on Fig. 145.

Mechanical freight handlers, or conveyors, are in use for loading and unloading vessels at Northern Steamship Company's wharf, Buffalo, adjustable to the height of tide and freeboard of vessel. Four continuous carriers, also adjustable, are used by Southern Pacific at New Orleans and 28 at Galveston. A saving of $48 per day was effected at New Orleans, which paid for the conveyors in a year—and in seven years repairs and maintenance did not exceed $500. A carrier, designed to handle tierces, barrels and sacks between a sugar refinery and shipping wharf at Chicago, 435 ft. long, with adjustable end, having a rise and fall of 16 ft., handles 75 bbl. of 700 lb. each, and will easily transfer 6,000 bbl. in 10 hours. An endless carrier 95 ft. long, 4 ft. wide, adjustable height, loads and unloads vessels of the Texas & Pacific at Donaldsonville, La. The Southern has a carrier at Port Chalmette, La., operated by electric motor, with a capacity of 500 bales of cotton per hour. A similar carrier is in service at Butler Brothers warehouse, St. Louis, length 132 ft. The Anchor Line has a freight conveyor at Chicago, arranged to handle freight direct or on trucks, for the purpose of eliminating the services of six or eight men who pushed loaded trucks from the steamer up a steep incline to the first floor of the warehouse. At Sydney, N. S. W., five inclined conveyors receive wheat in bags from cars, elevate and deliver them to a series of longitudinal conveyors, which, in turn, distribute the bags to piles and also deliver them from the piles to automatic ship loaders. These automatic loaders, four in number, receive wheat from the longitudinal conveyors and deliver it to holds of vessels. The capacity of the plant is 3,600 bags per hour. The Boston & Maine has at Charlestown, Mass., nine freight elevators—three in each warehouse—5- by 8-ft. platform, electric-motor-driven, with a capacity of 2,000 lb. on each.

Overhead cranes and gantrys are serviceable when heavy, bulky commodities are handled over constant routes and with slight variations in distances. Portable gantry cranes are used on the Hamburg docks— the best in Germany—which hoist the cargo from the hold of the vessel, swing the load through a section of a circle of 180 deg. and deposit it upon cars beneath the crane or upon car tracks between the crane and the shed, or upon drays, or upon the platform of the shed or warehouse. At the Kuhwaeder Dock, Hamburg, 134 portable gantry cranes are in use.

The average cost of unloading and swinging upon the dock varies. The power used is almost always electricity, and the cost of electricity is about 0.15 ct. per ton at 2 cts. per kilowatt-hour. These figures vary somewhat, depending upon local conditions and the cost of the electric current, which varies at European ports from 2 to 8 cts. per kilowatt-hour.

In some cases it is stated that as many as 40 movements have been performed within an hour, that is to say, 40 complete cycles. A complete crane cycle, often mentioned in German figures, consists in hoisting the load 50 ft., slewing 150 ft., lowering to the platform, raising, slewing back and lowering the hook to the starting point. Twenty cycles per hour can easily be accomplished. The number of cycles depends largely upon the operator.

Fig. 146.—Carrier system, Richmond, Va.—Old Dominion Steamship Co.

Carrier systems are becoming more numerous and in their development many of the difficult features are being overcome. Many concerns are now manufacturing them; some are prepared to install them in large houses, guaranteeing a saving in the cost of handling that will pay the entire installation cost in from one to two years, depending on the amount and kind of freight to be handled and the difficulties in construction.

An overhead runway system is in use at a steamship pier, and is to be used by the B. and O. A pair of trolleys riding on an elevated runway carry a frame with hoists for raising and lowering trucks or wheeled platforms. Current for electric traction is taken from an overhead wire, and an attendant riding with the machine controls the traveling and hoisting movements. This system has been in operation for about four years on the pier of the Old Dominion Steamship Company, at Richmond, Va. It handles 3-ton loads between the wharf and the railway warehouse and cars. Two views are shown in Figs. 146 and 147; in one, the hoist is seen elevating a load of 3.5 tons of sugar from the port of a steamship which the telpher conveys a distance of 500 to 600 ft. to the warehouse; in the other view, truck loads of bags in transit are seen, moving from warehouse for unloading alongside of cars. It is said to show a great saving in cost over the old hand-truck method, besides being able to handle freight more rapidly and with much greater ease. One operator does the work formerly requiring 16 men.

A telpherage installation has been designed for the Bergen freight house of the Erie Railroad. Sectional and detailed views are shown

FIG. 147.—Carrier system, Richmond, Va.—Old Dominion Steamship Co.

in Figs. 148, 149 and 150. This house has three platforms, each 1,400 ft. long, and three telpher tracks (one over the center of each platform) connected by loops at the ends. Ten telpher machines operating at one time on the three tracks, all machines following each other in the same direction around the loop, would provide for a movement of 1,000 tons of freight per day of 20 hours. Each machine is expected to make one round trip of 3,000 ft. in 6 min., at the rate of 10 trips per hour. The average speed would be 500 ft. per minute, including all stops and slow-downs, and the maximum speed of traveling 1,500 ft. per minute.

The Memphis Warehouse Company has overhead trolley tracks (Breck system) for handling cotton. The trolleys are not motor-driven, but the tracks have a slight grade, so that the load moves by gravity. The grade starts at the beginning of the inbound platform and extends

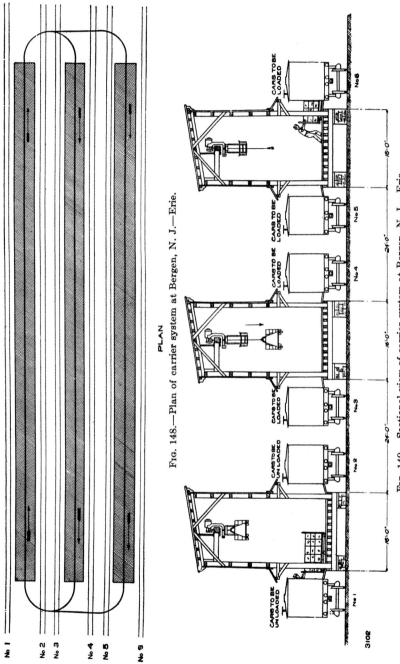

PLAN

FIG. 148.—Plan of carrier system at Bergen, N. J.—Erie.

FIG. 149.—Sectional view of carrier system at Bergen, N. J.—Erie.

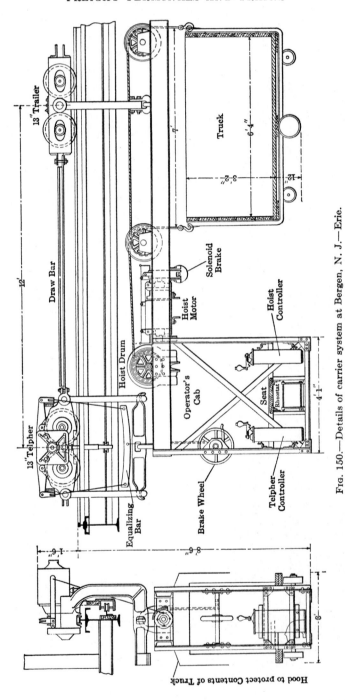

Fig. 150.—Details of carrier system at Bergen, N. J.—Erie.

through the plant to the end of the outbound platform, a distance of about 1.25 miles. The arrangement permits of placing four—or even six—trains of 25 cars each at the inbound platforms at one time, without "spotting." This makes it possible for one yard engine and crew to do the work, while ordinarily three or four engines would be required. There are about 3 miles of the trolley runway and 6 miles of railway tracks. The cost of handling by the telpherage system is said to be only about one-eighth of the cost of teaming. The company has an extensive cotton warehouse and compress plant, with storage capacity under cover for about 125,000 bales.

A development of the overhead trolley system, in an effort to reduce terminal costs, congestion and time of handling l.c.l. freight, is the installation in the double-deck St. Louis freight house of the Missouri, Kansas and Texas Terminal Company.

The ground floor is given over to cars and the one above to the receipt, delivery and storage of freight. Connection and transfer between the two floors and any point of the building are made by a telpherage system having monorail runways across the line of the tracks and suspended from the second-floor ceiling over hatchways leading to the lower floor. Transferring from one runway to another is done over leads at each side of the house. Telphers enter and leave the leads by means of automatic electric track switches. Seventy-five per cent. of the l.c.l. freight handled is outbound, and the design has been worked out to provide a capacity of 1,000,000 lb. in five hours. The present installation provides for the loading of 77 cars, and is arranged for easy expansion. Freight of a diversified character is handled at this terminal, including all the classifications and varieties of packages usually found in shipments to and from a large city.

This freight station is a two-story structural steel building having brick walls and reinforced concrete floors. It is 232 by 403 ft. in plan, and, with the 16 tracks, automobile shed and incoming switch tracks, occupies two and one-half city blocks.

On the ground or track floor the building is enclosed only on two street sides. Twelve stub tracks ending at Mullanphy Street enter from the open north end by a ladder system having four branches. Each track has a capacity of nine freight cars, but under normal conditions receives only eight. The tracks are spaced in pairs opposite 11-ft. island platforms between columns supporting the building. Trucking through the cars is thus eliminated and the column spacing of 38 ft. definitely fixed. The platforms are wide enough to permit two trucks to pass conveniently. Very little longitudinal trucking is anticipated, as transferring from car to car will be done by the telphers up through the hatchways and down to the receiving car, which may be in any part of the building. The 4,800 ft. of trackage under cover provides for 117 cars. Four team tracks to the east of the building for both in and outbound freight have a total capacity of 60 cars, 20 of which are served by a moving 12-ton gantry crane having a travel of 400 ft. These tracks are used to a large extent for shipments of heavy machinery and other bulky freight requiring an entire car for one or several pieces.

An interior view of the telphers on runways above hatches is shown in Fig. 151; the interior of team floor in Fig. 152, from which the arrangement of the hatchways in the platform over the train platform of the lower floor is clearly indicated. The small piles of freight are loaded

Fig. 151.—Telphers on runways above hatches, St. Louis terminal—Missouri, Kansas & Texas.

on wheeled platforms, which are picked up by the telphers. Several runways are shown; at the left of the view in Fig. 152 one of the switches may be seen connecting the longitudinal with the transverse runways.

On the second floor there are four driveways 38 ft. wide, extending across the width of the house. Adjacent to the driveways are four platforms, two wide ones, 82 by 230 ft., providing storage for inbound freight as well as for receiving outbound, and two narrow platforms, 42 by 217 ft., primarily for outbound freight. Driveways extend around the inside ends of the narrow platforms to facilitate the movement of drays.

Telpher runways pass longitudinally above the wagon platforms or in the direction across the tracks of the lower level, two runways being suspended over each of the two narrow platforms and one of the wide ones, and four runways over the remaining wide platform. Each of these runways connects with lead tracks at the two sides of the building. Hatchways through the wagon platforms are provided below the runways over each car platform in the lower level, so that there is a hatchway for every two cars.

Numerous experiments, observations and measurements have been made to determine unit movements by the old system of hand trucking. The methods successfully tried out are being adapted to the new conditions. Some of the results are given below. The 1,600-ft. total length

Fig. 152.—Interior of team floor, St. Louis terminal—Missouri, Kansas & Texas.

of platforms which is available to handle the 500 tons of freight in five hours, the capacity for which the station is designed, is more than double the length heretofore used. The driveways are placed the short way of the building, as it has been observed that short driveways do not become so congested as long ones. A width of driveway has been well established elsewhere at 38 ft. but was checked up in St. Louis by numerous measurements of drays both as to width and length. The unit movements ascertained by the new system are very uniform:

Average number of truck loads handled per day by each
man... 157
Average pounds on each truck....................... 225
Average tonnage loaded in each car................. 8 tons
Average number of cubic feet in each car............ 288
Average time weighing a truck load on beam scales...... 30 sec.
Average time weighing a truck load on automatic scales.. 10 sec.
Average length of teams and drays................... 18 ft.
Average width of drays............................. 6 ft. 3 in.
Maximum width of drays............................ 8 ft. 6 in.; minimum, 5 ft.

These averages are based on a total of 1,000,000 lb. of freight handled.

On a large New York pier, two motor trucks (Figs. 153 and 154), during a period of 26 working days, of 11 hours' service, each performed average daily service as follows:

Mileage....................................	13.6
Tons handled..............................	225.0
Tons per hour.............................	20.3
Loads handled.............................	230.0
Length of haul, average....................	1585.0 ft.
Pieces per load, average...................	29.8 lb.
Weight per piece, average..................	88.5 "
Time per round trip, average...............	2.89 minutes
Time to load, average......................	58.00 seconds
Time to unload, average....................	60.3 seconds
Men in gang...............................	8

The use of tractor and trailers in handling less-than-carload freight at Pennsylvania Station[1] at Polk street, Chicago, has shown excellent results. Introduced in July, 1920, and enlarged upon in the following year, the equipment and the system built around it has operated to accomplish marked economies. The amount of labor required for the handling of the freight has been reduced more than half and the tonnage handled per man has more than doubled. Greater elasticity in performance has obtained, while business is handled with greater dispatch and less demand on floor space.

The Polk Street terminal is a four-story structure, 450 ft. wide and 745 ft. long, which is built over 19 tracks with a standing capacity of 375 cars; the first or street level floor constituting the freight house proper and the upper three floors being utilized for storage by a warehousing concern. All merchandise is handled between the several floors and the track level platforms by 32 elevators, 8 of which are three-ton, 21 five-ton and 2 ten-ton.

The benefits which have arisen from the tractor operation are several. A comparison of the records for the last six months of this year with those for the six months immediately preceding the inauguration of the present system bring this out. As the table on page 373 shows, between these periods the average number of tons handled per trucker has been increased from 1,167 to 2,228, or 90 per cent., while the number of tons handled per man per hour has been increased from an average of 0.764 to 1.746 or 128 per cent., or if compared with the records of the last three months of the year from an average of 0.764 to above 1.80. This reduction in the forces actually handling the freight has also permitted some reductions to be made in clerical forces. The average size of the gangs receiving the freight from vehicles and of those loading or unloading the cars has been reduced from six or seven to two and three men. It has also been possible to cut down the distance through which the truckmen are required to operate from an average of 1,000 ft. or more to less than 50. Figures 155 and 156 illustrate typical uses of tractor and trailers.

[1] *Railway Age*, Jan. 21, 1922.

TRUCKING OPERATIONS AT THE PENNSYLVANIA'S POLK STREET TERMINAL BEFORE AND AFTER TRACTOR INSTALLATIONS

The six months period prior to tractor haulage

Month	Number of truckers employed	Trucker hours	Tons handled	Tons per man hour
January	195	43,651	37,038	0.85
February	183	48,763	34,940	0.94
March	328	85,023	56,611	0.66
April	155	37,739	22,926	0.61
May	199	49,785	38,104	0.77
June	256	69,674	55,107	0.79
Average men per month	219.3	334,635	225,726	0.764

The last six months of 1921 under tractor haulage

Month	Trucking force			Trucking hours			Tons handled	Tons per man hour
	Truck-ers	Tractor operators and helpers	Total	Truck-ers	Tractor operators and helpers	Total hours		
June	90	8	98	18,922	1,740	20,662	33,712	1.63
July	80	8	88	16,275	1,454	17,729	29,773	1.68
August	82	8	90	19,444	1,902	21,346	35,710	1.67
September	84	8	92	17,815	1,782	19,597	35,256	1.80
October	93	8	101	19,734	1,862	21,596	39,921	1.85
November	86	12	98	17,964	2,346	20,310	37,356	1.84
Average men per month	85.8	8.7	94.5	110,154	11,086	121,240	211,728	1.746

FIG. 153.—Electric freight truck entering a box car.

FIG. 154.—Electric freight truck unloading vessel.

Fig. 155.—Tractor and trailers at Polk St. Station, Chicago, Ill.—Pennsylvania system.

Fig. 156.—Tractors and trailers at Roanoke, Va.—Norfolk and Western.

The Merchants & Miners Transportation Company placed 20 electric trucks in operation on its Savannah, Ga., pier, of which the Superintendent of Agencies, said:

The performance records of 13 power-truck loads, after four weeks' operation, as compared with 13 hand-truck loads, handling similar commodities and traveling the same distances, were prepared by me personally. The average weight of electric-truck load was 1,531 lb.; distance traveled, 748 ft.; time consumed, 5 min. 23 sec.; 138 ft. distance per minute; while the hand-truck load

Fig. 157.—Inclined drop elevators, used by Merchant & Miner's Transportation Company.

averaged 400 lb.; time, 4 min., 46 sec.; 156 ft. per minute. The figures for average time were obtained by cutting out one power truck and one hand truck and timing them. The electric truck made seven stops, distributing freight around the houses, while the hand truck made but one stop. The results show 383 per cent. in favor of the electric truck, in weight handled, and 11.3 per cent. in favor of hand truck in time consumed. The electric truck handled about 8 tons per hour as against 2.5 tons for the hand truck. In moving freight from freight houses to the warehouses, an average trucking distance of 1,170 ft., the work was performed for a fraction over 9 cts. per ton, and at 17 cts. with the hand truck, a saving of 47 per cent., although these are conditions peculiarly favorable to the power truck, considering the long-distance run. At our Savannah terminal the average trucking distance is 637 ft., measured from center of the main discharging berth to average of all the warehouses. Varying tides produce inclines from ship's upper "between decks" to the pier surface, of anywhere from zero (level) to 37 per cent. ascending. On the extreme grades the trucks are assisted by inclined drop elevator for power economy. About 70 per cent. of our work can be done by power trucks; the remainder being handled by hand trucks. Cost for current has averaged 11 cts. per truck per day.

The view in Fig. 157 is of the inclined drop elevator referred to by him and in general use by the Merchant & Miners Company.

The present development in the general application of machinery to handling freight is not altogether satisfactory, but rapid strides are being made; and, with the more general use of electric power, the ease with which it may be transmitted and the flexibility with which applied, much will be done in this direction during the coming years. As a factor in reducing the cost of terminal handling, this machinery is important, and terminal handling must be looked to for the greatest opportunities.

CHAPTER XXIII

TRANSFER STATIONS

The daily amount of freight handled between two stations may be small, possibly consisting of one or two packages of 100 lb. weight each. Where these stations are located on the same district and on the line of a way freight's regular daily run, the packages would be loaded and unloaded to and from the peddler cars by the way-freight crew. Freight destined to or beyond the station at the end of the way-freight's run would be loaded into one or more cars for that station, and unloaded there by the station forces. At the larger intermediate stations, where a sufficient amount of freight originates, cars are loaded up for the station at the end of the run, or to a point beyond. These are usually termed "straight cars" and the contents are not handled by the train crew. The cars loaded or unloaded by the trainmen are variously known as "peddler cars," "way-freight cars," "scrap loads" or "local cars." To facilitate the handling of this l.c.l. freight, it is customary to establish transfer stations at convenient points where freight from various stations and converging lines centralizes and may be consolidated into straight cars—that is, solid car loads to stations for which enough freight may be running to justify such cars, and into local or peddler cars to be distributed over the various way-freight runs, and for other transfer stations which, in turn, may repeat this loading.

In England, "tranship" stations take the place of the American transfer station. Because of the small 12-ton-capacity "goods wagons" of Great Britain, there is little necessity there for rehandling the freight between the point of shipment and final destination, as straight car-load shipments are made in most cases where fast time is a desideratum. The heavy load and the large-capacity cars of American railways have their advantages, and likewise their disadvantages. Unless freight in considerable quantities is moving between two points, the large-capacity cars have to be loaded into and out of the many transfer stations which are necessary to enable the heavier loading of cars by consolidation of their lading. Each handling at a transfer station means an added expense in the freight handling and checking with the waybills, as well as extra expense in the yard-switching service. The opportunities for loss and damage to freight and for pilfering increase with the number of transfer points. Each transfer adds also to the delay in the movement of freight and cars. On the other hand, it permits the consolidation of car loads with regard to train service, and, in many instances, affords better time by enabling loading to final destinations.

In the handling of l.c.l. freight it is the general practice to load straight cars for stations to which the movement of traffic is large enough to justify them, and peddler cars for movement on diverging local or other designated trains. In addition, the larger shipping stations "scrap" load to transfer stations located at various operating terminals and junctions, shipments consigned to points on lines diverging from such transfer stations, to which the business is not heavy enough to justify the loading of a straight car for any one station. When these scrap loads are received at a transfer station, they are worked into that station's schedule cars, making straight cars for the heavier receiving stations, and peddler cars, loaded in station order for less important stations.

The transfer station is usually operated in conjunction with a freight station, although the larger and more important transfers are often operated independently. The organization, if operated independently, is planned after that of the ordinary freight station, except that straight gangs of truckers, each with a foreman, are employed; also checkers, who are responsible for checking both the inward and outward handling. A regular "set-up" is made daily at a transfer; the inward cars, when unloaded, ordinarily being utilized to make the outward "set-up," unless the unloaded car is routed by a different line or junction than the regular "set-up" car would travel.

The set-up may not be the same each day. Two-day and, at times, three-day cars may vary it. For points to which there is not sufficient freight to load a car daily, freight may be held two or even three days to obtain enough to secure a straight car, thereby avoiding delay and rehandling after the car leaves the transfer. This practice often makes it necessary to hold cars at the transfer for that purpose, unless storage room is available in which to care for it. Such storage room is usually provided, and should be in every instance, unless the transfer is a part of the regular freight station, in which case the freight-house room may be utilized.

To illustrate the general principles of a transfer set-up and its handling, assume a platform 20 by 560 ft. with two tracks on either side, giving length for 14 cars on each track and a set-up of 56 cars by working through the cars on the tracks next alongside the platform.[1] Cars may be placed on one track for a train of 14 cars, or by "doubling over" on two tracks for a train of 28 cars or less. If the cars are loaded with those on the head end of one track for first station reached, and so on, to the end of that track and following from the head end of the second

[1] That is, using the open doorways of the cars nearest the platforms and gang planks as a passageway to reach the cars on the second track.

track, and the first-track cars are drawn out and set over on the second, the train will leave properly made up.

The general organization, working force and methods of operating transfer stations are explained in Chap. XXV. Usually the freight house and transfer are adjoining and operated under one general head.

The largest transfer station in the East is that of the New Haven at Cedar Hill, near New Haven, Conn.

Before the opening of this transfer, eastbound merchandise cars received by the New Haven via the Harlem River gateway were handled at Westchester, N. Y., and transfer made at that point as far as the limited facilities would permit. Cars received in excess of that plant's capacity were sent further east, either to Bridgeport, Conn., or the New Haven Transfer and eastbound cars received via the Maybrook gateway were handled at Maybrook Transfer.

Westchester Transfer was operated under the gang and hand-truck system and handled from 15,000 to 20,000 tons of merchandise freight a month. Because of the diversity of destinations, and the lack of sufficient tonnage to warrant direct-to-destination cars, a large amount of freight handled there received a secondary handling at other transfer points. The gang and hand-truck system was also followed at Maybrook, where also the volume of business did not permit the making of direct-to-destination cars which good service demands.

By centralizing the cars received through both gateways at Cedar Hill, a direct-to-destination classification was made possible for approximately 75 per cent. of the freight handled there, thus insuring better service from the standpoint of time, and reducing the number of cars required for the service as well as the loss and damage resulting from a transfer of freight en route.

In addition to the Westchester and Maybrook plants, the road operated transfer plants at Bridgeport, and New Haven, Conn. These transfers accommodated approximately 100 cars each. Smaller transfers were operated at Danbury, Waterbury, Hartford and Putnam, Conn.; Springfield, Mass., and Poughkeepsie, N. Y. Because of the small tonnage handled at these points, only a limited number of classifications could be made and, in many instances, a second transfer was required before freight could be delivered at destination or to a connecting line.

All the transfers mentioned, except Westchester and Maybrook, were in cities originating a considerable local tonnage, and the local and the transfer plants were combined. As a result, delays to either the local freight or freight in transit were frequent.

Cedar Hill transfer was opened in July, 1920. Daily, 131 distinct classifications are made, and as many as 365 cars have been worked in one day, a normal daily performance being between 325 and 350 cars. The ability of the transfer to work this number of cars, with tractors and trailers, has resulted in the closing of the transfers at Westchester and Maybrook permanently. Furthermore, approximately 80 per cent. of the transfers at Bridgeport, and 50 per cent. of the transfers at Waterbury, Danbury and Poughkeepsie have been eliminated through the concentration of the transfer business on the west end of the line. In addition, the Cedar Hill plant handles business diverted from all of the other transfers mentioned.

Cedar Hill Transfer and its supporting tracks are located approximately in the center of the Cedar Hill yard, between the humps serving the westward and the north- and eastward classification yards, in a location convenient for the receipt of cars from the various New Haven lines converging at Cedar Hill, and for the delivery of northward cars to the various points from which trains depart.

The layout includes 15 tracks and 4 platforms with a set-up capacity of 402 cars. Beginning at the east, platform No. 1, which is 20 ft. wide, separates the four outside tracks, which are numbered consecutively, A, B, 1 and 2, from tracks 3 and 4. Platform No. 2 is also 20 ft. wide and is located between tracks 3 and 4 and tracks 5, 6 and 7. Platform No. 3 is 30 ft. wide and separates tracks 8 and 9 from tracks 5, 6 and 7. Platform No. 4 is 30 ft. wide and separates tracks 10, 11, 12 and 13 from tracks 8 and 9.

Each platform is 1,200 ft. long. Platform No. 1 is of wood construction and is covered with an umbrella-shed roof, with the post located in the center of the platform. Platform No. 2 is also of wood construction and is covered with a hip roof with the posts placed on the edges of the platform. Platform Nos. 3 and 4 are of concrete and steel construction.

Three lift bridges, 20 ft. wide, are provided between the platforms. The first bridge is located 200 ft. from the north end of the platform, the second, 600 ft. from the north end and the third, 200 ft. from the south end. The bridges serve as the main-line route between platforms for loaded trailers and trucks, while the door-to-door method of spotting cars provides for disposing of trailers after they are made empty without interference with oncoming loads.

An extension of 40 ft. on the platform level at the north end of platform No. 3 provides space for a charging station and a repair shop for the tractors as well as for the toilets and wash rooms for the laborers. Individual lockers, benches and tables for the laborers are in the basement of this extension. The space is also used for a rest room during lunch hour.

The standard classification provides for merchandise cars to be made for 148 different points. In several instances, however, more than one car is required for a destination. These are, of course, loaded in series on the same track, preserving the station and train order, so that at the close of each day's work the cars can be moved forward without delay. For instance, the daily tonnage for Boston and for Providence is sufficient to warrant a regular assignment of 10 cars for each of these cities. More than 148 cars are, therefore, required to fulfill the car requirements of the standard classification. Actually, the number of cars required for this purpose is in excess of 250 cars. Including the overflow cars, and the direct-to-destination cars, the total number of merchandise cars forwarded daily exceeds 275.

The platform equipment used at the transfer includes 31 electric storage-battery tractors, with 1,000 trailing units of various types, including both four-wheeled and three-wheeled trucks. With the latter it is possible to handle heavy packages, liquids in barrels, bales of cotton and other commodities which cannot be readily handled on four-wheeled trucks; and the joint use enables practically a 100 per cent. mechanical operation.

During a recent month, based on an 8-hour day, the transfer was operated with 464 employees per day, forwarding a total of 8,935 cars for the month, or an average of 343 cars daily. In the same month 7,995 loaded cars were received and unloaded, an average of 307 cars per day. The average daily tonnage handled was 2,381 tons, and in addition, 1,729 tons of "no-credit" tonnage moved out of the terminal in the original cars during the month.

The merchandise cars destined for the transfer arrive at both the east- and westward hump yards continuously throughout a 24-hour period. On arrival, the cars·are switched to classification tracks, where they are arranged according to the route to be followed when forwarded from the transfer, and are so placed on the transfer tracks.

The block-numbering system for cars at the house is simple and easily understood by the men. The last figure in the number indicates the number of the track, and the preceding figures the relative position of the cars on a track, the outward classification being confined to tracks 3 to 9 inclusive, with the other tracks accommodating the inbound loaded cars which are to be worked.

For example, the northerly car on track No. 3 receives the number 13; the corresponding car on track No. 4 receives the number 14; the second car from the north end of track No. 3 receives the block number 23 and so on up to block 263, indicating car 26 on track No. 3, numbered from the north. Block numbers are posted conspicuously on each platform.

The house organization is headed by an assistant agent, assisted by a general foreman reporting to the agent, and consists of a day and night force, the latter being limited to office help only.

Messenger service is maintained between the two hump offices and the transfer office for carrying waybill pouches. A book record of each pouch, arranged according to the last two figures of the car number, is kept. It includes the date of receipt of bills and the point of origin.

The record is completed later with the addition of the location or block number of the cars as placed at the platform and the date of handling. This is done so that tracing work, when necessary, may be expedited.

The daily layout sheet of the transfer is made up by the night force as the tracks are filled. The block numbers showing the location of cars to which the merchandise is to be transferred is noted on the waybills by the route clerks. This number serves as a guide to the tallyman and check clerks when the actual handling of the merchandise is begun. These men are also expected to check the waybills and detect any errors made by the route clerks.

Waybills pouches are assigned to tallymen by the foreman in charge of the platform where cars covered by the bills are located. The tallymen are required to check the freight as it is handled and note any exceptions as to condition or shortage. The tallyman also makes a check-over slip for any freight in the car not covered by a revenue waybill. Every package of freight, when placed on trailer, is chalked with the block number of the car to which the trailer is destined.

The contents of cars are loaded on trailer trucks, the trailers being held until the entire lading of a car has been handled. When the unloading of a car has been completed, the trailers are made up into trains of six or eight placed in location order—with the longest haul next to the tractor—and hauled to destination. Trailers are dropped from the train on the platform opposite the proper car and are taken into the car and unloaded by stevedores. The stevedores then push the empty trailers out of the cars, onto the platforms, where they are picked up by the tractors. The stevedores are assigned to the same cars each day, and become familiar with the destinations of the freight that belongs in their cars. They are required to examine both the markings on freight and the chalk marks placed on packages by check clerks, and to report for correction any freight trucked to them in error.

As an additional check on destination, three qualified tallymen act as inspectors. These men make the rounds of the cars and inspect the loading and stowing, to correct apparent errors.

Explosives, inflammables and acid shipments are handled specially, one man being assigned to this work. He is held responsible for the proper placarding of the cars.

As the cars are worked, tonnage on waybills is computed and totaled at the end of the day, the totals showing the tonnage actually transferred, tonnage traveling without revenue billing, tonnage left in cars and the amount checking short according to waybills. The latter two items are called "no-credit" tonnage and are not considered in arriving at the cost of handling.

The bills then pass on to the exception clerks, and any exception made by the tallymen are recorded. The bills are then racked, by the pouching clerks, and at the close of business are examined by the rack clerks before being pouched.   Each rack clerk is required to note the block numbers of cars he verifies, thus making it easy to place the responsibility for improper pouching.

At the close of business switching, requests are made on a standard form showing the track number, date, the initials and number of the cars as they stand on the tracks, the destinations, route, and other essential information.   Platform foremen are required to check the switching requests against their records, and the rack men are required to check the pouches against the copy of the switching request which is retained in the office.   The forms are then passed to the yard department.

Figures comparing the operation between Westchester Transfer, with two-wheel hand-truck, and Cedar Hill disclose the fact that 7.542 tons per man per 8-hour day were moved at Cedar Hill as compared with 4.454 at Westchester, an increase of 69 per cent.   This performance indicates the gratifying results that are possible from a tractor-trailer system of operation.

The proper arrangement of car loading, from freight houses, transfers and by local freight crews, to secure a maximum of car load with a minimum of car-mileage, and to reduce handling and other expense on a busy line, is a complicated problem.   Where a road is cut up by many side lines and junctions, any arrangement must have some disadvantage, and all require constant revision to meet changing conditions.

The system in use on the New Haven is necessarily elaborate, because it is planned to meet the most complicated and exacting conditions of handling package freight in this country.

General instructions are issued in booklet form, divisionally, showing how each station should handle the freight which it originates or transfers; they stipulate, that

To avoid transfer handling *en route* and to enhance movement of freight, the following minimums will govern in the loading of l.c.l. freight:

1. 20,000 pounds on eastbound business from western connections via Harlem River or Maybrook gateways, also from points on or via N. Y. C. R. R.

2. 10,000 pounds on business from points on or via B. & M. R. R., or C. Vt. Ry., also from local points on B. & A. R. R.

3. 7,500 pounds on business for points on or via connecting lines, also on local business moving between points on N. Y. N. H. & H. R. R. and C. N. E. Ry.

4. L.c.l. freight according to minimum, should be loaded and carded direct to several listed stations for certain combinations of adjacent stations.

General instructions read as follows:

1. Hours for receipt and delivery of l.c.l. freight will be arranged to meet prevailing conditions and must be such as will in a reasonably satisfactory way meet the requirements of shippers and receivers of freight.

2. L.c.l. freight should be loaded and forwarded the same day as tendered for shipment to the fullest practicable extent. Where way-freight movement is involved, agents will acquaint shippers with approximate time of departure of such service that shipments may be tendered sufficiently in advance to enable way-billing and loading thereof. Shipments offered after the departure of way freights should be promptly accepted when tendered within the prescribed hours and held for forwarding by next regular movement.

3. Where triweekly cars are in effect for purpose of avoiding a transfer *en route*, agents should arrange with shippers that, so far as practicable, freight for such cars may be delivered on the date car goes forward. If shippers prefer daily deliveries, freight should be accepted and forwarded according to arrangement.

4. L.c.l. freight must be loaded in accordance with routings shown on shipping orders or waybills and agents should see that this is understood by their freight-house forces accordingly.

5. Agents should observe both the inward and outward movement of l.c.l. cars and report to the Superintendent of Transportation on post card provided therefor any arranged cars the tonnage for which does not appear to warrant their continuance, or where freight has met with a delay *en route* to an extent that will cause loss of business to other means of transportation or complaint from shippers or consignees.

6. In order to avoid liability of damage resulting to such commodities as flour, sugar and other food products through the absorbtion of odors or by direct contact, shipments of oil, fertilizer, hides, tar, creosote and empty oil containers should, so far as possible, be transported in stock or rough freight equipment. In order to accomplish this, such freight may be held for consolidation.

Typical station loading instructions for the New Haven station at Fall River, Mass., are summarized in the following paragraphs:

All l.c.l. freight from this station loads to Cedar Hill Transfer, except such freight as is destined to specified territory which loads direct in straight cars.

In addition to way-freight cars for stations in the vicinity, scheduled daily cars are made for Taunton and Boston and for the transfer stations at Framingham, Middleboro, and Providence. Freight for points on other railroads travels in daily cars to Lawrence, Newport, and Nashua Transfers on the B. & M.; Waverly Transfer on the Pennsylvania; Manchester Transfer on the Lehigh Valley; Wayne Junction and Rockford, Del., for P. & R. freight; Port Morris Transfer on the D. L. & W. and West Albany Transfer for New York Central.

Tri-weekly cars are also made for North Adams on the Boston & Albany; Elizabethport Transfer on the C. N. J.; to Maybrook Transfer for all freight routed via the Erie; St. Albans Transfer for Central Vermont and Grand Trunk points, and Middletown, N. Y. for points on or via the N. Y. O. & W.

Figures 158 and 159 show forms for summarizing the record of station operations as used on the New Haven.

The transfer station and the transferring—in fact, the whole handling of l.c.l. is one of the increasingly difficult operating problems of the American railways. It may be termed one of those parasitic by-products of rail freight transportation; possibly a "necessary evil." The expense of handling the l.c.l. business is far in excess of that for handling car load freight. A question arises as to the best methods of caring for it and a doubt as to whether it is the best policy to carry on this losing game instead of discontinuing the handling or transferring it to some other agency thereby enabling the more remunerative straight carload traffic to be better and more economically cared for. The motor truck has entered the field; its effects and methods are mentioned in the chapters on British Freight Service and Integration of Freight Transportation. The whole problem immediately confronting the operating officers, as it relates to l.c.l. freight, with its allied transfer stations, is that of improving the service, and lowering the cost; a difficult and paradoxical situation, at best. In the preceding edition of this work in connection with this vital question, the author suggested the desirability of more progressive and intensive methods by urging that some thought be given to the possibilities of improved service at lower costs through the adoption wholly, or in part, of a more universal use of freight cars; of a system by which a car's contents and necessary delivering data would travel together and be available concurrently when they reach the point where the freight is physically available to the consignee; that more use be made of the piece-work and bonus systems in handling freight at freight houses and transfer stations and that a "store-door delivery" method be given consideration on plans similar to those followed by the Canadian roads or by some adaptation of such methods.

Much water has found its way over the dam since these thoughts were expressed, much has been done and a vast amount of experience gained through twenty-six months of Government operation of railways and many lessons have been learned but it has not been proven that car-pooling in all its branches makes for lower and better maintenance of equipment, nor shown that unification or joint operation of terminals is the long sought for panacea when considering the offsetting loss of competitive effort between railroads; the necessary detrimental effect on some of the lines involved and the loss of initiative of the individual.

That an advantage results through universal car use in the avoidance of switching and rehandling is obvious. The more general use of a "standard-length car" which perhaps more than a "standard car" appeals to the operating officer who knows what it means to place cars on adjacent tracks to be worked through and with it much switching might be avoided in "spotting" for freight house handling and other purposes. Progress is being made very rapidly toward the goal of a

Form 1861

THE NEW YORK, NEW HAVEN & HARTFORD RAILROAD CO.
CENTRAL NEW ENGLAND RAILWAY CO.

STATEMENT OF COST OF HANDLING FREIGHT THROUGH FREIGHT HOUSE

For Month of_____ 19_____ At _____ Station

KIND OF LABOR AND COST PER UNIT	NUMBER OF MEN								PAYROLL EXPENSE		
	THIS YEAR			LAST YEAR			Increase Decrease		This Year	Last Year	Increase Decrease
	No. Men	Man Hours	Rate Per Hr.	No. Men	Man Hours	Rate Per Hr.	No. Men	Man Hours			
FREIGHT HOUSE											
General Foreman											
Asst. General Foreman											
Foreman											
Asst. Foreman											
General Foreman Clerks											
Timekeeper											
Route Clerks											
Messengers											
Receiving Clerks											
Delivery Clerks											
Layout Clerk											
Tallymen											
Truckmen											
Truck Loaders											
Stevedores											
Others Handling Freight											
Coopers											
Car Cleaners											
Car Sealers											
Carders											
Watchman											
Total Over Time—Labor											
Total Over Time—Supervision & Clerks											
Total Short Time—Supervision & Clerks											
No. Days Freight House Operated ( )											
No. Hrs. Ft. House Oper'd per day ( )											
TOTAL (A)											
DEDUCTIONS											
NET TOTAL (B)											
COST PER TON (Divide "B by C")											

STATEMENT OF TONNAGE AND CARS

	Credit This Year	Credit Last Year	Increase Decrease	Previous Month	Increase Decrease	No Credit This Year	No Credit Last Year
Tonnage Actually Handled Through Frt. House by Frt. House Men:							
Tons Forwarded C. L.							
" " L. C. L.							
" Received C. L.							
" " L. C. L.							
" Transferred							
Number of bales of cotton handled through freight house ( )							
TOTAL (C)							

	THIS YEAR			LAST YEAR		
	No. Cars	Tonnage	Average Tons Per Car	No. Cars	Tonnage	Average Tons Per Car
All loaded Cars Forwarded and Rec'd.						
1. L. C. L. Cars Received						
2 C. L. Cars Received						
3 L. C. L. Cars Forwarded						
4 C. L. Cars Forwarded						

	THIS YEAR	LAST YEAR		THIS YEAR	LAST YEAR
1 Tons forwarded L. C. L. from Public Tracks.			3 Tons forwarded L. C. L. from private sidings.		
2 Cars forwarded L. C. L. from Public Tracks.			4 Cars forwarded L. C. L. from private sidings.		

INSTRUCTIONS

1. Actual pay-roll expense must be shown against each class of employees listed and the total inserted under (A) should correspond with the total freight house pay roll.

2. In computing the COST PER TON consider only the expense incurred in the actual handling of freight passing through the Freight House, deducting the actual time devoted to, and the wages paid for, the handling of carload freight and freight other than that which passes through the freight house, showing NET amount opposite (B). All deductions as provided for should be listed in detail on the back of this form showing class of employee; man hours, and amount paid.

3. The hours and amount lost account delay in setting up freight house should be shown on back of this form, but **must not be deducted** in arriving at the Cost Per Ton.

4. L. C. L. Tonnage Forwarded will include all freight received from consignor by dray or in Ferry Cars, also from Connecting Lines which is handled through Freight House.

5. L. C. L. Tonnage Received will include all freight received for delivery to consignee by dray or in Ferry Cars or for Connecting Line when handled through the Freight House.

6. Tonnage Transferred will include all freight transferred from car to car.
   One credit only to be taken for each ton handled regardless of the number of times actually handled. No Credit will be taken for freight which is left in cars. Such tonnage if handled or checked, together with the tonnage that is actually handled twice, will be shown under NO CREDIT TONNAGE.

7. In determining the number of men employed, use as a factor the hour basis on which Freight House is operated.

8. This report must be forwarded to Assistant to the General Manager on or before the 10th with copy to General Superintendent and Superintendent.

Correct: _____**Agent**

Fig. 158.

Form 1882*

THE NEW YORK, NEW HAVEN AND HARTFORD RAILROAD COMPANY
CENTRAL NEW ENGLAND RAILWAY COMPANY
COMPARATIVE STATEMENT OF OFFICE PAYROLL EXPENSE, VOLUME OF WORK HANDLED AND MISCELLANEOUS STATISTICAL INFORMATION

For Month of .... 192...   At .... Station ....

OFFICE FORCE	NUMBER OF EMPLOYEES				PAYROLL EXPENSE				VOLUME OF WORK	NUMBER OF ITEMS			
	This Year		Last Year	Inc.—Dec.	This Year	Last Year	Inc.—Dec.			This Year	Last Year	Inc.—Dec.

Supervision
Agent
Assistant Agent
Chief Clerk
Assistant Chief Clerk
Stenographers
General Clerks
Time Clerks
Messengers
Others
Over Time
Short Time

Cashier's Department
Cashier
Assistant Cashier
Window Clerks
Collectors
Ledger Clerks
Stenographers
Other Clerks
Over Time
Short Time

Accounting Department
Accountant
Audit Clerk
Register Clerk
Report Clerk
Posting Clerk
Stenographers
Freight Bill Clerks
Old Bill Clerks
Statement Clerks
Over Time
Short Time

Outward
1 No. shipping orders billed.
2 " prepaid freight bills made.
3 " local waybills made.
4 " foreign waybills made.
5 " astray waybills made.
6 " corrections issued on out billing.
7 " " charged by A. F. R. on out billing.
8 " " on hand unapplied

Inward
9 No. freight bills made.
10 " " received on unit billing.
11 " miscellaneous bills made (all except storage).
12 " storage bills made.
13 " station to station waybills made.
14 " corrections issued on in billing, ' local.
15 " " " " ' foreign.
16 " " charged by A.F.R. on in billing, local.
17 " " " " " foreign.
18 " " on hand unapplied.
19 " account astray shipments made and ap'd
20 relief claims made, short freight.
21 refunds created.
22 undercharges created.

Cashier's Department
23 No. over charges refunded.
24 " undercharges collected.
25 " freight bills on hand, freight short.
26 " shipments re-consigned.
27 " unclaimed and refused reports made.
28 " unclaimed and refused reports adjusted.
29 " unclaimed and refused shipments forwarded to Pier 1
30 " refused and unclaimed shipments on hand.

Claim Department

Way Billing Department
Chief Billing Clerk
Way Bill Clerks
Rate Clerks
Extension Clerks
Rack Clerks
Other Clerks
Over Time
Short Time

O. S. and D. Department
O. S. and D. Clerks
Trace Clerks
Other Clerks
Over Time
Short Time

Claim Department
Chief Claim Clerk
Other Claim Clerks
Over Time
Short Time

Car Record Department
Car Record Clerks
Demurrage Clerks
Other Clerks
Over Time
Short Time

Janitors and Porters
Total Over Time
Total Short Time
Total Office Payroll
Authorized No. of Clerks
Author. Am't of Pay Roll

31 No. claims carried over from previous month.
32 " reed. from F.C.Agts. including foreign lines.
33 " returned to F.C.Agts. including foreign lines.
34 " on hand.
35 " local claims presented by claimants.
36 " " " " " paid.
37 " " " " " not paid sent F.C.A.
38 " " " " on hand.
39 marked shipments received, over.
40 " over shipments matched.
41 " " " sent to Pier 1.
42 " " " on hand.
43 no-mark shipments received, over.
44 " over shipments matched.
45 " " " sent to Pier 1.
46 " " " on hand.
47 Total number of shipments on hand last inventory.
48 Date of last inventory.
49 No. over reports carried over from previous month, open
50 " " " closed.
51 " " " open.
52 " short carried over from previous month, open
53 " " " made.
54 " " " closed.
55 " " " open.
56 astray waybills received.
57 " " matched.
58 " " on which charges were assessed.
59 " " carried over from previous month.
60 " " on hand not matched.
61 " " " freight short.
62 " tracers issued outbound.
63 " requests for proof of ownership.
64 " tracers received and handled.

Miscellaneous
65 No. files received from the Accounting Department.
66 " " worked.
67 " " on hand.
68 " carloads received.
69 " " forwarded.
70 Amount of L.C.L. storage collected.

Agent

INSTRUCTIONS

The figures for last year must be shown in the payroll comparison section of the report and for all other items for which they are obtainable.
Under must show the number of hours for which the various classes are paid.
Under payroll expense show actual amount paid each class which will correspond with the amount shown on payroll.

A statement must accompany this report explaining in detail increase or decrease in number of employees or amounts as against authorized basis.
Short time not to include authorized holidays or time allowed under agreement.
Report must be signed personally by the agent and forwarded to the Assistant to the General Manager on or before the 15th of each month.
Carbon copy of the report to be furnished the General Superintendent and Superintendent.

Correct:

FIG. 159.

standard freight car; or, more accurately speaking a few selected standards.

During the period of close association and co-operation of the operating departments of the railroads preceding the governmental operation, much progress was made toward having all billing data accompany cars, and it was generally arranged and agreed that no interchange of loaded cars between roads could be considered a complete transaction unless such information was at hand with a tender of the car. This was doubtless a step in the right direction but there was much left to be done and there is still something to be accomplished.

As land values in large centers increase, and as freight business becomes heavier, it is essential that the handling of freight in houses shall be more rapid, and that the freight be moved through the houses and not stored in them. When a company does its own teaming, it increases its freight-house facilities. It is a very common experience to find teaming companies "lying by" on rainy days, or during ice and snow storms, when lighter loads have to be carried, or when they have an opportunity to obtain a few days' hauling at more remunerative rates. They argue that the outside contract may go to others while their railway works is always there for them to handle at their own convenience. The freight houses in the meantime become congested.

While this subject is more fully treated elsewhere, it may not be amiss to recall the nearly twelve months' study under the direction and guidance of one of the Commissioner's of the Interstate Commerce Commission in New York City with a view to establishing store-door delivery in New York City. It is believed that the Armistice and the ending of Government operation created an avenue of escape—possibly omitting the well known legend "Choose your exit now and in case of fire walk, (not run) to that exit." The report was that of all the associations, societies and combinations representing the shippers, and of the various trucking organizations, no two concurred; there was not even accord on any single important feature of the method. The one and only thing in which all these interests did agree was the wisdom of the decision to "forget it."

CHAPTER XXIV

THE FREIGHT AGENT

The duties devolving upon the station agent are complex. The kinds of stations and their importance vary; the qualifications of the men in charge must, therefore, differ. The large terminal station and the small country stopping place are two extremes; nevertheless, the agent at the small station is in many instances the most important member of the railway's family. His duties are as numerous and varied as those of the yardmaster and he is the medium through which the commercial part of the business with the public is conducted.

There is no one employee in a railroad's ranks who, in this one essential alone, can do more to make or unmake the status of the road's relations with the public. The passenger conductor may come next, but his position has an advantage over that of the agent. He runs into, or reaches, a general terminal as a rule and can, therefore, be readily directed or instructed by personal interview as well as by circulars and bulletins, and his duties are so uniform that a hundred conductors may be told the same thing. The freight agents, however, are scattered as to locality and their duties cover a very wide range. It is frequently difficult to interview them and, as each one has individual characteristics or is surrounded by peculiar local conditions, he must be treated separately. The traffic may be peculiar to his territory—as, for instance, in the case of granite quarries—and he has no near-by precedent to follow. The shippers may have peculiar ideas; they may have been permitted certain privileges which, if objectionable, must be withdrawn diplomatically; and local or state laws may affect the situation.

To enumerate the duties of the smaller agent would require a large book. The duties of the larger agent are even more exacting, although somewhat specialized. Both are required to meet the public and in their dealings with it must exercise discretion, patience and diplomacy. In the small towns especially, where the road's officers do not have many opportunities to coach him, the agent may be inclined wholly to the side of the public and forget his duties to his employer. He should always remember that his first obligation is to the road employing him, and that loyalty to the road does not in the least detract from his standard of citizenship. The greatest mistake, and probably one of the commonest, which an agent may make, is simply to answer questions, after declining something or discontinuing a privilege previously enjoyed by a patron, without carefully explaining the reasons or necessities. The simple statement, "Those are my orders," merely aggravates. A train may be late; a shipment fails to arrive; certain switching cannot be done; there is usually some reason—good or bad—for the failure. While the agent is not personally responsible for such failure, it will go a long way toward creating or strengthening good feeling between the company and its patrons if he will take a little time and trouble to explain the situation. Very few persons are so unreasonable as to find fault or hold a grudge against a railroad company if they know there is a reason for a failure and that the employees, as well as the officers, are sufficiently interested to explain it. It goes without saying that nothing should be misrepresented, but this does not mean that the blackest side alone should be presented. Agents should not be influenced or prejudiced one way or another because some unreasoning or unthinking person indulges in abuse of the road or its officers; they should remember that the custom of denouncing railroad corporations is a common habit of demagogues and others who are ignorant of true conditions, and who usually follow the lines of least resistance.

In an address to an association of agents, J. M. Daly, while General Superintendent of Transportation of the Illinois Central, said:

The position of agent is a very important one. You handle the entire business of the railroads. Every dollar that we earn is handled through your office. In the State of Illinois we have 417 industrial corporations that employ expert traffic managers to look after their railroad service. Most of these men formerly were employed by railroads. These gentlemen make a specialty of rates and service on from one to three commodities and devote their entire efforts to obtaining the best possible service at the lowest price. These industries keep a detailed record of the movement and service afforded each individual shipment; the small shipper or receiver of freight is equally anxious for prompt and efficient service and must receive the same attention. It is true that frequently unreasonable demands and requests are made on you . . . In winter the public moves its traffic by team during daylight hours, 8 a. m. to 4 p. m.—8 hours out of 24—and demands increased free demurrage time, whereas the shipper who is obliged to wait for cars (that are detained by the consignee) demands damages in the shape of reciprocal demurrage. In meeting these conditions, it is well to explain and make known our position. Shippers demand that we furnish our cars to load for distant points on foreign roads where we lose possession of them, the foreign roads holding and using our cars locally as long as desired. The average shipper and consignee does not understand and consequently cannot appreciate the difficulties we labor under, and the company must depend upon you, gentlemen, to make it known to them not with a view of finding fault, but in the same friendly manner that shippers make known their conditions to us.

If a patron asks you what train connections he can make with other roads, figure it out for him, and, if necessary, use the wire to get it for him. If a shipper asks you why it is that the rate on his hay or his live stock is 25 cts. per hundred, whereas the rate to the coal or lumber dealer is 5 or 10 cts. between the same points, reason it out with him; show him where coal loads 50 tons to the car and live stock only 10 tons; further, that live stock is moved in fast trains hauling less than 20 per cent. as many revenue tons as coal trains. The public is not informed on such matters and, if you are patient and careful in explaining, you make a friend to yourself as well as to the company. I have attended quite a number of investigations made by the different state legislatures, the state and federal commissions, and firmly believe these gentlemen aim to do what is just and fair, but they receive information on but one side of the case—that of the public—and their opinions are formed accordingly. Bear in mind at all times that a complaint from a patron shipping one car a year is as important as a complaint from a shipper giving us a hundred cars, and that the small shipper has an equal influence in any organization of which he is a member. If you, by giving him facts, convince him that we are doing our best to protect his interests, you will find that he will be our friend and cooperate with us. If the local agents will get together with the shippers and discuss their grievances carefully, I am satisfied that eight out of ten cases now brought before the commissions and legislatures could be disposed of in your conferences and never reach the commission. The average shipper is fair and wants only fair treatment, and when he is shown that he is receiving fair treatment he will be satisfied.

As the adjustment of a terminal to the conduct of the period of heaviest traffic, coupled with adverse weather and other conditions, measures the ability or efficiency of the road, so the true measure of the agent himself, his organization and his plant will show up most effectively during heavy freight movement, and particularly when this occurs during a period of unfavorable weather when teamsters postpone hauling freight out of house and cars, while the railroad must of necessity continue to haul it in. During such times of heavy pressure agents must exercise the utmost tact while firmly insisting on patrons removing freight promptly on arrival. Frequently, a careful explanation of the situation in a personal interview with a heavy shipper will result in securing prompt and hearty cooperation. The agent who has the respect of the community has no great difficulty in such cases; he is the agent who has made himself popular by being at all times courteous and considerate. He is not the one without the moral courage to defend his company and to state facts courteously but plainly when imposition is attempted or denunciation indulged in.

The conduct of the smaller, or so-called "one-man," station needs little instruction on the question of organization beyond a reminder, possibly, that even there much work may be saved and more satisfactory results achieved by working systematically, having a place for everything and keeping everything in its place; and a time, so far as practicable, to do certain work and keep ahead of the work. No freight should be delivered without a proper receipt. Freight unloaded should always be checked by the agent and conductor jointly and shortages, overs or damages certified to jointly and immediately. No "over" freight should be permitted to remain on hand any length of time without calling the claim department's attention to it. Tracers for lost freight should be given actual attention, not treated in a perfunctory manner. "Order-notify" shipments should be invariably held until the bill of lading is presented; waybills should be very carefully scrutinized to avoid over-looking these "order-notify" notations, which are the source of much trouble to the agent. Outbound freight should be inspected to see that proper classification is observed, that freight is properly crated and plainly marked, rules for handling of explosives and inflammables observed and the goods carefully and securely loaded into cars to prevent damage in transit.

Automatic couplers accompanied by increasing size and weight of locomotives and cars increase the liability of damage to freight and make necessary greater care in loading and in switching. Freight-house men must be taught to load large cars with package freight so as to prevent shifting. After part of such a car is unloaded, the remainder must be arranged to avoid shifting.

In attempting to reduce the damage to freight in transit—and it is a big field—the panacea is undoubtedly more inspection and supervision of a more intelligent character. British railroads employ many inspectors and their system is well worth imitating.

Among the smaller matters to which agents should look to reduce claims, and, what is more important, to satisfy patrons, is the loading. Recently killed meat has been known to be loaded on butter, covering the tubs with blood. Machinery has been loaded on flour or sacks of sugar. Agricultural machinery has been loaded on top of an automobile. Flour is frequently damaged by being loaded in a car with a leaky roof. Wet sacks of flour should be resacked, as usually only a small amount of flour is actually damaged, and should be handled promptly or it will become moldy. After unloading part of a car, the remainder should be broken down, so it will not fall and be damaged if the car is moved. An agent once left a piano under the eaves of a freight house, where it was damaged by rain.

There has been a tendency, on the part of shippers of late years, gradually to discontinue the full marking of packages. Nothing causes more loss of freight, or delay in reaching destination. There has also been a general indifference to proper crating; and weaker packages are being used. Boxes and sacks are made of thinner material, crates are substituted for boxes and sacks are used by some shippers for articles which should not be shipped in them. Every package, bundle or piece in an l.c.l. shipment should have:

Consignee's name in full.
Bill-of-lading destination in full.
State in which destination is located.

If there is more than one station in the same state of the same name, full name of county.

All previous shipping marks obliterated.

Shipper's name and location, with the word "From" preceding them.

A package may be fully marked in so far as name of consignee and destination are concerned, even the street address being shown; yet it may be more or less confused by being surrounded by a multiplicity of other information. This may cause the loss of the package or a delay in delivery.

The presence of the shipper's name is of assistance as a means of identification of a package and is of great value when it is refused or unclaimed by the consignee, as in all such instances the shipper can be promptly notified, and, if date of shipment and case number are shown, he can also be given this information, which will enable him at once to locate the particular shipment involved. When shipments are made at regular intervals or short periods, the presence of the date of shipment and the case number prevent any uncertainty as to which lot one or more packages belong, in case they check short and reach destination on the same date or subsequently to a later shipment.

An abridgement and modification of a number of leaflets issued by an intricate road[1] with a preponderance of high class l.c.l. traffic follows:

An outlay of $489.70—because of the shipper's failure to remove old tags and properly mark a reel of cable shipped from a local station to Buffalo, N. Y. Accessories to the crime were those "trailers" who usually appear; the man who receipted the bill of lading without comparing and verifying the marks on the reel with those on the bill of lading; the checking clerk at first transfer point reached, working under the old adage: "A rose by any other name would smell as sweet"—passed the reel to the trucker for the Olean, N. Y. car, without looking at (or for) marks; at Olean the checking clerk, not finding a reel marked for Buffalo, let it go at that, and marked the waybill "short." The reel not reaching Buffalo, a claim was made, and paid. True; the reel was found later; the amount recalled but that did not prevent much additional haulage; considerable extra handling and a vast amount of unproductive correspondence.

Another case of incorrect marking was that of two empty oil barrels from a Massachusetts station, for the Texas Company, Providence, R. I. They were loaded in a way car; checked short at Providence; claim filed. The shipping agent learned, by tracing, that two barrels were seen "astray" at Newport, Vt.— marked Texas Company, Port Arthur, Texas. At last accounts they were being trailed—much like Mark Twain's detective who following his subject on a street car and eventually learned that one street car never overtakes another.

We then come to the 480 baskets of apples shipped from New York State, on an order notify bill—that curse of railway operating vicissitudes—reaching destination under original seals. To permit inspection, seals were broken on

[1] Freight Claim Prevention Bureau of the New Haven.

one side; the "inspection" continued for three days, then it was rejected; it was reconsigned, and then checked out nineteen baskets short. A claim—of course. It then developed that the first consignee had taken nineteen baskets to his place of business for "further inspection." The claim was not paid but investigations and costs would have been avoided by proper record and protecting seal or lock at first point of entrance.

"Eternal vigilance is the price of safety,"—and emphasized by the story of a near-claim, caused, at the outset, by an error in billing. An item of "2 crates mop wringers and 1 empty crate wringer rack" was copied by the billing clerk as "3 crates and 1 empty crate." At the transfer point, notation—"checks 1 crate short"—at destination; "1 crate mop wringers short." First; the billing clerk blew up. The several claim clerks at the stations and elsewhere followed. The blind led the blind; result; expense; waste of time, effort, stationery, transportation.

The shipper prepares his bills-of-lading before the goods are packed and they are in the shipping room when the goods marked and ready to go are received there from the packing room The truckman makes up a load; takes the bills-of-lading and calls for corresponding packages. The truckman makes it snappy; he calls for "one for Jonesville"; not "one keg of shellac, Jones, Banjo Co., Jonesville, Mass." He got a box of paint; he did not get a keg of shellac valued at $46.50. It got by the usual procession of "accessories," in the good old-fashioned trailing way; the receiving clerk signed the bill-of-lading; the check clerk passed it up. When the box of paint was found "over," it was delivered according to marks and the prize-winner of the "fall-down" system, was the chap who signed a second bill-of-lading and "forced" a waybill which caused omission of the over report.

A record is no better than the man who makes it and the man whose records are good is himself a good man. The two cases of bronze wire worth $142.63 were to travel from one local station to another; both checked short at destination, and the claim was made. At the second transfer point, they had been left on the floor of the car and were received by a dealer's truckman with some other goods consigned to him—a "mistake" presumably. At this point they checked in and out correctly, according to the "records"; seal records perfect; "O.K." at destination. "One good turn deserves another."

Selecting an unsuitable car caused the burning up of $175. Better said; making no selection or inspection caused this economic waste. Fifty bags of powdered talc, to travel 30 miles, loaded into a car with a kerosene-saturated floor. The dark stains on the floor were noticed and it was covered over with wood chips but the kerosene soaked up through them, rendering the talc worthless. This notwithstanding repeated cautions as to oil, acid, tar, or other foreign substances or filth on car floor, and liability to damage flour, other foodstuffs, cotton piece goods, sacked or baled commodities.

The stevedore plays an important role; much depends on his skill and watchfulness. Stevedores are human; they prove it by erring occasionally. One of them loaded three burlapped bales containing white cotton yarn in a car which had charcoal dust on the floor and was therefore unsuitable. A leaky case of syrup loaded in close proximity to the yarn helped things along. The bill—$800. It is the stevedore who has the best chance to know if a car is right or not; he alone can keep various kinds of freight separated; he knows the various rules for stowing; he senses those points which the rules do not and cannot cover.

It cost the railway—and the public—$1,824.78 to make good the error in loading 37 bags of mohair tops (mohair is the trade name for goat wool; tops for mohair washed, cleansed, combed, and made ready for the spinner), into a car previously loaded with cement, although first weeping it out and loading a shipment of metal culvert pipe on the floor—the mohair on top of the pipe. The bridge by which you cross the steam dryshod does not serve as an umbrella; the car had probably as much cement in the cracks and crevices of the body as on the floor, and when in motion this cement began sifting down upon the bags and working through the burlap covering. At the transfer point, the pipe had to be removed; necessitating dragging the bags across the floor, thereby further grinding cement into them. At destination, the shipment was useless. "'Tis better to be safe than sorry."

Carelessness in not properly marking frequently causes misdelivery, as in the case not long ago of a bale of hay, to which no shipping marks were attached. There are various kinds and qualities of hay; the average shipper ships any of it as a "bale of hay," and it is so written in the waybill. When the local freight rolls up to a station after losing time—its usual habit—the conductor, hurriedly glancing over the waybills, sees there is a bale to be unloaded for John Smith.[1] The car door is opened; he sees three bales and, as all look alike to him, he unloads the handiest one and goes on. A little further down the road he unloads a second bale for Bill Jones and before reaching the end of the run he unloads the last for Tom Johnson. Now, in this special episode, John Smith ordered a bale of No. 1 timothy and when he received a bale of No. 2 he was mad clear through—thought the shipper was trying to cheat him, and so wrote him. Bill Jones had ordered a bale of No. 2 timothy and got the bale of clover that Tom Johnson ordered, and when Tom got the bale of timothy that John Smith ordered, both were hotter than hornets and took to letter writing. Before the affair was over everybody, including the claim agent, had hay fever—all arising from the lack of proper marking on the bales.

Some shippers of hay slip the tag bearing the marks under one of the wire bands, whereas it should also be tied to the band, as there is always the chance of its working out, thus leaving the bale without marks.

Figure 160 shows the ordinary method of shipping small orders of stoves. It is well known that cast iron is easily cracked or broken by a blow or falling article. Depict this article in a box car of 100,000-lb. capacity, surrounded and overtopped—for nothing can be piled on it—by a miscellaneous assortment of articles, ranging from an inoffensive sack of flour to a box of hardware stowed high above it, which may fall on it with

---

[1] This story and other information was obtained from a pamphlet, "Why Freight Is Lost or Damaged," by A. C. KENLY, President of the Atlantic Coast Line.

deadly effect at any minute, being thrown from its apparently secure position by the swing of the fast-moving train around a sharp curve or by the shock of the sudden application of the brakes.

The group shown in Fig. 161 represents another source of petty claims—broken chairs. Those of value should be crated; cheaper chairs should be shipped "knocked down" in full or part and then set up at

Fig. 160.—Ordinary method of shipping stoves.

destination. No unprotected article should be shipped unless of a nature to withstand the ordinary wear and tear of transportation.

Figure 162 shows the improper packing of spokes and applies to all similar articles, showing the condition in which a great many bundles reach their destination; many spokes are lost and claims necessarily follow.

The indifference of the ordinary manufacturer or jobber to proper and safe packing and marking is almost incredible. He will spend very large sums in extensively advertising his wares and in sending salesmen out, but after the goods are once sold he seems immediately to lose all interest in them. A pleased customer must be one of the most valuable assets to a manufacturer as well as to a railroad company; the customer

Fig. 161.—Improper method of shipping house-hold furniture.

who does not get his goods promptly and in good condition is certainly not satisfied. The agent has an extensive and important work to educate

Fig. 162.—Improper packing of spokes.

shippers at his station in these matters and to keep himself informed as to the company's rules relative to marking, crating and packing; and conveying such information to the shippers.

CHAPTER XXV

OPERATION OF FREIGHT HOUSES

At small stations the freight house is usually of the "combination" type, in which both inbound (arriving) and outbound (departing) package or l.c.l. freight are handled; while at large stations one or more houses may be in use for inbound, with similar separate facilities for outbound freight.

The administrative and supervisory organization of a freight house differs according to the size of plant, its general arrangement and the local method of conducting the business. In general terms, the agent (with possibly an assistant) requires the services of a chief clerk, a cashier, chief bill clerk and as many assistant clerks as the volume and character of the business demand. The larger stations are here considered because the smaller stations require so many and varied duties that each one may be a story in itself.

A general house foreman is in direct charge of the freight houses, and is usually assisted by a foreman for each inbound house, each outbound house and the transfer station, if they are extensive and separately operated. In smaller and compact layouts, one foreman may suffice for all. The "drop-truck system" of handling freight is described in Chap. XXII and, when combined with mechanical operation through use of tractors and trailers, effects the most efficient and economical operation possible. There are, however, many stations which still retain the "gang system" of operation, wherein each house, including the transfers, has one or more trucking gangs. The number of men in a gang varies according to the distance to be trucked, size of house, and other conditions. A stevedore is usually provided for each gang to stow freight into the car or load it on the trucks. A tallyman for each gang checks the freight with the waybills on inbound freight, and receiving clerks receive outbound freight from teamsters and check it with shipping bills, mark it and observe if the rules for handling explosives and inflammables are complied with and that the proper tariff classifications are followed. Usually more men are needed in the inward house during the forenoon and in the outward house during the afternoon, and it becomes necessary to balance the force carefully as may be required. In some instances men have been advantageously transferred 1 or 2 miles on street cars or by other means of conveyance, where the houses were that far apart.

Byers, in his "Economics of Railway Operation," estimates the value of some 30 freight stations, including tracks and driveways, at $12,000,000; these stations handled about 1,000,000 tons of bulk or car-load freight and 400,000 tons of house freight a month at an average expense of $166,000 for station forces and switching, to which was added $104,000 for interest and depreciation—10 per cent. on the value of the plant —giving an average expense per ton for handling freight:

	Cents
Interest and depreciation	28.6
Station force and shipping	41.5
Total	70.1

He concludes there is no general relation between freight-station areas and tonnage handled as affecting ton-cost and he cites a Baltimore freight station with an area of 330 sq. ft. per ton of freight handled— at a cost of 44 cts.; a New York house 150 sq. ft. and 56 cts.; a Jersey City house 170 sq. ft. and 95 cts.; a Chicago house 340 sq. ft. and 98 cts. a ton. Design and management seem to be the controlling factors, although with the best management the cost may be high, due to the peculiarities of the business at that terminal.

In figuring the cost of handling, interest and depreciation are not included. There are as many methods of computing cost of freight handling as there are of computing cost of car handling. One large railroad system has ruled that:

All freight-house labor that is employed in receiving, loading, unloading, delivering and transferring freight should be included; and the wages of house foreman, assistant foremen, receiving clerks, loading clerks, assistant loading clerks, delivery clerks, tallymen or checkers, stamp men, transfer clerks and checkers (not including men on records), sealers, stevedores and freight handlers or truckers.

The classification adopted some years ago by the Local Freight Agents' Association, provides as follows:

1. General supervision—consisting of general foreman, assistant foremen, clerks and such watchmen and sealers whose work extends over warehouse, platform and team yards.

2. Supervision and clerical work—consisting of:

(a) *Warehouse.*—Foremen, clerks, receiving checkers, loading and unloading checkers, delivery checkers, weighers, watchmen and sealers not included under "general supervision."

(b) *Platform.*—Foremen, clerks, loading and unloading checkers, watchmen and sealers not included under "general supervision."

(c) *Team Yards.*—Foremen, checkers, watchmen and sealers not included under "general supervision."

3. Labor—consisting of:

(*a*) *Warehouse.*—Loaders, packers, truckers, coopers.

(*b*) *Platform.*—Loaders, packers, truckers, coopers.

(*c*) *Team Yards.*—Laborers engaged in loading and unloading package freight on team tracks.

They also recommended the following tonnage classification:

Warehouse Freight.—General merchandise received and forwarded; includes handling from cars to teams and from teams to cars.

Platform Freight.—Freight transferred at platform from car to car or checked from and returned to same car.

Team-yard Freight.—Freight handled from cars to teams or taken from teams to cars, when supervision, checking or labor is furnished.

To arrive at the total number of tons handled, credit should be taken but once for the actual number of tons handled in receiving and disposing of the freight.

The cost per ton for handling is to be obtained by dividing the tonnage obtained as above into cost for labor at warehouse, platform or team track.

Total cost per ton for operation is to be obtained by dividing the tonnage obtained as above into the total cost for supervision, clerks and labor at warehouse, platform and team tracks.

The loading of freight at local stations is an interesting subject, modern methods being quite thoroughly discussed in Chap. XXII, on Mechanical Handling of Merchandise Freight. Yet, for comparative purposes, it would be well to outline methods still employed at stations which have not yet been equipped either with "drop trucks" manually operated or tractors and trailers.

Common practice is to assign certain doors of receiving houses for the receipt of freight for designated destinations, it being expected that drays will be loaded, so that freight can be unloaded in door order. The truck or dray assumes a delay when obliged to back to numerous doors. Freight is invariably unloaded by drivers by dropping it directly onto the freight-house floor or platform, and generally in the doorways. A receiving clerk next checks the shipment against the bill of lading and, upon satisfying himself of its correctness, signs and returns the bill of lading to the driver, retaining the shipping order, which is subsequently passed to the checker or tallyman, who, with his regulation gang of truck loader and four truckers, using two-wheeled trucks only, performs the actual loading of the freight into the designated cars.

The "gang system" involves at least two distinct operations as well as much lost motion through the necessity of pushing freight back to clear the doorways, increasing the possibilities of damage to freight, and the splitting of shipments. There is also a decided disadvantage through delay to outward billing, as shipping orders cannot be sent to the billing department until after the final check by the tallyman.

Wherever verification of the loading is made through the use of the veri- or affirmative check, as described later on, the operation is rendered decidedly slow, because the gang is necessarily held up until the veri-check can be issued by the checker or tallyman, which in the aggregate requires considerable time.

The " drop-truck" system, as shown, eliminates one operation entirely, that of the recheck by tallyman, as the freight is on wheels, and can be pushed back into the middle of the freight house, there to await proper disposition either manually or mechanically.

The so-called veri-check system of affirmative loading is designed to insure the loading of freight into proper cars and prevent its going astray.

A veri-check or ticket is issued to the trucker by the tallyman with each load, the ticket showing the block number to which freight is to be trucked, the number of pieces, the checker's name or number and the trucker's number.

Upon arrival at the car, after the freight has been dropped from truck, the trucker stamps the ticket with the number of the car (stamp pads and stamps are located in each car or location, and the number on the stamp is the block number of the car), which should agree with the number inserted by the tallyman. Upon return to the tallyman, he notes whether the two numbers agree. If they differ, wrong loading is apparent and can be corrected.

At some stations, a return ballot, or ticket with block number, can be obtained from the pad nailed to the side of the car, this ballot being used in place of a stamp but answering the same purpose, as the tallyman must check the two tickets and determine that the numbers are the same.

For inbound freight, under the tinker stamp system, it is practice at most stations of any size to stamp packages showing station name, date, car number, which information has been the means of securing the delivery of many pieces of freight that would otherwise have found their way into the pile of unclaimed freight and later into the "old-hoss" sale. Many packages may be traced to an originating point in this way, where the entire absence of marks would otherwise indefinitely "sidetrack" it.

The Chicago & North-Western has in operation in its Chicago freight houses a method of loading and unloading l.c.l. freight which has been worked out in minute detail. The principal freight houses are at State Street, Grand Avenue, Wood Street, 40th Street and 16th Street. The State Street house ships to the Galena division, and the Grand Avenue house, to the other two divisions and receives from all three. Wood Street is a transfer freight house for freight from connecting lines delivered in cars, and for industrial trap cars and freight from the Merchants Lighterage Company, for points on the North-Western and its western connections. Sixteenth Street is a transfer for connecting line freight except perishable for the North-Western delivered by teams. The mixed freight from the road for connecting lines received at 40th Street is there distributed into the proper foreign cars. Practically the only freight for

Chicago received at either Wood Street or 40th Street is that which has been mixed in with connecting line business except that Wood Street receives a considerable volume of business from eastern connections for delivery at Ravenswood, Oak Park, and other sub-stations in Chicago.

The State Street outbound freight house loads cars for all points on the North-Western Line west, large deliveries in l.c.l. lots being made at the house daily by teams. Perishable from connecting lines to western points is also received here. Six tracks with total capacity of 90 cars are loaded at a time. The 90 cars are divided into 18 "runs" a varying number of cars. The first run is made up of the first car on each of the five tracks; the second run comprises the second car on each of the five tracks; and so on, up to the last or nineteenth run. Each run is in charge of a stevedore who is entirely responsible for correct loading. It is also his business to examine each piece of freight for its actual destination instead of depending on the marker's chalk marks, which are intended solely for the direction of the trucker.

New York, Boston, Philadelphia, West Albany Transfer, Buffalo, Cleveland, Pittsburgh, Alliance, Columbus, the Erie Despatch, Lackawanna Despatch and Merchants' Despatch Transportation Company are among the eastern points and the fast-freight lines which load straight cars for Wood Street. These cars contain nothing but freight for points beyond Chicago proper on or via the Chicago & North-Western. Many overhead cars from connecting lines are received, if, via the Indiana Harbor Belt Railway they will reach the North-Western at Proviso, the great part of them will be picked up by transfer crews at the C. R. & I. Leavitt St., Yard and taken to 40th Street or Proviso. Most of the cars of mixed west bound freight are run into the freight house from the east end on a track running through the center of the house. They are then unloaded and their freight reloaded into cars for the road, those for the Galena division being on the five tracks at the north side of the freight-house and those for the Wisconsin and Milwaukee divisions on the six tracks at the south side. As the front cars in the house are emptied, the whole line is pulled through, the empty cars detached at the north end of the line and the whole process repeated. About 150 cars of such mixed-merchandise freight are received daily from connecting lines.

The accompanying loading plan shows the arrangement of cars loaded for the road at Wood Street (Fig. 163). Each numbered space represents a car. As will be seen from the chart, some 50 per cent. of the cars are way or pedler cars which run on through trains to the beginning of their respective territories and over their territories on way-freight trains. On these cars it is, of course, important that freight for the first station in the peddling territory be loaded next the door. Straight cars, on the other hand, such as the one for Elgin, Run 15, Track 2 or the nineteen for points west of Omaha, Tracks 4 & 5 are loaded with no care for any special arrangement inside the cars. The veri-check used in

Chicago and North Western Railway Company
WOOD STREET STATION
192

		TRACK ONE				TRACK TWO					TRACK FIVE		
Run	Sec	STATION	Car No.	Run	Sec	STATION	Car No.	Run	Run	Sec	STATION	Car No.	Run
44	1			7	1	CHICAGO SHOPS, ILL.		7					
43	1	OAK PARK, AUSTIN, RIVER FOREST AND RIDGELAND		8	1								
43	1			9	1								
41	1			10	1			10					
40	1	BREDA TO SARGEANT BLUFFS		11	1	DIXON							
39	1	Carroll to Crescent, Hooton, Audubon, Dabll, Herring to Oran		12	1	STERLING TO LIMESTONE							
38	1	LOW MOOR TO 'ONG POINT		12	1	STERLING, C B & Q							
27	1	BOONE, ONTARIO TO GLISDEN AND MOINGONA		14	1	ELVA TO SPRING VALLEY		14					
26	1			15	1	ELGIN		15					
25	1			16	1	DUNDEE TO CRYSTAL LAKE		16					
				17	1	WAYNE TO GARDEN PRAIRIE							
				18	1	BELVIDERE							
				20	2	FREEPORT TO CHERRY VALLEY		20					
21	1	16TH STREET		21	2	ROCKFORD, 7TH ST			21	5	COUNCIL BLUFFS TRF		
22	1	LA FOX TO CRESTON		22	2	ROCKFORD			22	5	COUNCIL BLUFFS		
23	1	McHENRY		23	2	ROCKFORD			23	5	OAKLAND		
24	1	TERRA COTTA TO WILLIAMS BAY		24	2	MAYWOOD & MELROSE PK			24	5	SEATTLE		
25	1	SYCAMORE, HENRIETTA AND HERBERT		25	2	ELMHURST TO GLEN ELLYN			25	5	BOISE		
26	1			26	2	WHEATON TO WEST CHICAGO			26	5	ELMHURST DURANT MTRS.		
27	1			27	2	BATAVIA			27	5	SAN FRANCISCO		
28	1			28	2	GENEVA TO ST CHARLES			28	5	SAN FRANCISCO		
29	1			29	2	AURORA AND NO. AURORA			29	5			
30	1			30	2	RACHUSA TO ROCHELLE			30	5	SALT LAKE		
31	1			31	2	CLINTON AND LYONS			31	5	OGDEN		
				32	2	CLINTON AND LYONS			32	5	LOS ANGELES		
				33	2	ALMONT TO ANAMOSA			33	5	COLORADO		
									34	5	GRAND ISLAND TRANSFER		

Run	Sec	TRACK ONE		Run	Sec	TRACK TWO		Run	Run	Sec	TRACK FIVE		Run
62	1	NORWOOD PARK TO DES PLAINES		62	2	DULUTH							
63	1			63	2	DULUTH							
64	1	MT PROSPECT		64	2	WINNIPEG VIA SUPERIOR							
65	1	ARLINGTON HEIGHTS		65	2	CHIPPEWA FALLS TO HANNIBAL							
66	1	PALATINE		66	2	Turtle Lake To Superior, Saupee and Bayfield		66					
67	1	BARRINGTON, FOX RIVER GROVE AND CARY		67	2	Eau Claire to Augusta, Clayton and Park Falls							
68	1	WILMETTE-WINNETKA		68	2	STILLWATER TO ELLSWORTH			68	5			
69	1	Lake Bluff, Kenilworth, Glencoe and Hubbard Woods		69	2	ST PAUL			69	5			
70	1	HIGHLAND PARK, HIGH-WOOD AND FT SHERIDAN		70	2	ST PAUL		70	70	5	NEW LONDON TO ELMHURST		70
71	1	LAKE FOREST		71	2	MINNESOTA TRANSFER, CHARLES STREET			71	5	WAUSAU TO McMILLAN AND MORRIS		71
72	1	NORTH CHICAGO AND GREAT LAKES		72	2	MINNESOTA TRANSFER EAST KENNEFIN AVE			72	5	ANTIGO TO CROATS AND SATURT		72
73	1	BEACH TO WINTHROP HARBOR		73	2	MINNEAPOLIS		73	73	5	RHINELANDER TO ODANAH		73
74	1	WAUKEGAN		74	2	MINNEAPOLIS		74	74	5	IRONWOOD TO MARENISCO		74
75	1	BERRYVILLE TO SOUTH MILWAUKEE		75	2	HAMLIN TRF. G. N			75	5			
76	1	KENOSHA TO TWIN LAKES		76	2	NORTHTOWN TRF., N. P.			76	5	Woodstock to Ridgefield and Hartland		
77	1	RACINE JCT.		77	2	SEATTLE, N P			77	5	HARVARD TO TIFFANY, HARLEM AND HEBRON		
78	1	RACINE		78	2	PORTLAND, N P			78	5	CALEDONIA TO BYRNE		
79	1	CUDAHY		79	2	SPOKANE, N P							
80	1			80	2	GREEN BAY, G B & W.		80					
81	1	SPARTA TO GLENDALE AND GALESVILLE		81	2	GREEN BAY							
82	1	LA CROSSE		82	2	Ansten to Saunders and Sanbelt, Incl., Ashland							
83	1	WINONA TO CHATFIELD, PLAINVIEW AND HAVERHILL											
84	1	ROCHESTER TO MERIDAN AND EUMBROTA											
85	1	WASECA TO NICOLLET VIA ST. PETER											
86	1												

FIG. 163.—Loading chart for Wood St. Station, Chicago—Chicago & North-Western.

guiding the truckers is shown in Fig. 164. A tin box with a number on it is hung on a nail in each car.

The unloading of each foreign car on the track in the center of the house is done by a gang of seven men, a checker, caller and five truckers.

The checker makes out a ticket for each piece of freight as it is brought out of the car. This the trucker takes along with him and drops into the box of the designated car when he deposits the freight in that car. Before the train leaves for the road, an inspector goes into each car and examines all tickets to see that no mistakes have been made. There is a stevedore for each run, who, although he does not himself truck the freight into the cars, is responsible for its being in the right car and for its arrangement in the car. The weight of each piece in each car, taken generally from the way-bill or as weighed when taken out of the foreign car, is recorded on a slip by a clerk in the office and the total tonnage unloaded from the car credited to the gang which did the work. Instead of being paid by the hour, as at State Street, the check clerks, callers and truckers are paid on a tonnage basis, the amount actually handled from each car being credited each to the checker and the caller and divided equally among the five truckers. A minimum day wage is paid in case the tonnage payment falls below that amount, but this seldom happens. The system is said to have worked satisfactorily both to the company and to the men. The same system has been applied at both 16th Street & 40th Street; 16th Street freight is received by teams, and there too it works satisfactorily. The base scale, of course, is different at each of the houses in order to meet the varying conditions, which make the handling more or less difficult. Further allowances are made, as for example, in trap car handling $1\frac{1}{2}$ tons is paid for each ton handled. By the tonnage system men are held in service. Probably Wood Street has as small a turnover of labor as any freight station.

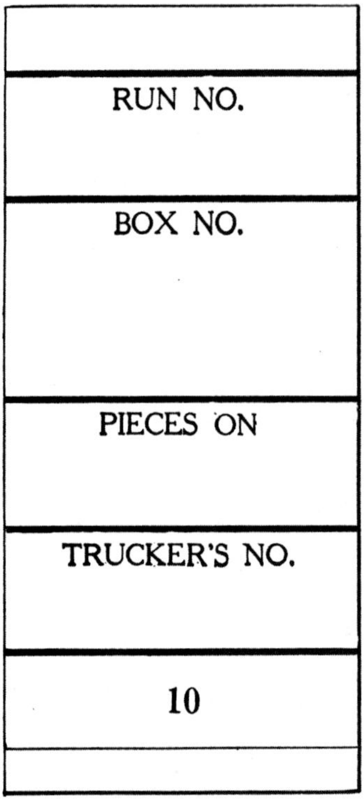

RUN NO.
BOX NO.
PIECES ON
TRUCKER'S NO.
10

FIG. 164.—Trucker's ticket used at Wood St. Station—Chicago and North-Western.

The 171 cars designated on the Wood Street loading chart are the very least number of cars loaded in any one day. The average at Wood Street is about 300 cars per day. The extra cars not designated on the chart (most of which are usually "straight" cars, for instance, extra cars for San Francisco or Minnesota Transfer) are set for loading on the tracks in places represented by the blank spaces on the chart or on available tracks at the east end of the freight house.

These 300 cars average from 30,000 to 35,000 pieces of merchandise daily. A careful record shows that the mistakes in lading amount at most to one-tenth of 1 per cent. This is quite remarkable in view of the fact that merchandise received at Wood Street comes out of foreign cars indiscriminately instead of as at freight houses used by the public where it is delivered at the most convenient door by a teamster who knows the arrangement of the house and the destination of his goods and who keeps his shipments separate for loading.

At 5 p. m. the boxes are taken out of the loaded cars, the doors are closed and sealed and the cars are ready for the road. Fast freights leave for the road at frequent intervals beginning at 7:15 p. m. Normally two trains go west each working evening from Wood Street, others leave from 40th Street and Western Avenue. In addition to the road cars loaded in the house, solid cars loaded on near-by team tracks go out of Wood Street.

A unique method of instructing illiterate truckers is successfully employed on the Panama Railroad. The truckers are of all nationalities. Ninety per cent. of them cannot read nor write but none are color-blind. At each terminal the steamship line and the railroad have checkers. A negro works with them calling freight, and, when traffic does not run heavy, he also marks it. He has a tin tray, a brush, holders and a number of small pots containing paints of different colors. A truck comes up containing a box for a certain destination, Callæ, for instance— and a stroke of yellow and one of green are applied. The trucker proceeds to the car on which a placard is hung with corresponding colors. A package going into the wrong car will show whether the painter or car stower made the error. At Balboa, crayons are being tried instead of oil paints.

The use of the Denver Veri-check system at the D. R. G. C. R. I. & P. house at Denver, a system of route cards of various shapes and colors, showed in 1923 only 121 errors in 1,552,265 packages loaded.

In unloading freight, the waybill check or blind tally may be used. Each method has its adherents. In the waybill check, the tallyman checks off each package or lot of packages opposite the waybill entry for same. It is possible, of course, for a careless checker to mark off packages or items for which the freight is not at hand, or to check off items mechanically before the freight is unloaded. In the blind tally, the tallyman uses a blank sheet upon which he enters the marks of all packages taken out of the car. The waybills are afterward checked with the sheet. A little more labor is involved, but those who favor this method claim that it insures a closer check than that afforded by the waybill check.

The practice as to weighing package freight differs. At some stations all shipments are weighed; at some stations it is the practice to weigh occasional or suspicious shipments, or those from shippers known to be unscrupulous; at other stations weighing is done spasmodically; at still other points there is practically no weighing done. Packages of known weight, such as flour in barrels, sugar, coffee, are seldom weighed. Weighing adds to the cost of handling and tends to delay shipments, but it should, nevertheless, be done, except for standard packages of known weight. At a western freight house, where package freight had not been weighed, it was found the estimated weights were nearly 20 per cent. too low. The loss to the road was enormous. The tendency of the times, backed up by the policies of the Interstate Commerce Commission, is to weigh all freight. The general question is fully discussed in Chap. XIV.

The ordinary process of handling inbound package, or l.c.l., freight is to place the cars opposite the house, unload the freight and truck it either to teams direct or to the proper section of the house. Bulk or car-load freight is handled on team tracks direct from cars to teams, or *vice versa.* The usual practice is to unload perishable freight first, *i.e.,* market produce, butter, eggs, etc. This is accomplished, as a rule, between 6 and 7 o'clock in the morning. The house is generally divided into sections alphabetically. The teamster hauling John Smith's freight will, for instance, go to the door nearest section S. In some cases his freight when unloaded is placed in the section nearest the car. This saves house trucking, but requires the teamster to go to different doors, and frequently to several doors, for one load. He then locates his freight by the information given on the freight receipt or at the cashier's office, where he pays the freight bill. In unloading from the car the freight is usually compared with the waybills accompanying it, checked and shortages, overcharges or damage noted. When the teamster gets his freight, he receipts for it to the delivery clerk.

Outbound freight is delivered at a certain door, the number of which indicates the destination. Large shipping concerns are usually furnished with a house layout, showing door numbers for different destinations. In this manner the hand-trucking distance from the team to the car is reduced and much cross-trucking in the house avoided. The receiving clerk signs the delivery receipt, which is the bill of lading. As the freight is loaded into the car, it is checked, and from this check slip it is billed at the agent's office; that is, the waybill is made. After the cars are loaded, they are sealed with the station seals, the numbers thereon showing where the car was loaded. A side card is placed on each side of the car, giving point of shipment, destination, car number and initial, weight and route, for the guidance of the yardmaster and conductors. The regular waybills, which show additionally the rates, amounts prepaid or to be collected, names of shipper and consignee, are usually mailed to the delivering agent or the transfer station direct and forwarded by passenger train.

The National Industrial Traffic League has distributed a circular among its members, containing this good advice about marking freight:

We desire to call special attention to the vital importance of having all packages of freight for less than car-load shipments legibly marked and so marked as not to be obliterated by the ordinary risks of transportation.

When necessary to use tags for marking, they should be strong and durable, made of rope manila, paper or linen, preferably the latter, and should be either sewed securely to the package or tied to it by a wire tie.

Also dray tickets and bills of lading should be made out in a clear and legible manner. Examination of the files at railway stations shows that excessive carelessness exists in this regard in very many firms, the shipping tickets being made out in the most slipshod fashion, so that in very many cases billing clerks must guess at name of consignee, destination and articles.

We are making complaint to the railways regarding the incomplete and sometimes illegible character of expense bills . . . We certainly cannot expect this reform to be accomplished unless we do our own part.

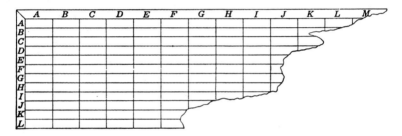

Fig. 165.—Cabinet for holding freight arrival records.

One of the troubles in a freight station is the enormous amount of impatient telephoning of inquiries regarding freight arrivals. This has been successfully met in the Toronto office of the Canadian Pacific, where the clerk at the telephone has constantly before him copies of the arrival notices made out for each consignee on the arrival of freight, and, as these are arranged alphabetically, he can usually answer a telephone inquiry from any person or firm in 20 sec. or less. The notices are classified not only under each letter of the alphabet, but also, when necessary, by subdivisions under each letter.

When waybills arrive, the clerk who makes the expense bills uses carbon sheets and makes four copies at one writing except where originating line uses a manifold waybill furnishing sufficient number of copies. One of these copies, the "No. 4," which is called the "office record," is handed at once to the clerk in charge of the cabinet at the telephone, who assorts all of the sheets received and puts them in the proper pigeonholes. Then, on receipt of an inquiry, for example, from the T. Eaton Company, as quickly as the clerk can turn and catch the letter E on the horizontal line (Fig. 165), and the letter A on the perpendicular line, he can locate the proper pigeonhole and get the necessary information. The "No. 4" being a carbon of the "No. 1," all information as to date of arrival, date of shipment, number and kind of packages, weight and charges are before him, so that all questions relating to the shipment can be answered intelligently. In the event of goods not being in and consignee wishing to be advised by phone when they do arrive, a pink slip is used, the information being inserted in it as to date shipped, kind and quantity of goods and the consignee's phone number. This "pink" also serves the purpose of a directory for keeping trace of inquiries made by transient persons when, together with the information above referred to, the street address is also inserted. When the goods finally arrive and the No. 4's are being distributed into their proper places, if a "pink" is discovered in a pigeonhole, the consignee is immediately notified.

The same consignee may phone, "When will our goods be delivered?" This may be answered as quickly as any of the other questions. When the delivery clerk passes over the sheets to the cartage company the "No. 3" is retained for the accounting department, but before these are passed to that department the inquiry clerk takes them and in spare moments takes out the corresponding "No. 4" and places it in the Z space at the bottom. All he then has to do when he fails to find a No. 4 in its proper place is to look in Z, and he is then in a position to know whether the shipment has passed out and is on its road for delivery.

At the close of the day the Z's are taken out, tied together, dated and sent to the record room. If taken from one pigeonhole after another in regular order, they will be found in alphabetical order when tied.

If a consignee has inquired several times and it seems desirable to start a tracer, the "pink," with the information obtained at the time of the first call, is still in the pigeonhole and is available for quickly making a memorandum which can be handed to the tracing clerk, thus saving the consignee all unnecessary trouble.

The work in the freight house includes that very large ingredient, the O. S. & D. (over, short and damage) clerical tracing either independently or in conjunction with and for the general freight-claim department. Unfortunately, there is a growing tendency to handle or trace claims in a most perfunctory manner. This is largely due to the lack of initiative or ingenuity displayed by the claim offices, and the ease with which they fall into the way of doing the work in a routine manner.

In Chap. XXI, the store-door delivery system of the railways of Great Britain is described. This method can be worked to advantage in many large freight terminals in this country, particularly where houses are frequently congested, because teamsters haul spasmodically or irregularly, being easily affected by weather conditions or opportunities to obtain more remunerative employment for a brief period of time. The freight house, they argue, can wait.

The most notable instance of actual operation of store-door delivery of l.c.l. freight in this country is the system which prevailed at Baltimore and Washington commencing in 1867 by the P. W. & B. Railroad (later absorbed by the Pennsylvania) and from 1886 by the B. & O. Railroad. This service provided free pick-up and delivery for certain classes of freight in both cities within designated delivery zones and freight rate charged by the railroads included terminal wagon service. It differed from the English system in that the freight rates were no higher than station-to-station rates so that the pick-up and delivery service afforded by the railroads was a charge on the rail line haul. This system continued in operation until 1913 when it was cancelled by the carriers, growing out of complaints made to the Interstate Commerce Commission respecting extensions of free delivery zones, and the Commission in its decision supported the position of the carriers that they were justified in withdrawing such free delivery service as unreasonable and discriminatory in that the cost of such collection and delivery had been included in the station-to-station rates. It seems obvious that had higher rates been named to take care of the collection and delivery service no such decision would have been rendered, and that had the practice been general everywhere of railroads furnishing free truckage, the charge of discrimination could not have been supported.

In Montreal, the Canadian National railway delivers and receives freight at the shipper's door, having a contract with a cartage company for that purpose. The system was evidently introduced because it was an English custom. The cartage company receives an average of 60 cts. per ton, of which 40 cts. is collected from the shipper, the railways paying the remainder. For instance, a package weighing 500 lb., on which the freight is 20 cts. per hundred, would be billed at 22 cts. or $1.10 for the shipment. The cartage company signs bills of lading for such freight as it collects and is responsible for it until delivered to the railway company at the freight house; and it receipts to the railway for inbound freight and assumes responsibility for it between the freight house and consignee's place of business.

The arrangement used by the Canadian Pacific and the Canadian National in Toronto is similar. As in Montreal, the cartage only applies to the first five classes. The rate charged the shipper is 2 cts. per hundred, with a 15-ct. minimum. The cartage company receives 2.5 cts. per hundred and 15 cts. minimum for small packages. The railway wins out in keeping its freight houses cleaned up. The cartage company is under obligation to furnish enough teams to keep freight moving rapidly from the houses; when short, it immediately employs outside teams to assist, for which it usually pays $5.00 per day. It is estimated each team will, under the rates in effect, earn $6 to $8 per day.

CHAPTER XXVI

REFRIGERATING, VENTILATING AND HEATING

The supply of ice used annually by railroads is enormous. It is required for cooling drinking water in depots, offices, shops and passenger cars and for icing refrigerator cars in transit. Independence of local or outside ice companies is essential. Unless manufactured ice or other artificial refrigeration is used, it is desirable to locate storage houses and icing plants on lakes or ponds and reship to consuming points as may be necessary. Care should be taken to locate the storage buildings where they will not interfere with future railroad development. Preferably locations should be at the source of supply, arranged to enable trains to pull away from and stand clear of the main tracks while being iced. From 1,000 to 4,200 lb. of ice is needed to charge a refrigerator car for a run of two days to a week, depending upon temperature and whether the car is in motion or standing.

In computing ice-storage capacity, allowance must be made for shrinkage. In brick or concrete houses, this will run about 10 per cent. In well-constructed frame houses it will be slightly more. Shrinkage in large houses is less than in small ones. If natural ice is depended on, short or missing crops must be considered.

In figuring on capacities and consumption, a cubic foot of sea-water ice weighs 64 lb.; rain-water ice, 62.3 lb. and pure, solid ice averages 58.7 lb. On the basis of 58.7 lb., 34 cu. ft. are equivalent to a ton of 2,000 lb.; or 38.25 cu. ft. to a ton of 2,240 lb. Ice is usually assumed to weigh 60 lb. per cubic foot, making 33.3 cu. ft. to a ton of 2,000 lb. Allowing for voids and irregular packing, 36 cu. ft. will be a better figure for estimates.

In construction of ice houses for the storage of ice, non-heat-conducting walls are essential. There should also be ample ventilation on top of the ice, good drainage of the bed and proper appliances and arrangements for handling and stocking the ice economically. The best designed houses have walls with air spaces, and spaces filled with cork, ashes or other non-heat-conducting material. The use of a good insulating material gives higher efficiency and prevents decay through absorption of moisture. Cork is also superior to shavings or sawdust in regard to fire risk. Less heat will be absorbed if the outside of the building is painted a light color or is whitewashed. Sawdust or salt hay are good materials for covering the top of the ice, to prevent contact with air.

Refrigeration plants are very generally used. Ice can, in many instances, be manufactured and sold cheaper than it can be harvested, stored and then transported to market. Mechanical refrigerator cars are used to a limited extent and have not been generally adopted, because of high first cost, the complicated arrangement and the care necessary for their successful operation. Stationary refrigeration plants require much supervision and, as the time of service is short, the railroads have generally left their construction and operation to shippers. Refrigeration is used only for the transportation of fruit, vegetables and meats, freight which is essentially seasonable in character. Perishable products are transported with ventilation or icing, or a combination of the two. For bananas the minimum temperature is 55°; for safety against chill with a usual refrigeration temperature of 58 to 60°. Other fruits require temperatures ranging from 34° to normal. Meats are often frozen.

Precooling plants for handling fruits—especially citrous and deciduous —are almost indispensable on roads with heavy traffic of that character, and several have been constructed. In one type of these stations, large quantities of air are cooled by being carried over cold brine or ammonia

FIG. 166.—General view, precooling plant, Roseville, Cal.—Southern Pacific.

piping, the air being then conveyed through troughs in the train shed, where it is injected through canvas ducts into as many as 50 cars at a time. The desired temperature is obtained in a few hours. Ice is objectionable because of the moisture it creates.

No precooling plants are used for bananas except as refrigerated ships answer the purpose in discharging precooled fruit for immediate loading in cars. Plants for heating and cooling were located at convenient railroad junction points in the interior but are now used for warming fruit in winter and the cooling process was dropped because the sustained refrigeration in transit afforded by icing was found to be better than intermittent cooling by treatment at these stations.

Sheds used for heating bananas in winter are operated at Mounds, Ill.; Dubuque, Ia.; and Rouses Pt., N. Y.

A precooling plant of the Southern Pacific Company, at Roseville, Cal., for cooling oranges for shipment, is shown in Figs. 166 and 167.

Fɪɢ. 167.—Roseville precooling plant in operation.

Cold air is blown through a large insulated tube leading from a bunker room in the storage plant to the ice trap in one end of the car. From a trap at the opposite end of the car, another tube leads back to the warehouse. One of the views clearly shows the method by which connections are made with the cars. The cold air is blown into the car at a temperature of 32° and, after passing through the car, is drawn back by an exhaust fan to the

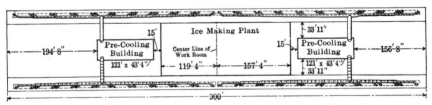

Fɪɢ. 168.—Ground plan, precooling plant, Colton, Cal.—Southern Pacific.

warehouse, where the moisture and gases from the fruit are frozen on the refrigerator pipes. The direction of the current through the car can be changed. With a powerful air current, it takes from 30 to 50 hours to cool the fruit in the center of the packages to 40°.

Figure 168 shows the ground plan of the Southern Pacific's precooling plant at Colton—an ice-making plant with a precooling building at each end, a track in each side and connections for 40 cars.

The precooling buildings, 43 ft. 4 in. by 121 ft., are built of reinforced concrete. The mechanical equipment is carefully arranged and includes the exhaust fans, which are motor-driven, the flexible piping and the brine coils around which the air is passed, and which are, therefore, enclosed in an air-tight chamber. The details of the false door, through which the cold air is forced into the car, are shown in Fig. 169.

In the vertical section, a deflector will be seen, placed opposite the mouth of the pipe, to throw the air current upward. The fruit is so

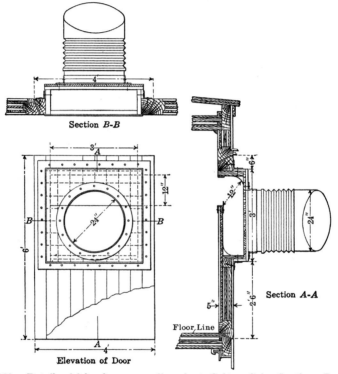

Fig. 169.—Details of false door, precooling plant, Colton, Cal.—Southern Pacific.

packed as to leave an open space at the top of the car opposite the door, and in this space a special deflecting device is placed during cooling, to direct the air currents among the boxes of fruit.

A typical icing station is that of the Pennsylvania at Huntingdon, Pa., with a productive capacity of 225 tons per day and storage capacity for 5,000 tons; the plant making both clear and opaque ice. Ice is conveyed from the plant to the icing platform by a link belt in under the tracks and up inclined joists to either level of the icing platform.

A combined ventilating, heating and refrigerating car has been developed and is said to be fairly successful. Exhaust ventilators on the roof of the car, operated and adjusted by levers on the roof, together with reversible hoods at each end of the car, control the ventilating features. Heating is accomplished by steam pipes connected to the locomotive, or a yard steam plug, in much the same manner as passenger cars are heated and kept warm. The usual refrigeration methods are employed; ice tanks are placed in each end of car with hatch openings, plugs and hatch covers.

Another car (the A B C) has been designed to operate with brine circulation between the overhead ice tanks at each end, the brine from melting ice being kept in motion through pipes by means of check valves worked automatically by the oscillation of the car. Floor pipes operate in the same manner for heating with hot brine in winter. This design is theoretically good in applying the refrigeration from over and the heat from underneath the load with a unit system not dependent on train line treatment. Ventilation is provided for in the usual way through hatches fitted with plugs and vent covers.

There is no difficulty whatever in designing units or train-line systems to supply heat or refrigeration to refrigerator cars. Some of these problems have been experimentally solved and partially solved in operation on European railroads under their refined operating methods in manners which have not been found practicable thus far in the American railroad service with its enormous tonnage, tremendous distances, and necessity for economical operation.

Refrigeration of freight in transit is affected by speed. At 25 m.p.h. and an external temperature of 68°, it is claimed that the interior of the car can be brought down to 32° or freezing, in from 40 to 50 min.

Few roads have any systematic method for the preservation of perishable freight while in transit. There is considerable variation in the temperature at which different commodities of a perishable nature are liable to damage, and they may be further affected by their condition when shipped, time in transit, time continually in motion, and similar conditions. With the use of the modern car, there is no good reason for permitting freight to become frozen. It is only during extreme winter weather that the use of the heater car becomes necessary. If produce has been exposed to low temperature for some time before being placed in a car, it is not in a condition to withstand cold. A car of produce, such as potatoes, will in all probability stand a lower temperature when the car is in motion than when at rest. With the outside temperature at 20°, perishable goods may be safely shipped in ordinary freight cars and in refrigerator cars down as low as 10° above zero. It is further claimed that these goods may be safely shipped in refrigerator cars with the temperature nearly 10° below zero, if the car is heated before being loaded and the goods, at the end of the trip, are immediately taken to a warm place without being handled any great distance in a dray. In the best refrigerator cars, perishable goods may be safely handled with the temperature as low as 20° below zero, provided they are not subjected to such cold for more than three or four days at a time; with the ordinary refrigerator cars the most perishable goods are liable to be damaged in zero weather. Before shipping fresh beef, it should be chilled to 36°, although 40° will suffice under favorable conditions. It is considered important that the beef be kept at a uniform temperature from the time it starts its journey until it reaches its destination, and the cars should, therefore, be at the same temperature as the chill rooms. In summer, cars need reicing frequently to maintain the proper temperature and no fixed rule can be established as to time or distance between reicings, these factors being governed by the outside temperature.

Heating cars by using ice has some possibilities, and the Government Weather Bureau has given the question consideration. A car has been designed to use ice with salt, in summer for the protection of perishable goods in transit, and in winter to prevent freezing. This car is constructed on the theory that ice, which is normal at 32° F., absorbs heat at a higher temperature and imparts heat at a lower temperature. Hence, when it is zero weather outside, the ice containers in a car act as stoves, helping to keep up the temperature inside. Another method for protection against freezing consists in throwing a stream of water on the car when the thermometer is near the zero point. The water freezes and forms a complete coat over the outside of the car. This coat prevents the warmer air from coming out of the car and so tends to keep up the temperature inside. In the winter, carload banana shipments are made in cars lined with paper and with large quantity of straw. Cars are preheated and heated while loading by means of stoves. There is no heating in transit other than stoves in bunkers provided for in the standard equipment used for bananas. The heating sheds referred to are only used in extremely cold weather and cars held for heating en route for a limited time in such sheds. No theory has, as yet, been suggested to account for the interesting phenomenon that perishable produce, such as fruit and vegetables, will stand a lower temperature when the car is in motion than when it is at rest.

The use of paper for protection against cold is increasing and its effectiveness is wonderful. Fruit wrapped in heavy brown paper will endue 15° more cold than without it. Potatoes are sometimes packed in barrels lined with paper, and when the weather is unusually severe the barrels are also covered with paper. Clams and oysters are similarly shipped in paper-lined barrels to keep them from freezing, and cars for transporting perishable merchandise are quite commonly lined with paper. There is said to be nothing like paper to keep out frost. Eggs shipped in crates with separate pasteboard divisions and covered with a layer of oat chaff will stand a low temperature. It has been found that pickled eggs are injured by cold more quickly than fresh ones.

Fruit products in cans or glass must not be shipped when the temperature is below freezing. A well-ventilated dry cellar is the best place to store apples, potatoes and vegetables generally, the temperature being from 30 to 45°. Apples are not made unfit for use by freezing, if they are allowed to thaw gradually. Tropical fruits in storage should be kept at from 60 to 70°.

The immensity of this problem may be comprehended by the statement that in 1921 New York alone received 141,000 car loads of fruit and vegetables; 103,000 of these—over 70 per cent—were brought in by rail. Of some 48,700 cars coming in by steamships, about 28,000 were sold in New York. The Pennsylvania and Erie handled about 70,000 car loads—or two-thirds of the amount coming in by rail. Citrus fruits pay the highest revenue per car of any commodity transported—$480.34, according to 1922 returns. Poultry follows, with a valuation of $382.67; fresh fruits, other than citrus, $325.70; automobiles, $210.26; wool, $194.20; wheat, $193.52; and so on down to logs, posts, poles and cordwood—the lowest—$28.81.

The Bureau of Chemistry of the U. S. Department of Agriculture, through its Food Research Laboratory,[1] conducted investigations of the transportation of perishables, which show great variations in the construction of refrigerator equipment.

Refrigerator cars are of two types of bunker—one known as the "box bunker," in which the ice rests directly against the end and sides of the car—and the other, known as the "basket bunker," in which the ice is held in a wire container 2 in. away from walls and bulkhead.

The box bunker usually has an open bulkhead of wood or metal. Sometimes there is a solid wooden partition open at the top and bottom. The basket bunker commonly has a solid wooden bulkhead, open 12 in. at the bottom and 14 in. at the top, and in the new cars this bulkhead is insulated with 1 in. of a recognized insulator. The new cars, also, have a rack on the floor, 4 in. in the clear, made of 2- by 4-in. runners and 1- by 3-in. cross-slats, 1½ in. apart. These racks are fastened to the sides of the car with hinged bolts, and are divided in the middle so they can be turned up against the walls when the car is cleaned. They are necessary for the safe carrying of perishable loads. Most of the cars now in use are without racks. Some have permanent strips on the floors 1 or 1½ in. in height. These strips are practically valueless. The insulation varies from a few layers of paper to 3 in. of some recognized insulator. In some, the layers of insulation are broken by spaces—in others, the insulation is massed. The cars in the experiments were from approximately 29 ft. between bulkheads to approximately 33 ft. Temperatures were taken by means of electrical thermometers inserted when the cars were loaded. The mechanism was such that neither the doors nor the hatches were opened to take records, nor was the car modified in any way.

The car factors which determine the size of the load which can be safely carried are insulation, bunkers and floor racks. The floor rack was first used as

[1] Dr. M. E. Pennington, St. Louis Railway Club.

a rough dunnage false floor by potato shippers and the raised floor or floor rack of portable design originated in the banana trade in New Orleans. The present permanent attached floor rack was an outgrowth of the portable rack. An experiment was conducted with three cars which had been in experimental service for about ten months. Cars A and C were provided with basket bunkers and floor racks; car B had a box bunker and strips on the floor. Cars A and B had 3 in. of insulation in the roof, 2 in. in side walls and ends and 2 in. of cork in the floor. Car C had 1½ in. in the walls and 2 in. in the roof and floor. Each

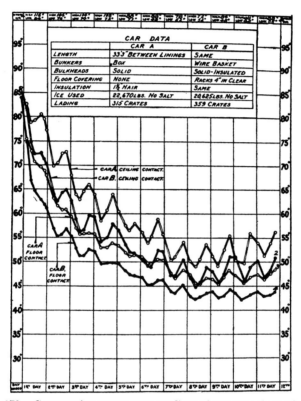

Fig. 170.—Comparative temperature readings of two cars of cantaloupes.

was loaded with 600 cases of eggs consolidated from pick-up cars, and each received the same amount of ice accurately weighed into the bunkers. About 12 thermometers were put into each car. The temperature of the eggs on the floor of car B, between the doors, was 66.5° F. on arrival; car C, in the same location, was 45.5° F. and car A 44.5° F. The packages between the doors on the top of the load—in this case five layers high—showed for car B, 64°, for car C, 56.6°, and for car A, 55.5° F.

Manifestly, car B is not a satisfactory carrier for a heavy load of eggs. Car A, on the other hand, has done its work well, and at first sight car C, having less insulation, appears to be efficient for a load of 600 cases of eggs during hot summer weather. Further study, however, shows that the packages around the

walls of car C came into destination over 6° higher than the corresponding
packages in car A, though when loaded they were but 3° apart but used about
1,000 lb. more ice than car A and, on the whole, did less satisfactory work, especially around the walls, where actual deterioration due to heat undoubtedly
occurred.

The performance of another poorly built car, said to contain 1½ in. of insulation throughout, as compared with a well-built car known to have 1½ in. of insulation (see Figs. 170 and 171), shows the temperature in cars in which cantaloupes

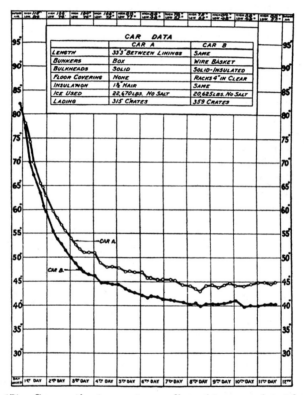

F<small>IG</small>. 171.—Comparative temperature readings of two cars of cantaloupes.

were hauled for 11 days across a hot territory. The top layer in car A, loaded six
wide and four high at the bunkers, was in such bad condition on arrival that
claims were filed for damage in transit. Car B, on the other hand, was in good
condition, although the load was seven cases wide and four cases high. In car A
the combination of a lack of cold-air circulation and of insulation proved disastrous, even though the load was light and open in character, and much easier to
refrigerate than a load of eggs.

Encouraging results have been obtained in refrigerating heavy loads of fruit
in the basket-bunker cars by adding salt to the ice in the bunkers. On a long
haul across a hot territory salt has been added to the ice at the first three icing
stations. By that time (the third day) the load was cooled and frequently no

more ice was needed, even though the haul continued for five to eight days. The air issuing from the bunkers is far below 32°, but the circulation is so rapid that there is no pocketing at the bulkhead. The insulated bulkhead also protects the load so that frosting does not occur. Salting ice in a box bunker, open bulkhead, merely freezes the load next to the bulkhead. The packages in the middle of the car are not benefited because of a lack of air circulation.

Investigation convinces that in the future ice and salt will be used for more commodities than fresh meats, poultry and fish. Indeed, it is the only way now known by which very perishable small fruits can be transported in good condition throughout the entire car. Of course, a definite routine for its application must be worked out.

The effect of poor insulation is clearly shown by comparing results obtained with two cars. One of the cars was of the paper variety—the other well insulated. There was a variation of more than 15° between the two cars. The floor of the one was often 6 or more degrees warmer than the ceiling of the other. The paper car follows the atmospheric temperature and the refrigerant in the bunkers is almost powerless. Yet again and again eggs, fruit, vegetables and dressed poultry have been shipped in these cars and sometimes they have been loaded almost to their cubical capacity!

The relative values of the air space and of paper as insulators may be further emphasized by comparing a car built with what is termed "a double-felt-lined" car. Such a car is considered to be a greater protection than a box car, but in no wise is it a refrigerator, it is not even provided with ice bunkers. The temperatures on the ceiling of such a car follow the atmosphere and there is a decided similarity in its performance compared with that of the paper car described before.

Summing up the results of such experiments as these lead to the following conclusions:

1. A combination of basket bunker, insulated bulkhead and floor rack produces a circulation of air which is not obtained in a car having a box bunker, open bulkhead and bare floor or permanent strips.

2. Such a basket-bunker car, approximately 33 ft. between bulkheads, can refrigerate the top and bottom of the load in the two middle quarters of the car, provided it is sufficiently well insulated and not overloaded.

3. Cars which depend for insulation on paper and air spaces should not be used for the transportation of such perishables as fruit, delicate vegetables, poultry, eggs and fish.

4. Cars having 1 in. of insulation will not carry eggs successfully during hot weather when loaded more than three layers high. Cars having 1½ in. of insulation in the side walls and 2 in. in the roof and floor will not carry eggs successfully during hot weather when loaded more than four layers high. Cars having 3 in. of insulation in the roof, 2 in. in the side walls and ends and 2 in. of cork in the floor will carry eggs five cases high, but not six. The box bunker car, regardless of quantity of insulation, does not refrigerate the two middle quarters of the load when it is tightly stowed. Even with an open load, the performance is unsatisfactory.

5. The use of salt with the ice in a well-insulated basket-bunker car will permit an increase in the load of from 25 to 40 per cent.

6. While each commodity must be studied separately in order to determin-
the maximum load, the principles of the relation between car efficiency and tone
nage of eggs as indicated in this discussion can be applied to perishables in general.

Care in operation is important; practical knowledge and application
are essential. Each commodity must be studied, packed, loaded, braced,
transported, unloaded, and exceptions recorded according to its peculiarities and needs. One road analyzed damage to perishable freight
due to broken packages alone and found lemons leading, with 57.7 per
cent. of all loss to that fruit chargeable to this cause; pears, canned 54.4;
grapes 47.0; oranges 43.1; apples 31.6; cantaloupes 28.3; vegetables 27.4
and peaches 24.3 per cent. A study of packing—and possibly containers
—is needed. Detailed instructions are desirable. Every agent and
yardmaster does not know the meaning of "row," "layer," "stack,"
"drain-pipes," "hatches," "plugs," "bunkers."

Those in charge of yard operations, icing or re-icing and refrigeration
plants should, first of all, inspect and record; should not open bunkers until
ready to ice; should sweep dirt and cinders from tops of cars before opening
plugs. The tamping bar alone will determine amount of ice required.

In icing banana shipments, large, full cakes of ice are used. The first
cake is broken into pieces which act as a cushion against the impact of
the full cakes subsequently loaded. Full cakes of ice are used as presenting the smallest possible contact with the atmosphere in relation to the
volume of ice, so as not to afford too much refrigeration. The comparatively high temperature applied to bananas in refrigeration (55°) is difficult to maintain, as the melting point of ice is 32°. Therefore, the vents
are carried open to some extent with regulated adjustment for the purpose
of providing interior circulation to dislodge any cold air which may
settle in the bottom of the load by gravitation and to assist in tempering
the interior atmosphere with outside air and to supply ventilation.
A fifty-cent thermometer cannot be reliable, in fact a very large percentage of the popular type of commercial thermometers are defective in one
or more of the details of manufacture. Many are found to permit play
between the tube and scale frequently due to the breakage of the tip of
the tube; others are found inaccurate in some parts of the scale, and the
bulbs of still others are made of inferior glass and thus become inactive
through changes in volume due to excessive contraction and expansion.

It must be kept constantly before all having to do with this important
feature of transportation that it is the quantity of ice melted, rather than
that remaining in the bunkers, that determines amount of refrigeration
supplied; ice that does not melt contributes little or nothing towards
lowering the temperature. A good refrigerator car is a high type of ice-
box, constantly being developed and improved, but it must meet conditions, and service, seldom full realized. It must stand all the shock and
vibration of movement besides variations in locality and it may be in
zero and 80° above temperature in one and the same day.

The shipment of vegetables, fish, and poultry in iced packages or with ice applied with or over the packages in the body of the car has grown to a great extent and causes great damage to the floor insulation of the standard refrigerator car, both by destroying the insulating power of the floor structure with moisture and by causing decay in the floor woodwork and sills. The effect of these concealed defects on service is obvious and all the more dangerous because the deficiency is not apparent on surface inspection.

The protection of bananas in transit is one of the greatest problems, both because of the susceptibility of this fruit to depreciation and because the shipments are enormous and increasing. Most of this fruit consumed in the United States comes from the West Indies, Central American Republics, Mexico and South America.

Fig. 172.—Horizontal conveyors delivering bananas to railway cars.

Of all the freight handled by railroads doubtless none is more susceptible to deterioration caused by extremes of heat and cold than the banana. It was first brought to this country in the early seventies in the form of a souvenir or a delicacy, wrapped in tin foil. In 1898 some 12,000,000 bunches were brought from the American tropics. Today the banana consumption of the United States is close to 50,000,000 bunches, of which about 30,000,000 are supplied by one company.[1] One of the conveyors used in loading bananas into cars is shown in Fig. 172.

The standard market bunch of bananas has nine "hands"—rows of bananas around the stem. Bunches of less than nine hands are classed

---

[1] The United Fruit Company, operating 90 steamships. The inland movement in the United States is handled by a subsidiary, the Fruit Dispatch Company, which handles upwards of 70,000 cars of bananas annually.

as seconds, and those having less than seven are not taken aboard ships. Each "hand" must have at least ten good fingers—*i.e.*, bananas. Smaller bunches, or hands, are said to be deficient in quality. An average marketable bunch weighs from 55 to 70 lb. Costa Rica has produced stems containing as high as 22 hands—"a veritable giant of tropical fecundity." The protection of this fruit aboard ship requires remarkable equipment and the continual attention of trained men. The fruit comes on board within a few hours after cutting and is stored without covering. The lowest bunches are laid with the stems vertical and a final layer is placed horizontally, this arrangement giving the best results in space utilization and freedom from damage. On the United Fruit Company's steamers, the ship's sides and bulkheads and the highest and lowest decks are insulated with granulated cork and wood boardings, forming a complete envelope about 7 in. thick. Cool air is conveyed through trunks along each side, formed by boarding, in which are openings with adjustable slides. Powerful electric motor-driven centrifugal fans, arranged in pairs, draw air from the fruit chambers, through suction chambers on one side, pass it over closely nested brine piping, thereby cooling and drying it, and returning it through the delivery trunks on the opposite side. The cooler pipes are electrically welded into grid form; there are no screwed joints except those in the headers and the brine flow is regulated by valves controlling a number of separate groups of grids. The two brine pumps are of the vertical duplex type, either one being of ample capacity in an emergency. On the outward—empty—trip, machines and fans are run during the last day or two, to cool the spaces preparatory to receiving the fruit. On the homeward voyage the plant is run continuously during the first two days, to extract the sun heat from the fruit and to retard ripening. The captain and his aïdes—all carefully trained—take temperatures and make general observations at frequent intervals—day and night. After a few days at sea the temperatures are well under control and the machines are slowed down—one of the compressors probably being disconnected—to avoid the risk of chilling. The temperature is maintained at about 55°. An error in the adjustment of temperature may result in great damage, possibly ruin, to a cargo of anywhere from 40,000 to 85,000 bunches of bananas.

The banana industry occupies a unique position among shippers. The extremely perishable nature of the commodity and the fact that it must be maintained at a temperature within narrow limits in successful transportation, made it necessary for the importer to follow through the transportation operation in detail with educational work and helpful assistance. The Fruit Dispatch Company, one of the largest banana distributing companies, marketing the importations of the United Fruit Company, maintains an equipment department which watches over the care of bananas and ships their cars, collaborating with transportation companies in the design and repair of refrigerator cars and maintaining a car-inspection service. The messenger department of this same company provides men (known as messengers) to travel in some cases with the trains to destination but who are more generally stationed at various division and junction points to cover matters of ventilation, refrigeration, and heating for the benefit of the consignee. It is doubtful whether this industry would have developed to this enormous extent and have become as efficiently operated if the transportation feature had not been covered by cooperation of this kind. The care which this industry has fostered carries the work of the importer still further in the transportation field to the point of assisting the jobber as to the process of ripening, and design of ripening rooms. As a result, in the railroad field, the claims paid on bananas are phenomenally low compared with other commodities transported.

CHAPTER XXVII

THE ENGINE HOUSE

The limitations of a work of this character do not permit of a discussion of engine houses ("roundhouses") from the viewpoint of locomotive repairs, beyond a reference to mere running repairs. The aim of this chapter is to describe the uses and abuses of engine houses as they relate to keeping a road's motive power in service and moving its traffic, with special reference to the location of the engine-house plant in its relation to the road, divisions and terminals; its accessories, such as the coal, ash, water and sand supplies, and the inspection pits, turntables and "wyes." These accessories are more fully considered in other chapters.

Engine houses were formerly built to shelter engines. As a rule, they are now used only incidentally for shelter and more particularly for making light repairs and for cleaning or washing out locomotives. Engines in active service need not, as a rule, be housed, although in northern climates it is difficult at times to care for engines properly in the open. Some motive-power people figure on providing engine-house capacity for 25 per cent. of the power in service. Small machine shops to care for more extensive repairs are generally annexed and form valuable adjuncts to engine houses. In the house one or more drop pits should be provided for taking out wheels.

In planning an engine house, consideration should be given to the number of engines to be cared for, including future possibilities, the materials available for construction purposes, the possibility of future electrification of the whole or part of the line, the climate and topography of the country and the available property and structures in the immediate neighborhood.

Types of construction may be divided into three general classes: square, rectangular and round.

Square houses, with one or more tracks entering from a ladder controlled by switches, are operated for a small number of engines, with the result that there is little delay because there are no breakdowns of turntables or other apparatus which are required in certain types of houses. The square house is exceedingly simple to construct, economical in first cost and durable. The liability of loss from fire is small. The foreman in charge has a good oversight of the layout and can, therefore, secure good operating results. The track approaches take up considerable land area. Provision for turning engines must be made where necessary.

A plan and cross-section of a typical square engine house is shown in Fig. 173, representing the Towanda, Pa., house of the Lehigh Valley, an old plant, but unique in its utilization of limited ground space lying

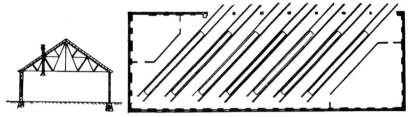

FIG. 173.—Section and plan, square engine house, Towanda, Pa.

adjacent and parallel to the main tracks. It is 63 ft. by 183 ft. Seven tracks enter the building at an angle of 46 deg. with the front, or entrance, side. Tracks are 13 ft. centers on the square, or 18 ft. on the skew, measured along the face of the building.

The view in Fig. 174 is that of a square engine house, called "steam-shed" or "running shed" at Crewe (England) on the London & North-

FIG. 174.—Square engine-house, Crewe, England—London and North-Western.

Western. It will be seen that engines are housed in tandem and are guided to their respective tracks by switches near the entrances.

Rectangular houses require the least ground space of any type of construction. Transfer tables are necessary, one of which may serve two houses. These houses are cheap and simple to design and construct. The oversight is excellent, they afford good light and ventilation and they may readily be extended as business increases. Ample and convenient space is provided for men, machinery and material for making repairs. One house may be built and served by a transfer table and later on a second house added, served by the same table, but a breakdown, derailment of engine or disabling of transfer table is likely to cause serious interference with train movements and, in case of fire, blockades may occur with disastrous consequences. In order to minimize this danger, engine houses of the square and rectangular type have, in some instances, been erected with descending grades on the tracks in the house and for some distance from the entrance, to facilitate the removal of engines in case of fire.

Round or polygonal houses require turntables to enable engines to reach or to leave their various stalls. They occupy comparatively little space and may be worked into oddly shaped land areas; they can be well lighted—this is not always done—and they give the greatest width at the head end of the engine, where room is most needed for repairs and handling of materials. On the other hand, however, they are costly to construct and very complicated both in construction and subsequent operation. The foreman's opportunity for supervision is limited; and a breakdown of a turntable, or derailment or disablement of an engine on or near the turntable often causes a bad blockade. These houses make a perfect trap in the event of fire, because every locomotive must pass out over the turntable. Houses of this type are usually planned for from 30 to 60 engines for the complete circle, but they are often constructed as a segment of a circle, because the shape of available land does not permit the full circle or because the present requirement does not demand it. In the latter case it is easy to add to the capacity of the house if the land is available.

In the engine house, with a turntable entrance, there are three arrangements of tracks in general use, as follows:

1. Omission of frogs altogether, arranging the outside of each rail to lie close alongside or just touching the rail of adjacent track at the edge of the turntable pit. This is by far the most satisfactory method from a Maintenance of Way standpoint. The table must be long enough to permit of this arrangement of tracks, which in itself seems sufficient argument for long tables. Thirty-six frogs represent an investment of about $3000, besides the cost of maintenance and adjustment. Tracks should leave the table pit at a 180-deg. angle, so they will match up at both ends in every case.

2. Running the two rails together to form a point at the edge of the pit, similar to frog construction—in other words, to form a frog without the wing rails. This permits—or compels—the use of a shorter table.

3. Adjustment of tracks to suit the selected angle for stalls, putting in frogs wherever a rail crosses another and, if necessary, introducing crotch frogs. The design must be carefully planned in this case, so that the

dead ends of rails around the turntable coping can be accommodated without interfering with each other, and so that the frog point nearest the pit is sufficiently distant from the pit to permit the frog to be put in and held securely to its place.

The width of the house to be constructed is determined by the length of the largest engine in service, with ample allowance to swing doors inwardly, if they are to be hung that way, and ample passageway width at the head end of the engine, along the inside of outer walls. As a heavy engine of modern design is 78 ft. long, over all,[1] the distance, clear, between the inner and outer walls, should be 92 or 94 ft., which will leave a space of 7 or 8 ft. at each end, as passageways.

Some houses are planned for engines to be backed in, standing with the front end toward the turntable pit. Aside from having the engine in position to head out and toward the table when required for service, there seems to be little in favor of this arrangement. It is decidedly better to have the head end, with the machinery part, nearer the outside wall, with the advantage of light, room, machinery, etc., for making repairs.

Much of the loss of engine service is likely to occur at the engine house and its tributary plants. A careful record was kept of one engine for 30 days, showing that it was held at the engine house (waiting to get over ashpit, cleaning fires, coaling, watering, in for repairs and minor delays) 22.6 per cent. of the entire time; in actual road-running service, 28.7 per cent.; delay on account not steaming, hot boxes, trouble with drawbars and brakes, 1.9 per cent.; while the remainder of the time—46.8 per cent.—was chargeable to the following items, in the order of the amount of time consumed: switching, wrecks, trains ahead, orders, cleaning fires on road, coal and water on road, waiting orders at engine house, yards blocked, passing trains, and sundry small delays.

A typical engine-house layout, with the usual facilities, is that at Jackson Junction, Mich., on the Michigan Central, shown in plan in Fig. 175.

Ashpit tracks Nos. 1 and 2 run to the turntable direct. The approach of the depressed track for ash cars is laid on a 2 per cent. grade. The coal elevator has a capacity of 500 tons.

The sanding boxes are placed on the corner of the coal elevator adjoining the ashpit tracks, on the corner of the sand house proper. The sanding is done by means of drop pipes handled by hostlers, the time for filling the largest boxes being about 15 sec. The sand house is equipped with three stove dryers; sand is elevated into sanding boxes

[1] The articulated (Mallet) type is often 88 ft. long. One built by the Baldwin Locomotive Company for the Pennsylvania is 88 ft. 2 in., engine and tender, with a total engine-wheel base of 57 ft. 5 in. The largest in service is an articulated compound on the Santa Fé, 108 ft. 1.5 in., with engine-wheel base of 66 ft. 5 in.

by means of compressed air. Storage is provided for about 12 car loads of wet sand, which is unloaded from cars placed on the sand house and storing tracks. The sanding box on ashpit track No. 2 is large, having a capacity of about 10 cu. yd., and out of this box sand needed for remote points is loaded by means of a drop spout or chute into cars placed on the sand-house track. Nine or ten yards of sand can be loaded in this way in a few moments.

Each of the ashpit tracks is provided with a 10-in. water column and tenders are filled very quickly, the filling of tenders being the last operation before engines are put on the turntable. This is not as the plant was planned, it being intended that the knocking out of the fire should be the last operation, but conditions of space made that impracticable.

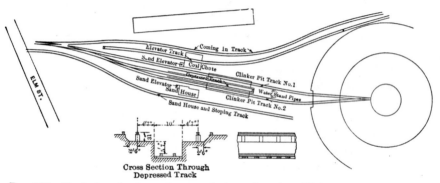

Fig. 175.—Typical engine-house lay-out, Jackson Junction, Mich.—Michigan Central.

The cross-section of the ashpit track shows the general plan, the inner rail supported on cast-iron piers jacketed with No. 10 iron, the remaining space on the inside filled with concrete and tie rods at 10-ft. spaces provided along the open space of the ash tracks to prevent the possibility of rails spreading. The ashpits and depressed track are of solid concrete and good drainage is provided. Two hydrants are arranged on each ash track for wetting cinders, and a steam pipe is provided for thawing out ash pans and grates when that is needed.

Engines arriving off the road are left on the "coming-in track." When they arrive in quick succession, as is the rule in winter or during seasons of heavy traffic, no attempt is made to coal all on the north side of the elevator, hostlers usually alternating, that is, one is coaled on the north side and the next on the south side, or, if necessary, several engines are taken off of the coming-in track at once and coaled on ashpit track No. 1. In this way it will be observed that, when, for example, it is necessary to remove the sixth engine in the line, the first five engines can be taken at once on the ashpit track No. 1, and the engine that is most desired can then be coaled on the coming-in track, after which it can be

Fig. 176.—Engine terminal Central New Jersey at Jersey City.

taken around onto ashpit track No. 2, sanded, fire-cleaned, watered and
housed, quickly after arrival.

Six hostlers and six ashpit men are regularly employed, three of each
for the day and night shifts respectively, and in addition to the duty of
cleaning fires, the ashpit men also attend the switches at the west end,
unload the green sand, run the dryers, elevate the dry sand to the sanding
boxes, attend to water columns and shovel the ashes on the cars on the
depressed track.

For the coal elevator there is one elevator man, one dumper and one
loader for each of the day and night shifts, or seven men all told, including
the fuel foreman.

One of the best engine terminals is that of the Central of New Jersey,
Jersey City (Fig. 176). The coaling station is shown in Fig. 202, the

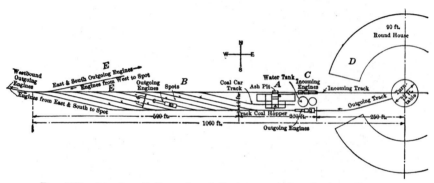

Fig. 177.—American Railway Association's suggested engine-house lay-out.

ashpits in Fig. 211. The "peak" requires the handling of over 250
engines a day. There are two roundhouses; with 32 and 34 stalls—each
with its 100-ft. turntable and electric tractor.

The plan which a committee of the American Railway Association
recommends is shown in Fig. 177. It provides a set of tracks upon
which incoming engines can be spotted by the road crew, where they are
left until the hostlers take them out for coaling, cleaning fires and housing.
The object of the spot tracks is to permit the last engine to be the first
one housed, if such is desired. This plan, it will be noted, requires
much space, longitudinally. It could not, therefore, be utilized at all
points.

The Association made the following general recommendations relative to the facilities which an engine house should have:

1. What is known in the yard language as a "spot"—a system of tracks
connected to the inbound track in the yard, also connected to the main coal
track leading to the roundhouse table; this system of tracks to be so designed
as to enable at least 10 engines to be delivered by inbound engine crews, any

one of which can be moved to the coal chute, in preference to the other nine, at any time.

2. An outbound "spot" track and a water crane, so that outbound engines may take a full tank of water just before leaving; also water cranes so that inbound engines may take water immediately after taking coal.

3. A double ashpit and means of wetting down and cleaning ash pans economically.

4. Method of loading ashes into the ordinary steel-car equipment by means of conveyors.

5. Turntable not less than 85 ft. with (preferably) an electric motor as power for handling same.

6. Door with at least 35 per cent glass for lighting purposes; also locks at top and bottom and posts so that the doors may be locked open as well as locked shut.

7. Smoke jacks so arranged that engines may be moved a quarter of a turn, and equipped with suction ventilators so that the harder the wind the stronger the up draft.

8. A system of ventilators on top of the roundhouse for catching the steam and other waste products from a locomotive.

9. Water pipes, air pipes, blow-off pipes, steam pipes and a good-sized steam supply pipe and taps for these for each pit.

10. A permanent, sanitary, dry floor; not a gravel or cinder floor, but a concrete foundation with wooden blocks set on edge, filled in between with tar and cement, and so fitted in as to drain any water into the pits.

11. A tool room for the care of all general roundhouse tools.

12. A wash room for engine crews, lockers for their extra clothing, etc.

13. A centrally located office, and telephone facilities for the foreman.

14. The low, flat roof of roundhouses is to be discouraged on account of the drippings in cold weather, and the impossibility of properly ventilating same.

The objections to the plan in Fig. 177 of the committee of the American Railway Association, as seen from an operating viewpoint, are:

(*a*) Too many switches to look after and too much switch cleaning for the engineering department to attend to at times, when, owing to snow storms and extreme low temperature, the limited number of men usually available for such purposes are kept busy keeping yard tracks open for operation.

(*b*) A switchman would necessarily have to be provided to attend "spot" switches.

(*c*) Conveyors for loading ashes are rather expensive, often out of order when most needed, and, as a rule, are unnecessary. The depressed track for ash loading is free from breakdowns and always in shape to use. Modern steel cars are not suitable for ash work, inasmuch as the bottom dumps provide a poor means of distributing ashes along the right of way for ballast, for which purpose, in most cases, they are used.

(*d*) The coal elevator and sand house should not be as closely adjacent as this plan provides, because of congestion likely to arise in handling and inability to expand, if necessary.

(*e*) The cinder, or ashpit, should be located on the house track as near to the door as possible, in order to curtail, to the minimum, the handling of engines without fire. It is often necessary to have fires drawn before an engine is put in house to enable repairs to be made in and about fire box.

(f) Incoming tracks and outgoing tracks should be as distinctly separate as possible, otherwise delays will be common to outgoing engines unless the tracks shown in the plan are double, in which event more switch throwing would be necessary—an operation that should be eliminated as far as practicable.

With the exception of the above features, the general idea shown in the committee's plan is good and would certainly provide a means of handling power very promptly.

A committee of the American Railway Engineering Association made the following recommendations in connection with the design and equipment of engine houses:

Clear opening of entrance doors not less than 13 ft. width; 16 ft. height.

Doors easily operated, to fit snugly, easily repaired and maintained, and admit use of small doors. Drop pits for handling truck, driving and trailer wheels.

General distribution of illumination between pits by arranging a number of lights to avoid shadows and to give good light for workmen at the sides of the locomotives; plugged outlets for incandescent lamps in each alternate space between pits.

Engine pits not less than 60 ft. length, convex floor, drainage toward the turntable, the walls and floors may be concrete, provision should be made for support of jacking timbers.

Floor should be of permanent construction, and crowned between pits.

At points where not more than three or four locomotives are housed at one time, and where it is more economical to provide a Y track than a turntable, or where it is not necessary to turn locomotives, a rectangular house, either with through tracks or with switches at one end only may be desirable.

Where a transfer table is used, a rectangular engine house served by the transfer table may be desirable—otherwise a circular form is preferable.

Heat should be concentrated at the pits, general temperature of house should be 50 to 60°. The recommended method for heating is by hot air driven by fans through permanent ducts, which should be under the floor where practicable. The outlets fitted with dampers so heat can be cut off while men are working in the pit. Fresh air supply should be taken from the exterior of the building and no recirculation allowed. It should be delivered to the pits under the engine portion of the locomotive. It should be heated as far as possible by exhaust steam, supplemented, as required, by live steam.

Hoists with differential blocks are generally used for handling heavy repair parts, and suitable provision should be provided for supporting them.

Stall along center line of track should be at least 15 ft. larger than the overall length of the locomotive, to provide a walkway behind the tender, a trucking space in front of the pilot and a certain distance in which to stop the locomotive or to move it to bring side rods or other parts into convenient positions.

In a circular house locomotive should stand normally with the tender toward the turntable.

The material used in construction of the house should be non-corrosive, unless proper care be taken to prevent corrosion. The additional security against interruption to traffic from fire warrants consideration of use of fireproof roof, and dividing the engine house into units of approximately 10 stalls by walls built of fireproof material. When roof is of reinforced concrete columns roof beams should be of same material. Reinforced concrete should be used for walls only where special conditions reduce its cost below that of brick or plain concrete. It should not be used for that portion of the wall directly in line of track where engine is liable to run into it.

The house should be equipped with piping for air, steam and water supply, and, where desired, piping for a washout and refilling system should be installed. Where this system is installed, the blow-off lines should lead to a central reservoir; where it is not used, the blow-off lines should lead to outside the house. Steam outlet should be located near the front end of the boiler. The blow-off pipe, the air, the wash-out and refilling water and the cold-water connections should be near the front end of the fire box. Connections need only be provided in alternate space between stalls.

Smoke jacks should be fixed. Bottom opening not less than 42 in. wide, and long enough to receive the smoke from the stack at its limiting positions, due to the adjustment of the driving wheels to bring the side rods in proper position for repairs. Bottom of jack should be as low as the engines will allow, and should be furnished with a drip trough. The slope upward should be gradual to the flue. Area of the cross-section of the flue not less than 7 sq. ft. Jack should be made of noncombustible material.

In an engine house without means of turning provided, it should preferably be equipped with smoke jacks at each end of engine spaces.

There should be facilities provided for hand tools and for the location of a few machine tools, preferably electrically driven.

Lead tracks to the turntable should line up with tracks of the engine house where possible. Tracks should be on a level grade and provided with stop blocks. Special fastenings of the track rails at the circle wall and on the turntable are desirable to prevent movement of rails, to give good bearing and to lessen damage from derailed wheels.

The turntables should be long enough to balance the engine when tender is empty. A deck turntable is preferable to a through table. At important terminals, tables are most economically operated by mechanical means. Where few and light engines are turned, hand operation may be desirable. Where electric power can be obtained at reasonable cost, an electric tractor is the most efficient means for operating a table, the cost of power is cheaper, and it is superior in continuity of service and maintenance. The first cost is approximately the same as an air motor of equal power and size. Power wires are brought to the table by either overhead or underground method. Overhead has advantage of accessibility for inspection and repair. Care must be taken to protect collector head properly from weather and gases and support collector rigidly, supporting framework to be fastened to steel frame of table and not to ties, and securely braced, the wires large enough to prevent breaking from sleet and supported to framework supporting collector. Lost motion at table increases at collector head. Wires should be brought to pole, close to curb of table, keeping lines as far distant from nearest wall of roundhouse as possible, to minimize the danger of destruction by fire. An underground system properly installed, has all exposed, non-current carrying parts permanently grounded, including the circular-track rail (the only part of system to repair is collector head); and non-interference from weather if table pit is properly drained. But the wires are not so easily repaired, and are more difficult to install, as they must be properly protected from water, and cannot be successfully laid in a fill or on ground where settlement or shifting takes place. Where table pit cannot be well drained, it cannot be used with success. It has the advantage of protecting power to run table in case of fire to engine house, especially in one of a nearly complete circle.

Compressed air tractors are frequently used. Ordinarily the power costs more than electricity and is less reliable. Where there is no power plant, a loco-

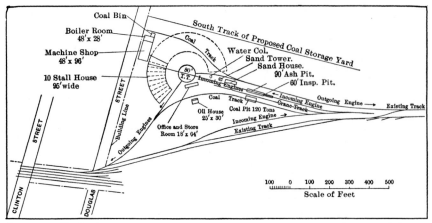

FIG. 178.—Engine-house and facilities, Collinwood, Ohio—New York Central Lines.

motive to be turned may furnish the compressed air, in which case an auxiliary supply should be maintained by providing a small air tank secured to the turntable for operating it before or after the engine is placed.

Deck on table should be wide enough to provide a walk on each side and should be protected with hand rails.

Most houses are of wooden roof construction, with the walls of brick, stone or concrete. The last is used in the form of blocks or solid construction. Stalls are seldom less than 80 ft. deep and many are deeper. Pits are from 50 to 60 ft. long, with the bottom sloping in either direction, as best suits the layout of the drainage system. The center of the pit floor is crowned, so the workman can have as dry a place as possible to stand on when under the engine. The depth of the pits varies considerably, but a fair average is 2 ft. 6 in. at the shallow end and 3 ft. at the deep end. Some form of hot-blast system of heating is now almost universally adopted. Because it assists materially in the ventilation of the building, it has met with great favor.

At the Collinwood, Ohio, engine house of the Lake Shore (Fig. 178) there is a duplicate arrangement of tracks and ashpits for the outside work, which permits of taking coal, sand and water from either side of the chute. There are two outgoing tracks with short pits on each. On each ingoing track is an ashpit capable of holding two engines. Over each pair of ashpits is a pneumatic hoist, each taking care of the ashes from a long and a short pit. A clam-shell bucket is used to receive the ashes from the engine. Next is a 4-in. washout line with 2.5-in. connections between alternate pits. Near the inner circle is a 1.25-in. air pipe with 0.5-in. outlets between alternate stalls.

Figure 179 is a plan of the complete shop, yard and engine-house layout of the Rock Island at East Moline, Ill. The plan gives an impression of roominess and easy movement into and out of the engine house and the various facilities.

Everyone realizes that an engine terminal is one of the most vital spots on the railroad, but it takes a first-hand knowledge of the actual time consumed by locomotives in terminals to bring us to a full appreciation of the tremendous import of terminal efficiency. That the performance of a terminal can be improved by additional mechanical facilities or a stronger operating personnel goes without saying, but the problem of the hour is that of getting better results with the facilities at hand. It is idle to talk about improving facilities until it is known that these are being utilized to the fullest extent. How much more readily would executives grant appropriations for terminal improvements if they could be assured that existing facilities were already being utilized to the utmost limit?

It may be said, then, that an accurate periodic statement of the performance of every engine terminal in terms of the time required to dispatch locomotives in a satisfactory condition would be of the greatest value to operating and mechanical officers. These figures are not a novelty by any means. Several American railroads have attempted a statement of this character and for years preceding the war these statistics were compiled regularly in Germany. The Operating Statistics Section of the Railroad Administration, and more recently the Interstate Commerce Commission, have required some very detailed information on this subject, but each railroad has been left to its own devices with respect to utilizing these figures locally, and because the compilation of this report has proved an onerous task for many railroads. The practical use of these data as an index to individual terminal conditions has been attempted by very few railroads.

It is perhaps due to the fact that a highly practical and economical method for obtaining an accurate account of the distribution of locomotive-hours eventually originated on the New York Central that a monthly report giving the time consumed by locomotives of each class at every terminal became a reality on that railroad. When, commencing in August, 1918, the Operating Statistics Section of the Railroad Administration called for a monthly report of the distribution of all locomotive-hours, the New York Central sought, as did many other railroads, to obtain this information through the mechanical and transportation depart-

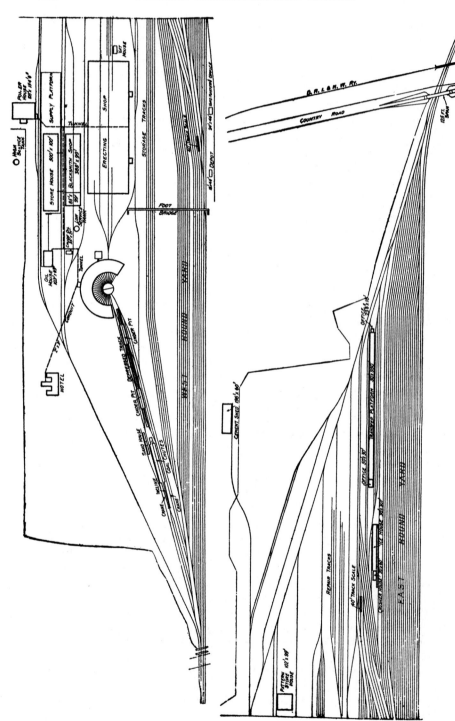

Fig. 179.—Shop, yard and engine-house, East Moline, Illinois—Chicago, Rock Island & Pacific.

ments, on whom was placed the responsibility for reporting the distribution of locomotive-hours within their respective jurisdiction. It was assumed that the mechanical department would secure a daily report from each engine terminal and that the transportation department could obtain the necessary data from the dispatcher's train sheets. It will be recalled, however, that the summer of 1918 was not a propitious moment at which to saddle so elaborate a report on any department of a very busy railroad. Washington had demanded the figures, but proposed no practical means for obtaining them and doubtless more than one railway executive in those busy war days wondered if "the charge of the light brigade" was not to be enacted over again.

It was estimated that, to furnish the required information on the New York Central alone would require at least two and in some instances as high as ten extra clerks on each operating division. After compiling the report for two consecutive months it was found that, in addition to proving an expensive burden, the statistical results were far from authentic. It was then that the officer in charge of statistics for this railroad hit upon a plan that soon resulted in simplifying the compilation of the data and made this report a source of the most valuable information relating to each locomotive terminal.

The originator of the plan, who had in mind a ticket which was attached to his automobile every time it was left at a garage and on which was recorded the time at which the car entered and left the garage, felt a similar card could be designed to follow every locomotive, on which could be recorded the time at which the locomotive was available for service, and other events in sequence.

Figure 180, Exhibits A and B, shows the card or locomotive waybill, which may be considered as the foundation of this system.

The first entry on the waybill is made by the engine dispatcher at the terminal from which the locomotive is to depart and states the time at which the locomotive is available for service. The second entry is made by the engineman and records the time that the locomotive left the terminal; that is, the time that the locomotive is delivered to the engineman. At this juncture the waybill is handed to the engineman, who later enters the time at which the train left the yard and retains the card until he reaches the destination of his run, when the time of arrival is entered. The time at which the locomotive arrives at the final engine terminal is then entered on the card, which subsequently goes into the hands of a designated employee at this terminal. The card is held here until this same locomotive is again ready for service. The time at which the engine is again ready for service constitutes the final entry on this card and is also used as an initial entry for the following card. Each succeeding card thus covers a complete cycle of locomotive events, as is shown in Exhibit A, and carries an overlapping figure to insure the proper sequence of events, as illustrated in Exhibit B. (Fig. 180.)

From the foregoing it will be noted that the figures which are to be used as a basis for the report are not only obtained directly at the source, but in such a manner as to avoid any additional clerical force. These are considerations of fundamental importance in connection with statistics of this character. To insure a complete report, the completed card waybills are first delivered to one of a number of checkers located at strategic terminals. These men have a tally

NEW YORK CENTRAL RAILROAD

DISTRIBUTION OF LOCOMOTIVE HOURS

Division *Hudson*

Locomotive No. *3383*

SERVICE. (Place X mark following service performed)

Passr.......Freight *X* Switch.... Mixed.... Work.... Special....

	Time: Hr.	Time: Min.	Time: AM or PM	Elapsed Time in Minutes (Not to be filled in): On Road or in Yard Switching Service (1)	At Terminals (2)	In Engine House: Mech. Dept. (3a)	In Engine House: Trans. Dept. (3b)
(A) Date *7-23-20* Available for Service	12	05	P				
(B) Date *7-23-20* Left Engine Terminal at *72nd St.* (Point)	2	00	P				115
(C) Left Yard with Train *7-23-20*	3	00	P		60		
(D) Arrived Final Terminal with Train	2	00	A	660			
(E) Date *7-24-20* Arr. Final Engine Terminal at *West Albany* (Point)	2	45	A		45		
(F) Date *7-24-20* Available for Service	2	00	P			675	

EXHIBIT A.

NEW YORK CENTRAL RAILROAD

DISTRIBUTION OF LOCOMOTIVE HOURS

Division *Hudson*

Locomotive No. *3383*

SERVICE. (Place X mark following service performed)

Passr.......Freight *X* Switch.... Mixed.... Work.... Special....

	Time: Hr.	Time: Min.	Time: AM or PM	Elapsed Time in Minutes (Not to be filled in): On Road or in Yard Switching Service (1)	At Terminals (2)	In Engine House: Mech. Dept. (3a)	In Engine House: Trans. Dept. (3b)
(A) Date *7-24-20* Available for Service	2	00	P				
(B) Date.... Left Engine Terminal at *West Albany* (Point)							
(C) Left Yard with Train....							
(D) Arrived Final Terminal with Train							
(E) Date.... Arr. Final Engine Terminal at .... (Point)							
(F) Date.... Available for Service							

EXHIBIT B.

FIG. 180.—Card or locomotive waybill.

sheet with a column for every locomotive operating within their territory, and it is their duty to see that an unbroken sequence of card waybills is submitted for every locomotive in active service. It is also their duty to see that a special monthly report submitted by the motive power department gives a full account of the number of hours that locomotives are held awaiting repairs and in the shops as well as stored. The figures reported by the motive power department are subject to check, as the total time acknowledged by this department must tally with the elapsed time as shown on the locomotive waybill cards issued just prior to and following the interval in the shop. The issuance of these waybills is discontinued during the time that the locomotive is held in the shop.

AVERAGE TIME - (BLANK) ENGINE TERMINAL

	Total dispatch-ments min.	In Enginehouse Mech.dept. hrs. min.	per cent	Trans.dept. hrs. min.	per cent	Initial terminal delay hrs. min.	per cent	Final terminal delay hrs. min.	per cent	On road hrs. min.	per cent
EAST DIVISION											
Passenger											
Last month	609	5 06	39.9	1 16	9.9	1 31	11.9	- 32	4.2	4 21	34.1
This month	667	5 09	42.8	1 23	11.5	1 33	12.9	- 26	3.6	3 31	29.2
Freight											
Last month	438	8 43	39.6	2 58	13.5	2 17	10.4	- 51	3.9	7 11	32.6
This month	593	7 28	37.9	1 22	6.9	2 27	12.4	- 54	4.6	7 32	38.2
Switch:											
Last month	3	13 02	48.8	3 40	13.0	- --	----	- --	---	10 13	37.8
This month	12	1 25	8.3	4 49	28.1	- --	----	- --	---	10 53	63.6
Other											
Last month	3	3 03	17.3	1 50	10.4	- 50	4.7	2 05	11.5	5 52	55.8
This month	2	4 30	22.5	2 13	11.5	1 15	6.2	1 15	6.2	10 45	53.6
WEST DIVISION											
Passenger:											
Last month	577	4 12	43.5	1 12	12.4	1 29	15.2	- 28	4.8	2 20	24.1
This month	602	4 13	39.3	1 14	11.5	1 25	13.2	- 36	5.6	3 16	30.4
Freight:											
Last month	414	7 37	32.6	2 18	9.8	1 33	6.6	1 02	4.4	10 53	46.6
This month	566	7 08	31.7	1 48	8.0	1 25	6.3	1 06	4.9	11 04	49.1
Pusher freight											
Last month	89	3 20	14.0	1 51	7.8	- 46	3.2	- --	---	17 48	75.0
This month	203	3 42	15.4	- 54	3.7	- 47	3.3	- --	---	18 40	77.6
Switch.											
Last month	1633	3 48	15.5	3 33	14.5	- --	---	- --	---	17 10	70.0
This month	1385	4 05	17.6	3 24	14.7	- --	---	- --	---	15 40	67.7
Other											
Last month	44	9 53	26.6	16 13	43.7	- 47	2.1	- 17	0.8	9 57	26.8
This month	21	8 58	18.6	28 36	59.4	- 48	1.6	- 25	0.9	9 23	19.5

FIG. 181.—Monthly locomotive report.

Having passed through the hands of the checker, the waybill cards are forwarded to the supervisor of statistics at the general offices in New York. Upon receipt of these cards, the first operation is that of computing the elapsed time between each event as recorded on the waybill. This information is entered in the four right-hand columns of the cards shown in Exhibit A. This operation is accomplished by skilled computers with remarkable rapidity, as one clerk can ordinarily compute and enter the time on 400 or more cards within a seven-hour day. An additional computer can check the accuracy of these figures by noting if the total time as computed on each of these cards tallies with the total elapsed time between the initial and final entries on the card. When all the required figures have been entered on the card, the work of summarizing these time intervals is greatly simplified by the use of mechanical tabulating machinery, although this method involves the perforation of a tabulating card for every waybill and is by no means essential to the successful operation of the system.

The monthly report summarizing the time locomotives of each class are held at each terminal by the mechanical and transportation departments, respectively, is prepared for distribution within 15 days after the close of the month. The report embodies a separate statement for each important terminal, of which Fig. 181 is a typical example.

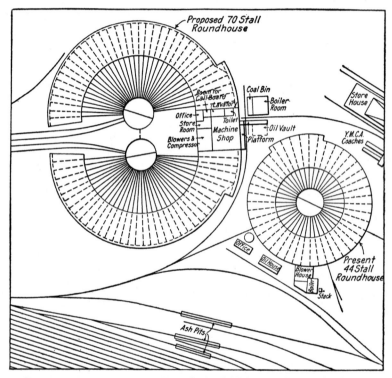

Fig. 182.—Engine terminals, West Springfield, Mass.—Boston & Albany.

There are about 386 engine terminals on the New York Central, serving 5,646 miles of railroad. The report printed does not include all of these, but the data is available from which the performance of any one of these terminals can be quickly determined, or the performance of any group or even any individual locomotive by a process of mechanically sorting and tabulating the cards. The report as compiled goes to the operating and mechanical officers of each of the 24 operating divisions on the New York Central and to as many subordinate employees as request a copy. It will be noted by glancing at Fig. 181 that where two divisions are served by an important terminal the performance of the locomotives assigned to each division is shown separately, and it will be appreciated by those who have ever been a witness to the disputes that frequently arise between the officials of adjacent operating divisions over the relative attention

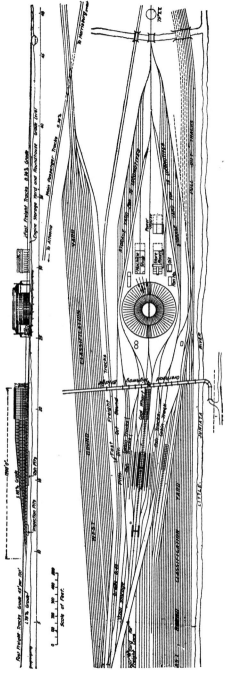

Fig. 183.—Plan and profile of East Altoona freight yards and engine terminal.—Pennsylvania Railroad.

accorded their power in a common terminal that this report will settle very definitely any argument of this character.[1]

The wasteful effect of poor designs may be observed at almost any engine terminal—as where men are found shoveling ashes from a pit to the ground and then rehandling to cars; where a turntable is just about the

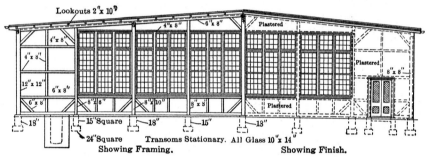

FIG. 184.—Elevation of end walls, Decatur, Ill., engine-house—Wabash.

length of the wheel base of the engines it turns and where engine houses have to care for engines so large that doors cannot be closed behind them.

Figure 182 is another unique development of Boston & Albany engine terminals, at West Springfield, Mass. One house with 44 stalls and another house, with two turntables, is shown, with a total additional

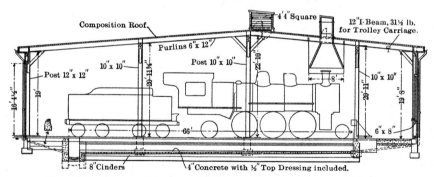

FIG. 185.—Cross-section, through Decatur, Ill., engine-house—Wabash.

capacity of 70 stalls. This plan is instructive in the study of the track layout and location of coaling plants, sand plants, ash tracks, repair shops, offices, etc.

The engine house in East Altoona, Pa., shown in plan and elevation (Fig. 183), is probably the largest engine terminal on the Pennsylvania

[1] F. A. Hasbrouck in *Railway Age*, July 30, 1920.

system and handles more engines than any similar plant in the country. The section through the roundhouse and the side elevation of the coal chute are shown in the upper part of the drawing. Outside of the engine house, there are two storage yards, having a capacity to care for 75 locomotives each, and so arranged as to reduce handling to a minimum. A fuller description of this plant is shown in Chap. XXIX, Engine Coaling Plants.

At Decatur, Ill., the Wabash has a good 42-stall engine house, which is similar to other recent standard layouts for the handling of many

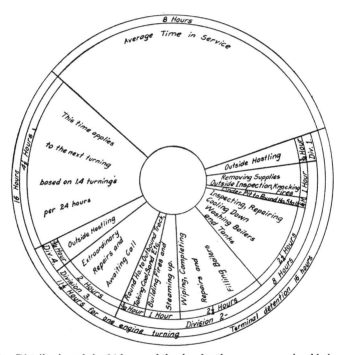

Fɪɢ. 186.—Distribution of the 24 hours of the day for the average serviceable locomotive.

engines of heavy design. The detailed drawings (Figs. 184 and 185) of the elevation of end walls and the cross-sections through engine houses are interesting.

An illuminating chart (Fig. 186) shows the distribution of the time for an average serviceable locomotive.[1] Such a locomotive is turned about 1.4 times every 24 hours—the average time required to

[1] L. K. Sillcox, General Superintendent Motive Power, Chicago, Milwaukee & St. Paul, in *Railway Age*.

turn it is 11.5 hours. There are four main operations constituting an engine turning, as follows:

	Hours
Movement of the engine from the train to the engine terminal....	¾
Roundhouse care and ordinary repairs.........................	8
Extraordinary repairs and awaiting call.....................	2
Movement from outbound track to train.....................	¾

Subdividing the first item, there is the outside hostling; for the second item—8 hours—the operations in their usual sequence are: (1) removing supplies, outside inspection and knocking fires, 1 hour; (2) movement from cinder pit into roundhouse stall, ¼ hour; (3) inspecting, repairing, cooling down and washing boilers and tanks, 2½ hours; (4) wiping, completing repairs and filling boilers, 2½ hours; (5) building fires and steaming up, 1 hour; and (6) movement from roundhouse to outbound track, taking coal, water, sand and supplies *en route*, ¾ hour. The third item is necessary to provide a period for overlapping, to take care of extra repairs and to compensate for slow operations at points where facilities are insufficient; it also allows for margin between the time the engine is ready and actually put in service—a joint responsibility of the mechanical and transportation departments. The fourth item is approximately the average time, after the engine is ready, that it is in the hands of the engine crew, from engine terminal to train yard, and varies according to distance and convenience of layout.

There are four fundamental factors relating to the proportion of time an engine is in service and out of service:

1. Mileage and time between terminals.
2. Demand for power.
3. Terminal layout and the location with relation to the train yard.
4. Facilities for conditioning engines for service.

There are two avenues open for studying the means for reducing the time involved in terminal detentions, with the consequent increase of time in road service: One is fewer and more properly spaced terminals; the other, adequate facilities for turning and repairing locomotives. Reference to the chart shows the proper spacing of terminals which, with a consequent reduction in frequency of terminals and lengthening of runs, would produce longer hours in service. If terminal facilities are available and the proper demand for power prevails, there will be a reduction in the time required at the terminal.

Regardless of the adequacy of any engine terminal, it cannot perform to its full capacity without proper management. To have a well-managed plant, it is necessary for those in charge to have a well-defined knowledge of every operation, considering time, capacity and cost. A diagram (Fig. 187) shows the relative costs of the various operations constituting an engine turning exclusive of repairs. With this, the man in charge should be able to regulate his output and expense in such a way as to operate his terminal economically and efficiently. The various elements constituting the several groups selected are as follows:

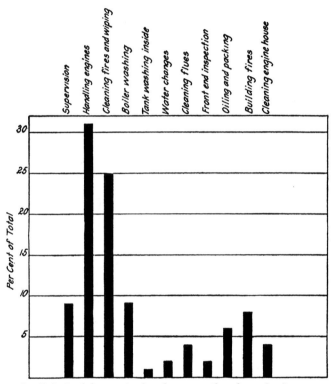

FIG. 187.—Relative labor costs of various operations in engine house expense.

Supervision—pro rata portion of salaries and expenses of foreman and clerks.

Engine handling—outside and inside hostling, watching outside of house, calling crews, drying sand and provisioning.

Cleaning fires and wiping—knocking or cleaning fires, ashpits, etc., and wiping engines and tenders.

Washing boilers, tanks and water changes.

Cleaning flues—and inside of front ends, fire boxes, brick arches, draining and cleaning air reservoirs and air equipment.

Inspecting front ends and ash pans.

Oiling and packing—labor only.

Building fires and watching in house.

Engine-house cleaning.

It will be seen that the cost of handling engines represents 31 per cent. of the total cost of turning (exclusive of repairs). This element is not within the full control of the men in charge. It is represented partly by items 1 and 4 of the chart, and rather reflects the relative location of the terminal layout with the train yard. The cost of cleaning fires and wiping engines, which in this case is about 25 per cent., reflects the efficiency of the cinder-pit operation, which is one of the operations that should be arranged to have proper facilities to keep the time and cost at a minimum. The cost of boiler washing represents 9 per cent. of the total, because boilers are washed on an average of once every four or five trips. This expense can be materially reduced with hot-water boiler-washing equipment and, in addition, such equipment will reduce the time required for this operation.

To the mechanical man, the engine terminal is a facility, or, in other words, merely a tool with which to perform a specific operation in detail. It is a double-edged tool, as it performs two functions. The first is the ordinary handling and care of the individual locomotive in the roundhouse; the other is repairs, both lighter classified and running. In the well-ordered performance of locomotives, it is necessary to divide the maintenance into running and classified repairs. The running repairs must of necessity be made in the roundhouses. It has been the usual practice to do the classified repairs in the back shops, but there is an increasing tendency to do the lighter classified repairs as well as the running repairs in the roundhouses, in order to get more intensive use of the power. Some carriers assign a certain mileage for a locomotive to perform between classified repairs, and, to operate locomotives at a minimum cost per mile, for all classes of repairs, it is necessary to obtain a consistent balance between the cost of classified repairs and repairs made in the roundhouses. The manner in which roundhouses are equipped with repair facilities determines the balance.

On many lines locomotives are sent to the back shop only when in need of heavy boiler repairs, taking care of all other work as due in the roundhouses. It is therefore, a function of the roundhouse, to obtain from the locomotive a specified performance in mileage and time, and to see that every engine leaves the terminal in proper condition to insure a successful trip.

Roundhouses usually perform maintenance work on locomotives to the extent of approximately 40 to 50 per cent. of the total cost of repairs and should, therefore, be equipped with this in mind. Any ratio ranging from 60 per cent. for classified repairs to 40 per cent. for running repairs on the one hand or from 50 per cent. for classified repairs to 50 per cent. for running repairs on the other hand, would seem practical. The ratio between the cost of repairs done in roundhouse and back shop depends largely upon the policy pursued with respect to the amount of work expected from the roundhouses.

It is more difficult to maintain the larger units of power that now predominate than it was to care for the smaller engines that were in use in the past. The modern engine is heavier and more complicated, and requires more consistent and frequent mechanical attention. The

Fig. 188.—Wrecking crane used on the Virginian.

various parts of the locomotive are larger and heavier and cannot be repaired quickly, if adequate facilities are not at hand with which to handle them. A modern locomotive represents a large capital investment and idle hours are of a relatively greater loss than in previous years.

A high performance in car-miles per day is not obtained by train speed, but by the promptness with which trains are broken up, assembled and moved through terminals. A terminal should be prepared to handle without delay any reassignment of power for seasonal loading or other reasons.

Besides maintaining locomotives, and other mechanical equipment, the engine house terminal, and organization—occasionally the car repair shops—house, care for, and man the apparatus essential to keeping the main tracks in passable condition or to open them after having been obstructed. Snow-plows and flanges are used to clear the line of snow and ice. Various types of derricks,[1] or cranes, for clearing tracks obstructed by accidents, landslides, or high water with drifted debris, are used.

The average cost of turning power is now approximately $6 to $8 per engine turning and the average number of turns is 1.4 per serviceable locomotive day. A revision of facilities reducing the time element of turning, would produce a reduction of 50 cents per engine turned and reduce the frequency of turning 0.1 turning per day (say from 1.4 to 1.3), will accomplish an annual economy on a complement of 2,000 locomotives to the extent of approximately $650,000, an amount that would pay interest at 5 per cent. on $13,000,000 which properly distributed, would provide for many time-saving features.

An ideal condition provides a schedule for each operation and then designs each facility in such a way that it will perform its allotted part of the total operation within the standard time.[2] For example, if a locomotive could be allowed 5 min. to take water, it would be necessary to provide apparatus to delivery 7,000 to 10,000 tal. in about 3 min. With the number of locomotives to be handled in a maximum day, the size of pipe, capacity of storage and size of water columns can be computed. If 5 min. were allotted to the taking of coal, the size of the chute, capacity of bins, capacity of hoisting apparatus and other dimensions could be figured.

As some of the operations require more time than others, they should be made the basis for proportioning the facilities of the plant. On account of the time required for cleaning fires and ash pans, the fire track will doubtless be found to be the governing facility outside of the roundhouse. This decided upon, the maximum number of locomotives to be handled in a 24-hour day should be determined and then a peak for some short period should be assumed, as, for example, 25 per cent. of this number in a 4-hour period. The design of the ashpit should provide for handling this peak load with an ample factor of safety, and then the designs of the other facilities can be worked out with capacities corresponding to or somewhat exceeding those of the fire track.

Engine tools are those carried on each locomotive. These usually consist of a hammer, wrenches, chisels, oil cans, lanterns, signals, scoops, firing bars, torches, etc. One of the problems is to check up these tools and to induce the enginemen and fireman to care for them properly. The small tools should be kept locked up in metal boxes, preferably

[1] The "Virginian" has a wrecking crane, Fig. 188, claimed to be the largest built It has a capacity on the main hoist of 400,000 lb. at a 17-ft. 6-in. radius with all outriggers in service, a capacity of 200,000 lb. at the same radius with end outriggers only in service and a capacity of 85,000 lb. at the same radius without the outriggers. On the auxiliary hoist, the capacities are 90,000 lb. at 24- to 30-ft. radii with the end outriggers only, and 60,000 lb. at a 24-ft. radius without outriggers.

[2] R. N. BEGIEN, *Railway Age.*

numbered to correspond with the number of the engine to which they belong. Where it can be done, the best plan is to have each engineman deliver his box to the tool room or other designated point, at the end of each trip, when the contents may be checked up. Where engines are regularly crewed, instead of being "pooled" it is not so difficult to keep up the equipment of small tools. The cost for tools and supplies will average about 20 cts. for each trip. The cost for tools alone will, on larger roads, range from $10 to $40 yearly for each engine in service.

Wiping or cleaning is one of the most neglected duties at the engine terminal—and not the least important. On some roads the engines handling the most important passenger trains are permitted to go out of terminals looking as though they had been rolling themselves in a clay bank. As the size of engines has increased, the fireman has been required to do less and less cleaning. Now he is usually required to clean only above the running board. Where engines are "pooled," the crews naturally take less interest in keeping them clean, the roads hesitate to incur the expense of wipers and the engines receive little attention. The cost of wiping an engine properly and thoroughly depends on its size and condition and, largely, on how often it is wiped.

Organization of the force is more essential in obtaining good results than anything else and without it the facilities provided will be useless in securing quick handling and turning of engines. This subject is treated more fully in another chapter. A good engine-house foreman must, of a necessity, be a good organizer, and upon his ability in this line will depend his successful operation of the plant in his charge. The usual form of organization gives the foreman complete control of all the terminal facilities for handling the engines, with the possible exception of the men at the coaling plant. These are sometimes handled by the operating department. At large plants, where the duties require it, the foreman has an assistant who handles the mechanics and distributes the work among them, seeing also that the work is properly done. It is also the usual practice to have a subforeman in charge of the engine dispatchers, ashpit men, wipers, etc. The foreman himself is thus relieved of much of the detail work, and can apply his labors to general duties, such as the assignment of engines and crews, investigations of breakages, making reports to the master mechanic and superintendent, and keeping himself generally informed as to the requirements of the service.

There is no such thing as an ideal engine terminal, or an ideal terminal operation. From the very poorest to the very best they are compromises. There are so many circumscribed elements affecting each point that, no matter whether built up by gradual expansion or constructed new, the final layout will always reveal some undesirable features. Financial stringency will retard development and restrict new construction. Precedent hampers relocation of existing facilities. A good labor market often overbalances other advantages and designates a location that is geographically or otherwise improper. A compromise must be reached and what is had or can be obtained must be used to the best advantage.

CHAPTER XXVIII

THE ENGINE-HOUSE FOREMAN

The successful railroad man must be large in every way; big in thought, brain and conception—an organizer and an executive; and broadminded. He must be a keen analyst—able to separate the wheat from the chaff and to use the kernel in the heart of the nut. The engine-house foreman must know and study the details of all departments, specializing in his own; he must select the right men, quickly and unfailingly and must, therefore, be a thorough student of human nature.

A well-known operating officer remarked that any division of a railway will give a good account of itself if the positions of engine-house foremen and yardmasters are filled by the right kind of men. The author suggests the inclusion of the chief train dispatcher to make the complete operating trio. With harmonious relations and thorough cooperation between them, the real problems of train service will be satisfactorily met.

The engine-house foreman is responsible to the mechanical and transportation departments for the care of the locomotive from the time it is delivered to him after being released from an incoming train at a designated point (usually at the entrance to the engine-house yards) until it is returned to the designated point for outbound road movement. During this time he must know that his subordinates clear the ash pan and clean the fire; inspect the boiler, tubes, fire box and machinery; make the necessary repairs; supply coal, water and sand; inspect the front end to see that everything is in good working order, and particularly that the front-end diaphragm and netting are properly placed, adjusted and in condition to prevent throwing fire; turn the engine on a wye or turntable; and clean it. He must also keep in close touch with the chief train dispatcher and yardmaster to know when trains are ready to move, so as to have power ready and engine crews on hand to man it. All this may have to be done in less than two hours on each engine handled, although in many instances it is attempted in less than half an hour.

Unfortunately for the engine-house foreman, it is almost invariably the case that the greater the need for the maximum number of engines in first-class condition the greater is the number of adverse conditions affecting his ability to fill the requisition. The heavier the business the less time is available for caring for engines between trips, and usually, too, the greatest demand for power comes in periods of snow storms and cold weather, when it is more difficult to keep locomotives in good condition,

453

and when the problem is aggravated by engine crews falling out on account of sickness.[1] In other words, the time that engine failures and train delays are most demoralizing to the service is just the time when it is hardest to prevent them.

It is necessary, therefore, that the engine-house foreman shall not only know how to make the best of a trying mechanical situation but he must also be somewhat of a diplomat. After hearing the engineman's story, which is usually far more intelligent than the brief and sometimes unreadable scrawl in the work book, he must decide quickly and irrevocably whether the engine is about to fall to pieces or can stand another trip. He must be an all-round mechanic, qualified to determine which work to do and which to slight. This ability is especially desirable during time of traffic pressures, when the good, quick, unerring judgment of the engine-house foreman may save the day. He must also be sufficiently broadminded to recognize that there is a commercial side to be considered.

A capable foreman should be given ample assistance; there is no real economy in paying him the necessary salary and then requiring him to perform the duties of a telephone clerk or a call boy. With the increasing weight and size of locomotives with their many new and complicated appliances, and with the more exacting demands of traffic in faster freight- and passenger-train movement, more time is required in the turning and handling power and more conveniences and better facilities should be furnished. "A stitch in time saves nine" was always true, but it may be raised to "nineteen" when a failure to keep everything keyed up may mean sending out the wrecking train to take down rods or do other work which the engineman and fireman could care for without assistance on the type of smaller engines of former days.

The late William McIntosh, when Superintendent of Motive Power of the Central of New Jersey, suggested the following as an advertisement for an engine-house foreman:

He must be neither too old nor too young.

Must have a good education and a thorough knowledge of handling and repairing locomotives.

Must know how to handle men successfully.

Must be diplomatic enough to keep on good terms with yardmasters, trainmasters, train dispatchers and others.

Must be of a cheerful disposition—an optimist preferred.

Must not object to being on duty 52 Sundays and 300 nights each year.

Must not be affected by climatic changes; must be willing to transact business out of doors in the absence of shelter.

Must be like "Mark Tapley"—cheerful under adverse conditions.

[1] This refers to steam locomotives. Electrical operation differs somewhat as explained in Chap. XXXI and in a chapter on Electrical Operation in "Passenger Terminals and Trains."

Must answer the train dispatcher pleasantly when he cannot furnish an engine that has not arrived.

Must explain how long it will take to put flues into the 99 and what is to be done with the 001.

Must not murmur when obliged to pull one engine apart to repair another, while awaiting the convenience of the storekeeper and purchasing agent to bring out supplies.

Must always have a few engines up his sleeve to meet emergencies.

A regular job and *steady employment* awaits the successful applicant.

While there should be the closest working relations between the engine-house foreman and the yardmaster, there is nothing more important than a well-defined line of demarcation between their territories. There should be no common or neutral ground, and preferably the engine-house foreman should take charge of the engine just after it leaves the yards or main tracks and before it reaches the ash tracks, or any of the other engine-house accompaniments. The point of delivery to the engine-house organization and the point of return from it to the yard organization should be clearly defined. A trustworthy and impartial employee located there should keep an accurate record of every engine movement in and out, upon which all statements should be based. This arrangement, carefully planned and conscientiously executed, will go far toward maintaining harmony between two very important operating heads and avoid the "Kilkenny cat" affairs too frequently indulged in and which some operating officers have tacitly encouraged.

One of the most important roads was starting its fast passenger trains late from one of its terminals. The thermometer had dropped to 16 below zero. The superintendent visited the engine house and found more ice than anything else. The engines were of the most powerful type, but under the conditions could not move themselves out of the house under their own steam. Their trucks were literally frozen to the tracks. Other engines were brought in to start them. About 20 per cent. of the men were absent, principally because of sickness. It was colder inside the house than outside; the steam escaping up in the roof trusses came down as water and snow and the floor was covered with ice. Even after the engines were gotten out by almost superhuman efforts, they were in no condition to handle fast and heavy trains. The principal trouble was that the engines had outgrown the house and doors could not be closed behind their tenders.

To secure the best results, the engine house should be kept as clean as conditions will permit, and by keeping the engines themselves clean it will be easier to inculcate neat habits in the enginemen, firemen and house employees. It requires constant vigilance on the part of the foreman and his men and of trainmasters and road foremen to break up the slovenly habits of enginemen and firemen who leave classification lamps or flags on engines after leaving their trains at terminals; who "forget" to take down marker and other lamps or flags and are almost as likely to have the headlights burning at high noon on a bright day as to light and keep them burning at night.

In a well-appointed and well-handled engine house, the pits are kept clean and the scrap is removed and properly sorted. All parts of the engine are examined each trip and the necessary repairs made; air-brake equipment and other appliances tested and repaired; and records kept by the inspector of all work reported as necessary by the engineman and of all work done. Boilers must be washed out as often as the condition of water necessitates and as required by the instructions governing the road or division. Under the federal regulations this is done once a month in the United States. A few states have laws regarding washouts, but it is to be hoped that such state legislation will be withdrawn, as it is extremely confusing and serves no good purpose, merely adding to the burdens of the master mechanics and the engine-house foremen, in requiring a large number of duplicated reports. Fire boxes and stay bolts must be tested periodically, flues must be maintained in good condition and all movable parts of the engine kept in proper adjustment. Stay plates or frame binders must be kept in place and should fit properly; shoes and wedges should be carefully adjusted; rods must be rebushed or lined when necessary; valves and pistons must be kept tight and in good condition; driving boxes, trucks and tender journal boxes should be carefully looked over and packed, oiled and adjusted.

Engines are ordinarily left by the enginemen on the incoming track, from which they are taken by the hostler and his helper to the coal chute, standpipe, sand house and ashpit before passing to the turntable and thence to the engine house. Before leaving the engine, the engineman inspects it and makes out a report of the work needed. He also reports the condition of the safety valves, injectors, air pump and brakes. This report is deposited by him in a box, to which only the foreman or his assistant have access. The report is used by the foreman as the basis for distributing the work among his force. The engineman then registers, in the book provided for that purpose, his name, his fireman's name, the engine number, the train number and the time of arrival. In some cases he also reports the time that he has been on duty and the amount of rest time that he must take according to the rules of the company.

After the engine is in the house, an inspector looks it over and reports the condition of the various parts. His report and that of the engineman should coincide, particularly as to the machinery. A boiler maker goes into the fire box and makes the needed repairs. The front end is opened and examined every trip in some localities; not so often in others— but this inspection is regular. Boilers requiring it are washed out. In some places a record of engines for washout is made on a board. The hostler or dispatcher, by referring to this board, can place and prepare the engine so that this attention can be given without confusion. Some roads have outside inspection pits, where the engine is inspected before going on ash pit, and it only goes into the engine house if repairs are needed. If no repairs are required the engine is stored outside.

When the engine is ready for service, it usually bears marks, made by the various mechanics, showing that the fire box, the front end, the machinery and all appliances are all right. Often this marking is done on a board provided for that purpose, to which the call boy and the foreman refer when they are called upon by the train dispatcher for engines.

One of the important duties for which the engine-house foreman is responsible is the proper condition of the fire when the engine is delivered to the engine crew. In these days of legislative agitation, inspection and supervision, it is essential to avoid unnecessary smoke. George H. Baker, in an address before the New England Railroad Club, Boston, said:

Fuel saving and smoke preventing on railroads is mostly a matter of *agitation* and *education*. One of these is as necessary as the other, but the best results follow the proper employment of both means of improvement.

Smoke from a standing locomotive is most objectionable when it is produced near a depot or an office building, and drifts to where it causes inconvenience or damage. It may be quickly suppressed at such times by opening the fire-box door and applying the blower slightly. Smoke from a running locomotive is most objectionable when it is produced in a dense volume, right after the throttle is closed. Then there are no exhausts to hurl it high in the air, and it trails back over the top and along the sides of the train. On passenger trains it enters the ventilators in the clearstory, or the open windows. On freight trains it obscures the vision of the trainmen. This should not be permitted. The smoke can be quickly dispersed by opening the fire-box door, and, if necessary, applying the blower for a few seconds. These movements on both standing and running locomotives result in the admission of a volume of fresh air above the surface of the fire, some of which engages in combustion with the gases liberated from the coal, burning some of these and diluting the balance so they escape through the stack nearly transparent.

Handling of the engine crew board, calling the men and manning the engines have become difficult and perplexing parts of the engine-house foreman's duties. The constant changes in the working agreements with the enginemen and firemen tend to confuse; and, as each change invariably further complicates and increases clerical work in connection therewith, this part of the foreman's work is not a bed of roses. He should be thoroughly conversant with the operating rules and the working agreements with the road- and shopmen, to prevent unnecessary controversies. The rosters of the enginemen and firemen, showing their ages in service and their seniority ratings, are usually made up once a year, in the office of the superintendent or master mechanic. The assignment of men to engines, unless "pooling" is in vogue, is also usually handled by the master mechanic and follows seniority lines.

"Pooling" engines—also termed "chain-gang" and "first-in-first-out"—consists of running all freight locomotives in turn, starting the first engine arriving on the first train departing, without reference to crews. By this method more engine mileage may be made, in theory at least, because engines may continue in movement, while crews are obtaining rest. Whether the additional mileage obtained offsets the loss due to lack of care in maintaining the machine, which regular crews almost invariably give, is a question on which the ablest managers differ. Sometimes "pooling" applies to locomotives handling ordinary freight only, regular locomotives being kept on the more important fast freight trains. "Pooling" has been done on passenger trains, and in a few instances attempts have been made to put passenger engines and freight engines into the same pool. In such cases a compromise type of engine for both kinds of service is essential.

Between 85 and 90 per cent. of the fuel used on railroads is consumed by the locomotives. Therefore, the importance of fuel conservation is apparent. Not all the fuel waste takes place on the line, although that part of the work must not be minimized. There is much fuel consumed in "stand-by" losses, much through unnecessary maintenance of steam pressure and a vast amount may be chargeable to indifferent or incompetent repair or maintenance work in shops and in roundhouses. The engineman and the fireman have no control over fuel waste due to cylinders out of round, valve gear out of square, leaky valve stems and pistons and other imperfections. Careful, painstaking preparation of the locomotive is necessary—first in the shop, then in the engine house. In considering roundhouse maintenance, sufficient time must be allowed for necessary repairs. The following remarks are pointed and pertinent:[1]

Transportation officer often requires the turning of the power so rapidly that locomotives do not receive needful repairs. One superintendent saw he was running his engines until the stack fell off and the bell rolled over into the field. He realized they were not fit to go, but gambled they might make a successful trip. He admitted he often had to send a second engine to get the first one in.

If the mechanical officer is to maintain locomotives in condition for economical and successful service, "the stitch in time" rule must apply—repairs must be made as needed. Locomotives are frequently hurried out and fail, necessitating the use of a second engine, which many times has to give up a train of inferior class to take a superior train to a terminal. Such practices cause delays and congestion on the railroad and could be avoided generally if locomotives received necessary repairs.

[1] Leslie R. Pyle, *Railway Age*, Jan. 23, 1920.

The maintenance of the boiler and firebox is the first consideration. The boiler should be kept clean by frequent and thorough washings, preferably with hot water. It is generally accepted that hot-water washout plants materially reduce the time required to wash boilers, and, by using waste steam to heat the water used for washing and filling, a direct fuel saving is accomplished.

Sufficient pressure should be used, with nozzles designed so that the water will reach all parts of the boiler. With well-located washout plugs it will be possible to clean the boiler thoroughly at each washout if where water contains scale-forming elements some form of water treatment is used.

There is a decided loss in heat transmission when boiler sheets are allowed to accumulate a scale deposit. Water treatment and thorough boiler washing will practically eliminate scale from locomotive boilers in any kind of water. When boilers are kept clean, it is comparatively easy to maintain the flues free from leaks.

An inspection of the flues should be made each trip, and when necessary they should be calked, or expanded and calked. Where flues are welded in, welding outfits should be maintained at terminals, so that when the welds break they can be rewelded. Fire-box leaks, even though they do not cause failures, waste fuel and, where locomotives are allowed to run with flues in a condition that causes failures or near failures, an excessive amount of fuel is consumed. Flues which will not make a successful trip should be changed.

Any neglect in the maintenance of any part of the grates or shaking apparatus discourages the intelligent use of grates by engine crews. They should be thoroughly maintained.

Frequent inspections should be made in the front end. When reports are made that the engine does not steam, no change in the draft appliances should be made. The steam pipes should be subjected to a hydrostatic test to determine whether there are any leaks in the superheater elements or return bends, steam pipes, at the base of nozzle stand or at the base of the nozzle tip. If everything is tight and set to adopted standard, someone should ride the engine to locate the trouble. The real trouble should be located. No change should be made in appliances or reduction in nozzle, except for weather or special fuel conditions.

It should be known by inspection that flues, both on superheated and non-superheated locomotives, are kept clean. Nearly all roads have flue-cleaning organizations, but it is necessary to check up the work of these men to insure their doing it thoroughly. The loss in fuel due to stopping up of large flues on superheated locomotives varies from 0.04 to 2.6 per cent. with five to seven flues plugged, to 21 to 24 per cent. with 18 flues plugged.

Valves out of square through lost motion in the valve gear or accident should be squared up immediately. A lame engine advertises itself to everyone.

Cylinder and valve rings should be renewed when necessary to prevent blows, which are exceedingly wasteful of steam and materially affect the hauling power of the locomotive. Many roads have adopted a 30-day inspection of cylinder and valve rings. Such inspection frequently develops worn rings which would not be reported. This practice is recommended. If an engine has been out of the shop for a long while and the cylinders have become worn $\frac{1}{8}$ in. or more, they should be rebored and fitted with packing rings turned to fit the rebored cylinders.

Hot-box reports should receive prompt attention. If a locomotive is equipped for the use of water on hot bearings developing en route, it should be known that there is no stoppage in the line of water travel to insure an available supply of water when the need arises. Water-cooling equipment on locomotives does not relieve the roundhouse from giving prompt attention to defects causing hot bearings.

Allowing locomotives due for the shop in two or three months to run with valves out of square, with cylinders blowing, with leaky flues or with some defect which materially affects the successful operation of the locomotive is expensive. Repairs are not made because at some time in the future the locomotive is expected to go in the shop. The money wasted by not making repairs which would have permitted the economical and successful operation of the locomotive would be saved many times over while an engine is waiting to go to the shop.

Auxiliary devices, such as bell ringers, head-light dynamos, fire doors, steam grate shakers, power-reverse gear, should be kept in good repair. Many of them are on to increase the economy of operation; unless maintained, the effect is the opposite.

Lost motion in power-reverse gear levers and connections and air leaks in the piping should not be permitted. These two things taken care of and the packing well maintained, there should be little trouble from reverse gears creeping. Usually, the engineer is relieved from oiling the reverse gear and oftentimes this is neglected in the roundhouse, resulting in a dry piston, which means a slow-acting gear.

Injectors should be maintained so that they will go to work without excessive attention on the part of the engine crew. One of the most annoying things with which an engineman has to contend is an injector which will not go to work unless fussed with for some time. This causes unnecessary safety-valve operation and oftentimes an actual neglect of the fire, all contributing to fuel waste.

Fire doors of the manually operated type should be evenly balanced, insuring ease of operation, and equipped with a good latch on the door to hold it open when the track is rough or when going around curves. It is impossible to fire well if the door closes while the fire is being put in. The chain should be hung so that the fireman can reach it and open the door with a minimum of effort; he should be able to open the door and close it between each scoopful of coal fired, and hardly know the door is there.

Safety valves should be coordinated with the steam gage so that the blow-back will not be more than 3 or 4 lb.

The apron between the deck of the locomotive and the shovel sheet should be level. An apron which is curved or bent in any manner makes it difficult for the fireman to stand securely while firing. To enable skilful firing, there should be no hindrance to a full, easy play of the muscles. Bent or curved aprons and roughed shovel sheets hamper the fireman materially. The shovel sheet should be level and free from any obstructions which will interfere with the movement of the shovel over the sheet and should extend back far enough into the coal to allow the fireman to get practically all the coal out of the pit. A coal guard should be placed in the right gangway to prevent coal from being pushed out.

Brick arches should be properly maintained.

Steam leaks around the locomotive are a federal defect and are wasteful of steam.

The air-brake system on a locomotive should be maintained free from leaks and the compressor should be in first-class condition.

It is necessary to use a drifting throttle on superheated locomotives to insure good lubrication, and the engineer should be provided with a throttle that will stay set in any position desired. Many throttles of necessity are shut off entirely or are nearly wide open and the engineer has to use a stick or try and hold the throttle in a drifting position, which cannot be done successfully.

Engineers must be encouraged to make out the necessary reports for the guidance of the roundhouse foremen in maintaining the locomotives. A locomotive inspector, preferably an engineman, to meet incoming engines while the crews are still on them, talk with the crew about the locomotive performance, help them make necessary tests to determine blows, and other defects, assist the engineer in making out his work report and possibly make out a separate one and then check the work done on the locomotive when it comes out of the roundhouse, can be of untold value to any mechanical organization, as these men not only uncover many defects but help educate the engineman to make out intelligent work reports, saving the mechanics considerable time in hunting for defects shown by vague reports.

After the actual mechanical work of preparing the engine for service has been finished, the transportation officer, cooperating with the mechanical officer, makes it feasible to place a definite order for the locomotive for a certain time. Definite printed instructions should be posted in every roundhouse showing just how far in advance of leaving time each class of power should be fired up and just how the fire should be built. The fire builders should follow this line-up.

To prevent pops opening in firing up, the blower should be shut off before the maximum steam pressure has been reached. This implies that the instructions to the fire builder provide against any heavy firing which would have built up too heavy a fire before leaving time.

When air-brake men test the air pump and brakes, they should not put more coal in the fire box and run the pressure up to the maximum, going away and leaving the pops blowing indefinitely.

Often, when the fire is built, an excessive amount of water is put into the boiler. When the engine is taken out of the house and placed on the storage track so full of water that it is impossible to work the injector, there is bound to be an excessive operation of the safety valves. When the engine crew arrives and the boiler is full, it is impossible for the fireman to build up the right kind of a fire without the loss of a great deal of fuel through the safety valves. The boiler should be filled with enough water to prevent any danger of low water before sufficient steam pressure is obtained to work the injectors. The fire should be built up gradually, using just enough fuel to raise the temperature sufficiently high to make all necessary tests before the engine goes into service.

From 20 to 30 per cent. of the total fuel consumed by the locomotive is used around terminals and there is room for real economy in the building of fires, if it is systematically supervised.

After the fire is built and the engine taken out of the house, just enough fire should be maintained to keep sufficient water in the boiler to prevent low water. With the boiler so supplied, it is possible for the fireman to build up a fire of the right depth without excessive popping.

Hostlers should be taught by demonstration the way the fire should look when the engine is taken out of the roundhouse, and inspection should be made of every fire before taking the engine out of the house.   When poor fires are being built, a report should be made to the roundhouse foreman to stop such practice.   Lack of attention to fire building, resulting in poor fires being turned out of the round-house, has caused many delays due to cleaning fires between terminals.

Cylinder cocks should always be opened and the engine started slowly when being taken out of the house or moved around the terminal by the engine watch-man or hostlers.   The cylinders nearly always contain water and, unless cylinder cocks are open and the engine is moved slowly, this water is worked directly through the cylinder and out the stack.   Many cylinder leaks are doubtless caused by working water through the cylinders around terminals.

When engines are placed on the outgoing track, all tools and oil cans should be on the engine in good condition, so the crew will not have to run around look-ing for supplies, which takes time away from their regular duty of preparing the locomotive.   Incoming locomotives should be despatched with the greatest possible speed to insure all of the time possible in the roundhouse for necessary work.   If the roundhouse is too small to handle the business, it is better to take out the engine which has been repaired and make room for an incoming engine needing repairs than to keep the incoming engine outside for several hours and then, when it is in the house, have to turn it out again without having time to do the necessary work.

There is a parallel between the emission of "black smoke" on the road and the methods of the roundhouse organization.   With the intensive growth of population adjacent to railroads and the increasing number of political aspirants who thrive by capitalizing the supersensitiveness of citizens of communities, the problem of preventing unnecessary—and reducing necessary—smoke is vital.   Many devices are used to reduce or prevent smoke; some are reasonably successful; others are detrimental from an operating point of view.   Undoubtedly, more agitation is leveled at the railroads on the smoke and noise questions than at industries. Cases are known where municipal officials "went after" railroads on both complaints on account of steam-operated trains that were within the town's limits but a comparatively short time, while industries near-by belched black smoke for periods of 20 to 30 min. at a time during nearly every hour of the day and night.   The explanation of this anomaly probably lies in the closer touch of citizenship, and the general tendency to bait the railroads.

A most thorough study of this smoke question in thickly settled com-munities is embodied in the report of a committee on Smoke Abatement and Electrification of Railway Terminals, in Chicago, covering a period of four years.   There were 17 members—9 named by the Association of Commerce, 4 by the railroads and 4 by the Mayor.   The relatively small proportion of the smoke nuisance caused by railroads is indicated in the committee's conclusions on this phase of its investigations:

1. *Visible Properties of Smoke.*—(a) Studies of visible smoke have led to the determination of a smoke-density factor for each fuel-consuming service, which

factor, taken in connection with the amount for fuel consumed by the service, has permitted the different fuel-consuming services to be rated on the basis of their relative contribution to the visible smoke of the city. The services recognized and the proportion of the total visible smoke contributed by each service in the city of Chicago are as follows:

	Per cent.
Steam locomotives.....................................	22.06
Steam vessels...	0.74
High-pressure steam stationary power and heating plants.....	44.49
Low-pressure steam and other stationary heating plants.......	3.93
Gas and coke plants....................................	0.15
Furnaces for metallurgical, manufacturing and other processes..	28.63
	100.00

(*b*) The production of visible smoke depends primarily upon the character of the fuel used. Assuming the use of Illinois coal, it is affected by the length of flameway, by draft, by rates of combustion and by the temperature of the furnace. It is affected also by the amount of excess air in the furnace. Smoke abatement is, under normal conditions, promoted by the use of brick arches and automatic stokers and by the exercise of care in the process of firing.

(*c*) Other things being equal, it is easier to abate visible smoke from large fires than from small fires.

(*d*) The loss in furnace efficiency attending the production of visible smoke is normally not great.

(*e*) Visibility, considered alone, constitutes an insufficient basis upon which to measure the extent of atmospheric pollution by smoke.

2. *Solid Constituents of Smoke.*—(*a*) The solid constituents of smoke, including soot, cinders and dust of varying composition, probably constitute the most important sources of atmospheric pollution arising from the combustion of fuel. The amount of the solid constituents of smoke discharged into the atmosphere of Chicago has been determined. The relative importance of the different fuel-consuming services as producers of solid constituents of smoke in Chicago is as follows:

	Per cent.
Steam locomotives.....................................	7.47
Steam vessels...	0.33
High-pressure steam stationary power and heating plants.....	19.34
Low-pressure steam and other stationary heating plants.......	8.60
Gas and coke plants....................................	0.00
Furnaces for metallurgical, manufacturing and other processes..	64.26
	100.00

(*b*) Not all the solids in smoke are of fuel origin. Of the total discharges of solid constituents of smoke into the atmosphere of Chicago, 41 per cent. are of non-fuel origin. These arise from furnaces used in metallurgical, manufacturing and other processes.

(*c*) All smoke arising from the combustion of solid fuels carries its burden of solids. The extent and character of the solid constituents are affected by various furnace conditions, especially by draft, rate of combustion and temperature of furnace. The fuel value of solids in smoke, under conditions which normally prevail, is small.

(*d*) The absence of visibility in smoke does not imply the absence of the solid constituents of smoke.

(*e*) The polluting effect of the solid constituents of smoke depends upon the size and the character of the particles emitted. The solids discharged by slow-burning, low-temperature fires consist largely of hydrocarbons carrying a large percentage of soot; solids from high temperature fires contain little or no soot, but are high in carbon and ash.

3. *Gaseous Constituents of Smoke.*—(*a*) The gaseous products of combustion consist of carbon and sulphur compounds and nitrogen. The extent of the sulphur gases is dependent upon the composition of the fuel. Smoke resulting from the burning of Illinois coal is relatively high in sulphur. The relative importance of the different fuel-consuming services as producers of the gaseous products of combustion in smoke in Chicago is as follows:

	Per cent.
Steam locomotives	10.31
Steam vessels	0.60
High-pressure steam stationary power and heating plants	44.96
Low-pressure steam and other stationary heating plants	23.00
Gas and coke plants	00.00
Furnaces for metallurgical, manufacturing and other processes	21.13
	100.00

(*b*) The relative importance of the different fuel-consuming services as producers of gaseous carbon constituents of smoke in the city of Chicago is as follows:

	Per cent.
Steam locomotives	10.11
Steam vessels	0.55
High-pressure steam stationary power and heating plants	40.68
Low-pressure steam and other stationary heating plants	23.06
Gas and coke plants	00.00
Furnaces for metallurgical, manufacturing and other processes	25.60
	100.00

(*c*) The relative importance of the different fuel-consuming services as producers of gaseous sulphur constituents of smoke in the city of Chicago is as follows:

	Per cent.
Steam locomotives......................................	18.22
Steam vessels..	0.45
High-pressure steam stationary power and heating plants.....	53.70
Low-pressure steam and other stationary heating plants.......	19.73
Gas and coke plants....................................	00.00
Furnaces for metallurgical, manufacturing and other processes..	7.90
	100.00

(*d*) The gaseous content of smoke consists of the gaseous products of combustion and of air. The effect of air in smoke is to dilute the products of combustion. This dilution is least in the case of smoke from steam vessels and from locomotives, and is greatest in smoke from domestic fires.

(*e*) The air dilution of the products of combustion tends to lower the visibility of smoke, and promotes a diffusion of the products of combustion in the atmosphere. The total volume of the products of combustion as compared with the volume of air moving over the city, by which it is absorbed, is very small.

The situation, which is undoubtedly duplicated in every large city in this country, is strikingly depicted by taking a typical block in the business district of Chicago in which the actual buildings are assumed to to give way to buildings of factory height and in which the existing smoke stacks and chimneys are assumed to remain at their present height. The drawing (Fig. 189) is an isometric projection; the numbers indicate power-plant stacks. It was estimated that within the city of Chicago there are approximately 17,000 high-pressure steam boilers served by not less than 11,000 smoke stacks.

Atmospheric pollution is one of the phases studied, and the conclusions reached by the committee were:

1. Streets and alleys represent approximately 20 per cent. of the entire area of the city; approximately one-half of the thoroughfares are unimproved.

2. Atmospheric dust is not entirely of fuel origin; much of it—probably one-third or more of the total—arises from street traffic and from other activities of the city.

3. The amount of city dust which enters as a polluting agency into the atmosphere is a function of efficiency in city sanitation; it depends upon the standards of cleanliness observed in the maintenance of streets and alleys, and upon methods employed in cleaning.

4. Atmospheric pollution cannot be reduced to a minimum through attention to smoke abatement alone; in order to accomplish its reduction

to a minimum, attention must be given to all of those processes and activities of the city which give rise to dust, or which deal with the collection and disposal of city dirt.

It was decided that the elimination of the steam locomotive from the Chicago railroad terminals, and the substitution of a system of electrifi-

Fig. 189.—Typical block in business section of Chicago replacing buildings with factories, but leaving existing smoke stacks and chimneys.

cation, would not reduce the amount of visible smoke discharged into the atmosphere by more than 20 per cent.; the amount of solid constituents of smoke (soot, ash and fuel particles) by not more than 5 per cent.; the amount of dust and dirt arising from all sources by not more than 4 per cent.; and the volume of gaseous products of combustion discharged into the atmosphere by not more than 5 per cent.

CHAPTER XXIX

ENGINE-COALING PLANTS

Arrangements for supplying coal, water and sand to locomotives, and for cleaning their fires, removing ashes from ash pans and cinders from front ends and for enabling thorough and prompt inspection of machinery and boiler to be made are essential; and such layouts, well located and suitably adjusted, contribute much to the smooth and economical handling of traffic. Without good locomotive service a railroad is helpless; and without suitable and ample engine-house accessories such service is extremely difficult.

The size of the appropriation to be made for a locomotive coaling plant should be governed primarily by the number of engines coaled and, secondarily, by the kind of coal used, whether the mixing of coal is necessary or not and the amount of coal to be supplied during "rush hours." Occasionally, the management may decide that it cannot afford to put in all the appliances needed at a large coaling plant. This impression is often due to a lack of knowledge as to conditions or to a lack of appreciation of the importance of such facilities; otherwise, the fact that it cannot afford to do *without* them would be apparent.

As an illustration: A fairly well-equipped coaling station in a northern climate was without provision for thawing coal in pockets or in cars to be dumped, although ample boiler capacity for generating steam was close at hand. The division officers were unable, for several years, to obtain authority to spend about $1,500 to install the necessary steam-pipe lines. A force of five men during the day and the same number at night took care of the work during the summer and in mild winter weather. During about three months each year, 20 to 25 men were required in the daytime and 10 to 15 men at night, picking the coal loose in the cars and pockets. This number was probably 20 or 25 men a day more than would have been needed had proper facilities been provided. About $7,500 was wasted each winter because $1,500 was not spent to save it and a great part of the latter amount represented material in the estimates which had a permanent value. The actual loss was far greater, since in the above no account has been taken of the waste of time to locomotives which could not be coaled promptly. There are many places where such conditions exist.

Another instance: An outlying small terminal coaled from six to eight engines a day. The plant consisted of a board platform at about the height of a car floor. The intention was to shovel the coal from the coal car to the platform and then from the platform to the tender of the engine. This was done, ostensibly, to release the coal car. Ordinarily, however, the coal was received in cars of 80,000- and 100,000-lb. capacity, which had sides so high that, after a part of the top of the load was shoveled off, the coal had to be dumped on the track and then shoveled from the ground to the platform and again to the engine tender. The difficulties were increased by snow and rain, and by the coal freezing in cold weather. The force employed was not only greatly increased, but frequently the engines could not be coaled in time for their runs. Occasionally, they were run to other coaling stations some distance away, where the men in charge already had troubles of their own. The division officers prepared plans for a coaling plant, taking advantage of high ground, at a cost not exceeding $10,000, which would enable all the work to be done with two laborers a day and not exceeding three during the coldest weather, as steam piping was provided for. As the old method required at times from 5 to 10 laborers, it was estimated that with the proposed plant a saving in wages of $7,500 annually would be effected, and a still more important saving in the time of engines and in avoiding disarrangement of schedules. The appropriation was not obtained.

A simple type of coaling station is that in which the coal is delivered on an elevated platform, loaded into barrows, carts or buggies, tracked to the edge of the platform and dumped directly into the tenders, the platform being about the level or slightly above the top of the tender. The ordinary barrow used for this purpose is 9 ft. long, 30 in. wide and 30 in. deep, with a capacity of 38 cu. ft.

In constructing a coaling plant, ample provision for storage should be made, so as to meet the conditions of irregular or intermittent supply often caused by labor troubles, temporary suspension of mining operations or road blockades. In northern climates it is desirable to store the bulk of the winter's supply before winter sets in, because weather conditions then render the movement of coal on rail and water lines unreliable; also because it avoids hauling the company's supplies during the season when roads are usually taxed to their utmost with revenue freight traffic. Storage plants should be roofed over to prevent the coal from being drenched and frozen solidly, making it difficult and costly to handle. Coal should be handled as little as possible not only to reduce cost of handling but to avoid breakage. In delivering to engines, it should be measured or weighed. As a general policy, a small number of well-located plants of ample capacity should be erected rather than a larger number of plants of less capacity, disadvantageously located. Coal should be taken only at division or run terminals.

The most primitive and expensive method of coaling is shoveling from cars into tenders. If the coal is frozen, the expense of handling is greatly increased. The use of coaling cranes and buckets is increasing and in this manner coal can be handled much cheaper than by hand. Elevating coal to inclined approaches and dumping in platforms level with the tops of the tenders and the use of chutes above the tenders, dumping by gravity enables the handling and the transfer of coal to the tenders at a low cost. The patented systems—such as various types of conveyors—require considerable machinery and the use of some form of local power, but are reliable and efficacious and enable a low cost when large quantities are handled.

For trestles or pockets requiring the elevation of coal in cars, inclines are constructed, usually from 400 to 600 ft. in length, with a rise of 3.5 to 5.0 ft. in 100, although in some instances these grades have been made as high as 8 or even 10 per cent. On grades above, say, 5 per cent., locomotives are not permitted to go on the incline, but use other cars to push with. By using cables and a "bunter" (sometimes termed a "Billy-goat"), cars may be pushed up much steeper grades—as high as an 18 to 22 per cent. grade.

To cause bituminous coal to run freely out of pockets, starting it from a standstill, a slope of 45 deg. should be arranged; in many cases the slope is made 50 deg., so as not to have less than 45 deg. in the valleys of the coal pile. For anthracite coal the angle of repose is considerably less; 35 deg. is usually deemed sufficient.

The approximate cost of handling fuel coal (from the car on which the coal is placed to the locomotive tender) by various methods has been given as follows:

	Per ton
1. Shoveling from railroad cars to tenders...................	50 cents.
2. Shoveling from cars to high platforms and again shoveled onto tenders...	50 cents to one dollar
3. Crane and bucket from storage platform..................	70 cents.
4. Shoveling from cars into bins from elevated trestle.........	20 cents.
5. Dumping from railroad car directly into bins and by gravity into tenders...	3 to 6 cents.
6. Hauling railroad cars by cable up steel incline and dumping directly into bins...	6 cents.
7. Dumping from railroad cars into pit and elevating by conveyors...	6 cents.
8. The same as above, but elevating by air hoist.............	10 to 20 cents.
9. Locomotive crane working from stock pile to bins or to tenders	3.5 cents.
10. Dumping through trestle to platform and tramming and dumping into tenders....................................	20 to 30 cents.
11. Dumping into pit in track and elevating skip by switch rope by engine taking coal....................................	10 to 20 cents.

It may readily be determined from the foregoing whether sufficient coal is handled at any one coaling station to enable the direct saving in cost of handling to earn 10 per cent. on the cost of a modern coaling plant, allowing 5 per cent. for the interest on the money invested and 5 per cent. for depreciation of plant. The company's profit would have to be found outside of this and would be made up, aside from the actual saving over and above 10 per cent. of the cost of the plant, in several ways, *viz.:* (1) quicker handling of locomotives, thereby to an extent reducing the number needed to move the traffic; (2) reliability and promptness with which the service is handled; (3) less deterioration in the value of coal; and (4) prompt release of cars. It must be remembered also that repeated handlings cause a loss in the fuel due to deterioration in breaking it up and to loss by wind gusts. Another loss occurs when unconsumed coal is carried through flues and stacks of locomotives.

Frequently, roads store coal to guard against interruption to traffic due to strikes and other causes. Usually, it is dumped on the ground and reloaded; occasionally, the reloading is done with steam shovels. Coal exposed to the weather and stored upon the open ground is unfavorably affected and the heating value depreciates quickly. Bituminous coal, stored in heaps exceeding 12 or 15 ft. in height, frequently ignites inside and near the bottom, through chemical action and high pressure; and, even though the fire may be extinguished, with much difficulty, by smothering, throwing heaps apart or forcing in steam through pointed, perforated pipes, the loss is often heavy. In loading, especially with steam shovels, a quantity of stones and natural soil is likely to be picked up. The depreciation of any kind of coal, and particularly bituminous, stored in the open is so heavy, and danger from self-ignition so great that the government Navy Department experimented at Key West, Fla., with coal submerged under salt water in concrete tanks. The storage of coal under salt water hermetically seals the gases in. Small pockets of combustion cannot be formed while it is under water. Fires in coal stored under water are impossible. Coal so stored is delivered damp and there is no loss of coal dust carried by the wind. Coal-storage methods are more fully discussed in Chap. XVII.

The kind and size of a coaling plant depend largely upon the kind of coal used. On account of the cost of anthracite the tendency is to use bituminous exclusively especially in freight service. With straight bituminous coal the plant may be simple, as provision need only be made for storing one kind of coal and dumping it directly in the condition in which it is delivered into the tenders of engines. In some instances coal is picked for engines on heavy or fast passenger runs. This only involves setting aside one or more pockets or bins for the purpose, unless the conveyor system is employed. On roads burning anthracite coal, the problem is more complicated. Such roads seldom use anthracite exclusively; nearly all mix more or less bituminous coal with it. They are compelled to use anthracite "lump" on important fast-passenger engines; anthracite "broken" or "egg" on others; and a mixture of bituminous and small-size anthracite on freight. Sometimes the coal is mixed in two or three different proportions for as many types of engines or kinds of service. Others use straight small-size anthracite, while some may burn straight bituminous. It will be seen that this practice complicates the coaling and it requires a well-arranged and rather extensive plant. While it has been attempted to furnish coal mixed in different proportions at "buggy" and "pocket-dump" coaling plants, the mixtures cannot be made with regularity and in uniformly maintained proportions. They will vary considerably and, as the number of engines to be coaled increases, the variation in the proportions will become greater. Where this mixing is not thorough and uniform, the efficiency of the engine's steaming qualities is impaired. This usually happens when the greatest number of engines has to be coaled, *i.e.*, when traffic is heaviest, and, consequently, at a time when engines are required to render their most efficient service. The difficulties encountered in heavy passenger or freight service are well understood. The fireman may run into a pocket of the inferior coal on his tender while ascending a heavy grade or when approaching some other point where the engine's utmost capacity is required. A conveyor plant, arranged so that the coal can be fed to the conveyor and the feed adjusted for each kind of coal, will give a thorough mixture in practically the proportions desired. With this system, ample storage capacity for each kind of coal is necessary.

The belt-conveyor system is expensive, but for plants where coal must be mixed it is probably the best. Where mixing is unnecessary the most economical results have been obtained in the ordinary gravity-dump pockets, where the loaded cars are pushed up an incline over the bins, dumped and from these bins run into the tenders by gravity. The author has handled coal at one of these plants, mixing it in various ways, at a cost of a fraction over 3 cts. a ton, while a conveyor plant may not load coal on the tenders for less than 5 cts. and more often doubtless for 8 to 10 cts. unless the amount handled is very large. The conveyor system, however, is the only one making a proper mixing possible.

A typical conveyor plant is that of the Lehigh Valley at South Plainfield, N. J., shown in Fig. 190.

Another conveyor plant which has been in service for many years is at Jersey City, on the Erie Railroad. It was designed to handle either lump anthracite, "run-of-mine" bituminous or bird's-eye and rice sizes of anthracite, using as a binder a small proportion of bituminous. Figure 191 shows a cross-section and Fig. 192 a skeleton elevation with the general arrangement of conveyors. The carrier is made up of a line of continuous overlapping buckets rigidly secured to two strands of chain, by which the coal is carried along the horizontal run and up the vertical leg without spilling.   Above the horizontal run and at the left of Fig. 192 where a

Fig. 190.—Coaling station, Plainfield, N. J.—Lehigh Valley.

coal car is shown are two track hoppers into which the coal to be stored is dumped from the cars.   Each of these hoppers is fitted with an automatic feeding chute, shown in Fig. 193.   These chutes have a pair of

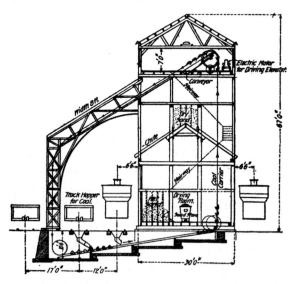

Fig. 191.—Cross-section of coaling plant, Jersey City—Erie Railroad.

small wheels which travel on the top edges of the overlapping buckets. As the buckets move forward under the chute, the wheels follow the serrated edges and the lip of the chute is alternately raised and lowered.

The amount of this movement is regulated by a hand wheel, which determines the amount of coal delivered to each bucket. The loaded buckets on reaching the head wheels of the conveyor are inverted and discharge

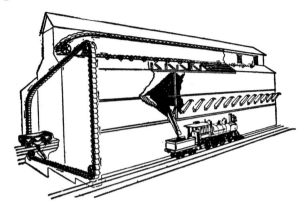

Fig. 192.—Skeleton elevation, showing conveyors, Jersey City—Erie Railroad.

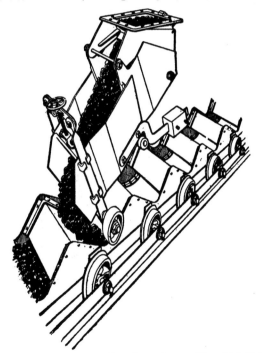

Fig. 193.—Mixing spout, coaling plant, Jersey City—Erie Railroad.

their contents into a chute leading to the horizontal conveyor running along the top of the storage pockets, which have a capacity of 2,500 tons. This is a double-strand, suspended flight conveyor, and by it the coal is deposited in any one of the 14 bins through gates in the floor of the trough which are opened and closed by hand wheels. The elevator and conveyor are driven with rope drives from a 36-hp. gas engine, located in a separate building.

The machinery will handle 90 tons of coal per hour. One of the track hoppers is used exclusively for anthracite and the other for bituminous, which makes it unnecessary to change the angle of the feeding chutes. The lump anthracite is stored in certain bins in the pocket and the bituminous in others. When it is desired to store the mixture of bird's-eye or rice anthracite and bituminous, the two automatic feeding chutes are run simultaneously, the hand wheels being adjusted to deliver the desired amount of each to each bucket in the elevator. When the buckets are dumped on the horizontal conveyor, the two kinds of coal are thoroughly mixed. The 14 bins are sloped at the bottom toward each side of the pocket and engines can be coaled from any one of the 28 chutes provided. Four engines may be coaled simultaneously on each side of the pocket in from 2 to 4 min.

A conveyor plant on the New York Central at Syracuse is shown in elevation and section in Fig. 194. This station is designed for coaling locomotives from overhead storage bins, and is built entirely of timber, with the exception of the beams carrying the tracks over the conveyor tunnel. It has four storage bins with a combined capacity of 820 net tons "run-of-mine" bituminous coal. Three of the pockets discharge directly into tenders of locomotives. The fourth, containing 265 tons, is held as an emergency supply and discharges through a chute into a conveyor delivering into the bins used for the daily supply. The conveying machine is of the "link-belt" design, consisting of an endless chain of 36- by 26-in. buckets. The elevating capacity is not less than 80 tons of "run-of-mine" bituminous or anthracite coal per hour. The conveyor passes under all tracks through a tunnel, up on one side of the structure, over all storage bins and down on the other side of the building. The two coal-car tracks are provided with large track hoppers, through which coal is automatically fed to the conveyor buckets, these automatic feeders being so designed as to deliver the exact amount of coal to fill each bucket as it passes, without waste.

Provisions have been made for storing 96 tons of dry sand in an overhead pocket from which it is delivered to locomotives on either track through flexible sand spouts. The sand is raised from the track level in steel buckets, on a belt conveyor, the elevating capacity being 20 tons of dry sand per hour. The sand bin is separated from the coal bin by partitions containing 12-in. air spaces, in which are located steam-pipe coils to prevent moist air from reaching the dry sand.

Winch heads are provided in each coal track for drilling coal cars. Any water which may accumulate in the conveyor tunnel is removed by a direct-connected electric pump. The entire plant is operated electrically on a direct current of 500 volts, and is lighted throughout by electricity. Eighty locomotives per day take coal and an average of 360 tons is delivered. The cost does not exceed 3.5 cts. per ton handled.

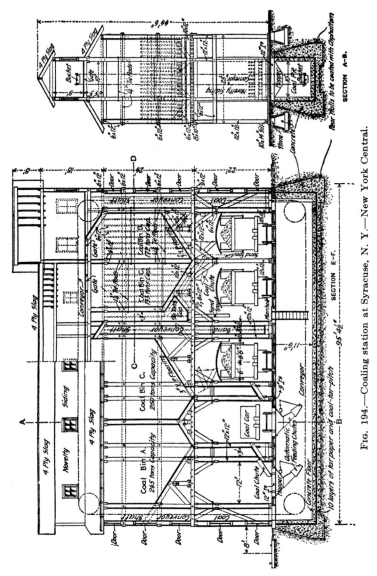

Fig. 194.—Coaling station at Syracuse, N. Y.—New York Central.

Engines are coaled and take sand at the same time. Both operations are completed, ordinarily, in about a minute.

For handling anywhere from 6 to 30 or 40 engines a day, there is in use on the Pennsylvania at Elmira, N. Y., Williamsport, Pa. and other places a method of coaling locomotives that is old but difficult to improve upon for the special purpose for which it is intended. Coal is dumped from hopper-bottom cars on a trestle just high enough to give clearance to a small car of metallic construction, running on a narrow-gage track under the trestle, each car having a capacity equivalent to that of the average tender to be coaled—about 6 tons. At these points the older and smaller engines predominate. When the small car is loaded, it is run on a lift which is elevated by compressed air power in a vertical runway to a point where gravity clutches, or chocks, hold it and from which the contents of the car are dumped into the locomotive tender. The small car is built to be dumped by tripping. Compressed air is used because it is usually convenient, but electric or other power may be

Fig. 195.—Coaling plant at Chicago—Chicago & North-Western.

substituted. At points where no other power is convenient, a very ingenious arrangement consists of a system of pulleys and cables by which the locomotive to be coaled lifts the platform on which the small loaded dump car has been placed. The locomotive is coupled to the end of a cable at a point on the approach track to the coaling lift. It is then moved forward a sufficient distance to lift the platform with the small loaded coal car to the desired height. At this point the platform is automatically caught and held. The lift, length of cables, etc. are so planned as to bring the tender just opposite the platform in position for coaling, when the platform is elevated sufficiently for that operation. The construction of a plant of this kind is not expensive and the cost of operation small.

A typical plant of the covered-trestle type is shown in Fig. 195, that of the Chicago and North-Western at Chicago. Essentially, it

FIG. 196.—Coaling plant at Elizabethport, N. J.—Central of New Jersey.

FIG. 197.—Conveyor Incline, Elizabethport coaling station—Central of New Jersey.

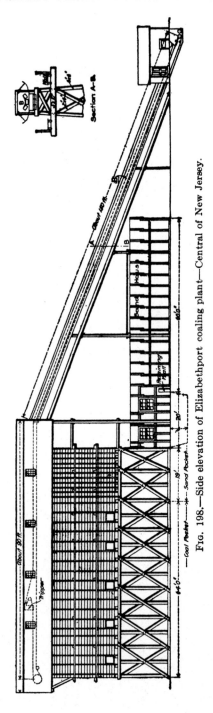

FIG. 198.—Side elevation of Elizabethport coaling plant—Central of New Jersey.

employs 24 "link-belt" undercut gates and hooded chutes, being particularly designed and adapted to the coaling of locomotive tenders of varying heights with run-of-mine coal and to avoid overflowing.

Figures 196, 197, 198 and 199 show perspectives on the stub end and the approach end; side elevation and cross-section of the Elizabethport, N. J., coaling plant of the Central of New Jersey.

This is of 800-ton capacity, is built of timber and includes a sand pocket. The coal pocket has partitions for the division of the several kinds of coal to be stored, and is provided with eight coal chutes, four on each side of the building. These chutes are operated from the engine tender. There are two sand chutes, one on each side of the sand pocket. Two 24-in. belt conveyors are used, which have a three-sixteenth pure rubber cover at their centers. The conveyor A is 35 ft.

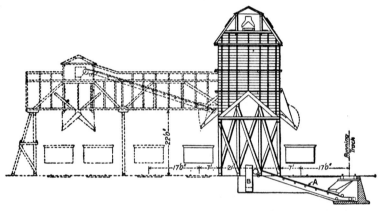

Fig. 199.—Cross-section of Elizabethport coaling plant showing proposed extension—Central of New Jersey.

between centers and is driven by a 5-hp. d.c. Sprague motor. Conveyor B is 240 ft. between centers and is driven by a 30-hp. motor. The coal is discharged from hopper-bottom cars into the track hopper, dropping down over a grizzly to a short conveyor A, which dumps at right angles on the long conveyor B, which, in turn, discharges into any part of the coal pocket desired by means of an automatic tripper. Any lumps of coal larger than 8 in. in diameter drop on a shaft at the lower end of the grizzly, where they are broken up and fall on the conveyor A. The troughing, return and guide idlers are of cast iron and run on hollow, cold-drawn steel tube shafts. These are lubricated by means of patent compression grease cups mounted on their ends. The tripper is of an automatic reversible type, and can be operated automatically by means of a lever on the side of the tripper and stops placed on the rails, or by hand from either side of the machine, the power being taken from the conveyor belt in both cases. The tripper can also be made to operate in a fixed position by throwing out the automatic attachment and clamping the machine to the rails. The carrying portions of the belts are kept clean by means of automatic rotary brushes. The driving pulleys at the conveyor ends have extra high crowns and are secured to the shafts by both keys and set screws, as are also the cast-iron gears. The track hopper and chutes are of yellow pine lined with steel. The sand pocket is lined with Paroid roofing paper and the floor is of 1.5-in. planks, doubled, with roofing paper placed between. The plant is electrically driven throughout, and the speed of the conveyor belt is 377 ft. per minute.

The view shown in Fig. 200 and plans in Fig. 201 are of the Pennsylvania coaling plant at East Altoona, Pa. The diagram (Fig. 183 on page 443) is self-explanatory. If an incoming engine needs no attention in the house it has the fires cleaned over the ashpit, takes coal, water and sand and is run around the house to the east end of the yard,

Fig. 200.—View of coaling plant, East Altoona—Pennsylvania Railroad.

turned and run in on the storage tracks to await call. The four ashpits are 240 ft. long and accommodate four engines each, or 16 in all—eight for the Pittsburgh division and eight for the Middle division. They are located about 280 ft. beyond the inspection pits, two on each side of the coal wharf. The track leading from the inspection pit turns out to two tracks spaced 30 ft. 4 in., center to center, which is the spacing at the ashpits. This allows room for a stub track for ash cars between the pits. A second ash-car stub track is laid next to the outside pit and an overhead traveling crane of 61-ft. 6-in. span covers all four tracks. This crane runs on a steel runway extending the entire length of the pits and has a capacity of 5 tons. The electric hoist has a speed of 85 ft. per minute, the trolley 150 ft. per minute and the bridge 400 ft. per minute. The operator's cab is hung from the bridge close to the runway at one side. The runway has 11 bents and is high enough to give a clearance of 21 ft. under the center of the bridge.

The pits are about 4 ft. deep and 4 ft. wide between the 12- by 6-in. oak stringers on which the rails are laid. The walls are of hard-burnt brick and the floor and foundations of concrete. In the bottom of the pit a narrow-gage (2 ft. 4¾ in.) track is laid on timber stringers to carry the ash-bucket cars. When an engine is run over the pits, three of these buckets, which have a capacity of about 48 cu. ft. each, are run under it, one under the front end and two under the ash pan, and the cinders and ashes are dumped into them. After the fires have been cleaned and the engine moved off the pit, the ashes are wet down in the buckets and the crane picks them up and dumps them into the ash cars on the adjacent stub tracks. The pits drain to sumps with perforated covers and removable perforated linings. These sumps extend 2 ft. below the center of

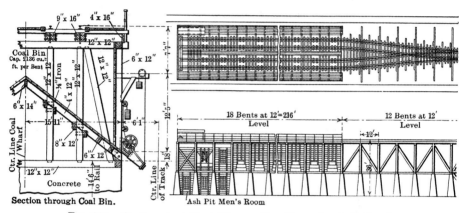

Fig. 201.—Coaling plant, East Altoona, Pa.—Pennsylvania Railroad.

the 10-in. drain pipe and all cinders washed down settle in the removable lining at the bottom, where they can be easily removed at frequent intervals.

The Jersey City coaling plant of the Central of New Jersey (Fig. 202; also see Fig. 176) is in duplicate; there are two dumping-track hoppers for unloading cars, two elevators, two belt conveyors; each outfit has a capacity of 100 tons an hour and each elevator can take coal for either hopper or handle coal from either elevator. Overhead bins of 1,600 tons capacity store and can deliver any one of three different kinds of coal to an engine on any one of ten tracks simultaneously. Bituminous coal and two sizes of anthracite are used.

The plant of the Terminal Railroad Association of St. Louis, shown in Fig. 203, is another good example of the conveyor type. It has a storage capacity of 1,000 tons and is so arranged that seven locomotives can take coal, sand and water and discharge ashes at one time, and 21 locomotives may be cleaned simultaneously. The average number of locomotives handled daily is about 200. The 13 auxiliary pockets, capacity 15 tons each, are mounted on registering beam scales.

Fig. 202.—Coaling Plant at Jersey City—Central Railroad of New Jersey.

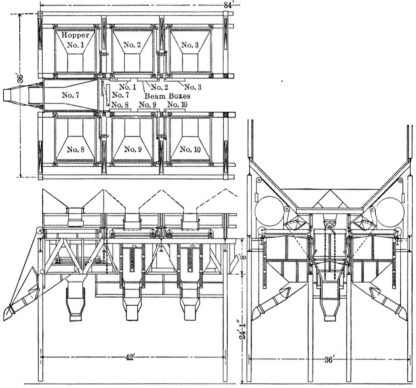

Fig. 203.—Coaling station of St. Louis Terminal Association.

Records of coal dumped, furnished locomotives, and related service should, so far as practicable, be kept without imposing much, if any, of the clerical work on enginemen, firemen or hostlers. Where these men are required to do much of this kind of accounting, it not only takes their minds from more important work but records are inaccurately kept and consequently are not reliable. Very few roads are equipped to keep a fairly accurate record of coal consumption, and to make an equitable disstribution of it. The "adjustments" at the end of the month or other time period are depended upon to balance the accounts. An engineman, fireman or hostler cannot be expected to estimate even approximately the amount of coal he leaves in a tender or the amount he finds there when he takes charge of the engine. Where the coal is dumped by gravity into the tender, a "guess" is made, which is usually far from accurate. In the absence of arrangements for weighing or measuring, the discrepancies are great. Where the barrow system is used—a barrow usually containing a ton—the amount may be more closely figured on, but that too is unreliable. The coal is then bought by weight and charged out by volume. Considering all the uncertainties, the most satisfactory system is that requiring the foreman at the coaling plants to keep the records of coal furnished. Enginemen, and others in charge of engines should not be asked to do anything beyond possibly certifying to the coaling plant foreman's ticket as to the amount of coal supplied.

One disadvantage of open-air storage in pockets or pits, is the liability of the coal and gates to freeze in cold weather. With the necessary tracks, pits and pockets, it will be found that this plant has a considerable first cost. Its operating cost depends upon the work which can be provided at spare times. Its value is great in emergency situations and at points where, because of impending changes, the construction of a permanent plant is unwise. With a large terminal where a conveyor plant is used, a locomotive crane may be very valuable to handle cinders and sand and also coal, during a possible breakdown of the conveyor. Then, again, not only can it unload direct from flat-bottom cars, handle ashes as well as coal and move to any spot where it is desirable to stop the locomotive, but, if superseded by a different system, can be easily moved to another point and utilized for the same or similar purpose. These cranes are always in demand at shop plants for lifting and conveying heavy pieces of machinery, and in freight yards to aid in loading or unloading heavy articles of freight.

A committee of the American Railway Engineering Association considered carefully the question of coaling stations. The principal factors to be considered in adopting a method, as given in that report, are:

1. To compare the relative economy of locomotive coaling stations properly, the cost per ton of handling coal should include charges for interest and depreciation on the investment, charges for maintenance and operation and a charge for the cost of such actual storage as is required in the daily operation of the coaling

station itself. The additional seasonal storage required in certain parts of the country is considered as a separate proposition. Most of these charges are included in accounts prescribed by the Interstate Commerce Commission. These prescribed accounts do not include the cost of switching cars onto trestle or coaling tracks, nor the cost of using cars for storage purposes, all of which should be included in figuring the cost per ton of handling coal.

2. Provision should be made for fire protection, the avoidance of damage to the coal and its delivery in the best possible condition.

3. The use of self-clearing cars should be made possible and ordinarily it should also be possible to shovel from flat-bottomed cars.

4. Storage for emergency purposes and fireproof construction are, in general, to be recommended. In some cases duplicate machinery is desirable.

Where coal is stored in summer for use in locomotive stations in winter, and where the amount stored is less than 75,000 tons, no special mechanical device is recommended, it being more economical to store it by unloading cars by hand or crane and reclaiming it by the use of tools that can be put to other use when not handling coal, such as locomotive crane, ditcher or steam shovel.

5. It is not possible to give absolute limits between which different types of coaling arrangements are recommended for use. Each installation must be considered as an individual problem. Before the selection of a type of coaling station can be based upon the least cost per ton of handling coal, consideration must be given to the extent to which investments in permanent structures and the adoption of fixed-track arrangements are warranted, and consideration should be given to price of materials, cost and character of labor, possible track arrangements, amount of coal desired, fire protection, power and attendance and shifting service available and the cost of maintenance.

(a) Where the quantity of coal handled is small, particularly at terminal points where locomotives lie overnight, it is recommended that the locomotives be coaled either directly from cars or by handling from cars to an elevated platform provided with a jib crane and 1-ton buckets, and from these buckets to the locomotive.

(b) A locomotive crane with suitable buckets is desirable at terminals under certain conditions, particularly where other work can be economically performed by the locomotive crane.

(c) For terminals larger than those previously described, the type of coaling station which should be selected as most desirable is dependent entirely upon local conditions. Where it is required that coal be delivered to not more than two tracks, and where the necessary ground space is available, a coaling station of the trestle or gravity type, with approximately 5 per cent. incline approach, where coal in cars is placed on top of the trestle by locomotives, the coal being stored in bins from where it is placed on the locomotives by gravity, is recommended. Where it is required to deliver coal to more than two tracks, or where the ground space for a trestle type is not available, a mechanical type is recommended.

CHAPTER XXX

ASH AND SAND PLANTS

The ash pans of a 100-ton freight engine, burning anthracite and bituminous coal mixed, or straight anthracite, will, after an average run with its full-tonnage rating, contain from 1.5 to 2 cu. yd. of ashes and clinkers. An engine of the same size burning bituminous coal will yield from 60 to 70 per cent. of that amount and will be very much easier to clean, as the ashes are lighter and will run out more readily. As there is, perhaps, no engine terminal which handles one type or class of engine only, an average weight may generally be figured on for the total number of engines at anywhere between 50 and 100 tons. This figure will give an average weight for all engines of between 75 and 90 tons each, it being assumed that the heavier engines predominate and that the proportionate number of such engines in service will increase. At a plant handling from 75 to 125 engines daily, or, say, 100 engines per day throughout the year, from 100 to 125 cu. yd. of ashes will be made and must be cared for on an anthracite road, and probably 80 to 100 cu. yd. on a bituminous road. This quantity will fill six to seven or five to six respectively of the old, light-capacity, low-side coal cars frequently used in this service which are usually not fully loaded. Many roads have found it advisable to purchase specially designed ash handling cars.

The fire of an engine burning bituminous coal may, under favorable conditions, be cleaned in from 10 to 15 min., running up to 30 min. for the large engines. A small engine burning a mixture of anthracite and bituminous or straight anthracite will require 20 min. to clean the fire; with the large engine the time will run from 30 to 40 min. There is hardly any limit to the time that may be consumed in freezing weather when the engine has been run through snow. Where no special arrangements are provided, it may take, and in extreme cases has taken, three or four men as much as four hours to get an engine ready. With the assistance of steam pipes or furnaces to thaw out the hopper slides and the ashes in the hoppers, it may run up to one and a half and two hours. When engines leak so as to have water in their fire boxes, the difficulty is increased. Leaky fire boxes and flues are among the aggravating conditions which accompany the already unfavorable combination of cold and stormy weather and increased demand for motive power. Men will not and cannot do their normal amount of work when the thermometer is at or below zero and accompanied by a high wind, with perhaps snow and darkness contributing further to the difficulties.

The "Brown-hoist," eight-wheel coaling crane of the Erie Railroad at Cleveland, Ohio, as well as the ashpit and track arrangement are shown in Fig. 204.   The coal being taken from the car is deposited in the tender; the crane also takes ashes from the pit and deposits them in cars on

Fig. 204.—Coaling and ash-track arrangement at Cleveland, Ohio—Erie Railroad.

Fig. 205.—Ash-track arrangement at Bellevue, Ohio—New York, Chicago & St. Louis.

adjustment tracks.   Figure 205 shows a similar installation using a four-wheel crane at Bellevue, Ohio, on the Nickel Plate.

The kind of ash track to be built depends on:

1. Number, kind and size of engines to be handled.
2. Kind of coal used.

3. Weather conditions existing when the maximum number of engines must be handled.

4. Physical characteristics and property limitations

5. Distance ashes are moved.

6. Amount of appropriation available.

Where the number of engines to be handled is small, a cheap arrangement, or even no arrangement beyond a spare track on level ground, may prove an economical one.

Ash Pits in use by the different railroads vary greatly in design, each being planned to best meet the particular requirements and to fit the location selected.

One road has recently built several pits of reinforced concrete lined on the sides with fire brick and on the floors with Belgian block pavement, the top of the walls being protected by $\frac{3}{8}'' \times 18''$ steel plates. These pits are of the single track type, a wall under each rail; inside dimensions 4-ft. by 4-ft. 2-in., the ashes being removed by "Brown-hoist" or "Gantry Crane" to ash cars on parallel tracks at the same level. They are arranged in pairs where there is need for more than one pit of from 150 to 200 feet in length with tracks between for hoist or crane and ash cars. One crane serving both pits. These pits cost approximately $44,000 per lin. ft.

If an average of 70 or more engines are handled each day, the decreased cost of handling will justify an initial expenditure of sufficient money to construct a serviceable ash track.

The author planned an ash-handling plant for a heavy terminal where a structure of considerable height, and necessarily of fireproof construction, enables the engines to be run thereon and the ashes dumped vertically into steel-body cars standing on an ash-car track directly underneath. This necessitates a span or opening through which the cars could be run under the track on which the engines stand; and preferably an entrance at each end to enable the empty cars to be shoved in from one end and the loaded cars taken out at the other end. Although the plant might be handled with an entrance at one end only, such plan would increase the cost for switching and lengthen the intervals between the placing of cars. The operation of such a plant may be greatly simplified by using gravity, the empty car track being on a grade sufficiently heavy to permit the cars to be dropped into position and the loads dropped out of the way. If a gravity empty-car track is not put in, other cars must be used to reach those to be taken out. The clearance on the low track, as a matter of course, cannot be made sufficient to permit an engine to go under the high track. This plan may seem expensive, but anyone who has knowledge of the actual cost of handling ash plants will not hesitate to recommend a comparatively large amount in first cost to enable engines to be handled afterward economically and expeditiously.

In small engine terminals a small bucket hoist makes an economical ashpit operation, but for a large operation the water pit is the most satisfactory. In designing a water pit, care should be taken to see that it is provided with a cover, so that men will not drown in it; that it will have a proper crane for handling the ashes. The principal objection to a water pit is that steam rises from the water in cold weather. This may obscure the men working around it and seriously interfere with the operation of the pit. However, on the whole, it is the most satisfactory from an operating standpoint for the following reasons:

1. It is possible to handle from 4 to 6 engines at once on the ashpit. While this capacity is not confined to a pit of this kind, it is one of the advantages of such a pit.

2. The pit has enough capacity to hold the ashes for a number of days without cleaning, so that, if it is not advisable because of switching or cold weather to clean the pit on any particular day, it need not be done.

3. The ashes are cooled, so they may be loaded into cars without damaging them.

4. Fire in the pit is prevented, so there is no danger of damage to the pit itself.

5. The operation may be conducted with a minimum number of men.

6. The force may be varied readily to correspond with the number of engines handled.

7. The capacity of the pit may be readily added to by increasing the force or varying the time between cleaning out the pit.

8. The capacity of the pit from a construction standpoint may be increased by adding to the length of the pit.[1]

The American Railway Engineering Association gives its recommendations as follows:

The ashpit is one of the most expensive structures on a railroad from a maintenance standpoint. Therefore, a great deal of thought should be given to the design.

The usual procedure at an ashpit is to drop or wash the hot ashes into the pit; this heats up the walls and other parts of the structure. Then cold water is thrown on the ashes to cool them. This rapid cooling causes contraction in the material of which the structure is built, and, when repeated many times, weakens and sometimes destroys the structure.

Another destructive element is the sulphuric acid produced by the water and sulphur in the ashes. This destroys the steel parts (coming in contact with it) at a rapid rate.

Most ashpits are built of concrete, in which limestone is a principal ingredient. Hot ashes cause this limestone to swell and disintegrate, and in a short time the concrete will begin to spall off.

Vitrified brick facing has been used, but, on account of the nature of the work and the tools used, experience shows that it is soon knocked off.

[1] R. N. BEGIEN, *Railway Age.*

Slag and gravel concrete has been used in place of limestone concrete and makes a good substitute. If trap rock is available, it makes a better concrete than either of the above materials.

All types of pits should be equipped with water supply to wet down the hot cinders.

To warn and prevent persons from falling into the pit proper, an extension floor should be placed under the track at both ends of all pits. This floor to be inclined on a 20 per cent. grade for a length of 15 ft.

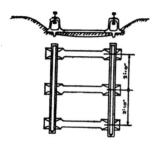

Fɪɢ. 206.—Cast-iron tie pit.   Fɪɢ. 207.—Track pit.

Where 25 or more engines are handled in 24 hours, the mechanical handling of cinders is recommended.

At outlying districts, where few engines are handled, cast-iron ties as shown in Fig. 206, approximately 12 in. high, are used to prevent burning wood ties. These should be located on spur tracks.

Pit located between the track rails of length (Fig. 207) to suit the business handled. The cinders are shoveled out on the track level and loaded by hand into cars or loaded into barrows and wasted at a convenient place.

These pits are sometimes fitted with buckets which are handled by stationary, traveling or gantry cranes. Where stationary cranes are used, the track is placed in the bottom of pit and buckets are equipped with trucks to permit of their being moved to the crane and loaded into cars.

Pit similar to Fig. 207, one side open, with depressed track alongside; the relative location of the top of the car with respect to the floor of the pit to be such as to give the easiest shoveling condition as shown in Fig. 208.

Depressed pit filled with water, into which the cinders are dropped, one feature being to design the pit so that cinders will drop directly into the water and reach the main body of the pit freely; another feature being the easy removal of the cinders by grab bucket operated either by a gantry, traveling or locomotive crane. This arrangement is shown in Fig. 209.

Depth of water in pit should not be more than 5 ft. below the drainage outlet.

Railing or iron posts with chains hooked between to be placed around pits, except across tracks where standard clearance diagram is to be followed.

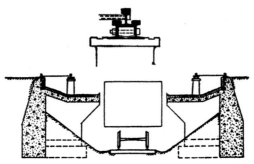

FIG. 208.—Depressed ash-car track.

Pit equipped with bucket or car located under the track and hoisted by mechanical means, the cinder bucket or car running on rails placed on an incline, car being run high enough to dump in a car located on a track parallel to and approximately 25-ft. centers from ash track, as shown in Fig. 210.

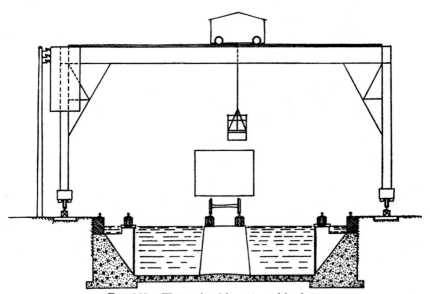

FIG. 209.—Water pit with crane and bucket.

In the Central of New Jersey's engine terminal, at Jersey City are four submerged cinder pits arranged in pairs each 200 ft. long; the traveling electric crane carrying the grab bucket spans all pits

(Fig. 211). One man loads the ashes in half a day with a grab bucket of 1.5-yd. capacity.

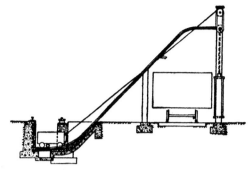

FIG. 210.—Track pit with bucket, power operated.

Comparative figures, taken from actual time studies, covering the cost of handling cinders by various means for a terminal averaging 40 engines per day, show the following results:

FIG. 211.—The ash pits have been adopted as standard by several railroads.

COST OF HANDLING CINDERS PER ENGINE, 40 ENGINES PER DAY

	Hand	Crane	Conveyor
Labor..	$0.26	$0.10	$0.06
Power..	00	.03	.01
Interest and depreciation..................	.02	.12	.04
Total..	$0.28	$0.25	$0.11

The interest and depreciation figures in the foregoing statement include those items for both the pit and the hoisting device.

For a terminal handling an average of ten engines per day, the figures would be as follows:

COST OF HANDLING CINDERS PER ENGINE, 10 ENGINES PER DAY

	Hand	Crane	Conveyor
Labor..............................	$0.26	$0.10	$0.06
Power.............................	.00	.05	.01
Interest and depreciation.................	.08	.48	.16
Total..............................	$0.34	$0.63	$0.23

A method largely in use on one trunk line is that of a pit under the engines containing ash buckets, which are lifted out by a crane or a compressed-air cylinder moving on a transverse crane. The bucket is carried directly over the empty car, into which it is dumped by tripping the hinged bottom. In some cases the buckets have small wheels under them running on a small track in the bottom of the pit. The bucket may then be readily run from the point where it received the ashes to the crane for dumping and from the crane, empty, to the point where the engine is to empty its hoppers.

One cinder conveyor for an ash track consists of an steel car running upon an incline track which enters the ashpit at the side. This incline track extends laterally over a depressed track, which is parallel with the pit and 18 ft. distant, center to center. The ash car is hauled up the incline by a cable and compressed-air cylinder and, as it arrives over the depressed track on which the receiving car stands, its bottom is automatically tripped and the ashes dropped.

The cross-section diagram in Fig. 212 shows the adaptation of a locomotive revolving crane for coaling engines, from cars or storage, and for taking ashes out of the ashpit and loading them onto cars.

Figure 213 shows an ash-handling plant built for the Baltimore & Ohio. It consists of a steel runway 95 ft. long, supported on steel columns securely braced laterally. On this runway is a 2.5-ton, direct-acting, air-hoist traveling crane of 28-ft. span and a lift of from 12 to 16 ft. It is moved along the runway by means of hand chains and the travel of the trolley on the bridge is accomplished by the same means. The entire structure is designed to handle full loads with a factor of safety of 5. The crane, bridge and trolley are fitted with roller bearings and the wheels have machined treads to make the travel as easy as possible. The traveling chain on the bridge projects beyond the runway, but this chain

can be located wherever desired on the bridge. The hoist is direct-acting
and is mounted on a universal swing bearing on the trolley. The working

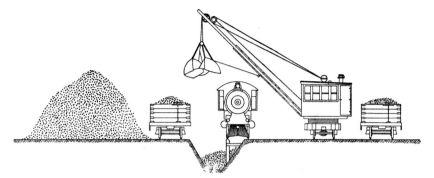

Fig. 212.—Power crane, coaling, storing and handling ashes.

pressure is 80 lb., the air being conveyed to the hoist by hose, carried
along the runway on small hose trolleys over which it is looped.

Fig. 213.—Pneumatic ash-handling plant for the Baltimore & Ohio.

In operation the ashes and cinders are dumped from the locomotive
into large metal ash boxes in the ashpit. These boxes are lifted out by
the crane and placed on a flat car alongside. The plant is cheap to build

and operate. If preferred, the bridge and trolley can be moved by air motors and, for those roads having electric power, electrically operated plants can be supplied. These are more compact than the pneumatic plants. The builders supply the runway in any span and length required, or the crane can be supplied alone, the buyer supplying the runway.

Two sets of ash tracks were put in for each of the engine houses of the New York Central at Elkhart, Ind. That for the freight engine house is 200 ft. long, and has two dumping tracks in addition to two short pits for yard engines and other engines coming from the house which require their ash pans cleaned. The passenger pits serve two tracks and are 120 ft. long. The design for both is the same, a depressed center track with concrete walls and floor. The dumping track is supported at the outer rail by a brick wall, and at the inner wall by cast-iron piers. There is a space between this and the wall of the depressed track, for the cleaners to stand on. All ashes are handled manually, there being space enough in the pit to clean a large number of engines, after which men shovel the cinders into cars on the depressed track. There are several water connections on either side of the pits and also a steam connection for melting out frozen ash pans.

From these suggestions, cheaper and simpler plants of somewhat similar types may be built for less important terminals. The system of columns described in the foregoing is frequently used without elevating the engine track beyond such elevation as is secured in the height of the columns and without depressing the empty-car track alongside. This necessitates shoveling and lifting all the ashes loaded and the removal of engines from the ash track, or a part of it, while shoveling ashes out.

Longitudinal stringers supporting the rails, with a slight depression between, the whole covered with fireclay, make a cheap and efficient ash track to care for a small number of engines.

Engine failures are frequently due to engines going onto the ashpit with low water. Before going on the pit, the boiler should be well filled and the engine kept in motion as much as possible while the injector is at work. Feeding water into the boiler while the engine is standing on sidings or over the ashpit will often cause flues to leak. If the engine is kept in motion, it causes the water to circulate more freely and prevents it from going to the bottom. If the engine is taken to the pit with its boiler filled, the fire may be knocked out, dampers closed, front end cleaned, and the engine then taken to the roundhouse without likelihood of leaks being started. When there is no work to be done on the engine, the fire should simply be cleaned and banked. When washing out the boiler is necessary, steam should be blown off and the boiler cooled through the check or injector pipe, with the blow-off cock open. In no case should water be allowed to drop below the crown sheet until the bare hand can comfortably rest upon the boiler head. , Many road troubles of engines may be traced to the carelessness or incompetency of handling at the ashpit.

Sand is used to increase the adhesion between the driving wheels of the locomotive and the rails, when required, and is at best a necessary evil. It is objectionable because it increases the wear on rails and tires and, when carelessly used on interlocking connections, clogs the movable parts and greatly increases the wear. On a bad rail—that is, one slightly moist with water or grease or frost—its use will often prevent the stalling of a train or enable a standing train to start. Occasionally, the too liberal use of sand, or carelessness in its application, will retard the train (by adding to the rolling resistance of the train) to an extent that will more than offset the advantage of increased adhesion.

On many roads enough consideration is not given to proper methods of supplying sand at the engine terminals and other places where it is required. The mistake is frequently made of not storing in the sand house (or near by) in summer or fall a sufficient amount of sand to last during the winter. In the absence of such foresight the sand is usually frozen in cars when received during the winter and can only be unloaded at enormous expense. In many instances the engine-house forces are unable to unload the sand, or when unloaded it is hard to dry it properly.

There are many methods of unloading the green sand, drying it, elevating it to the supply point and delivering it to locomotives. An elevated dry-sand arrangement, to enable the sand to be dropped into a locomotive sand box by gravity, has many features to commend it. It is possibly a little more expensive in first cost than when not elevated, but it is much less expensive to operate such a plant. There is less liability of the sand dropping on the guides, or other parts of the locomotive machinery, where its presence may produce bad results.

The green- or wet-sand bin should be large enough to hold the winter's supply. This is particularly desirable in cold climates where the cost of unloading and handling the frozen sand is high. The bins should be filled during summer or autumn when the sand may be handled readily, and when the car supply is more liberal and handling capacity of locomotives greater.

Where sand-drying stoves are used, which are economical but somewhat of a fire risk, the ordinary method is to build bins opposite one or more such stoves for the green sand, and hoppers for the dry sand. An elevated track—usually the coal-plant track—is used to unload the green sand by gravity into the bins. The dry-sand hopper is elevated sufficiently to permit the sand to be drawn from it by gravity through a spout inclining toward the engine on the side of the plant opposite the elevated track. The dried sand may be elevated into the hopper by compressed air, derrick or tackle, or by a windlass arrangement. In some instances electric power, close at hand, is used to advantage. A gasoline engine may also be economical.

Side elevation and cross-section of the East Buffalo, N. Y., sand plant of the Delaware, Lackawanna & Western are shown in Fig. 214.

The steam and drying bin is 6 ft. wide at top, 10 ft. long, with vertical sides extending 18 in. down from top. Below this, sides incline at an angle of 45 deg. to the bottom, leaving 12 in. flat surface on bottom, with the necessary opening for dry sand to pass through, detail of which is not brought out in the plan. Three sets of 1¼ gas pipe along each side and bottom of hopper, as well as through center of same, 9 ft. 6 in. long, with return bends, making 100 pipes on sides and bottom, and 31 in center, making a total of 131 in all. Underneath sand-drying hopper is suspended galvanized iron hopper, the top of which is full length of dryer, and 12 in. wide, reduced to 12 in. square at bottom. The hopper sheet is on the two ends only, in which are placed screens for screening sand, leaving a space of about 3 in. between the screens and sides of hopper on the bottom, through which sand passes, leaving gravel to pass over the screen. Two outlet spouts are provided, one for gravel, which is diverted outside of the building, and another for sand run by gravity to boot of elevator, where it is elevated into sand hopper, from which engines are supplied. The entire plant is 18 ft. wide, 62 ft. long; 25 ft. in length of which is used for green sand 12 ft. for sand dryer and the remainder for elevator and hopper, as well as dry-sand storage bin, which is located underneath the hopper. Track elevated 27 ft., where cars loaded with green sand are run and unloaded from drop-bottom cars through doors provided for that purpose in center of track, the bottom of green-sand bin being elevated 11 ft. above the track or ground surface, or 16 ft. below base of rail of elevated tracks. Top of sand dryer hopper 18 in. above green-sand bin floor. The outlet valve in bottom of dry-sand hopper is cone-shaped, running to a point in a vertical position, and inserted into the outlet spout inside the bin when desired to stop the flow of sand, being operated by lever attachments inside, and from the top of the bin, with suspended chain on outside, in easy reach of engineman. Outlet spout 3-in. galvanized iron, telescope pattern, suspended by weight attachment at outer end.

The cost given for handling and drying sand, based on experience, does not, as a rule, mean much because usually men in attendance at such plants perform additional duties and the labor expense is not always equitably apportioned. Some approximate figures may, nevertheless, serve as a guide. One master mechanic reports the cost of unloading green sand from cars to storage bin by hand shoveling, at $5.00 per car. The plant supplies about 70 engines every 24 hours. Adding the cost of power necessary to elevate the sand, it is placed on engines at a cost of about 10 cts. per engine. The average engine requires from 6 to 10 cu. ft. of sand each time it is supplied.

At another plant, of the ordinary storage type, the cost of labor is estimated at $5.00 per day, or, when other items of expense are included, about 20 cts. per engine.

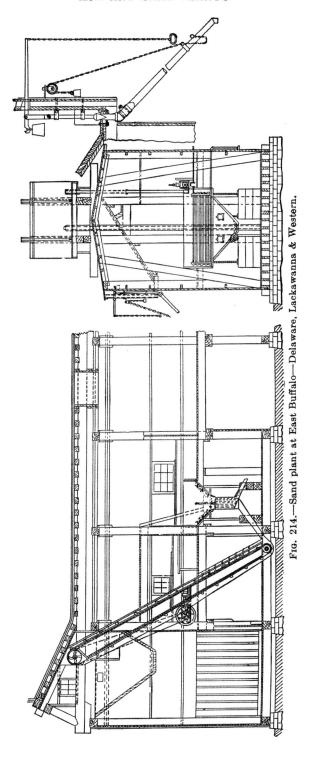

FIG. 214.—Sand plant at East Buffalo—Delaware, Lackawanna & Western.

At one engine house loading with sand boxes by gravity, the capacity of the dry-sand hopper is given as two car loads (24 cu. yd.) and the time required to sand an engine as 2 min.   The green-sand storage bin has a capacity of seven car loads (84 cu. yd.), and the cost for handling and, drying is said to be from 15 to 30 cts. per engine.

CHAPTER XXXI

ELECTRICAL OPERATION[1]

The electrification of steam railroads may now, after about twenty years' experience, be said to have passed the experimental stage, although much development work remains to be done. Improvements are being made in existing electrifications, while in new installations advantage is being taken of the recent developments and discoveries.

The principal systems used fall into four main groups: the low-voltage direct current, the high-voltage direct current, the three-phase alternating current and the single-phase alternating current and the principal characteristics of each are indicated in the table on p. 500.

The extent of electrification today is fairly well indicated by the fact that there are now some 2,200 electric locomotives in use by railroads in this and foreign countries, excluding light locomotives used for purely industrial purposes. Some 6.2 per cent. in number and 6.8 per cent. in horsepower use low-voltage direct current, 30.9 per cent. in number and 27.3 per cent in horsepower use high-voltage direct current, 40.7 per cent. in number and 36.2 per cent. in horsepower use single-phase alternating current and 22.2 per cent. in number and 29.7 per cent. in horsepower use three-phase alternating current. The distribution of the different types of locomotives is indicated in the table on pp. 502, 503 showing that, while the first three types are generally distributed, 98 per cent. of the three-phase locomotives are in use in Italy.

Experience in electric operation has not yet been sufficient to enable the adoption by the railroads of this country of a unified or standard system, in spite of the fact that in the United States alone upwards of 2,500 miles of track are now operated electrically. This is not surprising, in view of the complexity of the problem, but, until enough data have been accumulated, those responsible for the welfare of the railroads will necessarily feel reluctant to electrify unless they are obliged to do so by local conditions. The adoption of a standard system of electrification throughout the country is of nearly the same importance as was the universal adoption of a standard track gage. Joint terminal operation and the interchange of motive power will be of increasing importance

---

[1] Tables covering general electrical operation will be found in "Passenger Terminals & Trains," Chap. XXII; and information of a general nature respecting electrical train operation in Chap. XVII of that book. It is not deemed desirable to duplicate this data.

RAILWAY ELECTRIFICATION SYSTEMS

System	Primary		Secondary		
	Generation	Transmission	Conversion	Distribution and Contact	Locomotive
Low-voltage D.C.	Heat or hydro	3-phase at commercial or low frequency	At substations. Transformers and rotary converter or M. G. set or rectifier	Heavy feeder and single overhead wire or feeders and third rail	Low-voltage d.c motors.
High-voltage D.C.	Heat or hydro	3-phase at commercial or low frequency	At substations. Transformers and M. G. set or rotary converter or rectifier	Heavy feeder and single overhead wire	High-voltage d.c. motors M. G. set for auxiliaries.
Three-phase	Heat or hydro	3-phase at low frequency	At substations. Transformer	Feeder and two separate overhead wires	High-voltage 3-phase induction motors.
Single-phase	Heat or hydro	3-phase at commercial frequency	At receiving station. Frequency changer or phase balancer; and at substations. Transformer	Small or no feeder and single overhead contact wire	Low-voltage 3-phase induction motors with phase converter and transformer or low-voltage single-phase motors and transformer or low-voltage d.c. motors with M. G. set or rectifier and transformer.
		Single-phase at low frequency	At substations. Transformer		

as time goes on, and diversity of systems will increase operating difficulties, or even make impossible such desirable cooperation.

The necessity of the adoption of a universal electric traction system has been clearly felt in France, where much of the railroad mileage is controlled by the national government. High fuel costs indicated the advantage of an early change to electric operation on a large scale, and those responsible were called upon to make a decision in the face of admittedly inadequate information. Fortunately, such urgent necessity does not exist in this country and, when a decision is finally made and the universal system adopted, it will undoubtedly be on the basis of a full understanding of all the problems involved.

The choice in this country apparently lies between the 3,000-volt d.c. and the single-phase system at a voltage of 11,000 volts or more, although one important terminal electrification has recently been started on the basis of 1,500-volts d.c. Each of these systems makes use of an overhead trolley. The inherent limitations of the low-voltage third-rail contact distribution is now generally recognized, and, although some of the most important electrifications in this country have been installed on this basis, growth of this system will undoubtedly in the future be confined to necessary extensions of existing installations.

The 3,000-volt d.c. system has demonstrated its success very impressively in connection with the Chicago, Milwaukee & St. Paul electrification, where both passenger and freight services are handled economically and reliably over an extended territory and long grades, and where advantage is taken of the benefits of regenerative braking, to save power and for other obvious operating reasons. Some freight-switching service is also being successfully handled. Detailed records of cost comparison with steam operation on the St. Paul are shown later on in this chapter.

The 11,000-volt single-phase system in use in the New York, New Haven & Hartford, the New York, Westchester & Boston, the Pennsylvania and the Norfolk & Western has demonstrated that it can be used for extremely heavy freight service over mountain grades with regenerative braking; fast, heavy and frequent through passenger service; suburban service of an exacting nature—including heavy multiple-unit equipment—and freight and passenger yard switching on a large scale.

It is not within the province of this book to discuss the relative merits of the two leading electrification systems, but the author cannot refrain from pointing out—and he feels that all who are familiar with the subject must agree with him—that, while the 3,000-volt d.c. system may be flexible enough to handle adequately the various kinds of traffic problems which the railroad man must face, its scope thus far has, nevertheless, been limited to but a relatively small share of these problems and a very considerable amount of development remains to be accomplished before the high-voltage d.c. system can demonstrate that its flexibility

APPROXIMATE SURVEY OF ELECTRIC LOCOMOTIVES—BUILT AND BUILDING 1924

	D.C. high-voltage					A.C. single-phase				
	No.	Aggregate weight thousands of pound	Aggregate horsepower (one-hour)	Pounds per horsepower	Average weight per locomotive, thousand pounds	No.	Aggregate weight thousands of pounds	Aggregate horsepower (one-hour)	Pounds per horsepower	Average weight per locomotive, thousand pounds
Brazil	21	4,196	31,060	135	200					
Canada	6	996	7,680	130	166	6	792	4,500	176	132
Chile	42	8,446	68,420	124	201					
Mexico	10	3,090	27,360	113	309					
United States	131	37,863	247,300	153	289	199	57,845	359,450	161	290
Total American	210	54,591	381,820	143	260	205	58,637	363,950	161	286
Austria						84	12,259	99,250	124	146
England	11	1,898	12,800	148	173					
France	336	53,805	538,300	100	160					
Germany						290	61,029	486,054	126	210
Norway & Sweden						136	25,570	153,860	166	188

						A.C. three-phase				
Spain	12	2,220	19,320	115	185					
Switzerland						207	43,514	371,980	117	211
Total European	359	57,923	570,420	102	162	717	142,377	1,111,144	128	199
Japan	42	5,942	55,420	107	142					
Java	6	840	8,300	101	140					
New Zealand	5	537	3,400	158	107					
South Africa	78	11,400	93,700	122	146					
Total other countries	131	18,719	160,820	117	143					
Totals	700	131,233	1,113,060	118	188	922	201,009	1,475,094	137	218

	D.C. low-voltage					A.C. three-phase				
Argentina	2	295	1,840	160	148					
United States	128	31,815	261,090	122	248	4	920	6,000	153	230
Total American	130	32,110	262,930	122	247	4	920	6,000	153	230
Italy	10	1,520	13,600	112	152	492	76,580	1,197,730	64	156
Switzerland						6	913	9,369	98	152
Total European	10	1,520	13,600	112	152	498	77,493	1,207,099	64	156
Totals	140	33,630	276,530	122	240	502	78,410	1,213,100	65	156
Grand total D.C.	840	164,863	1,389,590	119	197					
Grand totals A.C.						1,424	279,419	2,688,194	104	196

is equal to that of the single-phase system and that all the operating problems which are now being successfully solved by th s system can be solved with equal reliability and economy by the high-voltage d.c.

The following excerpt from a report of an inspection of the New Haven electrification, made by engineers for the Connecticut Public Utilities Commission is of interest in the comparison of steam and electric propulsion:

In comparison with steam locomotive propulsion, the bulk of advantage appears to rest with its electrical contemporary. A few of the many obvious reasons for this may be cited as follows: With the electrical system of propulsion, any train can be brought to a stand-still anywhere on the line, in case of necessity not known on board; the operator in an adjacent signal-control tower simply, upon order or knowing of danger to be thus avoided, turns a knob and the controlling circuit breakers open; the power being thus cut off, the train cannot thus proceed to any considerable extent. No method has as yet been put into practical use that will similarly control a steam locomotive from a distance. The steam locomotive is unquestionably noisy; its objectionable vapor, noxious gases, odors, cinders, and ashes are seriously objectionable to.the traveler and the public generally. Its hot sparks are a source of constant danger to adjacent property; its requirement of watering and fueling stations, storage of fuel, the necessity of hauling a dead load tender, its inability to operate equally as well in either direction without being turned aound, and various other conditions peculiar to itself, are all objections common to it. The electrical system abates the noises incidental to the steam locomotive, makes but little noise of its own, entirely eliminates all the other objections named, and greatly simplifies train operation and handling. The vibration due to the reciprocating action of the steam locomotive which is communicated throughout the train, in consequence of the four dead centers to each revolution of its driving wheels, is done away with in the electric locomotive, by reason of its direct rotary motion. Thus the drawbar strain is more uniform and there is less liability of trains breaking in two with attendant disaster.

The possibility of controlling trains in emergency on electrically operated roads by shutting off the power from section or sections of the line might be useful. In connection with the non-observance of signals such a control might be worked out and possibly coupled with the use of some adaptation of the retarders used in hump yards as described in Chap. V. It seems within the realms of possibility that such a device might be worked out by means of electromagnetic control.

The new locomotives of the D. T. & I. and the New Haven are an interesting development of electric locomotive practice. The locomotive draws alternating current from the contact wire at 22,000 volts in the former and 11,000 volts in the latter installation, and by means of trans formers and motor-generator sets converts it into low-voltage direct current which is supplied to the motors. Each locomotive is, in fact, a separate power plant. Or as W. S. Murray expresses it "Thus we see a marriage between economic transmission and distribution of electric power."[1]

The arrangement of the electric apparatus is, of course, dependent on the general system of electrification for which the individual locomotive is designed, but there is a wide divergence of ideas upon locomotive design, even for a given system and for similar conditions of operation. This is perhaps due to lack of operating experience.

An electric locomotive, like a steam locomotive, has two main functions —that of an engine for developing drawbar pull and that of a vehicle. Its purpose is to develop tractive effort from standstill to and at certain speeds. In order to do so, it must be able to run safely over the track, tangent or curved, at agreed upon speeds, without undue stresses in its own structure or that of the permanent way, and without undue wear of rail or tires. The primary objective of the design is, of course, to secure both a good engine for developing drawbar pull and a good vehicle. This is relatively simple when operation is limited to low speeds and with little excess in curvature. When, however, high speeds or high speeds with heavy curvature, in addition to operation in both directions, must be provided for, it becomes more complicated, even with the great latitude in design and the possible combinations which the electric locomotive permits. The result is usually a compromise between what might be called the best engine for traction and the best vehicle.

The motive power units may have a single wheel base, or an assembly of short or long wheel bases, coupled together by cab, by hinges or by drawbars. Each individual unit may have or may not have auxiliary trucks for guiding or for bearing weight. Each unit may be an independent vehicle or it may be a vehicle whose guiding or stability is effected by the preceding or following unit through hinges. The cab structure may be integral with the locomotive frame or it may be independently borne, and attached to two or more wheel bases. The mechanical parts form the link between the electrical apparatus and the track and the adequacy of their detail design and the proper characteristics of the whole are essential to the success of an electric locomotive.

A large motor may drive more than one axle (collective drive), in which case a side-rod-drive direct or through gearing is required, or one or more motors may each drive a single axle (individual drive) through a direct connection or through gearing on side rods. Guiding or idle axles may or may not be used, depending upon the speed, curvature and track stress or the permissible axle loading.

The individual drive lends itself readily to both the d.c. and the a.c. series motors, except where very heavy tractive efforts are involved, or where motor-weight efficiency or axle loadings must be considered. Collective drives are adapted to these conditions, which are also the con-

[1] *Railway Review*, Oct. 25, 1924.

ditions most favorable to the use of the constant-speed induction motor. Representative types of individual and collective drives are shown in Fig. 215.

The simplest drive is the gearless, where the armature is either directly mounted on the axle revolving between two parallel pole faces which permit vertical movement of the armature, or is mounted on a quill, connected to the driving wheels by quill springs. This type of drive has found its most successful field in passenger service.

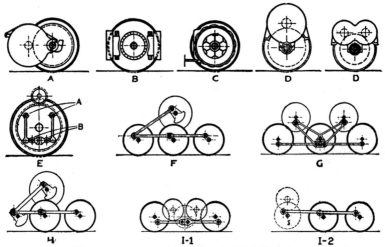

FIG. 215.—Types of drive for electric locomotives.

A, Axle-hung nose, suspended motors, single reduction, solid or flexible, single or twin gears   B, Direct gearless drive with the armature mounted upon an integral with the axle; the motor field integral with the locomotive frame.   C, Direct gearless quill drive, the armature mounted on a quill surrounding the axle, the connection to wheels through spring elements, permitting relative vertical movement; motor field mounted on locomotive main or truck frame.   D, Geared quill drive, the motors and quill frame-mounted; the quill surrounding the gear, connection to the driven axle through springs or mechanically flexible elements, these permitting relative vertical movement between motor and axle.   E, Geared flexible drive with motors frame-mounted, with or without quill gear connection through a flexible universal-driven wheel, to permit relative vertical movement between motor and axle.   F, Direct side-rod drive by which the torque is transmitted from the motor shaft by direct rod connection to the driving wheels.   G, Direct drive with Scotch yoke by which the transmission of torque to wheels is effected directly from the motor or motors, arranged to permit independent vertical movement of the driving pin and bushing.   H, Jack-shaft side-rod drive by which the torque is transmitted from the crank of one or two motor shafts through a main rod or rods to a jack or auxiliary shaft or shafts, and from the latter to the wheels through side rods.   The connection from jack shaft to side rods may be direct, or by yoke with or without flexible element.   I-1, Geared jack-shaft side-rod drive by which the torque from the motor shaft is transmitted to the jack shaft by solid or flexible gears and from the jack shaft to wheels by side rods direct or by yoke.   I-2, Geared jack-shaft side-rod drive similar to (I-1), except that the jack shaft is outside the driving wheels.

In freight service, the geared or side-rod drive or a combination of the two is used. The simplest form of gear drive, used extensively in multiple-unit equipment and light-switching locomotives, is the nose-and-axle suspension type, which is used with both rigid and flexible gears, and with gears at one or both ends of the motor shaft. Limiting factors to the use of this drive are gear reduction, clearance necessary about the motor and gearing, maximum safe locomotive speed and permissible dead weight on the axle.

The geared quill drive has been successfully developed for passenger, light-freight and switching service, the motor being directly mounted above the driving axle with spring supports between the motor and the wheel. This mounting, in addition to reducing track strains through higher center of gravity and spring-borne motors, affords opportunity to use larger motors than could be used in axle mounting. Like the axle-mounted motor, it is limited in length. It is not limited by clearance to the rail, however, but by space occupied in the cab. The motor may be limited in torque to the amount that may be transmitted through the quill spring and in speed by the velocity of the armature and

FIG. 216.—Partly assembled truck of 3,000-volt, d.c. locomotive used by the Chicago, Milwaukee & St. Paul Railroad.

other parts. This drive, when used with twin motors, quill-mounted, with the pinions on each armature meshing into a common gear, gives better weight efficiency. Because of the smaller diameter, more revolutions per minute are permitted, which, with suitable gearing, secures higher horsepower rating per axle.

With collective drives, using scotch yokes or side rods either directly connected to the driving wheels or connected by means of a jack shaft, the locomotives are not economical at low speeds, as the revolutions of the driving wheels are the same as the motor armature. By the use of gears and side rods combined, relatively higher armature revolutions are permitted.

Types of electric locomotives in use in this country are shown in Figs. 216 to 224 inclusive.

Essentially, in steam railway operation, each train has its own source of power, which bears no relation to the propulsion of the other

Fig. 217.—A 274-ton, 4,000-hp. electric locomotive on the Chicago, Milwaukee and St. Paul.

trains on the line; in electric operation, on the contrary, every train draws its power from one or more centrally located power plants. The power is

Fig. 218.—A 3,250-ton coal train hauled by electric locomotive on the Norfolk & Western.

transmitted from the power plant or substation to the trains either by means of a third rail which carries the current to the locomotive and then through the third-rail shoes into the locomotive, or by means of an overhead system of wires, with a trolley or pantagraph through which the current passes to the electric apparatus in the locomotive. The third-rail

Fig. 219.—Electric locomotive and train emerging from Hudson River tunnel of Pennsylvania Railroad.

system is used only when the electric power is of low voltage. When the power is of high potential, the overhead system must, for reasons of safety, be used. The use of a third rail in freight yards is undesirable

Fig. 220.—Boston & Maine electrification—freight train about to enter Hoosac tunnel

under any circumstances, on account of the interference with the work of the yardmen.

While rapid progress has been made during the past few years in the design of steam locomotives; improved by the introduction of feed-water heaters, brick arches, superheaters, stokers, and similar appliances, there has been a great advance in electric locomotives and in the economy

Fig. 221.—Typical catenary construction on New F ·rn Railroad, with train drawn by two gearless engines of the original type.

of power plants. Today axle loads of 65,000 lb. and continuous-capacity ratings upwards of 4,000 hp.[1] are found. The electric locomotive points

Fig. 222.—Latest type of passenger engine in use on the New York, New Haven & Hartford Railroad, 11,000-volt, a.c., and 600-volt d.c.

the way to solving many problems of the railroads; it is the most feasible means available for meeting problems incident to the continually increas-

[1] Manson's "Railroad Electrification."

ing traffic density where longer and heavier trains must be handled at higher speeds; where reliability of operation is important and flexibility of control is essential. Among its advantages is its certainty of continuous traction in cold weather, when heat radiation, so disastrous to the

FIG. 223.—Trucks and running gear of latest type locomotive used on New York, New Haven and Hartford's 11,000-volt, single-phase system.

steam engine, is beneficial to the electric locomotive. In other words, heat rather than cold, is a disadvantage to the electric locomotive, and it, therefore, can stand an overload, with less liability to damage, in cold weather than when high temperatures prevail, thereby more nearly rendering its effectiveness uniform during the 365 days of the year, because

FIG. 224.—Direct-current, third-rail locomotives of the New York Central lines.

it has greater power at a time when train resistance is increased. No time is lost in cleaning boilers or grates; taking water; lighting or banking fires. Stops for coal and water are eliminated. Two or more units may be coupled and placed under the control of one engine crew. Turntables or wyes are unnecessary, greatly reducing the space required for engine terminals. It also permits a better utilization of property available as the engine facilities can parallel the other tracks instead of diverging at an angle. Smooth and steady acceleration reduces damage to draft gear and other parts of freight equipment and to contents of cars. Operation from the front of the locomotive gives the engineman an unobstructed view. The tractive efforts desired may be more readily obtained without exceeding structural limits. Ruling grades may be met by increasing units without adding to crew, and at very moderate terminal expense. The safe descent of grades may be accomplished through regenerative braking. The use and value of real estate is increased along the railroad right of way. Terminal values may be increased on account of smoke elimination and by multiple-level operation. Coal consumption, and consequently the haulage and handling of coal, are reduced or eliminated. Locomotive-maintenance costs are materially reduced. The ratio of the effective to the total locomotive-hours is increased.

There is a variance of opinion as to the actual economies due to lessened coal consumption, per unit, in electric operation. To reach a reasonably safe conclusion, it becomes necessary first to agree on a satisfactory yardstick, and here again the time-worn arguments as to the use of "locomotive-mile," "train-mile," "car-mile," "gross-ton-mile" and "gross-ton-miles-per-hour"[1] are encountered.

A distinguished writer says.[2]

Ton-mileage is merely an expression of the product of weight and distance units, without relation to the characteristic features of freight rates and classification, of the varying proportion of dead weight to paying loads, of empty car to loaded car and train-mileage, or of other things which affect a comparison of the cost of service under different conditions and circumstances.

The data for the ton-mile average are obtained by multiplying the weight of each shipment by the number of miles that it has been transported. This information, obtained from the waybills, is aggregated in the railroad auditor's office and is then reported to the office of the Interstate Commerce Commission, where it is totaled and is used in establishing the ton-mile average for the railway system of the United States as a whole.

The term "ton-mile" may have one of four meanings: It may include the car and lading, or the lading only, or revenue freight only; or it may also include company freight; and the Committee on Statistical Inquiry of the American Railway Association proposed yet another in the "equated ton-mile," defined as "the sum of the weight of the car and lading and an allowance for the resistance offered by friction, grades and curves, multiplied by the mileage of the car." The ton-mile average is the official basis for comparisons of operative efficiency, and the unit of the long-haul and short-haul yardstick for the measurement of rates, yet it recognizes no distinction as to the relative weight, bulk, value or other

[1] This most satisfactory unit has been used by the New Haven since 1913 in its records of electric operation.

[2] HAINES, "Efficient Railway Operation."

qualities of the respective commodities transported, whether they be perishables, silk or coal.

There are other standards of measurement which are regarded as transportation units, besides ton-miles and passenger-miles. Freight is moved in car loads, and the cubic-content capacity of a car, as well as its weight capacity, causes the car-mile unit to correspond more closely to the qualities of commodities in general than is the case with the ton-mile unit. Freight in car loads constitutes a train load, and freight trains are rated as to the number of cars and their gross weight, and not as to the net weight of their contents. The ever-present problem for solution by transportation officials is the concentration of the most ton-miles in the fewest car-miles, and of the most car-miles in the fewest train-miles.

In brief, the objection to the first three units given are that the locomotive-mile unit does not give any indication of the comparative size of the locomotives, the train-mile unit does not distinguish between short and long trains and the car-mile does not make allowance for the proportion of empty and loaded cars, the different-sized cars and the extent to which they are loaded. The gross-ton-mile, although it does not take into account the grade and other operating factors, is the most convenient and satisfactory unit to use, as it reflects variations in both the weight of cars and contents and the distance moved.

The acceptance of any unit as between different roads or different divisions of a road is of doubtful value, but the use of the customary "1,000-gross-ton-miles," or of "ton-miles-per-hour" will give a reasonably true indication of the operating efficiency of a road or division as compared with itself, provided necessary adjustments are made.

The fuel consumption of electric operation as compared with steam operation is an extremely variable quantity among different roads and classes of service and between different periods on the same road, and each individual case must be carefully studied to arrive at a correct conclusion. The situation is further complicated by variation in power-plant operation. In general, it may be said that the saving in fuel may run up to 50 per cent. as a maximum, dependent on local conditions.

The result of making "two tons grow where one grew before" is frequently claimed. One of the ablest and most experienced railroad managers,[1] however, placed the percentage of economy as low as 3.7 and his reasoning, always interesting and illuminating, was:

The United States Geological Survey Professional Paper No. 123 gives the best fuel rate of eight large steam-electric plants, out of a total of 400 plants studied in 1919, as 2.14 lb. of coal, or 28,000 B.t.u., to produce 1 kw.-hr.; hence, as 1 kw.-hr. equals 3,413 B.t.u., the loss in converting the energy in coal into electric energy was 24,587 B.t.u., or 87.8 per cent.; in other words, out of 1,000-hp. potential

[1] The late Julius Kruttschnitt.

energy in coal, 878 hp. is lost in converting it into electric energy by the most modern and efficient steam boilers and engines driving the most efficient electric generators then known.   This leaves 122 hp. available.   In transmitting this power to motors of an electric locomotive, the average loss is 19 per cent., or 23.18 hp., leaving 98.82 hp. out of the original 1,000 available for work; but the internal losses of the electric locomotive will consume 15 per cent. of this amount, reducing to 84 hp. the energy to move trains.   The efficiency of the fuel from coal to driving-wheel contact with rail is but 8.4 per cent.   The corresponding efficiency of a modern steam locomotive with arches, superheater and feed-water heater is 8.1 per cent. under favorable conditions.   While under average conditions at the present time the advantage may be more than the 3.7 per cent. indicated in favor of the electric locomotive, the spread is hardly attractive enough to tempt capital to assume the expense of interest, depreciation, tax and maintenance expenditures that would have to be incurred in changing from steam to electricity generated in a steam plant.   The soundness of this conclusion was demonstrated by studies made of the Sierra Nevada and other heavy grades on the Southern Pacific, where trains are lifted 6,854 ft. in 86 miles.   Assuming the current generated in a steam station, the interest, taxes and depreciation on additional net plant required were demonstrated to be more than three times as great as the estimated savings in operating costs to be obtained from electric operation.

Other considerations, such as smoke prevention and increasing capacity on heavy grades, may influence the problem, but we cannot recall any instance of a change being made, where a steam-generated current was used solely for saving fuel.   The steam locomotive is by no means as obsolescent as the propagandists for electric traction would have us believe.   In an address, "The Last Stand of the Reciprocating Steam Engine," published in the Mar., 1920, edition of the *Journal of the American Institute of Electrical Engineers,* a fuel consumption of 100 lb. per 1,000-gross-ton-miles by electric locomotives is given as applicable "to conditions universally obtaining on regular profiles."   Data published by the Bureau of Railway Economics in September, 1921, show that the fuel consumption on 24,000 selected miles of steam railroad averaged but slightly over 100 lb. per 1,000 ton-miles.   Embraced in this mileage was the New York Central, Illinois Central, Chesapeake & Ohio, and St. Louis Southwestern.   On 3,142 miles, or 60 per cent. of the Southern Pacific main-line mileage, the fuel consumption in the same month was approximately 100 lb., while on the Salt Lake division, 543 miles, the fuel record in October, 1921, averaged 91 lb. per 1,000-gross-ton-miles, for all locomotives.

The foregoing, while valuable as representing the steam viewpoint, is somewhat extreme.   The figure taken as the unit coal consumption at power plants has been vastly improved in modern well-designed plants, which are comparable chronologically to the modern steam engine equipped with arches, superheaters and feed-water heaters.   Again, the assumed losses in transmission of electric power and in the electric locomotive are high, and most important of all, however, the comparison with the steam engine assumes favorable operating conditions for the latter and makes no allowance for stand-by losses, which, under some operations, are often equivalent to fuel consumed in useful work. Allowance for these factors would materially change the comparison.

A factor of no small moment, on the assumption that it resolves itself into a question of coal on the locomotive and coal in the power house— eliminating so-called "white coal"[1] from consideration for the moment— is the importance of using a comparatively high grade of coal on locomotives, with its ever-increasing cost, and the ability to burn an inferior grade of coal in a power house, with greater opportunity for increasing efficiency in that direction. A distinct advantage occurs, in this respect, when the central station is located on a water front.[2]

Another major advantage of electric operation lies in locomotive maintenance. This as well as the fuel-consumption figure, varies a great deal with conditions. The wear and tear due to heavy mileage and short intervals for inspection and repairs may mislead. The varying operating conditions encountered in the way of gradient, curvature, train rating, all affect the performance. Locomotives may run over more than one division. The schedule and actual speed maintained, the weight of train, the number and location of stops and the size of the locomotive are all-important features entering into the problem and requiring consideration. On the basis of a prorated figure, taking into account the weight of the locomotive, it may be said that the cost of electric-locomotive maintenance, including engine-house expenses, varies from 20 to 50 per cent. of that of a steam locomotive of equivalent capacity and under similar operating conditions.

On the other hand, mention should be made here of expenses in electric operation which are not met in steam operation. The power plant, or equivalent cost if power is purchased, must be taken into account. This item is so variable that no general figure can be given covering it. The operation and maintenance of the transmission and distribution system are expenses fundamental to electric operation, and, like the cost of power production, are difficult to translate into costs per 1,000-gross-ton-mile, unless all characteristics of operation are taken into consideration.

A study[3] of the comparative costs of electrical operation with that of previous operation with steam power indicates a saving on the Chicago, Milwaukee & St. Paul of $12,400,007 as a result of nine years' operation of 438 miles and five years' operation of 210 miles electrically, a total of 648 miles.

In this operation, alternating current is purchased at high voltage at taps in high-tension lines along the right of way and stepped down

[1] Term commonly used for hydroelectric power plants where water pressure is the source of power.

[2] The Interborough of New York City originally consumed 176,000 tons of coal in transporting 116,000,000 passengers; in 1922, with 704,000 tons it handled 993,000,000 passengers.

[3] Made by officers of the St. Paul and published in *Railway Age*, Feb. 28, 1925. This comparison however is made with the steam engines which were replaced and not with engines of a more modern type.

VARIATIONS IN TRAFFIC AND SAVINGS RESULTING FROM ELECTRICAL OPERATION, FIGURED ON PRICE LEVELS OF 1923

Years	Harlowton to Avery—Electrical operation began April and Nov., 1916		Othello to Tacoma—Electrical operation began March, 1920		All electrified sections	
	Volume of traffic—gross ton-miles, freight and passenger	Net savings by electrification	Volume of traffic—gross ton-miles, freight and passenger	Net savings by electrification	Volume of traffic—gross ton-miles, freight and passenger	Net savings by electrification
1916	[1]1,639,054,000	[1]$ 1,098,166	....	....	1,639,054,000	$ 1,098,166
1917	2,677,097,000	1,641,369	....	....	2,677,097,000	1,641,369
1918	2,759,178,000	1,734,687	....	....	2,759,178,000	1,734,687
1919	2,894,063,000	1,888,037	....	....	2,894,063,000	1,888,037
1920	2,710,745,000	1,679,623	[2]691,674,000	[2]$249,003	3,402,419,000	1,928,626
1921	1,812,714,000	658,651	664,238,000	12,363	2,476,952,000	671,014
1922	2,109,868,000	996,485	734,121,000	103,301	2,843,989,000	1,099,786
1923	2,247,102,000	1,152,508	746,405,000	119,285	2,993,507,000	1,271,793
1924	2,129,426,000	1,018,721	691,476,000	47,808	2,820,902,000	1,066,529
Total..........	....	$11,868,247	....	$531,760	....	$12,400,007

[1] Tonnage and savings for 6½ months.
[2] Tonnage and savings for 9 months.

from 100,000 to 2,300 volts and then converted by means of motor generator sets to 3,000-volt direct current for distribution to the trolleys. The comparison of costs were between the actual costs of electrical operation for the year 1923, and the actual costs for the last year of steam operation adjusted to the costs obtaining in 1923 of all expenses directly affected by the change in power.

The table on p. 516 shows for each year of electrical operation the operating savings from which the carrying charges on the additional investment required have been deducted and it will be noted that the net savings to date have aggregated more than three-fourths the cost of the electrification.

The tables on pages 518 to 521 show the detailed study of the operating expenses of the two sections according to Interstate Commerce Commission accounts, and the tables on pages 522 and 523 the detail of the capital investment required which aggregates in round numbers $23,000,000 against which is credited $7,000,000 as the investment in steam power replaced and retired, making a net capital investment of $16,000,000 or at the rate of $24,600 a mile.

As already stated there are, broadly, two general systems which may be employed:

1. Direct current, varying from 600 to 3,000 volts,

2. Alternating current, either single-phase or three-phase, 3,300 to 11,000 volts or higher.

There are limitations to the third-rail system. While in very dry climates 1,200 volts can be used on the third rail, it may be said in general that this system of distribution limits the voltage to 700 volts. The comparatively low voltage means an abundance of copper, frequent substations and other apparatus and materials to care for the heavy current necessary for the operation of numerous heavy trains over long distances and presents a difficult problem, especially in switching yards. A high voltage overhead contact system using direct current single-phase or three-phase alternating current, is required to eliminate the excessive use of copper and substations.

In typical single-phase systems, the power is transmitted at high voltage to the transformer substations, where it is transformed down to the trolley voltage desired for the service and is connected directly to the overhead contact system as single-phase current.

In the three-phase system, three-phase instead of single-phase power is delivered to the locomotives, necessitating two contact wires, insulated from each other, placed above the track, the rails of the track acting as a third wire.

The high-voltage d.c. overhead system is similar to the low-voltage d.c. third-rail system. The power is transmitted in the same way, con-

OPERATING EXPENSES DIRECTLY AFFECTED BY CHANGE IN POWER—HARLOWTON TO AVERY

I.C.C. accts. (1)	Classification of expenses—description (2)	Steam operation—Costs of the year 1915 adjusted to the price levels of 1923			Electrical operation—Actual costs of the year 1923		
		[1] Variable		[1] Constant freight and passenger (5)	[1] Variable		[1] Constant freight and passenger (8)
		Freight (3)	Passenger (4)		Freight (6)	Passenger (7)	
	Maintenance of way and structures:						
201	Superintendence			$ 94,472			$ 95,208
231	Water stations			23,800			
233	Fuel stations			9,930			33,927
235	Shops and enginehouses			42,383			47,671
249	Signals and interlockers			52,131			1,530
255	Power substation buildings						2,913
257	Power transmission systems						40,763
259	Power distribution systems						18,379
261	Power line poles and fixtures						847
271	Small tools and supplies (for Maintenance of Elec. Prop. only)						
	Total maintenance of way and structures			$222,716			$ 241,238
	Maintenance of equipment:						
301	Superintendence			$120,194			$ 105,440
306	Power substation apparatus						19,163
308–11	Locomotive repairs—train	$ 687,824	$218,725		$ 190,390	$135,349	
308–11	Locomotive repairs—switch	37,105			12,510	77	
314–17	Brake shoe and rigging, wheel and draft rigging wear	21,352	11,622				
326	Trolley maintenance cars—only						2,757
	Total maintenance of equipment	$ 746,281	$230,347	$120,194	$ 202,900	$135,426	$ 127,360
	Transportation:						
371	Superintendence			$ 70,240			$ 61,407
377	Yardmasters and yard clerks			17,055			17,055
378	Yard conductors and brakemen	$ 61,533			$ 27,174	166	

Account	Item						
379	Yard switch and signal tenders			1,189			548
380–81	Yard enginemen—yard motormen	39,644			17,990	110	9,489
382–84	Fuel for yard locomotives—yard switch, power purchased	43,315					1,053
383	Yard switching power produced						
385	Water for yard locomotives	1,257					
386	Lubricants for yard locomotives	777			394	1	
387	Other supplies for yard locomotives	808			302	1	
388	Enginehouse expense—yard	12,431			4,131	25	
389	Yard supplies and expenses			712			328
392–93	Train enginemen—train motormen	400,421	121,341		231,352	77,778	754,231
394–96	Fuel for train locomotives—train power purchased	886,009	270,693				87,135
395	Train for power produced						
397	Water for train locomotives	24,939	7,556		9,979	4,811	
398	Lubricants for train locomotives	14,534	3,360		4,831	2,470	
399	Other supplies for train locomotives	19,018	5,381				
400	Enginehouse expense—train	142,283	66,330		42,341	40,531	
401	Trainmen	317,041	94,649		197,067	94,649	
402	Train supplies and expenses (train—light and heat)					12,883	
404	Signal and interlocker operation			40,841			31,517
	Total transportation	$1,964,010	$569,310	$130,037	$535,561	$233,425	$962,763
	Work train expense—all other than included above in Maintenance of W. & S. adjusted to 1923 work train-miles			$74,721			$62,415
	Totals for operating expenses directly affected (Gr. Tot. Stm. $4,057,616; Gr. Tot. Elec. $2,501,088)	$2,710,291	$799,657	$547,668	$738,461	$368,851	$1,393,776
	Gross ton-miles in thousands—the work performed (Gr. Tot. Stm. 2,178,631; Gr. Tot. Elec. 2,247,102)	1,758,726	[2]419,905		1,827,197	419,905	
	Cost per 1,000 gross ton miles	$1.54105	$1.90438		$.40415	$.87842	

1 "Variable"—Expenses considered to vary practically directly with volume of traffic: "Constant"—Expenses considered to remain practically constant for all volumes of traffic within a reasonable range.

2 The actual for the period, 354,054,000, adjusted to the tonnage of electrical operation as the difference rests solely in the number of cars per train: Expenses adjusted to conform.

OPERATING EXPENSES DIRECTLY AFFECTED BY CHANGE IN POWER—OTHELLO TO TACOMA

I. C. C. accts. (1)	Classification of expenses—description (2)	Steam operation—Costs of the year, August, 1918 to July, 1919, inclusive, adjusted to the price levels of 1923			Electrical operation—Actual costs of the year 1923		
		¹Variable		¹Constant freight and passenger (5)	¹Variable		¹Constant freight and passenger (8)
		Freight (3)	Passenger (4)		Freight (6)	Passenger (7)	
	Maintenance of way and structures:						
201	Superintendence			$ 48,295			$ 49,777
231	Water stations			8,273			
233	Fuel stations			5,215			
235	Shops and enginehouses			16,234			12,513
249	Signals and Interlockers			33,202			31,343
255	Power substation buildings						2,047
257	Power transmission systems						5,179
259	Power distribution systems						19,723
261	Power line poles and fixtures						11,066
271	Small tools and supplies (for Maintenance of Elec. Prop. only)						365
	Total maintenance of way and structures			$111,219			$132,013
	Maintenance of equipment:						
301	Superintendence			$ 31,105			$ 22,306
306	Power substation apparatus						7,891
308–11	Locomotive repairs—train	$ 326,467	$129,174		$ 78,549	$ 60,703	
308–11	Locomotive repairs—switch	24,141			2,658		
314–7	Brake shoe and rigging, wheel and draft rigging wear	18,000					
326	Trolley maintenance cars—only		7,000				714
	Total maintenance of equipment	$ 368,608	$136,174	$ 31,105	$ 81,207	$ 60,703	$ 30,911
	Transportation:						
371	Superintendence			$ 35,097			$ 34,126
377	Yardmasters and yard clerks			6,708			3,268
378	Yard conductors and brakemen	$ 40,560			$ 10,038		

379	Yard switch and signal tenders						578
380–81	Yard enginemen—yard motormen	25,629		2,047	6,396		
382–84	Fuel for yard locomotives—yard switch power purchased	24,763					2,714
383	Yard switching power produced						447
385	Water for yard locomotives	603					
386	Lubricants for yard locomotives	506			105		
387	Other supplies for yard locomotives	526			44		
388	Enginehouse expense—yard	6,845			1,186		
389	Yard supplies and expenses			314		38,095	62
392–93	Train enginemen—train motormen	233,323	69,674		92,224		
394–96	Fuel for train locomotives—train power purchased	493,807	186,446				²319,634
395	Train power produced						53,301
397	Water for train locomotives	11,710	4,548				
398	Lubricants for train locomotives	5,606	1,758		4,804	2,171	
399	Other supplies for train locomotives	7,211	2,778		3,485	1,999	
400	Enginehouse expense—train	45,959	29,252		14,554	16,127	
401	Trainmen	264,338	60,644		107,183	47,698	
402	Train supplies and expenses (train—light and heat)			19,248		7,723	1,380
404	Signal and interlocker operation						
	Total transportation	$1,161,385	$355,100	$ 63,414	$240,019	$113,813	$428,510
	Work train expense—All other than included above in M. of W. & S. adjusted to 1923 work train-miles			$ 50,452			$ 39,676
	Totals for operating expenses directly affected (Gr. Tot. Stm. $2,277,-457; Gr. Tot. Elec. $1,126,852)	$1,529,993	$491,274	$256,190	$321,226	$174,516	$631,110
	Gross ton miles in thousands—the work performed (Gt. Tot. Stm. 1,014,511; Gr. Tot. Elec. 746,405)	805,830	³208,681		537,724	208,681	
	Cost per 1,000 gross ton miles	$ 1.89865	$2.35419		$ .59738	$ .83628	

1 "Variable"—Expense considered to vary practically directly with volume of traffic; "Constant"—Expenses considered to remain practically constant for all volumes of traffic within a reasonable range.

2 Constant up to a total of 906,097,000 gross ton miles for freight and passenger services; thence increased in freight service as estimated necessary for greater volumes of traffic: (The amount to be added at 1,014,411,000 G. T. M. is $38,307.00).

3 The actual for the period, 186,232, adjusted to the tonnage of electrical operation as the difference rests solely in the number of cars per train due to difference in train routing: Expenses adjusted to conform.

INVESTMENT IN AND CARRYING CHARGES ON THE PROPERTY PECULIAR TO EACH MODE OF OPERATION—HARLOWTON TO AVERY

(438 Roadway miles)

Items	Investment [1]	Carrying charges		
		Interest 5 %	Depreciation S. F. Basis 6 %	Total
Steam operation—fixed property:				
Fuel and water stations, cinder pitts, etc.......	$ 630,000	$ 31,500	$ 16,695	
D. C. signal system..........................	[2].........	....	....	
Totals, fixed property..................	$ 630,000	$ 31,500	$ 16,695	$ 48,195
Locomotives:				
Freight (incl. all pusher work service locomotives)...................................	$ 2,470,628	$123,531	$ 28,165	
Passenger................................	356,039	17,802	4,059	
Switch...................................	78,598	3,930	896	
Totals, locomotives....................	$ 2,905,265	$145,263	$ 33,120	$178,383
Totals, steam property..................	$ 3,535,265	$176,763	$ 49,815	$226,578
Electrical operation—fixed property				
Roadway buildings.........................	$ 89,545	$ 4,477	$ 2,382	
Power substation buildings..................	535,157	26,758	3,361	
Power substation apparatus.................	1,859,353	92,968	21,383	
Power transmission system.................	715,181	35,759	5,435	
Power distribution system.................	2,890,615	144,531	23,269	
Power line poles and fixtures...............	1,091,721	54,586	50,110	
A. C. signal system.......................	[2]197,446	9,872	1,374	
Engr.—Int. during construction and miscellaneous.................................	325,671	16,284	3,354	
Maintenance equipment....................	37,000	1,850	422	
Sub-total.............................	$ 7,741,689	$387,085	$111,090	$498,175
Rental of transmission lines—credit...........	....	Cr. $2,760	....	Cr. $2,760
Totals, fixed property..................	$ 7,741,689	$384,325	$111,090	$495,415
Locomotives:				
Freight (incl. all pusher and work service locomotives).............................	$ 2,881,112	$144,056	$ 32,845	
Passenger................................	927,408	46,370	10,573	
Switch...................................	111,564	5,578	1,272	
Totals, locomotives....................	$ 3,920,084	$196,004	$ 44,690	$240,694
Totals, electrical property...............	$11,661,773	$580,329	$155,780	$736,109
Increase in carrying charges—account electrification..	....	....	....	$509,531

[1] Electrical operating property at actual cost 1914–15–16: Steam operating property priced as of the costs obtaining during the same period (1915).

[2] Net increase in investment chargeable to electrification included under electrical operation.

INVESTMENT IN AND CARRYING CHARGES ON THE PROPERTY PECULIAR TO EACH
MODE OF OPERATION—OTHELLO TO LACOMA

(208 Roadway miles)

Items	Investment 1	Carrying charges		
		Interest 5%	Deprecia- tion S. F. Basis 6%	Total
Steam operation—fixed property:				
Fuel and water stations, cinder pitts, etc.......	$ 507,010	$ 30,421	$ 13,436	
D. C. signal system.........................	612,000	36,720	6,793	
Totals, fixed property....................	$ 1,119,010	$ 67,141	$ 20,229	$ 87,370
Locomotives:				
Freight (incl. all pusher and work service loco- motives)...............................	$ 2,135,785	$128,147	$ 24,348	
Passenger................................	430,231	25,814	4,905	
Switch...................................	144,224	8,653.	1,644	
Total, locomotives......................	$ 2,710,240	$162,614	$ 30,897	$193,511
Totals, steam property..................	$ 3,829,250	/229,755	$ 51,126	$280,881
Electrical operation—fixed property:				
Roadway buildings.........................	$ 114,215	$ 6,853	$ 3,027	
Power substation buildings..................	452,808	27,168	2,875	
Power substation apparatus.................	1,476,964	88,618	16,985	
Power transmission system..................	549,521	32,971	5,072	
Power distribution system..................	2,190,401	131,424	16,822	
Power line poles and fixtures................	966,563	57,994	40,596	
A. C. signal system........................	870,000	46,800	8,658	
Engr.—Int. during construction and miscellaneous	621,519	37,291	7,645	
Maintenance equipment....................	27,000	1,620	308	
Sub-total..............................	$ 7,178,991	$430,739	$101,988	$532,727
Rental of transmission lines—credit.........	....	Cr. $25,842	....	Cr. $25,842
Totals, fixed property....................	$ 7,178,991	$404,897	$101,988	$506,885
Locomotives:				
Freight (incl. all pusher and work service loco- motives)...............................	$ 3,065,280	$183,917	$ 34,944	
Passenger................................	1,035,690	62,141	11,807	
Switch...................................	48,520	2,911	553	
Totals, locomotives......................	$ 4,149,490	$248,969	$ 47,304	$296,273
Totals, electrical property...............	$11,328,481	$653,866	$149,292	$803,158
Increase in carrying charges—account electrifica- tion.......................................	....	........'.	....	$522,277

1 Electrical operating property at actual cost 1917–18–19: Steam operating property priced as of
the costs obtaining during the same period (1918).

verted by rotating machinery, but is fed at a higher voltage to an over-head conductor instead of to a third rail.

The electric operating data of the principal American railroads is shown in the table on p. 526. The mileage and power-consumption figures are for 1921 the latest comparative figures available, while the other data are for 1924.

It will be noted that the New Haven leads in passenger-service gross ton-miles. The Chicago, Milwaukee & St. Paul stands first in freight service performed, with the New Haven second, these two lines along with the Virginian, and Norfolk and Western, being the only ones handling a considerable freight traffic electrically. The Milwaukee has 440-mile runs while the New Haven's longest freight run is 68 miles.

A striking result of electric operation is in yard-switching service. A typical use of an electric yard engine is shown in Fig. 225. As an

Fig. 225.—Electric switching engines—New Haven.

example of the reliability and continuity of performance in such service on the New Haven, a typical—but not exceptional—record was selected, which shows an electric yard engine in continuous service for 25 days on three regular 8-hour shifts per day without leaving the yard. During this entire period the engine was out of service for only 1 hour and 40 min.—40 min. on one occasion to repair a worn pantagraph trolley shoe, and 1 hour on the other to replace worn brushes on the blower motor and a broken pantagraph. The mileage made was about 3,500 miles, or about 500 miles over the usual inspection schedule, and when the locomotive was inspected at the shop the only work found necessary was the usual lubrication of the bearings of the main motors and driving journal boxes. The 16 electric yard engines of this type in ten years' service have had only three main motors removed, none of which were taken out for rewinding.

A self-contained unit has recently been developed for use in yard switching. This locomotive (Fig. 226) contains an internal-combustion fuel-oil engine driving a d.c. generator, which supplies power to four motors, one geared to each axle.

The consistent mileage records of the electric passenger engines of the original gearless type—of which there are 41 on the New Haven Railroad—are also noteworthy. For some 17 years these engines have averaged about 170 miles a day, with no allowance for the time they were out of service for repairs and for changes found necessary in the original design. This mileage was, in the earlier part of this period, made on short runs—33 miles the longest—the longest run now being 73 miles ranging down to the shortest run of 16 miles, and of which there are many. As an example of the present-day mileage, the latest type passenger engines,

Fig. 226.—Oil-electric switching locomotive in use on West Street, New York City, in the steamship-pier section.

of which five have been in service about five years and twelve recently received, have made an average of 201 miles day in and day out. The cumulative mileage of the earlier type has been well over a million miles each, and of the later type nearly 400,000; covering 16 and about 4 years respectively.

It is interesting, from the standpoint of comparison with steam operation, to note that these 41 electric engines, some of which are 17 years old, have each made well over a million miles in service. Now, after such mileage in steam, assuming 30,000 miles as an average of the steam locomotive equipment per year, the age of a steam locomotive would be 40 years. The steam locomotive when 30, 35 or 40 years old would at least be retired to branch or secondary service, whereas these electric locomotives are still operating effectively on heavy express trains.

Reviewing the story of steam-road electrification, the New Haven completed the first such undertaking in 1895—the Nantasket Beach line[1]

[1] In Massachusetts.

ELECTRIC OPERATING DATA OF THE PRINCIPAL AMERICAN RAILROADS

Road	Mileage of road	Mileage of single track	Total kilowatt-hours per year	Number of locomotives — Passenger	Freight	Switch	Aggregate weight of locomotives passenger, freight switch. Tons	Multiple-unit cars — Number	Average weight. Tons	Gross ton-miles per year (trailing) — Passenger	Freight	Locomotive-miles per year — Passenger	Freight
Baltimore & Ohio	3.6	7.96	5,628,690	6	4	0	960	0					[b]232,786
Boston & Maine	7.92	23.80	7,250,640	[b]7			916	0		18,424,000	158,053,000	36,440	113,502
Butte, Anaconda & Pacific	28.00	90.50	18,749,189	2	26		2,240	0		13,879,260	200,149,124	83,524	609,280
Chicago, Milwaukee & St. Paul	646.70	860.40	[c]160,932,232	15	42	5	16,519	0		599,516,000	2,901,500,000	920,568	1,900,564
Detroit & Ironton					2		340						
Erie	34.00	40.00	2,042,843	[b]6			796	8	52	24,641,408	35,507,215	10,746	180,594
Grand Trunk	4.00	12.00	4,103,476	[b]6			460	0		4,280,156	8,411,067	26,424	46,320
Great Northern	4.70	6.50	3,003,700	[b]4			90	0		3,800,000			27,499
Long Island	[a]85.69	[c]227.08	105,450,000	0	1	0	1,080	634	46	1,073,388,277	60,408,000		243,907
Michigan Central	4.60	26.40	8,246,560	[b]10			8,669	0		14,067,000	3,991,000	48,525	893,511
New York Central	53.60	261.80		73				256	57	1,216,756,000		1,306,417	
New York, New Haven & Hartford	[a]87.86	530.58	[c]130,059,200	64	38	16	13,800	79	63	[c]1,254,678,065	1,123,694,301	[c]3,531,068	894,734
New York, Westchester & Boston	23.22	73.41	11,422,794	0	1	1	80	45	60	97,917,960		21,138	11,274
Norfolk & Western	35.38	108.26	50,503,450		16	0	5,256	0					330,536
Pennsylvania:													
New York Terminal	13.41	100.18	59,749,184	33		1	5,281	8	55	[d]595,438,539		1,462,994	592,496
West Jersey & Seashore	75.00	150.38	18,339,689					107	46	261,496,377			
Paoli & Chestnut Hill	30.00	117.40	23,653,205		3		870	115	59	171,835,943			
Southern Pacific:													
O. A. & B. Line	118.00	101.20						121	55	225,635,500			
Portland Line	146.32	141.70						49	51	100,148,000			
Virginian					18		7,740						

[a] Not including trackage rights into New York.
[b] Total passenger and freight.
[c] Includes D. C. zone.
[d] Includes weight of locomotive.
[e] Partial electric operation on part of zone.

—a seasonal summer operation. This was followed by the electrification of the B. & O. terminal at Baltimore in the same year and by the electrification, in 1901, of the Providence, Warren & Bristol (part of the New Haven system),[1] the first all-year-round electrification of a steam railroad for general service. The next important electrification was that of New York Central of its lines entering the Grand Central Terminal in 1906, followed by the New Haven's electrification of its line from Stamford, Conn., to the junction with the New York Central tracks. The latter has been described as

The first installation of single-phase; the most comprehensive electrification in America involving high-speed passenger service, multiple-unit service and switching service; now consisting of 590 track-miles; 11,000 volts on the trolley; an equipment consisting of 120 locomotives; 110 multiple-unit cars; altogether an undertaking that was most courageous; truly a pioneer, involving the determination of many features previously untried; among others, the generation of single-phase power in large steam-turbo units; high-voltage trolley exposed to steam exhaust; overhead conducting system on a four-track road; development of a selective system of circuit-breaker protection to handle short circuits of high capacity; first use of gearless single-phase motors; locomotives combining use of alternating and direct current; service inauguration of elements included in power house, line and locomotives and an extensive undertaking of electric service by a steam organization.[2]

In the years 1908 to 1911, several tunnel electrifications were put in service: the St. Clair tunnel of the Grand Trunk, the Cascade tunnel on the Great Northern, the Detroit River tunnel of the Michigan Central, the Hoosac tunnel of the Boston & Maine and the Pennsylvania's tunnel and terminal at New York. In 1912 the New Haven extended its electrification to the Harlem River branch, including its New York freight yards, and in 1914 from Stamford to New Haven. The other important electrifications commenced operations as follows; the Butte, Anaconda & Pacific in 1913; the Norfolk & Western, the Montana electrification of the Chicago, Milwaukee & St. Paul, the Paoli electrification of the Pennsylvania in 1915 and the Cascade electrification of the St. Paul in 1919.

In 1918 the Pennsylvania extended its suburban electrification at Philadelphia to Chestnut Hill. In 1925 the New Haven electrified its branch line to Danbury, the Long Island extended its electrification to Babylon, the Baltimore & Ohio electrified its line from St. George to Tottenville and South Beach, and the Norfolk and Western extended its electrification to Jaeger, West Virginia.

Important electrifications are under way, on the Virginian from Mullens, West Virginia to Roanoke, Va. (134 route miles) on the Illinois

[1] In Massachusetts & Rhode Island.
[2] F. H. Shepard, on the New Haven electrification.

Central in the suburban territory at Chicago, using 130 multiple unit motor cars and same number of trailers on a section of 20.5 miles of double track, 9 miles of four track, 3.75 miles of six track, and 4.5 miles of single track road with 1,500 volt direct current, and on the Detroit, Toledo and Ironton using new type of motor-generator locomotives operating from 22,000 volt trolley, and on the Great Northern in the Cascade Mountain region, and other important electrifications are under consideration.

The locomotives for the Virginian electrification are in three units with a total length of 152 feet, weighs 1,275,900 pounds and have a rating of 7,125 horsepower. They are the largest electric locomotives ever built.

In a previous chapter (page 159) the formulas for determining tractive power and other related data for steam locomotives are given. The tractive effort of an electric locomotive has a definite relation to the torque of the motors, and is affected by the mechanical connections between the motors and the drivers—these connections consisting of gearing, side rods or some combination of both.

After the fixed factors which enter into the calculation of the tractive effort, namely, the wheel diameters and gear ratios, are determined, the force from the motors, *i.e.*, the turning movement or torque, depends upon the electrical characteristics, which vary with the amount of current taken by the motor.

The torque of the motor is measured in pound-feet and is equivalent to the pull which it can exert at a 1-ft. radius from the center of the armature shaft, *i.e.*, at any point in a circumference of a circle 24 in. in diameter, from which it follows that the formula for the tractive effort of an electric locomotive is:

$$TE = \frac{T \times 24 \times G \times \text{mechanical efficiency} \times N}{D \times g}$$

Where TE = tractive effort in pounds.
T = torque of motor in pound-feet.
G = number of teeth in the gear.
g = number of teeth in the pinion.
D = diameter of the drivers in inches.
N = number of motors.

This formula is a general one and considers gearing as the mechanical connection between the motors and the drivers. When gearing is used, the speed of the driving axle is changed from that of the motor shaft according to the ratio $\frac{g}{G}$. As the power is the same at the motor shaft and at the driving axle, except for the gear loss and friction of bearings expressed in the formula as mechanical efficiency—the torque at the axle must increase according to the ratio $\frac{G}{g}$. Since the torque is measured at a 1-ft. radius, and the tractive effort at the wheel treads, the tractive effort will be to the torque as $\frac{24}{D}$. When side rods and no intermediate gearing are used, g and G are eliminated.

Much depends on the methods of locomotive inspection and maintenance. Those experienced in the science of transportation will heartily support the statement that efficiency and economy demand the best possible maintenance of the steam engine and its most rigid inspection, to that end, and they will readily admit that, even with indifferent inspection and maintenance, the engine may be kept going—or, in everyday parlance, it will "get by." The electric engine should be rigidly and regularly inspected and fully maintained to a high degree. It will then amply justify all effort and expenditure to that end, and abundantly reward those whom it serves. The experiences following the shopmen's strike of 1922 demonstrated that the reliability of the electric engine under trying conditions compared favorably with the steam engine. Steam locomotives are inspected at certain designated inspection points, while the inspection period of the electric engine is based on mileage run—usually every 2,000 or 3,000 miles. There is ordinarily a light inspection by shop forces after, say, 3,000 miles—requiring only a few hours—and a heavy inspection and overhauling requiring several days after every 100,000 miles. The engine crew consumes a few minutes looking the machine over before starting on a run.

In emphasizing the value of things done and things being done, the prediction is made, by a competent authority,[1] that it will not be impracticable to perform the transportation feat of handling 8,000-ton trains on 1 per cent. ascending grades at 20 miles an hour.

Not as an every-day all-around operating proposition, but to indicate some of the possibilities ahead, it may be recorded that, as far back as November 15, 1914,[2] a train of 201 cars (four loads, 197 empties and a caboose) 3,962 tons, was drawn by three a.c. locomotives (one engine crew) from New Haven, Conn., to Harlem River, N. Y.—68 miles. This is probably the longest train on record—its length being about 8,000 feet. What is believed to be the heaviest train was one loaded with ore handled by a Mallet engine on the Great Northern[3] in 1923. This engine hauled 125 loaded ore cars from Kelly Lake to Baden, Minn., a distance of 39 miles, where 25 more loads were added to the train and hauled to Allouez, a further distance of 64 miles. The total weight of the train was 16,360 tons.

[1] Manson.

[2] *Railway Age*, July 23, 1921.

[3] *Railway Age*, July 21, 1923.

CHAPTER XXXII

INTEGRATION OF FREIGHT TRANSPORTATION

The complete movement of freight from origin to destination, or from producer to consumer—sometimes called "store-door" or direct delivery —has today become, next to the general-terminal problem—and it is a part of that problem in its larger sense—perhaps the most vital issue confronting the railroads. The recent development of the motor truck has suggested its use in some one of several methods, with the various accompanying devices and appliances for loading, unloading and transferring, as a means of accomplishing this end.

Any study of self-propelled and self-contained freight carriers must be viewed from two diametrically opposed standpoints, which may be termed its uses and abuses. Motor trucking as a coordinate or supplemental means of transportation has its place, but as a competitor it produces an economic waste. In competing with the railroads over longer distance, the added wear and tear on the highways results in an increased expense to the taxpayers, chief and largest of whom are the railroads. This cost, however disguised or obscured it may be, is equivalent to a national subsidy, and works to the detriment and disadvantage of the railroads who now offer the best and most economical means of transportation yet evolved. In this respect the railroads of this country stand, and always have stood, without a peer. Considering such factors as the length of haul, fragility or perishableness of the commodity and the weight and volume of loads, the extent to which the motor truck is able to, and actually does, compete with the railroads is problematical. It is an indisputable fact, however, that the motor truck has developed an enormous freight traffic in a short time. This growth was fostered largely by war conditions, and by the dumping of many government-owned trucks on the markets at nominal prices.

The immensity of freight transportation is not always realized. A student[1] of this subject reminds that, while the railroads lift 2,200,000,000 tons per annum and transport each ton over an average haul of 181 miles[2] and also carry 1,250,000,000 passengers an average of 40 miles, one is naturally impressed by the thought of the 400,000 miles of railroad and terminal track 2,500,000 cars and the 66,000 locomotives required to haul this vast traffic. There are also 18,000,000 gross tons of American shipping, using 6,000,000 lin. ft. of wharfage and developed water front;

[1] J. Rowland Bibbins, Manager Transportation Department, U. S. Chamber of Commerce—address to New York Railroad Club, March, 1923.

[2] Based on average haul on each railroad. Allowing for duplication on through freight a higher average would be obtained.

45,000 miles of electric and interurban railway track in operation; plus the public roads, of which 186,000 miles (about 7 per cent.) of the total of 2,500,000 miles are designated as public-aid highways and on which the "rolling stock" includes some 12,000,000 passenger vehicles and 1,500,000 motor trucks. Probably 100,000,000 tons of surplus farm products are trucked to city destinations each year, which certainly cannot be classed as direct competition with the railways. Consider the vastness of the overall cost of all this freight movement, including the man handling, packing, crating and storing involved. There are also 2,250,000 tons shipped by parcel post annually, the average shipping weight having increased from 1.9 lb. per package in 1916 to 4.1 lb. in 1921, with a peak load, during the Christmas season, of over 30 per cent. above normal traffic. Then, too, there are 7,600,000 tons shipped annually by express, with an average weight of 85 lb. per shipment. Both of these services are high-class expedited freight. It is estimated that 190,000,000 express, 400,000,000 freight and 18,000,000 mail and parcel-post shipments are made annually.

The railroads are subject to what amounts to state-subsidized truck competition. We are not arguing for or against the present state highway policy in regard to trucks, but merely pointing out that for the movement of merchandise the railroads are of vastly greater importance to our industrial welfare, and yet we are playing favorites.[1]

The competition of motor trucks still continues during favorable weather to the lessening of railroad revenue and the detriment of the highways over which they run. There are signs that public opinion is coming to realize that if it is to have efficient rail transportation it must not handicap the railroads by subsidizing the motor trucks. Such a subsidy is created by maintaining highways free of any charge more than a nominal one, and by shifting to the taxpayers the expense of keeping up these highways, a considerable part of which falls upon the tax-paying railroads, who are thus handicapped by a subsidy which they pay to their competitors. Common justice should impose upon the operators of motor trucks, who offer themselves to the public as common carriers, the same duties and liabilities as are imposed upon common carriers by rail. The necessity of their operation in the public interest should be established by a state public-utility commission. The continuity of operation upon a regular schedule in bad weather as well as good should be imposed upon them as upon the railroads, and they should be made to pay for their use of the highways.[2]

Motor trucks reach after much long-haul business (100 miles or over), perhaps because of insufficient knowledge of the true cost of such service.

---

[1] From a report of the Joint New England Railroad Committee to the governors of six Northeastern states, published July 2, 1923.

[2] PRESIDENT E. J. PEARSON in the *Annual Report* of the New York New Haven & Hartford for 1922.

A very careful study of this was made in Connecticut and economic hauls of 50, 75 and even 100 miles were found possible, depending upon the commodity.

During August and October, 1921, the Connecticut Highway Department, in cooperation with the Bureau of Public Roads, made two 14-day counts on the two principal highways—one on the Hartford-Springfield Road at the State line (Massachusetts-Connecticut); the other on the Boston Post Road at Greenwich (New York-Connecticut). Essential conclusions were that overloading (in excess of the legal limitation of 25,000 lb.) was not confined to heavy material, such as sand, gravel, brick, but was almost universal. Violations included such commodities as apples, beer, butter, eggs, fish, furniture, groceries, paper, sugar and wire. Regular trucking vehicles were the offenders in 75 per cent. of the cases; 89.8 per cent. were overloads per capacity; and 39 out of 41 cases were loaded from 846 to 1,560 lb. per inch of width of tire on rear axle. Only 4.2 per cent. of the trucks were over 5-ton capacity; more 2-ton trucks were observed than any other—16.0 per cent.; followed by 5-ton, 12.7 per cent.; 1-ton, 12.2 per cent.; ¾-ton, 11.0 per cent.; there being only 0.4 per cent. of ¼-ton and 0.06 per cent. of 8-ton capacity—the two extremes observed. The least width of body was 5 ft.; the greatest 9 ft. 6 in. Every third truck, on an average, was loaded beyond the capacity of truck and tires; 37.5 per cent. were overloaded on rear axle; 40 per cent. on front axle. The 20 commodities noted in greatest bulk in the second census, the weight and the average haul of each were:

Commodity	Weight in pounds	Average haul in miles
Groceries	1,039,469	44.15
Furniture	553,545	71.47
Beer	421,665	72 92
Sugar	404,640	47.26
Household goods	375,495	99.81
Meat products	334,410	42.75
Rubber goods	279,020	82.96
Vegetables	176,893	37.68
Poultry	159,760	32.67
Cocoa beans	158,518	33.12
Merchandise	153,831	42.88
Wire	145,550	66.50
Grapes	141,220	48.56
Bananas	133,627	47.13
Dry goods	133,360	43.79
Feed	131,140	27.10
Silks	125,305	110.22
Lumber	119,805	35.51
Machinery	115,875	89.10
Litharge	114,370	106.25

The commodities on which the longest hauls were reported were boats, 840 pounds, 150 mile haul, and yeast 10,445 pounds and 150 mile haul, the shortest, charcoal, 2,150 lb., with an average haul of 3.5 miles; and milk, 4,725 lb., with a haul of 5.8 miles.

The summary of the Greenwich census, covering 15 days (only) and two nights —June 27 to July 11, 1922—shows a total of 54,249 passenger cars; 5,629 trucks; 330 motor cycles; 108 horse-drawn vehicles—a grand total of 60,312. Using Thursday, July 6, as a typical day—8 a. m. to 6 p. m.—the maximum hourly movements were, for eastbound passenger cars, between 5 and 6 p. m., 192; westbound, 3 to 4 p. m., 196; both ways, 5 to 6 p. m., 374; trucks, eastbound, 2 to 3 p. m., 33; westbound, 9 to 10 a. m., 34; both ways, 2 to 3 p. m., 58.

A study of the motor-truck movement in Connecticut[1] developed that the bulk of the motor-truck shipments in Connecticut are short hauls and are not competitive with railroads. Among the interesting facts are:

Rapid delivery and trade demands—and not lower rates than railroads —impel manufacturers to use trucks.

Improvement of rail service in Connecticut has decreased the use of trucks for the long haul.

That 80.5 per cent. of motor trucks handle 70.5 per cent. of the net commodity tonnage in door-to-door delivery.

The 5- to 7$\frac{1}{2}$- ton group of trucks carries 34.3 per cent. of the net tonnage the $\frac{1}{2}$- to 1$\frac{1}{2}$-ton group ranks second, carrying 26.3 per cent.

That 67.4 per cent. of freight is carried 29 miles or less.

More recently (Oct. 27, 1924) a count indicated 1,446 motor freight-carrying trucks alone passing over Mianus River near Cos Cob, Conn. for the twenty-four hours about one every minute, besides passenger automobiles and other vehicles.

The secretary of Agriculture says:[2]

In the Department of Agriculture we have come to feel the need of facts very keenly, because we have had imposed upon us by Congress the responsibility of administering the Federal highway act. We take that responsibility seriously. As we view it our job is not merely the building of a large mileage of road. We look upon the roads as a means to an end—not as the end itself. The end is the improvement of transportation.

To serve as a basis for the improvement of the roads, in co-operation with the state highway departments, we have made careful surveys of the use and the limits of use of the highway systems of Connecticut, Maine, Pennsylvania, California, Tennessee and Maryland.

One thing we know definitely—there is no basis for the fear that the motor truck is going to compete seriously with the railroads. The truck has found its place in the short haul, and it is not taking over any business that the railroads can do as well or better.

In Connecticut we have found that nearly 40 per. cent of the total tonnage is moved less than 10 miles and nearly 70 per cent. less than 30 miles. The movement which runs to 100 miles and over is largely a movement of furniture

[1] J. Gordon Mackay, Highway Economist, U. S. Bureau of Public Roads.
[2] Address at Chicago, May 28, 1925.

and household goods in which promptness of delivery and a minimum of handling are the controlling elements.

In that state we have found that two factors are, in general, responsible for the transportation of commodities by truck over 30 miles. The first is the lack of the rail service which would enable shippers to obtain rapid and dependable transportation of L. C. L. freight. The second is the one I have mentioned, that certain types of commodities, notably furniture, but including also groceries, meat and vegetables distributed from the cities to the smaller towns, are in their very nature adapted to motor truck shipments.

There was a time, no doubt, just after the war when enthusiasts thought they could see the truck taking the place of the railroad completely—at least they talked that way. But that time is past, and the reason for its passing is that the long haul doesn't pay—and truck operators know it doesn't. It has been tried. One of the most reputable haulage companies in the United States tried it and kept a careful record of the costs, and the result is discouraging. They operated a fleet of 35 trucks, averaging 3½ tons capacity, between Buffalo and Erie and Erie and Cleveland. The distance is about 100 miles in each case. They based their rates on the railroad tariff—a little more for the low class commodities, a little less for the high class, but averaging fairly close to the railroad rates. And, on the basis of a year's operation, with $200,000 gross revenue, their net loss was $14,000.

The service is distinctly a service of distribution from centers. In the main it is a service which neither the railroads nor any other inflexible carrier limited to a fixed line of travel—whether it be a rail line or a water line—can render. It is a service which does not aim to move large bulk day after day and year after year between the same points. Its loads are picked up everywhere and hauled anywhere within the short-haul limit.

Perhaps I may illustrate how the highways are being utilized by a brief reference to the situation we have found in respect to the transportation of milk. We have made special studies of the milk movement in the Chicago, Baltimore, Cincinnati, Detroit, Indianapolis, Milwaukee, Philadelphia, St. Paul and Minneapolis markets. In all these markets, with the exception of Chicago, Philadelphia and Baltimore, the studies show that approximately 90 per cent. or more of the milk now received is transported to them by motor truck instead of by railroad. Philadelphia receives only 20 per cent. of its milk by highway; Chicago, 32 per cent., and Baltimore, 45 per cent.; and in each case the lower percentage is probably accounted for by the fact that these larger cities, because of their heavy demands, must draw their supplies from an area so large that the shipping distances become too great for motor truck hauling.

Since we are in Chicago, suppose we take the delivery of milk to this city as an example. In 1910, 94 per cent. of the milk used in the city was transported by steam railroads, 2 per cent. by electric railroads, and 4 per cent. by wagons. Since then the growth of a circle of suburban towns and subdivisions around the city has gradually pushed the dairy farms back beyond a wagon's haul of the city, so that today more of the milk used by the city is delivered to it by wagon. But the motor truck now brings in 32 per cent. of the city's supply and the percentage transported by the 25 steam railroads has been reduced to 68. Electric railroad shipments have ceased.

Mere percentages, however, do not make clear what has taken place in this 15-year period of changing transportation methods. Although the percentage of milk delivered to Chicago by rail has dropped from 94 to 68, the quantity delivered remains today almost exactly what it was in 1910; and although the railroads have lost to the motor truck a considerable part of the business within the short-haul zone of 50 miles, they have gone out beyond the normal tracking radius to develop the new producing territory which the growth of the city demands. There has been a considerable extension of milk mileage by railroads operating in territories where motor truck competition is specially keen.

The transportation investment—roughly $50,000,000,000—is divided as shown in Fig. 227. In amount it is second only to agriculture—

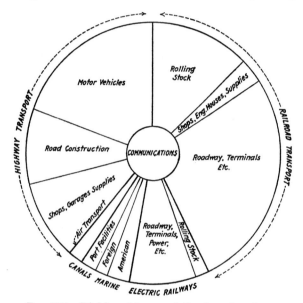

FIG. 227.—Division of transportation investment.

$80,000,000,000—and exceeds manufacturing, $45,000,000,000. It may be subdivided as, approximately—on a cost ratio—railroads, $21,000,-000,000; highways and motor transport, $19,200,000,000; electric railways, $5,000,000,000; merchant marine, $2,800,000,000; canals, $1,000,000,000; port facilities, $1,000,000,000.

Finished automobiles and parts shipped by railroad in the year 1924 aggregated 726,000 carloads. Tire shipments are some 50,000 carloads in addition.

Of the 7,780,625,085 gallons of gasoline consumed in this country in 1924, 80 per cent. or 6,225,000,000 gallons, was for automobile use. After allowing for local deliveries from refineries the shipping of the balance is estimated at 640,000 tank carloads.

Coal, steel and raw materials used in the manufacture of automobiles are also a factor. An instance of collateral business that helps the railroads is the move-

ment of road building materials, cement, sand and gravel. Total cement shipments in 1923 were 552,613 carloads, much of which went into roads and bridges.

If complete segregated data on this whole question were available it is estimated that 2,000,000 carload shipments could be credited as the annual contribution to the rail carriers through the manufacture and use of automobiles.

In 1923 finished automobiles and trucks shipped on the railroads paid over
142 million dollars freight revenue or 3.1 per cent. of the total revenue although
comprising but 0.7 per cent. of the tonnage.[1]

As a sample of the "groping-in-the-dark" methods, the interesting
fact was developed that a large percentage of California's concrete road
system had failed after a life of 4.29 years,[2] that 50 per cent. had failed
after 4 years and, in one instance at least, 4 years' up-keep equaled the
original cost. The motor truck was the cause. In 1922, the Federal
Government, the states, counties and municipalities spent $976,000,000
in building and improving highways—of the 2,800,000 miles of roads,
2,500,000 are yet to be "improved."[3]

The actual tons "lifted" by the larger railroads are 2,200,000,000;
by motor trucks, 1,400,000,000 (as estimated by the Automobile Chamber
of Commerce). Nevertheless, the ton-mileage was about 389,000,000,000
and 6,000,000,000 respectively, or, in other words, the truck ton-miles
were about 1.5 per cent. of the railroad ton-miles—notwithstanding the
present manifestly unfair policy of providing public highways over
which the truck may haul freight without paying anything for their use
except a nominal sum for licenses, while railroads must be built and maintained by private funds and pay a large proportion of the cost of maintaining highways as well. When trucks are required to pay a reasonable
part of the expense of maintaining the roads over which they run, the
situation may become less paradoxical.

The president[4] of an important New England road said:

The twenty years (1901–1920) were those in which the automobile industry
was attaining its present proportions, and it seems that the demand for seats in
railroad cars was growing along with the demand for seats in the flivvers. At the
same time, freight traffic was doubling, regardless of the great quantities of goods
transported over the highways by the trucks. This is not to be taken as meaning
that the motor vehicle has made no trouble for the managers of the railroads, or
that it has not taken from them profitable business. But it does go to show that
there is now greater need than ever before for the railroads, even if they are forced
to operate in competition with newer agencies of transportation. It is, perhaps,
to be regarded as indicating the coming of the day when the existing confusion

---

[1] J. S. Marvin, Assistant General Manager, National Automobile Chamber of
Commerce in *Railway Age*, March 28, 1925.

[2] Captain S. B. Moore, special engineer, Southern Pacific lines.

[3] Thomas H. MacDonald, Chief, U. S. Bureau Public Roads, American Road
Builders' Association, New York, May 16, 1923.

[4] J. H. Hustis of the Boston & Maine.

as to the proper fields of the old and the new will be removed and one will support and supplement the efforts of the other in keeping pace with ever-increasing demand.

Of 141,000 car-load lots of fruits and vegetables unloaded in the New York district in 1921, about 103,000 or over 70 per cent. came in by rail. The truck haul from the railroad yards on the Jersey shore to Manhattan points is estimated to cost a maximum of $28 per load.

It is claimed that New York has over 50 regular established motor express lines, tapping cities, towns and fields as far as 250 miles away. The problem of the integration of transportation is most acute in the great manufacturing and commercial centers, and some steps toward its solution have already been taken, particularly in New York, Chicago, Cincinnati, St. Louis, and from these something may be learned—and a note of warning sounded—of the possibilities of lack of uniformity in methods and standardization of equipment.

Each of these methods of transportation has its field. It is the transgression of the method—often stupidly; frequently blindly—into realms which carry it and its competitors to the wall which should be condemned. Perhaps the relative costs of service, as nearly as they may be ascertained, point the way. That the railroads of the United States, generally, are able to render transportation at a cost of a shade about 1 cts. a ton-mile, including their enormously high percentage for terminal valuation and operation, may be accepted as reasonably close.[1] Of the motor-truck cost less is known. It is generally accepted that there is a "stand-by" arbitrary of $20 a day; that the average load may run around 3.5 to 4 tons; that in cities a running speed of 6¾ miles an hour is attained; that the average profitable length of haul may be as much as 30 miles; that the terminal time for loading and unloading runs 60 min. (in one extended series of tests in a large center it was actually 54 min.), and, figuring it all down to a finality, the frequently used estimate, inclusive of all items, of 5 cts. a minute—running or standing during the hours of the working day—may be about as accurate as many extended and detailed studies will produce. The cost per truck-mile may, therefore, be anywhere from 40 cts. to a dollar. Some more detailed figures are given later on.

There are many methods of integrating freight transportation and they are, generally, in the embryonic state. Of those tried out, the container method is the oldest; the demountable-body method has seen several years' service, notably in Cincinnati; and the semi-trailer method is in service in St. Louis. Then there are the trailer, the motor truck in itself and the untried but strongly backed scheme of mobile bodies

---

[1] The story is worth repeating that, when a railroad officer answers a complaint, the 2-ct. postage stamp he affixes to the envelope alone represents more than the entire gross revenue derived for hauling a ton of freight 1 mile.

which can be lifted on railroad cars and placed at destination on a specially designed and constructed motor chassis or drawn or pushed on their own wheels.

The container is a large box, of wooden or metallic construction—usually steel—intended to move with its contents intact from producer to consumer. The shipper loads, locks and—if desired—seals it; the receiver opens it in his place of business. It is lifted onto a truck; then transferred to an open railroad car built to carry five to eight containers. At the unloading point it is again transferred to a truck. This method[1] is an old one, revived during the past two or three years. A thorough and painstaking

Fig 228.—The motor truck in railroad freight-station service speeds up movement of all freight by eliminating l.c.l. congestion and delays.

experiment is being conducted by the New York Central, using cars and containers specially built for this purpose, and specializing in handling U. S. mail and express. Consideration is also being given to a similar plan for handling milk shipments. As possible disadvantages, the weight of the container, the necessity of frequently lifting it and some empty-container movements may be mentioned. There are, on the other hand, possibilities in avoiding the use of heavy and costly packages and in securing the prompt movement and the certainty that the shipment will reach the consignee in the condition it left the shipper, pilfering being practically eliminated.

[1] The New Haven used containers, very similar to those of the present day, from 1847 to 1896—fifty years—on its rail and boat lines between New York and Boston via Stonington; between New York and Taunton via the Fall River Line, and other routes. An Old Colony Railroad report (1853) mentions as a part of that road's equipment, three 8-wheel platform cars 50 ft. in length and 25 containers, each of 160-cu. ft. capacity. Seven containers were loaded on a car—four for baggage and three for express. Each container had four wheels under it for "trundling" in transferring. The cars had hinged sides, which were turned up to prevent containers running off; there were also stout transverse pieces of timber on car floors, and short chains to keep the containers in place.

The New York Central is experimenting with handling brick in containers from Newton Hook and Hudson, N. Y., to Melrose Junction Yard, where it is dumped by cranes into the trucks. The containers are loaded twelve to a car and weigh about 7 tons. As a rule only ten containers on each car contain lading. The same road is using containers between several New York State points.

The demountable body has the advantage of adaptability—it may be used wholly between freight stations, or between stations and warehouses, and it may be operated on railroad cars and trucks. The generally voiced objection to it is the necessity—or desirability—of expensive hoisting and carrying machinery for placing the

Fig. 229.—Container nearly loaded—note stowage—insurance to carrier and shipper alike against l.c.l loss and damage.

bodies and contents where desired. In addition, platform space is required. Its advocates claim, contrariwise, that this first cost is soon offset by the possibility of using lighter carrying vehicles and the fuller, and perhaps better, utilization of the truck motive power. The best known and best tried use of this type of equipment is found in Cincinnati, where it operates between various railroad stations, in lieu of the "trap cars" formerly used on railroads. The system is a combination of motor truck, overhead electric traveling cranes and uniform containers. Freight cars are placed alongside freight stations in the customary manner; freight is unloaded and conveyed to containers, each being marked for one of the seven Cincinnati railroad stations. These seven stations serve 28 main and substations. The containers are wood and steel boxes, 17½ ft. long, 8 ft. wide, 7 ft. high—usually not exceeding 4 tons of load. They have wide side and end doors. Some are fitted with castors to enable them to be rolled over the floor. When filled, a crane lifts the container and places it on a motor-truck chassis; clamps are

set and tightened and it is hauled to the desired destination. Here it is
similarly removed and replaced with a return loaded container. Figures
228 and 229 show details of the operation.

The routing of trucks is in the hands of a dispatcher employed jointly
by the roads; he keeps a line on the truck movements and the work,
by private telephone connection with the various houses. It is claimed
that the average cost for handling under the "trap-car" method was
$1.718 per ton, while the new method is $1.37, losses in transit and claims
being materially reduced. To replace the some 200 freight cars, 225
demountable bodies, 66 electrically operated hoists, 13 hand hoists at
minor stations and 15 motor-truck chassis, were required.

Detailed operating figures for the months of January and February,
1923, follow:

Items	January	February
Average trucks used—per 8½-hour day.......	12.4	14.1
Average miles per truck—per 8½-hour day....	36.7	34.2
Average miles per truck—per 8½-hour day—per gal. gasoline..........................	2.38	2.28
verage miles per truck—per 8½-hour day—per gal. oil..............................	66.69	50.00
Average tons per truck—per 8½-hour day.....	52.56	47.6
Average percentage of loaded trips—per month..	51.65 per cent.	54.0 per cent.
Average percentage of empty trips—per month.	31.13 per cent.	31.0 per cent.
Average percentage of chassis trips—per month.	17.22 per cent.	15.0 per cent.
Average loaded trips per truck—per 8½-hour day...................................	13.62	12.2
Average empty trips per truck—per 8½-hour day...................................	8.21	6.9
Average chassis trips per truck—per 8½-hour day...................................	4.54	3.3
Average total trips per truck—per 8½-hour day...................................	26.37	22.4
Average railroad delay—per day—per truck (per 8½-hour day)....................	23.22 min.	30.0 min.
Average truck delay—per day—per truck (per 8½-hour day)....................	3.00 min.	13.0 min.
Average hoist delay—per day—per truck (per 8½-hour day)..............:....	1.00 min.	1.0 min.
Average body delay—per day—per truck (per 8½-hour day)....................	....	0.3 min.
Average total delay—per day—per truck (per 8½-hour day)....................	27.22 min.	44.3 min.
Percentage of total time worked chargeable to delays...................................	5.2 per cent.	7.6 per cent.
Percentage of delays chargeable to railroads....	82.0 per cent.	63.0 per cent.
Percentage of delays chargeable to trucks......	12.0 per cent.	33.0 per cent.
Percentage of delays chargeable to hoists.......	6.0 per cent.	3.0 per cent.
Percentage of delays chargeable to bodies......	....	1.0 per cent.

Trailers and semi-trailers in freight integration seem logical, economical and exceedingly efficient. This method accomplishes the maximum use of truck motive power, without heavy lifting and carrying installations. With it considerable hand trucking is necessary. The St. Louis—and East St. Louis—operation is doubtless the most extensive and thoroughly tested. Like the previously described Cincinnati

Fig. 230.—Off-track freight station at Eleventh and Spruce Streets.

method, this is an l.c.l. operation to and from freight houses and between the several roads involved. Eight off-track universal freight stations were established, the operating company serving 15 of the roads entering St. Louis. A view of an off-track station is shown in Fig. 230; also a line of loaded trailers at an east-side station in Fig. 231. Where the consignee desires store-door delivery, that is given, but this service

Fig. 231.—Trailers loaded at an east-side freight station

actually represents but a small percentage of the total tonnage. The terminal company assumes all the responsibility of a common carrier. Its revenue averages $2.14 to $2.25 a ton for outbound, $2.34 to $2.75 for inbound and $1.90 on interchange freight, averaging for 1923 from $2.15 to $2.23 per ton on all business handled with expenses of from $1.78 to $2.21, for which it provides facilities at off-track stations, and assumes all expenses at such stations and to or from the houses of the individual roads. It makes out all manifests; issues receiving notices, participates in the settlement of claims; and is governed by charges fixed in published tariffs which apply uniformly to all off-track stations. The motor trucks, as first used, proved unduly expensive because of terminal delays. Trailers were experimented with in 1919. At present 63 tractors and 197 ten ton trailers are in service; others will be added until the anticipated 125 tractors and 400 trailers will permit displacing all the 300 teams with which this service was previously handled. A tractor will

Fig. 232.—A 2½-ton truck and 4-ton trailer.

handle three or four trailers as fast as they can be loaded and unloaded— thereby reducing the non-productive time to a minimum—and averages 25 miles a day. An advantage to the roads lies in their ability, ordinarily, to truck freight direct from the car into the trailer, keeping most of it off the floor of the house. A trailer receives freight for one house only and its average load is 6 tons. When loaded, a central truck dispatcher is notified and sends a tractor for it (Fig. 232). The tractor driver is given a manifest of the load, and is thereby enabled quickly to detect over- or underloading. The average handling during March, 1923 was 3,000 tons a day; 15,000 individual shipments and the distribution was:

Tonnage outbound delivered to all roads on both sides of river. . 36,495
Total tonnage received at west-side stations. 10,270
Tonnage received at west-side stations for St. Louis. 3,737
Tonnage received at west-side stations for the west-side roads. . . 3,001
Tonnage received at west-side stations for the east-side roads. . . 3,538
Total tonnage received from east-side roads. 34,933
Tonnage received from east-side roads for St. Louis. 13,242
Tonnage received from east-side roads for the eastern roads. . . . 3,096
Tonnage received from east-side roads for the west-side roads. . 18,595

Intensive checking enables good use of freight houses, through close work on the part of consignees. The off-track houses handle an average of 2.68 tons of freight in and out per square foot per year—the roads get but 1.73 tons. With a heavy run of inbound freight, a road, to release cars, will frequently load as many as 50 to 60 trailers after the regular closing time.

Motor-truck operation has its field and its possibilities. There are many instances where heavy installations of either highway rolling stock, or heavy mechanical appliances in freight houses or on piers are not justified, because of varying commodities, volume of traffic, uncertainty of continuation of methods and routing of traffic. Less than 10 per cent. of the freight passing through terminals is handled by machinery; only 20 per cent. of our piers and 25 per cent. of our railway terminals have up-to-date mechanical handling appliances.

A courageous undertaking in trucking, with both motor and horse-drawn vehicles, at and to terminals, is that started in 1921 by the Erie at Jersey City and Manhattan. Off-track or "inland" freight houses were established at several points in New York (Manhattan), and ware-house facilities provided. A trucking company contracted to handle all l.c.l. freight in both directions between the yards in Jersey City and the New York stations. A uniform rate of 7 cts. a hundred ($1.40 a ton) is paid the trucking company, and, where an arrangement is entered into between the trucking company and the consignee for "store-door delivery," an additional charge of about 4 cts. is made. The trucks are transported across the North River on railroad ferries at the road's expense. A similar plan was started by the Lehigh Valley in 1924 using their own pier stations largely.

The New York Central is using motor trucks to handle l.c.l. freight between New York City and Brooklyn and the zone from Westchester Avenue to White Plains on the Harlem division and from Kingsbridge and Croton on the Hudson division. In this operation the l.c.l. freight is consolidated into cars for Yonkers—a central point—and trucked from there to the other freight stations, the trucks delivering freight to the freight stations in the morning and in the afternoon collecting freight and bringing it to Yonkers for loading. This arrangement has enabled a reduction to be made in way-freight crews and has reduced the number of freight cars used in the l.c.l. handling. Some 400 trucks are now in use by the New York Central in freight transportation.

The Pennsylvania has considered the use of motor trucks, dividing the problem into three progressive steps; first, in connection with short-haul l.c.l. traffic; second, motorization of terminals; and, third, the store-door delivery service.

The easiest plan to try, because it required less setting and less expense for the machinery, was the short-haul traffic of l.c.l. freight from large cities to suburban points. These include small lots loaded and unloaded by the carrier and transported by rail for distances up to 25 or 30 miles.

This was a peculiarly unprofitable business to the railroads, partly because about two-thirds of it was already handled by truck and the railroad was required to maintain full service to get what business it could on rainy days or some other day when the motor truck did not feel like operating for it.

And it was a tangled and expensive business for other reasons. Consider the processes:

Under the ordinary method of handling this traffic it was (1) loaded on the shipper's dray and hauled to the freight station; (2) unloaded at the platform; (3) picked up from the platform and loaded into a freight car; (4) transported generally to a transfer station, and unloaded on a platform; (5) loaded into a way-freight car; (6) unloaded at destination; (7) loaded onto the consignee's dray; and (8) unloaded finally at the door or warehouse of the consignee.

If it were conveyed entirely by motor trucks, loading at the shipper's door and unloading at the consignee's door, there would be but two handlings; and, at a time when labor is becoming an increasingly heavy factor in transportation costs, it requires little thought to observe the possible economies in substituting motor trucks for rail transportation for the handling of this short-haul small-lot freight.

There are other advantages in favor of the motor truck for these short hauls, such as less exacting packing than is necessary to protect the freight for movement by rail, as well as rapidity of service.

This method of substituting motor trucks for peddling way-freight trains in the distribution of l.c.l. freight is now in effect on 12 separate portions of the Pennsylvania, or, in 12 units, as we express it, as follows:

There are two units operating out of Pittsburgh: one over the Eastern division to Enon, Pa., and the other over the Monongahela division to Allenport, Pa., including the Ellsworth branch.

On the Pittsburgh division there are two units: one operating from Greensburg over the Alexandria branch to Andrico, and the other covering the territory between Youngwood and Uniontown.

Out of Philadelphia there are three units in operation: one over the Philadelphia division to Downingtown, and the other two on the Maryland division, one from Philadelphia to Wilmington and the other from Wilmington to Perryville.

In South Jersey there is one unit operating over the Atlantic division between Gloucester and Newfield.

Four units are in operation out of Trenton: one on the New York division to Rahway, including the Millstone branch; the other three on the Trenton division—one to Camden, one to South Amboy and one to Lambertville.

The above 12 units comprise between 400 and 500 miles of truck operation.[1]

Since this article, numerous other installations have been put in service and the total mileage of motor truck operation has reached 1,500.

The results of the experiment so far have been:

1. The elimination of the local way-freight train, with a saving of the out-of-pocket cost for its own operation, as well as its interference with other rail movements over that part of the division.

[1] The late Robert C. Wright, General Traffic Manager, Pennsylvania Railroad in *Nation's Business.*

2. The substitution of a more adjustable factor of transportation, with an immediate moderate saving, referred to above.

3. A reduced number of handlings of the freight, and a consequent saving in loss and damage.

4. A more prompt and satisfactory movement of the l.c.l. traffic.

Many instances of combined or correlated motor-truck and rail or water service have been developed. In a typical installation, the freight is assembled by motor truck in the eastern Massachusetts and Rhode Island territory, consolidated into car loads at selected rail shipping points, hauled to New York by the New Haven Railroad and then delivered by truck to destination. Similar service is also operated between the eastern New England section and Philadelphia, Baltimore, Washington and other points making the rail haul over the New Haven and Pennsylvania Railroads.

The B. R. & P. has also replaced way-freight service by a truck between Rochester and Silver Lake; the Long Island between Long Island City and Whitestone Landing, Port Washington; and the Lehigh Valley between Ithaca and Geneva.

In the New York Port District, the Pennsylvania, Delaware, Lackawanna and Western, Lehigh Valley and New York Central are handling some of their lighterage business by motor trucks.

The formation of subsidiary companies such as the Boston and Maine Transportation Company by the Boston and Maine Railroad, and the New England Transportation Company by the New Haven Railroad, are interesting recent developments. The former company is offering a trucking service between Boston and nearby points and the latter has mainly directed its attention to passenger bus operation.

Motor-trucking cost figures, at best, are elusive. Some approximations have been given and many "wise guesses" made. The manufacturers publish figures with an optimistic tinge; the owners are frequently operating on a small scale—and generally as a side issue—and all for service results, disregarding cost, and their figures are seldom kept on anything resembling uniformity. A distinct contribution to the limited knowledge on these lines is the study made by Col. Charles Hine[1] and includes the following typical formula for heavy-motor trucking:

[1] *Railway Age.*

	Dollars per working day (9 hours)	Cents per truck-mile, 100 miles a day (8 tons)	Cents per truck-mile, 20 miles a day (20 tons)
Amortization............................	4.38	4.38	21.90
Insurance...............................	1.60	1.60	8.
Taxes..................................	2.	2.	10.
Garage.................................	1.38	1.38	6.90
Office..................................	2.07	2.07	10.35
Driver..................................	7.	7.	35.
Helper.................................	5.	5	25.
Supervision.............................	3.50	3.50	17.50
Cargo insurance.........................	4.57	4.57	22.85
Fuel...................................	6.	6.	6.
Lubrication.............................	0.50	0.50	0.50
Tires...................................	5.	5.	5.
Repairs.................................	2.	2.	2.
Total.................................	45.	45.	171.
Per hour...............................	5.		
Per ton-mile............................	....	11.25	34.20

Interesting data are given showing the logical method followed in obtaining these figures. It is assumed that a 5-ton-cargo motor truck costing $5,000 has a life of five years; its expectancy of productive work is five 9-hour days a week, 260 a year—the other days idle, due to Sundays, holidays, shop work, painting and business shutdowns. For tires, $400 are expendable—chargeable to operation—leaving $4,600 for amortization. Depreciation over five years amounts to $920 per year, plus the interest charge for each of the five years in succession—$368, $294.40, $220.80, $147.20, $73.60, total $1,104, or total both, $5,704. For uniformity, divide this total by five years and again by 260 days. This gives $4.38 as a safe amortization charge for each working day. Insurance against theft, fire, accident and liability for damage to others amounts to $416 annually, or $1.60 per working day. Taxes, including license and registration, amount to $520, or $2 per working day. Garage costs, including washing and inspection, are $30 a month, $360 annually, or $1.38 per working day. An office headquarters, telephone service and the usual accompaniments are placed at $540, or $2.07 per day; and driver's wages, for owner or otherwise at, say, $7 a day, and a helper, or equivalent, in loaders at $5. With a fleet of two or more trucks, supervisory expense becomes necessary and may be allotted at $3.50 per truck, each working day. The foregoing elements of cost are designated as constant, being assumed as functions of time, and independent of miles run or tons hauled.

Variable elements, because they are assumed as functions of cargo and distance—of operating cost—are cargo insurance, fuel, lubrication, tires and repairs. Cargo insurance—said to be increasing and in some cases almost prohibitive—is assumed at $4.57 per working day. Fuel consumption varies with highways, trucks, cargoes, repairs and drivers, and runs from 4 to 7 miles a gallon of gasoline at a cost of from 4 to 7 cts. a mile, with 6 cts. a safe normal. Lubrication requires a gallon of oil, costing about 80 cts. for every 150 miles, which with some special lubricants gives about $\frac{1}{2}$ ct. a mile. Tires at $400 to $600 a set, with varying guarantees by manufacturers as to mileage, may be set at 5 cts. a mile as a safe normal. Repairs, including periodic overhauls, are found by experience to run about 2 cts. a mile. In congested city districts, with many sharp turns and much stopping and starting, repair costs may increase relatively faster than mileage and vary with time rather than with distance. These five variable elements may, for convenience in comparison, be equated in days or hours where warranted by sufficiently constant and uniform time performance.

Interurban trucks often make only 20 miles or less per working day and often handle only 20 tons of cargo a day. Interurban and suburban trucks seldom exceed 100 miles per day. A trip of about 50 miles, out and return, is normally the limit which can be undertaken and permit return to the home garage the same working day. Longer trips usually necessitate an allowance for garage en route and for meals, if not also lodging for driver and helper. Traffic is seldom balanced in direction. A 5-ton truck is lucky to handle 8 tons in a trip of 50 miles and return. The computations are based on high rather than low figures of cost, in estimating heavy trucking, and when actual figures are substituted for the assumed values given they may show the total cost as 10 to 25 per cent. lower, but the opinion is expressed that it is better for a truckman to base his costs on days than on miles, that neither the ton-mile nor the truck-mile is a safe unit, that, compared with a railway, his tons and his miles are relatively too few to absorb the wide fluctuations in individual cargoes and hauls, and that it is further apparent that some method must be introduced which will tend to reduce the standing time of the truck, to enable it to increase the tonnage handled per truck per day, and correspondingly reduce the cost per ton.

The electric truck is especially fitted for short-haul or frequent-stop routes. The American Railway Express Company, which operates some 1,800 electric vehicles, claims the following advantages for such trucks:

1. Electric trucks greatly reduce costs.
2. They are the fastest trucks there are on short-haul or frequent-stop routes.
3. The electric's simplicity makes it easy to run and easy to repair.
4. It is rugged and reliable, seldom breaking down on the road and becoming disabled less frequently than any other type of vehicle.

5. Electric trucks last a good deal longer than gas trucks.

6. The electric truck is clean, insuring immaculate and sanitary conditions for the goods it conveys.

7. The electric truck is quiet.

8. The electric truck is odorless.

9. It can be stored at loading platform, saving garage space.

10. It uses power with the minimum of waste.

11. It has all the speed that is consistent with prudence in city running and power economy.

12. Employer's control of the speed is inherent in the truck.

13. Its tractive power is greatest in proportion to the horsepower used.

14. Its hazard of fire, accidents and theft is lowest.

15. It costs less to run and maintain.

An interesting analysis of the cost of trucking service to meet the needs of a large wholesale grocery firm in New York is given in the table on page 549, showing the trucking costs to various near-by points in comparison with freight and express rates.

Of three typical present-day operations, each is different in its methods and in the work it performs. The Cincinnati installation uses the system of stationary hoists and demountable bodies; in St. Louis the trailer system is employed and the Erie-New York, which is essentially a motor-truck proposition, is experimenting with various types of horse-drawn vehicles, motor trucks and trailers. In Cincinnati, the problem is wholly one of transferring between the several roads; in St. Louis, it is essentially the usual freight-house operation, the trucking being virtually an extension of the rail lines' operations from the railheads; while the Erie has a movement into and out of Manhattan across the Hudson River, where it finds that the ferrying of motor trucks and other vehicles may be done at a lower cost than individual propulsion over highways for similar distances, and, in addition, it is enabled to substitute off-track or "inland" freight stations and warehouses for the exceedingly costly waterfront layouts.

An elaborate and comprehensive study of the freight and terminal problem at New York was commenced by the New York, New Jersey Port and Harbor Development Commission. This body was succeeded by the Port of New York Authority which continued the study. Their original check disclosed many interesting features of the trucking situation. Some 73 per cent. of the vehicles used were horse-drawn, but this percentage is becoming smaller as the use of the motor truck increases. Their study indicated trucking costs of $1.80 per hour to operate the average two-horse truck in railroad-pier service and of about $3.25 an hour to operate 5-ton motor trucks over the greater distances, as between Manhattan and the Bronx, or New York and Newark, where, on account of the longer runs and the smaller percentage of idle time, motor trucks are more economically justifiable than in the short-haul service in Man-

Towns	Mileage			Running time one way		Operating cost, 9 hrs.	Ferriage and overtime	Total cost	Cost per 100 lb for different truck loads			Freight rates		Express rates	Rate quoted per 100 lbs., cents
	Store to store	Garage to store	Total round trip	Hrs.	Min.				5-ton load	6-ton load	7½-ton load	First class	Second class		
Newark	12	5	34	1	45	20.65	2.30	22.95	23	19	15½	35	30	97	25
Orange	16	5	42	2	15	22.25	2.30	24.55	24½	20½	16½	35	30	89	30
Elizabeth	18	5	46	2	20	23.04	2.30	25.34	25½	21	17½	35	30	97	30
Rahway	23	5	56	3	00	25.01	2.30	27.34	27½	23	18½	35	30	1.03	35
New Brunswick	35	5	80	4	00	29.84	4.30	34.14	34	28½	23	35	30	1.25	40
Perth Amboy	34	5	78	3	30	29.44	4.30	33.74	34	28	22½	35	30	1.03	40
Plainfield	27	5	64	3	30	26.64	2.30	28.94	29	24	18½	35	30	1.03	35
Dover	44	5	98	4	30	33.44	5.30	38.74	39	32½	25½	45	30	1.03	45
Morristown	33	5	76	4	00	29.04	4.30	34.34	34½	28½	23	35	30	97	40
Jersey City	6	5	22	1	00	18.24	2.30	20.54	20½	17	13½	35	.....	97	25
Passaic	17	5	44	2	00	22.64	2.30	24.94	25	21	17	35	30	89	30
Patterson	21	5	52	2	30	24.24	2.30	26.54	26½	22	17½	35	30	.....	35
Montclair	18	5	46	2	20	23.04	2.30	25.34	25½	21	17	35	30	.....	30
Hackensack	12	5	34	2	00	20.64	2.30	22.94	23	19	15	35	30	89	30
Yonkers	13	5	46	1	15	23.04	.....	23.04	23	19	15	35	30	89	30
Tremont	12	5	34	1	00	21.64	.....	21.64	22	18	14½	35	30	.....	25
Mt. Vernon	18	5	46	1	15	23.04	.....	23.04	23	19	15	35	30	89	30
New Rochelle	21	5	52	2	00	24.24	.....	24.24	24½	20½	16½	35	30	89	30
White Plains	30	5	70	3	00	27.84	2.00	29.84	30	25	20	35	30	89	35
Tarrytown	26	5	62	2	45	26.24	.....	26.24	26½	22	17½	35	30	89	35
Ossining	33	5	76	3	15	29.04	2.00	31.04	31	26	20	35	30	89	35
Stamford	41	5	92	4	00	32.24	3.00	35.24	35½	30	23½	35	30	89	40

These figures were based on prices for 1921, and the present-day prices would not alter them appreciably. The freight and express rates have been changed.
This was figured on a tonnage sufficient to make one minimum load of 5 tons per day to each point.
The garage was located 5 miles from their place of business.

hattan. A time study of trucks delivering and receiving freight at rail-road piers is shown in the table below.

TIME STUDY OF RECEIVING AND DELIVERING FREIGHT AT NEW YORK CITY PIERS

	Receiving freight		Delivering freight	
	Hudson River piers	East River piers	Hudson River piers	East River piers
Number of trucks......................	4,232	1,253	3,270	1,308
Number of piers.......................	31	18	31	18
Tons of freight........................	8,662	3,374	2,987	1,997
Tons per truck........................	2.05	2.69	0.91	1.53
Time of truck, minutes essential time for papers...........................	6.05	6.05	1.00	1.00
Essential time travel on piers...........	5.00	2.66		
Essential loading or unloading time	22.52	21.54	10.24	12.07
Idle time.............................	9.44	6.91	8.80	7.10
Total time............................	43.01	37.16	20.04	20.17

The idle time at even $1.80 an hour—a low figure— would represent a loss of $1,500,000 annually at New York.

The mobile body—to coin a new term—is not new and there are various types. Many aspiring candidates are in and entering this field. In inter- and intraplant operation they worked wonders. All kinds, sizes and weights of so-called "trailer trucks" are used in and about freight houses. The efforts of some manufacturers to apply them to heavy-unit, outside, long-distance service have usually proved abortive. A unique but wholly untried device is entering the field and it commands attention because of the producers' (or promoters') standing in other successful ventures and the reliability and general financial ability of its backers. In its ambitions it reminds one of the old pre-war motto of the Hamburg-American Line—"*Mein Feld ist die Welt.*"[1] It aims to cure the ills of the country's greatest, most complicated and perplexing termi-nal problem[2] in its entirety. The method employed is an adaptation— if not a refinement—of that remarkable transportation achievement, the big-circus movement of wagons and cages on railroad cars, which, so far, is perhaps the only real, tried-out and successfully operated instance of "store-door-delivery" with "containers" intact, and which, therefore,

[1] "My field is the world."
[2] New York Harbor district terminals.

substantially reaches, in its own field, the goal of freight-transportation integration. It was this system that, many years ago, created a sensation during a tour of European countries.

In the adaptation, a specially constructed series of open rail cars is provided; containers of some 4 to 10 tons capacity, on wheels, with clear space below the body and between the wheels; and a motor-truck chassis with inclined side runners or running boards. The container is loaded, locked and sealed at the point of origin of cargo—the producer's establishment, freight house or other designated starting point. It is then drawn by horses, by motor or by hand to the end of the rail car or cars, drawn up on ramps, alongside and outside of the track, where it is let down onto the rail car body (floor), leaving its wheels suspended and clearing all obstructions. At the unloading or delivering terminal, the string of cars is drawn onto a track, provided with ramps outside the rails, which raise the mobile bodies in such a manner as to permit of the rail cars being withdrawn and the containers being moved separately. The container may then be again continued on its journey to its final destination by hand, horses, the specially designed motor or by an ordinary motor car. The motor chassis planned for this service draws the container onto the inclined runway by the power of its own engine. The undertaking has breadth and possesses splendid features. The investment required would be enormous and it is a question whether it would be justified in view of the method's lack of flexibility; the necessity for involing substantially all lines and, eventually as least, the carriers to and including other terminals; and the practical inability, after embarking on this enterprise, to step aside if it were demonstrated that it were not to the best solution. The "best possible" is the only method to be thought of when the installation demands a heavy outlay for permanent equipment or for unique individual types. Some of the methods described do permit of a "switch" with little or no loss, because the equipment used is adaptable to other purposes. After all, the whole field practically remains unexplored.

In its report dated Nov. 2, 1923, the special committee appointed by the Chamber of Commerce of the United States to consider the relation of highways and motor transport to other transportation agencies took up the question under the following headings:

Rôle of the motor truck within the terminal area,
Rôle of the motor truck outside the terminal area,
Passenger transportation,
Relation of motor transport to highway development and regulation of motor carriers, reaching the following conclusions:

1. The best interests of the public and the rail, water and motor carriers lie in cooperation between the various agencies of transportation rather than in wasteful competition.

2. The greatest opportunity for cooperation is at the points where the capacity of the railroads is most limited and expansion is most difficult and costly; that is, in the terminal areas of our great cities.

3. Store-door-delivery by motor truck, which would relieve congestion in these terminal areas and greatly increase the capacity of the freight stations, is undoubtedly the greatest contribution which can be made to the solution of the terminal problem.

4. Organized motor transport can also relieve the railroads of various forms of uneconomical service, such as trap-car service, switching between local stations and short-haul shipments within the terminal area. This will reduce yard congestion and release many cars for more profitable line haul.

5. To secure the fullest benefit from this organized motor transport will require the utilization and further development of modern technical equipment, such as demountable bodies, trailers and semi-trailers, containers and container cars, and mechanical handling appliances.

6. Outside of the terminal areas there are distance zones, varying in different localities and for different commodities, in which one type of carrier, the motor for short haul and the railway (or waterway) for long haul, is clearly more economical than the other, and intermediate zones in which competition is inevitable. The motor vehicle also has a wide field where there is no other agency available. Motor trucks and buses should be used to supplement the facilities of existing common carriers.

7. It is to the public interest, as well as to the interest of the respective carriers, that the economic limitations of each type of carrier be recognized, that the railroads be permitted to discontinue unprofitable service to which the motor is better suited, and that the motor abandon its efforts to handle general traffic over excessive distances. However, because of the public interest which affects the operation of railroads, they have performed and must continue to perform some service which is unprofitable, chiefly in territory where the performance of highway transportation would also be unprofitable. If the railroads are to be deprived of a substantial share of their more remunerative traffic through unfair and, to the trader, uneconomical methods, the traffic remaining to the railroads must take on an added burden in the form of higher rates or impaired service. In all cases where the railroad can handle traffic with greater or equal efficiency, all factors being considered, the public interest requires that it be allowed to do so. Unprofitable steam railroad service can in some cases be successfully replaced by the use of self-propelled railroad motor cars.

8. To insure to the public continuity and reliability of service, sound financial organization of motor transport is necessary, as well as public regulation of common-carrier motor service.

9. Passenger-bus transport should be so regulated as to secure the best service to the public, certificates of public convenience and necessity as already required in many states being a useful means of insuring reliable and continuous service. Rail lines can often advantageously extend or supplement their service by bus lines, and in states where this is now prohibited such restrictions should be abolished.

10. Regulation of traffic and of size, weight and speed of motor vehicles by states and municipalities having control should be made more uniform within

states and as between states.   Regulation of common-carrier operations of motor vehicles, including rate regulation, should be handled by the federal or state authorities, under the commissions which now control the operations of rail and water carriers.

11. Trunk highways in any area should be able to carry the normal vehicular traffic of that area, and, if the traffic economically justifies the use of especially heavy trucks, highways with stronger subbases must be provided.   This constitutes a problem requiring particular attention in the design of highway systems and in the regulation of traffic.   In other respects present types of highways, present routes connecting principal centers of population and production, and the present trend in size, weight and speed restrictions of vehicles using highways show a rational system of highway development that should be continued.

12. Investigations now under way by the U. S. Bureau of Public Roads, state highway departments and other agencies to determine more fully the economic rôle of the motor vehicle should be continued.

The results of an investigation, extending over a 6-month period, made by the National Automobile Chamber of Commerce in the latter part of 1924, show, that besides the twenty-three railroads using motor transportation at St. Louis and East St. Louis under contract with the Columbia Terminals Company, nine are employing motor trucks as part of their shipping service at various other points, six of these installations replacing local freight service and that in addition to the use made of the containers of the Motor Terminals Company at Cincinnati by seven railroads, two railroads are using containers at other points.

Summarization seems impracticable—with due regard to accuracy. There is a temptation to dismiss the whole subject with the oft and wisely expressed decision as to the electrification of steam roads—namely, each case has its own peculiar conditions to meet and overcome, in its own way. The terminal-freight integration must fit each case, or possibly a line of road or certain closely related and affiliated terminals.

The late President Harding said:

We have not fully appraised the evolution from the ox-cart to the motor age. The automobile and motor truck have made greater inroads on railway revenues than the electric lines with their intimate appeal to the local community.   There will never be a backward step in motor transportation.   But we shall do better if we find a plan to coordinate this service with the railways rather than encourage destructive competition.   Indeed, the motor transport already promises relief to our congested terminals through better coordination.   We have come to the point where we need all the statecraft in business, to find the way of making transportation in its varied forms adequate to the requirements of American commerce, to afford that transportation its due reward for service, without taking from production and trade a hindering exaction.

INDEX